Theory and Problems
of
Child Development

Theory and Problems
of
Child Development

DAVID P. AUSUBEL, M.D., Ph.D.

Bureau of Educational Research
University of Illinois

GRUNE & STRATTON · New York 1958

TO

MY PARENTS

Acknowledgments

THE WRITER wishes to acknowledge the courtesy of the following authors and publishers in permitting brief quotations from their publications:

American Psychological Association, for excerpts from D. P. Ausubel, "Relationships between Shame and Guilt in the Socialization Process," *Psychological Review 62*:378-390, 1955.

American Sociological Review, for excerpts from Allison Davis, "American Status Systems and the Socialization of the Child," *6*:345-354, 1941.

Child Development Publications, for excerpts from R. Q. Bell, "Convergence: An Accelerated Longitudinal Approach," *Child Development 24*: 145-152, 1953; from S. Escalona, M. Leitch, et al., "Early Phases of Personality Development," *Monographs, Society for Research in Child Development 17*: No. 1, 1952; and from H. Werner and E. Kaplan, "The Acquisition of World Meanings: A Developmental Study," *Monographs, Society for Research on Child Development 15*: No. 1, 1950.

Journal of Pediatrics, for excerpts from C. B. Stendler, "Sixty Years of Child Training Practices," *36*:122-134, 1950.

Little, Brown & Company, for excerpts from W. C. Boyd, *Genetics and the Races of Man*, copyright 1950.

The National Society for the Study of Education, for excerpts from Allison Davis, "Socialization and Adolescent Personality," *Adolescence, Forty-third Year-Book*, University of Chicago Press, copyright 1944.

Prentice-Hall, for excerpts from R. G. Barker, H. F. Wright, and W. A. Koppe, "The Psychological Ecology of a Small Town," *Readings in Child Psychology* (W. Dennis, Ed.), copyright 1951.

John Wiley & Sons, Inc., for excerpts from *Manual of Child Psychology*, Second Edition (L. Carmichael, Ed.), Copyright 1954, as follows: J. E. Anderson, "Methods of Child Psychology"; Kurt Lewin, "Behavior and Development as a Function of the Total Situation"; and Margaret Mead, "Research on Primitive Children."

Contents

vii

PART IV. SPECIAL ASPECTS OF DEVELOPMENT

Preface

A CURIOUS PARADOX characterizes the present status of child development as a field of specialization and professional endeavor. As the tremendous vogue of popularly written books about children has amply demonstrated, the general public continues to display an enthusiastic and ever-increasing interest in problems of child growth, care and behavior. Yet during the past decade or more a pervasive sense of gloom and uncertainty has steadily enveloped professional workers in the field regarding the proper place of child development in the total scheme of the biological and social sciences and its future as a justifiably distinct area of specialization. For although an impressive stream of empirical studies continues to inundate the scientific literature, the field as a whole shows unmistakable signs of diminishing vigor and impaired confidence in the promise of the course that has been charted. Under these circumstances public interest becomes a source of embarrassment rather than an impetus for growth.

The chief reason for this unfortunate state of affairs, in the writer's opinion, lies in the failure to develop a systematic body of developmental theory for ordering the vast accumulation of empirical findings. In the absence of such a framework these data remain disconnected, chaotic and unintelligible. It is not that there has been any dearth of theorizing or speculation: psychoanalysis, neobehaviorism, cultural anthropology and neo-Freudianism have had much to say about the nature of human development. The difficulty has been rather with the unsystematic, fragmentary and impressionistic character of these formulations—the reluctance to fit theory to data, to take seriously or come to grips with the basic theoretical issues in the field. As a result the unique role of child development as an area of specialization has been lost sight of, and its various interdisciplinary components have tended to drift back to the parent disciplines and subdisciplines from which they originated.

This book, therefore, is an outgrowth of the writer's conviction that the time is presently ripe for some systematic stock-taking in theory and problems of child development. Accordingly, an attempt has been made to organize and interpret the empirical findings in this field in relation to a general treatise on the nature of human development. Throughout, the approach has been to treat development as a process requiring explanation as well as description—to examine the factors that control and regulate it, the conditions under which it occurs, and its distinguishing properties and characteristics. Occupying a central place in the theoretical discussions in this book are such issues as the relative contributions of biological and social factors to the regulation of development, the existence and interpretation of "human nature," the meaning of maturation and "cultural relativism," continuity and discontinuity and reversibility and irreversibility in development, the nature of developmental regression, sources of uniformity and difference in developmental sequences, parallelism and unevenness in the component aspects of development, generality and specificity and integration and differentiation in the developing organization of behavior and personality.

The scope of the theoretical problems involved in issues such as these transcends characteristic doctrinal divisions among the different schools of psychological thought. Hence, the basic theoretical need is less for an organization or interpretation of data in terms of the general doctrinal orientations of various broad-based systems of psychology (or even in terms of an eclectic selection of doctrines) than for a body of relatively doctrine-free theory dealing exclusively with the major kinds of generalizations that can be made about the nature and regulation of development as a process. This would consist of an integrated and self-consistent set of propositions consonant with the empirical findings, the logical inferences, and the more self-evidently valid theoretical constructs in the various disciplines comprising child development. Thus it follows that although the views of numerous writers will be examined when appropriate to a particular discussion, this book does not purport to review and appraise systematically the major theoretical positions in the field; this latter task would constitute a volume in itself. Our primary concern is with the elaboration and exposition of a substrate of developmental theory for an interdisciplinary field of knowledge rather than with a history or critique of the application of general psychological theories to developmental problems.

This substrate consists of two recognizably distinct although not unrelated bodies of theory: (a) general principles dealing with the nature and regulation of development as a whole, and (b) principles of personality development. The former is wider in scope and includes personality as well as other areas of development. The latter attempts to provide a theoretical framework for the interpretation of those sequential changes in the more central aspects of personality structure (e.g., self-concepts, motives, values, interests, emotions, etc.) which accompany developmental fluctuations in biosocial status.

The organization of subject matter is based on the premise that cognitive learning represents a process of progressive differentiation of relatively un-differentiated fields of knowledge. We submit that human beings do not easily learn materials that are neatly segregated by virtue of topical or categorical homogeneity into discrete chapters and treated throughout at a uniform level of conceptualization. The ideational content of a particular field naturally imposes a logical sequence and mode of organization that cannot be summarily violated; but this does not preclude the simultaneous adoption of a scheme of presentation that attempts to conform to the actual cognitive steps by which facts and concepts are most effectively integrated into a coherent and stable body of knowledge. Hence, an overview of general principles is provided before more detailed information is intro-duced and previously presented concepts are reintroduced when they be-come relevant in new contexts. In this regard the writer has been deeply influenced by the impressively efficacious organization of medical textbooks of pathology in which the properties and characteristics of disease in gen-eral and of the main categories of pathological processes are discussed prior to a detailed consideration of the specific diseases of individual organs.

The argument for fluidity of boundaries between topics is further but-tressed by the obvious fact that single aspects of human development never occur in isolation from the total growth matrix. Nevertheless some artificial compartmentalization of material into separate chapters is self-evidently necessary for purposes of convenience, since everything cannot be simul-taneously discussed and related to everything else.

The two theoretical portions of the book already alluded to above are Part I, *Theoretical Foundations of Child Development,* and Part III, *Personality Development.* Parts II, *Beginnings of Development,* and IV, *Special Aspects of Development,* are concerned with less general problems and therefore contain fewer implications for development as a whole.

Part I deals with the general theoretical and methodological issues in child development: description and delimitation of the field, historical trends regarding the control and regulation of development, general issues involved in the interaction between heredity and environment, the nature of develop-mental processes, and research problems and methods in child development.

Part II considers the origins, raw materials and beginning status of behavior and capacity. It is concerned with such topics as the psychological aspects of pregnancy and lactation, prenatal development, the birth process, maturity at birth, neonatal behavior and capacities, and problems and issues of infant care and their implications for personality.

Part III deals with the general theory of personality development. Separate chapters are devoted to ego development, emotional development, parent-child relationships, values, interests, fantasy life, and moral development, the impact of culture on personality, and relationships with peers. Considerations of space made it necessary to abandon the original plan of including a chapter on the interpretation and management of the common behavior problems and disorders of childhood. However, in view of the abundance of opinion and the relative dearth of empirical data in this field of knowledge this chapter was considered most expendable in a volume devoted primarily to theoretical issues and problems in the normative aspects of child development.

Part IV is concerned with the following special aspects of development, which are relatively more peripheral and less ego-related than the topics listed in the preceding paragraph: physical growth and motor development, development of language, perceptual and cognitive development, and the growth of intelligence. In a larger sense, of course, these latter areas are also significant components of personality structure which constitute in addition extremely important independent variables affecting the more central stratum of personality development considered in Part III.

A word of caution is indicated regarding the applicability of the generalizations and empirical data in this book to practical problems of child rearing, child guidance, and curriculum development. Although such data and generalizations have obvious implications for these problems, immediate and wholesale extrapolation is not only unwarranted but also extremely dangerous. At the very best child development may be considered one of the basic sciences underlying these applied or engineering sciences—in the same sense that physiology and bacteriology are basic sciences for medicine or pediatrics. Thus, before the practical implications of child development can be legitimately and validly applied in guidance and educational settings, extensive preliminary research at the engineering level of operations is obviously required. The generalization that neuromuscular development proceeds in a proximo-distal direction to the detailed planning of a physical education curriculum is as far a cry as the antibiotic action of streptomycin in a petri dish and its therapeutic use in tuberculous meningitis. Partly to discourage the prevailing tendency toward rash and uncritical extrapolation, partly to conserve space, and partly because they are so frequently accepted as evidence rather than as interesting illustrative matter, case histories and anecdotal material have not been included in this volume.

Also, as a space conserving measure, and because of an impression that in many instances they serve more to simulate an atmosphere of scientific precision than to facilitate genuine conceptual understanding, figures and tables have been utilized only when it was felt that they could convey meanings more succinctly and effectively than could language. Considerations of space likewise precluded reference to all available empirical studies, thereby requiring the exercise of fallible subjective judgment regarding relative merit and significance whenever selective choice became necessary.

Finally, as should be abundantly clear from the material itself, there is need for great tentativeness and considerable humility in the statement of generalizations concerning psychological development. Compared to other developmental sciences such as embryology and geology, relatively little that is definite and conclusive is known about the psychological development of children.

This book is primarily intended as an advanced textbook for graduate students in psychology and education although in some instances it might be appropriately used by mature undergraduates with adequate preparation in psychology as well as in the biological and social sciences. It is intended too as a reference work for educators, pediatricians, clinical psychologists, psychiatrists, social workers and other persons whose professional work brings them into contact with children.

I am indebted to Grune & Stratton for permission to use materials from my *Ego Development and the Personality Disorders* (1952) and *Theory and Problems of Adolescent Development* (1954). Miss N. Catherine Hamrick was of invaluable help in the preparation of the manuscript.

DAVID P. AUSUBEL

Urbana, Illinois
September 1957

PART I

Theoretical Foundations

of Child Development

CHAPTER 1

The Field of Child Development

DEFINITION OF THE FIELD

AT FIRST BLUSH it might seem that the question of what constitutes the proper field of child development is a glaringly self-evident proposition. Closer inspection, however, reveals that the scope, concerns and objectives of this subdivision of knowledge are far from being a settled matter. For example, wide differences of opinion prevail as to whether child development is a natural or experimental science, whether description or explanation of development is desired, whether understanding, prediction and control of *individual* behavior is one of its legitimate concerns. Should child development specialists focus on the *behavior* of children at different age levels as an end in itself or merely as preliminary data from which growth trends may be abstracted and studied? In what sense are those "fundamental mechanics and dynamics of the developing person," that hold true irrespective of age level, appropriate matters of concern in child development?[1] To what extent is the developmental psychologist concerned with the reciprocal impact of organism and environment upon each other?[1] In measuring and explaining development, should emphasis be placed upon the overt and objective aspects of change in the organism or upon their subjective, psychological meaning to the individual?[8, 14, 18] Does child development encompass any unique content or goals that justify and make desirable the retention of its present status as a separate field of specialization or would scientific progress be better served if it were reabsorbed by its parent disciplines?

These and many other unresolved issues concerning the field of child development will be discussed below in an effort to arrive at some tentative and defensible conclusions.

Developmental versus "Contemporaneous" Sciences

By way of introduction a useful distinction may first be made between "contemporaneous" and developmental sciences, or more precisely between "contemporaneous" and developmental phenomena within a given science. Time is naturally a dimension in which both kinds of phenomena occur. But in the first instance it is only of nominal or incidental interest in relation to the phenomenon under investigation; whereas in the second instance,

3

change as a function of time is itself the phenomenon under investigation. Thus, for example, in the characteristic kinds of contemporaneous phenomena studied in chemistry, physics, physiology, psychology, sociology, ethnology, etc., scientists are concerned with describing and explaining events and relationships which for all practical purposes undergo no significant change during the conventional time interval in which they are considered. On the other hand, in each of these broad areas of science, when the focus of interest shifts to how and why matter, form, organisms, behavior, institutions, and civilizations are different from one point in time to another, we are confronted with such developmental phenomena as constitute the subject matter of geology, embryology, biological evolution, genetic psychology, philology, and history.

It is important to note that in this distinction the crucial consideration is not the duration of the time interval involved but whether change as a function of time is the primary phenomenon under investigation. Developmental phenomena may encompass less than a day (e.g., the life cycles of unicellular organisms) or millions and billions of years (e.g., geological events, biological evolution). And, similarly, as long as phenomenological constancy over time may be conventionally assumed for the purposes of a given investigation, tremendous variability may prevail with respect to the temporal span of events conceived as occurring within a contemporaneous frame of reference.

The Content and Goals of Child Development

In the light of the foregoing discussion, child development as a field may be best defined as that branch of knowledge concerned with the nature and regulation of significant structural, functional and behavioral changes occurring in children as they advance in age and maturity. However, the fact that it deals with the characteristics of children is not the essential reason for classifying it among the developmental sciences; childhood, after all, constitutes but a single segment in the total life cycle of the ever-developing human being. Thus, scientists who restrict the scope of their inquiries to this particular age period are not necessarily specialists in child development. They may simply be anatomists, physiologists, pathologists, psychologists, physicians or anthropologists who specialize in children.

Neither do attempts to establish the descriptive characteristics of children at different age levels necessarily imply concern with developmental processes. It frequently happens that the collection of normative data is regarded as an end in itself and leads to no subsequent effort to discern or account for growth trends. To be sure, such trends can only be abstracted from the measured properties and capacities of children occupying different positions on an age continuum. But unless the normative investigator takes the *further* steps of treating these temporally separated phenomena as successive stages of a continuous sequence in which the elaboration of each phase is lawfully related to its precursor, he is dealing less with the nature of change than with a discrete series of unrelated contemporaneous events. In short, the ultimate goal of child development is not simply to produce a series of composite portraits of the child at ages one, three, five, seven, or nine—his physical dimensions and bodily functions, how he eats, sleeps, plays, thinks, feels, and responds to others—but to identify the sequential steps between two levels of maturity, to explain how one is transformed into the other, to discover the variables that effect the transformation, the factors that either facilitate or retard its occurrence, and the uniformities and differences by which it is characterized.

By definition, therefore, the concept of development presupposes that some degree of lawful continuity prevails between successive stages of an ongoing growth process and that the properties of prior phases contribute in part to the form and substance of subsequent phases. Furthermore, in as complex a field as child development, in which innumerable overlapping areas are simultaneously undergoing change, it is evident that successive chronological ages are representative of more than a series of uniformly spaced points in time. They represent, in addition, progressive stages in the developmental status of the *total* organism* which are also lawfully related to subsequential phases in any *particular* aspect of growth.

The definition of the field formulated above also requires some restatement of several traditionally accepted goals of child development. If, for example, the nature of developmental change is made the primary focus of inquiry in child development research, it follows that the variables contributing to such change become legitimate objects of study only insofar as they are implicated in the developmental process, and *not* as ends in themselves. This holds true for both environmental factors and for such endogenous variables as the basic structural and functional properties of human beings that remain relatively constant over the age span. How these latter factors influence, direct and limit growth is obviously a matter of great concern to the child development specialist. But the "mechanics and dynamics" of these properties in their own right—how they are gov-

*These two different interpretations of the meaning of chronological age in the conventional growth curve (in which performance or capacity is plotted against age) introduce a possible source of confusion. Unless it is clearly appreciated that chronological age, when interpreted as representative of total development status, is only *one* of many independent variables operative during the time interval in which growth is studied, *all* of the measured change may be erroneously attributed to its influence.

erned and how they operate apart from their relationship to development—constitute "contemporaneous" phenomena which rightfully belong in the domain of anatomy, physiology, biochemistry and psychology.

A somewhat different but related question is the extent to which child development is concerned with the reciprocal influence of organism and environment upon each other.[1] Since environment is undoubtedly an exceedingly important collective variable participating in the control and regulation of development, one may properly refer to its "impact on the organism." It might be more precise, however, to conceive of the developmental influence wielded by the environment in more indirect terms—as constituting but one of many regulatory vectors which, by interacting, generate in turn the growth matrix that actually determines the direction of development. On the other hand, although the impact of the developing organism on the wider social environment is of great import in social psychology and sociology, it normally lies beyond the scope of child development. It becomes a matter of relevant interest only to the extent that by significantly influencing his more immediate environment in certain cases (e.g., parents, teachers, peers) the child contributes to the external factors shaping his development.

Lastly we would hold that the assessment of the *individual*, either genetically or at a given horizontal level,[1] is not a function indigenous to child development as a field. At this juncture we would invoke the well-established distinction between basic and applied sciences. Thus, as a basic science, child development is concerned with discovering—as an end in itself—growth trends that characterize a designated universe of children. Individual assessment, however, not only leads to no valid generalizations about children, but also implies primary concern with rendering such practical services as guidance, training and therapy. And although the child development specialist can hardly object to the collection of developmental data for single individuals and their subsequent utilization for practical ends, he should in all propriety leave these tasks to appropriately trained specialists in the applied disciplines.

Child Development as a Natural Science

Many of the characteristics of child development as a field, as well as many of its theoretical and methodological problems, stem from the fact that by virtue of its phenomenological content it is primarily a natural rather than an experimental science. Yet, as Barker and Wright[4] cogently point out, there has been and still is considerable resistance to the acceptance of naturalistic methods in developmental psychology. As a result,

no psychologist knows more than laymen about the sources, the frequency, the

degree and the behavioral effects of frustration and freedom, of reward and punishment, of conflict, of hostility, of social pressure, of success and failure in the lives
of men . . . [Hence] psychologists can do no more than speculate at the present
time about many important questions. What changes have occurred over the generations in the way children are reared and in the way they behave? How does
life differ for children in large and small families? Are American children disciplined differently from English and French children? If so does this affect the
national character of Americans, Englishmen and Frenchmen? How in psychological
terms does life differ for rural, town, and urban families? No accurate psychological
data bearing on these questions are available and they cannot be secured in
laboratories . . . For information about the actual behavior and life situations
of people we must go at the present time to novelists, biographers, diarists and
journalists.[4]

The experimental method has proven eminently satisfactory for the
solution of scientific problems in which the crucial variables involved could
first be clearly identified and then systematically varied under controlled
laboratory conditions. Unfortunately, however, it is neither possible nor
feasible to apply experimental procedures to many very significant problems in science. This is especially true when the phenomena under investigation are extremely complex, spatially gross, or of unusually long duration,
and when the conditions under which they occur are difficult to identify,
control, and reproduce—even by means of miniature scale models. Under
these circumstances, the scientist has no other choice but to describe,
measure and relate phenomena as they occur naturally in uncontrived situations. Geology, meteorology, astronomy, ecology, sociology and anthropology are typical examples of sciences in which such naturalistic procedures have been employed with great success.

Child development is a natural science for many of the reasons indicated
above. Apart from the great number and complexity of the variables involved
and the difficulty in identifying, isolating and controlling them under
experimental conditions,

it is impossible to create experimentally some conditions that occur in life situations. No laboratory can duplicate the frequency of repetition, duration, intensity
or complexity of psychological situations and behavior that are common outside
the laboratory.[4]

Some of the most significant aspects of human development—parent-child
relationships, the assimilation of cultural values, relationships with peers,
etc.—involve such extended periods of time, such a wide variety of situations, and the cumulative impact of so many repetitive and interlocking experiences, that adequate simulation by experiment would be physically and
administratively impossible.

But even if the latter feat were within the realm of human contrivance,
many practical considerations would still render the experimental method

unfeasible and ethically undesirable for such problems. We could not synthesize and manipulate human emotions, attitudes, values and interests at will for any length of time and still hope to simulate convincingly their real-life counterparts. Investigators could not in good conscience instruct mothers to reject some children and accept others, to overdominate one sibling and underdominate another, etc. And if they conceivably were rash and unethical enough to make the attempt, would mothers be able and willing to comply with such requests? Similarly, children could not be subjected experimentally to the prolonged and extreme experiences of physical deprivation, emotional frustration and social abuse that unfortunately occur so frequently under natural auspices. In all of these instances it would be sounder and more practicable to follow the lead of the epidemiologist who studies the incidence, distribution and etiology of naturally occurring diseases in relation to relevant, naturally occurring conditions.[4] This approach is so much more defensible and self-evidently valid that it is extremely unlikely that he ever toys with the idea of creating real epidemics in situ for research purposes or of simulating small scale models of epidemic conditions in the laboratory.

Serious misunderstandings have arisen in the past about the principal reason for the infrequent use of experimental methods in the natural sciences. It is not, as has so frequently been claimed, that the natural scientist has any deep-seated aversion to the fact of simulation per se, i.e., to the element of unnaturalness or artificiality that inheres in transferring a natural phenomenon to a laboratory setting. It is rather that he is unable to simulate *adequately* in his laboratory the conditions that are necessary for studying the significant problems in his field. From the standpoint of scientific method, the truly objectionable aspect of artificiality is not that natural events are contrived by man at arranged times and in arranged places, but that the attempted simulation is not complete or accurate enough to reproduce the essential features and conditions of the problem under investigation. Considered in this light, the more faithfully arrangements can be simulated, the less artificial they become.

Thus, no one looks askance at the artificiality of studying the life cycle and adaptive capacities of bacteria cultured in petri dishes. But should the comparable venture be attempted for tigers in zoos, the hue and cry that would be raised about artificiality would be deafening. And similarly, experimental methods in child development are not necessarily artificial just because they are employed in laboratories. They are only artificial when they are invalidly and inappropriately employed, that is, to the extent that they inadequately represent the conditions or phenomena they purport to simulate in the real-life problem under investigation.

As a matter of fact, as will be pointed out in Chapter 5, in the form of standardized tests, unstructured projective devices, manipulated stress experiences, etc., experimental techniques have an important place among the recognized research methods in child development. In accordance with accepted usage, however, the laboratory or test procedure is not designed to constitute in itself a representative sample of complex, prolonged or cumulative real-life situations, but either (a) to measure the *effects* of such naturally occurring situations on behavior, capacity, perception and response tendency, or (b) to simulate a relatively simple and episodic type of real-life situation.

Apart from the question of its intrinsic adequacy for these latter purposes in particular research studies, a related problem obviously bearing on the validity of the laboratory procedure is whether or not it *appears* artificial to children. But here the relevant criterion of naturalness or artificiality is not the degree of functional equivalence between simulated (laboratory) and natural experience or the extent to which the former is either realistically acted out with the customary props or merely "imagined." All that is required for the appearance of naturalness is sufficient congruence with the child's conception of the universe to permit a reasonable degree of self-involvement in the situation.

We may conclude, therefore, that although experimental techniques do have a legitimate auxiliary place in child development research, answers to the basic problem of how children actually develop in a complex interpersonal, social, and cultural environment will be obtained only as rapidly as adequate and sophisticated naturalistic methods of investigation are evolved. This requires greater acceptance of such methods in child development. It also means coming to grips with the following issues stemming from the status of child development as a natural science: (a) the avoidance of unsystematic, unprecise and biased observations. This problem will be discussed in Chapter 5; (b) the relationship between theoretical and empirical approaches; (c) the distinction between subjective and objective levels of analysis; and (d) the avoidance of unjustifiable extrapolation in the interpretation of naturalistic data.

Descriptive and Explanatory Levels of Analysis. Ecological investigations of children are not necessarily developmentally oriented simply because they deal with behavior in natural settings—even when they focus in normative fashion upon successive stages in the life cycle. The study of development first begins when normative data, naturalistic or otherwise, are *deliberately* collected or analyzed for the purpose of describing and explaining the *changes* that have occurred in the organism between various designated points in time. It is possible, therefore, to distinguish between two distinct levels of analysis: descriptive and explanatory.

Descriptive analysis takes place completely within the framework of frankly normative studies. Starting only with the assumption that development involves both continuity and a lawful process of transformation, data from single individuals or from entire age groups are first arranged in chronological sequence. The principal characteristics, both quantitative and qualitative, of successive age levels are then tabulated and described as coherently as possible. This preliminary procedure permits the abstraction of common trends and of sequential uniformities and differences between individuals. Similarities and differences between age levels may be pointed out or the data may be subjected to further analysis in terms of various characteristics of subgroups, situational contexts, etc.

Explanatory analysis begins with the questions raised but left unanswered by the normative data. How did the changes occur? What variables were responsible? How did the variables interact with each other and with the prevailing state of the organism? Were some factors more critical than others in effecting transformation? Did susceptibility to change vary from one stage to the next? Were some changes relatively more discontinuous and irreversible than others? Questions such as these lead to explanatory hypotheses and the design of new studies that can test them. Inability to manipulate variables experimentally is a disadvantage but does not necessarily preclude the planning and satisfactory performance of such research. By means of appropriate matching and statistical procedures, sufficient "control" may be established to uncover many significant explanatory relationships among naturally occurring phenomena. "Psychological experiments in nature are occurring every day and we need only the proper techniques and facilities to take advantage of them."[4]

Ordinarily, therefore, in the field of child development, descriptive analysis based upon normative studies must be considered logically prior to the planning of explanatory or hypothesis-based research. Before we can attempt to explain how or why certain changes take place during the course of development we need precise information about the actual changes that *do* occur. Otherwise we not only fail to identify the phenomena requiring explanation, but can also do little more than speculate about speculations (i.e., about the nature of hypothesized events) instead of testing hypotheses that might explain demonstrably occurring events. The futility of the latter procedure is illustrated by the tremendous amount of theoretical effort wasted in speculating about the nature of psychosexual development prior to the availability of a reasonably comprehensive and representative body of normative, naturalistic data such as were amassed by Kinsey and his co-workers.[11, 12]

Relationship between Empirical and Theoretical Approaches. It is possible in a sense to regard the preceding discussion as one aspect of the contrast between empirical and theoretical approaches. Explanatory hypotheses obviously deal with more theoretical matters and issues than the descriptive data from which they are derived. Ordinarily, however, a theoretical orientation refers to an organized structure of abstractions and propositions in relation to which a vast array of descriptive and explanatory data as well as interlocking hypotheses and postulates may be systematized and interpreted in meaningful fashion. Theories serve at least two important functions in science: (a) They make possible the orderly integration of seemingly miscellaneous and unrelated facts and fragments of knowledge under more inclusive generalizations. (b) They lead to a greater economy of research effort by structuring specific explanatory hypotheses along lines that are consistent with a larger body of interrelated principles and empirical findings. In this way hypotheses are both less likely to constitute aimless shots in the dark and to eventuate in data that are difficult to interpret and relate to other findings.

Of course, theoretical formulations in child development may themselves differ widely with respect to the level of generalization at which they are stated. They may deal with the developmental process as a whole or with a relatively circumscribed area or sub-area of growth. Somewhat intermediate between these extremes are theories that attempt to encompass and interrelate developmental changes in the more central, ego-related areas of personality that follow from or contribute to the shifting biosocial status of the individual in his social milieu.

As in all other sciences, empirical and theoretical approaches in child development are interdependent. Unrelated to a comprehensive theoretical framework, hypothesis-based research is wasteful and uneconomical; both the data from which it is derived and the findings it yields, considered as ends in themselves, are chaotic and unintelligible. On the other hand, specific explanatory hypotheses as well as larger bodies of theory that are not anchored to and continually corrected by empirical data are dealing with phenomena and problems the very existence of which is purely speculative.

Fruitful interaction between the two approaches occurs at still another point in the research process. After explanatory hypotheses are related to both descriptive normative data and to theory, preliminary exploratory studies may be profitably conducted before large-scale representative investigations of a longitudinal or cross-sectional nature are launched.[1] By testing both the general sense of the hypotheses and the feasibility of the proposed methods, this procedure may effect necessary and valuable improvements in conceptualization, design and measuring instruments. In this way the irrevocable commitment of excessive amounts of time, effort and money to theoretically unsound or practically unfeasible research ventures may be prevented.

In addition to being congruent with the implications of available data, adequate and fruitful theories in child development should conform to the law of parsimony and should be so formulated as to be testable by means of naturalistic investigation. Self-evident or face validity, as well as credibility in terms of the actual reactive capacities of *children,* are also highly desirable attributes of hypothetical constructs, especially in areas where empirical confirmation is difficult or impossible. Lastly, as Lewin[13] suggests, a fundamental objective of theoretical inquiry in a field such as child development is to identify "genotypic" clusters of antecedent regulatory conditions (or states of the organism) the developmental or behavioral products of which are relatively homogeneous in terms of basic origins, even if markedly different in terms of phenotype (i.e., overt appearance). Thus, for example, developmental disequilibrium, in periods of abruptly discontinuous personality growth, is a genotype which may alternately give rise to such diverse phenotypes as resistiveness and ultraconformity (see p. 487). And, on the other hand, the same phenotype of emulatory behavior may, at different stages of development, or in basically different personalities, be a manifestation of such different genotypes as the need for dependence and independence respectively (see p. 279). To use phenotypic similarity as the basis of classification is to reduce this essential tool of scientific systematization to little more than a convenient but arbitrary filing system, and to subvert its primary function of categorizing phenomena in accordance with their underlying commonalities.

Avoidance of Extrapolation. A serious methodological and theoretical hazard confronting all research in the behavioral and social sciences, naturalistic or otherwise, is the almost inevitable tendency to extrapolate unwarrantedly from one phenomenological level to another in observing and interpreting events and relationships. Nevertheless, the utilization of familiar frames of reference and conceptual models for understanding and ordering new sets of experienced relationships is an inescapable fact of cognitive life which hardly merits condemnation. When situations or phenomena are sufficiently comparable to warrant the tentative extension of generalizations from one area to another, new explanatory hypotheses are generated in the simplest possible fashion; and in any event before a decision can be reached that direct analogy is unwarranted and that radically new models or frames of reference are required, preliminary examination of similarities and differences and a genuine attempt at reconciliation are first necessary.

Hence, as an *exploratory* procedure in conceptualizing new relationships, extrapolation is by all accounts an unavoidable and desirable process. It is also perfectly legitimate in a more terminal sense if, on the basis of a reasonable degree of comparability between two situations, it leads to the formulation of analogous explanatory hypotheses. It first becomes objectionable (a) if the stage of preliminary and deliberate exploration is by-passed and analogies are accepted automatically or uncritically, (b) if analogous hypotheses are generated in the absence of sufficient essential comparability, and (c) if the extrapolated generalizations are regarded as self-evidently valid propositions rather than as hypotheses to be proven by further research.

The problem, therefore, of deciding whether the terminal phases of extrapolation are justifiable is very similar to the problem of deciding whether experimentally arranged conditions in the laboratory adequately simulate events in nature. An important difference, however, is the fact that in extrapolating one assumes, by definition, the existence of a greater gap between analogous situations as a result of the differential operation of one or more significant variables. Hence, the explanatory generalizations suggested by familiar and approximately comparable models not only always require confirmation by means of additional research in the new contexts to which they are applied, but the relevance (comparability) of the models is also more frequently open to question. The latter problem tends to arise when the introduction of significantly new or different variables creates a qualitatively different order of phenomenology which renders two situations no longer comparable and the application of the original explanatory principles pointless and unprofitable.

Variability in the relevance of conceptual models is illustrated by the relationship between animal and child development. Many of the same kinds of developmental conditions confront children and the young of infra-human mammals, e.g., in situations where the influence of culture is relatively minimal and where the unique reactive capacities of human beings are as yet undeveloped or are not fully called into play. Here generalizations respecting mammalian development may (in the form of explanatory hypotheses) be properly extended to children. But when neither of these conditions prevail, analogies are not apt to prove fruitful, since the mammalian principles when applied to children hold true only in a substrate sense and at a level of generality that has little explanatory value for the particular phenomenon under investigation.

Other typical illustrations of extrapolation in child development include (a) the interpretation of the child in terms of an adult frame of reference or in terms of a synthetic stereotype of a "primitive" adult, and (b) ethnocentric interpretation of the behavior of children in other cultures and subcultures. Thus, by attributing mature reaction capacities to infants and children, investigators have "observed" differentiated emotional responses in neonates,[17] have hypothesized the occurrence of anxiety in response to the implications of separation present in the birth experience,[6, 15] and have "perceived" the operation of complex, adult-like sex drives (including the object of libidinal interest) during the first year of life.[16]

Although it is probably impossible to rid completely the observation and interpretation of children's behavior from the contaminating influence of unwarranted extrapolation, two suggestions may be offered for minimizing it. First, *awareness* of the extrapolating process and *deliberate* use of it as a preliminary conceptualizing technique in the formulation of explanatory hypotheses undoubtedly serve to hold in check the tendency uncritically to accept far-fetched and basically untenable analogies. Second, if the development of children at a given stage of maturity is *first* interpreted from the standpoint of their known perceptual, cognitive, and reactive capacities, and in relation to the known environmental context in which it occurs, the aptness of using generalizations from other fields as the basis of explanatory hypotheses may be judged more explicitly, and appropriate modifications of the latter may be made.

Objective and Subjective Dimensions of Development. In studying the development of the child, it is possible to focus either on the more objectively observable aspects of growth (such as physical size and motor capacity, intellectual and language performance, and overt emotional and social behavior) or on the more subjective aspects of psychological experience such as perceptions, feelings, motives and attitudes.[8] Although the former can undoubtedly be investigated more directly and with greater validity, it cannot for this reason be considered more indigenous to the field. As a matter of fact, many of the more significant aspects of development are concerned precisely with these subjective meanings and reactions.

The subjective content of children's behavior and development may in turn be divided into two main categories of experience: (a) children's perceptions of the environment, and (b) their non-overt, conscious reactions to these perceptions. The perceptual world has been variously referred to as the psychological life-space[14] or habitat.[3] It, rather than the stimulus world, is the proximate external determinant of both the subjective and objective components of behavior. That is, the individual responds to the world as it exists for him, not to its objectively ascertainable stimulus characteristics. His subjective reactions to these perceptions are feelings, attitudes, values and aspirations. Thus, for example, loss or gain in social status is an objective event in the real world; but an individual only responds to it with subjective feelings of adequacy or inadequacy in terms of the status change that he *perceives*.

Subjective aspects of development may also be approached from the standpoint of descriptive or explanatory analysis. Normative investigation, for example, may establish that "the world in which the newborn, the one-year-old, and the ten-year-old child live are different even in identical physical and social surroundings."[14] The crucial explanatory problem, however, is to discover how and why the objective world is perceived differently at successive points in the life cycle. How do perceptual maturity, general developmental status, and personality factors interact with the stimulus properties of the environment to produce characteristic age-level differences in perception? Similarly, it is important to go beyond a simple statement of relationship and to ascertain how and on what basis certain perceptions interact with the existing capacities and personality structure of the individual to generate various feelings, motives, attitudes and values. This latter (reactive) aspect of subjective experience never involves a *direct* relationship to the "material-cultural world," although superficially this may seem to be the case since the intervening process of perceptual mediation is seldom observed.*

The investigation of subjective dimensions of development is naturally fraught with grave methodological hazards. The observer can never share directly the content of a child's experience but must always resort to inferences from his behavior and verbalizations. To really make contact with the subjective stratum of experience, however, he must attempt to relate himself to the child, to participate in his experiences, to empathize with him, to perceive the world through his eyes, and to react to such perceptions from the standpoint of the latter.[8] Observations made in this way are, of course, always subject to the contaminating influence of extrapolation, particularly from the observer's own experience and adult frame of reference. Here extrapolation already enters the picture at the stage of obtaining descriptive data, even before explanatory analysis is attempted. Other methods of investigation include direct verbal (introspective) reports from the child and the indirect elicitation of subjective content by means of projective devices. These techniques are discussed in Chapter 5.

Justification as a Separate Field of Specialization

In recent years the question of whether child development constitutes

*In a negative sense, however, the environment may be considered to exert a direct limiting influence on the subjective components of behavior. The absence of certain physical or social conditions in the lives of particular individuals or groups need not be perceived in order to be related to a corresponding lack of subjective reactive experience or growth.

a legitimate field of specialization has been raised with increasingly greater insistence. Are the interests of scientific progress best served by the present arrangement, or would it be more desirable to reorganize the subject matter it presently encompasses under the various component disciplines and subdisciplines from which it is derived? Answers to this question can only be framed in terms of such criteria as convenience, developmental trends in the history of science, and the potentiality of a given organizational scheme for solving significant problems in a unique area of scientific inquiry and, hence, for ultimately facilitating the solution of problems of practical importance in human affairs.

One familiar argument for abolishing child development as a separate field is based on the premise that, as human beings, children are subject to the same physiological and behavioral laws that govern all individuals irrespective of age. This, of course, is true for a great number of functions such as intracellular oxidation, the formation of urine in the kidneys, the basic optical phenomena underlying vision, and the temporal and reinforcement arrangements affecting the establishment of conditioned reflexes. On the other hand, there are a whole host of physiological, immunological, nutritional and behavioral phenomena which undergo marked qualitative as well as quantitative change over the course of childhood. The identification of these changes as a function of age and the discovery of their nature and regulation constitute the distinctive subject matter of child development, whereas the former category of phenomena belong in the realm of "contemporaneous" science. And as already noted above it is the concern with the properties of *change* rather than with children as an age category of characteristically functioning individuals that stamps the field as developmental in orientation.

A second type of argument disputing the desirability of retaining child development as a field of specialization does not challenge the easily demonstrable fact that many structural, functional and behavioral properties of children vary with developmental status. Instead the point is made that the changes attributable to age (like those related to other independent variables such as sex and socioeconomic status) could be adequately and more advantageously considered under other recognized fields of specialization, e.g., physical anthropology, medicine, psychology and its various subdivisions. However, while this arrangement would undoubtedly suffice for specialists in these other areas it would constitute a highly inconvenient, scattered, and fragmentary organization of knowledge for persons primarily interested in human development. It would hardly provide an integrated picture of how *many* different functions change with age, of the interrelationships among them, or of *total* developmental status at a given age level.

But perhaps the most serious disadvantage of all is the fact that studied adjunctively in this fashion, changes related to age would tend to be analyzed on a descriptive rather than on an explanatory level; and with developmental findings scattered over many fields, it would be difficult indeed to abstract general principles of development transcending particular functions.

Child Development versus Child Psychology. Although often used interchangeably to describe the same field, child psychology and child development are actually quite different in at least two important respects. First, child development covers a much broader and more interdisciplinary canvas, dealing with *all* facets of childhood, not merely with phenomena that are psychological in nature. Strictly speaking, therefore, it includes such topics as the physiological, nutritional and immunological changes occurring with increasing age, age changes in response to disease-producing and therapeutic agents, etc. However, because courses in child development are generally designed for students in psychology, education and home economics, these more medically oriented aspects of development are customarily reserved for treatises on pediatrics. Thus, although the actual field and technical literature are broader and more interdisciplinary than is apparent from text books in child development, the latter works are traditionally restricted to the different aspects of psychological development supplemented by a consideration of prenatal development, the birth process, physical (primarily skeletal) growth and motor development. Even so, they draw on data from such diverse fields as genetics, embryology, physical anthropology, pediatrics, psychology, psychiatry, education, sociology and ethnology. Second, the emphasis in child psychology more usually (although not necessarily) tends to be on the characteristic behavior and conscious processes of different age levels of children as ends in themselves rather than on the nature and regulation of the intervening changes. In this sense, a particular aspect of the child (i.e., the psychological) in contradistinction to its developmental history in childhood serves as the primary focus of concern and the distinctive feature of the specialty. In short, child development may be considered that branch of developmental anatomy, physiology, psychology, etc., dealing with the early phases of the life cycle, whereas child psychology deals with only one aspect of the child and not necessarily in terms of a developmental approach. As a field the latter is more comparable to pediatrics and child psychiatry.

Age Periods in Child Development. For purposes of convenience it has been found worthwhile to divide human development into the four age periods of childhood, adolescence, maturity and senescence. This classification, of course, is somewhat arbitrary, but can be rationalized on the grounds of the relative homogeneity of both biosocial status and of the rate of change characterizing development at each of these stages. On the basis of the same criteria, child development in turn may be subdivided into the following six age periods: *prenatal*, from conception to birth; *neonatal*, the first two to four weeks of life; *infancy*, the remainder of the first two years; *preschool*, ages two to six; *middle childhood* or primary school, ages six to nine; and *preadolescence*, age nine to the onset of adolescence.

Applications of Child Development

As a basic science, child development is concerned with the discovery of general laws in its area of special concern as an end in itself. Ultimately, of course, such laws have self-evident implications for the realization of certain practical goals which have social value, e.g., better understanding of individual children, more desirable methods of child rearing, the guidance and treatment of deviant children, and the improvement of education. However, because of widespread misunderstanding of the relationship between child development and these problems of *applied* science, much unwarranted and premature extrapolation of findings has taken place. It is necessary, therefore, to deal more explicitly with the limitations and hazards involved in applying such data and generalizations to the solution of problems for which they were not originally intended. Two separate issues involving different degrees of extrapolation require consideration here: (a) the utilization of child development generalizations for interpreting and predicting the development of the *individual* and evaluating his current behavior (This type of diagnostic and prognostic use is a necessary preliminary step in child rearing, guidance and therapy.); and (b) the application of knowledge from child development research in devising efficacious educational and guidance procedures for individuals or groups.

Interpreting and Predicting Individual Development. Many generalizations in child development are statements of uniformities and differences and of relationships between variables that apply to a designated universe of individuals. They are directly applicable to the understanding of the development of individual members of the universe for which they hold in the sense that prediction from one variable to another (e.g., from antecedents to consequences or vice versa) is possible within a certain margin of error. However, because we almost always deal with multiple causality in as complex a field as child development, predictions for individuals must be made from multiple regression equations. Thus, for example, assuming that the respective degrees of relationship between a majority of significant causal factors and the occurrence of a given outcome were established, it would be possible to predict, with a fair degree of accuracy, the probability with which the event in question would occur in a particular individual, providing that the specific values of these factors in the latter were known. This type of prediction, of course, is implicit in the original statement of relationship. Extrapolation is not required unless generalizations are invoked involving variables and relationships that are only indirectly related to the problem of development for which individual predictions are sought.

Unfortunately, however, the limiting conditions inherent in this modest statement of applicability are frequently ignored. Child development specialists are often embarrassed and dismayed when credited with omniscience by persons who seek precise developmental diagnoses and prognoses of children's behavior deviations on the basis of very inadequate data. At least five common misunderstandings are involved in this practice. First, it is seldom realized that more than one variable contributes to the condition under discussion; hence, no information is furnished about many other significant factors. Second, even if such data are available, reliable assessment of the status of all relevant variables in the particular individual is necessary before diagnosis or prognosis can be attempted. This implies first-hand evaluation by a trained person rather than casual judgment based upon hearsay evidence of unknown reliability by a presumed expert who may very well lack experience in the specific problem. Third, it is not fully appreciated that because child development is primarily concerned with general growth trends, most research findings are only highly tangential to many practical problems and developmental deviations in individuals. Thus, greater caution than is customarily employed is indicated if unwarranted extrapolation is to be avoided. Fourth, generalizations are not infrequently applied to individuals who cannot even remotely be considered members of the universe for whom they are valid. Lastly, many uncritical enthusiasts tend to accept diagnoses and prognoses as absolute pronouncements of fact rather than as the conditional statements of probability which they really are.

In addition to generalized statements of relationships, *normative* findings in child development are also directly applicable to the understanding of the individual child. In evaluating his *current* behavior, it is imperative that we first place it in its appropriate developmental setting, i.e., assess it in terms of the maturational standards and range of variability that prevail for children passing through the comparable period of development. Otherwise, gross distortions in interpretation are inevitable. However, this procedure obviously does not provide in itself a complete explanation of a given sequence of individual behavior. Other necessary information includes the unique personality attributes of the individual as well as significant characteristics of the immediate situation and of the wider cultural setting.

Relationship to Child Rearing, Guidance and Education. Somewhat more indirect than the application of child development research to the understanding of individual development and behavior, is its application to the *manipulative* aspects of child rearing, guidance and education. Developmental generalizations are obviously germane to the aims and methods of these applied sciences. In a very general sense, for example, they indicate the effects of different interpersonal and social climates on personality development and the kinds of methods and subject matter content that are most compatible with capacity and mode of functioning at a given stage of growth. But at the applied level, specific ends and conditions are added which demand *additional* research before such basic science generalizations become explicitly useful in practical situations. Thus, for example, the principle of developmental readiness in learning is of little practical value to the teacher unless rendered more specific in terms of different backgrounds, subject matters, levels of difficulty, and techniques of instruction.

On the more positive side, however, it can be stated that although child development findings do not ordinarily provide explicit answers to specific problems in these applied disciplines, they are extremely useful in other more indirect ways. First, as already indicated, they contribute to the evaluation of the individual child's behavior and development—a necessary precondition for employing rational child rearing, guidance and educational measures on an individual basis. Second, they constitute part of the basic theoretical background required for intelligent professional work in the above applied disciplines. Third, they provide a general theoretical orientation for devising research hypotheses and interpreting empirical data in the applied fields which ultimately raises the level at which such research can be performed.

Reasons for Studying Child Development

By way of summary the following reasons may be offered for studying child development:

First and foremost, an understanding of the nature and regulation of developmental processses in children based upon a critical interpretation of the empirical evidence is regarded as an important end in itself, quite apart from its applicability to practical problems. Such knowledge certainly holds as much intrinsic interest for most persons as do other developmental sciences (e.g., embryology, biological evolution) which are generally pursued without regard for their immediate utility in everyday life.

Second, provided that certain precautions are observed (see p. 19), generalizations in child development are applicable to the understanding and prediction of the development of particular children.

Third, normative child development findings make possible the evaluation of an individual's current behavior in terms of the maturational standards and of the distinctive developmental tasks and problems of his age group.

Lastly, by virtue of the previous two reasons, and because it provides a general theoretical orientation for professional and research workers in related applied fields, child development may be considered one of the basic sciences for such disciplines as child guidance, child psychiatry, pediatrics and education. Thorough grounding in the scientific literature of child development presumably fosters a cautious and critical attitude toward transitory fads in child care and promotes the search for sound and rational procedures in the management of practical problems. And because of developmental continuity, knowledge of child development is obviously valuable for educators, psychologists, psychiatrists, social workers and others whose professional concern is with adolescents and adults.

REFERENCES

1. Anderson, J. E: Methods of child psychology. *In* L. Carmichael, Ed., *Manual of Child Psychology*, ed. 2. New York, Wiley, 1954, pp. 1-59.
2. Barker, R. G.: Child psychology. In *Annual Review of Psychology*. Stanford University Press, 1951, pp. 1-22.
3. ———, and Wright, H. F.: *Midwest and Its Children*. Evanston, Ill., Row, Peterson, 1955.
4. ———, ———, and Koppe, W. A.: The psychological ecology of a small town. *In* W. Dennis, Ed., *Readings in Child Psychology*. New York, Prentice-Hall, 1951, pp. 552-566.
5. Dennis, W., Ed.: *Current Trends in Psychological Theory*. Pittsburgh, University of Pittsburgh Press, 1951, (Developmental theories, pp. 1-20).
6. Freud, S.: *The Problem of Anxiety*. New York, Norton, 1936.
7. Harris, D. B.: Why an interdisciplinary society for research in child development. *Child Development 24*: 249-255, 1953.
8. Jersild, A. T.: *Child Psychology*, ed. 4. New York, Prentice-Hall, 1954.
9. ———: Child psychology in the United States. *Teachers Col. Rec. 50*: 114-127, 1948.
10. Keller, F. S.: Animals and children. *Child Development 21*: 7-12, 1950.
11. Kinsey, A. C., et al.: *Sexual Behavior in the Human Male*. Philadelphia, Saunders, 1948.
12. ———, et al.: *Sexual Behavior in the Human Female*. Philadelphia, Saunders, 1953.
13. Lewin, K.: *A Dynamic Theory of Personality*. New York, McGraw-Hill, 1935.
14. ———: Behavior and development as a function of the total situation. *In* L. Carmichael, Ed., *Manual of Child Psychology*, ed. 2. New York, Wiley, 1954, pp. 918-970.
15. Rank, O.: *The Trauma of Birth*. New York, Harcourt, Brace, 1929.
16. Spitz, R. A.: Relevancy of direct infant observation. *Psychoanal. Stud. Child 5*: 66-73, 1950.
17. Watson, J. B.: *Psychology from the Standpoint of a Behaviorist*. Philadelphia, Lippincott, 1919.
18. Wright, H. F., Barker, R. G., et al. *Methods in Psychological Ecology: A Progress Report*. Topeka, Kansas, Ray's Printing Service, 1950.

CHAPTER 2

Historical Overview of
Theoretical Trends

BOTH ON HISTORICAL grounds and for purposes of convenience, the major theoretical issues in child development may be divided into two main categories: (a) issues dealing with the *control* and *regulation* of development, and (b) issues dealing with all of the other (i.e., *nonregulatory*) properties of the developmental process. The *first* category is concerned with the factors that determine development, their interaction and relative influence. Of paramount importance here is the regulation of developmental uniformities and differences prevailing between individuals exposed to similar and dissimilar cultural settings, and the respective contributions of heredity and environment to different developmental acquisitions. Subsumed under this general issue are such problems as the theory of recapitulation, the nature of maturation, the origin of drives, similarities and differences between animal and human endowment, and the meaning of human nature and cultural relativism. The *second* general class of theoretical issues, on the other hand, is concerned with such problems as continuity and discontinuity in growth sequences, individual differences in rate and patterns of growth, the maintenance of developmental individuality, reversibility and irreversibility in development, the organization of behavior, characteristics of transitional periods in development, parallelism and unevenness in the component aspects of growth, developmental regression, etc.

Both categories of issues will be discussed in every chapter of the book in relation to personality and various special aspects of development. But as already described elsewhere (see p. xi), for purposes of providing an integrated substrate for a general theory of child development, an overview of the regulatory issues will be presented in Chapter 3 and of other developmental principles in Chapter 4. The present chapter will be devoted to a brief historical survey of various trends and currents of thought dealing with the nature of the child and the control of development. It is primarily intended as a conceptual introduction to the more detailed discussion in Chapter 3.

The regulation of human development is still very much of a live and highly controversial issue. The nature-nurture controversy as such has abated somewhat in the sense that the two factors are now seldom regarded as

22

mutually exclusive or as operative on an either-or basis; interaction between them in determining the direction of growth is widely accepted in many quarters. Nevertheless much disagreement still persists, regarding their relative influence with respect to particular aspects of development, and very little is known about the mechanisms through which such interaction is mediated. Furthermore, the same basic issue of the regulation of development turns up in relation to many other theoretical problems in which it is often only dimly perceived as being relevant, e.g., the doctrines of maturation and recapitulation, psychoanalytic theories of personality, hypotheses regarding the nature of drives, various conceptions of cultural relativism, etc. For these reasons, therefore, more explicit consideration of the historical roots of and relationships between different ideological trends bearing on this issue may prove rewarding.

PREFORMATIONIST APPROACHES

Historical analysis shows that an interactional point of view regarding the role of internal and external determinants of development is of relatively recent origin. Over the past few centuries, and even in our own time, the theories of development that have wielded most influence have either stressed (a) an environmentally oriented *tabula rasa* approach or (b) a preformationist or predeterministic approach emphasizing the contributions of endogenous and innate factors.

The fundamental thesis of preformationism is a denial of the essential occurrence and importance of development in human ontogeny. The basic properties and behavioral capacities of man—his personality, values and motives, his perceptual, cognitive, emotional and social reaction tendencies—are not conceived as undergoing qualitative differentiation and transformation over the life span, but are presumed to exist preformed at birth. Nothing need develop as a result of the interaction between a largely undifferentiated organism with certain stipulated predispositions and his particular environment. Instead everything is already prestructured, and either undergoes limited quantitative modification with increasing age or merely unfolds sequentially on a prearranged schedule.

The origins of preformationist thinking are not difficult to trace. On the one hand, it is obviously related to theological conceptions of man's instantaneous creation and to the widespread belief in the innateness of the individual's personality and sense of unique identity as a person. A quaint pre-scientific embryological counterpart of this point of view is the formerly popular homuncular theory of human reproduction and prenatal gestation. It was seriously believed that a miniature but fully-formed little man (i.e., an homunculus) was embodied in the sperm, and when implanted in the uterus simply grew in bulk, without any differentiation of tissues or organs, until full-term fetal size was attained at the end of nine months.

On the other hand, the disposition to perceive the infant or child as a miniature adult is largely an outgrowth of the ubiquitous tendency toward extrapolation or anthropomorphism in interpreting phenomena remote from own experience or familiar explanatory models. What is easier than to explain the behavior of others in terms of one's own response potentialities? In order to extend this orientation to the interpretation of the child's behavior, it was necessary, of course, to endow him with the basic attributes of adult motivation, perceptual maturity and reaction capacities. Modern and extreme expressions of this tendency include such widely accepted psychoanalytic views that the prototype of all later anxiety lies in the psychological trauma of birth, [8, 26] that infantile and adult sexuality are qualitatively equivalent,[7] and that infants are presumably sensitive to the subtlest shadings of parental attitudes.

The theological variety of preformationism, allied as it was to a conception of man as innately sinful, inspired a rigid, authoritarian and pessimistic approach to education. Since ultimate form was assumed to be prestructed and complete in all of its essential aspects, one could at best only improve slightly on what the individual already was or was fated to become. Hence, it was unnecessary to consider the child's developmental needs and status, the conditions propitious for development at a given stage of maturity, or readiness for particular experience. Because he was not perceived as qualitatively different from the adult or as making any significant contribution to his own development, the arbitrary imposition of adult standards was regarded as self-evidently defensible.

Innate Ideas

Philosophically, in the realm of cognition, preformationism was represented by the doctrine of innate ideas, i.e., ideas existing independently of individual experience.* Vigorously combatted, by John Locke (1632-1704) and other empiricists, this notion consistently waned in influence and all but disappeared from view until revived and made popular by psychoanalytic theorists. Jung,[19] for example, postulated the existence in the "racial unconscious" of such inborn ideas as eternality, omnipotence, reincarnation, male and female, mother and father. And Freud's analagous "phylogenetic unconscious"[7] included—as the basis for resolving the Oedipus complex—an inherited indentification with the like-sexed parent prior to any opportunity for actual interpersonal experience.

*The content and validity of this and other historically important concepts will be considered more fully elsewhere in this chapter and in Chapter 3. Here we are only concerned with gaining historical perspective.

Human Instincts

On a behavioral level, preformationist doctrines have flourished in various theories of instincts and innate drives. Influenced by studies of inframammalian behavior and by the early nativistic implications of Mendelian genetics, psychologists, represented by such notable figures as McDougall[22] and Thorndike,[32] devised elaborate lists of human instincts, e.g., mating, maternal, acquisitive, pugnacious, gregarious. These were conceived as unlearned, complexly patterned, sequentially organized responses, perfectly executed on initial performance, that either unfolded in due course or were triggered off by appropriate environmental cues. But undermined by the rising tide of behaviorism in the 1920's, by demonstrations of numerous forms of conditioned responses, and by research findings in infrahuman primate development, ethnology, and sociology which pointed to the acquired, experiential basis of such behavior, this variety of instinct theory as applied to human behavior has long since passed into oblivion.

Primary and Libidinal Drives

Doctrines deeply rooted in cultural tradition do not die easily. Rejected in one guise, they subsequently gain reacceptance in other more palatable forms. Thus, instinctual theories reappeared respectively in stimulus or viscerogenic constructs of "primary drives" and in psychoanalytic conceptions of libidinal drives. The former notion, which was more compatible with the prevailing behavioristic and biologically oriented climate of psychological opinion, assumed the existence of a certain irreducible number of states of physiological disequilibrium which supposedly constituted in themselves the innate, energizing basis of motivated behavior. These states (i.e., primary drives) were, by definition, conceived as innate and inevitable since their operation was simply a function of the presence of persistent visceral or humoral stimuli within the organism or of intense external stimuli (e.g., pain) to which the organism invariably responded in predetermined ways.

Libidinal drives, in contrast, were conceptualized as innate, substantive sources of energy virtually independent of internal or external stimulation. Because the uninhibited expression of such drives seemed to engender a conflict of interest between biologically related needs of the individual and the mores of his culture, and because their sequential appearance was couched in terms of psychosexual "development," this point of view was more congruent than other instinct theories with the theoretical leanings of the more dynamically oriented psychiatrists, clinical psychologists and social anthropologists. Actually, however, no more development was envisaged than in any other orthodox, preformationist concept of instinct, for the energizing aspect of the libidinal drives, their locus, mode, and object of expression, and the sequential order of their appearance were all prestructured in advance; and although the emergence of later-appearing drives necessarily had to be latent at first, their eventual unfolding was assured without any intervening process of transformation or interaction with individual experience. Thus, despite their differences with respect to the source and nature of the fundamental drives, both "primary" and libidinal drive theorists agreed that the energizing basis of human behavior was innate and inevitable. Furthermore, both groups tended to regard the preformed drives as original and all other drives as derived from them through the various mechanisms of conditioning, symbolic equivalence, and sublimation. In other words, the environment was not conceived as capable of independently generating drives but only as repressing, modifying, differentiating and re-channeling innate drives.

Freud and his followers also derived the other two layers of personality, the ego and superego (i.e., conscience), from the libidinal instincts as they came into contact with a repressive reality and had to adapt to its demands. Similarly, character traits were conceptualized as symbolical derivatives of fixated libido at one of the stages of infantile psychosexual development following inordinate experiences of frustration or gratification. In all of these latter instances, it is true, preformationist concepts as such were not employed. Environment vicissitudes were granted a share in the developmental process, but only in the sense of modifying or accentuating a preformed product rather than of participating crucially in the directional regulation of new patterns.

PREDETERMINISTIC APPROACHES

In contradistinction to preformationism, predeterministic doctrines satisfy the minimal criteria for a developmental approach. Successive stages of the organism are not merely regarded as reflective of a sequential unfolding of preformed structures or functions forever fixed at conception or birth, but as the outcome of a process of qualitative differentiation or evolution of form. Nevertheless, because the regulation of development is conceived as so prepotently determined by internal factors, the net effect is much the same as if preformationism were assumed. Interaction with the environment and the latter's influence on the course of development is not completely ruled out; but its directional role is so sharply curtailed that it never crucially affects eventual outcome, accounting at the very most for certain minor limiting or patterning effects.

Hence, insofar as the essential and distinguishing features of development are concerned, theoretical violence is not perpetrated by referring to this approach as basically predeterministic. As will be pointed out later, the truly objectionable aspect of this point of view is its blanket or wholesale application to all aspects of development. In some cases it undoubtedly comes close to approximating the actual state of affairs (e.g., infantile locomotor and prehensile development), but in most other areas of human development it is recommended by neither evidence nor self-evident validity.

Rousseau and the Educational Philosophers

The first definitive predeterministic theory of child development was elaborated by the famous French philosopher, J. J. Rousseau (1712-1778). Rousseau postulated that all development consists of a series of internally regulated sequential stages which are transformed, one into the other, in conformity with a prearranged order and design.[28] According to this conception of development, the only proper role of the environment is avoidance of serious interference with the processes of self-regulation and spontaneous maturation. It facilitates development best not by imposing restrictions or setting coercive goals and standards, but by providing a maximally permissive field in which, unhampered by the limiting and distortive influences of external constraints, the predetermined outcomes of growth are optimally realized. Consistent with this orientation was Rousseau's belief that the child is innately good, that society constitutes the source of all evil, and that a return to a less inhibited and less socially restrictive method of child rearing would necessarily result in the unfolding of the individual's inherently wholesome and virtuous developmental proclivities.

The educational implications of these doctrines, which in essence were shared by such distinguished followers of Rousseau as Pestalozzi[25] (1746-1827) and Froebel[9] (1782-1852), were in marked contrast to those of the preformationists. Prominent recognition was given to the child's contributions to his own development, to his developmental needs and status, to his expressed interests and spontaneously undertaken activities, and to the importance of an unstructured, noncoercive instructional climate. This point of view has, of course, exercised tremendous influence on all subsequent educational theory and practice, and is essentially identical and, in a sense, historically continuous with present-day movements advocating a nondirective and child-centered approach to the training, education and guidance of children.

The Doctrine of Recapitulation: G. Stanley Hall

An especially fanciful but historically significant facet of Rousseau's (and later of Froebel's) conception of development was the theory that the child, in progressing through the various stages of his growth toward maturity, recapitulates the phylogenetic and cultural history of the human race. The analogy was only crudely drawn, but it served the purpose of providing a seemingly plausible explanation (a) for the hypothesized internal regulation of development, and (b) for the predetermined inevitability of its outcome in a direction which presumably paralleled the ascending spiral of cultural evolution. More than a century later, G. Stanley Hall (1846-1924) elaborated and refined this theory in great detail, postulating many ingenious and specific parallelisms between various hypothetical epochs in the history of civilization (e.g., arboreal, cave-dwelling, pastoral and agricultural) and supposedly analagous stages in the development of the behavior and play interests of the child.[15]

These speculations, which were advanced with great skill, comprehensiveness and internal consistency, acquired considerable vogue and many enthusiastic adherents. Their initial favorable reception was attributable, perhaps, to the fact that they were in accord with the prevailing evolutionary approach to cultural anthropology, and superficially, at least, seemed congruous with certain broad generalizations linking embryology and biological evolution. They were also bolstered by the prevalent beliefs that the thought processes of the civilized child are comparable to those of a stereotyped "primitive" adult (the "primitive mind" fallacy) and that the cultures of contemporary primitive peoples are analogous to the early stages of more advanced civilizations. Later, following more searching examination in the light of emerging data in comparative child development, and of changing concepts regarding the complex interrelationships between cultural environment, genic endowment and individual development, this theoretical orientation was no longer accepted as a parsimonious and potentially fruitful approach to problems in developmental psychology (see p. 35).

Arnold Gesell: Theory of Maturation[1]

With the collapse of Hall's elaborate theory of recapitulation, predeterministic theories of development received a serious setback, but they by no means disappeared from the scene. They simply assumed other forms more compatible with the prevailing theoretical climate. Perhaps the most influential and widely accepted of all present-day predeterministic approaches is Arnold Gesell's theory of maturation which reiterates Rousseau's emphasis upon the internal control of development, but discards the specific parallelisms between cultural history and individual development which made Hall's position so vulnerable to attack.

Gesell's theory also capitalized on its general resemblance to the empirically demonstrable concept of maturation which had gained considerable acceptance among behavior scientists, educators and the lay public. Actually, the latter concept dealt with the non-learning (as distinguished from the learning) contributions to enhancement in capacity, rather than with the more general issue of the relative importance of internal and external regulatory factors in development irrespective of the role of learning. Operationally it merely referred to increments in functional capacity attributable to structural growth, physiological change or the cumulative impact of incidental experience, in contradistinction to increments attributable to specific practice experience (i.e., learning). Gesell, however, used the term *maturation* in a very special and more global sense to represent the endogenous regulatory mechanisms responsible for determining the essential direction of *all* development, including that conditioned in part by learning and enculturation.

In essence, Gesell proposed an embryological model for all aspects of human growth—structural, physiological, behavioral and psychological—which "are obedient to identical laws of developmental morphology."[12] In *all* of these areas alike, a growth matrix consisting of endogenous factors supposedly determines the basic direction of differentiation and patterning, whereas "environmental factors [merely] support, inflect and modify, but . . . do not generate the progressions of development."[12] These intrinsic regulatory factors correspond to "ancestral genes" which in general reflect the evolutionary adaptive achievements of the race, but neither refer to specific epochs in cultural history nor condition the development of analagous ontogenetic phases.[11]

Because phylogenetic genes by definition have a species-wide distribution and are unusually potent in their effects, Gesell theorized that developmental sequences are relatively invariable in all areas of growth, evolve more or less spontaneously and inevitably, and show basic uniformities even in strikingly different cultural settings. Like Hall before him, he taught that certain undesirable stages in behavioral development were inevitable by virtue of the child's phylogenetic inheritance, and could be handled best by allowing them spontaneously to run their natural course without interference. Since comparable endogenous factors assured the eventual unfolding of more acceptable behavior, permissiveness and patience on the part of the parents, and self-regulation and self-discipline on the part of the child could be confidently relied upon to correct the situation. The application of parental expectations, demands, limitations and controls was not only regarded as unnecessary but also as calculated to increase negativism and to impair the parent-child relationship.[13]

This embryological model is basically tenable when applied to the development of structures, functions and behaviors which are phylogenetic in nature, i.e., which characterize all individuals of a given species. It would apply quite well to the total development of members of lower phyla, to the prenatal behavioral development of human beings and to much of the sensori-motor growth that occurs during human infancy. But as far as the greater part of postnatal psychological development in the human species is concerned, unique factors of individual experience and cultural environment make important contributions to the direction, patterning and sequential order of all developmental changes. Not only is there significantly greater variability in the content and sequence of development, but also the uniformities that do occur (both intra- and interculturally) largely reflect the existence of common problems of physical and social adaptation and common culturally derived solutions to these problems.

Supporting Biological Trends

Related biological trends influenced and bolstered predeterministic concepts of child development in at least two important ways. First, they helped create a general climate of scientific opinion which affected the acceptability of the latter theories. Second, various biological concepts suggested, modified or reinforced the specific content of predeterministic theories. That these supportive effects and conceptual resemblances were often based on popular misconceptions, outdated formulations, and even on basically irreconcilable contradictions with allegedly analogous biological models does not in the least minimize the historical fact or importance of their occurrence. The three fields of biology that exercised most influence on predeterministic theories of child development were evolutionary theory, embryology, and genetics—concerned respectively with the origin of species, prenatal development and the mechanisms of inheritance. In more recent years, advances in these fields have belatedly influenced a trend toward a more interactional approach to human development.

Biological Evolution. In 1859, Charles Darwin proposed the revolutionary theory that biological evolution was a consequence of gradual and cumulative developmental changes in species resulting from the selective survival and transmission of small inherited variations that furnished adaptive advantages in relation to prevailing environmental conditions. The environment, he believed, could not directly induce structural, functional or behavioral changes in the organism that were transmissible to its offspring*;

*According to J. B. Lamarck (1744-1829) and his followers, "acquired characters" *were* transmissible to offspring. This doctrine however is in conflict with modern genetic theory which holds that ordinary, environmentally-wrought changes in the phenotype are not accompanied by corresponding changes in the genotype. Although there is "no proof that Lamarckian inheritance is impossible . . . no incontrovertible evidence in favor of it has been brought forward."[4] Weismann's famous experiments (1889), which have been widely accepted as conclusively disproving Lamarck's hypothesis, actually did not adequately test it. The acquired traits, which were hypothesized by Lamarck as inheritable, were conceived as products of prolonged exposure or adaptive exercise over many generations, and could hardly be equated with such artificial, instantaneous insults as Weismann's snipping off of several generations of animals' tails.

it merely played a role in the determination of which of a number of naturally occurring variations was most adaptive and, hence, selectively favored for representation in future generations by virtue of a differential rate of survival and ultimate self-perpetuation. The impetus for and the regulatory mechanisms of organic evolution, resided, therefore, in existing and spontaneously occurring variability ascribable to hereditary endogenous factors rather than to environmental factors.

Applied to the development of human behavior, this latter principle was frequently misinterpreted in ways that supported the predeterministic position. It was not fully appreciated that although the environment could not directly induce changes that were transmissible to offspring and, hence, could not initiate phylogenetic differentiation (i.e., the development of new species), it could still influence ontogeny (i.e., developmental sequences in the life cycle of individual members of a species). Thus, the Darwinian position was frequently misrepresented to mean what was never intended, namely, that environmental factors were also incapable of exercising a direct effect on ontogenesis. Unfortunately this misinterpretation was reinforced and rendered more credible by the fact that it was not too far afield in relation to lower organisms with a more or less stereotyped pattern of adaptive behavior in response to environmental vicissitudes. Here individual experience *is* actually not much more crucial for the ontogeny than for the phylogeny of behavior. However in higher species, particularly in man, adaptation is characteristically a function of a learned and flexible organization of behavior modified by individual and cultural experience. Thus, the predeterministic tendency to discount the impact of experience on human ontogeny was seriously tainted with error and distortion. The preformationists, starting from the same position, denied behavioral development altogether, equating man's socially learned behavior in Western civilization with a catalogue of king-sized inframammalian instincts.

Embryology. Early knowledge of embryology also reinforced predeterministic doctrines by pointing to more or less invariable sequences of development regulated predominantly by endogenous factors. Even when slightly qualified by later research showing that gestational environment was not entirely inconsequential for the outcome of development, the embryological model as such, when projected into postnatal life, still proved highly inapplicable to most problems of human development. In the first place it dealt almost exclusively with developmental acquisitions that characterized the species as a whole. Second, it was concerned with development in a relatively constant physiological environment largely insulated from external stimulation. It was, therefore, an analogy heavily loaded in favor of predeterministic conceptions, thereby confirming the bias of theorists who, like Gesell, minimized the contribution of individual experience to ontogeny.

Actually these latter considerations interpreted in the light of numerous findings in experimental embryology should have led to precisely the opposite conclusions. All of the research of the past forty years indicates (a) that marked and even less extreme variations in the intrauterine environment such as rubella or advanced age of the mother are associated with developmental abnormalities in the fetus[5]; and (b) that structural growth and functional development of embryonic neural tissue are affected by many factors in the internal fetal and intrauterine environments. Much experimental work[3, 23] points to the conclusion that structural differentiation and the sequential development of function in different portions of the nervous system are influenced in part by differential concentrations of biocatalysts, by quantitative levels of various metabolites and hormones in the fetal blood stream, by mechanical and other external stimulation communicated to the child in utero, and by the presence and functioning of adjacent tissues. This last-mentioned effect has been variously explained in terms of regional differences in metabolic activity (gradients), the organizing potential of certain embryonic cells in promoting tissue differentiation (organizers), and the operation of electrodynamic fields induced by biological activity.

We may conclude, therefore, that the internal (intrafetal and gestational) environment plays an important contributory role in embryological development, and that the preservation of its constancy is important for uniformity of developmental outcome—even with respect to species characteristics. If this is so, it would be reasonable to expect that the directional influence of the environment on the development of intra-species *differences* would be infinitely greater once the individual were exposed to the tremendously wide spectrum of extrauterine variability in stimulation.

Genetics. The rediscovery of Mendel's laws in 1900 and the early subsequent work of geneticists had tremendous repercussions on theories of human development. The demonstration of a physical basis for heredity in the form of relatively stable, self-reproducing, discrete genes, which were resistant to ordinary environmental influences and which seemingly exercised an inevitable, unconditional, and one-to-one effect on the determination of specific traits, naturally favored prevailing predeterministic conceptions regarding the development of human behavior. And, of course, quite apart from this latter influence, the new science of genetics provided an urgently needed model for explaining the mechanisms underlying (a) *phylogenetic* inheritance as manifested in both biological evolution and in the embryological development of the individual, and (b) the *familial inheritance* operative in numerous studies of animal breeding, of the recurrent incidence of various "hereditary" diseases in certain human families, and of trait relationships between individuals differing in degree of consanguinity.

Later research in genetics showed that the model of single major genes with gross effects on variability, completely and invariably influencing the development of specific traits, was greatly over-simplified. It was convincingly demonstrated that "the phenotoype of an organism is not a mere mosaic of independently expressed single-gene effects . . . [but] depends on developmental interactions involving the entire aggregate of genic material."[5] Thus it is now known that the effects of many single genes are modified by other genes, and that most normal (and less extreme pathological) genic variability in human beings is produced by constellations of polygenes. The latter exert "individually minute but cumulatively appreciable [and] . . . quantitatively equivalent effects" resulting in continuous rather than in conspicuously discontinuous distributions of phenotypic variability."[5]

More important perhaps was the undermining of the older genetic view supporting the established belief (mistakenly derived from Darwinian theory and from exaggerated instinct approaches to animal behavior) that the environment does not appreciably influence ontogeny. Modern genetics fully supports the proposition that "the phenotype is always the resultant of the interaction between a certain genotype and a certain environment."[2] This, of course, does not mean that environmental factors ordinarily alter genes but that they alter the expression of genes.[2] The effect of genes on the development and patterning of morphological traits is frequently contingent upon the presence of a restricted range of such environmental conditions as moisture, temperature and diet; in other cases environmental influences are similarly operative only within a restricted range of genotypes; and sometimes the effects of heredity and environment on development are more nearly independent, additive, or complementary. Finally, "the effects of certain genes appear to be expressed with great uniformity within any range of environmental conditions"[5]; and, conversely, the effects of certain environmental conditions are manifested in practically all genotypes.

According to modern conceptions of genetics, therefore, the influence of genes on development is never complete or absolute, but always reflects to a variable extent the influence of the intracellular, intercellular, gestational or external environments. The phenotypic consequences of genic action are presently conceived of in such terms as probabilities of determination, degrees of regularity and completeness of expression, and limiting and threshold values of response and attainment. As will be pointed out later, this shift in theoretical orientation played an important role in resolving dichotomous views of the nature-nurture controversy and in generating an interactional approach to problems of human development. Nevertheless, exaggerated notions of the simplicity, specificity, prepotency and inevitability of genic effects continued to flourish and influence pre-deterministic formulations. For example, over-enthusiastic supporters of the latter point of view uncritically accepted much fragmentary and un-reliable evidence from pedigree studies which purported to show that an amazing variety of feeble-mindedness, mental disease, social delinquency, moral waywardness and personality inadequacy was exclusively or pre-dominantly the effect of genes inherited from a single and remote defec-tive ancestor.*[14]

The ultimate in emphasis upon the pre-eminent importance of genic factors in human development is embodied in the eugenics movement. Its program is predicated on the belief that the soundest and surest method for improving the lot of mankind lies in upgrading the genic endowment of large populations through the rigorous application of principles of se-lective and restrictive mating. However, even if men and women could be induced to choose their mates on the basis of eugenic considerations, it would still require vastly greater knowledge about the mechanisms of human genetics and evolution than is presently available before such a program could be successfully inaugurated. Furthermore, from the study of cultural history it is clearly evident that profound changes in the behavior of human beings and in the quality of their civilization can be effected by social, economic, technological, scientific and educational advances within several generations. On the other hand, comparable examination of human evolution indicates that significant changes in the genic basis of human behavior and capacity could only be expected over time periods measur-ing tens or hundreds of thousands of years. Negative eugenics, i.e., the re-duction and elimination of physical and psychological abnormalities by sterilizing the grossly unfit, is unfortunately not much more realistically grounded. Most of the more common and less extreme human defects that have an appreciable hereditary component are polygenically deter-mined; and the relatively few and uncommon defects that are attributable to the effects of single genes are extremely rare "recessives" the incidence of which would not be significantly altered by sterilization.

Relationships between Biological Evolution and Embryology. The exist-ence of many obvious parallels between biological evolution and embryo-logical development inevitably led to much speculation about how these two phenomena are related. As a result many biological and biocultural

*In reaching these conclusions little attention was paid to such obvious considera-tions as the representativeness of the sample, comparisons with a control population, the accuracy and equivalence of diagnoses made over an extended time span, the reliability of heresay evidence, and the influence of substandard family and social conditions which invariably accompany and compound such conditions.

concepts of recapitulation were elaborated, varying greatly in degree of empirical substantiation and theoretical credibility. The biological theory of recapitulation embodied in Ernst Haeckel's (1834-1919) famous proposition that ontogeny recapitulates phylogeny was predicated upon certain gross sequential parallelisms in morphogenesis between the biological evolution of a species in geologic time and the embryological development of its members. This proposition is compatible with the fact that biological evolution is characterized by both continuity and modification; that is, in addition to well-marked lines of divergence, there is also much structural and functional continuity between a given species and its evolutionary forbears. Genically speaking, therefore, it could be anticipated that each species would inherit and transmit genes reflecting such commonalities and divergences, and, hence, that its members would tend to recapitulate in their early ontogeny the course of its descent from earlier forms of animal life.

That such parallelisms are not exact and do not embody *all* previous stages is not at all surprising. In the first place, the line of descent typically zig-zags instead of following a directly vertical course. Second, considering the difference in the relative time scales involved in each process and the undoubted influence of the more recent genic material on older morphogenic sequences, considerable telescoping and modification of ontogenetic phases could reasonably be expected to occur.

However, *biogenetic* theories of recapitulation (e.g., Rousseau's, G. Stanley Hall's), although superficially resembling Haeckel's proposition, were actually an entirely different breed of cat. The analogy was extended to include the *cultural* history of the race and the *postembryological behavioral* development of the individual. We have already noted that the latter kind of development (in contrast to embryological morphogenesis) is both less insulated from environmental influence and is characterized more by intraspecies differences in ontogenesis resulting from unique individual experience. In addition, these theories are not substantiated by any convincing evidence, and are based on the untenable assumptions (a) that cultures universally undergo a parallel sequence of evolutionary changes, and (b) that such cultural acquisitions are genically transmissible, and hence universally recapitulated.

On both empirical and theoretical grounds, the once fashionable notion of universal stages of cultural evolution is now thoroughly discredited.[31] Some gross developmental sequences may conceivably be parallel in different cultures because of "recurrent causal relationships in independent cultural traditions."[31] For example, the evolution of certain levels of social organization may almost universally be dependent upon the prior attainment of supporting levels of technology.[31] However, apart from such limited parallels, and in the absence of significant cultural diffusion, the cumulative impact of differences in geography, climate, history, values, institutions, etc., typically leads to progressively greater divergence in the development of cultural forms. We must conclude, therefore, that all human beings, regardless of cultural membership, hold their biological descent in common and undergo the same embryological development but by no means share a cultural history which reflects the operation of substantially identical processes of social evolution.

But even if cultures everywhere did undergo the same evolutionary process, what effect would this have on the genic constitution of man? It will be remembered from the preceding discussion (se p. 30) that ordinarily only spontaneous, genically induced structural or behavioral variability is inheritable, and that the main contribution of the environment to phylogeny is its role in natural selection. Although environmental factors influence profoundly the development of the human individual during his lifetime,* the changes they induce do not effect his genes and, hence, are only culturally rather than genically transmissible to his offspring. It is clearly evident, therefore, that the genetic assumptions of biocultural recapitulation are incompatible with modern conceptions of biology.

Thus, despite the vast changes that have occurred in man's behavior and cultural level since the emergence of Homo sapiens a quarter to half a million years ago,

> it is hardly probable either on theoretic grounds or on the basis of inferences from human history and archaeology that the biologic basis of human abilities or behavioral potentialities has appreciably changed during this period.[5]

And it is even more certain that all contemporaneous groupings of human beings—irrespective of past cultural history—share the same genic potentialities for psychological and cultural development.

In a very limited and quite different sense of the term, concepts of psychocultural recapitulation might hold promise of manifesting somewhat greater face validity. If, for example, we conceive of a trend toward increased use of symbols and abstractions as characteristic of cultural development, it would appear that at later stages in the history of most cultures, the intellectual development of the individual would tend to be extended beyond the point which generally prevailed when the ideational level of the cul-

*It may be noted that predeterministic theorists tended to reject the quite modest proposition that the environment significantly influences human ontogeny. Yet, paradoxically enough, they accepted the primacy of certain internal regulatory factors, the very existence of which presupposed the validity of the much more extreme environmentalistic position that cultural experience directly influences phylogeny by affecting the genotype.

ture was lower. In a sense, therefore, the historically later-born individual might be said to be "recapitulating" the intellectual development of his culture as he gradually grows in intellectual capacity. However, parallel development would occur in this instance not because certain cultural sequences were written into his genes and merely needed to unfold, but (a) because a trend from concrete to symbolic ideation happens to characterize the course of intellectual development in both individual and culture, and (b) because the limits of individual growth are dependent in part upon the level of cultural achievement.

Thus, the greater attained intellectual capacity of individuals in more highly advanced civilizations would not be indicative of cultural alteration of genotypic endowment, but of the greater phenotypic achievement that is possible with a constant genotype under conditions of enriched cultural stimulation. Its occurrence would in no sense be inevitable but would be dependent upon actual ontogenetic exposure to the necessary experience. Hence, if twentieth century American children were artificially insulated from all ideational stimulation, their prospects for advanced intellectual development would hardly be brighter than those of prehistoric men.

"TABULA RASA" APPROACHES

In marked contrast to the preformationist and predeterministic doctrines we have been discussing are such movements as humanism, behaviorism, "situational determinism" and certain varieties of cultural relativism. If we consider the former approaches as constituting one extreme of a continuum embracing the various theories concerned with the regulation of human development, the latter ideological movements would have to be placed at the other extreme of the same continuum. They are referred to as *tabula rasa* (literally, "blank slate") approaches because they minimize the contributions of genic endowment and of directional factors coming from within the individual, and concomitantly emphasize the pre-eminent role of the environment in determining the outcome of development.* The analogy which likens the neonate to a *tabula rasa* is aptly representative of their general thesis that no fundamental predispositions are inherent in

*We have already referred to Lamarckianism as an example of the extreme environmentalist position in biology since it is based on the assumption that the genotype as well as the phenotype can be altered by prolonged exposure to certain environmental conditions. However, the most basic feature of the *tabula rasa* approach is its emphasis on the plasticity of human beings (i.e., the absence of significant or enduring predispositions) rather than on the importance of environmental determinants of development. Certain more recent *tabula rasa* orientations, e.g., client-centered therapy, stress the notion of plasticity, but assign the main directional control of significant personality change to self-directed cognitive and motivational processes.

the raw material from which behavior and personality develop, and that human beings are infinitely malleable. All of the patterning, differentiation, integration, and elaboration of specific and general behavioral content that emerges during the course of development is accounted for in terms of the unique stimulus conditions to which the individual is or has been subjected.

It should be noted, however, that the term *tabula rasa* is being used here in a very general sense, and only to denote such extreme environmentalist positions as described above. In the more specific sense of the term, as employed by John Locke, the "blank slate" only referred to the *ideational* state of affairs at birth and not to the *complete* absence of developmental predispositions; as a matter of fact in his discourses on education he placed much emphasis on the need for restraining the natural impulses of children. Furthermore, in the light of modern conceptions of cognitive and behavioral development, neither Locke's *tabula rasa* proposition nor more recent dissatisfaction with the notion of human instincts could be regarded as indicative of an extreme position with respect to the nature-nurture controversy. Hence, although theories of innate ideas, instincts and instinctual drives must be categorized as essentially preformationist in orientation, disavowal of these constructs does not necessarily constitute a *tabula rasa* approach to human development.

Humanism and Related Approaches

The humanistic movement in philosophy and education has consistently championed the environmentalist position that given proper conditions of nurturance, man's developmental potentialities are virtually unlimited in scope or direction. Implicit in this optimistic appraisal is (a) the belief that "human nature" is essentially amorphous and can be molded to whatever specifications man chooses to adopt as most compatible with his self-chosen destiny, and (b) unbounded confidence in the possibility of attaining this objective through appropriate educational procedures.

Of course, the humanistic conviction that man can deliberately select and take steps to insure the realization of whatever goals he chooses and, hence, is the master of his own fate, would be a perfectly defensible proposition *if* it were related to and qualified by the actual psychological capacities of human beings. More often than not, however, it is merely stated as an unqualified philosophical desideratum. This is especially detrimental to its acceptability since it is becoming increasingly more evident that the extent of developmental plasticity is no longer a question which can be settled by speculative fiat. Furthermore, it is extremely unlikely that one blanket generalization could ever suffice to cover all aspects of development. In the modern era this issue is more properly regarded as a matter for empirical determination. And regardless of the ultimate outcome of particularized research inquiry, any realistic statement of human objectives and potentialities should presently be formulated within the framework of the limitations imposed by man's genic endowment as currently conceived in the light of all relevant data.

Although predicated upon quite different theoretical premises, the humanistic program of education was strikingly similar in spirit and content to the preformationist (theological) approach already described above (see p. 24). Despite the fact that one school viewed the infant as a formless entity wholly at the mercy of his environment and the other conceived of him as essentially prestructured in advance, both were in agreement (a) that the individual himself contributes little to his own development, (b) that the child in essence is a miniature adult, and (c) that improvement of man's nature could be best effected through the imposition of a stern and rigorous regimen of training and education. Preformationists reached this conclusion by both denying that any significant developmental changes occur in the first place, and by conceding that some quantitative improvement of prestructured attributes could result if superimposed from without by proper authority. Humanists, on the other hand, arrived at the same position more directly by attributing all developmental changes in an originally amorphous creature to the all-important influence of environmental factors, and by conceiving of such changes as occurring in quantitative steps rather than by qualitative stages.

Typically, therefore, the humanistic approach to education was rigidly academic, traditional and authoritarian. Severe and arbitrary standards were imposed and strictly enforced by the application of physical punishment and other extrinsic motivational devices. If necessary, rationality and classical erudition were literally pounded into the resistive or reluctant individual. Age level differences in capacity and in developmental needs and status were largely ignored and little or no attention was paid to individual differences in ability or temperament. Humanistic educators did not seriously attempt to enlist the child's voluntary participation, encourage his spontaneity or appeal to endogenous motivation. The contribution of ongoing personality to behavior and cognitive development was regarded as inconsequential, and the learner was granted no directive role or responsibility in the educative process.

Behaviorism shared many of the environmentalist biases of humanism but conceptualized them in more psychological terms. Consistent with its *tabula rasa* emphasis upon behavioral plasticity was its denial of subjective experience (except as a form of subliminal behavior), its rejection of all developmental predispositions (except for reflexes and certain emotional responses) and its conception of the human organism as a noncognitive response mechanism subservient to the control of conditioned stimuli.[33] Similarly in the area of child care and education, its advocacy of impersonal handling, strictness, regularity, and the importance of habit training was strikingly reminiscent of humanistic practices.[34]

However, it need not be thought that a *tabula rasa* conception of human nature is necessarily or inevitably associated with a concomitant emphasis upon the pre-eminence of environmental determinants of development. The currently flourishing school of client-centered therapy,[27] for example, combines a clinical estimate of extreme human plasticity with an emphasis upon endogenously derived needs, goals, insights, responsibility, initiative for change, etc., in a maximally, permissive and nonauthoritarian therapeutic environment. As long as this relationship between endogenous and exogenous influences prevails, the possibilities for reorganizing personality on a more wholesome and constructive basis are held to be virtually unlimited, irrespective of existing personality structure or previous developmental history.

This point of view is obviously very close to the educational position of those predeterminist theorists (e.g., Rousseau, Hall, Gesell) who stressed the importance of permissiveness and self-direction in child rearing. Its principal point of departure from the older approach is that it conceives of these latter conditions as essential for the active *self-creation* of a personality with almost limitless possibilities for self-realization (or for the therapeutic reconstruction of an environmentally distorted personality) rather than for the optimal unfolding of a developmentally prestructured personality. However, we must reiterate again that the plasticity of the human personality and its responsiveness to reorganization are not issues that can be resolved by doctrinal assertion, but are matters for explicit empirical determination. And although self-direction is undoubtedly important for many aspects of both therapeutically facilitated and more normative sequences of development, there is little reason to believe that directional influences originating in the environment are unnecessary, unimportant or typically detrimental.

Cultural and Situational Determinism

The growth of empirical cultural anthropology during the first four decades of this century led to the formulation of a more explicit environmentalist position in conjunction with the conception of infinite human plasticity. Studies of modal behavior, socialization and enculturation in different primitive cultures impressed ethnologists with the remarkable homogeneity of these phenomena within cultures, with their tremendous diversity from one culture to another, and with the apparent absence of intercultural uniformities. The almost inevitable outcome of such conclusions was the emergence of a concept of cultural determinism, i.e., the notion that the human being is "well-nigh an empty vase into which culture and social prescriptions are poured,"[29] and that his behavior and personality development, therefore, are simply a function of the particular sociocultural stimuli which impinge on him. The personality-culture and the individual-society dichotomies were thus "resolved" by the simple expedient of virtually abolishing the categories of individual and personality.*

As long as intracultural differences in behavior were ignored, there was no pressing need to acknowledge the contributions of enduring response tendencies, selective perceptual sensitivities, and differential thresholds of reactivity established by the interaction between the individual's unique genotype and experiential history; and likewise, as long as cross-cultural similarities in development were disregarded, it seemed quite unnecessary to search for those panhuman regularities (of genic, physiological, psychological or interpersonal origin) that serve to limit and channel the impact of cultural influences on the human growth matrix along ontogenetic lines that are roughly parallel in terms of process from one culture to another.

Fortunately, expressions of this extreme *tabula rasa* version of cultural determinism are less commonly heard today. Most athropologists, although still not greatly impressed by intercultural uniformities, have become much

*We have already referred to social instinct theories which resolved the same dichotomies in opposite fashion by deriving culture and society from the preformed patterned behavior of individuals. Spiro[30] is representative of a new trend in social science theory which seeks to reduce *both* personality and culture to a unique configuration of cumulatively learned individual behavior in an interpersonal setting; hence, according to this view "there are as many cultures as there are personalities." This reductionism is based on the propositions that the *locus* of culture resides in the behavior of its individual members, that the acquisition of culture can only be conceived as a learning (internalization) process occurring in *particular* individuals, and that individuals typically modify their cultural heritage. However, one can accept all three propositions as valid without necessarily reaching the conclusion that personality and culture are one and the same thing. Although "culture" as such is an abstraction derived from a non-homogenous totality of individual behaviors, their interactions and products (and can obviously enjoy no existence independently of the persons who comprise, internalize, influence and are influenced by it), it still is a conceptually (if not functionally) independent phenomenon external to personality. The consensuses, commonalities and uniformities to which it refers are *real* (e.g., actual shared values, beliefs, social customs), distinguishable from those of other cultures, and are sufficiently stable to be studied as if existing in their own right.[18] They affect and are acquired by the individual as a result of influencing and being internalized by the particular cultural representatives (e.g., parents, teachers, peers) with whom he interacts in the course of his enculturation.

more cognizant of the importance of intracultural differences. However, the battle line they abandoned is still vigorously manned by various sociologists and sociologically oriented social psychologists who explain *all* such differences on the basis of subcultural membership or situational variables, and steadfastly deny the existence of stable, enduring antecedent predispositions to behavior or development. The situational *determinism* they advocate shifts the locus of personality structure from an organized system of underlying behavioral predispositions ("under the skin") to a series of behavioral *acts* manifested under specified socio-situational conditions. Whatever needs or motives are required to initiate or sustain behavior are derived intracurrently from the situation itself. Personality, as the more extreme of these theorists conceive it, is not a continuing, self-consistent structure exhibiting generality over situations, but a transitory configuration of individual behavior that is purely a function of the particular social stimulus conditions which evoke it.

This view of personality is rationalized on the grounds that since an individual's behavior does in fact vary *every time* the situational context is altered, it must therefore be determined by the latter variable *alone*. It is hardly necessary to point out however, that the demonstration of behavioral change associated with variability in one factor does not necessarily preclude the possibility that other variables are simultaneously operative. In fact, by simply reversing the picture, i.e., keeping the situation constant and varying the individuals exposed to it, one could just as easily emerge with the equally one-sided conclusion that only personality factors determine behavioral change. However, when a number of persons are studied in a diversity of situations, it becomes quite evident that both factors contribute to the obtained variability in behavior. This is shown by the fact that intercorrelations among behavioral measures in different situations are neither zero nor unity but somewhere in between, and that they tend to become higher when either the situations themselves or the subjects' degree of ego-involvement in them are made comparable (see pp. 102, 157, 309).

The situational approach to personality not only strips it of any explanatory implications, but also renders futile any search for the genotypic bases of behavior. If personality has neither stability nor generality, there is certainly little point in considering the possible effects it might have on behavior, and even less point in attempting to trace the course of its development. And similarly, if overt behavior cannot possibly be related to underlying predispositions in personality structure, behavioral taxonomy must be based entirely on phenotypic similarities and differences irrespective of their genotypic reference (see p. 12).

It might also be noted at this point that in practice (if not theoretically) nondirective schools of therapy tend to support the situational concept of personality. Although they do not explicitly deny the influence of antecedent response tendencies on ongoing behavior, they minimize their importance (a) by regarding them as almost invariably reversible, (b) by considering the discovery of their developmental origins as irrelevant for therapy, and (c) by placing major emphasis on the current adjustive situation.

Cultural Relativism

Viewed in historical perspective, cultural relativism must undoubtedly be reckoned the outstanding component and moving force behind the concept of cultural determinism discussed above. However, for purposes of conceptual clarity, it would be desirable for several reasons to consider the former movement separately. First, cultural determinists need only assume that the behavior of human beings is both plastic and crucially influenced by cultural factors; they need *not* accept the relativistic position that it is *completely unique* in every culture. In fact, if significant parallels of custom and tradition are demonstrable from one culture to another, to be perfectly consistent with the logic of cultural determinism one would have to postulate a corresponding parallelism in the area of behavior and personality development. Second, cultural relativism has been associated historically with an empirical, field study approach to ethnology and with a non-evolutionary, non-individualistic interpretation of cultural change* that are by no means indigenous to the position of cultural determinism. Third, because of these historical associations cultural relativism has come to represent an extreme point of view with respect to such issues as the plasticity, cultural uniqueness, intracultural homogeneity and intercultural heterogeneity of behavior, that is not necessarily inherent even in a relativistic position. Thus, many theorists who would readily agree that behavior and development are relative to and determined by the cultural environment in many important respects still hold views on these latter issues

*Since we are only concerned here with individual development, this issue naturally lies outside the scope of our inquiry. However, it is important to point out that the methodological approach of the relativists, which emphasized the empirical study of *behavior* in particular cultures (as opposed to the logical analysis of cultural institutions and products in relation to a universal concept of cultural evolution) predisposed them toward a conception of uniqueness in considering the impact of culture on behavior and personality.[30] Their non-evolutionary view of cultural change similarly predisposed them in this direction; but since similarity in cultural development is only one of many factors affecting cross-cultural uniformities in personality, the two positions (the anti-evolutionary and the relativistic) are not necessarily co-extensive.

that are much less extreme than is implied in a more doctrinaire statement of cultural relativism.

Cultural relativism, of course, provided a much needed corrective against the ethnocentric social instinct and biogenetic doctrines that flourished during the same and preceding decades. It rejected the notion that complex social behavior is ever innately patterned by virtue of universal instincts, or that intra- and intercultural uniformities ever reflect the operation of an identical species-wide genotype with prepotent and invariable directional influence on the content and sequence of development. In accounting for behavioral regularities within a culture, it pointed to the obvious importance of considering commonalities in social conditioning; but in explaining cross-cultural similarities, it advanced the less convincing hypothesis of cultural diffusion. Most important, however, by demonstrating that the cultural patterning of innumerable aspects of behavior and development is characterized by an extremely wide range of variability, it completely demolished the ethnocentric preformationist view that distinguishing features of personality structure in Western civilization are manifestations of an immutable "human nature" and hence must be universally distributed. Instead it advanced the thesis that the unique values, traditions, institutions and historical development of each culture gives rise to a distinctive personality type. In so doing it established the beginnings of the now flourishing research area concerned with empirical investigation of the personality-culture problem.

Of course, even cultural relativists could not assume complete behavioral plasticity. Certain limitations imposed by man's species membership and by his biological and psychological needs, capacities, and mechanisms were recognized as constraining the impact of culture on behavior. But within the framework of these highly general limits, all patterning, differentiation and selectivity in behavioral development was considered a function of cultural variables. Thus, for example culture was conceived as determining the kinds of stimuli evoking a particular emotion and the manner in which it is expressed, and as selecting through differential rewards and punishments which potential capacities and personality traits of man are either emphasized or neglected in a particular cultural setting.

Relationship to Psychoanalytic Theory. To a very great extent the full impact of cultural relativism on conceptions of personality development was blunted by the considerable influence exerted by psychoanalytically oriented ethnologists and by psychoanalytic theorists concerned with the problem of the individual in society. The partial fusion of these two currents of thought (i.e., psychoanalysis and cultural relativism) probably reflected the prevailing absence of a satisfactory body of competing psychological theory in the area of personality as well as some dissatisfaction with the extremeness of the relativistic view. In any event it occurred despite the presence of the following serious conceptual incompatibilities between the two positions*: First, psychoanalysis reintroduced the anthropologically suspect doctrine of instinct in the somewhat more palatable form of patterned psychosexual drives, and established the latter as the new basis of intercultural uniformities. Nevertheless, this conception of drives as innately prestructured and biogenetically transmitted entities was in direct conflict with the relativistic principle that all significant and detailed psychological patterning is determined by unique factors of cultural conditioning; and projected universally as it was from an unrepresentative sample of neurotic individuals in our own society, it naturally ran afoul of the rigorous relativistic strictures directed against ethnocentrism. Second, the psychoanalytic view of society as basically frustrating was incompatible with the proposition implicit in any form of cultural determinism that the social order not only provides the means of gratifying the individual's biologically instigated drives but is also capable of independently generating in its own right highly significant drives of interpersonal origin. Lastly, the psychoanalytic school explained intercultural differences in personality structure almost exclusively on the basis of differential parental practices influencing the course of psychosexual development. Cultural relativists, on the other hand, have necessarily taken a much broader view of the potential range of interpersonal and sociocultural factors in a given society that are significant for personality development, and have recognized that aspects of personality structure other than erogenous impulses are subject to societal influence.

IMPLICATIONS OF HISTORICAL TRENDS FOR MODERN CONCEPTIONS OF DEVELOPMENT

We can summarize most helpfully the implications of the foregoing historical trends for modern conceptions of developmental regulation by indicating briefly in what general ways both predeterministic and *tabula rasa* approaches to human development are theoretically untenable. These considerations will point up the desirability of adopting the emerging interactional approach that will be presented in Chapter 3. Since the main issue here is the extent of behavioral plasticity, we may properly subsume preformationist views under the predeterministic category.

*Basic incompatibilities in viewpoint with respect to the development of cultural institutions are not pertinent to the present discussion. In general, however, Freudian interpretations of cultural forms and practices as institutionalized mechanisms of repressing or symbolically expressing psychosexual drives have not won as much acceptance from ethnologists as have psychoanalytic formulations regarding the influence of culture on personality development.

Summary Critique of Predeterministic Approaches

1. Except for simple responses of a reflex nature, there is little substantial basis in either logic or empirical data for the belief that *any* psychological aspect of human functioning is preformed at birth, *completely* independent of subsequent enviromental experience. Even the initial, unpatterned psychological repercussions of intense visceral and hormonal stimuli (i.e., drive states) are influenced by the effects of prior experience and by concurrent internal and external stimulation; and under extremely unfavorable social auspices, it sometimes happens that certain "primary" drives (e.g., sex) may *never* be generated, regardless of the adequacy of gonadal output (see p. 226). Where complex patterning is involved, the possibility of prestructured psychological entities is, of course, still less credible. But although the existence of human instincts is no longer taken seriously by most behavior scientists, the quite comparable notion that patterned affectional-sex drives exist preformed in a biogenetically inherited id has won much acceptance in many quarters.

The most anachronistic of all present-day preformationist thinking is exemplified in the psychoanalytic theory of innate ideas (e.g., cosmic identification, reincarnation, omnipotence) lodged in a phylogenetic unconscious. Supporters of this doctrine point to the widespread occurrence of these themes in the mythologies of historically unrelated cultures and in the ideational outpourings of deeply regressed psychotics. The first phenomenon, however, is more parsimoniously explained by the independent cultural generation of common ideological solutions to such universal problems as death and supernatural control of the environment, and the second by regression to an earlier ontogenetic stage of ego development (see pp. 284-287).

2. Equally unsubstantiated is the embryological model of psychological development which is not predicated upon preformationism, but asserts nevertheless that developmental sequences and outcomes are basically predetermined and inevitable because of the prepotent influence of internal (genic) directional factors. Actually this conception only holds true for the relatively few and simple behavioral acquisitions which in terms of specificity of content and sequential appearance characterize every member of the human species (e.g., locomotion). For all other behavioral traits, the contribution of unique environmental conditions to developmental regulation is considerably greater; and, hence, both the kinds of growth changes that take place and the sequence in which they occur are more variable by far. It is quite erroneous, therefore, (a) to underestimate the impact of culture and individual experience on almost any psychologically significant aspect of human development; (b) to minimize the extent and

significance of culturally conditioned diversity in individual development; and (c) to overlook cultural commonalities operative in the life histories of individuals, and attribute all observed developmental uniformities both within and between cultures solely to the influence of similar genic factors.

Biogenetic theories of recapitulation hypothesizing specific parallelisms between successive stages in the psychological development of the individual and various inferred stages in the cultural evolution of mankind are insupportable on both empirical and theoretical grounds. They rest on the discredited assumptions that cultures everywhere evolve in parallel sequence and that the cultural acquisitions of a people are genically transmissible to their offspring.

Summary Critique of "Tabula Rasa" Approaches

1. Not content with having successfully cast doubt on the validity of preformationist and predeterministic doctrines, *tabula rasa* theorists unfortunately veered to the opposite extreme and asserted that human behavior is infinitely plastic and malleable to environmental influences. Although they were probably correct in assuming that *some* aspects of behavior (e.g., social roles and attitudes) are almost entirely determined by cultural variables, they stood on palpably less solid ground in refusing to recognize that other facets of psychological development are patterned in many significant ways by various selective predispositions, limitations, capacities and potentialities arising from within the individual. Because these internal factors (which either directly or indirectly have a genic basis) do not characteristically exercise solitary, highly specific and invariable effects on the content and sequence of development, *tabula rasa* theorists fallaciously concluded that they do not even operate as partial or general determinants.

2. Hence, for example, extreme cultural relativists and situational determinists failed to appreciate (a) that many intracultural differences in behavioral development are conditional by genotypic diversity as well as by subcultural, familial and individual differences in background experience; and (b) that numerous intercultural uniformities in psychological development are undoubtedly determined in part by various aspects of man's genic endowment which both relate him to and differentiate him from other species.* Thus, the unique ontogeny of human beings is more than a reflection of their uniqueness in being the only species in nature whose development happens to be systematically molded by a culture. It is also a reflection of the fact that they are the only species *genically capable* of responding

*See p. 65 for a listing of both genic and environmental factors contributing to intercultural uniformities in development.

to cultural stimuli in ways that characterize the development of a cultural organism. No amount of cultural stimulation could possibly make chimpanzees develop like human beings.

3. In addition to overlooking the genic basis of intercultural uniformities in behavioral development, cultural relativists also failed to appreciate that many of these uniformities (e.g., general stages in personality development) are induced by numerous "common denominators" in culture itself. The latter in turn are derived from universal features in man's physical and interpersonal environment and from his adaptations thereto, as well as from panhuman biological and psychological characteristics.[21, 24]

4. As will be pointed out in later chapters, many cultural relativists (under the influence of psychoanalytic and stimulus theories of drive), paradoxically relapsed into some of the most serious errors they berated in their adversaries. For example, in assuming that sex drives are either preformed or inevitably generated by gonadal hormones, they surprisingly underestimated the characteristic plasticity of human beings in responding to factors that induce and pattern drive states (see p. 226). And in defining a basic human capacity such as guilt in terms of the particular conditions under which it arises and the specific forms it adopted in our own culture, they reached the surprising ethnocentric conclusion that individuals in most other cultures exhibit shame rather than guilt (see p. 403).

REFERENCES

1. Ausubel, D. P.: *Theory and Problems of Adolescent Development.* New York, Grune and Stratton, 1954.
2. Boyd, W. C.: *Genetics and the Races of Man.* Boston, Little, Brown, 1953.
3. Carmichael, L.: The onset and early development of behavior. *In* L. Carmichael, Ed., *Manual of Child Psychology.* New York, Wiley, 1954, pp. 60-185.
4. Carter, G. S.: The theory of evolution and the evolution of man. *In* A. L. Kroeber, Ed., *Anthropology Today.* Chicago, University of Chicago Press, 1953, pp. 327-342.
5. David, P. R., and Snyder, L. H.: Genetic variability and human behavior. *In* J. H. Rohrer and M. Sherif, Eds., *Social Psychology at the Crossroads.* New York, Harper, 1951, pp. 53-82.
6. Dennis, W., Ed.: *Current Trends in Psychological Theory.* Pittsburgh, University of Pittsburgh Press, 1951 (Developmental theories, pp. 1-20).
7. Freud, S.: *The Ego and the Id.* London, Hogarth Press, 1935.
8. ——: *The Problem of Anxiety.* New York, Norton, 1936.
9. Froebel, F.: *The Education of Man.* New York, Appleton, 1896.
10. Fuller, J. L.: *Nature and Nurture: A Modern Synthesis.* New York, Doubleday, 1954.
11. Gesell, A.: Maturation and the patterning of behavior. *In* C. Murchison, Ed., *A Handbook of Child Psychology,* ed. 2, rev. Worcester, Mass., Clark University Press, 1933, pp. 209-235.

12. ——: The ontogenesis of infant behavior. *In* L. Carmichael, Ed., *Manual of Child Psychology*, ed. 2. New York, Wiley, 1954, pp. 335-373.

13. ——, and Ilg, F. L.: *Infant and Child in the Culture of Today*. New York, Harper, 1943.

14. Goddard, H. H.: *The Kallikak Family*. New York, Macmillan, 1912.

15. Hall, G. S.: *Adolescence*. New York, Appleton, 1904, 2 vols.

16. Hallowell, A. I.: Culture, personality, and society. *In* A. L. Kroeber, Ed., *Anthropology Today*. Chicago, University of Chicago Press, 1953, pp. 597-620.

17. Harlow, H. F.: Levels of integration along the phylogenetic scale: learning aspect. *In* J. H. Rohrer and M. Sherif, Eds., *Social Psychology at the Crossroads*. New York, Harper, 1951, pp. 121-144.

18. Herskovits, M.: *Man and His Works*. New York, Knopf, 1948.

19. Jung, C. G.: *Contributions to Analytical Psychology*. New York, Harcourt, Brace, 1928.

20. Kardiner, A.: The concept of basic personality structure as an operational tool in the social sciences. *In* R. Linton, Ed., *The Science of Man in the World Crisis*. New York, Columbia University Press, 1945, pp. 107-122.

21. Kluckhohn, C.: Universal categories of culture. *In* A. L. Kroeber, Ed., *Anthropology Today*. Chicago, University of Chicago Press, 1953, pp. 507-524.

22. McDougall, W.: *An Introduction to Social Psychology*. Boston, Luce, 1914.

23. McGraw, M. B.: Maturation of behavior. *In* L. Carmichael, Ed., *Manual of Child Psychology*. New York, Wiley, 1946, pp. 332-369.

24. Murdock, G. P.: The common denominator of cultures. *In* R. Linton, Ed., *The Science of Man in the World Crisis*. New York, Columbia University Press, 1945, pp. 123-142.

25. Pestalozzi, J. H.: *Leonard and Gertrude*. Boston, D. C. Heath, 1895.

26. Rank, O.: *The Trauma of Birth*. New York, Harcourt, Brace, 1929.

27. Rogers, C. R.: *Client-centered Therapy*. New York, Houghton Mifflin, 1951.

28. Rousseau, J. J.: *Emile*. New York, Appleton, 1895.

29. Sherif, M.: Introduction. *In* J. H. Rohrer and M. Sherif, Eds., *Social Psychology at the Crossroads*. New York, Harper, 1951.

30. Spiro, M. E.: Culture and personality: the natural history of a false dichotomy. *Psychiatry 14*: 19-56, 1951.

31. Steward, J. H.: Evolution and process. *In* A. L. Kroeber, Ed., *Anthropology Today*. Chicago, University of Chicago Press, 1953, pp. 313-326.

32. Thorndike, E. L.: *Educational Psychology*, vol. 1. *The Original Nature of Man*. New York, Teachers College, Columbia University, 1919.

33. Watson, J. B.: *Psychology from the Standpoint of a Behaviorist*. Philadelphia, Lippincott, 1919.

34. Watson, J. B.: *Psychological Care of Infant and Child*. New York, Norton, 1928.

CHAPTER 3

The Regulation of Development: Interaction Between Heredity and Environment

THE NATURE-NURTURE CONTROVERSY is much less acrimonious today than a consideration of the historical trends in Chapter 2 would indicate. As a result of research and theoretical progress in the fields of embryology (see p. 32), genetics (see p. 33), intellectual growth (see pp. 597-607) and social anthropology, current formulations of the respective roles of heredity and environment in development are couched in less dichotomous and more interactional terms. Nevertheless, as long as the interactional position is restricted to a general statement of bipolar determination, the hub of the controversy merely shifts from "all-or-none" propositions to conflicting estimates of over-all relative importance. *The pseudo-issue underlying the controversy can only be eliminated by specifying in more precise and detailed fashion how the interaction takes place and the relative weight of each factor in determining the course and outcome of particular kinds of development.* When this approach is adopted, the irrelevancy of dichotomous or overall estimates becomes apparent, and we are left with a genuine scientific problem which can be formulated in terms of theoretical postulates that are both meaningful and empirically testable.

In the present chapter, therefore, we shall attempt an interactional interpretation of the problem of developmental regulation that deals more explicitly with the directional influence, mode of operation, and relative weight of both genic predispositions and environmental conditions. We shall first consider these regulatory factors systematically and relate them to the similarities and differences in developmental sequence to which they give rise. Then, reversing the procedure, we shall survey intercultural uniformities, intracultural regularities, and intracultural differences, and try to identify their determinants. Lastly, we shall conclude the chapter with a discussion of two issues traditionally associated with the heredity-environment problem, namely, maturation and the neutral correlates of development.

INTERACTIONAL BASIS OF DEVELOPMENTAL REGULATION

In studying the development of children, the concepts of heredity and

50

environment are no more than convenient abstractions or categories of variables that only theoretically can be disentangled from each other. What we actually observe as development takes place is change in a given direction when certain internal or external influences impinge on an individual with existing properties and predispositions. The latter already represent the resultants of innumerable prior interactions between hereditary and environmental factors. What was once originally environmental or outside the inherited genic material is now inextricably bound up with it as the organism's contribution to the course of development.

In the first portion of the present section, therefore, we shall examine this interdependency between heredity and environment which renders them phenomologically inseparable and guarantees the bipolar determination of all developmental processes. At a purely abstract level of analysis, however, it is legitimate to inquire about the "relative contribution of variation in genes and variation in life history to variation" in developmental outcome[20]; and we shall, immediately afterwards, turn our attention to this aspect of the problem.

Bipolar Determination of Development

Human development is always a product of continuous interaction between various stimulating factors and a prevailing growth matrix consisting of selective predispositions both to undergo change and respond to the environment in particular ways. This latter matrix naturally encompasses directional tendencies representing the total outcome of all preceding developmental history. It is synonymous with the genotype of the individual only at the moment of conception. Thereafter, it itself, as well as the developmental progressions it generates, are always interactional products.

Genotype, Phenotype, Growth Matrix and Constitution. The "genotype" of the individual refers to his genic endowment or to the totality of all his inherited elements. It consists of the potentialities inherent in the 24 chromosomes inherited from each of his parents and represented in every somatic cell of his body. Barring exposure to such atypical stimulation as massive doses of x-rays, the genotype remains intact, throughout the life span of the individual. At any given point during this period, and especially during the prenatal and early postnatal phases of development, it constitutes a major determinant of the growth matrix. But although it itself remains unchanged, the directional influence it contributes to the growth matrix is naturally modified in varying degrees from the very beginning of the organism's existence. Strictly speaking, therefore, the predispositions established by genes are never absolute or inevitable in their effects on development; their actualization is always a function both of their relative strength and of various environmental considerations. Thus, regardless of whether final phenotypic outcome closely approximates or is far removed from genic endowment, it can never be said that genes determine traits and capacities, but only that they determine the potentialities for developing traits and capacities.

It is not always apparent that the impact of the genotype on development is operative over the entire life history of the individual. In many cases, of course, the consequences of its influence are overtly observable at birth and in the developmental sequences that progressively follow. In other cases, however, the initial products of genic determination are either years in the making (e.g., gonadal maturation) or cannot be manifested until a certain level of development is already achieved. Thus, for example, considerable time must elapse from birth before any but the grossest kinds of genically conditioned temperamental traits became evident in personality structure.

The "phenotype" on the other hand, is a "description of the organism in terms of its observable qualities."[20] "The phenotype is always the resultant of the interaction between a certain genotype and a certain environment."[5] Although the latter cannot alter the properties of genes, it not only limits and modifies their expression but also independently initiates many directional trends of its own.

> The end result depends upon both factors . . . The genotype determines [in part] the reaction of the organism to its environment, but does not determine the external environment . . . Different genotypes may react in some environments to produce similar phenotypes; therefore, similarity of phenotypes under identical environment is not always proof of identity in the genotypes. On the other hand, the same genotype may react differently in different environments and produce dissimilar phenotypes. So dissimilarity of phenotypes is not necessarily proof of dissimilarity of the genotypes.[5]

As already indicated, the "growth matrix," like the phenotype, is a product of all prior interactions between heredity and environment. It not only consists of "the immediately observable qualities of the organism" (i.e., the phenotype), but also of all covert factors within the individual which at any given time predispose the nature of his response to the environment and contribute to the current direction of his development. The products of the latter event, in turn, include new phenotype, new developmental predispositions and, hence, a new growth matrix.

The term "growth matrix" was introduced in this discussion because the special meaning to which it refers is conceptually distinct from that of both genotype and phenotype. The genotype is a stable, ordinarily unmodifiable structural entity which in an abstract sense is synonymous with all of the inherited potentialities of the organism; but the particular directional predispositions to which it contributes and which are *actually* operative at any given stage in the course of development are reflective of genotypic endowment *alone* only at the moment of conception. Thereafter, it is not pure genotypic tendencies which interact with current stimulating conditions to determine developmental outcome, but the former tendencies as modified by extragenic protoplasm, by other bodily tissues and agents, and by prior influences from gestational and external environments. The phenotype, which is an interactional product and describes the manifest appearance of the organism at a given point in its life cycle, comes closer than the genotype to indicating what is meant by the growth matrix; but it only includes overt properties of the individual entering into the interactional process, and makes no reference to the equally important *covert* developmental predispositions.

Within the framework of the particular developmental sequence in which it is operative, the growth matrix manifests the same regulatory properties as the hereditary and environmental factors that determine it. That is, it exerts limiting, directive (patterning), and selective influences on development. And its modifiability is similarly dependent upon its own resistance to change and upon the strength of the environmental variables with which it interacts.

In the entire field of genetics and development, there is no more confusing term than that of "constitution." It has been variously defined as synonymous with the genotypic endowment of the individual, with all of his phenotypic characteristics, with multifactorial protective elements in his genic organization that facilitate his adaptation to the environment and increase his resistance to disease,[45] and with his "basic physiological makeup . . . at a given time."[51] In the broadest sense of the term, however, its meaning is most adequately and consistently conveyed by the concept of growth matrix as delineated above.

Constitution, therefore, refers to the totality of the individual's relatively stable predispositions, at a given point in his life history, to respond in particular ways to environmental influences affecting his structural, functional, or behavioral development. By virtue of traditional usage, however, it is usually restricted to predispositions established by body type, by physiological characteristics (especially those related to metabolic, endocrinologic and autonomic functions), by genically conditioned aspects of temperament and susceptibility to different physical and mental disorders, and by the various interrelationships among these latter factors. It includes those aspects of personality with strong genic loading as well as response predispositions that are morphological, biochemical, immunological, etc., rather than behavioral or psychological in nature. Existing correlations between these different categories of constitutional variables have been explained on the basis of (a) "pleiotropic or linked genes," (b) genically regulated mediating mechanisms (autonomic nervous system, endocrines) with dual effects on psychological and bodily functions, and (c) experientially established reciprocal relationships between certain physical and temperamental traits such as muscular hypertrophy and enjoyment of motor activity (see p. 76).

Manipulation of Developmental Regulation. The problem of developmental regulation also has important practical implications. As our knowledge of the relevant determinants expands, it becomes increasingly possible to manipulate them in ways that are most conducive to optimal or desired outcomes. If we rule out eugenic procedures at the present time (see p. 34), attempts at manipulation must necessarily assume the existence of a constituted and fixed genotype. For this reason, only in relation to the environmental determinants of a given trait, can intervention be effected *directly* and with hope of achieving significant *positive* changes in patterning or level of functioning. It is only necessary in such cases—to the extent that is compatible with the plasticity of the trait and with the possibility of modifying the physical, interpersonal and social environments—to provide those environmental conditions that are correlated with optimal development* in the desired direction.

The above statement conflicts in no way with the previous description of genotypic predispositions as subject to modification. It must be realized, however, that when such modification occurs, it is effected indirectly by the operation of the environmental determinants of a given trait rather than directly by any change in its genic basis. Also, the environment can, at best, mitigate or circumvent the negative consequences of genotypic inadequacies. It cannot exert a more positive influence on development by generating *genic* predispositions that do not already exist as, for example, it can generate new exogenously derived predispositions. To counteract the effects of genic insufficiency, either optimal environmental conditions can be brought to bear on development, or phenotypic deficiencies can be compensated for nondevelopmentally by employing substitutive measures (e.g., supplying diabetics with the insulin they can't produce) or by surgical procedures.

Regulatory Functions of Heredity and Environment in Development. The respective roles of hereditary and environmental factors in the bipolar regulation of development may be summarized in the following listing of the ways in which each participates in the developmental process:

*What are optimal conditions for development will, of course, apply generally to only certain kinds of growth; for other types of growth these conditions will vary for different categories of individuals. Genic determinants of traits, on the other hand, cannot be influenced directly or in the same positive sense.

1. Genic factors set absolute *limits* of growth for both individual and species which cannot be exceeded in any environment, as well as determine capacity for profiting from environmental stimulation. Environmental factors similarly *limit* the extent to which existing genic potentiality can be realized in individuals or species. In a generally optimal environment, phenotypic actualization of the genotype is enhanced for everyone, and the prevailing range of variability is widened.

2. Both factors in varying degrees contribute to the *patterning* of traits, i.e., determining the direction, differentiation, content and sequence of development.

3. Genic variables make the individual *selectively* sensitive to or more prone to prefer certain aspects of the environment to others. Environmental variables, on the other hand, in accordance with cultural needs and values, differentially *select* from the total range of genic potentiality certain capacities and traits for maximal development and others for relative oblivion.

4. To a certain extent, the genically conditioned temperamental characteristics of an individual help determine his environment by differentially affecting the attitudes and reactions toward himself of significant persons in his interpersonal milieu.

Determination of Relative Influence

Now that we have defined the different interactional variables and products involved in the developmental process, we are ready to consider the relative contributions of hereditary and environmental factors. Our aim is to go beyond the indisputable but unilluminating generality that all development is the product of heredity *and* (rather than *or*) environment. Obviously, as abundant research data have already demonstrated, there is and can never be any over-all solution to the question of relative influence. The weight of each factor in the resulting phenotype is not only different for every conceivable trait, but also for every individual in a given population. However, if we wish to derive some meaningful generalizations from data bearing on such relationships, it will first be necessary to deal with the "average effects [of heredity and environment] upon individual differences", and to establish various quantitative classes of relative influence, i.e., categories of development regulated predominantly by either factor or by varying proportions of the two factors. The next step is to establish criteria for traits that may be placed in each of these categories and to relate them to different models of genic organization* and of heredity-environment interaction.

Before attempting these latter tasks, it will be helpful to note that in general the greater the relative influence of genic factors is upon the develop-

---

*The detailed properties, organization and effects of genes are obviously beyond the scope of this volume.[5, 9, 20, 89]

ment of a given trait the less variable it tends to be in its phenotypic expression. This inverse relationship between degree of genic regulation and extent of expressed variability is a function of two related factors. First, more potent genic effects are, by definition, more resistant to environmental influence than relatively less potent genic effects. Hence, the resulting phenotype tends to reflect mostly the impact of genic sources of variability in the former instance and of both genic and environmental sources in the latter instance. Second, traits referable to more prepotent, environmentally resistant genic effects generally illustrate the operation of single or major genes which genotypically exhibit very little variability and phenotypically are distributed in either uniform or dichotomous fashion among members of a species (e.g., almost all human beings have two eyes which tend to be blue or brown in color). On the other hand, traits referable to less prepotent and more environmentally susceptible genic effects are generally polygenic in nature (see p. 33) and, hence, are genotypically more variable from one individual to another (except in monozygotic twins), and phenotypically are continuously distributed (e.g., height, I.Q.). Thus, traits that are more heavily determined by hereditary factors tend to be less variable on two counts: they not only reflect less the influence of environmental variability but also are less variable in terms of their genic components.

It is true, of course, that traits predominantly influenced by environmental factors also only reflect a single source of variability. However, this solitary source of variability is usually greater than in the analagous situation of traits determined predominantly by heredity, since the latter traits tend to be expressions of single-gene effects. Nevertheless, although environmental diversity is more striking than genotypic diversity (even where polygenes are involved), it is quite obvious that there are uniformities as well as differences in the environments of individuals, and that all developmental uniformities cannot be ascribed to genic factors alone.

The Ontogenetic-Phylogenetic Continuum. The bottom row of figure 1 presents a classification of categories reflective of varying relative weights of heredity and environment (modified from Boyd[5]) arranged in the form of a continuum. At one end of the continuum are traits that are so prepotently determined by heredity that they appear almost invariably in any environment favorable enough to sustain life. At the other end of the continuum are traits that are analagously determined in prepotent fashion by the environment. In between are categories of traits the developmental direction of which is either (a) primarily determined by one factor, contingent upon certain restrictive conditions in the other, or (b) the additive or vectoral resultant of more nearly independent influences provided by both factors.

In relation to this continuum, a useful qualitative distinction can be drawn between two great classes of traits—phylogenetic and ontogenetic—under which can be placed the entire spectrum of phenotypic characteristics (morphological, physiological and behavioral) manifested by a given species. *Phylogenetic* traits are fundamental developmental acquisitions that are both characteristic of the species as a biologically distinct class of organisms and essentially independent of individual experience. Hence, they are essentially identical for all members of the species. *Ontogenetic* traits, on the other hand, are also present or potentially present in almost all members of the species, but differ from one individual to another in accordance with both genic and environmental sources of variability. They constitute the entire range of characteristics by which individual representatives of the species can be distinguished from each other in contradistinction to the fund of characteristics they share in common.

As illustrated in figure 1, phylogenetic traits tend to be homogeneously determined by single-gene effects that are highly resistant to environmental influence and, both genotypically and phenotypically, are practically identical for all individual members of a given species. Ontogenetic traits, on the other hand, are extremely heterogeneous with respect to the degree of their genic determination. They include (a) single-gene effects, only slightly susceptible to environmental influences, that are expressed with considerable regularity and completeness and result in dichotomous phenotypic distributions; (b) polygenic effects, moderately susceptible to environmental influences, that are irregularly and incompletely expressed and result phenotypically in relatively wide continuous distributions; and (c) traits almost completely determined by environmental factors.

The acquisition of phylogenetic traits by the individual is extremely important for the realization of "his racial inheritance."[23] In human beings, the vast majority of such traits develop during prenatal life and early infancy and include morphological, physiological and behavioral characteristics essential for viability or species membership. Behaviorally, they are for the most part restricted to reflex, sensory, sensori-motor, and neuromuscular acquisitions (e.g., tendon reflexes, vision, sitting, walking, vocalization). On the whole, these traits develop "autogenously," i.e., without the benefit of cultural tutelage;[15] and, barring unusual environmental pressures, they emerge at approximately the same age and in the same sequence in all sociocultural environments, thereby rendering the basic developmental features of infancy universal in spite of tremendous diversity in child-rearing practices.[15] Even a practice as severe as cradling, for example, does not materially delay the age of walking among Hopi infants,[11] and pronounced socioeconomic differences do not affect the acquisition of neuro-

GENIC MECHANISM	Identical single-gene effects	Dichotomous single-gene effects	Polygenic	Polygenic	Polygenic
SUSCEPTIBILITY OF GENOTYPE TO ENVIRONMENTAL INFLUENCE	Practically zero	Slight	Moderate	Great	Very great
PHENOTYPIC RANGE OF VARIABILITY	Practically zero	Dichotomous	Continuous with moderate range	Continuous with wide range	Continuous with very wide range
RELATIVE DETERMINATION OF PHENOTYPE	Genetic for almost any environment	(a) Genetic within a restricted range of environmental conditions	(b) Bipolar (additive or vectorial effects of heredity and environment)	(c) Environmental within a restricted range of genotypes	(d) Environmental for almost any genotype

PHYLOGENETIC TRAITS — ONTOGENETIC TRAITS

FIG. 1. Schematic representation of a hypothetical ontogenetic-phylogenetic continuum showing relative influence of heredity and environment on the development of a given trait.

muscular and sensori-motor capacities during the first 36 weeks of life.[26] On the other hand, marked cultural pressures and taboos may effect some changes in the sequential patterning of locomotor development. Balinese infants do not crawl in the course of learning to walk, and unlike American infants squat before they are able to stand.[66] Severe emotional deprivation, such as occurs in institutionalized infants, may also retard phylogenetic aspects of development.*[26, 88]

At either extreme of the ontogenetic-phylogenetic continuum, literal insistance on the bipolar determination of development is confusing, although, as the aforementioned examples indicate, some interaction always takes place. Throughout the greater range of the continuum, however, the bipolar determination of such ontogenetic traits as temperament and intelligence is clearly evident. Sometimes, nevertheless, when one determinant is not completely prepotent and the directional influence of the other is only minimal, the latter's contribution to development is overshadowed and tends to be disregarded entirely. Hence, the fact that a given trait is not universally distributed but appears to be determined by specific cultural factors does not definitively eliminate the possibility that relatively weak panhuman genic predispositions might be operative but overwhelmed by sociocultural variables. It is similarly easy to overlook the contribution of relatively noncrucial environmental factors when hereditary influences appear all-important. Thus, although cross-cultural universality of a behavioral trait, coupled with occurrence among infrahuman primates, is strong presumptive evidence of considerable genic determination, much of the uniformity may be a product of universally limited environmental or social possibilities.

Intra-species Uniformities, Differences and Limits of Variability. From the foregoing considerations, it is evident that the following sources of developmental *uniformity* exist within a species: First, all members of a species develop phylogenetic traits that are almost identical in sequence and detailed content because of the operation of prepotent identical genes. Second, uniformities with respect to *general* process and sequence of development arise as a result of commonalities in polygenic make-up. Superimposed on these uniformities, however, are genically conditioned individual differences in rate of growth, ultimate level of attainment, and detailed content and sequence of development. Lastly, commonalities in environmental conditioning give rise to comparable kinds of process and sequence uniformities in the development of ontogenetic traits. It is extremely im-

*These instances of slight variability in the patterning of "phylogenetic" behavioral traits suggest that they may be determined by relatively potent polygenic effects rather than by single-gene effects.

portant to note at this point that because phylogenetic traits pertaining to behavioral aspects of development are relatively rare in human beings beyond the first year of life, few developmental generalizations about the behavior of children could ever be formulated if these latter two sources of uniformities did not exist. We would, otherwise, have to regard development in each individual as practically unique and as a law unto itself.

Intra-species *differences* in phenotypic outcome are similarly attributable to both hereditary and environmental factors. Differences of genic origin are either dichotomously distributed in the case of single-gene effects or continuously distributed in the case of polygenic effects. Environmentally conditioned differences, in turn, reflect variation in familial and cultural setting as well as in the idiosyncratic experience of individuals, and are characteristically distributed within a wide range of continuous variability.

The limits of developmental variability within a species are determined by the interaction between two factors: (a) a characteristic range of genotypic diversity for a given trait setting maximal and minimal points of potential attainment at the extremes of the distribution*; and (b) the prevailing range of environmental diversity, which both determines the degree of realization of genotypic potentialities that is possible and more independently influences the patterning of traits. In instances of minimal genic determination of development, the potential range of phenotypic variability is as unlimited as environmental variability itself, subject, of course, to constraints imposed by limitations in other relevant traits.

Methods of Determining Relative Weight. The precise determination in quantitative terms of the proportionate influence of heredity and environment upon the development of a given trait is naturally fraught with serious difficulties. In the first place, all empirical approaches to this problem presuppose the possibility of working with known and measurable degrees of genotypic and environmental similarities and differences. Actually, this requirement can at best be met only indirectly and approximately for both kinds of variables. The genotype, for example, can never be measured directly; its properties must always be inferred from its effects, which invariably, even at the moment of birth, have already been influenced to an undeterminable extent by fetal, gestational and external environments. Even in the case of monozygotic twins it is unwarranted to assume complete genotypic equivalence. And when it comes to equating or estimating environmental variability, the difficulties of establishing adequate controls and obtaining accurate measures are even greater. Second, in many research areas such as the development of intelligence, personality, and be-

---

*The adult stature of most human beings, for example, varies between four feet, ten inches and six feet, eight inches.

havior disorders, the above methodological hazards are further compounded by the unavailability of completely reliable and valid measures of the trait under investigation.[43] Finally, the quantitative estimates of the relative influence of heredity and environment can only be validly applied to populations that are reasonably comparable (in terms of level and variability of the two factors) to the sample from which they were derived.[43] And since these highly fallible estimates naturally refer to "average effects upon individual differences or to differences between groups,"[43] their probable errors, when applied to particular individuals must obviously be high enough to impair seriously their usefulness for prognostic purposes.

All methods* of determining the proportionate weight of heredity and environment attempt to ascertain the variation in a given trait attributable to variability in each of the two factors. In the most commonly used method, variability with respect to each factor is introduced separately while the other is held constant; whereas in analysis of variance designs it is possible to take account of variability in both factors concomitantly. Thus, for example, when the former method is employed, the relative influence of heredity would be adjudged greater than that of environment (a) if *much* variation occurred in the outcome of a trait as genic constitution was varied in a relatively homogeneous environment, and (b) if *little* variation occurred in trait outcome as environmental setting was varied for relatively homogeneous genotypes. In the first instance, holding family environment for sibling pairs constant, small mean intra-pair trait differences would be associated with relative genotypic equivalence (monozygotic twins), and large trait differences with genotypic diversity (like-sex dizygotic twins); whereas, in the second instance, holding heredity constant, extremely divergent environmental settings would *not* be associated with much larger mean intra-pair trait differences than would relatively similar environmental settings (monozygotic twins reared together versus monozygotic twins reared apart).

The available range of genotypic variability between siblings that can be utilized in such studies includes identical twins, fraternal twins or full siblings, half siblings, and foster siblings. A similar continuum of environmentally determined intra-pair variability within the same family setting (taking both gestational and external environments into consideration) can be constituted as follows: identical twins, fraternal twins of like sex, fraternal twins of opposite sex or ordinary siblings of like sex, and siblings of opposite sex. If intrauterine environment could be ignored, the place-

*Discussions of different quantitative methods in this research area are available.[5, 20, 39, 43, 45, 71] Cattell, Blewett, and Beloff also describe a new "multiple variance analysis" approach in the *American Journal Human Genetics 7*: 122-146, 1955.

ment of half and foster siblings on this continuum would be determined on the same basis as that of full siblings, i.e., on the basis of age and sex differentials. It is obvious, of course, that the occurrence of significant mean differences between various categories of sibling pairs (e.g., identical and fraternal twins) does not necessarily preclude the possibility that in certain traits as great or greater variability may exist between paired individuals in the *same* category. This *within* category variability occurring in the same family environment is attributable to both genic differences and to idiosyncratic individual experience. Even monozygotic twins whose parents take great pains to rear them exactly alike, must inevitably be differentially exposed to a wide variety of interpersonal situations. If the investigator wishes to widen the range of environmental variability affecting the trait outcomes of his different categories of paired subjects, he may go beyond the intrafamilial setting, and, for example, compare identical twins separated from early infancy.

More specific findings illustrating the use of these various research methods will be provided later in this chapter and in the discussion of the nature-nurture problem as it relates to intellectual development (see pp. 597-607). For our present purposes it will suffice to give several examples showing that the relative influence of heredity and environment varies greatly depending upon the particular trait under investigation. Preliminary evidence from twin studies, in which both genic and environmental sources of variability were considered, indicates that physical traits (except for body weight and muscular development) are least affected and that intellectual attainment and personality traits (especially those associated with values and interests) are most affected by environmental variability.* Somewhere between these two extremes are such psychological characteristics as intelligence and temperamental traits related to susceptibility to personality disorder. Environmental variability results in relatively small differences between separated monozygotic twins in both the incidence of schizophrenia[47] and (except when radical discrepancies in education exist) in measured I.Q.[71]

DETERMINATION OF INTRA- AND INTERCULTURAL UNIFORMITIES AND DIFFERENCES

In the preceding section we have seen how it is possible to integrate meaningfully a large number of complex interrelationships among genic mechanisms, relative potency of heredity and environment, and degrees of expressed phenotypic variability by postulating the existence of a con-

*Similar findings are reported by P. J. Clark in the *American Journal Human Genetics* 8: 49-56, 1956.

tinuum of ontogenetic-phylogenetic traits (see fig. 1). This paradigm defines in highly general terms the interactional nature of developmental regulation for a wide range of traits and species representation along a phyletic scale. It is this very generality of its applicability, however, that makes it unsuitable for conceptualizing the regulatory relationships governing the vast majority of developmental phenomena considered in this volume. Human development is characterized by various special features that make desirable the introduction of additional organizing concepts. The latter, however, supplement rather than supplant or invalidate the previously established biological classification.

The unmodified ontogenetic-phylogenetic paradigm cannot handle adequately problems of human development for the following reasons:

First, because human beings are biologically unique in undergoing development under distinctive cultural auspices, it is not very meaningful to talk about *intra-species* uniformities and differences as such. It is more illuminating to inquire why and in what ways development (a) is alike in all cultures, (b) differs from one culture to another, (c) is essentially similar for most individuals within a culture, and (d) varies for individual representatives of a particular culture.

Second, relatively few of the uniformities characterizing human behavioral development can be referred to the phylogenetic end of the continuum. Hence, in contrast to infrahuman, and especially infraprimate species, the overwhelming proportion of uniformities that do occur involve ontogenetic traits, are more variable in sequence, are both genically and environmentally determined, and are more reflective of process than content of development.

Third, within the range of ontogenetic behavioral traits, environmental factors are much more important determinants of both developmental uniformities and differences among human than among infrahuman individuals. At the lower phyletic levels, more of the basic patterns and processes of behavioral development are regulated by genic effects that are relatively resistant to environmental variability, thereby limiting the potential impact of the environment to comparatively inconsequential developmental sequences. This pre-emption of the more significant aspects of infrahuman behavioral regulation by genic factors obviously reduces the possible incidence of environmentally conditioned uniformities more than it does that of environmentally conditioned differences—since uniformities, unlike differences, characteristically occur at the level of general process rather than at the level of specific details of patterning. Furthermore, environmentally conditioned behavior in animals tends to be quite idiosyncratic to the individual. In human beings, on the other hand, not only are more basic patterns of behavior susceptible to environmental influence, but the culture also standardizes and institutionalizes the environment. We may conclude, therefore, that environmental factors primarily give rise to developmental differences in behavior among infrahumans, whereas among humans they also constitute a significant source of intra- and intercultural uniformity. The very same behavioral plasticity of human beings also accounts for their potentially greater range of environmentally conditioned developmental differences (both intra- and intercultural). In the absence of this plasticity, the greater environmental variability induced by cultural factors could never be reflected in behavioral development.

In order to deal more adequately with these special developmental characteristics of human behavior, the following supplementary classification will be employed to categorize traits in terms of uniformities and differences exhibited within and between cultures: (a) The term *psychobiological* will refer to intercultural uniformities in development. Except for phylogenetic traits, which exhibit both process and content similarities, this category ordinarily includes only those ontogenetic traits that manifest a certain amount of genically and/or environmentally determined panhuman uniformity in the process of development (irrespective of specific differences in form, content or degree attributable to cultural variation). (b) The term *psychosocial* will encompass intercultural differences and their reciprocal intracultural uniformities in development. It refers to those relatively more plastic and environmentally determined ontogenetic traits that reflect the influence of the particular or unique customs, values, institutions and social conditions prevailing within a given culture. It is self-evident, of course, that the very psychosocial traits that differentiate individual behavioral development from one culture to another (i.e., interculturally) constitute *intraculturally* the uniformities characterizing the development of individuals who share the same cultural membership. (c) The term *idiosyncratic* will refer to all of the differences in developmental outcome and process among individuals within the same culture. It includes ontogenetic traits which are either not completely plastic to environmental influences or which reflect the impact of that unique combination of experiences which is idiosyncratic for each individual representative of a particular culture.

Sources of Psychobiological Traits

In general, intercultural uniformities in behavioral development (i.e., psychobiological traits) are determined by the interaction between (a) certain genic predispositions and potentialities which all human beings share in common, and (b) certain universal features of their physical, interpersonal and cultural environments. At the outset, however, it should be noted that the concept of psychobiological traits is a far cry from the theory of universal cultural evolution. In the first place, the former concept refers to successive changes in the life cycles of *individual* representatives of the culture and not to historical changes in cultural forms and practices. Second, cultural evolution ordinarily refers to a complicated chain of events set off by intricate social and economic phenomena. The processes of cultural change are, interculturally, much more divergent than they are similar; and insofar as they influence individual development, they tend to give rise to psychosocial rather than psychobiological traits.

Man differs in his development from infrahuman species not only in being uniquely stimulated by a rich cultural environment, but also in possessing a genic endowment that enables him to acquire culture and to respond to it in particular ways. This same endowment, of course, enables him to invent and acquire a culture in the first place, and to continually modify and expand it. The essential culture-giving attributes of his genic make-up are: (a) the fact that so many of his basic behavioral adaptations are not prepotently determined by hereditary influences, thereby leaving room for invention and making his survival dependent upon it; and (b) the fact that he possesses the cognitive and other capacities that make possible the original invention and transmission of learned adaptations within a cultural framework and their subsequent acquisition by later generations.

Table 1 presents in highly condensed form the sources (determinants) of psychobiological traits. Actual examples or manifestations of such traits

TABLE 1.—*Sources of Psychobiological Traits*[*]

I. GENIC SOURCES

A. *Patterning Predispositions*

1. Predispositions toward relatively invariable process and content ("phylogenetic") uniformities in development (e.g., locomotion, prehension).
2. Predispositions toward more variable ("ontogenetic") process uniformities:
   a. General predispositions governing sequence of development in motor, emotional and cognitive development (e.g., the "concrete-to-abstract" trend in cognitive development).
   b. Predispositions resulting in unlearned sensory preferences (e.g., sweet over bitter) and hierarchies of drive-reducing responses (e.g., sucking over kicking in hunger).
   c. Predispositions toward various responses to particular endocrine stimulation (e.g., selective lowering of thresholds for perceptual and behavioral responses; increased motility and irritability).
   d. Predispositions toward random, general activity.
   e. Predispositions to react to certain kinds of situations (e.g., frustration, pain, perceptual disorientation) with emotional instability.

---

[*]Based on reference data.[28, 31, 50, 51, 54, 70, 79, 87] The listing of the various sources of psychobiological traits is intended to be illustrative rather than exhaustive.

f. Predispositions toward specific motor expression of various emotional states (e.g., facial expressions in anger, fear, joy).

g. Predispositions to respond to frustration and anxiety in particular ways (e.g., perseveration, sterotypy, regression; defense and escape mechanisms).

h. Predispositions toward certain primate temperamental-social traits: gregariousness; tendency to form social aggregations*; desire for companionship; dislike of social isolation; curiosity; imitativeness, etc.

B. *Potentialities for Developing Various Capacities*

1. Potentialities for developing species-characteristic capacities and mechanics of biological and psychological functioning that are basically stable over the life span (e.g., most reflex activity).

2. Potentialities for acquiring species-characteristic capacities that fluctuate more on a developmental basis: ranges of sensory sensitivity; gross motor skills; perceptual, memory, discriminative functions; primary drives and emotions.

3. Potentialities for developing certain kinds of social behavior exhibited by primates, e.g., affection, loyalty, identification, helpfulness, mutual dependence, rivalry, possessiveness, differentiated interpersonal roles and status.

4. Potentialities for various types and mechanisms of learning, e.g., conditioning and problem solving; incidental, intentional goal-directed, and drive-reduction learning; imitation and identification, etc.

5. Potentialities for developing unique human capacities making possible and facilitating the invention and acquisition of culture.†

   a. Unusual capacity for behavioral plasticity, i.e., for learning major behavioral adaptations to the environment (e.g., for improvising mechanisms of satisfying biological needs, institutionalizing social relationships, inventing tools).

   b. Greater capacity for mechanical dexterity (dependent in part upon opposing thumb and erect posture).

   c. Capacity for inventing and acquiring language,‡ making possible more com-

---

*Harlow[31] observes that in contrast to New World primates, the Old World primate stock (from which man and the anthropoid apes are descended) exhibits many antisocial temperamental traits, such as brutality, aggressiveness, self-centeredness, and ruthless dominance patterns, which are not ideally suited to the functioning of complex social organizations. However, even if such predispositions are operative at the human level, they are obviously not singly determinative as evidenced by the tremendous intercultural variability in the expression of these traits.

†It is generally agreed that human culture, in contradistinction to animal societies, is characterized by more variable, learned adaptations; the institutionalization of interpersonal relationships; the possibility of indirect (other than face-to-face) communication between individuals and groups; continuity of learned adaptations from one generation to another; an invented symbolical language; inter-group relationships, etc.

‡Studies of chimpanzee and human infants reared alike[32, 48] show that their rate of acquiring habits is quite comparable with respect to such learnings as use of the toilet, utilization of eating utensils, dressing, etc. The former, however, exhibit little spontaneous vocalization and, for all practical purposes, fail to acquire linguistic sounds and language. In evaluating the comparability that does exist, it should also be borne in mind that the chimpanzee matures more rapidly and ordinarily attains adult maturity at a much earlier age.

plex conceptualization, commonality of meanings and values, indirect communication of ideas, and continuity of traditions (dependent upon spontaneous vocalization, superior mimicry and ability to articulate sounds, and superior symbolical intelligence).

d. Greater capacity for higher order conceptualization and problem solving involving the manipulation of symbols.

e. Capacity for symbolical adjustive mechanisms (e.g., rationalization).

f. Greater capacity for time perspective, delay of overt response, and anticipation of consequences.

g. Greater capacity for self-awareness, making possible complex ego attitudes and motivations (e.g., self-esteem, levels of aspiration) and self-evaluation in relation to internalized group norms (necessary for conscience formulation).

II.   ENVIRONMENTAL SOURCES

A. *Universal Interpersonal Problems, Needs, and Conditions of Adaptation to the Physical and Social Environments*

1. Intrafamilial needs, problems, and conditions of adaptation:

   a. Ocurrence of early development within nuclear family group assuming responsibility for child's physical survival, rearing and enculturation.

   b. Basic structural conditions of family organization: two sexes; more than one child; individuals of different age, sex, status and capacity in the same group.

   c. Long period of biosocial and emotional dependence on parents facilitating socialization, identification, and internationalization of parental norms.

   d. Necessity for intrafamilial differentiation of roles and status, regulation of sexual access, and socialization of child.

   e. Universally limited possibilities in basic dimensions of parent attitudes (e.g., accepting or rejecting; over- or underdominating, etc.); uniformities in modification of parental demands and expectations with increasing maturity of child.

   f. Uniform shifts in kinds of biosocial status (derived or primary) available to child at different stages of maturity, with accompanying transitional stages in personality development.

2. Social or extrafamilial needs, problems and conditions of adaptation:

   a. Satisfaction of group's biological needs and problems of physical survival; regulation of sexual access.

   b. Invention of stable and organized systems of social interaction and differentiation of roles and status (e.g., division of labor, privileges, responsibilities).

   c. Need for socialization and personality maturation of child in the direction of greater independence and frustration tolerance, inhibition of immediate impulses, self-subordination to group norms, internalization of moral obligations, acceptance of social responsibility.

   d. Integrative system of communication, some mutuality of values, minimal reciprocity of behavior and expectations.

B. *"Universal Categories of Culture" and Cultural Needs*

1. Commonality in customs, practices and adaptive solutions (e.g., the universality of kinship systems, codified language, incest taboos, institutionalization of status relationships and of child rearing practices, division of labor).

2. Needs for cultural survival: protection against external threats and internal disruption, recognition of limited life span, provision for indoctrination and training of younger generation.

will be considered later under the heading of "human nature." Two general categories of determinants, genic and environmental, are delineated. The former in turn are broken down into (a) predispositions toward specified kinds of developmental patterning, and (b) potentialities for developing certain capacities or mechanisms of biological and psychological functioning that both limit and make possible the kinds of development that can take place. Some of the predispositions and capacities are shared with man's primate relatives; others are unique to man and account for culture as a biological emergent. They are deduced from developmental comparisons between man and other primates in their natural habitat, in controlled situations, and in simulated human environments. It must be borne in mind, however, that genic predispositions toward various temperamental traits are much more plastic in man than in other primates and are subject to cortical modification in the light of all kinds of situational and cultural variables. Nevertheless they are still operative as partial determinants and at least furnish the alternatives from which cultural selection is made.

The environmental sources of psychobiological traits are grouped under *interpersonal* (both intra- and extrafamilial) and *cultural* categories. The former category includes universal *needs, problems* and *conditions* of adaptation to the physical and social environments that are characteristic of man as a social animal and both antedate and coexist with culture. Cultural sources of psychobiological traits, on the other hand, consist of a common body of customs or adaptive *solutions* to the above needs and problems as well as universal new needs generated by culture itself. The "common denominators" of culture, as already noted, reflect the operation of the same genic and interpersonal uniformities giving rise to psychobiological traits. In addition, they are attributable to universal features of the physical environment, to common limitations in available solutions, and to certain gross parallels in cultural development.*

Human Nature. The conception of psychobiological traits,† i.e., intercultural uniformities in development transcending specific differences in cultural conditioning, corresponds to what has traditionally been referred to as "human nature." This latter concept, however, has long since fallen into disrepute because of certain unwarranted assumptions that had been made about the source of these uniformities. Predeterminists accounted for

*We are only concerned here with "universal categories of culture" as determinants of psychobiological traits. Sophisticated discussions of the factors generating these universal categories are available in this chapter[28, 50, 70] and in Chapter 2.[31]

†Examples of psychobiological traits include developmental sequences in locomotion and prehension, directional gradients in neuromuscular coordination, gross stages in personality development, general characteristics of personality maturation (see Chapter 9), general trends in cognitive development (see Chapter 17), etc.

them on the basis of prepotent, genically determined predispositions for all human beings, irrespective of cultural milieu, to develop in uniform ways. Preformationists invoked the concept of hereditary, prestructured, species-wide instincts. Further difficulty was generated by the ethnocentric tendency to identify as panhuman behavior (i.e., as part of human nature) some of the distinctive subcultural or psychosocial traits prevailing within our own culture (e.g., competitiveness, desire for prestige). Thus, when it became evident that such ethnocentric projections had no intercultural basis in fact, that no complexly patterned behavior is ever preformed, and that many intercultural uniformities are environmentally determined, these conceptions of human nature became insupportable. Unfortunately, however, the baby was discarded with the bath. Instead of merely rejecting the untenable theories of human nature, the valuable and necessary concept of human nature itself was dismissed as invalid.

Much of the difficulty with the concept of human nature arose from a failure to distinguish between intercultural behavioral uniformities and their sources or determinants. Both were loosely referred to as "human nature." From the restricted perspective of instinctual or predeterministic theory, the distinction between uniformities of innate origin and innate determinants of uniformities was obviously not very important. However, when environmental determinants entered the picture, the broader distinction could no longer be logically ignored without giving rise to serious misunderstandings. Hence, it was not always as clear as it should have been (a) that if the term, *human nature,* were to be applied to developmental uniformities, *both* genic and environmental determinants had to be recognized, and (b) that if it were still desired to reserve the human nature concept for the "raw material" or hereditary basis of human behavior, the term could not refer to panhuman commonalities in behavioral development but only to their genic determinants.

In choosing between these alternative meanings, we decided to use the term *human nature* to refer to psychobiological traits, i.e., to the uniform ways in which human beings actually develop everywhere, irrespective of cause, for the following reasons: (a) This connotation is somewhat more consistent with historical usage. (b) Intercultural uniformities in development can be identified directly by conducting cross-cultural research, whereas their genic determinants can only be inferred indirectly and tentatively from inter-species comparisons.* For example, the similarities observed be-

*The methods of determining the relative influence of hereditary and environmental factors described above (see page 61) can only be applied intraculturally where it is possible to work with relatively known and measurable degrees of genotypic and environmental variability.

tween human beings and chimpanzees, each in their own habitat, could be caused by comparable interpersonal variables as well as by genic commonalities; and the differences between human and chimpanzee infants reared in the same environment are not necessarily determined by uniquely human genic potentialities, but could be attributed, in part, to the disadvantages experienced by chimpanzees in being exposed to an environment structured for and by human beings.

The method of cross-cultural comparison can only be used to identify a human nature defined in terms of intercultural developmental uniformities. It cannot be employed to provide data about an original nature referable to genic endowment. In conducting such comparisons, all we are doing is separating that which is culturally universal (psychobiological) from that which is specific to particular cultures (psychosocial). Since it is true, as Margaret Mead points out,[63] that we are holding "human nature constant" here, it is valid to infer that observed intercultural differences are culturally determined. But at the same time we cannot conclude that the residual intercultural uniformities are genically determined. What we are holding constant is not just genotypic endowment alone, but also the interpersonal and cultural determinants of panhuman uniformities.

Because human nature can nowhere be observed apart from its cultural or even from its interpersonal determinants, the concept of extracultural or extrasocial human nature must forever remain a hypothetical construct. Even if it were possible, as Leuba [54] has proposed, to isolate unwanted children on a tropical island and to observe in their development the "human nature" that is supposedly a direct product of the interaction between genic endowment and the physical environment, these observations would hardly throw much light on the raw (genic) material that the human being contributes to his development. They would simply reflect the operation of genic endowment under very atypical (extrafamilial and extrasocial) conditions that render impossible the expression of many genotypic capacities and predispositions; for nowhere do children develop in such an impoverished physical and interpersonal environment with no possibility for succorance or rearing by adults. The offspring of the survivors of such an experiment might possibly enjoy the benefits of a familial and social setting; and very soon thereafter, some semblance of culture itself would be operative. It would seem, therefore, (a) that human nature can be most meaningfully studied by means of cross-cultural comparisons as a composite product of its various determinants, and (b) that the separate contributions of the latter determinants could be derived more profitably from inferential analysis of inter-species comparisons than from essentially unfeasible empirical investigations using "culture-free" or "family-free" human subjects.

In accordance with our usage of the term, the only criterion that can be employed for designating a particular developmental sequence as characteristic of human nature is virtual universality of occurrence. This universality simply indicates that either genic or environmental commonalities (or the interaction between them) are sufficiently salient to induce process uniformities in development despite cultural diversity. The absence of universality, therefore, does not necessarily signify that particular hereditary or environmental factors are not operative but that they are insufficiently potent to be overtly determinative of psychobiological traits.

Observable changes in human nature, as we have defined it, are, of course, inconceivable in terms of the usual historical time scale of centuries and millenia. But fortunately, neither the progress of civilization, significant betterment in the development of individuals, nor substantial improvement in interpersonal and intergroup relationships are as dependent upon the modification of human nature as is frequently alleged to be the case. The constraints imposed upon behavioral development by the determinants of human nature must certainly be realistically reckoned with, but they need not be exaggerated out of all proportion to their actual influence. Despite the virtual constancy of human nature, tremendous change and diversity in cultural forms have occurred—even in the relatively infinitesimal fraction of evolutionary time that is spanned by recorded history. It is quite apparent, therefore, that such changes must be brought about by complex social, economic, scientific, technological and ideological factors that exhibit an impressive range of variability within the framework of a stable human nature. And since man's psychosocial traits can be altered in the space of a single generation by conspicuous cultural change, considerable room for rapidly shifting variability in human behavioral development prevails within the same framework of psychobiological constancy.

Sources of Psychosocial Traits*

Now that we have examined the determinants of pan-human uniformities in development (i.e., psychobiological traits), the analagous problem may be raised in relation to psychosocial traits. Why is it that individuals who

*The term, psychosocial, customarily refers to the psychological accompaniments or consequences of social phenomena. In this volume, however, its meaning is restricted to those aspects of development that reflect the operation of practices unique to a given culture or group of cultures. Hence, depending on the level of generality (universality) involved, social factors may give rise to either psychobiological or psychosocial traits.

share the same cultural tradition also share certain developmental commonalities that set them apart from individuals in other cultures? What properties of culture* account for the relative intracultural standardization of so many features of behavior and development? At this point we shall only be concerned with the different *sources* or determinants of psychosocial traits and not with the *mechanisms* whereby the distinctive customs, values, and institutions of a particular culture find uniform representation in a corresponding set of developmental processes, content, and outcomes among its individual members. The actual *mediating* mechanisms responsible for the acquisition of cultural norms (e.g., external sanctions, imitation, identification, internalization of obligations, prestige suggestion) and for their selective perpetuation once acquired (e.g., canalization reaction-sensitivity, perceptual structuralization, symbolization) will be elaborated in succeeding chapters. Only by the study of these latter mechanisms can we learn how and why "the members of society . . . *want to act as they have to act* and at the same time find gratification in acting according to the requirements of the culture."[19]

In consequence of the growth of empirical cultural anthropology and the correction of earlier ethnocentric bias, many features of development that were formerly regarded as genically determined and universally distributed can now be categorized as psychosocial in origin. Nevertheless, so influential has the doctrine of maturation been, that many developmental uniformities are still widely accepted as inherently and inevitably characteristic of "Five" or "Nine," even though they could be much more credibly attributed to the fact that the children to whom they refer all happen to grow up in American middle-class families living in a medium-sized New England city.†

*Because "persons who live in the same culture are more likely to have the same genes than are persons who live far apart," it is theoretically possible that some psychosocial traits are genically determined.[51] Actually, however, the possibility is quite remote since the only type of inheritance conceivable in the case of these relatively plastic characteristics is the polygenic variety; and the degree of genic segregation necessary for the uniform expression of polygenically determined traits within a culture never occurs in the absence of natural selection except in extremely small and isolated populations.[9] We are quite safe, therefore, in attributing the source of psychosocial traits to environmental (predominantly cultural) factors.

†However, even the correction of ethnocentric bias in this case would not totally eliminate the maturational fallacy. If cross-cultural studies revealed that some of the developmental uniformities were psychosocial in nature, the doctrine of "internal ripening" would merely be shifted to psychobiological traits. To date, this doctrine has been tested on a cross-cultural basis only in relation to those early locomotor and other phylogenetic sequences[66] in which it is most tenable and on the basis of which most of the unwarranted extrapolation has been made.

On the other hand, the concept of psychosocial traits must be qualified in several important respects. First, all of the developmental uniformities found within a culture are not necessarily of psychosocial origin. In the absence of cross-cultural investigation, it is impossible to distinguish definitively between regularities conditioned by the specific intracultural standardization of the environment and regularities that are panhuman in scope. Second, the same psychosocial traits could be anticipated in all cultures in which similar kinds of institutionalized role and status relationships prevail.[51] In instances where certain generalized aspects of these relationships approach universality (e.g., some dimensions of parent-child interaction), we would, in fact, be dealing with psychobiological traits. Last and most important, because culture itself is only an abstraction referring to *modal* behavior, values, norms, etc., the developmental uniformities it induces can only be regarded as approximate rather than as identical. Herein lies the source of many of the idiosyncratic traits to be discussed below. "Few institutions apply without exception to every member of a society."[29] In addition to "universals," i.e., beliefs, values, and aspirations shared by practically all members of a culture, there are "specialities" (skills, values and behaviors restricted to a particular age, sex, status or occupational group) as well as culturally tolerated *alternative* value systems that cut across these latter groupings.[56] And if one looks closely enough at the norms that hold for any one of these three categories, discrepancies will almost certainly be found from one situation to another and between the officially professed ideology and the actual behavior that prevails.

The non-universal properties of culture give rise to psychosocial traits in two ways—by limiting and patterning the course of individual development. Because the level of cultural stimulation to which human beings are exposed limits the actualization of their genic endowment, cultures differ quantitatively among each other in the extent to which various potentialities are realized in the modal individual. The differential level of cultural achievement itself may either be determined by technological and historical factors, or may be reflective of a prevailing set of cultural values which influence the selection of certain human capacities (e.g., art, motor skill, mechanical invention) for maximal development in preference to others.

The second inevitable outcome of cultural diversity—and source of psychosocial traits—is differential cultural patterning of the content, sequence and outcome of development: (a) By virtue of cultural tradition, certain aspects of drive and emotion are uniquely differentiated with respect to eliciting stimuli, mode and conditions of expression, adequacy of opportunity for gratification, need for repression, etc. Sensory preferences and favored modes of adjustment within a culture are similarly determined. (b) Each culture has its own way of institutionalizing relationships with respect to age, sex, status and occupational differentiation. The particular choices it adopts have profound implications for such aspects of personality structure as security and adequacy feelings, levels of aspiration and anxiety, and attributes of masculinity and femininity. (c) The central values of a culture, i.e., whether emphasis is placed on mercantile, artistic, spiritual, competitive, or cooperative endeavors, shape the goals of its members and help determine which personality traits are encouraged and rewarded. The *modal or basic personality type* of a particular culture is partly determined by these latter two factors and partly by various technological, economic, political, and historical considerations that influence the frustration and anxiety levels of individuals and the quality of interpersonal relations.

Sources of Idiosyncratic Traits

Since all of the individuals within a culture do not develop in the same way or reach the same terminus of development, we propose to examine briefly in this section both the genic and environmental sources of idiosyncratic traits and the different mechanisms mediating the influence of genes on behavioral and personality development.

Genic Sources. Geneticists are in agreement that genotypically (apart from some physical traits), the populations of different cultures are substantially alike with respect to the range and central tendency of most individual differences. Hence, it is quite defensible to assume that genic factors are not responsible for intercultural differences or intracultural uniformities in behavioral development. But this does not mean, despite frequent claims to the contrary, that genotypic diversity plays no role whatsoever in determining differences among individuals *within* a culture. It is obvious, of course, that genic factors are not singly determinative of behavioral, intellectual, and temperamental differences,* that they interact with environmental variables at every stage of development, and that the significance of their phenotypic effects is contingent upon cultural values. Thus, although many genically determined temperamental predispositions are undoubtedly eclipsed by and subordinated to the influence of more weighty cultural factors, others are sufficiently potent to modify appreciably the impact of the social environment on individual development, and sometimes even to produce a personality who deviates seriously from the expectations of his culture (see p. 98).

*We shall not consider here genic determinants of physical variability which indirectly influence personality development by affecting the social acceptability of an individual, since the ultimate outcome of such variability is almost completely a function of sociocultural factors.

The most obvious genic source of idiosyncratic traits are hereditary factors influencing such capacities as intelligence, gross motor skills, mechanical dexterity, artistic ability, various sensory acuities, etc. Genic differences not only limit the terminal level of attained capacity and the relative rate of growth in these particular areas of development, but also differentially influence the individual's interests and responsiveness to various kinds of environmental stimulation and the quality of his adjustment and interpersonal relations. It is also conceivable that in certain extreme cases, quantitative differences in capacity may give rise to qualitative differences in the processes of development (see p. 592).

Many opportunities are also present for genically determined *temperamental* differences to influence the course of personality development. It could be anticipated, of course, that greater leeway would exist for the operation of such differences in those areas of behavior that are "relatively less institutionalized, more variable from generation to generation and socially less consequential."[29] The influence of culture is truly pervasive; nevertheless innumerable aspects of private life are left relatively uncharted by social norms. But even in more highly institutionalized aspects of behavior, "each person's selection from and reaction to cultural teachings have an individual quality."[51] In accordance with his temperamental proclivities he interprets cultural prescriptions slightly differently from his neighbors and improvises minor variations of his own on major cultural themes; and as long as his deviancy is passably discreet and conforms overtly to accepted ways, it is usually accorded a reasonable measure of social tolerance. In still other instances, culturally institutionalized alternatives are available, making it possible for him to choose values and activities most compatible with his temperamental inclinations.

Human beings, therefore, are more than helpless puppets dangling from the ends of cultural strings. In the formation of their personalities, innate temperamental characteristics always interact with social pressures; and depending upon the relative strength of the variables concerned, complete or partial conformity or outright resistance and rebellion ensue. And in a sense their peculiar temperamental qualities even help determine their social environments by eliciting differential responses from significant individuals in their interpersonal orbits.

Types of Evidence for Genic Determination of Individual Differences in Behavioral Development. In some areas the evidence for the contribution of genotypic diversity to intracultural differences in behavior is conflicting, ambiguous, and difficult to interpret. In general, however, there can no longer be any serious doubt about the fact that some of the observed variance in psychological capacities, behavior, and personality structure must be attributable to genic differences. *Direct* and relatively unequivocal evidence comes from pedigree studies of such rare causes of feeble-mindedness as amaurotic idiocy, sex-linked idiocy, phenylketonuric amentia, and microcephaly [9, 90]; from pedigree and twin studies of such behavior disorders as epilepsy,[53] Huntington's chorea,[9, 90] schizophrenia,[45, 47, 84] male homosexuality,[46] and general neuroticism[17]; and from twin studies of such nonpathological behavioral traits as intelligence,[71] numerous verbal and motor abilities,[90] and locus and degree of autonomic reactivity.[44]

Indirect sources of evidence for the genic determination of behavioral development are much more equivocal when considered individually but are quite convincing in their totality: (a) The finding of consistent individual differences among neonates in such temperamental factors as kinetic level, irritability and reaction to stress (see p. 112) can only be explained on a nongenic basis if all of the variability is ascribed to such factors as the uterine environment. (b) Lower mammalian species can be selectively bred for many temperamental traits including emotionality, spontaneous activity, tameness and aggressiveness.[27] Although analagous genic predispositions in man are undoubtedly subject to greater experiential and ideational modification,[9] in the total context of evidence from related sources it is highly improbable that they are not operative at all. (c) Meaningful relationships between various personality traits and variability in endocrine and autonomic functioning (see below) can be explained most plausibly by assuming the existence of genically regulated differences in the reactivity of the latter mechanisms (or their "target" tissues) with resulting parallelism in their behavioral and physiological effects. (d) Obtained correlations between body-type, on the one hand, and temperament,[2, 30, 75, 77, 80, 82] neurotic and psychotic trends, [75] and hormonal and autonomic functioning[75, 77, 80] on the other hand, suggest that the relationship between body type and temperament* is mediated either by "linked genes" (with direct effects on physical characteristics and the neuroendocrine basis of temperament) or through genically regulated hormonal and autonomic mechanisms with parallel secondary effects on morphology and behavior.

Mediation of Genic Influences on Behavior. Except for some of the

---

*Some reported correlations between body-type and temperament have undoubtedly been inflated by (a) "halo effect" in rating, (b) the fact that the temperamental traits under investigation (e.g., "active," "energetic") are stereotyped psychological equivalents of bodily characteristics (e.g., well-developed muscles), and (c) experientially determined mutual reinforcement as a result of conforming to socially stereotyped expectations (e.g., "fat and jolly") or of a circular relationship between organ (muscular) hypertrophy and frequent, satisfying (motor) activity. Nevertheless, significant but lower correlations still remain when the first two sources of spuriousness are removed.

relatively rare neuropathological causes of amentia and behavior disorder (e.g., amaurotic idiocy, Huntington's chorea), variability in the normal and in the more common of the abnormal behavioral traits is undoubtedly related to polygenic rather than to single-gene inheritance.[9, 20] Individual differences in such traits, therefore, reflect the cumulative effect of many positive and negative factors. However, in certain instances, the phenotypic appearance of a trait (e.g., schizophrenic symptoms) may depend upon exceeding for a given environment a critical threshold value of the polygenic influences concerned. Such all-or-none phenomena may "obscure the continuous nature of the susceptibility gradient."[20] If, for example, an individual's genic threshold for psychotic breakdown were high, much environmental stress would be needed to precipitate a psychosis; if it were low, the opposite would hold true. In the more medain ranges of susceptibility, relatively small shifts in environmental stress would be determinative of phenotypic outcome.

As in the case of any other trait, genes do not influence behavioral development in some mystical fashion but through a series of intermediate mechanisms. The latter are probably initiated by "some effect [of genes] on chemical reactions and rates of reaction in the developing organism."[5] Preliminary evaluation of available evidence indicates that the following kinds of intermediate mechanisms may be operative between genic effects and behavior: Most directly, in the case of single-gene inheritance, behavioral defects may be caused by "the defective structure of an intracellular enzyme" (phenylpyruvic amentia),[20] by cerebral agenesis, or by gross organic brain lesions (amaurotic idiocy, Huntington's disease). More indirectly, the effect of genes may be mediated through the autonomic nervous system. Young infants, for example, vary in their degree of visceral or somatic response to excitatory stimuli.[42] Even the locus of maximum autonomic reactivity may be genically determined as shown by the greater resemblance between monozygotic twins than between siblings in autonomic patterning,[44] and by individual consistency in type of autonomic response to different kinds of stress.[52] Wenger has demonstrated that parasympathetic (as contrasted with sympathetic) predominance in autonomic balance is associated with such traits as diminished emotional excitability, less fatigability and suggestibility, and high dominance.[97]

A similar type of mediating mechanism may be provided by endocrine secretions. The relationships between general activity and thyroid functioning, between motherliness and blood levels of prolactin and estrogen[3, 55] are well known. Benedek[4] has been able to relate psychological aspects of sex drive to different histological phases of the menstrual cycle. More recently, the tissue-damaging and tissue-protecting roles of various humoral responses to stress situations have been elucidated.[81] The possibility that genically determined hyper-reactivity in the destructive aspects or of deficiency in the defensive aspects of reaction to stress is related to incidence of psychotic breakdown is suggested by the facts that (a) schizophrenics do not respond adequately to stress tests with enhanced corticosteroid output,[18] (b) that schizophrenic patients with poor prognosis and poor response to shock therapy do not respond therapeutically to ACTH,[18] and (c) that normal children and children with behavior problems differ in their EEG and autonomic response patterns to physiological stress stimuli.[16] It is quite conceivable, however, that in the case of both endocrine and autonomic mechanisms, differential reactivity is related to genically determined differences in the responsiveness of "target" tissues rather than to differences in the level of stimulation per se. Clues regarding the mechanisms mediating many other genically regulated predispositions are presently unclear. In this category belong differential sensitivity to stimulation in particular sensory modalities; differences in intelligence and in motor, mechanical and artistic abilities; and many temperamental differences such as self-sufficiency, self-assertiveness, etc.

We are by no means suggesting that these genically determined capacities and temperamental factors operate *directly* in influencing the course of personality development or the genesis of behavior disorder. However, it does not seem unreasonable to suppose that they interact with other interpersonal, situational and cultural factors in differentially determining personality outcomes. It is not difficult, for example, to appreciate how the temperamental traits of dominance, self-assertiveness, and strength of hedonic drives might affect ease of socialization and disposition to assume dependent or independent roles. Such traits as level of affectivity, self-sufficiency, and being "tender" or "tough-skinned" are self-evidently related to introversion-extroversion, ability to relate to reality and to other persons, and to choice of escape and defense mechanisms. Similarly, frustration tolerance, level of energy and intelligence, and availability of other adaptive resources affect the quality of an individual's adjustment and his susceptibility to behavior disorder.

Environmental Sources. The social and cultural environments both limit and furnish the ways in which individuals can differ from each other intraculturally. Irrespective of the degree of genotypic diversity that exists, variability can never be expressed phenotypically in the absence of those environmental determinants essential for the development of a given trait or capacity. The culture also establishes the limits of tolerance for deviancy and provides the necessary instrumentalities for the expression of individual differences, whether these are tailor-made, institutionalized alternatives or uniquely improvised innovations. Even "the political revolutionary does not refuse to cast his revolutionary songs in the modal structure and the scale progressions of the culture he is in the process of changing."[33]

The environmental sources of idiosyncratic traits are interpersonal, cultural and situational. No culture can ever institutionalize interpersonal relationships so thoroughly that all of the temperamental qualities of the participants as well as their affective reactions to each other are completely squeezed out of the transaction. Especially in their early formative years, and to a lesser extent in adult life, individuals are continually influenced by these culturally unstandardized aspects of the feelings and personalities of parents, siblings, and other associates. Furthermore, no two persons are ever ground through the same cultural mill. Each of us is exposed to a unique conception of cultural reality by the biased sample of cultural representatives we encounter in the course of our experience.

Even the most conventional teachers will give culture a certain personal flavor in accord with their constitution and peculiar life experiences. The culture may prescribe that the training of the child shall be gradual and gentle, but there will always be some abrupt and severe personalities who are temperamentally disposed to act otherwise.[51]

Lastly we must consider situational factors, i.e., unplanned events that "just happen to people." Such situations are by definition unique in their "number, kinds and temporal order" for any particular individual.[51] When to this situational uniqueness is added a unique genotype, a unique familial upbringing, unique exposure to the institutionalized aspects of culture, unique interpersonal transactions with others, and the unique resultant of the interaction among all of these various factors, it is difficult indeed to appreciate how the existence of intracultural differences in development could have ever been seriously denied.

MATURATION

Maturation has long been the central theoretical issue in child development dealing with the nature-nurture problem. However, ever since the concept was first introduced, its meaning has been clouded by ambiguity and by the diversity of connotations with which it has been endowed. The latter are presently predominantly predeterministic in accordance with the immense influence on professional and lay opinion wielded by Gesell and the Yale school who regard the term as descriptive of a process whereby *all* development is essentially regulated by endogenous factors, (see pp. 28-30, 73). Most other writers have taken a less global position, equating maturation with either the acquisition of "readiness" in *certain* capacities as a consequence of internally directed "ripening", or with changes in the anatomical and physiological substrate of behavior. Because of the resulting semantic confusion it might even have been advisable to dispense with the term altogether. But in view of its great historical importance in the theory and research of child development, it was deemed preferable to redefine it rigorously in operational terms and to clarify its meaning in relation to such concepts as development, growth, learning and readiness.

The Meaning of Maturation

We shall use the term, "maturation," to refer to any instance of development (i.e., change in the status or underlying process of a behavioral trait) that takes place in the demonstrable absence of specific practice experience.* It should be noted that so defined it is neither restricted to development occuring independently of environmental influence (internal ripening), nor is uniquely identified with enhancement in capacity resulting from alteration of the neuroanatomical or neurophysiological substrate of behavior. Also, in contrast to Gesell's usage of the term, this definition does not equate maturation with an endogenous process regulating all development (including that in which learning is operative); it simply designates those particular components or aspects of a developmental sequence in which the influence of specific practice can be operationally or logically excluded, in contradistinction to those aspects in which it is a determining factor. Apart from historical considerations the main justification for retaining the concept of maturation is that this distinction has obviously important implications for education and other related disciplines.

Since most developmental sequences consist of both maturation and learning, it is frequently difficult to distinguish between the two components. Nevertheless, in most instances it is possible and practically useful to order various developmental sequences in accordance with the relative contributions of genic factors, incidental experience, and specific practice to increment or change in capacity. Categorization of traits on this basis can, in turn, be related to the ontogenetic-phylogenetic and psychobiological-psychosocial continua discussed above. (a) At one end of the continuum (psychosocial traits), specific practice is always essential, genic factors are of negligible significance, and incidental experience may or may not be important. (b) At the opposite end of the continuum (phylogenetic traits), development is largely regulated by prepotent genic factors, specific practice is not involved, and incidental experience similarly plays a supportive role.

*Maturation has a special meaning in biology, designating the process whereby the number of chromosomes in the ovum or sperm are reduced in half as a result of one member of each homologous pair being segregated into each of two daughter cells. In personality theory, maturation usually refers to the child's gradual acquisition of the character traits typical of adult members of the culture.

(c) Between these two extremes, in the case of psychobiological traits that are ontogenetic in character, the regulatory picture is more variable: all three determinants are implicated, and their relative importance varies with the nature and complexity of the particular developmental sequence involved.

Hence, under the heading of maturation can be subsumed that portion of any increment or change in capacity referable to genic influence and/or incidental experience. Development in phylogenetic traits is wholly maturational with emphasis upon the former component. The latter component assumes greater salience in the ontogenetic variety of psychobiological traits and also plays a role in psychosocial traits. Learning (specific practice), on the other hand, is the most important determinant of psychosocial traits, does not influence phylogenetic traits at all, and is of variable significance in psychobiological traits that are not phylogenetic.

Differentiation from Development, Growth and Readiness. One important source of confusion regarding the meaning of maturation has resulted from the failure to distinguish between two entirely independent dimensions of development. The first, dealing with the participation and relative importance of specific practice (learning) versus genic influences and incidental experience (maturation) as determining factors, has already been discussed. The second concerns the question of whether or not structural and functional changes in the nervous system accompany developmental modifications of "overt behavior."[62] In a strictly technical sense the term, *growth,** may be used to designate relatively permanent changes in the neuroanatomical and neurophysiological substrate of behavior. Development is inclusive of both dimensions of behavioral change—of substrate and overt aspects as well as of maturation and learning. Growth, on the other hand, only refers to the substrate correlates of overt developmental change irrespective of whether it is attributable to maturation or learning.

Many writers have attempted to differentiate between maturation and learning by identifying the former with the substrate changes we have just defined as growth. However, this distinction is unwarranted because such changes occur in both maturation and learning; in the first instance they are effected by genic factors and incidental experience, and in the second instance by practice. In both maturation and learning, the achievement of substrate adequacy is an essential prior or limiting condition for the emergence of any nontransitory overt change in behavioral development. However, this does not necessarily mean that "structure precedes function"

---

*As used here, *growth* refers only to substrate changes associated with behavioral development. Obviously, much anatomical and physiological growth, both inside and outside the nervous system, has no effect whatsoever on behavior.

since both incidental experience and practice contribute to as well as reflect substrate adequacy. The fact that the existing status of a capacity affects its responsiveness to regulatory influences requires the introduction of still another term. *Readiness* signifies that the current developmental status of an organism is such that a reasonably economical increment in capacity may be anticipated in response to adequate stimulation—irrespective of how this status is achieved or the type of stimulation that is applied. In either case, maturation, learning or a combination of the two factors may be involved. Thus, for example, because of inadequate readiness, an individual may fail to profit from either practice or incidental experience; but the deficiency in readiness may be reflective of insufficient learning as well as of insufficient maturation. On the same grounds, although the outcome of most developmental sequences depends on the operation of both maturation and learning, it is inaccurate to state that the two processes are necessarily mutually interdependent. Either one could occur in the absence of the other if sufficient readiness ascribable to one of the two factors alone prevailed.

Evidence Regarding Maturation

By controlling the opportunity for and the timing and amount of specific practice affecting development, it is possible to demonstrate empirically that maturation does occur. However, since nonspecific environmental determinants are operative from the very moment of conception, the relative contributions of genic influences and of incidental experience can only be estimated approximately. In certain instances the organism seems ready and able to perform a given behavior at the very first opportunity without the benefit of prior experience. Relatively complex behaviors of this type do occur in lower phyla and are called instincts. These are not preformed, but for all practical purposes are predetermined, developing during embryonic life. In man, however, only simple responses of a reflex nature are fully organized at birth. Undoubtedly, in the case of such developmental acquisitions, as well as in the case of phylogenetic traits acquired postnatally, environmental factors play a supportive rather than a crucially determinative role. But beyond these primitive developmental sequences of early infancy, the relative importance of incidental experience increases tremendously.

In general three kinds of empirical data support the occurrence of maturation: (a) evidence of developmental progress when opportunity for practice is experimentally or otherwise restricted; (b) evidence indicating that specific practice has no effect whatsoever on development until a certain stage of readiness is achieved in the absence of intervening practice; and (c) evidence indicating that when intervening practice is excluded, training at a later age is more efficacious than at any earlier age.

Restriction of Practice. The consistent emergence in unvarying sequential order of such neuromuscular acquisitions as movement of various bodily parts, prone progression, sitting, and postural adjustment[24, 61, 83] lends support to the view that these phylogenetic traits are acquired through maturation. It is true, of course, that in these instances the possibility of specific practice is not experimentally excluded. Nevertheless, there is little reason for believing that a significant degree of parental tutelage is furnished in any culture. Furthermore, cross-cultural studies[15,66] indicate that (barring extreme deprivation or cultural pressures) these as well as several simple social and emotional developmental sequences are substantially identical from one culture to another in the first year of life in spite of considerable diversity in child rearing practices (see p. 57).

More rigorous evidence is provided in an experiment by Dennis in which fraternal twins were reared under conditions of artificially restricted practice and minimal social stimulation. Despite lack of encouragement, reward, example, or opportunity for the usual degree of self-initiated experience, only slight retardation in motor development occurred, the latter being attributed to deprivation of self-directed activity.[12] In the same vein are findings that cradling does not delay the onset of walking,[11] that smiling appears spontaneously in the absence of social example,[15] and that the facial expressions of laughter, fear, and anger develop no differently in blind than in seeing children.[93]

More drastic and controlled restriction of practice has naturally been possible in animal experiments. In general these studies show that many phylogenetic capacities develop almost normally despite restriction of function "beyond the expected period of [their] manifestation", although they do not necessarily "emerge at a peak of perfection" (e.g., pecking in chickens).[62] The latter qualification, of course, does not invalidate the maturational hypothesis since incidental experience falls within the scope of maturation. Typical of these experiments is Carmichael's demonstration that the swimming capacity of salamander embryos is not adversely affected as a result of immobilization in an anesethic solution during the period in which bodily movements ordinarily develop.* It should be noted, however, that deprivation of ordinary environmental experience impedes development in certain functions and can cause retardation in any area if prolonged "beyond a critical period."[62] For example, pigeons do not develop optokinetic nystagmus in the absence of vision,[69] infant chimpanzees isolated from normal tactual stimulation show defective kinaesthetic learning

*For a review of animal studies, see McGraw.[62]

and cutaneous localization,[72] and chimpanzees reared in darkness fail to
fixate or recognize familiar objects or to blink in response to a threatening
object.[76] Examples of more permanent retardation following severe deprivation will be given later (see p. 87).

Effects of Premature Practice. The occurrence of maturation can also be
demonstrated by showing that practice which is useless or relatively ineffective at one stage of development becomes more efficacious at a later stage
despite isolation from a given activity in the intervening period. McGraw
has shown that specific practice has little if any effect on the acquisition of
phylogenetic traits; development simply proceeds at its own pace in response
to genic influences and incidental experience. She gave systematic daily
toilet training to one member of each of two sets of identical twins after
the first few weeks of life. Nevertheless, they failed to achieve bladder
control any earlier than their co-twins whose training was postponed until
they indicated responsiveness to same.[60] Similarly, in a pair of fraternal
twins, Johnny and Jimmy, practice in such activities as sitting, walking and
standing did not accelerate Johnny's development and only modified minor
aspects of sequence and patterning.[58] On the other hand, practice was
found to be essential in the acquisition of psychosocial skills and to accelerate
their development provided that it was administered when the child was
maturationally ready for it; prior to such time it was just as ineffective as
in the case of phylogenetic traits. Much variability prevailed from one skill
to another with respect to the age at which readiness developed. For example,
Johnny was an accomplished skater by sixteen months but profited little
from early practice in tricycling.[58]

Numerous experiments have been conducted in which practice or training at an early age have been shown to be much less efficient than at a
later age when increased readiness attributable to maturation was present.
In such studies an experimental group or identical twin is given extended
early practice, whereas an equated control group or co-twin is given a
shorter period of practice at a later age. The relative superiority of the
latter procedure (i.e., the same gain in capacity after considerably less
practice) has been demonstrated for such motor activities as buttoning,
stair and ladder climbing, cutting with scissors, tossing rings, cube building,
and throwing a ball at a moving target.[25, 34-37] It is also more effective for
tasks of a more cognitive nature such as learning vocabulary[91] and memor-
izing digits.[21, 37]

Neural Correlates of Behavioral Development

Corresponding to all overt changes in behavioral development are substrate changes in the nervous system.* The latter constitute the character-

*Reviews and reports of original investigations are available in this area.[6-8, 61, 62, 86]

istic form of growth associated with behavior, in the same sense that certain quantitative and qualitative changes in bone and muscle mark the course of skeletal development. Depending on the level of behavior involved (i.e., phylogenetic, ontogenetic, psychosocial), neural growth may reflect genic influences, incidental experience or specific practice.

Unfortunately, the determination of the neural correlates of behavioral development is beset by numerous difficulties. One approach is to measure the electroencephalographic changes that occur with increasing age.[49] However, at best, this furnishes an extremely limited and superficial picture of neural organization and functioning. A much more basic approach is through elaborate histological analysis of the brains of children who die at various ages. The disadvantages of this method are (a) the enormous technical labor involved, and (b) the impossibility of obtaining behavioral and morphological data from the *same* subjects.[62] Nevertheless such studies.[7, 8, 61] have identified many histological developments that take place in the course of neural maturation. Already at birth, an orderly laminated arrangement of cells, divisional differentiation of function, and fissurization are present. During the ensuing months, cortical cells become increasingly more differentiated, their processes became longer and more elaborate, further localization of function takes place, and the presence of myelin and neurofibrils becomes more evident. In general, these changes are demonstrable at an earlier age in those regions of the cortex that become functional first in terms of overt behavior, appearing earlier in the motor than in other areas, and earliest in the cephalic portion of the motor cortex.*

On the basis of these findings and correlative observations of infant behavior, McGraw has formulated a credible neurobehavioral theory of early motor development.[61] She holds that behavior in the first few months of life is essentially regulated by subcortical nuclei, and increasingly thereafter by the cerebral cortex. In support of this view is (a) the earlier neural maturation of the lower centers, (b) the fact that acephalic monsters manifest normal neonatal behavior,[14] and (c) the fact that certain reflexes (Moro, Babinski, grasp), which conceivably have vestigal phylogenetic significance, are active shortly after birth but are then inhibited and replaced by more mature responses. On the other hand, it is difficult to reconcile evidence of learning, conditioning and localization of cutaneous stimuli

*Although there is general agreement that these histological changes are characteristic of neural maturation, difference of opinion prevails regarding which structural changes are *essential* for functioning. Tracts tend to become myelinated in order of their phylogenetic development and functional readiness, but function may antedate myelinization. Different workers have attributed "the essential basis of functional activity in the nervous system" to the appearance of neurofibrils, to differential thresholds at the synaptic junctures between neurons, or to critical concentrations of choline esterase in neural tissue.[6]

in neonates with the *complete* absence of cortical functioning.[74] However, the greater participation of the cortex in subsequent behavioral development is unequivocally evident in the inhibition of primitive reflexes (which may reappear after cortical injury), the emergence of voluntary motor sequences, and the parallelism between the cephalocaudal trend in neuromuscular development and the order in which different portions of the motor cortex reach maturity. The successive stages of subcortical reflex dominance, cortical inhibition, and voluntary cortical control postulated by McGraw are in agreement with empirical findings regarding the development of swimming movements, prone progression and postural adjustment.[61, 62] Sitting, however, which "is of recent phylogenetic origin" starts at a cortical level.[62]

The Principle of Readiness: Educational Implications

The principle of readiness, that attained capacity (irrespective of how it is achieved) limits and influences an individual's ability to profit from current experience or practice, is one of the conceptual corner stones of child development with important implications for education and other applied disciplines. Unfortunately, however, because of the predeterministic connotations associated with the term, it has been seriously misinterpreted to mean that readiness is solely the product of maturation and that it is fixed by an endogenous (genic) timing mechanism wholly unresponsive to external influences. In the following propositions we shall attempt to summarize the implications for education which we feel can be validly derived from the principle of readiness.

1. From the standpoint of developmental psychology, the effects of practice depend upon the readiness of the individual, the nature of the task and the type of practice employed. We have already given many examples of activities, in which practice is ineffective because of insufficient readiness. On the other hand, training is surprisingly effective at a very early age in such specialized functions as roller skating[58] and the singing of tones, phrases and intervals.[40, 94] Thus, although practice has no effect on phylogenetic acquisitions, it may significantly accelerate the attainment of a *particular* ontogenetic skill if introduced at an age level when children are ready for it.

In some instances the benefits of practice do not become evident unless the task is sufficiently specific and complex to provide children with an advantage over and above what they would ordinarily derive from endogenous neural maturation and incidental experience. Mattson found that in maze learning the advantage of the trained over the untrained group of subjects was directly proportional to the complexity of the maze pattern.[57] The amount and type of practice may also make a difference. The relative efficacy of early practice in tasks such as singing and roller skating may be attributable in part to the fact that *guided* practice (*training*) utilizes most efficiently whatever readiness is present. These latter considerations suggest that before it is concluded that practice is inefficient at a given age level, the task in question be varied for difficulty level and method of instruction.

2. The relative permanence of the effects of practice is exceedingly variable. Whether a particular skill acquired at one stage of development will be intact at a later stage in the absence of intervening practice depends in part upon the extent to which the original neuromuscular integrations are disrupted by changes in size, strength, body proportions and center of gravity. In the case of roller skating, but not tricycling, these changes are sufficiently great from two to six to require almost complete re-learning.[59]

3. Apart from being wasteful and inefficient, premature practice is educationally unsound for other reasons. The child's interest and cooperation cannot be secured, irritability and negativism are aroused, and experiences of frustration may engender negative and avoidance attitudes toward particular activities.

4. Training should not be postponed merely on the theory that an older child can invariably learn anything more efficiently than a younger child. Optimal readiness rather than age per se is the relevant criterion. Waiting too long wastes valuable and often unsuspected learning opportunities. Also, on the basis of animal evidence there is good reason to believe that postponement beyond a certain critical point results in permanent retardation. If buzzards are caged for ten weeks their flying ability is permanently impaired.[13] Similarly, if newly hatched chicks are isolated from the hen for more than ten days, they fail to respond to her call, and if prevented from pecking beyond eight days, no longer peck at single grains.[73] Although comparable evidence is lacking for human infants, this suggests that certain kinds of learning may be more difficult or even impossible at a later age, and that a linear relationship does not necessarily prevail between the age of a child and his readiness for a given activity.

5. Except for phylogenetic traits, the mean age of readiness can never be specified apart from a given set of environmental conditions affecting development. When we state that reading readiness develops at 6.6 years,[68] all we mean is that the modal child in contemporary America first demonstrates ability at this age to profit from currently employed methods of instruction in reading. It does not mean that Scotch, German or Samoan children necessarily develop readiness at the same age or that age of readiness would not be altered by a radical change in teaching methods. Even within our own culture we know that reading readiness can be

accelerated by the preliminary introduction of relevant background experience.[96] Middle-class children are ready to read at an earlier age than lower-
class children because of the greater availability of books and because
they are "read to" and 'taken places" more frequently.[67] Also, since reading
readiness is related to mental age[68] and I.Q.,[10] children with high I.Q.'s
may be expected to profit from instruction prior to the age of six and
one-half, and to progress more rapidly than older but duller children of
the same mental age.

6. The educational implications of readiness illustrate beautifully the
gap between basic science and applied knowledge referred to in Chapter 1
(see pp. 18-20). Before this principle could become practically useful to
teachers they would first have to know when readiness develops in relation
to each subject matter area, to different levels within an area* and to
different techniques of teaching the same material. Teaching methods and
materials would also have to be developed to take optimal advantage of
existing degrees of readiness and to increase readiness wherever necessary
and desirable. Valid answers to such questions cannot be derived from
speculative extrapolation or provided by administrative fiat, but require
meticulous applied research in a school setting.

REFERENCES

1. Ausubel, D. P.: *Theory and Problems of Adolescent Development.* New York,
Grune & Stratton, 1954.
2. Bayer, M., and Reichard, S.: Androgyny, weight and personality. *Psychosom.
Med. 13:* 358-374, 1951.
3. Beach, F. A.: Body chemistry and perception. *In* R. R. Blake and G. V. Ramsey,
Eds., *Perception: An Approach to Personality.* New York, Ronald Press, 1951.
4. Benedek, T.: *Psychosexual Functions in Women.* New York, Ronald Press, 1952.
5. Boyd, W. C.: *Genetics and the Races of Man.* Boston, Little, Brown, 1953.
6. Carmichael, L.: The onset and early development of behavior. *In* L. Carmichael, Ed., *Manual of Child Psychology,* ed. 2. New York, Wiley, 1954, p.
60-185.
7. Conel, J. Le R.: *The Postnatal Development of the Human Cerebral Cortex.
I. The Cortex of the Newborn.* Cambridge, Mass., Harvard University Press,
1939.
8. ——: *The Postnatal Development of the Human Cerebral Cortex. III. The
Cortex of the Three-month Infant.* Cambridge, Mass., Harvard University Press,
1947.
9. David, P. R., and Snyder, L. H.: Genetic variability and human behavior. *In*
J. H. Rohrer and M. Sherif, Eds., *Social Psychology at the Crossroads.* New
York, Harper, 1951, pp. 53-82.

*The unpredictable specificity of readiness is seen in the fact that at eighteen
months children are ready to roller skate but not to use a tricycle,[58] and at four
to five years of age can profit from training in pitch but not in rhythm.[40, 41]

10. Davidson, H. P.: Experimental study of bright, dull and average children at the four-year mental level. *Genet. Psychol. Monogr. 9*: 119-289, 1931.

11. Dennis, W.: The effect of cradling practices upon the onset of walking in Hopi children. *J. Genet. Psychol. 56*: 77-86, 1940.

12. ———: Infant development under conditions of restricted practice and minimum social stimulation. *Genet. Psychol. Monogr. 23*: 143-189, 1941.

13. ———: Spalding's experiment on the flight of birds repeated with another species. *J. Comp. Psychol. 31*: 337-348, 1941.

14. ———: Is the newborn infant's repertoire learned or unlearned? *In* W. Dennis Ed., *Readings in Child Psychology.* New York, Prentice-Hall, 1951, pp. 46-53.

15. ———, and Dennis, M. G.: Does culture appreciably affect patterns of infant behavior? *J. Soc. Psychol. 12*: 305-317, 1940.

16. Ellingston, R. J.: Response to physiological stress in normal and behavior problem children. *J. Genet. Psychol. 83*: 19-29, 1953.

17. Eysenck, H. J.: Neuroticism in twins. *Eugenics Rev. 43*: 79-82, 1951.

18. Friedlander, J. H.: Some comments on the relationship of the responsivity of the adrenal cortex in schizophrenia. *Psychiat. Quart. Suppl. 25*: 76-80, Part I, 1951.

19. Fromm, E.: Psychoanalytic characterology and its application to the understanding of culture. *In* S. S. Sargent and M. W. Smith, Eds., *Culture and Personality.* New York, Basic Books, 1949, pp. 1-10.

20. Fuller, J. L.: *Nature and Nurture.* New York, Doubleday, 1954.

21. Gates, A. I., and Taylor, G. A.: An experimental study of the nature of improvement resulting from practice on a mental function. *J. Educ. Psychol. 16*: 583-592, 1925.

22. Gesell, A.: Maturation and the patterning of behavior. *In* C. Murchison, Ed., *A Handbook of Child Psychology.* Worcester, Mass., Clark University Press, 1933.

23. ———: The ontogenesis of infant behavior. *In* L. Carmichael, Ed., *Manual of Child Psychology,* ed. 2. New York, Wiley, 1954.

24. ———, and Halverson, H. M.: The daily maturation of infant behavior. *J. Genet. Psychol. 61*: 3-32, 1942.

25. ———, and Thompson, H.: Learning and growth in identical infant twins. *Genet Psychol. Monogr. 6*: 1-24, 1929.

26. Gilliland, A. R.: Socio-economic status and race as factors in infant intelligence test scores. *Child Development 22*: 271-273, 1951.

27. Hall, C. S.: The genetics of behavior. *In* S. S. Stevens, Ed., *Handbook of Experimental Psychology.* New York, Wiley, 1951, pp. 304-329.

28. Hallowell, A. I.: Culture, personality, and society. *In* A. L. Kroeber, Ed., *Anthropology Today.* Chicago, University of Chicago Press, 1953, pp. 507-523.

29. Hanks, L.: The locus of individual differences in certain primitive cultures. *In* S. S. Sargent and M. W. Smith, Eds., *Culture and Personality.* New York, Basic Books, 1949, pp. 107-123.

30. Hanley, C.: Physique and reputation of junior high school boys. *Child Development 22*: 247-260, 1951.

31. Harlow, H. F.: Levels of integration along the phyletic scale: learning aspect. *In* J. H. Rohrer and M. Sherif, Eds., *Social Psychology at the Crossroads.* New York, Harper, 1953, pp. 121-141.

32. Hayes, C.: *The Ape in Our House.* New York, Harper, 1951.

33. Herskovits, M. J.: Cultural and psychological reality. *In* J. H. Rohrer and M. Sherif, Eds., *Social Psychology at the Crossroads.* New York, Harper, 1951, pp. 145-163.

34. Hicks, J. A.: The acquisition of motor skill in young children: a study of the effects of practice in throwing at a moving target. *Child Development 1*: 90-105, 1930.

35. ———, and Ralph, D. W.: The effects of practice in tracing the Porteus diamond maze. *Child Development 2*: 156-158, 1931.

36. Hilgard, J. R.: Learning and maturation in preschool children. *J. genet. Psychol. 41*: 36-56, 1932.

37. ———: The effect of early and delayed practice on memory and motor performances studied by the method of co-twin control. *Genet. Psychol. Monogr. 14*: 493-567, 1933.

38. Hofstaetter, P. R.: The rate of maturation and the cephalization coefficient: a hypothesis. *J. Psychol. 31*: 271-280, 1951.

39. Hogben, L.: *Nature and Nurture.* New York, Norton, 1933.

40. Jersild, A. T., and Bienstock, S. F.: The influence of training on the vocal ability of three-year-old children. *Child Development 2*: 272-291, 1931.

41. ———, and ———: Development of rhythm in young children. *Child Development Monogr.,* No. 22, 1935.

42. Jones, H. E.: The galvanic skin reflex. *Child Development 1*: 106-110, 1930.

43. ———: The environment and mental development. *In* L. Carmichael, Ed., *Manual of Child Psychology,* ed. 2. New York, Wiley, 1954, pp. 631-696.

44. Jost, H. and Sontag, L. W.: The genetic factor in autonomic nervous-system function. *Psychosom. Med. 6*: 308-310, 1944.

45. Kallman, F. J.: Modern concepts of genetics in relation to mental health and abnormal personality development. *Psychiat. Quart. 21*: 535-553, 1947.

46. ———: Comparative twin studies on the genetic aspects of male homosexuality. *J. Nerv. Ment. Dis. 115*: 283-298, 1952.

47. ———: *Heredity in Health and Mental Disorder.* New York, Norton, 1953.

48. Kellogg, W. N., and Kellogg, L. A.: *The Ape and the Child.* New York, McGraw-Hill, 1933.

49. Kimura, T.: Studies on the electroencephalogram of the newborn. *Iryo 5*: 6-11, 1951.

50. Kluckhohn, C.: Universal categories of culture. *In* A. L. Kroeber, Ed., *Anthropology Today.* Chicago, University of Chicago Press, 1953, pp. 507-523.

51. ———, and Murray, H. A.: Personality formation: the determinants. *In* C. Kluckhohn and H. A. Murray, Eds., *Personality in Nature, Society and Culture.* New York, Knopf, 1949, pp. 35-48.

52. Lacey, J. I., Bateman, D. E., and Vanlehn, R.: Autonomic response specificity and Rorschach color responses. *Psychosom. Med. 14*: 256-260,1952.

53. Lennox, W. G.: The heredity of epilespy as told by relatives and twins. *J.A.M.A. 146*: 529-536, 1951.

54. Leuba, C.: *The Natural Man.* New York, Doubleday, 1954.

55. Levy, D. M.: Psychosomatic studies of some aspects of maternal behavior. *Psychosom. Med. 4*: 223-227, 1942.

56. Linton, R.: *The Study of Man.* New York, Appleton-Century-Crofts, 1936.

57. Mattson, M. L.: The relation between the complexity of the habit to be acquired and the form of the learning curve in young children. *Genet. Psychol. Monogr. 13*: 299-398, 1933.

58. McGraw, M. B.: *Growth: A Study of Johnny and Jimmy*. New York, Appleton-Century, 1935.

59. ———: Later development of children specially trained during infancy: Jimmy and Johnny at school age. *Child Development 10*: 1-19, 1939.

60. ———: Neural maturation as exemplified in achievement of bladder control. *J. Pediat. 16*: 580-590, 1940.

61. ———: *The Neuromuscular Maturation of the Human Infant*. New York, Columbia University Press, 1943.

62. ———: Maturation of behavior. *In* L. Carmichael, Ed., *Manual of Child Psychology*. New York, Wiley, 1946.

63. Mead. M.: Anthropological data on the problem of instinct. *Psychosom. Med.*, 1942, 4, 396-397.

64. ———: Educative effects of social environment as disclosed by studies of primitive societies. *In* T. M. Newcomb and E. L. Hartley, Eds., *Readings in Social Psychology*. New York, Holt, 1947. pp. 151-157.

65. ———: On the implications for anthropology of the Gesell-Ilg approach to maturation. *In* D. Haring, Ed., *Personal Character and Cultural Milieu*. Syracuse, Syracuse University Press, 1949, pp. 508-517.

66. ———, and Macgregor, F. C.: *Growth and Culture*. New York, Putnam, 1951.

67. Milner, E.: A study of the relationship between reading readiness in grade one school children and patterns of parent-child interaction. *Child Development 22*: 95-112, 1951.

68. Morphett, M. V., and Washburne, C.: When should children begin to read? *Elem. Sch. J. 31*: 496-503, 1931.

69. Mowrer, O. H.: "Maturation" vs. "learning" in the development of vestibular and optokinetic nystagmus. *J. Genet. Psychol. 48*: 383-404, 1936.

70. Murdock, G. P.: The common denominator of cultures. *In* R. Linton, Ed., *The Science of Man in the World Crisis*. New York, Columbia University Press, 1945, pp. 123-142.

71. Newman, H. H., Freeman, F. N., and Holzinger, K. J.: *Twins: A Study of Heredity and Environment*. Chicago, University of Chicago Press, 1937.

72. Nissen, H. W., Chow, K. L., and Semmes, J.: Effects of restricted opportunity for tactual, kinesthetic, and manipulative experience on the behavior of a chimpanze. *Am. J. Psychol. 64*: 485-507, 1951.

73. Padilla, S. G.: Further studies on the delayed pecking of chicks. J. *Comp. Psychol. 20*: 413-443, 1935.

74. Pratt, K. C.: The neonate. *In* L. Carmichael, Ed., *Manual of Child Psychology*, ed. 2. New York, Wiley, 1954, pp. 215-291.

75. Rees, L.: Body build, personality and neurosis in women. *J. Ment. Sci. 96*: 426-434, 1950.

76. Riesen, A. H.: The development of visual perception in man and chimpanzee. *Science 106*: 107-108, 1947.

77. Sanford, R. N.: Physical and physiological correlates of personality structure. *In* C. Kluckhohn and H. A. Murray, Eds., *Personality in Nature, Society and Culture*. New York, Knopf, 1949.

78. Schneirla, T. C.: The "levels" concept in the study of social organization in animals. *In* J. H. Rohrer and M. Sherif, Eds., *Social Psychology at the Crossroads*. New York, Harper, 1951, pp. 83-120.

79. Scott, J. P.: Implications of infra-human social behavior for problems of human relations. *In* M. Sherif and M. O. Wilson, Eds., *Group Relations at the Cross-*

roads. New York, Harper, 1953, pp. 33-73.

80. Selzer, C. C.: The relationship between the masculine component and personality. *Am. J. Phys. Anthrop. 3*: 33-47, 1945.

81. Selye, H.: Stress and the general adaptation syndrome. *Brit. M. J. 1*: 1383-1392, 1950.

82. Sheldon, W. H.: *The Varieties of Temperament.* New York, Harper, 1942.

83. Shirley M. M.: The sequential method for the studying of maturing behavior patterns. *Psychol. Rev. 38*: 507-528, 1931.

84. Slater, E.: Genetic investigations in twins. *J. Ment. Sci. 99*: 44-52, 1953.

85. Spalding, D. A.: Instinct: with original observations on young animals. *Macmillan's 27*: 282-293, 1873.

86. Sperry, R. W.: Mechanism of neural maturation. *In* S. S. Stevens, Ed., *Handbook of Experimental Psychology.* New York, Wiley, 1951, pp. 236-280.

87. Spiro, M. E.: Culture and personality: the natural history of a false dichotomy. *Psychiatry 14*: 19-56, 1951.

88. Spitz, R. A.: Hospitalism. *Psychoanal. Stud. Child 1*: 53-74, 1945.

89. Stern, C.: *Principles of Human Genetics.* San Francisco, Freeman, 1949.

90. Strandskov, H. H.: Some aspects of the genetics of human behavior. Paper read at a meeting Am. Psychol. Assoc., New York, September 1954.

91. Strayer, L. C.: Language and growth: the relative efficacy of early and deferred vocabulary training studied by the method of co-twin control. *Genet. Psychol. Monogr. 8*: 209-319, 1930.

92. Tanner, J. M.: Growth and constitution. *In* A. L. Kroeber, Ed., *Anthropology Today.* Chicago, University of Chicago Press, 1953, pp. 750-770.

93. Thompson, J.: Development of facial expression of emotion in blind and seeing children. *Arch. Psychol. 37*: No. 264, 1941.

94. Updegraf, R., Heiliger, R., and Learned, J.: The effects of training upon the singing ability and musical interests of three-, four-, and five year old children. *Univ. of Iowa Stud. Child Welf. 14*: 83-131, 1938.

95. Washburne, C.: *Child Development and the Curriculum,* 38th Yearbook, Nat. Soc. Stud. Educ., Part 1. Chicago, University of Chicago Press, 1939.

96. Waters, D.: Pre-reading experiences. *Education 54*: 308-312, 1934.

97. Wenger, M. A.: Preliminary study of the significance of measures of autonomic balance. *Psychosom. Med. 9*: 301-309, 1947.

CHAPTER 4

The Nature of Developmental Processes

THIS CHAPTER is concerned with the general characteristics of development as a process apart from its determinants or from the factors that control and regulate it.

CONTINUITY AND DISCONTINUITY

Second only to the nature-nurture controversy in historical importance has been the great debate over whether development is a process of gradual, quantitative and continuous change or whether it is characterized by abrupt, uneven and discontinuous changes which are qualitatively different from one another. However, in recent years, paralleling in large measure the fate of the first great controversy, this issue has all but disappeared from the current theoretical arena. In both instances, the decline in interest and theoretical salience has resulted from general appreciation of the fact that each issue as originally stated constituted a false dichotomy; but unfortunately, in the excess of enthusiasm over this discovery, both the genuine as well as many of the "pseudo" aspects of these issues were discarded. For even after the "either-or" and "all-or-none" formulations are rejected as untenable, the tasks of determining the relative contributions of heredity and environment in particular developmental sequences and of identifying those aspects of the latter that are relatively continuous or discontinuous still remain.

No living organism is ever in a state of complete developmental equilibrium. Nevertheless, the changes that transpire from one interval to another are hardly homogeneous in either kind or degree. For both practical and theoretical reasons it is important to distinguish between periods of intra- and interstage development. Both types of change are equally characteristic of the developmental process; and whether growth is quantitative and continuous or qualitative and discontinuous is partly a function of the rate at which it is taking place. When the rate of change is slow, development tends to occur within a framework of qualitative constancy. Old forms are consolidated or modified slightly to meet new conditions, and new elements are incorporated without any necessity for fundamental reorganization. A state of relative equilibrium and stability prevails.[40] But when the rate of change is more rapid, qualitative differentiation also

93

tends to occur. Established patterns must either be discarded or undergo radical revision. Together with recently introduced components, they are reorganized into a qualitatively different Gestalt which is discontinuous with the antecedent condition of the organism; and until consolidation occurs, a state of relative instability and disequilibrium exists.[40] In other instances, however, because of the operation of cushioning mechanisms, qualitative, interstage growth is accomplished gradually without abruptness.

Factors Making for Development Continuity

The greater portion of any developmental process tends to be continuous rather than discontinuous in nature. When, for example, height, strength, masculinity-femininity or androgenic-estrogenic secretion are plotted against age, the resulting growth curves are smooth except for one or two indications of marked acceleration or deceleration. Other growth curves (e.g., general intelligence) appear to be completely continuous, although this is partly attributable to the fact that they represent the *average* attainment of many individuals with respect to a battery of heterogeneous functions. Nevertheless, even if a given sequence can be divided into several qualitatively different phases, it is self-evident that the total duration of intra-stage growth will usually exceed that of transitional periods of development.

Apart from the absence of conditions that precipitate sudden rapid growth, many factors inherent in the developmental process operate either to cushion the abruptness of discontinuous change or to maintain continuity. The first possibility is illustrated by the fact that a sharp line of demarcation can seldom be drawn between the relinquishment of an established pattern and the acquisition of a new pattern of behavior. Instead, a long period of coexistence tends to be the rule. Creeping and walking occur alternately in varying proportions until the latter practice predominates and gains ascendency. Sometimes a preview of the more mature behavior appears sporadically long before it is ready to function. A ten month old infant may take several steps and then not make another attempt at walking for another month. Eventually, however, the new pattern becomes a subsidiary accompaniment of the old and undergoes gradual perfection before partial and later total replacement occur. In a sense the earlier phase of a new activity may be regarded as a preparatory stage of the terminal phase. This sequence of events not only takes place autogenously in nature, but is also deliberately induced as an instrument of parental or cultural child rearing policy. For example, much of the training which children receive is not intended for immediate application but as an investment in the future—to be available when needed in adult life. In either case, however, this overlapping of current and future patterns mitigates the abruptness of developmental discontinuity.

Cushioning of the content as well as of the execution of discontinuous change is also possible. This occurs when an old behavior pattern can be retained or reestablished but requires radical restructuring because of significant alteration in the larger setting in which it takes place. This would apply to the relearning of roller skating (see p. 87), to sex behavior, to the quest for primary or derived status, and to many forms of dependent and immature behavior that are acceptable at a later stage of development provided they are recast in a qualitatively different form. Nevertheless, the change is not nearly as discontinuous as would be the case if the content were completely new.

A more fundamental source of continuity that goes beyond mere cushioning of abrupt qualitative change inheres in the possibility of perpetuating established patterns of behavior in quantitatively different contexts *without* any basic need for reorganization of content or process. For example, most of the motor skills of early childhood (e.g., swimming, bicycling) are retained intact for a lifetime despite gross changes in size, strength and body proportions. Similarly, the moral and religious values of adults are fundamentally identical in content with those of children despite marked shifts in the basis of acceptance.

Factors Making for Developmental Discontinuity

Because biological and behavioral equilibria are maintained by a complex system of regulatory devices, once established they are not easily disrupted. Generally speaking, organisms react to changing conditions by modifying themselves or the environment in ways that tend to perpetuate the constancy of the prevailing adaptive mechanisms. In the absence of compelling reasons for drastic change, only minor and qualitatively homogeneous adjustments are made; and even when coercive reasons are operative, the cushioning factors described above frequently temper the abruptness of change. Hence, the only *essential* criterion of discontinuity is a qualitative break in the content, organization, or functional basis of a phenomenon. It need not necessarily be ushered in abruptly or represent a complete departure from previous practice, although acceleration in the rate of change obviously fosters disequilibrium and reorganization.

Crises in personality development satisfy both criteria of discontinuity. They are generated by the relatively sudden introduction of compelling new variables with a catalytic or consummatory impact on an ongoing developmental process (see pp. 104 and 288). Threshold phenomena— developmental acquisitions that do not become overtly functional until a certain critical level of substrate change is exceeded—offer another case in point. Many long-range learning processes and endocrinological changes illustrate this type of development. Here the occurrence of gradual continuous change merely results in quantitative, nonfunctional modification over the greater portion of a given range of variability. Then, with the reaching of threshold value, the last unit of quantitative change generates a qualitatively discontinuous state of affairs culminating in the apparently sudden emergence of a new function.

When the determining factors of development are less dramatic or when cushioning is more effective, discontinuity in process or content still occurs but the mode of transformation or the extent of change is less abrupt. In response to new demands, expectations, or developing capacities, qualitatively different levels of functioning are achieved by the cumulation of small continuous changes. Many successful and highly rewarding behavior patterns of long standing (e.g., creeping, hand feeding, executive dependence on parents) are gradually abandoned or revised in this manner. The change-over itself is effected gradually and continuously despite the fact that the new patterns are qualitatively distinct from and even antithetical to the old. In phylogenetic activities such changes may occur quite spontaneously without any cultural pressure, but it cannot be assumed that the same holds true for ontogenetic traits as well. The abruptness of change in other instances is lessened by the duplication of content even though extensive qualitative restructuring is required.

Criteria for Stages of Development

Much controversy exists regarding the legitimacy of identifying different stages of development. Yet, if certain wholly gratuitous criteria are excluded from the definition of a "stage," the issue is easily resolved. Following logically from the above discussion of continuity and discontinuity, the designation of developmental stages merely indicates that qualitative distinctions in process or content can be identified during the course of growth. For stages of development to exist it is neither necessary to assume (a) that they are the spontaneous and inevitable products of endogenous factors nor (b) that *no* overlapping of process occurs among children of different ages. For example, it is fashionable nowadays to dismiss Piaget's description of different stages of causal thinking on the grounds that both mature and immature responses are found at all age levels. Considerable overlapping, however, is inevitable in any ontogenetic developmental process where great variability necessarily prevails in both genic endowment and environmental stimulation. Thus, to demonstrate the existence of developmental stages it is only necessary to show that certain qualitative differences in process arise consistently at definite points in a developmental cycle which differentiate the greater mass of children at a given age level from adjacent age groups.

LONG-RANGE STABILITY OF INDIVIDUALITY

A related but different kind of developmental continuity from the type we have just been discussing has to do with the long-range stability of individual differences. Here we are not concerned with the continuity or discontinuity of normative developmental sequences but (a) with the problem of whether individuality in personality organization is maintained over extended periods of time, and if so, (b) with the factors responsible for same.

Evidence of Stability

Examination of the available evidence points unequivocally to an affirmative answer to the first question raised above. Shirley,[90, 91] Gesell,[39, 41] and others have shown that temperamental differences in children are both marked at birth (see p. 113) and exceedingly stable throughout infancy and the preschool period.* The relative positions of five infants ranked on fifteen personality traits at one year of age remained constant or showed little change when they were ranked again at age five.[38] Longitudinal studies by McKinnon[71] and Paulsen[79] have yielded comparable findings for the age periods from three to eight and two to twelve respectively. Individual differences in general approach to social situations and in Rorschach variables were maintained despite developmental changes implicating the group as a whole; and where shifts occurred, they were in the direction of tendencies that were evident but less pronounced at an earlier age. Follow-up studies of Shirley's infant subjects[75] and Gesell's infant twins T and C[41] 15 and 13 years later indicated that many of the earlier differences in total personality pattern or style of life were still maintained. Even more remarkable was the finding that ratings of children on 30 out of 35 character traits remained approximately the same when they were independently rated on the same traits 50 years later.[94]

These data by no means point to the life-long "freezing" of childhood personality structure. In fact, as we shall indicate shortly (see p. 265), many of the more desirable personality outcomes of favorable early upbringing can be partly vitiated by undue deprivation, severe interpersonal conflict, or crippling disease in later childhood, adolescence and adult life. Nevertheless, they do indicate that a sizable nucleus of stubborn individuality remains relatively intact in the face of environmental vicissitudes.

Sources of Stability

How can such consistency in individual personality development be

*The persistance of many single temperamental traits, such as laughing, crying, smiling, aggressiveness, perseveration, etc., during this period has been reported by several investigators.[2]

explained? Three kinds of factors seem to be involved: those originating from within (a) the child himself and (b) his environment, and (c) various integrative and self-perpetuating mechanisms involved in the organization of personality. The child furnishes a cluster of genically determined temperamental predispositions (see p. 112-113) which, in accordance with their strength and resistiveness to environmental modification, help perpetuate the sameness of his response to social experience. These predispositions may even be strong enough in certain cases to persist despite considerable training and cultural pressure in the opposite direction.[90, 91] In addition, different children respond differently to the same pattern of parental behavior, and thereby serve either to change or reinforce the latter. A self-assertive child, for example, reacts differently than an apathetic child to parental overdomination. Lastly, the child's temperament in and of itself selectively evokes differential responses from significant persons in his environment; and to the extent that his genically conditioned traits and the reactions of parents, teachers and associates to same are relatively consistent, an additional source of long-range continuity is provided. Everyday experience indicates that irritability or peevishness in a child "tends to arouse impatience and annoyance in others, and by so doing . . . helps to produce an environment that fosters his peevish ways."[56]

The parent contributes to the continuity of the child's individuality by providing a relatively constant interpersonal environment during the important formative years of the latter's personality development. This constancy, of course, is a function of the longitudinal consistency of the parent's own personality and child rearing attitudes. It is true that sooner or later the child is directly exposed to extrafamilial values in the culture which are at variance with those of the home; but in general, by virtue of prior conditioning and differential exposure, he tends to be selectively influenced by the particular value judgments emanating from the social class and other institutional affiliations of his parents.

Perpetuation of the formative effects of early (post-infantile) experience may be attributed in part to their initially deep entrenchment. The family-biased sample of the culture exerts disproportionate influence on the child's personality development because the restricted nature of his early environment and the unstructured condition of his major value and attitude systems make him maximally susceptible to any form of recurrent, pervasive and affectively toned patterning influence. Then, once established, canalization and reaction-sensitivity tend to impose further restrictions on the theoretical array of behaviors open to any individual. What would otherwise constitute just one of many potentially adequate ways of meeting a need or solving a problem becomes the *only* adequate way.[74] "Habitual modes of reaction," in turn, "sensitize" the individual "to certain aspects of his experience and dull him to others. When he enters new surroundings and meets new people, he is more ready to respond in one direction than another, and this readiness itself acts selectively to bring him more of similar kinds of experience."[21]

Once organized on a stable basis, distinctive personality structure, like any developmental equilibrium, tends to remain intact in the absence of substantial cause for change. The child does not start from scratch in each new situation, but brings with him a precipitate of all past learnings. He attempts to maintain the same orientations, habits, adjustive mechanisms, and modes of striving and interacting with others that he used before. Even if change occurs in the objective properties of a situation (e.g., parent attitudes), habitual apperceptive sets may be strong enough in certain cases to force altered stimulus content into preconceived perceptual molds* (perceptual constancy"). When this kind of perceptual manipulation is precluded by major change in the environmental situation, the child attempts first to respond in terms of his existing personality organization and to utilize habitual adjustive techniques found successful in the past before he ventures to reorganize his personality or to improvise basically new patterns of behavior. Extreme conservatism in this regard leads to the perpetuation of immature behavior patterns that are no longer appropriate or acceptable at higher age levels, e.g., temper tantrums, "baby talk," enuresis, motor helplessness in an eight year old.

Finally, the longitudinal continuity of individuality can be attributed to the fact that certain central dimensions of personality play a crucial integrative role in its development and organization.

> As a result of characteristic ways of interacting with significant persons in the environment, more or less permanent constellations of ego needs and habitual modes of self-evaluation arise. Examples of such constellations are differential feelings of security and adequacy, and needs for ego status and independence that emerge in crucial developmental sequences like satellization† or failure to undergo devaluation. These constellations give rise to propensities for characteristic modes of learning, aspiring, socialization, ego-defense, and attitudes toward authority and group demands.[5]

---

*This "freezing" of perception despite change in stimulus content is facilitated further by the acceptance of general categorical propositions which dispose individuals to ignore the information supplied by first-hand experience. Once general categories of objects and relationships are established, the properties of currently experienced stimuli are simply inferred on the basis of their categorical membership.

†A form of dependent identification with superordinate figures as a result of which an individual acquires derived status if he is accepted and intrinsically valued by the former. See p. 279.

It would be surprising indeed if the prior existence and operation of such salient aspects of individual uniqueness did not leave some functional residue in personality structure. The latter could affect directly the kind of current biosocial status an individual seeks and the basis on which he assimilates values. "Thus, for example, although an adult who satellized as a child obtains most of his current status from primary rather than from derived sources, some satellizing patterns [could] still remain operative in adult life and furnish a subsidiary source of status, e.g., satellizing-like relationships with boss, spouse, pastor, physician, membership group, etc."[6] In addition, a residue of prior satellizing experience could conceivably constitute an inner core of self-acceptance which would be independent of situational success and failure. Although this would not function as a subsidiary source of currently generated status, it cold exercise a substrate influence serving to keep his ego aspirations within realistic limits and to protect him from catastrophic impairment of self-esteem (see page 329).

CONTEMPORANEOUS CONSISTENCY IN PERSONALITY ORGANIZATION

Even more basic perhaps to the concept of personality than the longitudinal continuity of individuality is its internal consistency at a given horizontal level. It is self-evident that the former can be no more than a developmental outgrowth of the latter. As already pointed out, the entire concept of personality would be meaningless if it did not refer to a relatively stable and consistent organization of individually unique behavioral predispositions (see p. 42); behavior could otherwise be explained completely in terms of general reaction capacities, situational determinants, and transitory motivations generated in the course of current experience.

Both contemporaneously and longitudinally, consistency in personality structure is largely a function of the fact that behavioral traits become organized and hierarchically ordered in relation to certain of its central unifying gradients or core aspects. In human beings, the *ego*, a functionally interrelated constellation of attitudes, motives, values, aspirations, and orientations toward other persons and groups—all having significant self-reference—plays this crucial integrative role in personality organization and development.[5, 74, 88] It constitutes in itself a self-consistent, integrated, and enduring system; and further consistent development is insured by the tendency to assimilate new trait trends compatible with it and, hence, with each other. As a result, generality in responding to a host of objects, persons, values, and institutions in an unending variety of concrete situations becomes possible,[88] and syndromes of functionally and developmentally meaningful personality traits can be identified.

Evidence of Limited Consistency in Children

In children, for reasons which we shall examine shortly, the evidence indicates that although a nucleus of horizontal consistency does exist, considerable tolerance for inconsistency in personality organization is also present but probably diminishes with increasing age. Sanford and others were able to identify twenty meaningfully constituted personality syndromes in school children based upon intercorrelations among traits that averaged about .5 within each syndrome.[84] However, these syndromes were quite phenotypic in nature, the intersituational generality of the various trait measures was unknown, and relatively little stability over a three-year period was maintained. Hartshorne and May obtained correlations of .4 to .5 for different objective measures of deceit within the same kind of situation but considerably less generality of function from one situation to another.[47] On the other hand, comparable studies by Slaght[93] and Barbu[10] showed a fair amount of intersituational generality in children for truthfulness and honesty respectively. In studying satellizing and nonsatellizing trends in such related areas as explanations of moral behavior, agreement with perceived parent opinions, identification with heroes, and notions of omnipotence, Ausubel and others found relatively high inter-item generality for each instrument but low intercorrelations among the different variables in a population of ten year olds.[8, 9]

Moral, character and value traits, however, probably provide too rigorous a test of trait generality in children. Much of the inconsistency is undoubtedly indicative (a) of insufficient cognitive ability with which to subsume specific situations under general value propositions, and (b) of the chaotic and conflictful state of moral education in our culture (see p. 399). In contrast, extremely high generality over trials was obtained for such motivational measures as goal discrepancy scores (level of aspiration),[8] goal tenacity scores,[8] and responsiveness to prestige incentives,[3] and for responsiveness to prestige suggestion;[9] and in the case of the first three variables, generality coefficients of .4 to .9 were found, depending on the degree of similarity between the tasks used.[6, 8]

Sources of Inconsistency

Consistency is a measure of the compatibility of parts with the whole and with each other. Hence, since the child's personality is relatively unformed and is changing rapidly, there is obviously less basis for consistency than in the adult. Until a crystallized and stable representation of individuality is achieved, many divergent trends are compatible within the existing total organization. Furthermore, since the child requires some experience with a given kind of behavior before he can judge its congruence with his major goal and value systems, he is apt to give many ultimately unsuitable patterns a "provisional try" before he finally rejects them. With increasing age, however, a more characteristic portrait of the individual emerges and a clearer standard for guaging compatibility becomes available. Many alternatives experimented with on a tentative basis are found wanting and are sloughed off. Thus, by a process of progressive "acquisition of dislikes by individuals whose initial attitude is favorable toward everything," personality organization becomes increasingly more integrated and self-consistent. Even in the turbulence of adolescence such character traits as honesty, responsibility, and moral courage acquire considerably more generality than in childhood.[51] And the adolescent and young adult who consistently over or underestimates his forthcoming performance does likewise with his past performance,[7] I.Q.[42] and sociometric status.[85]

We do not wish to imply that judgments of consistency are necessarily deliberate; very frequently they are made quite incidentally. Yet with advancing age, as the child's personality takes more definite shape and as he develops a clearer conception of it and greater capacity for perceiving incompatibility, the need for preserving self-consistency gradually increases. Unlike the young child, the older individual employs a conscious monitoring system which, by virtue of selective assimilation, retention, and rejection, helps maintain congruence between his personality structure and his self-concept;[6] but since unbiased conscious control is often insufficient for this purpose, he also utilizes such supplementary mechanisms as perceptual and logical distortion, repression, and the isolation of beliefs in logic-tight compartments. Nevertheless, even the well-integrated adult displays considerable tolerance for consciously appreciated inconsistency. The widespread belief that *all* inconsistency must necessarily be "unconscious" or below the threshold of awareness is one of the major psychological myths of our time.

Relatively recently it has also been recognized that *some* of the apparent lack of trait generality in children, as well as in adults, is spurious because of the failure to hold ego-involvement constant. It stands to reason that trait behavior in different situations is not comparable unless degree of self-implication is approximately equivalent. For example, level of aspiration in laboratory[48, 69, 80] and "real-life"[7] tasks, tendency to cheat,[3] responsiveness to prestige incentives,[3] memory for completed as against incompleted tasks,[82] level of confidence in a variety of tasks,[59] and tenacity of vocational goals,[7] all increase with magnitude of ego-involvement.

Lastly, some of the apparent inconsistency in children's personality structure is merely a reflection of the grossness and invalidity of existing measuring instruments. In the absence of subtle measures capable of penetrating beneath (a) normative commonalities characterizing all children at a particular stage of development, and (b) different phenotopic expressions of the same genotypic tendency, spurious inconsistency is inevitably added to that which already exists. Originally it was thought that projective techniques might provide the needed methodological tools, but many difficult problems still remain to be solved with respect to feasibility of administration, reliability, validity, and applicability to many important personality variables (see p. 160). The crucial importance of the problem of measurement is also underlined by the fact that to date, longitudinal continuity in children's personality organization has only been demonstrated for gross temperamental traits,[39, 41, 90, 91] total personality patterns,[71, 75] highly general Rorschach variables,[79] and a mother's impressionistic ratings of character and temperament.[94] More structured thematic materials used in the investigation of specific trait trends have shown inadequate interinstrument or intersituational generality in many instances[8] as well as little long-range continuity.[84]

TRANSITIONAL PERIODS OF DEVELOPMENT

We have already indicated that one of the chief types of developmental discontinuity is brought about by significant and relatively rapid shifts in the individual's biosocial status. The periods in which qualitatively new and discontinuous (inter-stage) changes in personality organization are being formulated may be designated as transitional phases or developmental crises. "During these transitional periods the individual is in the marginal position of having lost an established and accustomed status and of not yet having acquired the new status toward which the factors impelling developmental change are driving him."[5] He is not without any status whatsoever, but that which he does enjoy is "vague, ambiguous and rapidly changing."[5]

Causes of Developmental Crises

What is responsible for critical shifts in biosocial status and the developmental crises they precipitate? Although it is true that some of the determining factors may be endogenous or the product of incidental experience, no transitional period is ever completely divorced from external pressures or solely a reflection of "spontaneous maturation."* It is also important to bear in mind that preparatory or predisposing influences are usually operative for a long time before consummatory or catalytic factors are brought into play, and that the factors responsible for inaugurating developmental crises are not necessarily the same ones required for their satisfactory resolution.

*In some nonpersonality areas of development (e.g., neuromuscular development in infancy), transitional periods may be conceived of as maturational.[70]

In general, transitional stages in personality organization are precipitated by two kinds of factors:

(a) an urgent need within the culture for a fundamental modification of the social and personality status of an entire group of individuals who are in a given stage of developmental equilibrium; (b) the occurrence of marked changes within the individual, changes in physical make-up, basic drives, competencies, perceptual ability, which are so crucial that present status becomes incompatible with his altered appearance, capacities, needs and perceptions.[5]

An example illustrating the operation of and interaction between these variables is afforded by the crisis of devaluation separating infancy from childhood. It

is precipitated by the consolidation of sufficient motor, intellectual, and social skill to make possible a greater measure of self-help and conformity to parental direction. The parents in turn are motivated by a desire to gain the volitionally ascendent role in the relationship that the conditions of dependency warrant, and to rear their child in the traditions of the culture. And lastly, the child's perceptual capacity becomes sufficiently acute to appreciate more realistically his role and status.[4]

Characteristics of Transitional Periods

There are many reasons for believing that transitional periods in personality development must be difficult and productive of stress. First, an individual's biosocial status provides an over-all frame of reference for the organization of his attitudes, values, goals and standards of conduct. Hence, it is quite understandable that profound *disorientation* should occur when it is abruptly cast aside and replaced by another. As he is thrust into "new and uncharted psychological fields the landmarks . . . of which are obscure and hazy," the familiar and differentiated roles that he had learned in relation to an earlier pattern of social expectations and the cues that he had employed with confidence in interpreting his interpersonal environment suddenly become useless and confusing. Second, considerable *anxiety* is engendered by the threat to self-esteem inherent in forfeiting current status while the attainment of new status is still uncertain. He is required to discard a painfully acquired portion of his identity, the security of established roles and status prerogatives, and frequently a sheltered and protected position; and in return he is permitted to strive for a potentially more satisfactory type of biosocial status. But in connection with this striving looms the ever-present threat of disappointment and failure, the pull of conflicting loyalties and the awesome responsibilities of freedom and autonomy.*[56] And whenever he is forced to choose between two alternatives,

*It also seems likely that the aura of uncertainty regarding the acquisition of potential status is deliberately fostered by the culture in order to encourage a high and sustained level of individual motivation in meeting new social expectations.

each of which offers advantages as well as disadvantages (e.g., parents or peers, dependence or conformity, conformity or individuality), a decision in favor of one inevitably frustrates needs and inclinations referable to the other and gives rise to regret and self-recrimination.

A third source of the stressfulness of transitional periods is the inevitable abruptness with which they are inaugurated. The very suddenness of discontinuous changes in the rate or direction of development adds to disorientation and anxiety and affords insufficient opportunity for the acquisition of adaptive responses; "and when the developmental process is sufficiently complex to encompass several constituent aspects, discrepancies in rate of growth are practically inevitable"[5] (see p. 109). Fortunately, however, the abruptness of developmental crises is often mitigated by the cushioning mechanisms described in the first section of this chapter.

Marginality of status is a characteristic feature and still another source of transitional stress. It is a product of natural overlapping in developmental sequences (as when preparatory or training periods coexist with older patterns of behavior), of inertia and resistance to change, and of developmental regression. Inertia refers to the various regulatory devices that tend to perpetuate sameness of personality organization and to adapt established response patterns to new conditions, i.e., canalization, reaction sensitivity, perceptual constancy, the preferential use of habitual adjustive techniques, and the tenacity of central organizing dimensions of personality. Resistance to change arises from anticipated anxiety and disorientation in connection with developmental crises, from threatened loss of immediate status, from ambivalence about exchanging an established and familiar status for one that is insecure and uncertain, and from resistiveness to insistent environmental pressures. By opposing irresistible forces impelling redirection of development, it makes the transition more traumatic and conflictful. Lastly, regression (see following section), a common adjustive response to the hazards and frustrations of developmental transition, reinstates outmoded behavior patterns and prolongs the period of overlapping.

Marginality—whether of overt status or of needs and loyalties—generates an uncomfortable and unstable state of psychological ambiguity, tentativeness, uncertainty and indecision. Unquestionably,

many conflicts in childhood are due to forces corresponding to the various groups to which the child belongs. Such conflicts are particularly important for children in marginal positions, that is, for children who are standing on the boundary between two groups. . . . Uncertainty of the ground on which the child stands leads to an alternation between the values of the one and of the other group, to a state of emotional tension, and to a frequent fluctuation between overaggression and overtimidity.[65]

Transitional periods of personality development, in which biosocial status and major identifications and anchorages are substantially marginal and indefinite, are necessarily self-limited in duration. Beyond a period of weeks or months they become intolerable. Hence, if further prolongation is required, as, for example, during adolescence in most complexly organized cultures, "it becomes necessary to formalize a definite *interim status*" with various distinctive characteristics of its own. This acquires relative stability, and "provides the adolescent with some recognized social standing, an opportunity for acquiring some current self-esteem, and a tangible frame of reference for selectively accepting certain attitudes, values, and goals and rejecting others."[5]

DEVELOPMENTAL REGRESSION

The term "regression" refers to development that is opposite in direction to the prevailing trend of growth. It indicates that after attaining a more advanced, complex, or highly differentiated level of behavior or personality organization, an individual reverts to an earlier and more primitive level characteristic of younger or less mature persons. Regression may occur both as a manifestation of behavioral disorganization or as an adjustive response to frustration. We shall not be concerned here with transitory regressive reactions to situational frustration[11] but with longer-lasting regression in connection with typical developmental sequences in personality development.

Pseudo-regression

Regression is frequently and mistakenly confused with two other common developmental phenomena, namely, agenesis or fixation, and incomplete consolidation. The important differentiating criterion is that before regression can be said to exist, a more advanced level of development must have previously been attained. For example, the *simple* schizophrenic who at the age of 25 is passive, dependent, preoccupied with hedonistic gratification, and unconcerned about normal adult goals has not essentially undergone regression; for the most part, he simply never *progressed* beyond the preadolescent stage of personality maturation.

A common cause of personality agenesis (in addition to whatever genic predispositions may be operative) is insufficient environmental pressure, in the form of appropriate demands and expectations, to overcome resistance to and ambivalence about change. The underdominated child, for example, frequently fails to learn responsibility and frustration tolerance because he does not feel that they are expected of him. Lack of adequate stimulation or opportunity for practice may also result in agenesis, as illustrated by developmental retardation among institutionalized children, and by the failure of overdominated or overprotected children to acquire normal volitional independence and peer group socialization.* Less serious forms of fixation or persistence of developmentally inappropriate behavior may be induced by undue frustration at an earlier stage, (e.g., thumbsucking [see p. 240]), or by excessive gratification, e.g., if temper tantrums are made too rewarding.

Incomplete consolidation of newly learned behavior patterns may also bear some superficial resemblance to regression. Actually, however, the path of developmental progress seldom takes an undeviatingly upward course; zig-zag fluctuations are characteristic until equilibrium is established. For example, before foolproof sphincter control is finally achieved, occasional "slips" are not uncommon—even after apparent mastery has been attained. Also, everyday experience confirms the fact that vestiges of ostensibly discarded behavior continue to appear until their underlying attitudes are completely eradicated. And even when outmoded attitudinal substrates are finally abandoned, time must be allowed for deeply ingrained fragments of old roles to wither away and for the nuances of new roles to become habitual ("developmental lag").

Another characteristic pseudoregressive feature of transitional phases of development is the loss in efficiency that occurs when a more primitive but highly practiced activity is superseded by one at a qualitatively higher level of performance. "The creeping child moves faster through space than his contemporary who is learning to walk."[4] This apparent retrogression and "the see-saw fluctuations" that occur until consolidation is complete have been referred to by Gesell as the "spiral of development."[38, 40]

True Regression

Genuine regression is a general manifestation of the altered state of reactivity accompanying any form of gross behavioral disorganization induced by serious frustration, conflict or disorientation. As a result of a generalized lowering of response thresholds, behavior becomes less specific and adaptive and more primitive and undifferentiated. Thus, regression is frequently characteristic of the behavioral disequilibrium found in all normative developmental crises[38, 40, 70] as well as in the more personal crises in individual experience. Regressive behavior may also serve an adjustive function. It can be utilized as an escape from the hazards of threatening new situations to the security of more familiar roles, or as a certain means of obtaining gratification and insuring success when an individual is blocked at a higher level of performance. For example, the six year old who is terrified at the prospect of beginning school may relapse

*The subject of personality maturation and agenesis is discussed fully in Chapter 9 (p. 300).

to babyish ways in the home; the socially unpopular child who is rejected by his peers may revert to "kid" games and playing with younger children. Sometimes, regressive behavior (e.g., loss of sphincter control, enuresis), may be employed consciously or "unconsciously" as an attention-getting device, i.e., as a means of competing with a younger sibling, or as a technique of expressing aggression and punishing parents.

A special type of regression occurs occasionally as a reflection of developmental preoccupation with a new phase of growth.[56] For example, in his initial fascination with the new activity, a child who is first learning to talk may become practically oblivious of everything else in the environment. As a result, other older developmental acquisitions, such as sphincter control or use of eating utensils, may go by the board.

PARALLELISM AND DIVERGENCE IN COMPONENT ASPECTS OF DEVELOPMENT

There can be little argument about the fact that different aspects of development must of necessity be *interrelated*. Since any organism functions and develops as a whole rather than as a collection of discrete and isolated capacities, growth or retardation in any one area obviously affects (i.e., stimulates or limits) growth in all other areas.* However, even though such interrelatedness makes for a significant degree of functional and developmental interaction, and limits the extent of disparity between component rates of growth, it does not necessarily insure *parallelism* between different functions. In effect this means that although physical and intellectual development, for example, mutually influence each other, there is no necessary relationship between their respective rates of growth in a *particular* individual. Thus, if Johnny is physically advanced for his age, the probability that his intellectual development will be similarly accelerated is little better than chance.

The Evidence

Studies of the relationship between physical status and motor ability, on the one hand, and intelligence or intellectual ability, on the other hand, show negligible or zero correlations throughout adolescence and adult life.[1, 57, 77] Relatively high positive correlations are found during infancy,[12, 89] but these decline consistently with increasing age.[1, 12, 13] Moreover, even the initially high relationship is largely spurious. Since intelligence has few cognitive outlets in infancy, many of the tests of "intellectual" ability included in infant intelligence scales really measure sensori-motor or

*Illustrations of interrelatedness in development are found on pages 288, 320, 464, and 516.

neuromuscular skills. The positive relationship between intelligence and physical-motor status demonstrated at the extremes of intellectual ability also reflects the operation of extraneous factors. In extreme cases of intellectual deficit, children frequently do not possess sufficient general intelligence to learn even simple motor skills; and intellectually gifted children tend to be taller and heavier, and to become pubescent earlier[92, 102] largely because the same superior socioeconomic status they tend to enjoy provides both better nutrition and more intellectual stimulation. A direct test of the organismic age concept in children at three grade levels showed no tendency for acceleration in mental age to be accompanied by similar acceleration in weight, age or dental age.*

In view of these findings, the widely accepted generalizations reached by Olson and Hughes that "a child's growth and achievement show a 'going-togetheredness' " and that "achievement is a function of the organism as a whole", hardly seem justified.[76] That they are supported by isolated cases selected from a given population proves little indeed since such occasional concomitance could be expected merely on a chance basis. Furthermore, much of the obtained parallelism can be accounted for by the presence of common general factors *within* the two main categories of functions measured by these workers. For example, it is hardly surprising that reading age, spelling age, language usage and educational age are positively intercorrelated, or that height, weight, strength of grip, skeletal age, and dental age are similarly related to each other.

Factors Making for Divergence

Logical analysis confirms the empirical findings cited above. Since each area of development is regulated by a different set of determinants, there is no *a priori* reason for supposing that parallelism should exist. "It is extremely unlikely that the particular constellation of genic and environmental factors regulating the development of any given trait or capacity would completely overlap the set of regulatory factors involved in the development of any other trait or capacity."[5] During transitional periods of development, discrepancies between the relative status of different functions tend to widen since all components are not equally sensitive to the factors precipitating developmental crises. Skeletal and neuromuscular growth, for example, are extremely conspicuous during infancy, level off in childhood, and enjoy another spurt in adolescence. Emotional and social development are also marked by periods of slow and rapid growth, whereas the course of intellectual development is relatively smooth and even.

The general trend in development is toward increasing divergence of

*See P. Bloomers, M. Knief, and Stroud, J. B., *J. Educ. Psychol. 46*: 142-150, 1955.

existing differences in the component capacities of an individual. In intellectual development, for example, intelligence becomes increasingly more differentiated, as shown by the decreasing intercorrelations among the subtests of intelligence scales as children advance in age.[36] Another indication of the progressive trend toward differentiation of abilities is the fact that ten year old boys of high socioeconomic status make higher scores than ten year old boys of low socioeconomic status on tests of both verbal and mechanical ability, but at age sixteen are only superior on the verbal tests.[50, 55]

This trend toward differentiation and divergence reflects the operation of a selective process which accentuates initial acceleration or retardation in a given function. Since all potential abilities cannot be maximally developed, individuals tend to exercise those capacities in which they excel and succeed, and to avoid those activities in which they are relatively inferior and experience failure. Thus, as a result of a circular relationship between use and proficiency, original discrepancies in ability are progressively widened.*

Factors Making for Parallelism

As already suggested, although the interrelatedness of development does not necessarily insure parallelism, it does limit the extent of divergence that is possible. Serious intellectual deficiency, for example, inevitably spreads to all other aspects of development. Another type of limiting effect is illustrated by the fact that acceleration in one area must frequently be halted until growth in other supportive areas catches up sufficiently to permit further progress. Thus, relative to his limited motor and verbal capacities, an infant's social behavior is quite precocious; but until he learns to locomote and communicate more efficiently, more mature forms of social experience are beyond his reach. Rapid development in one area may also serve to stimulate growth in another, thereby tending to reduce the discrepancy between them. This sequence of events is seen during transitional periods of development that are precipitated when the capacities of an age group are seriously at variance with the type of biosocial status it enjoys. The period of infancy, for example, is brought to a close when parents decide that a child is mature enough in a motor and cognitive sense to surrender some of his volitional independence (i.e., to submit to their direction) and to manifest more executive independence (self-help).

Parallelism in rate of growth of capacities within an individual sometimes occurs because of particular social values or stereotypes. Since educa-

---

*In compensating for deficiencies it is only natural to seek success in conspicuously different activities. Conformity to such cultural stereotypes as athlete *or* scholar also helps to promote dichotomization and divergence in the development of abilities.

tional and motor retardation affect adversely a child's social acceptability among his peers, it would be reasonable to expect that this retardation would spread to the social sphere as well. Similarly, by virtue of expectations generated by the cultural association of leadership ability with a commanding appearance, tall, well-built children are more apt to seek and be chosen for positions of leadership (see p. 484).

INDIVIDUAL DIFFERENCES IN RATE AND PATTERNING OF DEVELOPMENT

In the present section we shall consider some *general* issues concerned with individual differences in development. This discussion, of course, deals with much different problems than the advisability of using the individual as a source or subject of application of developmental data and insights (see pp. xiii, 18 and 141).

Normative Growth versus Individual Differences

Despite the occurrence of individual differences and overlapping between age groups in rate, sequence, and patterning of growth, many uniformities characterize development as a process. Except for phylogenetic traits, these regularities are attributable to commonalities in polygenic make-up and in environmental influences. If they did not occur, few generalizations indeed could ever be formulated about the development of children, and each child's growth would have to be considered completely unique. Fortunately, however, it is possible to discover developmental laws that express in equation form the relationships of different variables to each other. In relation to such laws "individual differences have to be conceived of as various, specific values which these variables have in a particular case."[65]

It is equally important to emphasize the converse of the above proposition. That is, despite the existence of normative uniformities, it is possible to identify both wide variations within the range of normality and innumerable individual patterns of development. As children advance in age, they tend to maintain their individuality as well as to undergo the normative changes that characterize their respective age groups. This is easily demonstrable in many areas where the relative status of an individual's capacity can be expressed in quantitative form, e.g., I.Q.; in other instances normative changes of a qualitative nature are so salient that in the absence of extremely subtle measuring instruments, individual differences are completely obscured. In any case, however, it is never safe to assume qualitative equivalence between the mean status of a given age group and the status of accelerated younger or retarded older individuals. For example, the intellectual status and functioning of children aged four, eight, and sixteen who possess the same mental age of eight are hardly comparable (see p. 592. Similarly, an extremely independent preadolescent is not necessarily self-assertive on the same basis as the modally independent adolescent.

Because of the strikingly more rapid rate of development in children than in adults, both variance from one age level to another and uniformity within a given age level *appear* much more conspicuous than intra-age group variability. For example, the fact that all ten year olds in our culture enjoy an overtly dependent biosocial status which is not commensurate with their biosocial competence does much to obscure and confound marked and possibly consistent individual differences.[8] However, this restricted range of intra-age group variability in children is actual as well as relative to greater inter-age group variability, since the former tends to increase with age in most functions.[15] The widened range of variability in older individuals can be explained by the greater differentiation within a given stage of development that is possible when the rate of growth decreases, and by the greater cultural tolerance for nonconformity in adults than in children.

Developmental norms are valuable because they provide a standard or frame of reference for evaluating and interpreting the status or current behavior of an individual. They can be abused if the range of variability is overlooked; if expectations for *all* children are geared to group averages; if substantial parallelism is expected between component rates of growth; if they are unwarrantedly applied to individuals who could not be included in the sampling population; and if individual guidance is predicated upon normative comparisons alone to the exclusion of information regarding individual patterning. They are also abused if they are regarded as inevitable and immutable products of maturation or as necessarily desirable. But because an instrument is subject to abuse is no reason for declaring it value-less or urging its abolition as some over-zealous but misguided exponents of the "clinical" approach have suggested.

Early Manifestations of Individuality

There is no such thing as absolute identity in nature. Behavioral differences are demonstrable in infants from the very moment of birth—even in monozygotic twins.[37, 39] Such differences are determined by polygenic factors, uterine environment, length of gestation, type and duration of delivery, and perhaps, by minor variations in early handling. Genotypic diversity is probably the most important determining factor in the case of ordinary siblings and unrelated children, and cannot be discounted even in the case of single-egg twins.

Six main categories of distinct and stable individual differences have been identified in infants during the early months of life. These may be grouped as follows: (a) placidity and irritability[33, 90]; (b) activity level and distribution of activity[27, 28, 33, 90]; (c) tone, length and vigorousness of crying[39, 41, 90]; (d) tolerance of frustration or discomfort and reaction to stress situations and over-stimulation[27, 28, 30, 33, 39, 41, 90]; (e) differential sensitivity to stimulation in various sense modalities[28]; and (f) social responsiveness.[39, 41] The demonstration of differences such as these does not, of course, preclude the existence of other genically conditioned differences in temperament (e.g., introversion-extroversion) which can first be manifested after a certain stage of maturity is reached. However, at a later age it is more difficult to prove their genic origin because of the operation of environmental factors during the interim.

Individual Differences in Rate of Growth

Normative investigations which concentrate on *mean* changes in capacity or behavior with increasing age frequently tend to obscure individual differences in rate of growth. However, in longitudinal studies, where repeated measurements of the same subjects are made over an extended period of time, and where individual scores as well as measures of central tendency are plotted against age, individual patterns of development are clearly evident.[15, 30] Except for extreme cases of mental deficiency, few individuals are uniformly accelerated or retarded in all growth functions. Even within a single area such as intelligence, most children achieve basal age scores on some subtests and over- or underage scores on others.

In general, three principal methods of expressing rate of growth are currently utilized: (1) an individual may serve as his own unique basis of comparison, (2) his status may be compared to that of the *mean* child of like age, or (3) his status may be assessed in terms of the progress achieved by the particular sub-group of his age mates in which his level or rate of growth in a given function place him. In the first instance, the individual's status at a particular stage of development is represented by the percentage of his adult or maximum growth attained at that age level. This expression does not indicate his relative status or rate of growth in terms of his age group but in relation to his own terminal achievement. It is undoubtedly the most meaningful way of assessing an individual's developmental progress in the light of his own idiosyncratic pattern of growth.

In the second method, the child's current status is generally expressed as a *developmental age* (e.g., skeletal age, mental age) or as a *developmental quotient* (e.g., I.Q.). An individual's developmental age in a given function corresponds to the chronological age at which the mean attainment of a representative sample of children equals his current status in that function. If this expression is divided by his chronological age, a developmental quotient is obtained. Needless to state, developmental age units for a given function are not comparable (equivalent) from one period to another unless differences in variability at successive age levels are taken into account. Otherwise, they artificially tend to impose an appearance of straight-line progress on basically uneven growth sequences.[15] For the same reason, uncorrected developmental ages cannot be used in comparing an individual's relative status and rate of growth with respect to different functions, or cannot be averaged to yield an expression such as Olson's and Hughes' *organismic age.*[76]

By using standard scores,* relative status can be rendered comparable from one age level or function to another. Nevertheless, additive treatment of component individual scores representing different areas of development is still unwarranted. Since the latter are largely independent of each other, both functionally and in terms of their determinants,[15] there is no defensible basis for using a standard score version of the organismic age concept which implies that the constituent elements are qualitatively homogeneous or that their rate of growth is regulated by a common set of factors. The major disadvantage of using standard scores is that because of the restricted range of variability in the early years of life, relatively small differences in capacity can give rise to relatively large differences in score values. This tends to magnify the effect of any adventitious situational or testing variable operative for one series of measurements but not for another, and hence to give an exaggerated impression of instability in rate of growth.

The third method listed above represents a compromise between the normative and uniquely individual approaches. Several typical patterns of development in a given function are first identified, and then the individual's growth is appraised sequentially in relation to the particular category in which he falls. The Wetzel grid technique of evaluating nutritional status operates essentially on this principle (see p. 505).

Each of the three methods of expressing the current developmental status and rate of growth of an individual provides valuable information from a particular standpoint of assessment. Used conjunctively, they supplement each other in the task of interpreting and evaluating the processes of growth in children.[15]

Constancy of Individual Rate of Growth. How constant is an individual's rate of growth in a given function? Does he tend to retain the same relative status among his age-mates from one age level to another? Here we are referring to quantitative longitudinal constancy, not to long-range consistency in personality traits or in the organization of personality. We

*A standard score is the difference between individual score and group mean divided by the standard deviation of the group.

shall return to this topic again in chapters 15 and 18 respectively in discussing growth in stature and intelligence. It will suffice to point out here that individual rates of growth in these functions tend to remain relatively constant (probably because of the relative stability of their genic and environmental determinants), and that whatever inconstancy does exist tends to be normally distributed. That is, with respect to a given function most individuals tend to be only slightly variable in rate of growth from one age level to another, a smaller number tend to be moderately variable, and a still smaller number tend to be extremely variable.*

Fluctuations in rate of growth may be caused (a) by factors relating to the standardization, reliability and validity of the measuring instrument or to situational variability associated with test administrations (see p. 596), (b) by significant changes in environment, and (c) by idiosyncratic irregularities in the processes of growth that occur even in a relatively constant environment. At this point we shall only consider the second and third factors. Mention has already been made of the genuine inconstancy that is indigenous to extremely rapid periods of growth, and of the spurious appearance of inconstancy attributable to restricted intra-age group variability. Both of the latter conditions apply to infancy and early childhood and account for much of the striking instability of most functions during those age periods (e.g., intelligence).

In general, such fluctuations in the environment of children as frequency of illness, health status, nursery school attendance, and separation from parents are not significantly correlated with measures of general intelligence.[13] However, the impact of these variables on the intellectual growth of individual children could conceivably be obscured in the correlational analysis of group data by the simultaneous operation of compensatory factors. Furthermore, as Bayley points out,[13] the effects of such environmental conditions may vary greatly from one individual to another. By carefully studying individual mental growth curves and accompanying life histories, various investigators[13, 25, 76, 81] have shown that conspicuous fluctuations in intelligence test scores frequently correspond in time to incidence and recovery from emotional and environmental peturbations. However, a note of caution in accepting these latter findings at face value is indicated by the demonstration that the reported fluctuations in one of these studies[25] do not differ significantly from the deviations in test scores that could be ordinarily anticipated on the basis of test unreliability.[46]

Much of the idiosyncratic patterning in rate of growth can undoubtedly be attributed to individual differences in genotypic makeup or experiental

*Approximately one-half of the I.Q.'s of elementary school children do not deviate more than five points from original score on retesting.

background. For example, in analyzing the mental growth careers of 48 children over a period of nine years, Bayley found that eight children maintained a fairly constant rate of growth, eight lost and eight gained ground consistently, eight maintained a decelerating pace in early childhood and an accelerating pace in later childhood, eight did just the opposite of the latter, and eight did not conform to any recognizable pattern.[14] Characteristic patterns in the velocity of mental growth also appear to be related to the intellectual status of children. In comparison to their brighter contemporaries, dull children tend to gain a larger proportion of their eventual intellectual attainment during the early years.[15]

THE NORM VERSUS NORMALITY

Were it not for the widespread influence of the mental measurement movement which has fostered a statistical concept of normality and abnormality, it would hardly be necessary to make explicit the distinction between the norm and normality. *Normality* is an evaluative term, implying a desirable, wholesome, or constructive state of affairs. The *norm,* on the other hand, is merely a descriptive statement of current central tendency in a given population. It may be good or bad, desirable or undesirable, constructive or destructive.

It is also unjustifiable to assume that the children constituting either or both extremes of a distribution of scores on a personality test are necessarily abnormal or that they are qualitatively homogeneous with individuals suffering from a phenotypically similar pathological entity. The behavior may appear identical symptomatically, but the underlying mechanisms may be entirely different. For example, extreme instances of normal situational anxiety in well-adjusted children and ordinary instances of neurotic anxiety originating in atypical personality development have little in common except for some superficial overt manifestations (see p. 329).

REVERSIBILITY AND IRREVERSIBILITY IN DEVELOPMENT

Physical, chemical, biological and psychological reactions vary tremendously in the extent to which phenomenological change is reversible. The factors affecting the occurrence of reversibility, the conditions under which it occurs, and the nature of the developmental processes that render it possible or impossible are obviously matters of the greatest theoretical and practical importance. For, depending on the outcome of research findings in this crucial area of inquiry in developmental psychology, many issues affecting child rearing, guidance, education and therapy will be resolved.

Reversibility commonly has two quite different meanings. In the physical sciences it refers to the possibility of reversion to an antecedent or alternalive condition. In the behavioral sciences reversibility more usually refers to the possibility of modifying the direction of behavior or personality development once a given type of conspicuous change has taken place; the former meaning is conventionally considered under the heading of regression (see p. 106). Reversibility may also be classified with respect to whether it is partial or relatively complete, peripheral or central, covert or overt. Some developmental changes, for example, repudiate almost completely antecedent phases of growth (e.g., walking, the acquisition of adult executive independence). Other developmental experiences, such as satellization in early childhood, leave a permanent residue in personality structure that either affects adult behavior covertly or is perpetuated more overtly as a current form of adult status-seeking activity.

General speaking, few developmental phases in human beings are ordinarily irreversible, especially in those instances in which environmental determinants are influential. Despite the tendency for personality equilibria to resist reorganization, the typical course of development is for one stage to be succeeded by another as significant changes in biosocial status occur. This is less true for development in infrahuman species and in embryonic life; here it is more difficult for subsequent experience to alter the direction of development because of the relatively prepotent influence exerted by genic factors.

Types of Irreversibility

Three fundamentally different mechanisms help account for developmental irreversibility in animals and human beings. First, relative irreversibility of behavioral organization may be a function of extreme susceptibility to specific kinds of stimulation during those brief critical periods in ontogeny when "certain types of behavior normally are shaped and molded for life."*[16] Learnings established during such periods may be maximally resistive to change because of the unstructured state of the organism's behavior, the absence of competing responses, and the pre-emptive effects of canalization; and once established, "certain types of early experience influence later behavior by structuring the individual's perceptual capacities."[16] Also, since he lacks an adequate experiential background and adjustive repertoire with which to interpret and respond to environmental trauma and frustration, the younger individual is more vulnerable to the damaging

*This hypothesis is logically and historically related to research findings in experimental embryology which indicate that the developmental susceptibility of transplanted tissues to the cellular environment in which they are embedded is limited to relatively restricted periods of time. However, it would be unwise to extend this analogy too far since few developmental sequences in postinfantile human beings are as prepotently determined by genic factors.

effects of such experience than the mature member of the species provided, of course, that he is sufficiently mature to be susceptible in the first place. And by the same token, if he is deprived of necessary stimulation during the critical period when he is maximally susceptible to it, in terms of actualizing potential capacities or developing in new directions, it is quite conceivable that some degree of retardation will result.

A second source of relative developmental irreversibility lies in diminished plasticity or increased rigidity of personality structure. Aside from factors already mentioned as enhancing resistance to personality reorganization (see p. 99), Kounin has demonstrated that "degree of rigidity is proportional to chronological age and hence to degree of feeblemindedness for any given mental age level."[60] Although the latter writer infers that degree of rigidity and differentiation increase independently as a function of advancing age, it is just as plausible to hypothesize that growing rigidity is largely a reflection of the restricted range of variability that necessarily results as behavior and potential genotypic capacity become progressively more committed in specific directions during the course of differentiation.

Lastly, some aspects of personality structure are relatively irreversible because of the strength of their genic determinants, the recurrent aspects of certain interpersonal experience, and the operation of various perpetuating mechanisms in personality organization. The latter have already been considered in discussing the long-range continuity of individuality (see p. 99). It is important not to confuse irreversibility of such origin with the type that results from the persistent influence of less continuous but more dramatic experience during critical periods of susceptibility.

Factors Affecting Reversibility

In the light of the foregoing mechanisms accounting for relative developmental irreversibility, what variables must be considered as affecting behavioral modifiability? First is the matter of *susceptibility* at the time of original exposure to the experience in question. In the absence of minimal psychological susceptibility, the most traumatic of experiences can have little lasting effect. Thus, because he is insufficiently mature in a cognitive sense to appreciate the meaning of threat, the young infant is insulated from much psychological trauma; and even if he were sufficiently mature, there would still be no definite ego to which threat could be referred. Since he cannot distinguish among persons[100] and offers no resistance to or fear of inoculation before the age of six months,*[64] it is fanciful indeed to suppose that "birth trauma," hunger, or separation from the original

*Naturally, the designation of such normative ages does not imply applicability to *all* infants since individuals undoubtedly differ in degree of susceptibility to particular kinds of experience.

mother figure can leave permanent emotional consequences. In general, it is safe to assume that until he gains in perceptual maturity the young infant will be susceptible to only the grosser aspects of interpersonal relations, and will not be affected by subtleties of parent attitude; in this respect he is even less susceptible than mammals of comparable chronological age who already display a relatively keen sense of social perception. And even beyond this age, retention of specific experience is bound to be poor unless it is recurrent or singularly dramatic (see p. 555).

A second important factor affecting reversibility of development is the particular trait or experience involved. For reasons that will be elaborated in later chapters, there are credible grounds for believing that the effects of extrinsic valuation by parents are less reversible than those of rejection, and that failure to learn adequate techniques of self-assertion is more permanently damaging than is the learning of excessive self-assertion (see pp. 367 and 372). Much depends also on the importance of a given type of experience for over-all personality development at the particular stage in the life cycle when it occurs. In general, one would expect unfavorable experience to be most damaging when it interferes with the dominant personality changes taking place at a given phase of development. Hence, gross emotional neglect and loss of succorance are most serious in their consequences in the last quarter of the first year and in the second year of life when initial socialization occurs; more subtle rejection and extrinsic valuation by parents are most damaging in the preschool period when satellization ordinarily takes place; and parental overprotection and underdomination have most detrimental after-effects in middle childhood and pre-adolescence when they impede the preparatory phases of adult maturation. In all of these instances, of course, duration and severity of trauma, and constitutional and normative differences in resistance to stress are crucial variables.

Finally, we must take into account the nature of subsequent experience that counteracts the impact of previous events. It makes a difference whether such experience (e.g., re-education) occurs early or late, within or beyond the period of maximum susceptibility; whether it is consistent or sporadic, intensive or superficial, gentle or insistent; whether the organism is rigid or retains a reasonable measure of plasticity in responding to particular environmental influences.

Animal Studies

Numerous studies with animal subjects illustrate the operation of the foregoing mechanisms and factors affecting the reversibility of development. However, because of the generally slower rate of maturation and the greater importance of environmental determinants in children, care must be taken against indiscriminate extrapolation of research implications from infra-human species.

For explanatory purposes, most of the research findings in this area can be subsumed under the "critical period" hypothesis. In its simplest form, this hypothesis is exemplified by "imprinting" in domestic fowl.[67] This refers to the phenomenon in which incubator hatched fowl, exposed to human beings shortly after hatching, follow the latter in filial fashion in preference to the mother bird of the same species. "Imprinting" is reflective of the fact (a) that a behavioral predisposition to respond in a particular way is so prepotent that the organism reacts to even a highly generalized version of the typical eliciting stimulus, and (b) that this susceptibility to environmental stimulation is so great that the *first* stimulus to evoke the response in question soon becomes the only adequate stimulus that can do so. The critical stage is confined to an extremely limited period of time (e.g., 6 to 24 hours), and once established, the resulting behavior pattern is relatively irreversible. This remarkable degree of canalization is facilitated by the fact that the newly hatched fowl are insulated both before and after "imprinting" from other competing evocative stimuli. Very comparable to "imprinting" are the frequently observed phenomena that birds exposed to the songs of other species early in life fail to develop the typical song of their own species,[16] and that chicks reared by hand tend to ignore the food calls of the hen.[22]

Evidence of critical periods in development is also found in mammalian species. For example, newly born domestic lambs reared on a bottle and isolated from sheep for ten days, experience difficulty later in adjusting to the flock and tend to graze by themselves.[86] Puppies, on the other hand, can be isolated from other dogs for the first nine weeks of life and still adapt socially to them. According to Scott and Marston,[87] the period between the third and tenth weeks is crucial for socialization in puppies. The earlier in this phase that they are removed from the litter and establish a relationship with humans, the tamer they become. If untamed before three months of age, they remain relatively wild and difficult to tame.

The persistent traumatic or structuring effects of early experience in areas other than socialization also point to developmental mechanisms characteristic of "critical periods." Laboratory rats subjected to partial starvation for 15 days immediately after weaning show a greater tendency to hoard food in adult life than do control animals if the starvation experience is repeated.*[53] This does not occur if the rats are older at the time of the original food deprivation.[53] Similarly, mice trained to compete

---

*Recent experiments do not confirm these findings completely and indicate that the hoarding behavior is related in part to a more rapid rate of eating in rats starved as infants.[72]

for food in infancy also tend to compete as adults even in the absence of hunger[32]; and the younger the age at which infant mice are subjected to the attacks of a trained fighting mouse, the greater is the tendency for nonaggressive withdrawal to persist in a fighting situation in adult life.[58] The protective effects of early favorable experience are illustrated by an experiment in which rats gentled in infancy gained more weight and were better able to survive starvation stress than were nongentled rats.[103] Abundant early perceptual experience in a spacious and heterogeneous environment with various types of problems apparently facilitates adult learning ability[45, 52, 54]; and the exploratory tendencies of adult rats are enhanced if they are reared in larger rather than in small cages.[78] The lasting developmental retardation induced by serious deprivation of visual, pecking and flying experience in different animal species has already been discussed (see pp. 83 and 87).

Infant Deprivation*

Less precisely controlled but more relevant for our purposes are numerous studies of infant deprivation. Many of these studies are extremely impressionistic and subjective in nature; others have ingeniously taken advantage of uncontrived deprivation occurring in foundling homes or resulting from wartime dislocation, and are reasonably well controlled. Although the basic findings have been confirmed by independently conducted research in many parts of the world, considerable controversy still rages regarding their interpretation and implications for child rearing.

The evidence is clear that after six to nine months of age, prolonged or severe deprivation of maternal care or abrupt separation from the accustomed mother figure during the first three years of life often (but not necessarily) leads to extremely serious developmental consequences. In the preschool period these may be described as follows: (a) retardation in motor, language, and intellectual development[35, 49, 95, 96, 97, 98]; (b) malnutrition and an unusually high infant mortality rate despite excellent medical care (marasmus)[95, 98]; and (c) a behavioral syndrome of agitation and weepiness followed by apathy, passivity, disinterest in the environment, stereotyped rocking movements and head banging, and increased susceptibility to infection.†[31, 83, 99] The latter syndrome, designated as "anaclitic depression" by Spitz and Wolf appears typically after abrupt separation from the mother and generally disappears shortly after her return.[31, 99]

Children hospitalized in foundling homes from the earliest months to three

*Judicious reviews of studies in this area are available.[20, 101]

†Other symptoms of separation from parents include loss of sphincter control, overeating, autoeroticism, resistiveness, and hostility. See Heinicke, C. H., *Human Relations 9*: 105-176, 1956.

years of age and then placed with foster parents were followed through adolescence and compared with matched controls who had not been subjected to the institutional experience.[43] The former tended to have a persistently depressed I.Q. (median of 75); exhibited special retardation in language skills and conceptualization; were distractable, unable to concentrate, hyperactive, and uncontrollable; showed little ability to anticipate the consequences of their behavior or to acquire normal inhibitory control; and displayed temper tantrums and aggressive, impulsive, antisocial behavior without appropriate anxiety. Their emotionality and interpersonal relationships were shallow, they demanded attention and affection indiscriminately, they adjusted poorly to their peers, and showed conspicuous lack of executive and volitional independence.[43] The same characteristics were found clinically in juvenile delinquents with psychopathic personalities who have a history of inadequate maternal care.[17, 19] In one follow-up study of 38 adolescents who had been institutionalized in foundling homes during the first three years of life, 4 were diagnosed as psychotic, 21 as suffering from character disorders, 4 as mentally retarded, 2 as psychoneurotic, and only 7 as normally adjusted.[18] Another investigator, however, found the results of maternal deprivation to be less serious, inevitable and irreversible.[66]

In interpreting these data, some investigators have concluded that the young infant is sensitive to the most subtle nuances of parent attitudes, that permanent psychological damage results unless extremely high levels of mothering are maintained, and that post-infantile experience has little effect on personality development (see p. 255). It is important, therefore, to bear the following qualifications in mind: First, the effects of emotional deprivation have not been reliably established prior to six months of age; and most observers agree that the period from nine months to three years is the most crucial in this regard.[17, 19, 20, 95, 96, 99] Prior to this time insufficient perceptual maturity exists for the infant to enter into significant interpersonal relationships or to appreciate the meaning and consequences of deprivation.

Second, the effects of maternal deprivation can be avoided by providing the infant with only a minimal amount of stimulation, personal attention and individualized care,[23] or by arranging for daily visits by the mother.[20] Thus, it seems more likely that *inadequate* mothering (as represented by completely impersonal attention or gross neglect) is detrimental rather than that constant or extreme mothering is necessary or desirable. Furthermore, the effects of deprivation are reversible if adequate maternal care is provided after the first year of life, that is, if the mother returns or if a satisfactory substitute is provided.[20, 31, 95, 99]

Third, it is important to distinguish between rejection and outright neglect. The former attitude does not necessarily imply lack of personal attention or inadequate stimulation, and can only be perceived by older, more perceptually mature infants.

Finally, it should be realized that "like biological heredity, infant experiences, while placing certain constraints upon personality give mainly potentialities. Whether these potentialities become actualized or not, or the extent to which they become actualized, depends upon later social and other conditions which structure the individual's experiences. Only an external condition of adult life brings out fully a predisposition, the basis for which has been laid in the experiences of infancy and early childhood."*[73]

ARE DEVELOPMENTAL PROBLEMS PERMANENT OR PHASIC?

As a result of different connotations and usages in developmental and clinical psychology, the definition of what constitutes a behavior problem has become increasingly more difficult. Developmentally oriented psychologists tend to think of behavior problems in children as essentially phasic or transitory in nature. Clinical psychologists and psychiatrists, on the other hand, tend to take a more pessimistic view of the genesis and prognosis of such problems. Actually the two approaches are not mutually incompatible. Depending on the particular problem involved, either point of view may be essentially correct. Certain personality and behavioral disturbances are characteristic of the developmental needs, tasks, and pressures confronting a given age group in a given cultural setting† But at the same time, *in addition* to these phasic normative disturbances, some children display behavior pathology that is a function of their own unique experience and constitutional make-up. For our present purposes it will suffice to give a brief general answer to the question, "Do children inevitably 'grow out' of behavior problems?"

The answer is sometimes "yes" and sometimes "no." If the difficulties are simply indicative of immaturity appropriate to a given age level, it is obvious

*If the data regarding "wild children" reared by animals could be accepted at face value, and if it could be assumed that such children were not feeble-minded to start with, we could conclude that "the socialization which ordinarily takes place during the early years is readily lost upon close contact with animals (and) that animal influences are relatively permanent."[21] However, the writer agrees with Dennis that "rather than accept these conclusions it seems better not to attempt to draw generalizations concerning childhood from data so tenuous as the reports on alleged animal-reared children."[24]

†Some problems are relatively specific to particular age periods. For example, the incidence of thumb sucking and enuresis decline sharply with increasing age, whereas nail biting, overt temper tantrums, fears, jealousies, and oversensitiveness increase at four and one-half and then decline in frequency.[73]

that as children grow older they simultaneously shed their immaturity unless there is a compelling reason to the contrary. For example, most children at ages three and five respectively have managed to overcome urinary incontinence and have abandoned solitary or parallel play for cooperative play. These developments tend to take place even in the absence of rigorous environmental pressures because they are largely dependent upon enhanced neuromuscular and cognitive capacity. Other problems symptomatic of disequilibrium during transitional stages of development (e.g., negativism at two and one-half) also tend to disappear once the developmental crisis is over. "No child is completely free of adjustive devices that get labeled as problem behavior."[68]

On the other hand, children just do not "grow out" of problems reflective of marked developmental retardation, extreme personality deviation, or aberrant parent-child or peer group relationships. They do not ordinarily "grow out" of feeblemindedness, cleft palate, cretinism or mongolism. Neither do they grow out of excessive introversion, the impact of persistent parental overprotection, or the effects of long-standing rejection by their peers. Finally, they do not necessarily "grow out" of phasic immaturity if they are "just left alone." Whereas much neuromuscular, perceptual and cognitive development takes place quite incidentally, i.e., without the exercise of deliberate cultural pressure, stages in personality development that depend upon radical changes in biosocial status do not occur automatically. They are induced in large part by altered expectations and demands reflective of cultural norms regarding appropriate behavior, responsibilities, and prerogatives as children move from one age level to another.

REFERENCES

1. Abernathy, E. H.: Relationships between mental and physical growth. *Monogr. Soc. Res. Child Development* 1: No. 7, 1936.
2. Anderson, J. E.: Personality organization in children. *Am. Psychologist* 3: 409-416, 1948.
3. Ausubel, D. P.: Prestige motivation of gifted children. *Genet. Psychol. Monogr.* 43: 53-117, 1951.
4. ——: *Ego Development and the Personality Disorders.* New York, Grune & Stratton, 1952.
5. ——: *Theory and Problems of Adolescent Development.* New York, Grune & Stratton, 1954.
6. ——: The relationship between social variables and ego development and functioning. *In* M. Sherif and M. O. Wilson, Eds., *Emerging Problems in Social Psychology.* In preparation.
7. ——, Schiff, H. M., and Zeleny, M. P.: "Real-life" measures of level of academic and vocational aspiration in adolescents: relation to laboratory measures and to adjustment. *Child Development* 24: 155-168, 1953.

8. ——, et al.: Perceived parent attitudes as determinants of children's ego structure. *Child Development 25*: 173-183, 1954.

9. ——, et al.: Prestige suggestion in children's art preferences. *J. Genet. Psychol.,* 85-93, 1956.

10. Barbu, Z.: Studies in children's honesty. *Quart. Bull. Brit. Psychol. Soc.* 2: 53-57, 1951.

11. Barker, R., Dembo, T., and Lewin, K.: Studies in topological and vector psychology: II. Frustration and regression. *Univer. Iowa Stud. Child Welfare 18*: No. 1, 1941.

12. Bayley, N.: *The California First Year Mental Scale.* Berkeley, Calif., University of California Press, 1933.

13. ——: Factors influencing growth of intelligence in young children. *Yearbook Nat. Soc. Stud. Educ. 39* (II): 49-79, 1940.

14. ——: Mental growth in young children. *Yearbook Nat. Soc. Stud. Educ. 39* (II): 11-47, 1940.

15. ——: Individual patterns of development. *Child Development 27*: 45-74, 1956.

16. Beach, F. A., and Jaynes, J.: Effects of early experience upon the behavior of animals. *Psychol. Bull. 51*: 239-263, 1954.

17. Bender, L.: Anxiety in disturbed children. *In* P. H. Hoch and J. Zubin, Eds., *Anxiety.* New York, Grune & Stratton, 1950.

18. Beres, D., and Obers, S. J.: The effects of extreme deprivation in infancy on psychic structure in adolescence: a study in ego development. *Psychoanal. Stud. Child 5*: 212-235, 1950.

19. Bowlby, J.: *Forty-four Juvenile Thieves: Their Characters and Home Lives.* London, Balliere, Tindall and Cox, 1946.

20. ——: Maternal care and mental health. *World Health Org. Monogr. Ser.* No. 2, 1951.

21. Cameron, N.: *The Psychology of Behavior Disorders: A Biosocial Interpretation.* Boston, Houghton Mifflin, 1947.

22. Collias, N. E.: The development of social behavior in birds. *Auk 69*: 127-159, 1952.

23. Dennis, W.: Infant development under conditions of restricted practice and minimum social stimulation. *Genet. Psychol. Monogr. 23*: 143-189, 1941.

24. ——: A further analysis of reports of wild children. *Child Development 22*: 153-158, 1951.

25. Despert, J. L., and Pierce, H. O.: The relation of emotional adjustment to intellectual function. *Genet. Psychol. Monogr. 34*: 1-56, 1946.

26. Eggan, D.: The general problem of Hopi adjustment. *Am. Anthropologist 47*: 516-539, 1945.

27. Escalona, S. K.: The use of infant tests for predictive purposes. *Bull. Menninger Clinic 14*: 117-128, 1950.

28. Escalona, S.: The influence of topological and vector psychology upon current research in child development. *In* L. Carmichael, Ed., *Manual of Child Psychology,* ed. 2. New York, Wiley, 1954, pp. 971-984.

29. Escalona, S. K., and Leitch, M. E.: *Psychoanalytic Study of the Child,* vol. 3. New York, International Universities Press, 1949. (The reaction of infants to stress).

30. ——, ——, et al.: Early phases of personality development: a non-normative study of infant behavior. *Monogr. Soc. Res. Child Development 17*: No. 1, 1952.

31. Fischer, L. K.: Hospitalism in six-month-old infants. *Am. J. Orthopsychiat.* 22: 522-533, 1952.
32. Fredericson, E.: Competition: the effects of infantile experience upon adult behavior. *J. Abnorm. Soc. Psychol.* 46: 406-409, 1951.
33. Fries, M. E.: Psychosomatic relationships between mother and child. *Psychosom. Med.* 6: 157-162, 1944.
34. ———, and Lewi, B.: Interrelated factors in development: a study of pregnancy, labor, delivery, lying-in period and childhood. *Am. J. Orthopsychiat.* 8: 726-752, 1938.
35. Freud, A., and Burlingham, D.: *Infants Without Families.* New York, International Universities Press, 1944.
36. Garrett, H. E., Bryan, A. I., and Perl, R. E.: The age factor in mental organization. *Arch. Psychol.* No. 175, 1935.
37. Gesell, A.: *Infancy and Human Growth.* New York, Macmillan, 1928.
38. ———: The ontogenesis of infant behavior. *In* L. Carmichael, Ed., *Manual of Child Psychology,* ed. 2. New York, Wiley, 1954, pp. 335-373.
39. ———, and Ames, L. B.: Early evidences of individuality in the human infant. *J. Genet. Psychol.* 47: 339-361, 1937.
40. ———, and Ilg, F. L.: *Infant and Child in the Culture of Today.* New York, Harper, 1943.
41. ———, and Thompson, H.: Twins T and C from infancy to adolescence: a biogenetic study of individual differences by the method of co-twin control. *Genet. Psychol. Monogr.* 24: 3-121, 1941.
42. Gilinsky, A. S.: Relative self-estimate and the level of aspiration. *J. Exper. Psychol.* 39: 256-259, 1949.
43. Goldfarb, W.: Psychological privation in infancy and subsequent adjustment. *Am. J. Orthopsychiat.* 15: 247-255, 1945.
44. Hallowell, A. I.: The use of projective techniques in the study of socio-psychological aspects of acculturation. *J. Proj. Tech.* 15: 26-44, 1951.
45. Harlow, H. F.: The formation of learning sets. *Psychol. Rev.* 56: 51-65, 1949.
46. Harris, R. E., and Thompson, C. W.: The relation of emotional adjustment to intellectual function. *Psychol. Bull.* 44: 283-287, 1947.
47. Hartshorne, H., and May, M. A.: *Studies in the Nature of Character.* Vol. I. *Studies in Deceit.* New York, Macmillan, 1928.
48. Harvey, O. J. and Sherif, M.: Level of aspiration as a case of judgmental activity in which ego-involvements operate as factors. *Sociometry 14:* 121-147, 1951.
49. Hasselmann-Kahlert, M.: Einige Beobachtungen bei entwurzelten Kleinst-und Kleinkindern. *Prax. Kinderpsychol. Kinderpsychiat.* 2: 15-18, 1953.
50. Havighurst, R. J., and Janke, L. I.: Relations between ability and social status in a mid-Western community. I. Ten-year-old children. *J. Educ. Psychol.* 35: 357-368, 1944.
51. ———, and Taba, H. *Adolescent Character and Personality.* New York, Wiley, 1949.
52. Hebb, D. O.: *The Organization of Behavior.* New York, Wiley, 1949.
53. Hunt, J. McV.: The effects of infant feeding-frustration upon adult hoarding in the albino rat. *J. Abnorm. Soc. Psychol.* 36: 338-360, 1941.
54. Hymovitch, B.: The effects of experimental variations on problem solving in the rat. *J. Comp. Physiol. Psychol.* 45: 313-320, 1952.

55. Janke, L. L., and Havighurst, R. J.: Relations between ability and social status in a mid-Western community. II. Sixteen-year-old boys and girls. *J. Educ. Psychol. 36*: 499-509, 1945.

56. Jersild, A. T.: *Child Psychology,* ed. 4. New York, Prentice-Hall, 1954.

57. Jones, H. E.: *Motor Performance and Growth.* Berkeley, University of California Press, 1949.

58. Kahn, M. W.: The effect of severe defeat at various age levels on the aggressive behavior of mice. *J. Genet. Psychol. 79*: 117-130, 1951.

59. Klein, G. S., and Schoenfeld, N.: The influence of ego-involvement on confidence. *J. Abnorm. Soc. Psychol. 36*: 249-258, 1941.

60. Kounin, J. S.: Intellectual development and rigidity. *In* R. G. Barker, J. S. Kounin and H. F. Wright, Eds., *Child Behavior and Development.* New York, McGraw-Hill, 1943, pp. 179-198.

61. Lecky, P.: *Self-Consistency: A Theory of Personality.* New York, Island Press, 1945.

62. Leighton, D., and Kluckhohn, C.: *Children of the People.* Cambridge, Mass., Harvard University Press, 1941.

63. Levitt, E. E.: Cognitive distortion and ego-involvement. *J. Personality 19*: 212-220, 1950.

64. Levy, D. H.: Observations of attitudes and behavior in the child health center. *Amer. J. Pub. Health 41*: 182-190, 1951.

65. Lewin, K.: Behavior and development as a function of the total situation. *In* L. Carmichael, Ed., *Manual of Child Psychology,* ed. 2. New York, Wiley, 1954, pp. 918-970.

66. Lewis, H.: *Deprived Children.* London, Oxford University Press, 1954.

67. Lorenz, K.: Der Kumpan in der Umwelt des Vogels. Der artgenosse als auslosendes moment sozialer Verhaltungsweisen. *J. Orn. Lpz. 83*: 137-213, 289-413, 1935.

68. MacFarlane, J. W.: Study of personality development. *In* R. G. Barker, J. S. Kounin, and H. F. Wright, Eds., *Child Behavior and Development.* New York, McGraw-Hill, 1943, pp. 307-328.

69. McGehee, W.: Judgment and the level of aspiration. *J. Gen. Psychol. 22*: 3-15, 1940.

70. McGraw, M. B.: *The Neuromuscular Maturation of the Human Infant.* New York, Columbia University Press, 1943.

71. McKinnon, K. M.: *Consistency and Change in Personality and Behavior Manifestations—as Observed in a Group of 16 Children During a Five-year Period.* Child Development Monograph. New York, Teachers College, Columbia University, 1942.

72. Marx, M. H.: Infantile deprivation and adult behavior in the rat: retention of increased rate of eating. *J. Comp. Physiol. Psychol. 45*: 43-49, 1952.

73. Mowrer, O. H., and Kluckhohn, C.: Dynamic theory of personality. *In* J. McV. Hunt, Ed., *Personality and the Behavior Disorders,* vol. 1. New York, Ronald Press, 1944, pp. 69-135.

74. Murphy, G.: *Personality: a Biosocial Approach to Origins and Structure.* New York, Harper, 1947.

75. Neilon, P.: Shirley's babies after fifteen years. *J. Genet. Psychol. 73*: 175-186, 1948.

76. Olson, W. C., and Hughes, B. O.: Growth of the child as a whole. *In* R. G.

Barker, J. S. Kounin and H. F. Wright, Eds., *Child Behavior and Development.* New York, McGraw-Hill, 1943, pp. 199-208.

77. Paterson, D. G.: *Physique and Intellect.* New York, Appleton-Century, 1930.

78. Patrick, J. R., and Laughlin, R. M.: Is the wall-seeking tendency in the white rat an instinct? *J. Genet. Psychol. 44*: 378-389, 1934.

79. Paulsen, A. A.: Personality development in the middle childhood years, a ten-year longitudinal study of 30 public school children by means of Rorschach tests and social histories. Unpublished Ph.D. dissertation, New York University, 1953.

80. Preston, M. G., and Bayton, J.A.: Correlations between levels of aspiration. *J. Psychol. 13*: 369-373, 1942.

81. Richards, T. W.: Mental test performance as a reflection of the child's current life situation: a methodological study. *Child Develop. 22*: 221-233, 1951.

82. Rosenzweig, S.: Need persistent and ego defensive reactions to frustrations as demonstrated by an experiment on repression. *Psychol. Rev. 48*: 347-349, 1941.

83. Roudinesco, J.: Severe maternal deprivation and personality development in early childhood. *Understanding the Child 21*: 104-108, 1952.

84. Sanford, R. N., et al.: Physique, personality and scholarship. A cooperative study of school children. *Monogr. Soc. Res. Child Develop. 8*: No. 1, 1943.

85. Schiff, H. M.; Judgmental response sets in the perception of sociometric status. Unpublished Ph.D. dissertation, University of Illinois, 1953.

86. Scott, J. P., Fredericson, E., and Fuller, J. L.: Experimental exploration of the critical period hypothesis. *J. Personal. 1*: 162-183, 1951.

87. ———, and Marston, M.: Critical periods affecting the development of normal and maladjustive social behavior of puppies. *J. Genet. Psychol. 77*: 25-60, 1950.

88. Sherif, M.: The concept of reference groups in human relations. *In* M. Sherif and M. O. Wilson, Eds., *Group Relations at the Crossroads.* New York, Harper, 1953.

89. Shirley, M. M.: *The First Two Years: a Study of Twenty-five Babies.* Vol. 1. *Postural and Locomotor Development.* Minneapolis, University of Minnesota Press, 1931.

90. ———: *Ibid.* Vol. III. *Personality Manifestations.* Minneapolis, University of Minnesota Press, 1933.

91. ———: Impact of mother's personality on the young child. *Smith College Stud. Soc. Work 12*: 15-64, 1941.

92. Shuttleworth, F. K.: The physical and mental growth of girls and boys age six to nineteen in relation to age at maximum growth. *Monogr. Soc. Res. Child Develop. 4*: No. 3, 1939.

93. Slaght, W. E.: Untruthfulness in children: its conditioning factors and its setting in child nature. *Univ. Iowa Stud. Charact. 1*: No. 4, 1928.

94. Smith, M.E.: A comparison of certain personality traits as rated in the same individuals in childhood and fifty years later. *Child Develop. 23*: 159-180, 1952.

95. Spitz, R. A.: Hospitalism: an inquiry into the genesis of psychiatric conditions in early childhood. *Psychoanal. Stud. Child 1*: 53-74, 1945.

96. ———: The role of ecological factors in emotional development in infancy. *Child Develop. 20*: 145-155, 1949.

97. ———: Environment versus race: environment as an etiological factor in psychiatric disturbances in infancy. *In* G. B. Wilbur and W. Muensterberger, Eds., *Psychoanalysis and Culture.* New York, International Universities Press, 1951, pp. 32-41.

98. ——: The psychogenic diseases in infancy. *Psychoanal. Stud. Child 6:* 255-275, 1951.

99. ——, and Wolf, K. M.: Anaclitic depression; an inquiry into the genesis of psychiatric conditions in early childhood. *Psychoanal. Stud. Child 2:* 313-342, 1946.

100. ——, and ——: The smiling response: a contribution to the ontogenesis of social relations. *Genet. Psychol. Monogr. 34:* 57-125, 1946.

101. Stone, L. J.: A critique of studies of infant isolation. *Child Develop. 25:* 9-20, 1954.

102. Terman, L. M., et al.: *Genetic Studies of Genius.* I. *Mental and Physical Traits of a Thousand Gifted Children.* Stanford, Calif., Stanford University Press, 1939.

103. Weininger, O.: Mortality of albino rats under stress as a function of early handling. *Canad. J. Psychol. 7:* 111-115, 1953.

104. Wile, I., and Davis, R.: The relation of birth to behavior. *Am. J. Orthopsychiat. 11:* 320-324, 1941.

CHAPTER 5

Problems and Methods of Research in Child Development

In THIS CHAPTER we propose to discuss some general methodological problems and issues of a theoretical nature that confront the research worker in child development. It should be understood at the outset that we cannot possibly deal here with (a) the design of psychological studies, (b) the various types of research methods and measuring instruments available in psychology, or (c) all of the many specific research techniques that have been designed for obtaining data about the behavior and development of children. Many excellent textbooks and monographs covering these latter areas are currently available.[5-7, 22, 36, 42, 46, 47, 51, 57, 64, 69, 101, 115] Considerations of space only permit discussion of crucial methodological issue indigenous to child development as a field,* and of selected research methods employed in research with children that are not covered adequately in treatises on psychological measurement.

GENERAL PROBLEMS OF METHOD

The scientific standing of any field of knowledge depends upon the reliability, validity and definitiveness of the empirical evidence on which its generalizations are based. Depending on these criteria, the latter are qualified by varying degrees of tentativeness, assuming the status of laws, theories, or hypotheses. Historically speaking, two poles-apart approaches to the problem of evidence have been adopted in child development. On the one hand, extreme "empiricists" have been engaged in the collection of discrete data and isolated measurements unrelated to any comprehensive or systematic theories of development. On the other hand, psychoanalytic theoreticians, unconstrained by rigorously obtained data from representative populations of children, have enjoyed a speculative field day in developmental psychology. Theories that are not founded upon or testable by naturalistic

*Many of these issues have already been discussed in defining the field of child development, namely, its status as a natural science, the appropriateness and difficulty of exercising experimental control, descriptive versus explanatory levels of analysis, the relationship between theory and data, the problem of extrapolation, objective and subjective aspects of development, and the hazards associated with investigating the latter (see pp. 6-15).

data are not far removed from idle speculation and have little heuristic value. And data that are not derived from integrative hypotheses can hardly be expected to shed much definitive light on crucial problems.

Desired Kinds of Generalization from Data

The principal aim of child development research is to formulate—as ends in themselves—generalizations about different aspects of the development of children. Although such generalizations may be employed for making diagnoses and prognoses about the development of *particular* children, this use represents an application outside the ordinary scope of the field and should be restricted to properly qualified clinicians. It is true, of course, that research workers in child development expend much effort in studying individual growth patterns. However, their interest stems from concern with discovering general principles regarding individuality and variability in different areas of development rather than from concern with understanding a particular child as such or with influencing his development.

Although many investigators in the past "have worked backward from behavior outcomes to antecedent factors", more satisfactory generalizations could be obtained if studies moved "from context to behavior, not from behavior to context."[6] The "backward-working" approach has been traditional in clinical and ethnological studies. However, even in these areas, more careful research planning and control of relevant variables would be possible if the independent variables (environmental conditions) were ordered first and the dependent variables (behavioral outcomes) measured later in the research sequence. This latter approach offers the additional advantage of avoiding the serious pitfalls associated with the retrospective collection and interpretation of data (see p. 133).

Realistically oriented research in child development also avoids seeking generalizations based upon the "fallacy of the single cause."

> Behavior at any moment is the resultant of the child's history and of the stimulation present. The concept of simple and single causes must be replaced by concepts of multiple causation, reciprocal relations, and the progressive cumulation of effect.[6]

Appropriateness of Method for Age Group

To a very great extent, the appropriateness of a given research method is a function of the age of the children under investigation. In the case of infants and young children, direct observation is the most feasible method. The investigator is greatly handicapped by the limited language ability of the young child, the difficulty with which he follows directions, his frequent unwillingness to cooperate, his distractibility and limited span of attention, and by his disconcerting tendency to respond to other aspects of the stimulus field than the ones designated by the experimenter. Also, to elicit a satisfactory number of meaningful responses test stimuli must be relatively concrete and highly structured. Older children are more cooperative and attentive, can respond better to more abstract and unstructured stimulus situations, can be tested by procedures requiring reading and writing, and can report verbally their perceptions, attitudes, feelings and emotions. On the other hand, they are less ingenuous and more disposed and better able to conceal responses that they feel will meet with disapproval.

Difficulties in Obtaining Evidence in Child Development

Difficulties Shared with Psychology. Human behavior is so extremely complex that it is very difficult even to identify the relevant variables that are operative in a given situation. Furthermore, the great number and complexity of the variables involved makes it difficult to keep some factors constant while varying others. But even when control is theoretically possible, humanitarian considerations rule out the imposition of many experimental conditions that are injurious to children (e.g., extreme deprivation, frustration, etc.). Partly for this latter reason, ecological methods are mandatory in many areas of developmental research (see p. 7).

The phenomenological content of psychology also makes for research problems not found in other disciplines. Most important of these is the difficulty of obtaining reliable and valid measures of behavior or conscious processes. First, many psychological functions and traits such as intelligence, motivation, interest, anxiety, etc., must be measured *indirectly* by eliciting responses to a representative sample of stimuli that are supposedly indicative of the trait or function in question. However it is often somewhat questionable to what extent such instruments measure what they purport to measure since criteria of validity are usually just as indirect as the measures themselves. In many instances, also, the subject's sincerity, honesty, cooperativeness and ability to communicate his actual feelings and ideas are difficult to evaluate, although in recent years many ingenious devices have been employed to check objectively these aspects of his test behavior. Second, because human behavior is so complex and is influenced by so many transitory factors, measurements tend to be unstable and inconsistent from one session or test component to another; and because of the tremendous range of intra-group variability characterizing most behavioral indices, measures of central tendency tend to have relatively large standard errors. Finally, before many kinds of psychological findings can be generalized to a wider population, it is necessary to choose an experimental sample that is reasonably representative of the population about which generalizations wish to be made. Consideration must be given to a veritable host of socioeconomic and other variables that could influence behavior or development differentially. Such serious sampling problems do not ordinarily arise when the properties of molecules, bacteria or muscle fibers are under investigation.

Special Difficulties in Developmental Research. In addition to the foregoing difficulties, special methodological problems arise in developmental studies. First, since behavioral change over *extended* intervals of time is the phenomenon under investigation, experimental control is obviously much more difficult than when a relatively contemporaneous or situational event is studied, even if it were possible and desirable to simulate nature successfully. Second, if it is necessary to make use of retrospective data, there are problems of simple and selective forgetting, purposeful and "unconscious" distortion, and the sheer impossibility of an adult recalling and interpreting childhood events as they actually appeared to him at the time of their occurrence; and even if it is possible to collect and record data contemporaneously, they are not easy to interpret five, ten, or twenty years later in a changed context, especially if the personnel of a research project has turned over several times in the interim. Third, because developmental studies are usually intensive and extensive in scope and involve repeated and frequent measurements, practical difficulties frequently arise in obtaining an experimental population. Parents, teachers and school administrators are reluctant to contribute the necessary time, often fail to appreciate the value or ultimate usefulness of such investigation, or object to "using children as guinea pigs." Fourth, sampling considerations are more important in developmental studies than in other types of psychological research because of concern with making normative statements about various age groups of children and interpreting the nature of the developmental differences between them. For many types of contemporaneous phenomena, on the other hand, when higher order relationships between variables or basic processes are under investigation, almost *any* subjects are equally representative of human beings.

Finally, the measurement of change and rate of change presents many serious methodological problems. Suppose that we wished to determine whether three- and four year old children differ significantly with respect to a given capacity or type of behavior. The significance of the measured difference would vary depending on the size and composition of our sample, the degree of variability among our subjects, and the discriminating power of our instrument (e.g., whether it was an "all or none" measure or reflected partial or subliminal status, whether it provided adequate "ceiling" for the older groups, etc.). The age difference itself could also be an important factor. It is quite conceivable that by simply using six months older children in both groups or by increasing the age difference slightly, significant results could be rendered nonsignificant or vice versa.*

Moreover, the determination of age differences assumes that the measuring instrument yields scores that are comparable in the sense of measuring qualitatively equivalent capacities or behavior. If, for example, we use one battery of sub-tests for measuring intelligence at age four and different batteries at ages six, eight, ten, twelve and fourteen, plotting scores against chronological age assumes that all of the batteries are equally representative of general intelligence. On the other hand, if the *measures* do not vary in content from one age level to another, they may for this very reason provide a distorted picture of growth if the *capacities* or behaviors in question undergo qualitative change over the age span (see p. 587).

Even if the foregoing assumptions with respect to the measurement of behavioral change are adequately satisfied, the mean performances of different age groups may still *not* be comparable (a) unless relevant environmental factors are relatively equivalent for the two age groups, and (b) unless measures are expressed in units that are quantitatively equivalent at all points on the scale. Thus, it makes considerable difference whether developmental status is expressed in terms of raw scores, age scores, standard scores, or percentages of mature capacity. Raw scores and age scores are obviously not comparable from one age level to another since degree of variability does not remain constant from infancy to adolescence. All the criteria that affect the validity of measured differences between adjacent age groups naturally apply also to comparisons made in the *rate* of developmental change or to the slope of the growth curve.

When units of measurement are available that are quantitatively and qualitatively comparable, meaningful growth curves may be constructed by plotting successive scores of individuals or groups against chronological age. If such units are *not* available, marked differences in the form of a given growth function will result depending on the instrument and type of score employed. Age scores (e.g., mental age), for example, will by definition yield linear growth curves since one year of functional gain is calibrated in terms of the mean increment attained in a calendar year. However, when intellectual status is measured as a percentage of total adult achievement, several studies show similar negatively accelerated curves despite sampling differences and differences in the type of measuring instrument used.[62] The same findings are reported for growth curves based on standard deviation scaling.[80, 88, 105, 108]

---

*Of course, by reducing the interval between two measurements sufficiently it would never be possible to obtain a significant indication of growth. Hence, the *consistency of a trend* in a given direction is more important than the significance of a difference between any two points on a growth curve.

Although a negatively accelerated curve is characteristic of growth in many different areas of development, it can by no means be considered *the universal* growth curve that Courtis[32, 33] claims it to be. Some types of growth (e.g., skeletal, genital), for example, are marked by spurts and plateaus; others show a gradual or precipitous decline after maximum attainment. Also, because of tremendous diversity in the underlying processes of growth in different areas of development as well as in the relative importance of different determinants, the search for a generalized curve of growth holding true for all developmental functions and at all age levels would, on theoretical grounds alone, seems doomed to failure.

Another important theoretical issue involved in the measurement of developmental change has to do with the determination of true zero and terminal points of development. Implicit in all measures of behavioral capacity is the assumption that the designation of a given developmental level represents a degree of attainment that can be specified in relation to a developmental zero and terminus respectively. It is further assumed that the latter reference points can be located at opposite extremes of a scale composed of equivalent units. True zeros cannot be determined by direct measurement. They are calculated by extrapolation, i.e., by extending the lower end of an empirically determined growth curve and assuming that the same trends and factors will be operative for the unknown as for the known portion of the curve. Although there is considerable difference between mental tests in the chronological age at which the mid-point of intellectual status is attained[8, 59, 88, 104, 105, 108] extrapolation from the lower end of all tests places the zero point of intelligence at or shortly before birth.[107] Thurstone's method of calculating developmental zero is based on the premise that zero capacity exists when no variability is present in the group. This is determined by extrapolating the lower end of the curve when means of Binet items are plotted against standard deviations for the age group from three to fourteen.[107]

Evaluation of Difficulties. The research problems described above certainly complicate the task of obtaining valid developmental data, but by no means remove child development from the realm of science. The least common denominators making for research difficulty are the variability and complexity of human beings. Because of these factors it is difficult to identify and control relevant variables, to construct reliable and valid measuring instruments, and to obtain representative and statistically significant findings. However, these problems are not unique to developmental psychology. In varying degrees they characterize all sciences. Identity does not exist in nature—not even in the case of two sodium atoms. In ascending order of the complexity and variability of their phenomenological content, the different sciences may be ordered as follows: physics, chemistry, biology, psychology and sociology.

Hence, comparable difficulties may be found in all sciences. Absolute control is a research ideal that can be approached but never attained. At best one can hope to control the most important and relevant variables. Sampling errors occur even in physics and chemistry but are sufficiently small to be ignored safely. The same applies to errors of measurement obtained with micrometers and stop watches. Statistical significance can also never be more than a statement of probability that defines the *relative* degree of confidence which may be placed in a given finding. In child development these problems are more serious than in the physical and biological sciences. However, by the use of judicious sampling techniques, special control procedures, ingenious measuring devices, and large groups of subjects, it is possible to obtain research findings that satisfy the criteria of scientific data.

Problems of Sampling

The reasons for the greater importance of sampling problems in child development than in other areas of psychology have already been discussed (see pp. 133-134). Although child development specialists always wish to generalize beyond their experimental population, this does not necessarily mean that generalizations applying to *all* children are always sought. More frequently, because of the practical considerations involved, it is necessary to restrict the scope of applicability to a particular culture, subculture or socioeconomic group. Sometimes also, an investigation is concerned with a special kind of population, e.g., physically handicapped, intellectual gifted, or socially maladjusted children. In the latter instances, care need only be taken to choose a sample representative of the particular subpopulation.

Sampling considerations are not as important in some aspects of child development as in others. Normative investigations of children and of developmental changes in capacity obviously require highly representative experimental populations. Before certain emotional, social, cognitive, and psychosexual behaviors can be characterized as typical of designated age levels of children, much greater attention must be paid to problems of sampling than Gesell and Freud and their followers have acknowledged as necessary. The same holds true for many of the conditions and factors affecting development. However, certain physiologic and phylogenetic aspects of development (see p. 57) and many higher order relationships between antecedent conditions (e.g., parent attitudes) and personality outcomes are relatively uninfluenced by cultural and socioeconomic factors. For example, anterior pituitary and gonadal hormones probably influence skeletal development, and *gross* emotional deprivation probably affects personality development in much the same ways in all cultural settings; but height and child rearing norms and their relationship to social adjustment obviously vary tremendously from one culture to another. Hence, rigid insistence on sampling control of the *same* variables (e.g., intelligence, socioeconomic status, paternal occupation) in *all* studies is just as indefensible as is total neglect of sampling in purely normative investigations.

The operation of numerous selective factors in the social and cultural environments makes it extremely difficult to obtain a representative sample by merely choosing children at random.[6] By procuring subjects solely from within a given socioeconomic level, from a particular section of a city, or from either exclusively rural or urban areas, it is quite possible to select a highly distorted sample of the population for which an estimate of capacity or a statement of relationship is sought. Randomized sampling is only feasible when either extremely large experimental populations are employed or when there is substantial reason for believing that variability in the function under investigation is not distributed selectively, i.e., is relatively unaffected by social stratification. Ordinarily, therefore, the experimental sample should be deliberately stratified in advance so as to duplicate as nearly as possible the major characteristics of the total population.

Statements regarding the statistical significance of differences between age levels or other groups of children are obviously misleading if they are based upon data secured from unrepresentative samples. Although it is true that the standard error of a mean varies inversely with the square root of the number of cases, it is important to add the qualification, "provided the sample is adequate."[6] Also, since

> most scientific workers are under practical limitations of time, money, and availability of subjects, it . . . becomes desirable so to design and arrange a study that the results will be significant without undertaking a great deal of unnecessary experimentation . . . A small sample selected in accordance with criteria rigidly laid down in advance gives more significant and meaningful results than a larger sample the characteristics of which are unknown.[6]

Thus, it is desirable to use as large an experimental population as is reasonably available and expedient to use as small a sample as will yield definitive data for the type of problem under investigation. This naturally varies with the complexity and variability of the functions and relationships involved, the extent of control that can be exercised in designing the study, and the reliability and validity of the measuring instruments.[6] In any event, the greater the representativeness of the sample employed the smaller it need be to provide significant findings.

The categories used as a basis for selecting a stratified sample of a particular age level of children vary with the relationship that are being studied. In general, stratification need only be concerned with population characteristics that might be expected to influence the variables under investigation.

Since the two sexes differ significantly with respect to many developmental functions, it is always advisable to use an equal number of boys and girls and to analyze the data separately by sex. Socioeconomic status affects so many developmental phenomena that it is usually desirable to stratify the sample by paternal occupation in accordance with the percentage of employed males found in each of the seven broad categories of male occupations reported by the United States Census Bureau.[6] In some studies, the experimental sample should take into account the additional factors of race or ethnic origin, religion, geographical location, and urban or rural residence. Although sampling differences in these latter categories show a consistently diminishing trend,[6] they still cannot be ignored in many kinds of research problems. School grade and I.Q. are also relevant sampling considerations in a substantial number of studies.

MEASUREMENT OF DEVELOPMENTAL CHANGE

In addition to the difficulties already discussed as complicating the measurement of developmental change (see pp. 133-136), another major problem still remains to be considered. Since behavioral development refers to change in performance or capacity occurring between two designated points in the life cycle, it is essential that successive age levels of experimental subjects be comparable in all respects except for chronological age. Two different approaches may be employed here—*cross-sectional* and *longitudinal*. The former investigates the growth of a particular function by comparing mean measurements of *different* groups of children varying in age. The latter approach utilizes successive mean measurements made on the *same* individuals at regularly prescribed intervals.

Cross-Sectional Approach

The cross-sectional approach offers many attractive advantages. First, it is relatively easy to obtain access to large groups of subjects for short-term research projects particularly in large urban centers. Second, cross-sectional studies are relatively inexpensive and require no continuity of or long-term cooperation between research workers. Third, data need not be "frozen" over long periods of time until subjects complete their development before interpretation and publication are possible. Lastly, "uniform sampling procedures can be used throughout the age or level series"[6]; selective loss of subjects does not occur as in a longitudinal population.

However, carefully executed stratified sampling is necessary before successive age levels of different subjects can be rendered truly comparable. "Matching different groups for even the important identifiable variables can at best be only approximate . . . In school populations increasing age itself tends to operate selectively in such important variables as intellectual ability" since many duller pupils become academic casualties.[11] Furthermore, "because children grow at different rates and reach similar developmental levels at different times, a cross-section study places together at the thirteen-year age level many girls well past puberty and many girls months away from puberty."[6] Finally, social change renders noncomparable the respective backgrounds of different age groups of children. Consider, for example, a cross-sectional study of negativism performed in 1941. Because of the occurrence of World War II, a ten year old born in 1941 would hardly be likely to have had the same kind of family environment during the first three years of his life as a three year old born in 1948. "The former is almost completely a product of the turbulent war and post-war years, whereas the latter grew up . . . in a period with conditions affecting American family life relatively stable."[11]

Longitudinal Approach

In longitudinal studies, although the comparability of serial age levels of the *same* individuals is affected by selective loss of the residentially less stable subjects, it is obvious that in all other respects greater comparability prevails. Hence, not only is matching of different groups unnecessary, but also many different studies can be performed on the same population. It is also possible with longitudinal data to plot individual growth curves and increments and to analyze in detail "the interrelationships between growth processes, both maturational and experiential, because all data have been obtained on the same children."[6] This is especially important in studies of the cumulative effect of antecedent conditions on the personality development of children, where there is no satisfactory substitute for intensive longitudinal measurement, particularly if individual growth curves are desired. A further advantage is that longitudinal findings allow one

> to trace the development of special subgroups within the total population, thus pointing up differential trends that would otherwise become obliterated in computing measures of central tendency for the group. It is also possible, of course, to use cross-sectional data in studying the development of subgroups, by first identifying and making comparable in other respects varying age samples of the subgroups; but unless the criteria for identification are relatively unambiguous and homogeneous in nature (e.g., race, sex, physical characteristics), such comparisons cannot be relied upon to provide as accurate a picture of differential development as would be possible were data on the *same* group of special individuals available over a period of years. If, for example, we wished to study the social development of [preadolescents] who as children were rejected by their parents, it would not be very satisfactory to obtain our data from different age groups of rejected children. In either instance, however, comparison with a control group would be necessary before a significant differential trend could be concluded.[11]

Lastly, longitudinal data enable the investigator to measure more adequately the impact on development of events (e.g., pubescence, confirmation, initial school attendance, death of parent) which do not occur at the same age for all children. For example, with longitudinal data the emotional or intellectual status of individuals one, two, three or four years after pubescence can be measured and the data pooled regardless of whether pubescence occurs at age 10 or 17.

The longitudinal approach is also not without serious disadvantages. From a practical standpoint, it is much more expensive, requires continuity of research personnel, and postpones publication of findings for many years. Furthermore, it is difficult to obtain a cooperative population which is willing to be studied intensively and repeatedly for a decade or more; and almost by definition, such a population constitutes a highly unrepresentative sample. Original errors in sampling or in the omission of crucial variables, hypotheses, and newly originated methodological devices can never be corrected.[6, 23, 46] Many subjects drop out because of illness, death, removal from the area, financial catastrophe, or simply because they are "fed up." Those who remain come from atypically cooperative and stable families or may be affected by repeated measurement per se[23] and, hence, are no longer representative of the population at large; and unless the original data of subjects who drop out are discarded, the different age levels are also no longer comparable. Finally, if the span of years covered by the research includes an unusual social or economic phenomenon such as war or depression, growth curves may be distorted.

In any event it is clear that elaborate longitudinal studies as well as refined sampling techniques are wasteful before meaningful and testable hypotheses related to a comprehensive theoretical orientation can be formulated.

> In the absence of specific questions to be asked of the data, all kinds of information that could be obtained about the subjects of the study have at times been unselectively accumulated. When the data were subsequently analyzed and reported, much of the available information held but little interest to the investigator, to wit, the files upon files of developmental data still gathering dust in many places. More frustrating yet, it has been a common experience that after a number of years investigators found that they lacked the very facts which they would currently find of greatest interest but which played no significant part in their thinking when the longitudinal study was begun.[46]

It is highly desirable therefore first to test, redefine and reformulate preliminary hypotheses and measuring instruments by cross-sectional methods on less precisely selected populations. "If a hypothesis . . . can find no support from cross-sectional data, it is probably not one which should be used in subsequent studies . . . Comprehensive cross-sectional data should

[also] . . . suggest new relationships among phenomena [and] . . . enable us to examine not only the specific relationship between two factors as hypothesized, but numerous additional variables which may modify, inhibit or facilitate the emergence of the behavior in question."[46]

> Thus, the development of a theoretical model in the area concerned moves much more rapidly than would be the case in a longitudinal approach in which the hypotheses are developed over a longer period of time and cannot be adequately tested within the framework of the study as originally formulated.[23]

Bell has originated a promising "convergence approach" which attempts to overcome the shortcomings of both the longitudinal and cross-sectional methods. In essence,

> cross-sectional studies are made of different age groups so spaced in age that remeasurement of the same groups after a period of time provides information on the nature of changes occurring over the entire age period as well as data which will permit an answer to the question of whether the shorter curves for each span may reasonably be combined into a curve covering the entire age period . . .
>
> The convergence approach appears to have greatest utility in two types of situations: (a) in investigations basically oriented toward a cross-sectional approach but in which there is reason for concern over the comparability of the experimental groups relative to the dependent variables on factors other than age, and in which it is possible to make limited remeasurements of these groups; (b) for investigations oriented toward the longitudinal approach but faced with problems of transient or less cooperative groups or with possibilities of undesirable contamination of the experimental population by extensive observation.[23]

Other similar, essentially cross-sectional approaches that include longitudinal components are (a) Mead's method of studying different age levels grouped about a transitional phase of development[76] and (b) Lasswell's method of "interlapping observation" in which transitional phases between different adjacent age groups are observed.[68] Because the focus of attention is on developmental phenomena that occur relatively rapidly, much valuable intra-group longitudinal data can be collected in the space of a single year to supplement the data on inter-age group differences.

Case Study Approach

The case study method may be considered a special variant of the longitudinal approach. Here, too, emphasis is placed on accumulating developmental data—both measurements of antecedent conditions and of outcomes —on the *same* individuals over a span of years. Ordinarily the unit of study is an individual rather than a group of subjects, and the purpose of the study is to shed light on some problem of adjustment for which diagnosis, therapy and prognosis are desired. Hence "a much greater quantity of personal data from a wider diversity of sources is [usually] assembled for a single case study than ever becomes available for an individual subject in a longitudinal group."[11] Not only are more biographical and interview data utilized in addition to the usual objective measures, but also the focus of inquiry is the unique growth pattern of a single individual rather than developmental trends characterizing children in general.

> From the intimate knowledge thus gained of the interrelationship between significant aspects of an individual's developmental history, personality structure and overt behavior, it is often possible to acquire valuable insights into the nature of personality development and behavioral adjustment. But apart from their applicability to the individual from whom they are derived, such insights enjoy at best the status of hypotheses which can be tested either by an analysis of a *series* of case studies or by normative group studies.[11]

Simple application of the methodological principles elaborated above indicates why—"although the attempt is frequently made . . . no definitive generalizations about human development can be drawn from one individual."[11] First is the matter of sampling. Case studies are not typical of children generally but largely of maladjusted children whose parents are either financially poor enough to qualify for free treatment in clinics or sufficiently wealthy to afford the high cost of private therapy.

> The value of the concept of the lawfulness of the individual's own history and the practical value of earlier data in predicting later outcomes for the particular individual is not to be confused with using a single case as a basis for generalization to wide populations. In the former case prediction is justifiable; in the latter the representatives of the case must be demonstrated, which is literally an almost impossible task.[6]

This applies to anthropological as well as to clinical case studies. Although it is far better, as Margaret Mead points out, to use a small sample whose place in the whole is well understood than a large sample whose relationship to the total population is unknown, adequate sampling, whether of the "pure" or "deviant" case variety[76] can never be achieved in a single case. Too much variability prevails in the non-physiological aspects of human development for any single individual—irrespective of how typical he may appear to be—to serve as representative of his culture.

In relation to a single case it is also impossible to determine whether an obtained difference or finding of relationship is statistically significant or is merely a chance occurrence. One reads, for example, that delinquent Johnny came from a "broken home." But it is very simple to cite case studies of children from broken homes who never became delinquent and of children from intact homes who did. It is also self-evident that in the absence of systematic control of other relevant variables, which is impossible in the single case approach, no statement of relationship or causal inference can be generalized to a wider population.

Another limitation of case-study methods only applies when the data involved are derived from retrospective reports of the subject.*

It is undeniable that an adult's account of his early memories and childhood experiences furnish valuable data on the way in which adults see childhood experience, their own and other peoples'. However, these are essentially data upon how the narrator feels and what significance those experiences have for him in the present, not data upon his actual development in the past. This distinction has been lost sight of because for therapeutic purposes a false memory is often as good as a real one. When our object is the study of the growth of personality, data derived from these introspective accounts must be taken with the greatest caution.[76]

Thus it is very easy for an adult male undergoing psychoanalysis retrospectively to interpret childhood hatred for a harsh rejecting father as sexual rivalry, or for an adult female to "remember" childhood sexual experiences with an affectionate father, particularly if they are familiar with psychoanalytic theory. However this neither proves the existence of an Oedipus complex in the first instance nor establishes the historical authenticity of incestual relationship in the second. In ethnological studies, life histories must also be interpreted cautiously since native informants frequently have little notion of historical sequences and often fail to distinguish between what *has* and what *might have* occurred.[56]

Psychoanalytic investigations of children overcome to some extent the objectionable aspects of retrospective case studies. However,

as one who knows normal young children reads, it becomes clear that the child is approached from a particular theoretical point of view and that the responses are fitted to that point of view. Little attempt is made to evaluate, no statistical or quantitative material is presented, and no complete statements or records of the analyst's speech and actions or of the child's responses are given. Some of the content seems to be directly or indirectly suggested to the child. Younger children are very markedly suggestible. No attempt is made to control the sampling of children subjected to analysis, nor are precise data over a span of years made available as to the success or failure of the . . . treatment. The great difficulty with psychoanalysis as a scientific method lies . . . in its acceptance of intuition as a valid method of securing basic data.[6]

A final criticism of the case study method relates to an extremely widespread practice which, however, is not necessarily indigenous to this ap-

*Some case-studies, e.g., cumulative records, "simultaneous life histories,"[6, 56, 76] utilize data in which subjects offer contemporaneously recorded verbalizations regarding current aspects of their life situation. Such accounts can be checked against the memories of other persons for historial accuracy and related to objective indices of behavior.

proach. This is the common error of citing single case studies as proof rather than as illustrative of a given theory of personality development. Were this error not multiplied countless times every year it would hardly bear repetition that genuine empirical evidence in support of a theoretical orientation can only come from empirical studies concerned with such matters as sampling, control, reliability and validity of instruments, tests of statistical significance, and exclusion of alternative theories. Permitted to select a "typical" case of their own or even using the very same case material, psychologists of ten different schools could find equally credible support for their particular theories.

Part of this difficulty stems from a failure to distinguish between the respective primary aims of research and therapy. The clinician's focus of interest is in ameliorating the adjustive difficulties of the individual child, not in establishing valid generalizations about children. He may, therefore, use intuition and unvalidated diagnostic instruments, or instruments that work for him but for nobody else—if nothing better is available—in diagnosing and treating behavior disorders. He may even be quite successful without being able to identify the factors responsible for his success. Such success is laudable and should not be disparaged, but it does not yield scientific generalizations about the development of children. The fact that certain therapeutic methods "work" does not prove the theories on which they are allegedly based. Actually, of course, some valid underlying theoretical principles *are* operative, but not necessarily the ones that are invoked. For example, *if* it were shown that psychoanalysis benefits neurotic children or adults significantly more frequently than would happen by chance, this would in no way substantiate the theory of psychosexual instincts, the doctrine of sublimation, or the Oedipus hypothesis. It would only demonstrate that ventilation, catharsis and transference have therapeutic value. No other psychoanalytic principles are actually tested in psychoanalytic therapy.

In conclusion, the *single* case study is useful only as a source of hypotheses or as an illustration of a particular theoretical viewpoint or previously validated generalization. *Series* of case studies, on the other hand, can be used in much the same way as longitudinal data, provided, of course, that the usual methodological requirements are observed.

METHODS OF MEASUREMENT

In this section we shall consider some of the more important methods of psychological measurement utilized in child development research. Naturally, many of the same measurement techniques and considerations applying to adult behavior apply to children as well. Hence the more general aspects of these methods will not be discussed unless deserving special emphasis.*

Observational Techniques

The key role of observation in all natural sciences, including child development, has already been considered at length (see pp. 6-8). But whereas systematic and rigorously controlled observation yields valuable scientific data, the scientific value of incidental and impressionistic observations (except for suggesting new hypotheses) is practically nil. Most anecdotal "baby diaries" kept by fond parents fall into the latter category. The early baby biographies written by such famous figures in the early history of child psychology as Tiedemann,[109] Preyer,[85] Pestalozzi,[38] and Shinn,[98] were handled somewhat more systematically and provided a continuous, longitudinal, and "multivariable picture of the molar and molecular aspects of behavior and situations."[19]

Nevertheless, these biographical efforts suffered from many of the understandable methodological shortcomings that could be expected at this early stage in child development research. Observations were often made haphazardly and at irregular intervals, resulting in biased selection of incidents. The kinds of behavior to be observed were not determined in advance, and the precision of observations in terms of setting, antecedent conditions, and properties of eliciting stimuli were not always adequate. Common criteria for recording a given instance of behavior were the special and often fluctuating interests of the observer and the uniqueness or precocity of the performance. The latter tendency was enhanced by the fact that the biographers were usually highly educated and proud parents whose objectivity and comparability to the population at large were obviously open to question. Much of the recording was also done retrospectively and was subject to selective forgetting; and since observations were not always distinguished from interpretations, the former were distored by preconceived notions, particularly by the attribution of adult response capacities to children. Lastly, these data shared all of the disadvantages of single case studies, insofar as generalizability to wider populations was concerned.

Ecological Observation. Ecological observation is concerned with the description of behavior in natural or uncontrived situations in which the observer does not attempt to manipulate the stimuli impinging on the

*No attempt, also, will be made to consider rating, ranking, questionnaire and interview methods definitively. These are handled adequately in the references.[4, 6, 36, 57, 101] Inventory methods and standardized tests will not be considered at all since they are usually treated quite exhaustively in courses on psychological measurement. Infant developmental scales and preschool tests of mental ability are discussed in Chapter 18.

subject. Strictly speaking it is limited to in situ field studies in our own or other cultures.

Adequate ecological techniques demand attention to the following methodological points: First, the range of situation and behavior to be observed should be explicitly defined and limited in advance to prevent undesirable dispersion and nonuniformity of observational efforts. Observations should also be conducted at regularly determined intervals and under uniform conditions of time, place and setting. Second, it is essential to use trained and unbiased observers; and to make possible an estimate of observer reliability, several different observers should be used. Complete absence of bias, of course, is an unattainable ideal. Appraisals of the same behavior vary considerably from one observer to another because of differential projection of observer attitudes into behavior settings.[103] Hence, "an important part of the training of observers lies in techniques of minimizing and holding constant the involvement of the observer in the subject's behavior."[19] Barker and Wright also recommend half-hour observation periods for a single observer because "the alertness required to perceive and remember the multitude of simultaneous and sequential occurrence is fatiguing."[19]

Third, observations should be recorded in full *immediately after* they are made from notes taken *during* the observation period. Retrospectively recorded observations, are not only less accurate and more biased but also are "only as valuable as the questions which were already formulated in the investigator's mind . . . Simultaneous records, on the other hand . . . contain a great deal more spontaneous observation and may yield to analysis and reanalysis not only by the investigator but also by other investigators."[76] Ambiguities and omissions in the observational report can be corrected by later interrogation of the observer.[19]

Fourth, long rather than short behavioral sequences maximize the continuity in behavior and minimize the possibilities of biased selection and interpretation of incidents.[19] *Immediate* inferences regarding the motivations and feelings of the subject should also be made. "One who is concerned about the objectivity of records must face the fact that he has to deal with the direction, the goals and the meaning of behavior when he studies psychosocial development, and that these can never be perceived directly. By recording long sequences of both directly observed and inferred behavior the best basis for constructing a final 'true' record is laid."[19] However, although observations and inferences may be recorded simultaneously in time they must be carefully distinguished from each other. Also, all interpretation other than first order inferences from the behavior itself should be excluded from the record.

Fifth, "the influence of the observer must be kept minimal and constant.

The observer is almost always a part of the subject's psychological situation and hence influences his behavior in some degree. This is an inevitable limitation of most naturalistic observations.[19] Some but not all of this contamination can be reduced by allowing for an initial period of habituation. One-way screens and hidden microphones are useful for this purpose but can only be utilized in relatively few natural (non-laboratory) settings. Records may also be supplemented by simultaneous sound moving pictures.[76] However, this adds greatly to the technical difficulties and expense of the operation and accentuates the presence of the observer and the self-consciousness of the subject.

The ecological method is exemplified best by field studies. In long-range investigations concerned with the evolution of interpersonal and intergroup relationships, group structure, and role behavior,[72, 110] it is advantageous for the observer to serve as a participant in the community activities of the population of subjects under observation. This enables him to gain access to much data and to acquire many insights that would ordinarily be inaccessible to a detached observer. In studies involving more circumscribed kinds of behavior[67, 115] non-participation of the observer is more appropriate.

If in certain instances more direct and immediate quantification of observational data is desired, behavior can be appraised and rated in relation to an evaluative scale*[18, 31] *Time sampling*[81, 82] also enables the investigator to quantify his data readily and to determine the generality of observed behavior. He simply enumerates the number of times a particular type of recurring behavior (e.g., quarreling, cooperative behavior, aggression) is manifested by a given child in a constant, systematically spaced interval of time. It must be borne in mind, however, that such enumerations of response patterns, independent of context, may lump many genotypically diverse behaviors into the same phenotypic category. Also, the descriptive data they yield do not necessarily shed any light on the nature of the behavior or on the determining factors involved.

From a methodological standpoint, the ecological approach in child development has been employed most definitively by Barker and Wright. [19, 21, 115] These investigators defined a large number of discriminable "psychological habitats" which tend to arise uniformly in particular kinds of "behavioral settings." For example,

the Sunday school, the day school, a basketball game, the drug store . . . Such community situations coerce the children who enter them to behave in relatively homogeneous ways regardless of the individual characteristics of the children . . . [They] form a link between the non-psychological milieu of a child and his

---

*See also the schedules for measuring child-adult interaction in Bishop, B. M.: *Psychological Monographs 65*: No. 11, 1951; and Moustakas, C. E., Sigel, I. E., and Schalock, H. D., *Child Development 27*: 109-134, 1956.

psychological habitat . . . A behavior setting [therefore] may be defined as a physical or social part of the non-psychological world that is *generally* perceived as appropriate for particular kinds of behavior."[19]

The "psychological habitat," on the other hand, represents the psychological life-space or situation of a *particular* individual in a behavior setting. Barker and Wright[19, 115] studied the psychological habitats of different age levels of children (and hence their "psychosocial development") by observing meaningful, goal-directed behavior units ("episodes") occurring in such standardized behavior settings, and by making judgments of children's subjective reactions, to various objective determinants of frustration, satisfaction, success, failure, and constraint.

Controlled Observation. A modified form of ecological observation results when a limited degree of control is imposed on the situation in which subjects are observed. This may vary from the extremely general kinds of constraints placed upon behavior, as would be implicit in the physical and social arrangements found in nursery schools and playgrounds, to much more specific attempts at manipulating the types of stimuli and situations to which children subjects are exposed (e.g., play techniques, experimental situations, psychometric and personality tests). A great deal of the normative data in child development is a product of the former approach.[29, 52, 99] In infant and nursery school laboratories, the typical use of one-way vision screens makes the children unaware of the fact that they are being observed. Sound motion pictures have also been used extensively in the Gesell Institute of Child Development to supplement the observational record.

When situations and stimuli are selected, structured or manipulated more specifically, the method of controlled observation tends to shade into the laboratory type of experimental investigation. For example, if number, age, and sex of children, and type and number of toys are systematically varied in order to determine the relationship of these variables to ascendent behavior,[60] if controlled variability in "social climate" is related to group cohesiveness and expression of aggression,[71] if regressive behavior is induced by observer manipulated frustration,[20] the essential features of the ecological approach are largely replaced by those of experiment. *Such experiments, of course, can yield valuable data about the social, emotional, and intellectual behavior and development of children, particularly when the impact of situational variables is studied or when the experimental setting is used to *elicit* and measure *existing* response tendencies and capacities. By means

*The problem of design of experiments—the use of control groups, matched pairs of children, co-twin control,[53] etc., and of experimental and statistical methods of systematically varying, holding constant, replicating and analyzing the effects of and interaction between various determinants of behavior—is beyond the scope of this volume.[5-7, 42, 57, 64]

of carefully designed experiments it is possible to determine the effects of and interaction between particular variables that are not likely to be operative frequently in isolation under natural auspices. However, the futility of attempting to use experimental situations to simulate the cumulative *effect* of many kinds of complex, recurrent and long-term aspects of the natural interpersonal environment has already been discussed at length (see pp. 8-9).

More structured than controlled observations, but less rigidly controlled than experimental situations, are various *play techniques*. These differ from other *projective devices* in presenting a wider and less controlled range of stimulation that evokes more spontaneous responses. Originally employed in the diagnosis and treatment of emotionally disturbed children, this method has also been used for a decade or more as a research tool for investigating the normal child's perceptions, concepts, feelings and attitudes. Its chief advantage is that it makes possible the elicitation of existing attitudinal and response tendencies in simulated real-life situations that could otherwise not be elicited at all because of limitations in the young child's verbal capacities. Standardized stimulus objects and figures (e.g., doll families and furniture) are utilized to enable the subject to dramatize in fantasy the type of behavior he might ordinarily express (or repress) in relation to the actual figures represented by the dolls.

As a source of valid generalizations about children's behavior and attitudies, the use of play techniques is warranted to the extent that careful attention is paid to such matters as standardization of materials, experimenter-child interaction, duration of play sessions, conditions preceding play sessions, recording of observations, reliability and validity of measures,* etc. For example, doll-play aggression in young children has been reliably observed and validated in terms of everyday habits of aggression[17, 93, 96]; and differences in this behavioral index have been significantly related to such factors as age, sex, sibling status and father's absence.[93]

Extreme caution, however, is indicated in the interpretation of children's responses to play interviews. Specific and invariable relationships between a child's handling of play materials and particular aspects of child rearing cannot be expected. For example, the same attitude of parental rejection may in different children (or under different conditions in the same child) give rise to overt play aggression against the offending parent, to displaced aggression directed against self or another adult, or to complete inhibition of aggressive response.[112] It is also important to guard against projection of observer bias or theoretical orientation. Psycho-

*Treatment of these methodological problems are available in the references.[4, 16, 78, 93, 94, 112]

analytically oriented play therapists tend to generalize impressionistic interpretations of isolated play session episodes to all children.[37, 44, 45, 49, 50, 65]
Ignoring such obvious considerations as sampling, observer reliability, statistical significance, the laws of parsimony, and exclusion of alternative
hypothesis, they present *illustrations* of doll play dealing with erogenous
zones as "evidence" for the Freudian theory of psychosexual development.
For the less doctrinaire observer, however, there is no self-evident connection
between a little boy pushing a miniature auto into a toy garage and
incestuous desires for sex relations with his mother, or between the "oral
and anal stages of personality development" and the ubiquitous interest
of four year olds in nursing bottles and toy toilets.

   Cross-Cultural Studies. Cross-cultural investigations represent a special
variant of intracultural field studies. Although mainly utilized in the past
to disprove ethnocentric overgeneralizations regarding child development,
they can serve the more positive function of extending "our knowledge of
the possible range of human behavior,"[76] and thereby lead to empirical
differentiation between those aspects of development (psychiobiological)
that are universal in distribution and those aspects (psychosocial) that are
referable to unique factors of sociocultural conditioning (see pp. 64-65).
In this regard they offer the following special advantages[76]: (a) they include
a broader sample of child rearing practices and other conditions affecting
personality development than is available in our own culture; (b) they
encompass "varieties of social systems which we could neither produce
experimentally nor derive by extrapolation from known forms"[76]; (c)
focusing as they do on "small groups of preliterate peoples sharing a
common culture, [they make it] possible to deal with the individual within
the whole society, in relation to his total culture, in a way that is not
possible in large groups, in a stratified society, characterized by great
heterogeneity of culture."[76]

   The failure of cross-cultural studies to measure up to their earlier promise
is largely attributable to two factors. First, there has been a lack of adequate
conceptualization in terms of which broad hypotheses with respect to personality development and socialization could be formulated, tested, and
related to the vital distinction between psychobiological and psychosocial
processes and mechanisms of development. This step should obviously
precede the organization of long-term and expensive field studies in which
precise observations and measures are brought to bear on relatively specific
problems.[76] Instead, ethnologists have been preoccupied with disproving
ethnocentric overgeneralizations or stereotypes of "the primitive mind" or
with finding discrete illustrations of child rearing practices or outcomes
that "prove" or "disprove" various aspects of Freudian theory.[76]

Second, and equally important, has been an incredible degree of methodological naivité regarding the nature of scientific evidence. Numerous investigators have made sweeping generalizations about the relationship between various specific items of infant care and adult personality on the basis of impressions gleaned from a single culture or from a small unrepresentative sample of cultures. [40, 55, 63, 66, 70, 89] These impressions have also been used to "prove" (rather than illustrate) various psychoanalytic formulations regarded as self-evidently valid. In general they have ignored such elementary considerations as adequate sampling, statistical significance, and control of other relevant variables. They have failed to consider the possibilities of accidental concomitance and of multiple causality. Observations have frequently been recorded retrospectively and developmental generalizations made from the retrospective accounts of older individuals, the authenticity of which could not be checked.

Finally, considerable vagueness often prevails with respect to the sample of individuals used, the methods of obtaining data, observer reliability, and the statistical operations through which conclusions are reached from data. Since interpretations seem to be a product of intuitive selection and weighting of obtained data rather than a product of objective, fully described, and rigorously designed procedures which could be repeated by other investigators, it is extremely difficult to assess the scientific value of such studies. In any event it is evident that they do not constitute definitive findings about human development and require confirmation by more rigorous methods.*

Because of difficulties in communication, ecological and controlled observation, nonverbal psychometric tests, projective devices, play techniques, infant developmental scales, and physiological measures are the most feasible methods of investigation in studying the development of primitive children. Care must be taken to devise test materials and scoring criteria that are not limited to our own culture, and to base quantitative and qualitative interpretations of psychometric and projective materials

*The above paragraph does not purport to characterize *all* psychological research in ethnological settings but only the rather numerous studies making extreme claims and overgeneralizations about the ultimate personality outcomes of particular aspects of child rearing. In their cross-cultural survey of child training practices as related to personality outcomes, Whiting and Child used pooled and reliable ratings of each type of variable in a wide variety of cultures.[111] Although these judgments took into account the larger context of cultural meanings in which the specific behaviors occurred, satisfied criteria of adequate sampling, and were treated by correlational techniques that permitted an estimate of statistical significance, the investigators were admittedly unable to arrive at any definitive conclusions with respect to hypothesized casual relationships between antecedents and consequents.

on the norms of the particular culture being studied.[76] Since satisfactory "culture free" tests of intelligence can never be constructed, the results of such tests should only be used for obtaining cross-cultural or intracultural information about cognitive capacities and processes and not for making comparative quantitative estimates of over-all intelligence.

Rating Methods

In quantifying observational data on the behavior of children, an almost inevitable step involves the abstraction of discriminable traits or capacities and rating them on a quantitative continuum of frequency, more or less, better or worse, etc. If the original observations were not made in reference to an evaluative scale or in accordance with a "time sampling" technique, the rating is done at a later date on the basis of a series of prior observations. Sometimes, and preferably, the ratings emerge from comparative content analysis of simultaneously recorded protocols of systematically observed behavior. More frequently, however, they represent a cumulative impression in which the rater reviews retrospectively in his mind the behavior of the ratees as he remembers it, or expresses a mere formulated judgment of the trait in question. This latter type of rating is naturally more contaminated by subjective bias, retrospective error, and lack of consistent, systematic and temporally equivalent relationships to the actual behavior of the different subjects being rated. Hence, ratings should not be used when more direct measures or more objective indirect indices of behavior or capacity are available.

Ratings are more valid when raters are trained in advance (i.e., briefed on the nature of the trait; permitted to ask questions, to make a trial run of ratings, to compare and discuss their ratings with others; instructed on how to distribute their ratings over the entire scale). The rater must be in a position to observe subjects frequently with respect to the trait being measured, and the trait itself should be tangible, accessible to observation, and objectively assessable on the basis of concrete behavior considered in its situational context. "Halo effect" can be minimized by having the rater judge each item on the scale for the entire group before proceeding to the next item. A mean rating by five observers is more reliable than a single rating; if this is not possible, a mean of successive ratings by a single observer should be used. Reliability may be determined by intercorrelating the ratings of different observers or the successive ratings of the same observer.*

*A methodological discussion of rating and ranking procedures is available in the references.[5, 36, 57, 101]

Self-Report Methods

A major departure from observational techniques, objective and psychometric tests, experimental situations, and rating methods is taken by procedures which rely on information that is provided by the subject himself rather than being inferred from observation or measurement of behavior and performance. Although such data present serious difficulties with respect to the sincerity, honesty and authenticity of the data supplied by the subject, promising attacks have been made on many of these problems.*

Furthermore, self-report methods frequently constitute the only *direct* approach to the investigation of the subjective life of human beings, their attitudes, values, motives, beliefs, perceptions, etc. Natural science methods that ignore these crucial areas of human behavior and development would, by definition, be ruling out some of the most important aspects of the phenomenological field. The distinctive feature of the ecological approach is not the fact that it relies on observational techniques but its concern with studying behavior in naturally occurring settings. In subhuman species, observation and experiment are the only feasible methods of investigation because animals cannot verbalize their subjective experience. Among human beings, however, not only is such verbalization possible, but the kinds of subjective experience that can be verbally communicated also happens to be the most significant aspects of their *behavior* broadly conceived.

The use of self-report methods in child development presupposes that the child is sufficiently mature in a cognitive sense to supply the desired kinds of information. Hence, they are inapplicable to infants and can only be employed in a very limited sense in the preschool child. These methods include the face-to-face interview, the questionnaire, inventory, diary and perceptual inquiry. Sometimes pictorial materials may be used to illustrate the concepts about which inquiry is made, e.g., race relations, awareness of interpersonal relations.[41, 86]

Interview. Interviews may either be structured or unstructured. The latter are conducted informally; appropriate questions are asked at opportune moments. To avoid inhibiting the subject, only brief notes are made if at all. In recent years, with the advent of sound recording devices, such interviews are usually transcribed and then studied or analyzed at a later

---

*To a very great extent, the same problems also apply to observational data. Parents, for example, are motivated to impress observers favorably regarding their child rearing practices. The identical issue of whether a parent's verbal *report* of his attitudes toward his children represents a true sample of his *actual* attitudes arises when the validity of observations of his child rearing *behavior* is examined. In neither case is there a genuinely independent or direct validating criterion available.

date. Although they make for better rapport and often yield richer data, they present serious disadvantages when used for research rather than for clinical purposes. The same ground is not covered and questions are asked in a different sequence and situational context for each subject. Since there is no standardized way of phrasing questions, variability in response will be indeterminably influenced by such difference in phrasing. Difficulty also arises in quantifying the data. The only possible method is to subject the protocols to content analysis and obtain independent ratings from qualified judges which can then be inter-correlated for a determination of reliability.[95]

Structured interviews correspond more to questionnaires except they make possible more detailed responses, and tend to discourage indifferent and careless replies. They do not generate as much rapport as do unstructured interviews, but, on the other hand, yield more uniform, comparable and quantifiable data. Subjects are generally more inhibited and suspicious and are often disturbed by the verbatim recording of their replies. The interviewer also has to adhere closely to his schedule of questions and is unable to pursue unexpected leads.

Questionnaire. The questionnaire is a frequently used and abused research instrument in child development. However, it can provide valid data if certain precautions are rigorously observed. The questions should be tangible, precise, specific and unambiguous. Unless opinions and attitudes are the objects of investigation, questions should refer to matters of fact that are accessible to the subject and recent enough to be remembered accurately. It is also essential that respondents be sufficiently mature and intelligent to grasp the meaning of questions and under no undue pressure to give particular kinds of answers. Some measure of the authenticity and sincerity of replies should be used. This may consist of a spot check against available objective records or the use of built-in devices that detect insincerity and carelessness in responding. It goes without saying that careful sampling is necessary before any reliance can be placed on normative or interpretive findings.

A very common error in the interpretation of questionnaire data is the investigator's tendency to equate frequency with saliency. For example, children may be asked to mention the school subjects or games they like best, the reasons for selecting particular vocational choices, etc. Responses are then tabulated and ordered in frequency of mention. Thereupon the unwary investigator may conclude that the most frequently mentioned items or reasons are the most important. It is entirely possible, however, that because of purposeful forgetting, repression, lack of insight, desire to impress the examiner favorably, or miscellaneous situational factors, frequency of report reflects conventionality rather than saliency of subjective content. Hence, some independent index of sincerity of response is essential before much credence can be placed on questionnaire data.

Inventories are more complete, detailed and standardized questionnaires dealing with the attitudes, interests, personality traits, or adjustive behavior of respondents. However, the data they provide are not used as ends in themselves but to furnish an indirect measure of a more generalized trait or ability. Hence, they correspond to psychometric and indirect personality tests.*

Diaries. Diaries provide useful sources of developmental data if a sufficient number of such autobiographical accounts are available to make possible the application of suitable sampling criteria and tests of statistical significance. Quantification by means of content analysis is only possible if the diaries are "written under essentially the same conditions and for the same purposes," and if particular categories of events and subjective reactions occur with sufficient frequency.[6]

Direct Subjective Inquiry. Direct subjective inquiry includes a wide variety of methods in which the subject reports his own perceptions, attitudes and judgments. He may rate perceptions of himself or others on a scale (e.g., self-ratings, predictions of individual or group responses), express interpersonal attitudes or preferences (e.g., sociometric choices), categorize prepared statements on a judgmental continuum into discriminable steps in terms of a designated criterion or dimension of subjective experience (Q-sort), select persons who best fit a given description ("guess who"), or compare his own perceptions or judgments systematically to each other (method of paired comparisons). Customarily, these methods are shorter and more restricted in scope than the questionnaire or interview, but obviously have much in common with the latter techniques. They differ from projective devices in yielding data (perceptions, judgments or attitudes) which constitute in themselves the phenomena under investigation rather than *indirect* measures of more global capacities or traits. Hence, since they are not "tests" in the usual sense of the term, the customary criterion of validity, i.e., the extent to which they accurately reflect or sample the larger and more general universe of behaviors they purport to measure, does not apply. The only relevant question that can be raised regarding their validity is the extent to which "verbal reports of subjective content correspond to actual subjective content."[15] Correspondence to objective stimulus reality is not a relevant criterion of validity since perceptual instruments only purport to measure perceptions, not the stimuli that evoke them. But since

*A discussion of the principles of test construction, scaling, reliability and validity is available.[5, 6, 36, 57]

no genuinely independent measure of the actual content of perception can ever be obtained, the best available criterion of validity is test reliability as measured by stability over successive administrations or by generality over items.

Perceptual measures are especially important in studies of children's personality development. For example, in studying the impact of parent attitudes on children's personality growth it is reasonable to suppose that "although parent behavior is an objective event in the real world it affects the child's ego development only to the extent and in the form in which he receives it."[15] Second, there is reason to believe

> that children's perceptions of parent behavior and attitudes can be measured more validly than these latter phenomena themselves. In relation to such emotionally loaded issues as acceptance-rejection and intrinsic-extrinsic valuation, both verbal responses by parents to structured or unstructured interview questions and ratings of actual parent behavior by observers are inevitably contaminated by the parents' understandably strong motivation to perceive their role behavior in a favorable light and similarity to impress others. Furthermore, the intent of such inquiries can be more effectively disguised from children; and because of their relative inexperience in such matters, the responses of the latter are less likely to be devious representations of actual feelings.[15]

By means of an attitudinal inquiry device such as sociometry,[61] it is possible to obtain valuable developmental data regarding group structure, social distance, and interspersonal relationships within peer groups. Patterns of choices, social stratification, clique formation, leadership, popularity, sex and race cleavage, deviancy, reciprocity, etc., can be studied effectively by means of sociograms. It is important to realize, however, that sociometric choices vary depending on the particular activity for which one child selects another. A child's sociometric status also varies depending on whether it is computed from the number of times he is chosen or from the mean social distance (acceptability) rating he receives from *all* members of the group.[13] Sociometric scores show both stability over time and generality over persons[13, 27, 28, 61, 84]; and since they are direct measures, they are as valid as they are reliable.[84]

If children are asked to predict the attitudes or responses of others, and if measures of the latter are available, various other dimensions of interpersonal perception can be investigated. For example, at the same time that children rate each other sociometrically, they can predict the sociometric ratings they will receive from their age mates as well as the sociometric status of the latter. It then becomes possible to measure accuracy in perceiving own and others' status, tendency to over- or underestimate own and others' status, the degree to which individuals actually reciprocate acceptance and tend to assume that such reciprocity exists, and the extent to which an individual is both similar to the group in accepting or rejecting other persons and tends to assume similarity in this respect. Such measures of interpersonal perception in peer groups (socioempathy) have been shown to possess considerable generality over persons and to be significantly correlated with other judgmental aspects of personality.[10, 12, 13, 92]

Objective Tests of Behavior and Personality

Objective tests of behavior and personality differ from projective and psychometric tests in being direct measures, and from direct subjective inquiry in dealing with overt behavior. Unlike the former, the behavior measured is the actual object of measurement and not an indirect representation of a more generalized trait or capacity. In common with projective techniques, however, the purpose of the test is generally concealed, thereby increasing the likelihood that obtained responses are genuinely representative of actual response tendencies. Hence, test data constitute samples of everyday behavior which are difficult to obtain in uncontrived situations either because they occur infrequently under relatively standardized conditions or because they tend to be disguised to avoid censure and punishment. In the former sense they are quite comparable to experimental situations, differing principally in elaborateness of standardization and concealment of purpose and in emphasis upon yielding reliable *individual* scores.

Typical of objective measures of conduct are Hartshorne and May's tests of deceit in which subjects are given an opportunity to steal, cheat or lie and are led to believe that detection is difficult or impossible.[58] Objective measures of motivational behavior include level of aspiration techniques,[15] measures of goal persistence (length of time in persevering in an exceedingly difficult or impossible task,[15] responsiveness to prestige versus anonymous[9] or to cooperative versus competitive motivational conditions,[74] and goal tenacity (tendency to maintain high levels of aspiration in relation to prior success-failure experience).[15] These tests manifest very high inter-item generality, but intersituational generality is significantly less, especially in tests of moral behavior. Much of the apparent lack of generality, however, not only reflects the actual tentativeness of personality structure in children, but also such spurious determinants of specificity as inability to generalize abstract moral propositions and variability in ego-involvement (see pp. 101-102). For example, degree of responsiveness to a prestige incentive depends on degree of ego-involvement in the type of test material employed. Thus, although the trait itself may be general in nature and the objective measure of it perfectly adequate, an individual child's scores will naturally vary from task to task unless ego-involvement is kept constant. The solution to this problem is not to discard objective measures of personality but to construct tests utilizing a wide variety of situations and to weight subscores in accordance with degree of ego-involvement. This weighting may be done on the basis of the subject's own ratings, or if subscores are converted into standard scores and then combined into a composite standard score, they are automatically weighted in terms of ego-involvement (subjects make higher standard scores in tasks in which they are highly ego-involved and vice versa).

The great advantage of objective over projective tests of personality is the directness of the former: there is no ambiguity regarding the trait or dimension of personality being measured, the aspect of the stimulus field to which the subjects are responding, the *particular* character in a story or picture with which he is identifying, and whether the identification is mild or intense, positive or negative. The widely cited disadvantage of situational specificity has been greatly exaggerated. As already pointed out, much of the apparent specificity reflects an actual lack of generality in children's character structure, and much of the remaining test specificity is spurious and correctable. A more inferential objective test of personality in children is illustrated by the use of physiological indices (e.g., pulse rate, blood pressure, respiration rate, psychogalvanic reflex) and a behavioral rating scale (e.g., non-adjustive activity, substitutive responses, withdrawal, regression) to measure frustration tolerance in children.[102] Since such behavioral and physiological indicators are never specific to a single motivational or emotional state or to a particular personality trait, they can only be used when the personality variable under investigation can be inferred unambiguously from the test situation or when it is desirable to corroborate or scale in intensity test responses derived from other methods.

Projective Personality Measures*

In recent years projective personality techniques have been used with increasing frequency in child development research. In fact, the uncritical enthusiasm with which they have been greeted in some quarters—as a panacea for all methodological difficulties—has many of the earmarks of a fad. To a certain extent this enthusiasm reflects the influence of clinical

*A volume in itself would be required to present pertinent descriptive and evaluative data on the tremendous number and variety of projective techniques currently available. Hence, the following discussion will only consider general methodological problems and issues involved in the use of projective techniques in child development research—their distinguishing characteristics, their general limitations, the special difficulties they present with children, and the distinctions that should be made between clinical and research uses. General discussions of projective methods in developmental research,[1, 5, 6, 15, 22, 36, 57, 69, 91, 100] Rorschach test,[3, 14, 25, 35, 48, 83, 90] thematic tests,[15, 24, 26, 34, 73, 97, 100] children's art work and other special techniques,[2, 30, 43, 54, 69, 75, 79, 87, 114] are available.

approaches, especially psychoanalysis. In part it reflects disillusionment with objective personality measures and other techniques for investigating personality such as paper and pencil inventories, which have adhered more closely to traditional psychometric principles. Because of their relatively nonverbal nature, projective devices also have unique appeal to investigators working with young children.

Like any other measure of personality, the usefulness of projective techniques in child development research depends on their ability to delineate different age levels or stages of personality organization, to indicate the nature of the changes that occur from one stage to another (and the determinants and conditions thereof), and to identify individual differences among children at the same level of development. Only if both inter- and intra-age level differences are distinguishable is it possible to differentiate between what is uniquely characteristic of the individual child and what is characteristic of his age group; and only in the light of the norms referable to his *own* age level is it possible to evaluate and place in perspective the developmental deviations that occur in any particular child.

General Characteristics. Like objective personality tests and play techniques, the purpose and psychological significance of projective measures are disguised from the subject. They are designed to elicit personality trends that are covert or not immediately observable, to make self-revelation possible with a minimum of awareness, repression, dissimulation and self-embellishment. Although they typically present subjects with a more restricted or standardized range or stimulation than do play techniques, they too are relatively unstructured in three important respects. First, the stimulus content itself is relatively ambiguous (lacks explicit meaning), and hence is subject to wide variability in interpretation. This does not mean, of course, that external test stimuli play no role whatsoever in determining perceptual responses. It simply means that because the external determinants of perception are indefinite in form and structure, the influence of internal personality determinants is maximized; and since standardized stimulus cues are presented to all subjects, individual differences in response presumably reflect variability in the internal determinants of perception. Subjects either react differentially to the same set of cues or respond selectively to a different constellation of cues in the stimulus field.

A second aspect of unstructuredness inherent in projective tests is the fact that they permit the subject to react *simultaneously* to many different, nonspecific attributes of the stimulus field. Hence he tends to reveal various generalized aspects or organizing features of his personality structure rather than specific traits or attitudes with substantive content. Projective measures, therefore, are especially useful for providing a global picture of the person as an interrelated whole, for sketching in broad outlines the uniqueness of his individuality. They indicate the quality of his adjustment and his adjustive resources; his organizing potentialities and his characteristic way of attacking problems; his level of integration; his awareness of reality; the extent to which he is original, spontaneous and creative or rigid, inhibited and restricted; his drive and emotionality; his relatedness to other persons; the characteristic degree of tension under which he is operating.

A third related feature of projective measures that contributes to their unstructuredness is the freedom they allow the subject in organizing his responses. Since he is neither required to focus on a restricted portion of the field in deriving his perceptions nor to direct his perceptual impressions along specified lines, many different dimensions of personality are simultaneously implicated.

Research Limitations. The very features of projective measures that make them valuable for certain kinds of research problems (i.e., for providing a generalized portrait of personality as an interrelated whole, for crystallizing trends that are not easily observable) constitute limitations and create difficulties for other types of personality research. All three components of their unstructuredness make for a lack of denotative specificity that complicates tremendously the task of interpreting responses to projective material. In the first place, the contribution of personality factors to perceptual form or content is never explicit, direct or self-evident. As a matter of fact, since we have little or no knowledge regarding the reasons why certain aspects of personality structure lead to particular perceptual elaborations of unstructured stimuli (or of the mediating mechanisms involved), interpretation becomes a function of related personality theory (on the basis of analogy or metaphor) or of empirically established concomitance between known personality trends and frequently occurring perceptual patterns; and even if interpretative schemes are derived from a general theory of personality (rather than from sheer empirical concomitance), empirical validation is still necessary before projective devices can yield valid measures. In either case, however, it is evident that a table of personality-perception equivalents can only represent *mean* values for a given age-sex group in a given cultural milieu.* If it is true that personality influences perception, then the true meaning and psychological significance of any response on a projective test can only be validly interpreted in the light of the unique personality trends, life experiences and current situation of a *particular* individual. Hence, projective tests are much more suitable for identifying longitudinal changes within a single individual or average differences in personality

*Cultural differences in projective test responses not only reflect differences in personality structure but also other culturally conditioned cognitive factors that influence perceptual response to unstructured stimuli.[39]

organization between age, sex and cultural groups than for identifying variability within a group.

This does not mean, of course, that individual differences within a homogeneous category of persons cannot be validly interpreted. It does mean, however, that a large element of subjectivity is introduced into the interpretive process. The examiner must consider the subject's life history and current situation in evaluating the significance of any particular response or score; and since single responses or scoring categories on a projective test are always interdependent, he must relate each of them to the total pattern. Hence the validity with which an individual's pattern of responses can be interpreted depends a great deal upon the examiner's empathic sensitivity and ability to discount his own personality biases.* And since diagnostic skills are only in part dependent upon experience, it follows that much variability will prevail from one experienced examiner to another in the validity and research usefulness of data from projective techniques.

Further complications in interpretation stem from the difficulty of inducing comparable sets among subjects regarding the purpose of the test procedure and of insuring that the stimulus content *itself* has comparable psychological significance to individuals of varied experiential backgrounds.[25, 100]

A second research limitation of projective measures springs from the globality and generalized nature of the personality dimensions with which they deal. This makes the technique unsuitable for determining the substantive content or detailed nature of particular conflicts, relationships, identifications, attitudes, etc. If, for example, a ten year old boy is asked to make up a story from a picture of a father and a son we have no reliable way of knowing with which character he is identifying, the intensity or nature of the identification that exists, or whether the dramatic construction mirrors the boy's perception of his own current relationship with his father, his brother's or friend's relationships with their fathers or the type of relationship he would like to have with his father.

To a certain extent cues about substantive meaning can be derived from knowledge of the subject's life history. Such interpretations, however, are highly subjective and are greatly influenced by the particular theory of personality to which the investigator subscribes. Frequently several different and sometimes mutually exclusive interpretations are equally credible so that theorists of several different schools can use the same projective and case history materials to bolster their own theoretical positions. Therefore, no particular interpretation or theoretical orientation is truly supported

*In comparing two groups of records, pattern analysis can be an objective statistical procedure. However, it is impossible to avoid some element of subjectivity in analyzing the pattern of scores within a single record.

unless alternative explanations are excluded and unless the basic theoretical assumptions of the general theory are actually tested. For example, certain types of erogenous content may appear in the thematic responses of subjects, may show significant sex differences, and may even be correlated with personality variables in a direction predicted by psychoanalytic theory.[26]; nevertheless one cannot conclude therefrom that the same erogenous factors are necessarily *causally* related to the evolution of the character traits involved or that an innately structural sequence of psychosexual drives is operative over the life span. Hence interpretations of substantive content from unstructured projective measures are highly suspect for research purposes— even when supplementary life history data are available.

Still another limitation inherent in projective techniques is the difficulty of isolating a single personality dimension for research study. Because subjects are free to respond in perceptually undirected fashion to stimuli that simultaneously implicate many different dimensions of personality, their responses are not necessarily pertinent to the personality variable under investigation. This gives rise to the difficult problem of sorting relevant from irrelevant responses as well as to the distinct possibility of not obtaining any relevant responses whatsoever.[100]

It is also extremely difficult to ascertain the reliability and validity of projective measures. It is hardly surprising, therefore, that these requirements have not been adequately met as yet in many instances or have been found wanting in others. Test-retest reliability (stability over time) is frequently spuriously high over short intervals because of memory factors, or spuriously low over longer intervals because of actual developmental changes. The all-important criterion for personality instruments of generality over test items cannot be meaningfully tested since items ordinarily are not sufficiently homogeneous so that when divided according to some systematic plan they yield two halves of a test that are quantitatively and qualitatively equivalent. Another often used approach to measuring reliability, by determining degree of interpretive agreement among different examiners, is not completely satisfactory since some (although not necessarily all) of such agreement may merely represent commonality in theoretical orientation to the interpretation of projective responses.

The determination of validity presents comparable difficulties. Because of the global nature and interrelatedness of the traits with which they deal, the most satisfactory method of ascertaining validity is to measure resulting degree of correspondence when "blindly" interpreted records are *matched* on a total *pattern* basis with independently derived personality descriptions, Binet I.Q.'s, or case history materials. Substantial degrees of agreement are reported for some projective techniques like the Rorschach when this validating procedure is employed.[3] However, Benton suggests that such identification may be possible on the basis of trivial personal idiosyncracies rather than on the basis of fundamental personality trends.[25] Varying degrees of validity (from much to little or none at all) are obtained for different projective methods when single subscores, patterns of scores, or total records of contrasting groups of subjects (e.g., adjusted versus maladjusted; intellectually retarded versus intellectually normal; schizophrenic versus nonschizophrenic; anxious versus non-anxious) are compared, or when subscores or whole records of individuals are compared with clinical judgments, teachers' ratings or psychiatric diagnoses.[3, 30, 34, 75, 79] Least satisfactory indications of validity are obtained when particular subscores of projective devices are *correlated* with I.Q. and with scores on other tests purportedly measuring the same dimensions of personality.[3, 30, 73, 75] Projective tests, therefore, seem to be most valid when interpretations are made on the basis of total pattern of responses and for detecting differences in global traits between grossly contrasting groups.

Several possible explanations may be offered for the frequently disappointing results obtained when projective techniques are subjected to different validating procedures—apart from the possibility that intrinsic validity may be lacking. First, if subscores are scrutinized in isolation or if tests are used to measure substantive content rather than various global dimensions of personality, the technique is being misused or required to serve a function for which it was not originally designed. Second, the validity of such validating criteria as psychiatric diagnoses, paper-and-pencil tests of personality and teachers' ratings, is seriously open to question. Third, it is possible that the actual traits measured by the different tests may be phenomenologically quite different although bearing similar labels.[3] Fourth, projective tests may be measuring different components or dimensions of the same trait than are measured by self-perceptions or by the perceptions of others. Thus, the enduring response tendencies reflected in the particular ways in which an individual perceptually structures ambiguous stimuli are not necessarily the same things as his own or other persons' judgmental *perceptions* of these tendencies.[14, 73] For example, projective test measures of achievement motivation are not significantly correlated with self-estimates or clinical estimates of same,[73] and Rorschach measures of adolescents' adjustment do not correlate with teachers' ratings or with MMPI adjustment scores.[14] Lastly, because of subjectivity in interpretation and differences in diagnostic astuteness, the validity (and to some extent reliability also) of any projective test is largely a function of the experience and skill of the particular clinician or investigator.

Special Limitations in Use with Children. One of the chief difficulties encountered in using projective techniques with children is the relatively meager, matter of fact responses they give to unstructured stimuli. This is partly a reflection of their relative lack of responsiveness to non-concrete materials and partly a reflection of the minimal degree of generality and self-consistency characterizing their personality organization (see pp. 101-103). On a priori grounds alone, one could hardly anticipate richness of response to the more diffuse and less well organized aspects of the stimulus field that ordinarily implicate the global, organizing features of more mature personalities. Of course, where differences between groups are great enough, as in normative studies, relative impoverishment of response is not as serious a drawback as in relational studies of personality organization within a restricted age range. In the latter instance individual differences tend to be obscured by commonalities referable to the group as a whole. Nevertheless, a significant range of individual variability is found within each of the age levels on the Rorschach test[3, 83]; and as children mature they not only participate in the age level changes shown by their fellows but also tend to maintain with some consistency earlier evidences of individuality with respect to many of the global traits measured by this instrument.[3, 83]

In order to overcome this and other disadvantages many investigators have modified the projective method by both making the stimulus content more explicit and highly structured and by restricting freedom of response. For example, instead of merely asking the subject to invent a story about an ambiguous picture, the investigators may supply much of the narrative content and then ask specific open-ended questions or provide several alternative endings or interpretations from which the subject is required to choose the one that seems most appropriate to him. In addition to tapping individual differences more effectively, this approach involves less subjectivity of interpretation and yields data more relevant and specific to the particular variables under investigation. It also permits inquiry into the more substantive aspects of personality and makes determination of inter-item generality possible. By definition, however, less global features of personality are evoked in this type of perceptual response, and the purpose of the test becomes more transparent. Furthermore, although inter-item generality is satisfactory for some instruments measuring achievement motivation, vocational tenacity, moral values, and defensive behavior,[15, 73, 100] it is notably inadequate in others, e.g., children's perceptions of parent attitudes.[15]

Research versus Clinical Use. Because many of the research disadvantages of projective instruments do not apply to clinical use, clinicians tend to be less conversant than research workers with their limitations. Clinical diagnosis is admittedly a highly subjective process involving special skills and sensitivities. Hence, for clinical practice, it is less important to eliminate subjective diagnostic instruments requiring special intuitive talents than it is to eliminate practitioners who lack these talents. Also, since more abundant life history data are available in clinical settings, subjective interpretation (even of substantive content) tends to be more valid and individual differences within an age group more identifiable. Furthermore, in clinical practice, isolation of relevant variables is not important since the object is to obtain a view of the individual as an interrelated whole and not to compare individuals on a series of personality traits for relational purposes.[100]

In any event as long as projective tests are only used as supplementary sources of information or as adjunctive diagnostic tools they can obviously be no more invalid than the very procedure of clinical diagnosis itself. In a sense they can be considered a diagnostic short-cut for the interiew method, especially in the clinical handling of children where difficulties in communication are formidable indeed. However, it is one thing to use instruments of questionable validity in a setting where the exigencies of the situation demand that something be done immediately for a disturbed individual (and nothing better is available) and quite another to use them as sources of purportedly valid generalizations about intra- or inter-age group differences among children.

In conclusion, unstructured projective techniques are most suitable for clinical practice and for normative and longitudinal research study of children. They are inappropriate for isolating substantive personality variables and their reliability and validity are not easily established. Nevertheless, they are less adversely affected by limited degrees of reliability and validity and by meagerness of response, and require less subjectivity of interpretation when used for measuring normative and intra-individual longitudinal trends than when used for identifying intcrindividual differences within an age group. As screening devices, for differentiating between grossly contrasting populations, they find ready applicability to many research, clinical and personnel problems. Obviously a much higher order of reliability and validity is necessary before dependable individual predictions can be made with respect to smaller and more subtle personality differences. For reasons indicated above, *structured* projective instruments appear to be more promising than unstructured devices for investigating interindividual personality trends of a substantive nature in children. In any event because of the relative trait specificity, the relatively uncrystallized state of children's personality organization, and the all pervasive influence of normative similarities within an age group, methodological difficulties constitute the principal bottleneck in research on children's personality development. Hence it has not yet been possible to devise sufficiently valid, reliable and subtle instruments that reveal the individuality of children in many of the crucial substantive aspects of personality organization.

REFERENCES

1. Abt, L. E., and Bellak, L., Eds.: *Projective Psychology.* New York, Knopf, 1950.
2. Altschuler, R. H., and Hattwick, L. A.: *Painting and Personality: A Study of Young Children.* Chicago, University of Chicago Press, 1947.
3. Ames, L. B., et al.: *Child Rorschach Responses.* New York, Hoeber, 1952.
4. Ammons, C. H., and Ammons, R. B.: Research and clinical applications of the doll play interview. *J. Personal 21*: 85-90, 1952.
5. Anastasi, A.: *Psychological Testing.* New York, Macmillan, 1954.
6. Anderson, J. E.: Methods of child psychology. *In* L. Carmichael, Ed., *Manual of Child Psychology,* ed. 2. New York, Wiley, 1954, pp. 1-59.
7. Andrews, T. G., Ed.: *Methods of Psychology.* New York, Wiley, 1948.
8. Arthur, G.: *A Point Scale of Performance Tests.* New York, Commonwealth Fund, 1930.
9. Ausubel, D. P.: Prestige motivation of gifted children. *Genet. Psychol. Monogr. 43*: 53-117, 1951.
10. ——: Reciprocity and assumed reciprocity of acceptance in an adolescent group, a sociometric study. *Sociometry 16*: 339-348, 1953.
11. ——: *Theory and Problems of Adolescent Development.* New York, Grune & Stratton, 1954.
12. ——, and Schiff, H. M.: Some intrapersonal and interpersonal determinants of individual differences in sociempathic ability among adolescents. *J. Soc. Psychol. 41*: 39-56, 1955.
13. ——, ——, and Gasser, E. B.: A preliminary study of developmental trends in sociempathy: accuracy of perception of own and others' sociometric status. *Child Develop. 23*: 111-128, 1952.
14. ——, —— and Zeleny, M. P.: Validity of teachers' ratings of adolescents' adjustment and motivation. *J. Educ. Psychol. 45*: 394-406, 1954.
15. ——, et al. Perceived parent attitudes as determinants of children's ego structure. *Child Develop. 25*: 173-183, 1954.
16. Bach, G. R.: Young children's play fantasies. *Psychol. Monogr. 59*: No. 2, 1945.
17. ——: Father-fantasies and father-typing in father-separated children. *Child Develop. 17*: 63-80, 1946.
18. Baldwin, A. L., Kalhorn, J., and Breese, F. H.: The appraisal of parent behavior. *Psychol. Monogr. 63*: No. 4, 1949.
19. Barker, R. G., and Wright, H. F.: Psychological ecology and the problem of psychosocial development. *Child Develop. 20*: 131-143, 1949.
20. ——, Dembo, T., and Lewin, K.: Frustration and regression: an experiment with young children. *Univ. Iowa Stud. Child Welf. 18*: No. 1, 1941.
21. ——, Wright, H. F., and Koppe, W. A.: The psychological ecology of a small town. *In* W. Dennis, Ed., *Readings in Child Psychology.* New York, Prentice-Hall, 1951.
22. Bell, J. E.: *Projective Techniques.* New York, Longmans, Green, 1948.
23. Bell, R. Q.: Convergence: an accelerated longitudinal approach. *Child Develop. 24*: 145-152, 1953.
24. Bellak, L., and Bellak, S. S.: *Children's Apperception Test.* New York, C. P. S. Co., 1949.
25. Benton, A. L.: The experimental validation of the Rorschach test. *Brit. J. M. Psychol. 23*: 45-58, 1950.

26. Blum, G. S.: A study of psychoanalytic theory of psychosexual development. *Genet. Psychol. Monogr. 39*: 3-102, 1949.

27. Bonney, M. E.: The constancy of sociometric scores and their relationship to teacher judgments of social success and to personality self-ratings. *Sociometry 6*: 409-424, 1943.

28. Bronfenbrenner, U.: A constant frame of reference for sociometric research. II. Experiment and inference. *Sociometry 7*: 40-75, 1944.

29. Bühler, C.: *The First Year of Life*. New York, John Day, 1930.

30. ——, Lumry, G. K., and Carrol, H. S.: World test standardization studies. *J. Child Psychiat. 2*: 2-81, 1951.

31. Champney, H.: The measurement of parent behavior. *Child Develop. 12*: 131-166, 1941.

32. Courtis, S. A.: Maturation units for the measurement of growth. *Sch. & Soc. 30*: 683-690, 1929.

33. ——: *Measurement of Growth*. Ann Arbor, Mich., Brumfield & Brumfield, 1932.

34. Cox, B., and Sargent, H.: TAT responses of emotionally disturbed and emotionally stable children: clinical judgment versus normative data. *J. Proj. Tech. 14*: 61-74, 1950.

35. Cox, S. M.: A factorial study of the Rorschach responses of normal and maladjusted boys. *J. Genet. Psychol. 79*: 95-115, 1951.

36. Cronbach, L. J.: *Essentials of Psychological Testing*. New York, Harper, 1949.

37. Davidson, A., and Fay, J.: *Phantasy in Childhood*. New York, Philosophical Library, 1953.

38. De Guimps, R.: *Pestalozzi—His Life and Work*. New York, Appleton, 1906.

39. Dennis, W.: Cultural and developmental factors in perception. *In* R. R. Blake and G. V. Ramsey, Eds., *Perception: An Approach to Personality*. New York. Ronald Press, 1952, pp. 148-169.

40. Dillaway, N.: *The Lesson of Okinawa*. Wakefield, Mass., Montrose Press, 1947.

41. Dymond, R. F., Hughes, A. S., and Raabe, V. L. Measurable changes in empathy with age. *J. Consult. Psychol. 16*: 202-206, 1952.

42. Edwards, A. L.: *Experimental Design in Psychological Research*. New York, Rinehart, 1950.

43. Elkisch, P.: Children's drawings as a projective technique. *Psychol. Monogr. 58*: No. 1, 1945.

44. Erikson, E. H.: Studies in the interpretation of play. *Genet. Psychol. Monogr. 22*: 557-671, 1940.

45. ——: Sex differences in the play configurations of preadolescents. *Am. J. Orthopsychiat. 21*: 667-692, 1951.

46. Escalona, S., and Leitch, M.: Early phases of personality development: a non-normative study of infant behavior. *Monogr. Soc. Res. Child Develop. 17*: No. 1, 1952.

47. Festinger, L., and Katz, D., Eds.: *Research Methods in the Behavioral Sciences*. New York, Dryden Press, 1953.

48. Ford, M.: *The Application of the Rorschach Test to Young Children*. Minneapolis, University of Minnesota Press, 1946.

49. Freud, A.: *Introduction to the Technique of Child Analysis*. New York, Nervous & Mental Disease Pub. Co., 1928.

50. Fries, M. E.: Play techniques in the analysis of young children, *Psychoanal. Rev. 24*: 233-245, 1937.

51. Gesell, A., and Amatruda, C. S.: *Developmental Diagnosis: Normal and Abnormal Child Development.* New Yorker, Hoeber, 1947.

52. ———, and Ilg., F. L.: *Infant and Child in the Culture of Today.* New York, Harper, 1943.

53. ———, and Thompson, H.: Learning and growth in identical infant twins: an experimental study by the method of co-twin control. *Genet. Psychol. Monogr. 6*: 1-124, 1929.

54. Goodenough, F. L., and Harris, D. B.: Studies in the psychology of children's drawings. II. 1928-1949. *Psychol. Bull. 47*: 369-433, 1950.

55. Gorer, G.: Themes in Japanese culture. *Tr. N. Y. Acad. Sci. 5*: 106-124, 1943.

56. Gottschalk, L., Kluckhohn, C., and Angell, R.: *The Use of Personal Documents in History, Anthropology and Sociology.* Bull. No. 53. New York, Social Science Research Council, 1945.

57. Greene, E. B.: *Measurements of Human Behavior,* New York, Odyssey, 1952.

58. Hartshorne, H., and May, M. A.: *Studies in the Nature of Character.* Vol. I. *Studies in Deceit.* New York, Macmillan, 1928.

59. Heinis, H.: A personal constant. *J. Educ. Psychol. 17*: 163-186, 1926.

60. Jack, L. M.: An experimental study of ascendent behavior in pre-school children. *Univ. Iowa Stud. Child Welf. 9*: No. 3, 1934.

61. Jennings, H. H.: *Sociometry in Group Relations; A Work Guide for Teachers.* Washington, D. C., American Council on Education, 1948.

62. Jones, H. E., and Conrad, H. S.: Mental development in adolescence. *Yearbook Nat. Soc. Stud. Educ. 43*: 146-163, 1944.

63. Kardiner, A.: *The Psychological Frontiers of Society.* New York, Columbia University Press, 1945.

64. Kempthorne, O.: *The Design and Analysis of Experiments.* New York, Wiley, 1952.

65. Klein, M.: *The Psycho-analysis of Children.* New York, Norton, 1932.

66. La Barre, W.: Some observations on character structure in the Orient: the Japanese. *Psychiatry 8*: 319-342, 1945.

67. Lafore, G. G.: Practices of parents in dealing with preschool children. *Child Develop. Monogr.* No. 31, 1945.

68. Lasswell, H. D.: The method of interlapping observation in the study of personality and culture. *J. Abnorm. Soc. Psychol. 32*: 240-243, 1937.

69. Lerner, E., et al.: Methods for the study of personality in young children. *Monogr. Soc. Res. Child Develop. 6*: No. 30, 1941.

70. Lewis, C.: *Children of the Cumberland.* New York, Columbia University Press, 1946.

71. Lippit, R.: An experimental study of the effect of democratic and authoritarian group atmospheres. *Univ. Iowa Stud. Child Welf. 16*: 43-195, 1940.

72. Lynd, R. S., and Lynd, H. M.: *Middletown in Transition.* New York, Harcourt, Brace, 1937.

73. McClelland, D. C., et al.: *The Achievement Motive.* New York, Appleton-Century-Crofts, 1953.

74. Maller, J. B.: *Cooperation and Competition: An Experimental Study in Motivation.* New York, Teachers College, Columbia University, 1929.

75. Martin, W. E.: Identifying the insecure child. II. The validity of some suggested methods. *J. Genet. Psychol. 80*: 25-33, 1952.

76. Mead, M.: Research on primitive children. *In* L. Carmichael, Ed., *Manual of Child Psychology,* Ed. 2. New York, Wiley, 1954, pp. 735-780.

77. Moloney, J. C.: Psychiatric observations in Okinawa-Shima. *Psychiatry 8*: 391-399, 1945.
78. Moustakas, C. E.: *Children in Play Therapy: A Key to Understanding Normal and Disturbed Emotions.* New York, McGraw-Hill, 1953.
79. Napoli, P. J.: Finger-painting and personality diagnosis. *Genet. Psychol. Monogr. 34*: 129-230, 1946.
80. Odom, C. L.: A study of the mental growth curve with special reference to the results of group intelligence tests. *J. Educ. Psychol. 20*: 401-416, 1929.
81. Olson, W. C., and Cunningham, E. M.: Time sampling techniques. *Child Develop. 5*: 41-58, 1934.
82. Parten, M. B.: Social play among preschool children. *J. Abnorm. Soc. Psychol. 28*: 136-147, 1933.
83. Paulsen, A. A.: Personality development in the middle childhood years, a ten-year longitudinal study of 30 public school children by means of Rorschach Tests and social histories. Unpublished Ph.D. dissertation, New York University, 1953.
84. Pepinsky, P. N.: The meaning of "validity" and "reliability" as applied to sociometric tests. *Educ. Psychol. Measurem. 9*: 39-51, 1949.
85. Preyer, W.: *The Mind of the Child.* New York, Appleton-Century, 1888.
86. Radke, M., et al.: Social perceptions and attitudes of children. *Genet. Psychol. Monogr. 40*: 327-447, 1949.
87. Ravin, J. C.: *Controlled Projection for Children,* ed. 2. London, H. K. Lewis, 1951.
88. Richardson, C. A., and Stokes, C. W.: Growth and variability of intelligence. *Brit. J. Psychol.* No. 18, 1935.
89. Roheim, G.: Racial differences in the neurosis and psychosis. *Psychiatry 2*: 375-390, 1939.
90. Rotter, J. B.: The present status of the Rorschach in clinical and experimental procedures. *J. Personal. 16*: 304-311, 1948.
91. Sargent, H.: Projective methods: their origins, theory, and application in personality research. *Psychol. Bull. 42*: 257-293, 1945.
92. Schiff, H. M.: Judgmental response sets in the perception of sociometric status. Unpublished Ph. D. dissertation, University of Illinois, 1953.
93. Sears, P. S.: Doll play aggression in normal young children: influence of sex, age, sibling status, father's absence. *Psychol. Monogr. 65*: 1951.
94. Sears, R. R.: Influence of methodological factors on doll play performance. *Child Develop. 18*: 190-197, 1947.
95. ———: Relation of fantasy aggression to interpersonal aggression. *Child Develop. 21*: 5-6, 1950.
96. ———, Pintler, M. H., and Sears, P. S.: Effect of father separation on pre-school children's doll play aggression. *Child Develop. 17*: 219-243, 1946.
97. Seaton, J. K.: A projective experiment using incomplete stories with multiple-choice endings. *Genet. Psychol. Monogr. 40*: 149-228, 1949.
98. Shinn, M. W.: *The Biography of a Baby.* Boston, Houghton Mifflin, 1900.
99. Shirley, M. M.: *The First Two Years; A Study of Twenty-five Babies.* Vol. 1. *Postural and Locomotor Development.* Minneapolis, University of Minnesota Press, 1931.
100. Swanson, G. E., Miller, D. R., McNeil, E. B., and Allinsmith, W.: *Learning Psychological Defenses.* New York, Holt. In press.
101. Symonds, P.: *Diagnosing Personality and Conduct.* New York, Century, 1931.

102. Thiesen, J. W., and Meister, R. K.: A laboratory investigation of measures of frustration tolerance of pre-adolescent children. *J. Genet. Psychol.* 75: 277-291, 1949.
103. Thomae, H.: Beobachtung und Beurteilung von Kindern und Jungendlichen. *Psychol., Prax.* No. 15, 1954.
104. Thorndike, E. L.: *Adult Learning.* New York, Macmillan, 1928.
105. ——, et al.: *The Measurement of Intelligence.* New York, Teachers College, Columbia University, 1926.
106. Thurstone, L. L.: Scale construction with weighted observations. *J. Educ. Psychol.* 19: 441-453, 1928.
107. ——: The absolute zero in intelligence measurement. *Psychol. Rev.* 35: 175-197, 1928.
108. ——, and Ackerson, L.: The mental growth curve for the Binet tests. *J. Educ. Psychol.* 20: 569-583, 1929.
109. Tiedemann, D.: *Beobachtungen über die Entwicklung der Seelenfahrigkeiten bei Kindern.* Altenburg, Bonde, 1787.
110. Warner, W. L., and Lunt, P. S.: *The Social Life of a Modern Community.* New Haven, Yale University Press, 1941.
111. Whiting, J. W. M., and Child, I. L.: *Child Training and Personality: A Cross-Cultural Study.* New Haven, Yale University Press, 1953.
112. Winstel, B.: The use of a controlled play situation in determining certain effects of maternal attitudes on children. *Child Develop.* 22: 299-311, 1951.
113. Witkin, H. A., Lewis, H. B., Hertzman, M., Machover, K., Meissner, P. B., and Wapner, S.: *Personality Through Perception.* New York, Harper, 1954.
114. Wolff, W.: *The Personality of the Preschool Child.* New York, Grune & Stratton, 1946.
115. Wright, H. F., and Barker, R. G. *Methods in Psychological Ecology: A Progress Report.* Topeka, Kan., Ray's Printing Service, 1950.

PART II

The Beginnings
of Development

CHAPTER 6

Prenatal Development and the Birth Process

SURVEY OF PRENATAL DEVELOPMENT

IN SEARCHING for the origins and early developmental phases of behavior we must start with the fetus, not with the neonate. Before the baby is born many of the raw materials of behavior have already been patterned in certain very definite ways to constitute the antecedents of later forms or the "true zeros" of development.* By studying these antecedents the nature of subsequent developmental processes becomes more comprehensible, providing that we do not assume that *all* aspects of "later performance [are necessarily] implicit or hidden in earlier types of response"; much can intervene in the interim to account for essential features of more mature behavior that were not even suggested in beginning phases.[9]

Although genic predispositions present at conception are modified somewhat by fetal, gestational and external factors during the course of prenatal development, their influence still tends to be prepotent. Thus the embryological model of development fits well: the environment is relatively constant, and even if variability does occur it has little effect unless extreme. During this period of development, the acquisition of "phylogenetic" traits (intraspecies uniformities referable to identical single gene effects) is most conspicuous. Nothing is preformed, but since the genic contribution to the growth matrix is disproportionately great, the basic outlines of development are virtually predetermined. Growth is not independent of environment, but environment, within very broad limits, does not play a crucially determinative role in the regulation of development.

Methods of Study

Four general methods are available for studying the prenatal development of human behavior: (1) observation of development in infrahuman species, the embryos of which are more accessible to observation (e.g., birds) and from which large samples of individuals at various stages of growth can be obtained at will; (2) observational and motion picture study of

---

*Much of this early behavior can be observed and measured directly. In relation to other aspects of behavior, however, which only become measurable at more advanced stages, zero points can only be derived by extrapolation (see p. 135).

nonviable human fetuses removed surgically under local anesthesia while still alive (for medical reasons) and placed in saline solution at body temperature; (3) study of prematurely born, viable human fetuses delivered spontaneously or operatively; and (4) study of the spontaneous or induced activity of the intact unborn fetus and of its responsiveness to stimulation from reports of the mother and by means of apparatus (e.g., stethoscope) applied to her abdominal wall.

Each of these methods has its advantages and limitations. When the data they yield are pooled they provide complementary and confirmatory evidence from which a coherent picture of prenatal behavioral development can be constructed. Animal specimens are more available and sometimes more accessible to observation; but the viviparous species which most closely resemble the human are equally as inaccessible. In any event, the problem of extrapolation invariably arises, particularly in the case of the oviparous lower species which offer the advantage of greater accessibility. Surgically removed fetuses can be stimulated and observed directly but obviously under conditions quite different from those of uterine life. Instead of being suspended in amniotic fluid under constant pressure and temperature, and largely insulated from stimulation, they are placed in a different, more variable, and generally more stimulating environment. Even more important perhaps is the impact of recent operative insult and the effects of gradual asphyxiation that first increases and then inhibits the very activity which the investigator is seeking to elicit in response to controlled stimulation.

These latter disadvantages are absent when the spontaneously delivered, viable premature infant is studied. On the other hand, the disparity in this instance between uterine and external environments is even greater; and fetal-maternal circulatory, respiratory, alimentary and excretory arrangements are not merely disrupted but are replaced by a modified set of independent arangements. Furthermore, viability is generally impossible before the fetus is twenty-six weeks old, and relatively little new development, especially in the motor sphere, occurs between that age and full-term. All of these contaminating factors can, of course, be avoided by studying the unborn fetus in utero; but the barrier to direct stimulation and observation imposed by abdominal and uterine walls and by fetal membranes is formidable indeed, especially in the early months of pregnancy.

Another difficulty common to all methods is the impossibility of ascertaining accurately the age of the fetus. If age is inferred from fetal length, using a table of mean age-length equivalents, two sources of error enter into the determination of the age of a particular fetus—variability in rate of growth and the original error in estimating age in the sample of fetuses used in constructing the table. Hence it is more straightforward to determine fetal age by simply using whatever method is employed in making the estimate in the first place. *True* age, of course, would be measured from the moment of conception; but since there is no way of ascertaining when this occurs, it can only be inferred from the date of ovulation preceding fertilization. Unfortunately, however, the occurrence of this event cannot be determined directly with any exactitude. In practice, therefore, it is necessary to use a formula which, on the basis of related histological and biochemical evidence, assumes that the ovulation prior to pregnancy occurs two to three weeks after the first day of the last menstruation. Moreover, in addition to the possible error of one week stemming from variability in the time of ovulation, uncertainty about the date of effective insemination and about the viability span of both ova and spermatazoa contribute further to the error of estimate.

Timetable of Embryological Highlights*

By way of general orientation to fetal behavioral development, the following overview of major embryological highlights based largely on studies of surgically removed fetuses may be offered:

By the end of the *third week* humoral integration of the organism is made possible as the fetal circulatory system becomes functional. Neural development is marked by the appearance of the medullary groove and of the cerebral and optic vesicles. Limb buds are already in evidence, and maternal-fetal circulatory interchange is firmly established through the placenta and umbilical vessels. By the *second month* the fetus becomes recognizably human; almost all bodily organs, including the special sense organs are present. The muscles respond to direct electrical stimulation, but no neurally mediated responses are possible as yet.

At the beginning of the *third month* all of the components necessary for neuromuscular behavior at the simple, segmental reflex arc level are functionally available. The earliest neurally mediated response to tactile stimulation occurs when the oral-nasal regions innervated by sensory fibers of the trigeminal nerve are stimulated; but the response is highly diffuse, implicating practically all effector units that are functional at this time. Whether or not *spontaneous,* generalized movements of an uncoordinated nature precede or follow this diffuse type of response to stimulation is still an open question.[9, 34, 35] During the course of this month practically all of the various kinds of motion possible at each of the joints appear. The fetus responds to proprioceptive and vestibular stimulation and palmar and plantar reflexes can be elicited. The mature form of the kidney is present and minimal function is indicated by the appearance of urea in the amniotic fluid.

*Based on available references.[9, 24, 34, 35, 72, 81]

During the *fourth month* tactile stimulation at any point on the body surface becomes capable of eliciting reflex response. By this time most of the discrete responses manifested by the neonate (including swallowing and abdominal reflexes) are at least partially developed except for functional "respiration, voice, grasp, suctorial response, tendon reflexes, and special sense responses."[34] A wide repertoire of both spontaneous and elicited responses appear which are also less mechanical, generalized, and stereotyped and more specific, graceful, and delicate.

Unequivocal and gross signs of fetal activity in utero become evidence during the *fifth month*. The mother "feels life" and the fetal heart beat becomes audible. Grasp and Babinski reflexes appear and weak respiratory movements can be evoked by applying stimulation to the thoracic wall. During the *sixth month* synergetic movements and tendon, sucking, Moro, and corneal reflexes make their appearance. Toward the end of this period and the beginning of the *seventh month* the fetus becomes viable and is able to cry weakly. In terms of response capacities, little change occurs during the last two months of pregnancy. The fetus gains principally in strength, fat, and volume of neuromuscular activity. Individual differences in degree of spontaneous fetal activity may have some initial prognostic value inasmuch as more active fetuses tend to rank higher six month postnatally in motor development, as measured by the Gesell Developmental Schedule.[57] By eighteen months, however, significant correlations are no longer obtained.[56] In comparison to full-term infants the visual responsiveness and ocular movements of the prematurely born are poorly developed.

Influence of Gestational Factors

Through what mechanisms does uterine experience influence fetal behavior and contribute (along with the genotype) to the growth matrix regulating the direction of development? How crucial is the influence of extragenic, environmental factors during the prenatal period? Four different categories of gestational variables must be considered: (1) humoral communication between mother and fetus through the placenta; (2) the uterine environment—considered as both a gestational habitat and as a source of stimulation; (3) external stimuli penetrating the uterine wall and impinging upon the fetus; and (4) stimuli originating within the fetus itself. Also, apart from whatever other effects it may have on fetal development, receptivity to intrafetal, uterine and external stimulation, introduces the possibility of acquiring new behavior patterns (learning) or modifying existing patterns.

Communication through the Placenta. The placenta is a special organ of circulatory interchange derived from both the uterine mucosa and from the chorionic villi of the fetus. These villi, vascularized by terminal branches of the umbilical artery and vein, penetrate branches of the uterine artery. Through this semipermeable barrier, selective interchange of practically all substances found in plasma occurs between the circulatory systems of mother and fetus. This includes water, blood proteins, glucose, amino acids, blood fats, oxygen, carbon dioxide, non-protein nitrogen, hormones, vitamins, antibodies, antigens, electrolytes, drugs, viruses, bacteria, etc. In this way it is possible for the mother to supply the fetus' needs for oxygen and nutritive elements and to remove carbon dioxide and nitrogenous wastes. Nevertheless, a certain amount of selectivity of interchange is maintained: the concentration of various substances (e.g., vitamin E, glucose, antibodies) is less in fetal than in maternal blood,[26, 76, 81] and the opposite is true in the case of fructose.[26]

Ordinarily the placental barrier is not permeable to the formed elements of the blood, i.e., red and white corpuscles and platelets. This is indeed fortunate since it reduces by almost twenty times the incidence of erythroblastosis in mothers whose own red blood cells do not contain the Rh factor (Rh negative) but whose offsprings' red blood cells do contain this factor (Rh positive). In this disease Rh agglutinogens in fetal red blood cells manage to penetrate the placental barrier and enter the maternal blood stream. Since the mother does not have the Rh agglutinogen in her red cells, it acts as an antigen and stimulates the production of specific antibodies (agglutinins) capable of agglutinating Rh positive red cells. These agglutinins have no difficulty in entering fetal circulation and destroying large numbers of red blood corpuscles. Severe anemia and jaundice results, and sometimes lesions in the basal ganglia, abortion, and fetal or neonatal death. It is evident, however, that in all instances in which the placental barrier is normally impermeable to red blood cells this disease will not occur despite disparity between mother and fetus with respect to the Rh factor.

The concentration of metabolites in the fetal blood stream maintains a remarkable degree of constancy despite great variability in maternal diet and nutrition. The fetus obtains much more than its proportionate share of nutritive elements when maternal diet is inadequate. Nevertheless, because it is developing and growing at such a rapid rate, it apparently suffers more than the mother from the consequences of malnutrition.[7, 18, 75] Unsatisfactory nutrition in the mother is associated with lower fetal and infant weight, the occurrence of fetal rickets, and with a higher incidence of abortion, stillbirth, malformations, infant mortality, and of such diseases as infant rickets, anemia and tetany.[7, 18, 44, 50, 68, 75, 78]

Because of maternal-fetal circulatory interchange, the development of the fetus is affected by many pathological conditions in the mother which influence the composition of her blood plasma. It may develop allergies from allergens in her diet. Large doses of quinine, morphine and barbiturates may have an adverse effect on the fetus. Such infectious diseases as measles, mumps, chickenpox, erysipelas, syphilis, tuberculosis and rubella (German measles) are transmissable through the placenta. The last mentioned, when occurring in the first trimester of pregnancy not infrequently results in stillbirth, premature birth, abortion and in such abnormalities as cataract, deafness and mental deficiency. [71, 79] Various non-infectious maternal conditions such as hypertension and diabetis are associated with a higher incidence of abortion, stillbirth, neonatal death, and oversized infants. [2, 10, 23]

It is also entirely conceivable that through the "neurohumoral bond between them," [47] maternal activity, fatigue, emotion and personality may influence the irritability, activity level, and autonomic functioning of the fetus. [30, 66, 67] Excessive activity and fatigue in the mother alters the lactic acid and carbon dioxide levels of fetal blood, thereby increasing fetal activity and pulse rate. Fear, rage and anxiety in the mother have similar effects on the fetus by virtue of the sympathomimetic effects of adrenalin and its tendency to lower all response thresholds. In fact, prolonged and intense maternal anxiety may cause autonomic imbalance and dysfunction in the immature and susceptible fetal gastrointestinal tract as well as chronic lowering of response thresholds. This may carry over into neonatal life in the form of pyloric spasm, cardiospasm, diarrhea, hyperactivity, excessive irritability, and increased frequency of allergic reactions. [27, 65, 66, 67] Indirectly, abnormal emotional states in the mother decrease her intake, absorption and utilization of food, thereby affecting adversely the nutritional status of the fetus. [63, 67] And insofar as cultural variables influence the activity level and emotional responsiveness of expectant mothers, it is possible to account for some of the discrepancies between cultures in the typical amount of fetal activity reported by pregnant women.

Uterine Environment. The gestational habitat provided by the uterus, fetal membranes and amniotic fluid tends to provide a relatively stimulus-free environment under constant pressure and temperature. A more important source of intrauterine variability, therefore, consists of various endocrine and local tissue factors that enable the mother to maintain the fetus intact throughout the gestational period, inhibit premature contraction of the uterus, and prevent disintegration or premature separation of the placenta. Thus, older mothers who presumably are less adequate in these respects, conceive fetuses who are more predisposed toward abortion, stillbirth, neonatal mortality, hydrocephalus and Mongolism. [40, 45, 48] Substantiating this interpretation is the fact that the last mentioned condition also tends to occur more frequently in infants whose mothers have a prior history of menstrual and hormonal abnormalities, difficulty in becoming pregnant, uterine pathology and habitual abortion.[3] Abnormalities of fetal position and knots in the umbilical cord may also result in deformities and strangulation.

Responsiveness to Intrafetal and External Stimulation. Evidence regarding fetal responsiveness to stimulation comes from surgically removed fetuses, from prematurely born fetuses, and from studies of fetuses in utero. All such evidence is pertinent in considering the extent to which the fetus *could respond* to particular kinds of stimulation. This is one question which we will want to consider. An entirely different issue, however, is the extent to which intrafetal and external stimulation influence the course of fetal development. This depends not only on absolute sensory capacity but on whether and to what degree the fetus actually *does respond* to various types of stimulation under typical conditions of intrauterine life. Hence, in evaluating the pooled data presented below as it relates to the latter issue it is necessary to bear in mind that extrauterine sources of tactile, pressure, vibratory, pain and auditory stimulation are largely buffered or muffled by fetal membranes, amniotic fluid, uterus, and maternal abdominal wall; that these various layers are completely impenetrable by light; that adequate stimuli for taste, smell, pain and visceral sensation rarely if ever impinge on the fetus; and that the range of variability in intrauterine temperature is extremely small and never discriminable.

In view of all these formidable barriers to stimulation from without, it seems likely, therefore, that the fetus itself serves as its own principal source of sensory experience. Most effective stimulation during the gestational period originates with the fetus and is picked up by proprioceptive, vestibular and visceral interoceptors. Of the extroceptors, only the non-distance tactile receptors are actually functional in prenatal life; and for the most part tactile stimulation is provided as moving fetal parts come into apposition with each other. Energy changes in the environment for which the human organism has no adequate receptors will not be considered here, although such phenomena (e.g., massive doses of x-ray) may have deleterious effects on development, gestation, and on the genotype itself, giving rise to malformations, abortion and imbecility.[49, 50] In the present atomic age, these potential consequences of radiation need to be taken more seriously.

Proprioceptive receptors in muscles, tendons and joints are well developed in the early months of prenatal life.[9, 35, 81] A continuous source of proprioceptive stimulation is provided by normal muscle tonus, movement of bodily parts, and by shifts in postural tonus induced by positional changes of the entire fetus. The latter postural shifts, including accompanying eye movements, are probably mediated by vestibular stimulation, although it is difficult to exclude the contribution of proprioceptive stimuli associated with changes in positional orientation. Because of adequate fetal experience, prematurely born infants respond just as adequately as full-term infants to both kinds of stimulation. Rhythmic activity and tonus changes in the nonstriated muscles of respiratory and gastrointestinal systems probably account for some visceral-proprioceptive stimulation in utero, but this is obviously minimal compared to what is generated when these systems become functional after birth. Nevertheless, since the receptors themselves are well developed, the premature infant is highly responsive to visceral stimuli.

The tactile components (touch and pressure) of cutaneous sensibility are both well developed and well exercised during prenatal life. Beginning in the oral-nasal area in the third month, the acquisition of sensitivity spreads rapidly and is almost complete by the fourth month. A wide variety of reactions of both reflex and nonreflex nature occur in response to tactile stimulation, and gradually become more specific and localized with age. Fetal responsiveness to pain, however, is minimal both because of little actual uterine experience with pain and because of the important role of cortical, apperceptive and emotional factors; for the latter reasons, responsiveness is not markedly increased shortly after birth in either premature or full-term infants. In the case of thermal sensitivity, on the other hand, the afferent mechanism is well developed and quite functional in the premature infant, but fails to be stimulated in utero. The same holds true for taste and smell: amniotic fluid is not a good medium for transmitting olfactory stimuli, and does not vary sufficiently in chemical composition to provide adequate gustatory stimulation.

The auditory apparatus is also ready to function during the last two months of fetal life and in premature as well as in full-term infants. However, because of closure of the external auditory meatus and Eustachian tubes and the presence of a gelatinous substance in the middle ear, sounds of ordinary intensity are not effective prior to birth. Loud music, a doorbell buzzer placed close to the fetal head, and pure tones transmitted through air to the maternal abdomen evoke convulsive, startle-like responses in the fetus and result in cardiac acceleration[4, 69, 81]; but it is not clear whether these responses are caused by auditory or vibratory stimulation.[4] Development of the visual mechanism starts early in fetal life, but the morphological changes involved are not completed until after the normal gestational period.[9, 81] Thus, although the prematurely born neonate can differentiate between light and dark and responds to illumination with the iris reflex he does not manifest pursuit, pupillary distance, and convergence responses.[9, 81] Even if light could penetrate the uterus the fetus would be relatively unresponsive to it.

Importance of Gestational Factors. To what extent is this summary of the evidence dealing with the effects of gestational influences on prenatal development compatible with our preliminary conclusions that genotypic factors are relatively prepotent during this stage of growth? We have seen that for the most part the fetus is enveloped in a relatively constant gestational environment and is exposed to very little variability in stimulation, either through the placental circulation or through penetration of the fetal habitat by extrauterine stimuli. This degree of variability is both too great to account for the remarkable uniformity prevailing in the development of phylogenetic traits and too little to contribute much to the development of ontogenetic traits. Hence, it seems likely that intra- and extrafetal gestational factors ordinarily play a supportive rather than a crucial directional role in development. Only when these factors are extreme or pathological in nature do they seem to make a difference; and even then their effect tends to be negative. That is, instead of providing a *new* direction for growth, they merely produce malformations by retarding or arresting development or else create conditions that are unfavorable for continued fetal life or gestation (stillbirth, abortion, premature birth, fetal and neonatal death or disease).

Furthermore, even if gestational variables are extreme their detrimental effects on fetal development still seem to be partly contingent upon the presence of other special factors. In the case of phylogenetic traits, pathologic conditions affect principally those organs or organ systems which are developing most rapidly at the time when the disturbance is operative; or stated conversely, susceptibility to the adverse effects of gestational pathology in a given organ is largely limited to a brief critical period when developmental differentiation is most rapid. Thus, by knowing the time table of fetal development and the date when uterine disturbance occurs, it is possible to predict the site and type of developmental malformation that will result.* German measles, for example, produces defects chiefly in certain portions of the central nervous system and in the auditory and visual apparatus; however, it will only do so if the mother contracts the disease in the early months of pregnancy when these regions are in a critical stage of development. In view of the highly damaging effects of anoxia, particularly in the central nervous system and in rapidly devel-

*For a comprehensive survey of the evidence in support of this theory, see T. H. Ingalls: *Journal of the American Medical Association 161:* 1047-1051, 1956.

oping tissues, it is possible that oxygen deprivation in the common mechanism through which the damaging effects of many different pathological conditions are mediated.[47]

Ontogenetic traits are more responsive to extreme variability in the gestational environment than are phylogenetic traits, and are also more affected by less extreme degrees of variability. There is reason to believe, however, that uterine disturbances primarily affect prenatal development in instances where a strong genic predisposition toward disease or dysfunction already exists in the first place. The stronger an unfavorable genic predisposition is, the less intense and prolonged the cumulative environmental insult must be before the defect in question becomes overtly manifest. Thus one would tend to suspect strong genic loading in those neonates showing marked symptoms of hyperirritability and autonomic imbalance following exposure to maternal anxiety during gestation; genically determined inadequate ACTH response to stress (maternal adrenalin) could conceivably fail to protect organs against damage and dysfunction, particularly physiologically immature organs (e.g., gastrointestinal) which first begin functioning after birth. It is also possible that strong genic predispositions may be responsible for most fetal and neonatal deaths. This is indicated by the fact that whereas environmental improvement over the past forty years has resulted in a phenomenal drop in infant mortality, the corresponding reduction in neonatal mortality has been negligible.[6]

Because sensory experience in utero is so restricted it is hardly likely that it plays a significant directional role in prenatal development. Some sense modalities are quite well developed but fail to provide the fetus with much sensory experience since adequate stimuli are not available. This applies to taste, smell, hearing, temperature, and visceral sensibility; in the case of vision and pain, not only are adequate stimuli lacking, but responsiveness itself is highly limited. Only the proprioceptive, vestibular and cutaneous modalities are reasonably functional during prenatal life, and these, do not furnish the type of sensory impressions from which clear percepts can be formed. Hence it seems reasonable to infer that stimuli impinging on these modalities mostly evoke available responsiveness, and only to a very meager extent give rise to clearly defined mental content that influences the course of behavioral development.

Development of Prenatal Behavior

Learning versus Genic Regulation. In the previous section we have considered intrafetal and extrauterine sources of stimulation as factors evoking available sensory and motor responsiveness and as potential determinants of conscious experience. Implicit in this discussion was the assumption that the determination of which patterns of response are associated with which types of stimulation is a matter that for all practical purposes is controlled by genic factors and is not essentially influenced by specific experience. This proposition, as suggested earlier, follows from the remarkable degree of intra-species uniformity in prenatal behavior development in the absence of sufficiently determinative and uniform regulatory influences from without.

Nevertheless, in view of the fact that receptivity to stimulation and potentiality for establishing sensori-motor connections exist in the fetus, it is necessary to examine more fully the position of Holt[33] and others that the neonate's behavioral repertoire is largely acquired as the product of specific intrauterine experience. In support of this notion, Holt presents the development of the grasp reflex as a paradigm illustrating how purportedly unlearned reflexes could conceivably be acquired by a process of conditioning. As part of the fetal posture of generalized flexion, the muscles of the hand are flexed, generating proprioceptive impulses which tend to perpetuate finger closure. Concomitantly, the tips of the fingers touch the palm. Eventually, according to Holt, after many contiguous occurrences, the tactile stimulus alone becomes adequate for eliciting the grasp reflex. That this type of conditioning is theoretically possible was demonstrated by Spelt in fetuses 26 to 34 weeks old. After about twenty contiguous presentations of a loud sound and tactile vibration to the maternal abdomen he was able to elicit fetal movement with the latter (originally inadequate, conditioned) stimulus alone.[70]

Dennis,[14] however, lists many convincing reasons for not regarding such evidence as adequately substantiating the thesis that fetal behavior is learned. First, the grasp reflex is the only possible illustration that can be offered where this theory fits easily; applied to any other instance of fetal behavior it is highly implausible. Second, although certain conditioned reflexes can be established *experimentally* during fetal life, the minimal conditions essential for conditioning are not ordinarily present in utero. Auditory and vibratory stimulation, for example, are seldom intense enough to arouse fetal responsiveness and do not normally occur with sufficient contiguity or repetitiveness to make conditioning possible. Only proprioceptive and tactile stimuli are reasonably adequate during fetal life and only in the case of the grasp reflex does contiguity occur frequently and regularly enough to lend credence to this explanation. Third, many reflexes can be elicited perfectly or nearly perfectly at birth even thought the neonate had not previously been exposed to the evocative stimuli in question, e.g., ocular pursuit movements in response to a roving visual stimulus, crying in response to intense heat, cold, or smell. This eliminates any possibility of learning or conditioning. Fourth, for a conditioned response to be established the response itself must be available so that it can be associated with an originally inadequate stimulus; but some responses, like crying, do not appear until after birth.

Fifth, even if the conditioning hypothesis were applicable in some instances it would still not account for *all* fetal stimulus-response behavior patterns, since an unconditioned response must obviously exist before conditioning itself is possible. Sixth, the suggestion that the behavior patterns developed in the last few months of antenatal existence are conditioned derivatives of earlier developed responses is not very convincing because most discrete responses, except for sucking, crying, respiration, and tendon, grasp and visual motor responses, are already present by the fourth month; and since in the latter instances (except for the grasp and tendon reflexes) neither the responses nor the adequate stimuli are available, learning is out of the question. To hypothesize that the early tactile reflexes are themselves learned would assume that learning is possible nine weeks following conception.

Finally, the absence of significant cortical participation in fetal and neonatal behavior patterns, as demonstrated experimentally and in the case of acephalic monsters, makes the learning hypothesis extremely unlikely. Subcortical learning is difficult indeed in human beings. The few acephalic monsters who do survive after birth show no evidence of learning. Thus, "if prenatal development occurs by virtue of a sort of subcortical learning, one wonders why such learning [does] not continue to occur in [the] acephalous infant."[14]

In conclusion, therefore, the weight of the evidence indicates that the emergence of fetal and neonatal behavior patterns is a function of neural maturation. It is regulated for the most part by prepotent genic predispositions for particular kinds of afferent input to be linked with designated types of efferent output. Except for certain isolated instances, the conditions of fetal existence are not propitious for the uniform acquisition of such connections on the basis of specific experience.

Organizational Trends. Quite apart from the relative contributions of genic and experiential factors to the development of fetal behavior capacities is the long-standing and controversial issue of sequential trends in the organization of these capacities. Are independently controlled part activities individuated out of total responses of the entire organism or are single part activities combined to form more complex whole activities? From his study of behavioral development in the salamander, Coghill concluded both that the direction of organization is invariably from total to part activity and that the original total responses are integrated from the very start. He showed that swimming movements implicating the entire organism precede independent motion of single limbs and that lateral rotation of the entire body in response to a stimulus in one visual field precedes simple rotation of the eyeballs alone.[12, 13]

These findings were later applied by Coghill and others to encompass the direction of behavioral organization in all species. Critical examination of the evidence, however, indicates that the generalizations holding true for the salamander probably do not apply to human beings: too much disparity exists between the two species in rate of behavioral development and in degree of cortical control over integrated activity. The developmental situation, therefore, is much more complicated in the human infant. First, although individuation of part activities out of total responses does precede the knitting together of simple parts into more complex wholes, the latter type of organizational trend (e.g., coordinated and sequential reflexes, learned motor performance) is *also* very characteristic of human behavioral development. Second, the original form of total activity is uncoordinatedly diffuse rather than integrated. Individuation proceeds from a diffuse type of mass activity; and integration is only achieved subsequently—when the individuated parts are synthesized into a new coordinated whole.

Furthermore, qualitatively different kinds of individuation seem to take place and to occur at different rates. The earliest type of diffuse response to stimulation is apparently replaced by discrete, and invariable stimulus-response connections; this sequence corresponds to the development of simple reflexes and is presumably regulated by potent genic factors. On the other hand, stimulus elicited behavior that is more variable in nature, spontaneous behavior, and finally volitional behavior, appear to be individuated from a different type of precursor. Development in these instances does not follow the seemingly predetermined and inevitable pattern of attaining greater discreteness and invariability; instead diffuseness is replaced by greater specificity, directedness and localization, but never by a stereotyped set of responses. This type of individuation also begins later and is by no means completed in fetal life.

Other directional trends in prenatal behavioral development are axial in nature. The emergence of neuromuscular responsiveness, control, and coordination follows a proximodistal and cephalocaudal sequence. That is, sensori-motor function appears earlier in cranial than in sacral areas of innervation, and sooner in muscle groups that are close to rather than distant from the longitudinal axis of the body. These axial trends also persist in postnatal motor development.

PREGNANCY, CHILDBIRTH, LACTATION AND MATERNAL BEHAVIOR

Maternal behavior begins before the child is born. Genetically speaking it starts as soon as the mother-to-be as a child forms her first concept of parenthood. More proximately it begins with her reactions to ongoing pregnancy and anticipated childbirth. Here the dominant considerations are factors that increase or decrease the desire for motherhood. After birth takes place the problem of caring for an infant who is now an insistent reality elicits actual parent behavior that is determined by a related but different set of physiological, cultural, personal and situational variables.

Psychological Reactions to Pregnancy

In all cultures powerful social and psychological forces operate to increase a woman's desire for motherhood and to generate positive attitudes regarding pregnancy. Wherever children are supportable, they are desired for a wide variety of reasons: to help in the economic support of the family; to perpetuate the culture; to carry on the family name; to enhance the dignity and social standing of the parents; to succor them in their old age; to attend to their burial; to mourn for them, and to care for their departed spirits; and, especially where the material level of the culture is high, children are also desired for their own sake—for the psychological joys and satisfactions of parenthood. The sterile woman is frequently an object of cultural scorn. Sterility creates dissatisfactions in marital life, undermines the woman's position in the home, and frequently jeopardizes the very legal status of her marriage.

Because motherhood fulfills important biological and social sex roles in a woman it constitutes a source of considerable ego satisfaction that tends to place pregnancy and its successful culmination in a very favorable anticipatory light. It enables her to prove her biological adequacy and to achieve parity with other women,[59] to satisfy an unconscious desire for immortality,[15] to avoid the cultural reproach of sterility,[15] and to look forward to a companion whose personality she can mold. It is no wonder then that pregnancy is a period of pride, exhilaration and increased zest for many women and is regarded as the beginning of a rewarding and challenging experience.[37] Nevertheless, even for the normal woman who looks forward with enthusiasm to motherhood, pregnancy gives rise to many stresses and tensions; and for the woman who is emotionally unstable or who abhors the prospect of maternity, it is a period of genuine crisis.

How a woman will respond to the stresses and strains of pregnancy is naturally a function of the personality structure she brings with her into this experience. It is reasonable to expect a continuation of the same level of adjustment and of the same type of adjustive devices that prevailed prior to this time. Hence, pregnancy may be regarded as a period of more or less stress that tests the adequacy of the prepregnancy personality rather than as a discontinuously new and unpredictable cause of behavior disorder. Deviant psychological reactions to pregnancy are seldom unheralded in the past history of the expectant mother.[8, 15, 31, 59, 77]

Sources of Tension during Pregnancy. Counteracting the more positive motivations and wholesome attitudes regarding pregnancy and maternity are numerous other factors that make for tension and conflict. The social stigma attached to sterility (the blame for which is almost invariably placed on the woman) may be great enough to coerce a woman into a pregnancy for which she is not quite ready or create undue apprehension about its successful outcome. A comparable type of unwholesome situation exists when pregnancy is perceived as necessary to retain the husband's affection or to rescue a faltering marriage. Under such circumstances the felt need for pregnancy may be sufficiently intense to precipitate pseudocyesis, a hysterical condition in which a non-pregnant woman believes she is pregnant and presents such characteristic signs and symptoms of pregnancy as cessation of menses, morning sickness, sensation of fetal movements, enlargement of breasts, uterus and abdomen, and labor pains.[52, 59] In instances where a woman has doubts about remaining married to her husband, pregnancy often carries implications of finality and is, therefore, resented for restricting her freedom of decision.

Even in the absence of unusual pressures, expectant motherhood has its characteristic hazards and adjustive difficulties. For every woman there is always the statistical possibility of protracted illness, disability and death in connection with childbirth; of abortion or fetal death; of giving birth to a monster or an idiot, to a deformed infant or a child with a dread hereditary disease.[74] All pregnant women have to face the ordeal of labor and delivery—both the genuine, tissue sources of pain and the emotional sources derived from fearful anticipation of these events as they are represented in the embroidered tradition of folklore. For prudish women there is the additional shame and humiliation of exposure before physicians and nurses and of discussing signs and symptoms of an intimate bodily nature.[74] Motherhood invariably brings new duties and responsibilities, the curtailment of personal freedom, and limited opportunities for enjoying rest, relaxation and leisure time activities. In many instances it creates serious financial difficulties* and interrupts or even ends a woman's vocational career. As a matter of fact, in terms of the practical and emotional read-

*That reluctance for children in marriage is less often a function of actual financial incapacity than of social class values, competing vocational ambitions, and high standards of what constitutes an acceptable minimal family income is shown by the inverse relationship between socioeconomic status and number of children in the family.

justments involved, parenthood makes more of a difference than marriage in the lives and daily routine of most persons.

Expectant motherhood may also reactivate latent conflicts and guilt feelings that a woman experiences in the course of her relationship with her own mother.[15, 16] It signifies the expression of emotional independence and the enactment of a mature adult role that is directed toward the establishment of new primary attachments. Hence it carries implications of disloyalty and threatens the dependency ties of an overdependent woman to her own parents; whereas in the case of women who are still resentful of their parents' former authority, the same situation provides a consummate opportunity for self-assertion. This latter motivation plus the desire to inflict punishment on the parents are often found in cases of repeated illegitimate pregnancy.[8] The stigma attached to such pregnancy in our culture commonly leads to acute anxiety, shame, guilt, and resentment, frequently culminating in self-induced or illegally committed abortion, infanticide, suicide, hysterical denial of pregnancy, or psychotic states.[52]

The most serious types of disturbed psychological reactions to pregnancy (persistent vomiting and gestational psychosis) occur in women who by virtue of personality structure are strongly predisposed to regard prospective motherhood with apprehension, anxiety, ambivalence, or outright rejection. The characteristic symptoms of these syndromes (e.g., vomiting, denial of or amnesia for the act of parturition, delusions of infant death, fear or projection of own homicidal impulses toward the child, oversolicitude) are generally interpreted as reflective of extreme disinclination for motherhood.[8, 31, 52, 77] Psychiatric study shows that one or more of the following personality trends underlie such reactions: (a) narcissistic self-preoccupation, (b) resentful rejection of the feminine role in life as incompatible with basic ego aspirations, (c) an immature attitude of passive irresponsibility and parasitic dependence on others, and (d) feelings of anxiety and depression stemming from lack of self-confidence in handling the anticipated responsibilities of motherhood.[15, 16, 31, 52, 77]

Reactions to Childbirth. A woman's anticipations of and actual experiences during childbirth are, of course, determined in part by the actual content of the three stages of labor (uterine contractions and dilatation of the cervix, expulsion of the fetus, delivery of the afterbirth).* In large measure, however, it is also influenced by culturally determined concepts and practices of childbirth. The intensity of pain experience, for example, depends in part on the degree of threat perceived in a given situation and

---

*Such experience naturally varies in duration and severity depending on the size and position of the fetus; pelvic dimensions; condition of uterine, perineal and abdominal musculature and of other soft parts; parity of the mother, etc.

on the degree of emotional response made to such threat. Hence, in accordance with the traditions of their culture, women react to the same physiological experience of childbirth in a large variety of ways. At one extreme, childbirth is accepted very casually: expectant mothers work in the fields until active labor begins, are unattended throughout, sever the umbilical cord by themselves, walk home with the infant immediately after delivery, and then go about their daily routines. At the other extreme, as in our culture, pregnancy has more or less the status of a debilitating disease, childbirth is regarded as an excruciatingly painful ordeal and as a hospital or quasisurgical procedure, and elaborate prenatal and postnatal measures are observed.

In recent years a new concept of "natural childbirth" has arisen in obstetrical practice.[25, 46, 55, 73] It is based on the premise that pregnancy and childbirth can be made less fearsome and more emotionally satisfying experiences by counteracting cultural factors that heighten *emotional* determinants of pain and discomfort. Despite popular misconceptions to the contrary, no claim is made that labor and delivery are "naturally" free of all pain and discomfort, or that the latter experiences are *entirely* emotional in origin. It is pointed out, however, that the tissue basis of pain is enhanced tremendously by such culturally derived sources of fear as anxious anticipation of unbearable pain, lack of knowledge of what to expect in the course of labor and delivery (due to ignorance of the underlying anatomy and physiology and of hospital routines), isolation of the "patient" from others in the delivery room, the absence of opportunity to explore her fears with informed persons, and the conspiracy of silence surrounding her condition and progress during labor. These emotional components of fear are combatted psychologically by an appropriate program of education during pregnancy, by the continuous attendance of and sympathetic reassurance from trained personnel throughout labor, and by keeping the patient informed of her progress. The pain and discomfort of pregnancy and labor are also reduced by an adjunctive program of breathing control, muscular relaxation, and exercises that relieve the postural backache of pregnancy and strengthen the abdominal muscles for pushing during the second and third stages of labor. These procedures generally make it possible for the obstetrician to eliminate entirely or to reduce considerably the need for anesthesia or analgesia during labor. As a result, although consciousness during delivery is not necessary for the success of this method, it is often achievable, thereby eliminating amnesia for the experience of childbirth and allowing the woman to cooperate more actively. She is able to enjoy the exhilaration that comes from immediate contact with the child, and from immediate and first-hand knowledge that partly through her own efforts her pregnancy has been brought to a successful conclusion.

Initial Maternal Behavior

The nature of early maternal behavior in the human female is still a highly unsettled and controversial matter. The once fashionable notion of "maternal instinct," either in the sense of an innately determined "drive" or of a ready-made pattern of complex behavior inevitably released at childbirth, has long since fallen into disrepute—even for explaining the post-pregnancy behavior of infrahuman mammals.[58] Tremendous variability from one culture to another in the basic characteristics of the mother's early behavior toward her offspring demonstrates quite unequivocally that social variables determine in large measure both the genesis and intensity of maternal drive and the specific content of maternal behavior. Nevertheless, despite widespread belief to the contrary, this does not mean that culture is the *only* determining variable. Physiological, personality, experiential and situational factors all play supportive and sometimes extremely significant roles; and in the case of the first two variables mentioned, genes (both "phylogenetic" and "ontogenetic") are also regulatory factors.

Physiological Aspects and Lactation. The relationships between maternal behavior and lactation are complex indeed. Both phenomena are determined in part by the same physiological factors; but although lactation occurs in the general context of and probably enhances maternal behavior, there is no evidence to indicate that maternal attitude influences the mother's *ability* to breast-feed her infant. The breasts of the non-pregnant woman do not ordinarily contain sufficient glandular tissue to make lactation anatomically possible. During pregnancy, however, this defect is remedied as estrogens and progesterone, secreted by the placenta, act as priming agents stimulating the necessary tissue growth. Thus, by the end of pregnancy the breasts are able to produce milk when stimulated adequately by prolactin, a hormone secreted by the anterior pituitary. Nevertheless, because of the inhibitory influence of high blood levels of estrogen and progesterone on the secretory *function* of the breast, lactation does not occur until about 24 hours after birth, when removal of the placenta allows the blood levels of these hormones to fall.* If the infant is placed at the breast immediately after birth, his sucking may help stimulate later milk flow, but at the time he obtains colostrum, not milk.

In addition to stimulating lactation, prolactin also tends to lower the

---

*Sometimes even the infant himself secretes milk since his breasts may be both enlarged from prenatal exposure to placental hormones and functionally stimulated by removal from these hormones at birth.

threshold for the elicitation and acquisition of maternal attitudes and behavior. That is, it facilitates the release of maternal tendencies and responses that have already been acquired by cultural indoctrination or actual experience, as well as facilitates the elaboration of maternal responses from initial bodily and suctorial contacts. It does not establish by itself any recognizable pattern of maternal behavior.[58] The breast feeding situation in turn leads to such mutually stimulative and tension-relieving effects as the provision of bodily warmth, the satisfaction of hunger, and the reduction of mammary gland engorgement. In infrahuman mammals this constitutes a nucleus of highly rewarding behavior, in part reflexly and physiologically determined, which under the influence of prolactin facilitation can be expanded into a more complex pattern of learned maternal responses.[41, 58] At the human level, the satisfying experiences associated with breast feeding undoubtedly reinforce existing and promote the acquisition of new maternal dispositions; but because human maternal tendencies and practices are part of the cultural heritage and do not have to be fashioned anew by each individual from personal learning experience superimposed upon more or less inevitable tactual-suctorial mother-child interactions, their acquisition is not dependent upon the latter core of experiences.

Since prolactin is a common determinant of both lactation and maternal attitude, and since the breast feeding situation probably enhances maternal responsiveness, it is hardly surprising that women who are judged as more motherly in attitude also produce more milk.[51] It is unjustifiable, however, to conclude from this positive relationship that motherliness necessarily increases milk flow, although it may obviously influence disposition (rather than ability) to continue breast-feeding.

Other Determinants. Cultural standards and concepts of maternal role crucially influence the development of the mother's attitudes toward the neonate. Such standards of what constitutes appropriately maternal attitudes, duties, functions, and responsibilities are related in turn to more general moral and religious values in the culture and to the cultural valuation of children and of child rearing. In certain extreme instances they even provide moral sanction for such apparently unmaternal practices as infanticide and child barter.[39] Although some intracultural variability does prevail in these latter practices and in the extent to which consanguinity (i.e., biological motherhood as opposed to adoption) is regarded as important for the development of maternal feelings, most of the variance in the expression of such behavior seems to be inter- rather than intracultural.

In most aspects of maternal behavior, however, considerable intracultural variability is the rule. The perceived cultural norm constitutes the ideological core of the individual's maternal value system, but this core is modified substantially by personality and idiosyncratic experiential factors; and in the actual expression of maternal behavior, the situational and physiological considerations operative at the moment must also be taken into account. A woman's first concept of motherhood is based upon her perceptions as a child of her *own* mother's behavior. In accordance with her affective reaction to these perceptions and memories—matter-of-fact acceptance, idealization, or rejection—she tends to impart to different components of the cultural prescription her own peculiar emphases and personal flavor. Motherliness, to a certain extent, is also a reflection of a constellation of temperamental traits bearing on the individual's capacity for bestowing affection, tenderness and solicitude on a helpless creature who is dependent on her. Since it is positively correlated with duration of menstrual flow,[42] these traits are probably determined in part by level of estrogenic secretion, as well as by other genic and experiential factors. Their expression is also undoubtedly influenced by such ego-related personality traits as level of ego aspiration, acceptance of feminine role in life, tendency toward narcissistic self-preoccupation, level of anxiety, feelings of adequacy, notions of volitional and executive independence, ability to postpone hedonistic self-indulgence, and sense of moral responsibility. Depending on the strength of some of the latter trends, the infant will be accepted warmly for his own sake, rejected as a nuisance or as a barrier to the mother's vocational career, overprotected, or regarded as a potential source of vicarious ego aggrandizement. Women with pronounced anxiety reactions and attitudes of rejection toward motherhood not only tend to have more physical and emotional symptoms of maladjustment during pregnancy and delivery, but also experience more difficulty in adjusting psychologically to their newborn infants.[83]

Numerous situational factors also impinge on the evolution of maternal behavior from the moment the child is born. Absence of breast-feeding deprives the mother of the initial reinforcement of maternal impulses that this satisfying, tension-relieving experience ordinarily effects. Isolation of the infant in the hospital nursery may leave her with a sense of strangeness and remoteness about the reality of her relationship to him, and may generate overwhelming feelings of apprehension or inadequacy about her ability to cope with the routines of child care when she is home on her own with no immediate source of help or advice.[20] In addition, upon arriving home from the hospital she must face again the countless household responsibilities from which she had been given a temporary respite, as well as satisfy other demands on her affectional resources. The emotional needs of her husband and other children must somehow be integrated with her care of the newcomer, or he may be justifiably regarded as an intruder and become an object of resentment. Then too, she has her own dependency needs as a wife and as a person who has just passed through what the culture generally regards as a harrowing, crisis-like experience in her life.[20] She wants to receive emotional support as well as extend it, to lean on others, and to be relieved of some of the responsibility of caring for her child. Because she feels entitled to some self-indulgence she may resent the actual or perceived unwillingness of relatives to shoulder part of her new burdens.[20] If her family situation is essentially wholesome, such problems are inevitably resolved in the course of time. If, on the other hand, it is beset by marital discord, these problems tend to become worse, to aggravate existing relationships with her husband, and eventually to involve the child as a pawn, a scapegoat, a compensatory source of affection, or as an object of competition between his parents.

An integral part of the immediate situation shaping the mother's early attitudes toward the neonate emanate from the latter himself. His very helplessness is in a sense his greatest ally but his apparent fragility may also constitute a source of considerable maternal anxiety. He also helps or hinders his own cause, as the case may be, depending on whether his sex and general appearance conform to what had been desired and anticipated. Because of the mother's lack of sophistication about infant care or her susceptibility to the more morbid insinuations of baby folklore, she may become unduly alarmed about such natural occurrences as startle reactions or the shallowness of his breathing.[20] For similar reasons she may exaggerate the hazards of bathing and the dangers of suffocation, or blame herself unreasonably about her inability to interpret the uninterpretable and predict the unpredictable, i.e., the significance of and the reason for all of his crying.[20]

In conclusion, therefore, it seems likely that cultural factors furnish the substantive and ideological core from which maternal attitudes are fashioned, and account for both some major intercultural uniformities as well as some conspicuous intercultural differences. Within a given culture, variability in maternal attitudes is related to idiosyncratic individual experience, to temperamental, physiologically determined and ego-related personality traits influencing motherliness, and to specific situational factors emanating from the marital and family situations, from the lying-in experience, and from the infant himself. In all cultures hormonal variables facilitate the expression of existing maternal dispositions, determine ability to lactate, and indirectly provide reinforcement for maternal behavior through the tension-relieving properties of the breast feeding situation. However, neither hormonal facilitation nor the nursing situation necessarily insure the development of maternal behavior in the human female; and evidence from the child rearing behavior of foster mothers and from fathers generally indicates that psychological parenthood is possible without the facilitating influence of hormones, breast feeding, or the notion of consanguinity.

THE BIRTH PROCESS

Birth represents a transition from a parasitic type of sheltered existence in a relatively invariable environment to a physiologically autonomous existence in a less protected and highly variable environment. During the course of less than a day the fetus is catapulted from a restricted fluid world of constant warmth, darkness and muffled sounds to a vastly expanded world of air, light, noise, taste, smell, and temperature, as well as ever-present contact with stimuli outside himself. He is suddenly required to obtain his own oxygen, ingest and digest his own food, excrete his own wastes, and regulate his own temperature. Hence, many organ systems and sense modalities, although capable of functioning at an earlier date, are first brought into actual use at this time, thereby facing an initial period of adaptation before they can operate efficiently. Another group of organ systems and sensory mechanisms, on the other hand, (e.g., cardiovascular, endocrine, neuromuscular, vestibular) have already been functioning effectively for some time and merely undergo varying degrees of adjustment to changed conditions of life.

Major Physiological Changes

Respiration. The sudden need for obtaining his own oxygen supply at birth makes the inauguration of functional respiration a critical condition for the continued survival of the neonate. More than half of all natal day deaths are attributable to asphyxiation.[6] After some preliminary gasping,[53] breathing movements become strong enough for the first time to inflate the lungs and permit oxygen to pass from the pulmonary air spaces to the infant's blood stream. They are initiated both (a) by cutaneous and thermal stimulation from the environment, and (b) by the humoral stimulation of the medullary respiratory center that results when disturbance of the placental circulation during delivery increases the carbon dioxide content of fetal blood. The first functional inspiration is accompanied by mechanical stimulation of the vocal cords, causing them to vibrate. This is the physiological basis of the well-known "birth cry" which marks so dramatically the onset of the infant's career as a physiologically autonomous organism. At birth, respirations are mostly of the abdominal type, and even during sleep average about thirty-two per minute as compared to twenty in the adult.[29]

The change from fetal to natal respiration also happens to be adaptive at this time because the former method is not adequate for the full-term fetus' intracellular tissue needs. As embryonic tissue becomes more mature, it shifts to a more aerobic type of respiration in which a greater percentage of the source of energy (glucose) is oxidized completely into carbon dioxide and water rather than being converted to an intermediary product such as lactic acid. Although this results in a more economical utilization of glucose and makes possible a reduction in caloric intake per pound of body weight, it necessitates an increase in oxygen supply. During the last few weeks of prenatal life, however, the amount of oxygen available from the placental circulation becomes insufficient to satisfy these increased demands, leading to severe anoxia if pregnancy is prolonged beyond term.[11] To compensate in part for the relatively low oxygen tension, the number of circulating red blood corpuscles increases. After birth, when the oxygen supply is adequate again, the additional red cells are no longer needed and are destroyed releasing a rich supply of iron for future use and sometimes sufficient bile pigment (bilirubin) to create a mild, temporary condition of jaundice.

Circulation. The two major cardiovascular changes at birth are (a) termination of the placental circulation that links maternal and fetal blood systems, and (b) obliteration of the shunts that channel fetal blood away from the lungs. In prenatal life, since fetal oxygen requirements are taken care of by the mother, and since the lungs in any case contain no air, pulmonary circulation of blood is unnecessary and is by-passed by means of two shunts that divert venous blood directly from the right side of the heart into the systemic circulation. At birth, when the fetus is obliged to oxygenate his own blood and the lungs are inflated with air, these shunts are obliterated and pulmonary circulation commences. The trend toward increased cardiac output that begins in prenatal life continues after birth and is reflected in a progressively increasing blood pressure and decreasing pulse rate. Neonatal pulse rate is approximately twice as rapid as that of the adult,[29] and blood pressure is correspondingly only half as high as the adult's.

Nutrition and Excretion. For all practical purposes, ingestion and digestion of food occur for the first time after birth when nutritive elements are no longer available to the infant from the mother's blood stream. Prior evidence of gastrointestinal activity, such as fetal stools, is attributable to the swallowing of amniotic fluid. Neonatal stomach contractions tend to be more vigorous than in the adult and to occur about three hours after nursing despite the fact that the stomach takes four to five hours to empty.[53] Emptiness of the stomach, therefore, does not seem to be essential for gastric contractions; and as we shall see later, gastric contractions, themselves, are not the only determinants of hunger. The neonate typically loses weight during the first few days of life but tends to regain his birth weight by the end of the first week. The weight loss is probably a reflection of dehydration due to initial restriction of fluid intake and inefficient absorption of what fluid is ingested.* The kidneys also become functional at this time since nitrogenous wastes can no longer be disposed of through the placental circulation. In the total absence of sphincter control it is not surprising that an average of nineteen urinations and four to five defecations occur in the course of a day.[28]

Physical Trauma

Even normal uncomplicated birth is a prolonged and violent phenomenon. It involves much pushing and squeezing through extremely narrow quarters and a sudden drastic change in environment and in basic physiological processes. Yet there is no reason to believe that it ordinarily exceeds the infant's capacity for withstanding stress or that it leaves lasting consequences. Instances of prolonged and difficult labor, however, (especially when forceps are applied high in the birth canal) are quite another matter. Asphyxia is a common complication under these circumstances, and such serious injuries as skull fracture, intracranial hemorrhage and cerebral laceration may result. If the infant survives the neonatal period, initially delayed respiration and anoxia apparently have no residual effects.[38] Intracranial injury may lead to convulsive disorders, cerebral palsy and mental retardation.[17, 43, 45] Less serious consequences, e.g., loss in auditory acuity[53] and disturbed osseous growth,[68] may occur in cases of difficult and protracted labor in which no obvious signs of injury or dysfunction are present at birth. Mild degrees of cerebral damage may also have delayed effects in later years. For example, the behavior disorders of children with a history of operative delivery tend to be characterized by hyperirritability and general motor hyperactivity[60, 80]; and in monozygotic twins suffering from mental disease, the member of a twin pair with the more serious form of the disorder is more likely to have had the more difficult birth experience.[64]

Lest the significance of physical trauma at birth be exaggerated, the foregoing facts should be qualified by the following considerations: First, the vast majority of deliveries are not unduly protracted or difficult, and fall well within the infant's capacity for withstanding trauma. Second,

*As fluid intake increases, some of the initial, extreme dehydration (and weight loss) is reversed. In general, however, gradual but progressive dehydration of the tissues is a regular concomitant of the aging process.

many of the typical manifestations of birth injury may also be caused by other, entirely unrelated conditions. For example, marked vitamin K deficiency in the mother may give rise to intracranial hemorrhage in the fetus, hereditary cerebral agenesis is responsible for much cerebral palsy, and nuclear jaundice (associated with incompatibility of the Rh factor) results in varying degrees of spasticity. Lastly, even in those instances in which labor and delivery are unduly difficult, other predisposing factors such as prematurity or genic susceptibility to disease may be operative. If this were not the case, *all* children exposed to a given degree of birth trauma would be adversely affected by it.

Psychological Trauma

Less credible than the possibility of physical trauma at birth are the metaphysical claims of psychological birth trauma advanced by the psychoanalytic school. It is alleged that uterine existence is experienced as a paradisaic state in which the fetus shares a mystical and undefined "oneness" with the mother; that a nostalgic desire for return to the serenity of the womb pervades behavior until death; that birth is catastrophically traumatic because it interrupts the Nirvana-like bliss and separates the child from unity with his mother[54]; and that the "helplessness" and "insecurity" experienced as a result of the separation constitute the primal basis for and the prototype of all later anxiety.[22, 54] Clinical "evidence" of the reality of these feelings, desires and reactions is even brought forward from the dreams of adult patients.[21]

It hardly needs to be pointed out that before an individual could conceivably appreciate the blissfulness of the womb, enjoy "oneness" with the mother, or react traumatically to the implications of separation, he would first require a varied background of experience, much cognitive sophistication, and the speculative abilities and proclivities of a philosopher. Life in the uterus might appear very attractive to a battle-weary and philosophically minded veteran of life. Unfortunately, however, the neonate has neither the experiential perspective nor the intellectual equipment to enjoy his alleged good fortune. As is true of the vaunted "peace of the grave," prenatal existence could be enjoyable indeed—*if* only the necessary sensibilities for enjoyment were available. Furthermore, reactions of helplessness, insecurity and anxiety presuppose that the neonate possesses functional concepts of self and self-esteem, appreciates his own executive incompetence, is mature enough to feel threatened, and is able to think in terms of the future. As we shall see later (see p. 325), unequivocal evidence for even the much simpler emotion of fear is not present before the fifth month of life.

MATURITY AT BIRTH

Because of variability in the length of gestation and in the rate of prenatal development, children naturally vary in degree of maturity at birth. Although the precise duration of the gestational period can never be ascertained for a particular child (see p. 174), the *mean* length of gestation is estimated to be 280 days, with an upper limit of 334 and lower limit of 180 days.[9] The lower limit is set by the age of viability and corresponds to the minimal degree of structural and functional maturity necessary to sustain life outside of the uterus; in accordance with the generally observed "margin of safety" characterizing most biological processes, this occurs well in advance of the age at which parturition typically takes place. The upper limit is set by the inability of the placenta to satisfy increased fetal needs for food and oxygen, especially in the wake of degenerative changes that develop after full-term. Approximately one-third of all postmature infants fail to survive if the mother is primiparous and over 26 years of age.[11]

In actual practice when we refer to "prematurely born" infants, what we actually mean is that they are "immature." The commonly employed criterion of prematurity is not reduced length of gestation (which can only be estimated), but developmental status inferior to that of a full-term infant. Such immaturity, of course, could be caused by slow rate of development as well as by delivery prior to term. Since the characteristics and management of this condition are the same irrespective of the cause, it is not too important to make the distinction provided that "immaturely-born" is understood when the conventionally accepted term, "prematurely-born" is used.

The Prematurely Born Infant

Prematurely born infants constitute five to ten per cent of all live births.[1] With very few exceptions viability is not possible prior to 26 weeks of age or under a birth weight of two and one-half pounds. Thereafter, if special care is provided such infants may be kept alive, their chances of survival varying directly with weight and gestational age. Prematurity is associated with primiparity and advanced age of the mother[48, 61]; with maternal rubella, congenital syphilis, and incompatibility of the Rh factor[1]; with congenital anomalies of the fetus such as anencephaly[1]; and with inadequate maternal nutrition.[18] For the latter reason the incidence is higher among Negroes and in lower socioeconomic groups.[5] As might be expected, the mortality rate among prematurely born infants is exceedingly high because of their susceptibility to asphyxia and intracranial hemorrhage. Birth trauma is less important here than immaturity of the respiratory center, capillary fragility, and softness of the skull and brain.[1] Prematurity is a causal factor in more than half of all neonatal deaths.[1]

Characteristics. From the standpoint of response capacities, the viable, prematurely born infant is relatively well developed. All of the discrete responses of the full-term infant are elicitable, but level of general activity is lower and the more recently acquired responses tend to be rudimentary in nature. Thus, his respirations are shallow, his cry is weak, and he is unable to suck and swallow well or to regulate his body temperature efficiently. For reasons already indicated (see p. 180), his sensory status except for vision, does not compare unfavorably with that of the full-term fetus. In general, although he is less well developed than the full-term infant at birth (because he is one to three months younger), he is more highly developed nine months after conception than is the latter because of exposure to the more stimulating environment outside the uterus during the last few months of this period.

The actual diagnosis of prematurity is made on the basis of various physical signs, the most important of which is birth weight under five and one-half pounds. Other physical criteria include softness of the cartilages of the nose, absence of centers of ossification in the lower extremities, crown-rump length less than 32 cm., head circumference less than 33 cm., and scalp hairs shorter than 2 cm.[19]

Special Care. The prematurely born infant requires a special environment designed to compensate for his adaptive immaturity and to satisfy his distinctive metabolic needs. Because of his poor temperature control and precarious breathing, a constant, warm atmosphere high in oxygen and low in humidity is necessary. He must be spoon-fed because of inadequate sucking and swallowing responses. Unlike the full-term infant, his relatively anaerobic intracellular oxidation requires a daily caloric intake of 120 rather than 45 calories per pound. His diet should be rich in calcium and vitamins C and D because ossification of bone normally begins in the last two months of prenatal development; and since he does not experience the typical compensatory increase in red blood corpuscles in the latter weeks of intrauterine life (followed by their destruction after birth with release of iron), he is more dependent upon dietary sources of iron (see p. 195).

Later Development. Prematurely born infants tend to overcome their initial immaturity and to "catch up" gradually to their full-term contemporaries. Infants under four pounds at birth are still retarded one or more months at 18 months of age; whereas babies weighing four to five pounds at birth are fully caught up by the age of nine months.[61] The retardation is primarily in the postural, locomotor and manipulative areas. As a matter of fact, Shirley's premature group was significantly advanced in sensory acuity and in social responsiveness.[61, 62] In the preschool period these children manifest significantly more behavior problems than full-term children. Such problems include hyperactivity, later acquisition of bowel and bladder control, enuresis, excessive distractibility, shyness, thumbsucking, negativism and hypersensitivity to sound.[32, 61, 62] Some of these symptoms (hyperirritability, hyperactivity, distractibility) point in part to the possibility of mild but diffuse brain injury at birth. Inconsistency in handling may also be a determining factor, since such children tend to be overprotected at first and then overstimulated and pushed into catching up with their peers.[61]

REFERENCES

1. Arey, J. B., and Dent, J.: Pathologic findings in premature infants. *Am. J. Clin. Path. 20*: 1016-1025, 1950.

2. Barns, H. H. F., and Morgans, M. E.: Prediabetic pregnancy. *Brit. J. Obst. & Gynaec. 55*: 449-454, 1948.

3. Benda, C. E.: Prenatal maternal factors in Mongolism. *J.A.M.A. 139*: 979-985, 1949.

4. Bernard, J., and Sontag, L. W.: Fetal reactivity to tonal stimulation: a preliminary report. *J. Genet. Psychol. 70*: 205-210, 1947.

5. Block, H., et al.: Reduction of mortality in the premature nursery. 2. Incidence and causes of prematurity: ethnic, socio-economic and obstetric factors. *J. Pediat. 41*: 300-304, 1942.

6. Bundesen, H. N.: Natal day deaths: the long neglected field of infant mortality. *J.A.M.A. 153*: 466-473, 1953.

7. Burke, B. S., et al.: Nutrition studies during pregnancy. *Am. J. Obst. & Gynec. 46*: 38-52, 1943.

8. Cappon, D.: Some psychodynamic aspects of pregnancy. *Canad. M. A. J. 70*: 147-156, 1954.

9. Carmichael, L.: The onset and early development of behavior. *In* L. Carmichael, Ed., *Manual of Child Psychology*, ed. 2. New York, Wiley, 1954, pp. 60-185.

10. Chesley, L. C., and Annetto, J. E.: Pregnancy in the patient with hypertensive disease. *Am. J. Obst. & Gynec. 53*: 372-381, 1947.

11. Clifford, S. H.: Postmaturity—with placental dysfunction. *J. Pediat. 44*: 1-13, 1954.

12. Coghill, G. E.: *Anatomy and the Problem of Behavior.* New York, Macmillan, 1929.

13. ——: Integration and motivation of behavior as problems of growth. *J. Genet. Psychol. 48*: 3-19, 1936.

14. Dennis, W.: Is the newborn infant's repertoire learned or instinctive? *Psychol. Rev. 50*: 203-218, 1943.

15. Deutsch, H.: *The Psychology of Women.* New York, Grune and Stratton, 1944.

16. ——: An introduction to the discussion of the psychological problems of pregnancy. *In* M. J. E. Senn, Ed., *Problems of Early Infancy*, Transactions of Second Conference, 1948. New York, Josiah Macy, Jr., Foundation, 1949, pp. 11-17.

17. Doll, E. A.: The feeble-minded child. *In* L. Carmichael, Ed., *Manual of Child Psychology*. New York, Wiley, 1946, pp. 845-885.
18. Ebbs, J. H., et al.: The influence of improved prenatal nutrition upon the infant. *Canad. M. A. J. 46*: 6-8, 1942.
19. Ellis, R. W. B.: Assessment of prematurity by birth weight, crown-rump length, and head circumference. *Arch. Dis. Child. 26*: 411-422, 1951.
20. Escalona, S.: The psychological situation of mother and child upon return to the hospital. *In* M. J. E. Senn, Ed., *Problems of Infancy and Early Childhood*, Transactions of the Third Conference, 1949. New York, Josiah Macy, Jr. Foundation, 1950, pp. 30-51.
21. Fodor, N.: *In Search of the Beloved: a Clinical Study of the Trauma of Birth and Pre-natal Conditioning*. New York, Hermitage, 1949.
22. Freud, S.: *The Problem of Anxiety*. New York, Norton, 1936.
23. Gaspar, J. L.: Diabetis mellitus and pregnancy. *West J. Surg. 53*: 21, 1945.
24. Gesell, A.: *The Embryology of Behavior*. New York, Harper, 1945.
25. Goodrich, F. W., Jr.: *Natural Childbirth*. New York, Prentice-Hall, 1950.
26. Hagerman, D. D., and Viller, C. A.: The transfer of fructose by human placenta. *J. Clin. Invest. 31*: 911-913, 1952.
27. Halliday, J. L.: *Psychosocial Medicine*. New York, Norton, 1948.
28. Halverson, H. M.: Genital and sphincter behavior of the male infant. *J. Genet. Psychol. 56*: 95-136, 1940.
29. ———: Variations in pulse and respiration during different phases of infant behavior. *J. Genet. Psychol. 59*: 259-330, 1941.
30. Harris, D. B., and Harris, E. S.: A study of fetal movements in relation to mother's activity. *Hum. Biol. 18*: 221-237, 1946.
31. Harvey, W. A., and Sherfey, M. J.: Vomiting in pregnancy, a psychiatric study. *Psychosom. Med. 16*: 1-9, 1954.
32. Hirschl, D., Levy, H., and Litvak, A. M.: The physical and mental development of premature infants: a statistical survey with a five-year follow-up. *Arch. Pediat. 65*: 648-653, 1948.
33. Holt, E. B.: *Animal Drive and the Learning Process*. New York, Holt, 1931.
34. Hooker, D.: Reflex activities in the human fetus. *In* R. G. Barker, J. S. Kounin, and H. F. Wright, Eds., *Child Behavior and Development*. New York, McGraw-Hill, 1943, pp. 17-28.
35. ———: The development of behavior in the human fetus. *In* W. Dennis, Ed., *Readings in Child Psychology*. New York, Prentice-Hall, 1951, pp. 1-14.
36. ———: *The Prenatal Origin of Behavior*. Lawrence, University of Kansas Press, 1952.
37. Jersild, A. T., Woodyard, E. S., and del Solar, C.: *Joys and Problems of Child Rearing*. New York, Teachers College, Columbia University, 1949.
38. Keith, H. M., and Norval, M. A.: Neurologic lesions in the newly born infant. I. Preliminary study. II. Role of prolonged labor, asphyxia and delayed respiration. *Pediat. 6*: 229-243, 1950.
39. Klineberg, O.: *Race Differences*. New York, Harper, 1935,
40. Kuder, K., and Johnson, D. G.: The elderly primipara. *Am. J. Obst. & Gynec. 47*: 794-807, 1944.
41. Leuba, C.: *The Natural Man*. New York, Doubleday, 1954.
42. Levy, D. M.: Psychosomatic studies of some aspects of maternal behavior. *Psychosom. Med. 4*: 223-227, 1942.

43. McKhann, C. F., Belnap, W. D., and Beck, C. S.: Late effects of cerebral birth injury. *J. Mich. Med. Soc. 50*: 149-152, 1951.
44. M'Gonigle, G. C. M., and Kirby, J.: *Poverty and Public Health.* London, Gallancz, 1936.
45. Malzberg, B.: Some statistical aspects of Mongolism. *Am. J. Ment. Def. 54*: 266-281, 1950.
46. Mandy, A. J., et. al.: Is natural childbirth natural? *Psychosom. Med. 14*: 431-438, 1952.
47. Montagu, M. F. Ashley: Constitutional and prenatal factors in infant and child health. *In* M. J. E. Senn, Ed., *Symposium on the Healthy Personality.* New York, Josiah Macy, Jr. Foundation, 1950, pp. 148-175.
48. ——: *An Introduction to Physical Anthropology,* ed. 2. Springfield, Ill., C. C. Thomas, 1951.
49. Murphy, D. P.: The outcome of 625 pregnancies in women subjected to pelvic radium roentgen irradiation. *Am. J. Obst. & Gynec. 18*: 179-187, 1929.
50. ——: *Congenital Malformation,* ed. 2. Philadelphia, University of Pennsylvania Press, 1947.
51. Newton, N. R., and Newton, M.: Relationship of ability to breast feed and maternal attitudes toward breast feeding. *Pediat. 5*: 869-875, 1950.
52. Parks, J.: Emotional factors in early pregnancy. *In* M. J. E. Senn, Ed., *Problems of Early Infancy,* Transactions of Second Conference, 1948. New York, Josiah Macy, Jr. Foundation, 1949, pp. 22-27.
53. Pratt, K. C.: The neonate. *In* L. Carmichael, Ed., *Manual of Child Psychology,* ed. 2. New York, Wiley, 1954, pp. 215-291.
54. Rank, O.: *The Trauma of Birth.* New York, Harcourt, Brace, 1929.
55. Read, G. D.: *Childbirth Without Fear,* rev. ed. New York, Harper, 1953.
56. Richards, T. W., and Nelson, V. L.: Abilities of infants during the first eighteen months. *J. Genet. Psychol. 55*: 299-318, 1939.
57. ——, and Newberry, H.: Studies in fetal behavior. III. Can performance on test items at six months postnatally be predicted on the basis of fetal activity? *Child Develop. 9*: 79-86, 1938.
58. Schnierla, T. C.: A consideration of some problems in the ontogeny of family life and social adjustments in various infra-human animals. *In* M. J. E. Senn, Ed., *Problems of Infancy and Childhood,* Transactions of Fourth Conference, 1950. New York, Josiah Macy, Jr. Foundation, 1951, pp. 81-124.
59. Schopbach, R. R. Fried, P. H., and Rakoff, A. E.: Pseudocyesis: a psychosomatic disorder. *Psychosom. Med. 14*: 129-134, 1952.
60. Schroeder, P. L.: Behavior difficulties in children associated with the results of birth trauma. *J.A.M.A. 92*: 100-104, 1929.
61. Shirley, M. M.: Development of immature babies during their first two years. *Child Develop. 9*: 347-360, 1938.
62. ——: A behavior syndrome characterizing prematurely-born children. *Child Develop. 10*: 115-128, 1939.
63. Sieve, B. F.: Vitamins and hormones in nutrition. V. Emotional upset and trauma. *Am. J. Dig. Dis. 16*: 14-25, 1949.
64. Slater, E.: Genetic investigations in twins. *J. Ment. Sci. 99*: 44-52, 1953.
65. Sontag, L. W.: The significance of fetal environmental differences. *Am. J. Obst. & Gynec. 42*: 996-1003, 1941.

66. ——: Differences in modificability of fetal behavior and physiology. *Psychosom. Med.* 6: 151-154, 1944.
67. ——: Some psychosomatic aspects of childhood. *Nerv. Child 5:* 296-304, 1946.
68. ——, and Harris, L. M.: Evidence of disturbed prenatal and neonatal growth in bones of infants aged one month. *Am. J. Dis. Child. 56:* 1248-1255, 1938.
69. ——, and Richards, T. W.: Studies in fetal behavior: I. Fetal heart rate as a behavioral indicator. *Child Develop. Monogr. 3:* No. 4, 1938.
70. Spelt, D. K.: The conditioning of the human fetus in utero. *J. Exper. Psychol. 38:* 338-346, 1948.
71. Sivan, C.: Rubella in pregnancy as aetiological factor in stillbirth. *Lancet 1:* 744-746, 1948.
72. *The Miracle of Growth.* Urbana, University of Illinois Press, 1950.
73. Thomas, H.: *Training for Childbirth.* New York, McGraw-Hill, 1950.
74. Thompson, L. J.: Attitudes of primiparae as observed in a prenatal clinic. *Ment. Hygiene 26:* 243-256, 1942.
75. Tisdall, F. F.: The role of nutrition in preventive medicine. *Milbank Memorial Fund Quart. 23:* 1-15, 1945.
76. Vahlquist, B., Lagercrantz, R., and Nordbring, F.: Maternal and foetal titres of antistrepolysin and antistaphylolysin at different stages of gestation. *Lancet 259:* 851-853, 1950.
77. Victoroff, V. M.: Dynamics and management of para-partum neuropathic reactions. *Dis Nerv. Sys. 13:* 291-298, 1952.
78. Warkany, J.: Etiology of congenital malformations. In *Advance in Pediatrics.* New York, Interscience, 1947.
79. Wesselhoeft, C.: Rubella (German measles) and congenital deformities. *New England J. Med. 240:* 258-261, 1949.
80. Wile, I. S., and Davis, R.: The relation of birth to behavior. *Am. J. Orthopsychiat. 11:* 320-334, 1941.
81. Windle, W. F.: *Physiology of the Fetus: Origin and Extent of Function in Prenatal Life.* Philadelphia, Saunders, 1940.
82. Wright, S. W., Filer, H. J., Jr., and Mason, Karl E.: Vitamin E blood levels in premature and full term infants. *Pediat. 7:* 386-393, 1951.
83. Zemlick, M. J., and Watson, R. I.: Maternal attitudes of acceptance and rejection during and after pregnancy. *Am. J. Orthopsychiat. 23:* 570-584, 1953.

CHAPTER 7

Neonatal Behavior and Capacities

THE NEONATAL PERIOD is generally regarded as comprising the first two
weeks or month of postnatal life. It is a transitional phase of physiological
and psychological adaptation from a parasitic fetal to a more autonomous
postembryonic existence, "a period of adjustment and perfection of newly
acquired vegetative functions."[57] In most respects the study of the neonate
merely carries us one *continuous* step beyond the fetus in the search for
the antecedents of behavior. No new organic developments take place,
essentially no new sensory or response capacities emerge, and subcortical
centers continue to dominate behavioral activity. The principal change is
in exposure to a new environmental milieu which requires the exercise of
latent vegetative capacities, and provides more frequent and adequate
stimulation and greater freedom of movement for the activation of available but hitherto unused or little-used sensori-motor functions.[57]

Nevertheless, despite this exposure to a richer and more variable environment, genic factors continue to play nearly the same prepotent role in the
regulation of development as they did in prenatal life. In fact since "infancy
is the period in which the individual realizes his racial inheritance",[26] the
unique human capacities for behavioral plasticity, learning and social
responsiveness first became significant determining factors in development
during the second and subsequent years of life. And since the rate of early
development appears to be inversely proportional to the eventual complexity of and degree of cortical control over behavior,[32] the period of
subcortical dominance is more prolonged in human infancy than in the
infancy of any other species.

In some respects the behavior of neonates may be studied with greater
facility than the behavior of older infants and children. Experiential backgrounds are more nearly equal, the current environment is more restricted
and easier to control, differential social and interpersonal factors need not
be considered, and behavior is relatively simple and, therefore, more amenable to complete observation, description, and analysis. On the other hand,
since the neonate is unable to verbalize his sensations, perceptions and
feelings, we are dependent upon inferences from behavior for clues about
the subjective content of his experience. This naturally opens the door wide
to anthropomorphic and metaphorical reasoning.

GENERAL APPEARANCE AND PHYSICAL CHARACTERISTICS

The first month of postnatal existence is by far the most dangerous period of life.[74] Reduction of neonatal mortality, particularly in the first few days, has been substantially less over the past four decades than one might have anticipated from the dramatic lowering of infant mortality in general. This discrepancy, however, is not surprising when one considers that the effects of such factors as prematurity, birth injury, difficult labor, initial delay in respiration, congenital malformation, and genically determined susceptibility to stress are primarily reflected in the neonatal death rate. It is true, of course, that the higher incidence of neonatal mortality among non-white groups in the United States[9, 74] suggests that some of these early deaths could be prevented by better prenatal care, by more careful management of labor, and by improved handling of the prematurely born. Nevertheless, even under optimal conditions an irreducible number of severely unfavorable initial predispositions, stemming from genic factors, immaturity, birth trauma and structural deformity will inevitably develop; and one can reasonably expect less benefit to accrue from environmental manipulation in such instances than in the case of infants who succumb at a later age because of malnutrition or disease.

The neonate's general appearance is by no means prepossessing. His head and eyes are disproportionately large and his trunk and limbs disproportionately small in relation to later childhood standards. As a result of "molding" of the skull bones and subcutaneous swelling or hemorrhage (due to pressure contact in passing through the narrow birth canal) his head may be misshapen. Not the least disappointing to an unprepared mother is the red, wrinkled and ill-fitting skin covered with a cheesy substance. Fortunately at this point positive maternal attitudes are facilitated by the secretion of prolactin.

Mean weight at birth is between seven and seven and one-half pounds and mean length is 20 inches. Consistent average differences prevail between various racial and ethnic groups. Male infants are slightly heavier and larger in all bodily dimensions[15]; and first-born infants tend to be smaller at birth than the infants they precede in birth order, although this relationship is reversed in later childhood.[54] Probably because birth weight and size are affected adversely by poor maternal health and nutrition,[19, 31] infants from lower socio economic levels tend to be smaller and lighter at birth.[5, 8, 28]

BEHAVIORAL ORGANIZATION AT BIRTH

The organization of behavior in the neonate is a reflection of organizational changes occurring during the preceding prenatal period (see p. 184).

The distinction between reflex and non-reflex activity (see pp. 207 and 209) which is quite apparent even in fetal behavior and development becomes sharper after birth. Because of the conventional tendency to lump together all fetal and neonatal behavior (reflex and non-reflex) under the ambiguous term "response" (often used interchangeably with "reflex") incalculable conceptual confusion has arisen in the past. This looseness in terminology obscures basic differences in rate, patterning and regulation of development, as well as the salient generalization that motor development as it is generally understood is an outgrowth of non-reflex activity.

Because individuation of reflex activity has almost reached completion, a large number of discrete reflexes may be elicited in the neonate. Individuation of non-reflex activity, of the type of behavior that will eventually be voluntary and cortically controlled, has first begun. It is characterized by much diffuse mass activity and by relatively little and only partially localized specific movements. Hence, until more precise control of these latter movements is attained, much integrated whole behavior on a non-reflex basis cannot be expected; most of the integrated behavior displayed by the neonate consists of coordinated reflexes. Thus, the general picture of neonatal behavioral organization is epitomized by the striking contrast between the highly developed segmental and coordinated reflexes regulated by spinal and subcortical centers and the relatively diffuse, amorphous non-reflex responses that have yet to be brought under efficient cortical control.

Non-Reflex Behavior

Mass Activity. Much of neonatal behavior may be described as an "ungainly amalgamation of movements" or as an "amorphous mass of activity."[33] It occurs at a very rapid rate, making observation and analysis in detail extremely difficult. This type of behavior tends to increase in quantity during the first ten days of life, particularly after initial adjustment to the feeding situation takes place.[33] Most observers attribute it to the absence of the degree of cortical inhibition and control that is necessary both for precise and directed specific movements on a non-reflex level as well as for integration and coordination of such movements into more complex patterns.[33, 57]

In relation to its instigating stimulus (internal or external), mass activity is extremely nonspecific in nature. It consists of highly generalized and largely irrelevant movements.[57, 58] The whole body or large parts of it are simultaneously involved. Head, trunk, hips, arms, legs, hands, feet, toes and fingers are all moving at once to the accompaniment of sucking or smacking movements of the lips or violent crying.[33] This activity is very diffuse, unprecise and amorphous in form, and exaggerated in intensity.[33] Although either internal or external stimuli may release mass activity, the greater part of it seems to be instigated by viscerogenic or humoral excitants, particularly by those originating in or related to gastrointestinal functions. This is evident from the intensification of general motility during bowel evacuation, intestinal disturbance and regurgitation,[33] and from its progressive increase during the interval between feeding.[35] Intense, abrupt, prolonged or noxious stimuli from without also increase mass activity[57]; whereas mild external stimulation (such as provided by clothing or by moderate and continuous illumination or sound) tends to reduce it,[38, 39, 77] possibly by inhibiting viscerogenic excitation.

Full appraisal of the meaning of the apparently random and disorganized nature of mass activity demands consideration of contributing factors (other than lack of cortical control) that help determine its distinguishing properties. First, the extent to which responses are specific or generalized is partly a function of the intensity of stimulation involved[20]; less intense stimuli tend to be associated with more specific movements. Thus, some of the wide spatial dispersion of mass activity must certainly be attributed to the intensity ordinarily characterizing visceral stimulation. Second, since such stimulation tends to be diffusely distributed (and is localized with difficulty even by adults), it is not surprising that (in the absence of compelling reasons to the contrary) the responses thereto should be equally diffuse and irradiated. Third, general bodily activity is undoubtedly facilitated by the general lowering of all response thresholds associated with humoral factors operative during hunger and excitement.

Furthermore, "mass activity and specific movements . . . are not to be rigidly considered as contradictory or as mutually exclusive categories." [33] Reflective of some beginning progress toward individuation, mass activity is not completely disorganized but is characterized by some degree of patterning and by the inclusion of some segmental responses.[20, 57] Although many unrelated responses are also included in the generalized reaction to a particular stimulus, the most relevant response seems to be the most pronounced of all. Even the generalized reduction of response thresholds, resulting from the operation of visceral determinants of drive states, shows some adaptive selectivity. The degree of threshold reduction of a particular response that takes place under conditions of drive corresponds to its position in a hierarchy of potentiality or relevance for satisfying the tissue need determining the drive in question. For example, under conditions of hunger the threshold for eliciting the sucking response is lowered more than the corresponding threshold for kicking. Although this original hierachy of need-reducing responses is subject to modification in accordance with later experience, the fact that it exists at birth suggests that it is genically determined.

Specific Movements. In contrast to the mass activity described above, specific non-reflex behavior "involves a localized or segmental response of the organism, . . . exhibits precision and nicety of movement,"[33] and occurs at a rate slow enough to be observed and analyzed in detail. It includes the following kinds of simple segmental responses: rolling of the trunk; all of the varieties of motion that are possible about any of the joints of the extremities (e.g., extension, flexion, abduction, adduction, rotation); backward, forward, and sideway movement of the head; opening and closing of the eyelids; pursing, licking, and smacking of the lips; sucking; whimpering, sighing and vocalizing.[21, 33] Most of the utterances of the neonate, however, are crying sounds which do not occur alone but as accompaniments of mass activity.[33] In addition, the neonate's behavioral repertoire contains several more complex, specific movements that involve some bilateral, contralateral or intersegmental coordination such as sucking, smiling, pursuit movements of the eyes, a characteristic sleeping posture, and alternate extension and flexion of the legs.[21, 33] Like mass activity, specific movements are also instigated by both internal and external stimuli. According to Irwin, however, "nonamorphous, integrated behavior patterns in [neonates] are infrequent . . . when external stimuli are constant."[33]

Both on the stimulus and response sides, specific behavior in the neonate is not nearly as specific as the name implies.[40, 57, 58] The lack of specificity to which we are alluding here is not variability in locus and occurrence of stimulus-elicited response but rather to *irrelevancy* in stimulus-response connections; for by definition non-reflex behavior is variable in both former respects. Some segmental responses are triggered off by completely irrelevant stimuli; and conversely, a single stimulus may evoke several irrelevant as well as relevant responses. The *sucking response,* for example, may be elicited by pulling the infant's hair or by punching his toes[40]; and leg flexion may be accompanied by sucking and thrashing of the arms when the sole of the foot is stimulated. Nevertheless a specific movement tends to be elicited most reliably by its normally appropriate stimulus. And although other irrelevant movements may be implicated in the segmental response to a particular stimulus, they tend to be less vigorous than the relevant components of the behavior in question.

Reflex Behavior

Reflex behavior shares many of the aforementioned properties of the more specific variety of non-reflex behavior. It too consists of precise, clearly defined and isolatable units of activity that are localized and segmental in nature. The stimulus-response connections, however, appear to be more strongly predetermined by genic factors and are more specific and stereotyped. They are also more invariable, both with respect to the locus and type of response to a particular stimulus and with respect to the elicitation of the response (provided, of course, that the stimulus is adequate). Furthermore, reflex behavior is stimulus-bound in the sense that it can only be initiated by stimulation, never volitionally, and is not ordinarily or completely subject to voluntary inhibition.*

Although individuation of reflex responses is quite far advanced prior to birth, some terminal aspects of the process remain to be completed during the neonatal period. Further shrinkage of reflexogenous zones takes place, and with increasing age there is "progressively less involvement of the organism in the response."[57] Reflex activities in the neonate, however, are not nearly as nonspecific as even the more specific components of non-reflex activity. And far from being substantially complete at this time, individuation of non-reflex behavior is a continuing aspect of motor development, both in the early "phylogenetic" stages dominated by neural maturation and in the later "ontogenetic" stages dominated by practice.

Regional Survey. By way of illustrating the large repertory of reflex behavior in the neonate, the more important and commonly observed reflexes will first be listed and described briefly. Three of these reflexes (plantar, grasp and Moro), which have been the object of particularly extensive investigation and which undergo significant developmental changes during early infancy, will then be described in greater detail.

The following is a summary of reflex responses in the neonate classified according to region of the body[21, 33]: (1) *Eyes:* eyelid closure in response to illumination or a blast of air; pupillary contraction and dilatation in response to change in illumination or in the distance of the object of fixation from the eyes; nystagmus in response to bodily rotation or to cold stimulation in the external auditory meatus; imperfect coordinate movements of the eyes; imperfect convergence of the eyeballs in fixating an approaching object. (2) *Upper respiratory and gastrointestinal tract:* salivation, swallowing, sneezing, coughing, yawning, gagging. (3) *Abdominal and pelvic viscera:* hiccoughing, vomiting, urination and defecation.† (4) *Head and neck:* balancing movements of the head in response to change in bodily position; tonic neck reflexes in the supine position.[26] (5) *Arm and hand:* arm flexion in response to a sudden blow against the hand;

*Some neonatal reflexes, although never brought under voluntary control, are regularly and permanently inhibited some months later by higher neural centers, thus disappearing from the behavioral repertoire of older infants. Reflexes, therefore, are not necessarily fixed or permanent.

†Only the reflex aspects of these activities are referred to here. Both the urethral and anal external sphincters, currently non-functional, are brought under voluntary control during later infancy.

the grasp reflex. (6) *Trunk:* abdominal and cremasteric reflexes (contraction of the recti muscles and retraction of the scrotum respectively in response to tactile stimulation of the lower abdominal wall and of the inner surface of the thigh). (7) *Leg and foot:* knee and ankle jerks in response to tapping of the patellar and Achilles tendons; stepping movements when the neonate is supported under the armpits with the soles of his feet touching a hard surface; the plantar reflex. (8) *Coordinate responses:* creeping and swimming movements of the neonate when lying prone with resistance offered to the soles of his feet; the Moro reflex.

The plantar reflex per se consists of flexion of the big toe when the outer edge of the sole of the foot is stimulated. In neonates and young infants, such stimulation often evokes extension of the big toe and fanning of the other toes (the Babinski reflex) and frequently retraction of the foot, leg and thigh (mass reflex).[52, 57, 60, 66] The relative frequency of the Babinski and plantar reflexes in the neonate, and the age until which the former reflex can be elicited in normal infants, are matters of some dispute. Discrepancies between equally competent observers may be attributed to differences in the type of stimulus employed, to variability in the posture of the toes prior to stimulation, and to differences in the wakefulness of the subjects.[58, 60, 66] It does seem clear, however, that with increasing age both the mass and Babinski reflexes become progressively more infrequent until only the plantar reflex is elicited.[58, 60, 66] Since the Babinski reflex reappears following lesions of the pyramidal tract, and since extensive neural maturation of the cortex takes place during the early period of postnatal life (see p. 85), we may infer that the developmental waning of this reflex is reflective of cortical inhibition.

The grasp or palmar reflex exhibits a developmental history that is very similar to that of the Babinski reflex. Descriptively, in stimulus-response terms, it is homologous to the plantar reflex; the palm and four fingers (but not the thumb) close in response to tactile stimulation. Approximately ten per cent of all neonates can support their own weight by grasping a thin rod in this fashion.[66] Gradually, during the first four to six months of postnatal existence, the grasp reflex is replaced by volitional grasping which is both less invariable and characterized by conspicuous involvement of the thumb.[29] This developmental trend may also be interpreted as an indication of increased cortical control and of inhibition of a subcortically regulated reflex, especially since the grasp reflex may be reactivated after injury to the premotor area of the cortex.

The Moro reflex is still another in this group of subcortically mediated reflexes which are progressively subjected to cortical inhibition. It is a coordinate response, more complex than the grasp or Babinski, consisting of initial bilateral extension of the arms and legs, followed by bowing and return to the middle line of the body. The response is elicited by jarring, loud noises, or by any sudden, unexpected stimulus. The same kind of stimulation, may also evoke the startle reflex, which is more of a restrained flexion response and has a somewhat shorter latency time[46, 53]; but whereas the Moro reflex tends to disappear after four to six months of life, the startle reflex remains indefinitely.[17, 46, 53] Although reminiscent of fear, it is improbable that either the Moro or the startle reflex per se are accompanied by any subjective emotional content; the latency time between stimulus and response is much too short and the organism returns much too instantaneously to its prior motor and visceral state. This does not mean, however, that these reflexes and generalized excitement (or at a later date, fear) are necessarily mutually exclusive. If the eliciting stimulus is sufficiently prolonged or intense, the Moro reflex in the neonate may be followed by all of the bodily signs of excitement including crying[53]; and similarly if the older child perceives the stimulus evoking the startle reflex as threatening, he reacts shortly afterwards with fear.

Subsequent Organizational Trends

Once maximal specificity and discreteness are attained, reflex behavior undergoes relatively little developmental change after the neonatal period. The vast majority of discrete reflexes remain intact throughout the life span. From time to time, of course, depending on particular idiosyncratic experience, conditioning may occur. As already indicated some subcortically regulated reflexes, especially those which are intersegmental (mass reflex, Moro reflex) and which are suggestive of vestigial prehensile (grasp reflex) and locomotor (stepping, swimming and creeping movements) functions, are subjected to cortical inhibition; they are replaced by more segmental or restricted reflexes (plantar, startle), and by voluntary, cortically controlled prehensile and locomotor responses.[53] But except for chronological antecedence and superficial resemblance in the kind of behavior involved, the subcortical reflex stage of these activities bears little relationship to the cortical voluntary stage which follows. The latter is not a functional outgrowth of the former, but merely a later occurring, phenotypically similar activity dependent upon intervening neural maturation.

All other behavioral change generally subsumed under motor development occurs in the area of non-reflex activity which includes both stimulus elicited and voluntary responses. With increasing age such responses become more localized, economical in extent of involvement, and relevant in relation to their eliciting stimuli, but never as invariable or as stereotyped as true reflexes. However, this narrowing down of the range of stimuli that can elicit a particular response and of the range of responses that are made to a particular stimulus cannot be interpreted in strictly quantitative terms. Actually, in the course of learning, many new and originally inadequate stimuli tend to become adequate as a result of conditioning, and many new and different responses are made to familiar stimuli. Hence the restriction that occurs constitutes an increase in the selectivity rather than a decrease in the quantity of stimulus-response connections. It is true that the number of irrelevant connections decreases, but at the same time new learning experiences continually establish new relevancies. And taking place concomitantly or alternately with this process of individuation in the acquisition of new motor skills is the complementary process of integration of individuated activities into new complex patterns.[51]

In interpreting the meaning of "stages" in later motor development, it is important to distinguish between phylogenetic and ontogenetic acquisitions. In the first place, the occurrence and sequence of stages is much more invariable in the phylogenetic group; deviations from a panhuman norm will only be minor in nature except under extremely atypical environmental conditions. Second, whereas incidental learning and practice are important for *both* the inter- and intra-stage changes occurring in ontogenetic traits, they can only account for *intra*-stage changes in phylogenetic traits. Before the organism can go on to a new stage in the development of the latter traits, a higher level of neural organization must first be achieved. Thus, in the development of phylogenetic traits, although lower stages of neural integration are sometimes (but not necessarily) prerequisite for the emergence of higher stages of neural integration, lower stages of *performance* cannot be considered functionally prerequisite for the emergence of higher stages of performance. In other words, the individual could conceivably proceed from one stage of motor development to another solely on the basis of neural maturation, without actually having experienced the performance aspects of the earlier stage. In the genesis of ontogenetic motor traits, on the other hand, discontinuously new (inter-stage) changes in performance are developmental outgrowths of and functionally dependent upon prior levels of performance at the time of their emergence.

MAJOR NEONATAL BEHAVIORAL PATTERNS

Another approach to the behavior of the neonate, apart from analyzing it in terms of its differential organizational elements, is to identify the major functional areas in which his response patterns are distributed. Here our concern is with describing and interpreting those aspects of his behavior that constitute the greater portion of his activity day as a total functioning organism. Four such salient patterns that dominate neonatal behavior are crying, feeding responses, sleeping, and response to pain.

Crying

Crying in the neonate is part of a general pattern of undifferentiated excitement that is aroused by any persistent or intense noxious stimulus. It is the major type of vocal response made by the newborn, and is almost invariably accompanied by mass activity.[33] Observers are unable to distinguish reliably between the cries evoked by such different stimuli as hunger, pain and cold,[11] and show little agreement in identifying "the emotional state" accompanying crying unless they know what the evocative stimuli are.[63] Nevertheless, crying is the most effective response the infant can make in relieving discomfort caused by unsatisfied bodily needs or by noxious stimulation; it is an unlearned adaptive response that summons help from his interpersonal world. At this point it is completely involuntary; but later on as its causal relationship to need reduction is perceived, it is employed deliberately for this purpose.

A stereotyped pattern of pre-crying behavior precedes actual vocalization by several seconds. The forehead wrinkles, the jaws are depressed, the eyes are shut tight, tongue and nose are flattened, the mouth opens and unilateral kicking begins.[4] If these pre-crying cues are recognized and the infant's needs promptly satisfied, it might be possible to forestall both the early involuntary and the later volitional crying.[61] During the first week of life infants cry on the average about two hours a day,[1] but wide individual differences prevail with respect to amount, loudness and intensity of crying.[2] Sound analysis at this time shows that front vowels predominate over the rear vowels and that consonants are infrequent.[36] Hunger accounts for approximately one-third of all crying, the incidence of crying being greatest just prior to feeding; observers have attributed the cause of the remainder equally to wetting and soiling and to unknown factors respectively.[2] Contrary to general belief the crying of one infant in the nursery does not tend to stimulate crying on the part of other infants.[1] Crying ceases when the discomfort which evokes it is removed directly (e.g., by feeding or change of diapers), or when substitutive satisfactions habitually associated with or signalling the immenence of need reduction (e.g., holding by adult) are provided. It increases when parents or other attendants are too busy to identify the cause of discomfort and to remedy it either directly or indirectly.[1, 70]

Feeding Responses

When stimulated in the oral-facial region, the neonate turns toward the stimulus, opens his mouth and begins to suck. Stimulation of the lips is most effective in eliciting this series of responses, other stimuli varying in effectiveness with distance from the lips.[58] Hunger selectively facilitates feeding responses. A fully satiated infant will not respond at all to even the most specific stimulus whereas a hungry infant will respond to remote and totally irrelevant stimuli.[57] The nature of the contact stimulus that initiates sucking is relatively nonspecific. The infant will suck on anything that is soft. It is sheer anthropomorphism, therefore, to attribute to him any initial purposive searching for the breast as such or any foreknowledge of its function. Human mothers place their infants at the breast; but the young of other mammalian species reach this goal through purely trial and error efforts (as would the unaided human infant), and perish if they are unsuccessful. Indicative of the importance of the sucking mechanism for survival is the fact that the pad of fat constituting the sucking cushion is selectively resistive to absorption, remaining intact even after the body as a whole is thoroughly emaciated.[25]

Each infant tends to maintain a characteristic and regular sucking rhythm that is coordinated with breathing and swallowing. Hence, for swallowing to take place it is unnecessary for either breathing or sucking to cease.[57] During sucking the thoracic cavity typically expands, the abdominal cavity contracts,[30] and general motility decrease.[40] With continued exercise of the feeding responses, various signs of inefficiency attributable to initial use tend to disappear. As lip control improves, leaking of milk from the corners of the mouth decreases.[27] The older neonate sucks more vigorously and is less responsive to irrelevant stimuli[57]; and eventually the young infant learns to swallow food without simultaneously swallowing air.

Hunger is an extremely salient experience in the neonate. Strong gastric contractions are probably related to hunger pangs, but are typically induced by humoral factors (low blood sugar, "hunger hormone") rather than by emptiness of the stomach.[59, 73] However, since typical hunger behavior can be induced in a satiated gastrectomized animal by the injection of blood from a starved animal, it seems evident that humoral substances can effect this behavior by *directly* lowering response thresholds as well as by indirectly increasing the amplitude of gastric contractions.* The behavioral response to hunger is three-fold: (a) increased sucking and responsiveness to stimuli inducing sucking[49, 57,] (selective lowering of response threshold); (b) increased mass activity[33, 35, 48, 49] (generalized lowering of all response thresholds); and (c) undifferentiated excitement, including crying.[1, 49] As

*A summary of recent experimental literature dealing with hunger is available.[65] The secretion of adrenalin in response to lowered blood sugar may also play a role in hunger behavior. Subjective aspects of hunger experience obviously cannot be investigated in infants.

previously noted, interpretations of hunger cries as indicative of rage, fear or insecurity are undoubtedly anthropomorphic projections. With increasing age, hunger contractions decrease in frequency[73] and, accordingly, infants on a "self-demand" schedule demand food less frequently.[27, 67, 68] This evidence, plus the fact that neonates on a three-hour feeding schedule are less restless than neonates on a four-hour feeding schedule[48] seems to indicate that a flexible regimen of progressively less frequent feedings is more compatible with the physiological needs of the newborn infant than a fixed regimen. Nevertheless, even in the neonatal period infants appear capable of adapting to a four-hour feeding interval; by the tenth day of this regimen, the typically sharp increase in activity and crying between the third and fourth hours tends to diminish. This is in marked contrast to the abrupt rise in activity that occurs during the same interval when infants habituated to a three-hour schedule are suddenly shifted to a four-hour regimen.[48]

Sleeping

Although the neonate is judged to be asleep about twenty hours of the day,[58] the state of sleep is peculiarly difficult to define. Even more so than in the adult, sleeping and waking states are not dichotomous and must be described in terms of *relative* degrees of irritability and motility. The most precise physiological criterion of sleep is an abrupt increase in the minimal intensity of electrical stimulation necessary to elicit a given response. This criterion is highly correlated with *amount* of measurable motility.[57] On the basis of extent and duration of reactivity to different stimuli, Wagner has designated various postural, motility and response patterns as indicative of seven different gradations of depth of sleep[75]; according to Pratt, however, these patterns are not consistently related to thresholds of irritability and degree of motility.[57] In actual practice, closure of the eyelids is the most commonly employed criterion of sleep and is probably satisfactory enough for most purposes.

Despite the fact that the neonate spends the preponderant portion of his day in sleep, individual periods of sleep are relatively short, approximating three hours in duration.[58] Motility is greatest just before nursing and least immediately afterwards, but the greatest incidence of sleep, according to the judgment of observers, occurs midway between two nursing periods.[33] With increasing age, the sleeping and waking states tend to become more dichotomous, and the total amount of time spent in sleep decreases; most of this decrease occurs during the first three months of life.[13] In addition, individual periods of sleep and wakefulness become longer in the older infant.

Response to Pain

Sensitivity to painful stimuli increases rapidly during the first four days of life. This is shown by the marked decrease in the minimal intensity of stimuli (e.g., number and depth of penetration of needle jabs) necessary to evoke a response.[66] Sensitivity is greater in the cephalic than in the caudal region of the body [65, 66] and is appreciably diminished when the infant is asleep or nursing.[57] From the available evidence, therefore, there is little reason to doubt that painful experience associated with noxious and intense stimulation (typically of visceral origin) is a major cause of excitement, mass activity, and crying in the neonate. Nevertheless, from the fact that operations such as circumcision are performed at one week of age without anesthesia and do not precipitate surgical shock, we can infer that the experience of pain is less intense in the neonate than in older individuals.

Various theoretical considerations also lead to the same conclusion. First, because of immaturity of the cerebral cortex and paucity of apperceptive background, the cortical threshold for pain perception is probably high; much pain sensation is undoubtedly experienced at a crude thalamic level. Second, pain experience is not enhanced by anticipatory anxiety or by emotional reaction to the threatening implications of pain, since it is unlikely that the neonate is sufficiently mature to perceive threat; and even if he were able to do so, he has no functional concept of self to which a perception of threat could be referred. Finally, because he is asleep most of the day and nursing a good part of the remainder, his threshold for pain is typically much higher than its lower physiological limit.

SPECIAL SENSES

Except for late occurring anatomical and physiological changes in the visual apparatus, the sensory *capacities* of the neonate are little different from those of the viable fetus (see pp. 179-181). The main difference inheres in the greater degree of exposure to adequate stimuli in postnatal life.

The investigation of sensory experience in the newborn is fraught with numerous methodological difficulties. Foremost among these is the unavailability of verbal reports of subjective experience and the necessity for relying completely on overt responses to stimuli. It is evident, therefore, that the neonate's failure to respond to a given stimulus may be less indicative of sensory incapacity than of the inappropriateness of the experimental arrangements for peculiarities in his sensory, response, and attentional capacities. Interpretation of overt responses is further complicated by the simultaneous occurrence of mass activity and specific movements induced by internal stimuli.

Vision[57]

The readiness with which the neonate responds to illumination leaves little doubt about his visual sensitivity. Intense stimuli of short duration elicit pupillary contraction, eyelid closure, the Moro and startle reflexes, the ocular-neck reflex and changes in circulatory and respiratory responses.[57] *Continuous* illumination, on the other hand, tends to inhibit mass activity, the degree of inhibition increasing (within limits) with the intensity of stimulation; minimal intensities of continuous illumination cause much *more* general motility than do either darkness or moderate intensities.[39, 77] Following a period of dark adaptation, less intense stimuli are required to release visual reflexes.

It is one thing, however, to show that light can release various subcortically regulated responses in the neonate, and quite another to define the properties of his visual experience. Does he visually apprehend discrete objects, how clear are the images he "sees," does he experience different colors? At the very best, answers to such questions can only be tentative and inferential. Presumptive evidence of object fixation comes from coordinate "pursuit" movements of the eyes in response to a moving stimulus, from concurrent immobility of the eyes as movement of a roving stimulus is temporarily halted, and from convergence of the eyes upon a bright light.[10, 16] Such responses, although imperfect, are found in the first week of life,[10, 16] and undergo rapid improvement, especially with respect to the correction of strabismus.[65, 66] It is not known whether the lens can accommodate to distance, but the presence of retinal hemorrhages, and of physiological myopia (attributable to the relatively long diameter of the eyeball) probably precludes the occurrence of clear retinar images.[57] Depth perception is also improbable since binocular coordination is not yet good enough for fusion of separate images. The most unsettled issue of all has to do with color vision. However, the ability of the neonate to pursue a spot of color moving against the background of another color equated for brightness[16] provides presumptive but not definite evidence of color discrimination.

Hearing

The neonate is more responsive than the full-term intrauterine fetus to auditory stimulation. His auditory acuity, however, is still relatively poor, probably because of the presence of amniotic fluid or mucous in the middle ear, external auditory meatus and eustachian tubes. Paralleling the effect of visual stimulation, when auditory stimuli are of short duration, an increase in their intensity tends to release more overt responses such as eyelid reflexes, general bodily movement, crying, changes in respiration and circulation, and the Moro or startle reflex[57, 58, 71]; continuous auditory stimuli, on the other hand, especially when more intense, inhibit general motility.[77] The crying infant is least responsive to auditory stimulation and the awake but inactive infant is most responsive.[71] "With successive repetitions of . . . auditory stimuli the gross muscular components decline in extent of involvement . . . There is no indubitable evidence that neonates possess either differential responses to varying frequencies of vibration [pitch discrimination] or the possibility of acquiring them during the neonatal period."[57]

Taste and Smell

Compared to adult standards, gustatory and olfactory sensitivity in the neonate is minimal despite exposure to more adequate stimuli than in fetal life.[58] The neonate reacts positively (i.e., by continued sucking) to sweet solutions, whereas salt, bitter and sour solutions induce cessation of sucking, negative facial grimaces and irregularities in respiration and circulation.[40, 58] It is doubtful whether differentiation of the four taste qualities exists as such apart from this distinction between positive and negative reactions. Taste discrimination tends to improve during the neonatal period[58] and to be sharper in a moderately full than in a hungry infant.[40]

Because of methodological difficulties, evidence regarding olfactory sensitivity in the neonate is less definitive. In the absence of a calibrated sucking indicator, only grossly negative reactions to odorous substances (e.g., crying, squirming, withdrawal, grimaces, changes in respiration and circulation) are unequivocally indicative of responsiveness. Such reactions can only be elicited by ammonia and acetic acid[58]; but since these substances, also irritate the nasal mucosa, it is entirely possible that their behavioral effects are wholly or partly produced by the activation of pain receptors. A greater percentage of response to stimulation is reported for a variety of odorous responses than for pure air, but the responses to different odors are indistinguishable from each other and from those made to pure air.[23] Some observers report positive mimetic responses, licking, and sucking to some volatile oils (anise) and negative mimetic responses to others (oil of chenopodium). In general, however, evidence of olfactory sensitivity in the newborn is neither impressive nor definitive, and indicates that at the very best a gross type of discrimination between noxious and pleasant stimuli is made.

Thermal Sensitivity[57]

Neonates respond to thermal stimuli that deviate markedly from physiological zero, i.e., from the temperature of the body surface that is being stimulated. Both the upper and lower thresholds beyond which thermal stimuli first become adequate are relatively distant from physiological zero but vary considerably for different parts of the body.[57, 58] Although threshold values also vary widely from one individual to another, they tend to be quite stable within a particular individual[40]. Generally speaking the neonate is relatively insensitive to small differences within the range of adequate thermal stimuli, but here too there is much variability among individuals. The major response to thermal stimulation consists of movements of the body part which is stimulated, but other more generalized movements may also occur as well as changes in respiration and circulation. When the oral cavity is stimulated thermally, the sucking rhythm becomes irregular.[40] Warm stimuli lead to adient responses whereas cold stimuli more usually result in withdrawal.

Ability to maintain a constant body temperature is relatively deficient in the neonate. He is less able than the older child or adult to adjust to extremes of environmental temperature, especially to heat. Since increased motility is one way of adjusting to cold, body activity tends to be inversely related to room temperature. Because of inefficient temperature control and a relatively large body surface for his weight (both of which factors promote heat loss) the neonate's basal metabolic rate is high.

Other Sense Modalities

Cutaneous, proprioceptive and vestibular sensitivity in the neonate is little different from that previously described for the fetus (see pp. 179-180). By virtue of early structural and physiological development and frequent exercise in intrauterine life, these modalities are highly developed at birth. As already indicated in the discussion of mass activity, hunger and crying, visceral stimulation becomes an important determinant of behavior when gastrointestinal and excretory systems become physiologically autonomous subsequent to birth.

EMOTIONS

The distinguishing characteristic of emotion is a special kind of intense subjective experience consisting of strong feeling tones. This experience is usually accompanied by some perceptual awareness of the instigating stimulus and is followed by a generalized lowering of response thresholds and by visceral and somatic reactions. Afferent reports of the latter responses, in turn, reinforce, enhance, perpetuate and modify the original subjective state. But precisely because emotion is primarily a subjective experience, evidence of its existence in the neonate can at best be presumptive. Nevertheless, it is a fair inference that the evident excitement (violent mass activity and crying) exhibited by infants when they are aroused by intense, noxious and prolonged stimuli is analagous in intensity of feeling tones to the emotional states of older individuals. It is equally clear, however, that this excitement is completely undifferentiated with respect to quality of feeling tones (fear, rage, anxiety), instigating agents, and mode of expression.

Watson's theory of three innate emotions, rage, fear, and love[76] (aroused respectively by restraint, loud noises or loss of support, and stroking of the skin) is only remembered today as a vivid illustration of anthropomorphic interpretation of infant behavior. Sherman demonstrated conclusively that observers show little agreement in identifying specific emotional patterns in neonates unless they are aware of the instigating stimuli.[62, 63] Dropping an infant only rarely causes crying,[34, 72] and loud noises do not evoke any consistent or distinctive pattern of response.[72] The Moro and startle reflexes are frequently released by loud noises but can also be evoked by other abrupt and intense stimuli; furthermore, they are elicited and dissipated much too instantaneously to have any emotional content. Restraint also fails to evoke any consistent type of response.[72] If it is rough it precipitates undifferentiated excitement as does any intense stimulus[22]; if it is mild (such as the effect of clothing) it has a quieting effect.[22, 38] And finally, what Watson called "love" can be most parsimoniously interpreted as quiescence or physiological satiety. It is extremely doubtful whether the initial feeling of pleasantness associated with this latter state is sufficiently intense to qualify as the emotional reciprocal of excitement, as Sherman has asserted.[64] The writer, therefore, agrees with Bridges[12] that excitement is the only emotional state found in the neonate.

That patterned emotions should be absent in the neonate is entirely consistent with theoretical considerations pertaining to ego development. First, it is highly improbable that differential emotional responses could be made to threat, frustration, or protection against threat in the absence of sufficient cognitive sophistication to perceive and understand the significance of these conditions that ordinarily determine the distinctive quality of feeling tones. The neonate's undeveloped cortex and limited apperceptive background do not improve matters here. Second, unless a functional concept of self is available to which perceptions of threat and frustration can be referred, such perceptions lack the salient implications necessary to arouse strong feeling tones. Obviously, if a neonate does not have a sense of identity he cannot be frightened by threat even if it were possible for him to perceive and appreciate its significance.

It is interesting to note that in young infants slightly past the neonatal period, the intensity of the visceral components of emotional response (as measured by the psychogalvanic reflex) is not highly correlated with the vigorousness of the motor and vocal components.[42] Since this correlation is much improved in preschool children,[43] it appears that integration of the different aspects of emotional expression is dependent in part upon maturation (substrate growth and incidental experience). This evidence also suggests that the degree of excitement inferred from the violence of the neonate's crying and bodily activity is often exaggerated since it is not necessarily accompanied by the extent of visceral involvement necessary for reinforcing and prolonging emotional reactions.[42]

LEARNING

Since ability to learn is pre-eminently a cortically regulated function (see p. 183) we cannot anticipate impressive evidence of learning in the neonate. However, if learning is broadly defined as more or less permanent modification of behavior caused by repeated exposure to similar experience, the newborn individual undoubtedly manifests it to a limited extent. This indicates that either some learning can occur on a subcortical level[47] or that the neonate's cortex is not completely lacking in function. Two kinds of learning in the neonate—simple association and temporal conditioning —have already been alluded to in the discussion of crying (p. 213) and feeding (p. 215). The infant who ceases to cry when held, even before he is fed, has learned to associate preliminary contact with the feeding situation. Being held, therefore, serves as a signal of imminent need reduction and may even result in some anticipatory satisfaction. In due time, by virtue of repeated association with actual reduction of hunger, contact may also acquire some substitutive satisfaction value in its own right apart from heralding the approach of food. Temporal conditioning is shown by neonates who gradually learn to "expect" food every three hours after nine days of habituation to such a schedule.[48] The adaptation of neonates to a hour-hour schedule, on the other hand (see p. 215) involves the learning of tolerance for an initially frustrating situation (as a result of habituation) as well as temporal conditioning.

The occurrence of another type of learning in neonates, namely, classical conditioning, is much more controversial. Through the usual method of successive concomitant presentations with adequate (unconditioned) stimuli, the following responses have been successfully conditioned in the first ten days of life to originally inadequate stimuli: (a) leg withdrawal (electric shock as unconditioned stimulus) to a buzzer, pure tone, tactual vibration, and light[78, 79]; (b) eyelid closure (bright light as unconditioned stimulus) to tactile vibration of the foot[78]; and (c) sucking (nipple in mouth as unconditioned stimulus) to a buzzer.[47] In the last mentioned study, after conditioning was established the buzzer alone also induced less crying and general activity. Such typical conditioning phenomena as experimental extinction and spontaneous recovery have also been demonstrated in neonates.[78, 79]

For a number of reasons these findings must be regarded as equivocal and lacking in definitiveness. First, in the case of one group of studies,[78] particularly in view of overlapping between experimental and control groups, the number of subjects employed was inadequate. Second, Marquis' findings regarding conditioned sucking[47] failed to be unequivocally confirmed by Wenger.[78] Third, although Wickens and Wickens[79] were able to condition leg withdrawal to a buzzer by first pairing the latter originally inadequate stimulus repeatedly with electric shock, members of a control group who received the shocks *alone* (unpaired with the buzzer) during the training period also responded positively to the buzzer alone when tested for conditioning. These workers suggest that after repeated elicitation of leg withdrawal by shock, the response becomes "sensitized"; the muscles involved "are in a state of readiness and may be tripped off [by] almost *any* [extraneous] stimulation," and not necessarily by the particular inadequate stimulus repeatedly associated with the adequate stimulus in the past. The two explanations (conditioning and sensitization), however, are not necessarily mutually exclusive. The fact that a buzzer previously unintroduced in the training period, and operating as a purely extraneous stimulus, may release a "sensitized" withdrawal response does not necessarily rule out the possibility that under other circumstances, when the buzzer is appropriately paired with the unconditioned stimulus during the training period, it may later operate as a specific conditioned stimulus in eliciting the response in question.* Finally, in comparison with older age groups the conditioned response in neonates is difficult to establish (requires an inordinate number of pairings), is relatively unstable (easily extinguished), and cannot be established in all individuals.[79]

The status of the conditioned sucking response is further complicated by the fact that it is somewhat more analogous to instrumental conditioning or to associative learning in the holding-feeding situation than to classical conditioning. That is, the sucking response made to the conditioned stimulus (buzzer, holding) is not merely an acquired response to an originally inadequate stimulus but also leads to need reduction as well. Hence, the buzzer, in addition to being a conditioned stimulus for sucking, may also (by signalling imminent need reduction) provide some anticipatory satisfaction, or may even acquire some substitutive satisfaction value of its

*This interpretation is strengthened by the finding in Marquis' study of conditioned sucking that her control subjects who *did* experience the buzzer during the training period, but *not* concomitantly with the nipple, failed to develop a conditioned sucking response to the buzzer alone.[47]

own. It is also understandable that in as much as satiety ordinarily raises the threshold of the sucking response in relation to its unconditioned stimulus, it also does so in relation to a conditioned stimulus. Thus in infants six weeks to four months old, Kantrow found that the conditioned sucking response is rarely elicitable immediately after nursing.[45]

ORIGIN AND NATURE OF DRIVES

Implicit in the foregoing discussion of such neonatal behavior patterns as response to pain, hunger, and noxious stimuli, has been the notion that shortly *after* birth both specific movements and general bodily activity fluctuate periodically because of the operation of drive states. We have also assumed (see table 1, p. 65) that because of various universally distributed genic predispositions, physiological processes, and environmental conditions, all individuals may *potentially* develop certain drives but do not necessarily acquire all of the drives that they potentially could. Thus, some of these psychobiological drives develop in all human beings. Others are found in almost all cultures or in all cultures with the exception of certain groups or individuals. And finally some drives are unique to particular cultures (psychosocial) or to particular individuals within a culture (idiosyncratic). In any event, our position has been that no drives are innate or completely independent of experience (p. 46).

If we adopt the view that all drives are developmental products acquired through experiential interaction between internal and external factors, two main kinds of questions may be raised at this point: (a) What is the nature of drive as a condition inducing transitory fluctuations in behavior? What determines drives? Are drives stimuli or states? (b) How do drives change as a function of increasing age? How are new drives learned and how are existing drives differentiated with respect to goal objects and goal-seeking activities? Do new drives develop autonomously or are they derived from pre-existing drives? Many different approaches have been taken to these problems and many different kinds of explanatory models have been proposed.* But in our present state of knowledge there can be no empirical testing of alternative formulations geared at this level of abstraction. Since a definitive discussion of motivational theory would be out of place in this volume, only a single point of view consistent with the general theoretical orientation adopted thus far will be presented. Hence, both the choice of terminology and of constructs will be admittedly and unavoidably arbitrary. This section is intended as a general introduction to

*References [7, 18, 44] which discuss various theoretical issues and formulations display little general agreement in this area of inquiry.

the problem of drive in *developmental* psychology. Other more specific issues will be raised in later chapters.

The Nature of Drive

Stimulus or State? Drive is an inferred neurobehavioral state that accounts for transitory fluctuations in the organism's propensity for responding to stimulation with its available repertoire of reaction tendencies. We have already observed that sucking and head orientation can be elicited more readily in the hungry than in the satiated neonate and that the hungry infant is also more prone to thrash about, cry, and manifest general excitement. This momentary difference in reactivity may be attributed to the existence of a state of drive (hunger) consisting of a partly generalized but nonetheless selective lowering of response and perceptual thresholds in accordance with their relevance to or capacity for terminating the drive state that is operative. What we wish to emphasize at this point is that drive is *not* a persistent afferent or humoral *stimulus* but a *multiply determined neurobehavioral state coextensive with the lowering of response thresholds.* It is necessary, in other words, to distinguish between drive as a transitory state of altered reactivity and the various determinants (including stimuli) that induce it. Drive is always a summated (net) resultant of the threshold changing effects (both raising and lowering) of its numerous determinants.

This distinction between drive states and drive determinants is theoretically useful for many reasons: (a) it allows for the multiple determination of a drive and for variability in its occurrence; (b) it helps explain why particular responses may fluctuate from time to time in the ease with which they may be evoked despite constancy in the strength of their underlying reaction tendencies; (c) it enables us to separate more unambiguously the role of stimuli in eliciting responses through neural excitation from their role as drive determinants in altering behavioral reactivity; and most important of all from a developmental standpoint (d), it clarifies the issue of whether "primary" drives* are innate and inevitable.

The multiple determination of drives, even of hunger, is evident from the moment of birth. Although the effects of internal physiological determinants (humoral factors, gastric contraction) are undoubtedly crucial in the generation of the hunger drive, it also makes a difference whether the neonate is quiescent or excited, whether he is asleep or awake, whether he is subjected to auditory stimulation that is mild and continuous or

*In this section the term *primary* refers to drives in which the more salient drive determinants and responses (and the relationships between them), not the drive states themselves, are innate (i.e., relatively independent of experience, predetermined by genic factors).

intense and of short duration. Other determinants also become operative shortly afterwards. As a result of temporal conditioning, of habituation to frustration, of exposure to associated stimuli that herald the imminence of need reduction, of memory for various antecedent-consequence relationships, a background of experience is accumulated that gradually makes cognitive interpretation of drive determinants possible. Thus in the older neonate, before the drive determining (threshold changing) effects of humoral and situational factors, of emotional excitement, of memories and anticipations of need satisfaction are summated to constitute a drive state of hunger, they are first filtered through an interpretive screen which, to be sure, is relatively primitive at this stage of development. In the total need satisfaction sequence some (preparatory) internal and external stimuli play a sensitizing role in lowering response thresholds whereas other (consummatory) stimuli actually elicit the responses in question. The intensity of the drive tends to be proportionate to the net psychological salience of the determinants that induce it. In the case of primary drives, however, this does not always correspond to the strength of the visceral or humoral stimulus, since the drive determining effects of the latter may be counteracted by other factors raising response thresholds and, in any event, are always subject to cognitive interpretation.

Innate and Inevitable? Whether stimuli per se are regarded as drives or merely as determinants of drive states also has marked relevance for the issue of whether or not primary drives are innate and inevitable. According to the conception of drive as stimulus, primary drives are innate by definition since the organism need only be exposed to designated internal or external stimuli to which he responds in invariable and predetermined ways for corresponding drives invariably to be operative; they are inherent in the possession of a stomach or bladder wall, of pain receptors, and of a circulatory system that transmits humoral substances. Also, if drives are considered to be innate they must necessarily be inevitable in the sense that they must be generated sooner or later.*

According to the "state" conception of drive, on the other hand, primary drives are never innate but may or may not be inevitable. If humoral conditions or afferent stimulation are only regarded as *partial* determinants

*Even more incompatible with the notion of drive as an acquired, multiply determined neurobehavioral state is the psychoanalytic doctrine of instinctual or libidinal drives. These drives are conceptualized as basically independent of not only experiential determinants but of physiological stimuli as well. Moreover, instead of becoming operative periodically when instigated by appropriate and adequate determinants, they are conceived of as enjoying more or less permanent substantive form which is prestructured in advance with respect to locus, object choice, mode of expression, and sequential appearance.

of a summated drive state that is complexly determined by all kinds of external, visceral, situational, and cognitive factors, the generation of drives must always be considered acquired or dependent upon particular past and present experience rather than innate or invariable. The inevitability of a primary drive, on the other hand, depends upon how essential it is for the maintenance of life and upon the extent to which it is cortically and environmentally regulated. Since external (e.g., cultural) inhibitory conditions may sometimes be more potent than internal (hormonal) facilitating conditions, primary drives are not necessarily inevitable. The sex drive, for example, which is not essential for the maintenance of life and which in human beings is largely regulated by situational and experiential determinants may fail to develop in all post-pubescent individuals. In this case it is more parsimonious to speak of agenesis than to invoke the concept of repression.

Drives and Emotions. Although by by means synonymous, emotions and drives are closely related. In the first place, as we have already seen in the case of pain and hunger, many of the determinants of drive also (but not necessarily) tend to generate emotion; but even if drives and emotions are not simultaneously determined by the same factors, subjective repercussions of drive states and of their associated responses and outcomes (need satisfaction or denial) are often productive of emotion. In either case the subjective and visceral components of emotion, and frequently the need or desire to prolong or terminate its affective qualities, constitute additional drive determinants influencing the continuation or cessation of drive states. Second, even when emotions are aroused independently of any connection with drives, one of their main consequences is to lower response thresholds in selectively generalized fashion. Thus, although the determinants of drives and emotions do not overlap completely, if emotion is aroused, whether in association with drive determinants or effects or entirely apart from drives, it itself invariably serves as a drive determinant.

Developmental Aspects of Drive

Developmental aspects of drive refer both to the ways in which various aspects of primary drives become more finely differentiated with age and to the acquisition of essentially new drives. In the latter case, however, since learning refers to a more or less permanent change in responsiveness and drive is only an induced and transitory neurobehavioral state, it would be more precise to speak of an acquired capacity for generating drives that certain basically new drive determinants develop, that is, the capacity for lowering the thresholds of particular patterns of responses and perceptions. It is not really meaningful to speak of drives per se as being learned. The learned aspects of drive include (a) drive determinants (acquired needs, goal objects), (b) surrogate determinants (memories, anticipations) derived from conscious repercussions of drive states and their consequences, and (c) drive responses. The differentiation of drives also occurs through such learnings, generally in a social context, but requires no basic or qualitative change in the kind of drive involved.

In the sense that the new drive determinants and drive responses (and the relationships between them) of later acquired and more experientially determined drives are predominantly learned rather than innate, it is not objectionable to refer to the latter as *secondary*. The term does become objectionable, however, when, as is frequently the case, it connotes inferior potency, dependability or importance for the direction of behavior. Actually it is common knowledge that secondary drives are frequently more insistent than primary drives.

Derived or Autonomous? An even more seriously objectionable connotation of secondary drives is the widely held belief[24] that they are characteristically and necessarily derived from primary drives. Libidinal drive theorists recognize only a single source of drive from which all other drives are derived, whereas behavioristically oriented proponents of the traditional view of primary drives recognize a limited but irreducible number of original drives. It is conceivable, of course, that under certain conditions analagous to conditioning, secondary drives may sometimes be derived from primary drives. Through simple contiguity of presentation with an adequate drive determinant (or more indirectly by virtue of symbolical equivalence), an originally neutral cue may gradually acquire drive determining power. Similarly one drive determinant may sometimes replace another if the two are experienced as alternatives and one is habitually rewarded whereas the other is systematically followed by punishment* However, even if a given drive should originate on a derived basis in the remote past, its connection with the "original" drive rarely enjoys any functional significance in the present[3]; during the interim the new determinant acquires drive instigating powers in its own right that are functionally independent of its previous association with the primary determinant. It also seems more parsimonious (in the absence of any self-evident demonstration of the derived nature of most secondary drives) to assume that although new drives may occasionally arise on a derived basis, they more typically tend to emerge independently of any connection with prior drives.

In opposition to the traditional concept of secondary drives as derived

*This mechanism is not at all similar to the Freudian concept of *sublimation* which presupposes the direct and automatic transformation of blocked, socially unacceptable drive energy (sex) into a more acceptable form, rather than the gradual investment of a neutral cue with drive determining power as a result of differentially rewarding conditioning experience.

entities, and making increasingly greater headway in recent years, is the view that new drives constantly emerge in the course of new experience, in the further development of personality, and in the acquisition of new values and capacities[3, 41, 50, 56] According to this view, the exercise of learned capacities and the pursuit of satisfying activities connected therewith are, generally speaking, wholly autonomous needs in their own right from the very beginning of their availability.* Thus, while the child matures in perceptual, motor, cognitive, emotional and social abilities, and in the experience of his own individuality, he simultaneously develops needs to explore and manipulate the environment, to master and understand it, to feel secure and adequate, respected and desired, to obtain status and belongingness in groups, to achieve self-actualization, to give and receive affection. In explaining why these goals and activities are pursued it need only be assumed that they are usually found satisfying. Attempts to show that they are derived from primary drives by way of conditioning are tortuous and far-fetched in most natural settings and in conflict with commonsense observation.

Positive or Negative Origins. The proposition that secondary drives are largely autonomous in origin and inherent in the satisfying exercise of capacities also conflicts with the notion implicit in "derived" formulations of such drives (stimulus or libidinal) that motivations arise in predominantly negative contexts. Since primary drives are most commonly represented as instigated by conditions of physiological disequilibrium (hunger, thirst, sex) or by painful, noxious or threatening stimuli from without, it necessarily follows that the motivated behavior that they and their hypothesized secondary *derivatives* induce is regarded as directed principally toward the restoration of homeostatis or toward escape from distressing noxious stimulation. Such negatively oriented drives, both primary and secondary, undoubtedly exist and influence behavior in important ways. However, if secondary drives can arise autonomously from emerging capacities it seems extremely far-fetched to ascribe most exploratory, investigatory, affectional or social activity to the need for avoidance of or escape from unpleasant stimuli (hunger, pain, fear, anxiety) rather than to the quest for positive satisfactions associated with such activity. The libidinal theory of drive follows a similar tack in denying that most human activities are pursued because they are found interesting, satisfying or self-fulfilling; it differs,

*Some so-called secondary drives (e.g., sensory, activity) are really primary since they arise from sensory and motor capacities that are unlearned, i.e., mostly dependent on genically regulated growth. They have been widely regarded as secondary, however, because of the restricted concept of primary drives as only embracing viscerogenic, humoral and noxious external stimuli.

however, in insisting that secondary drives come into being solely as culturally sanctioned compensations for libidinal drives that are outlawed or frustrated by the social environment. The assertion that the main function of these drives is to provide vicarious gratification for the denial of sex drives enjoys no more self-evident validity than the view that the mainsprings of human activity are to be found in the avoidance of pain, threat and distress.

Nevertheless, just because capacities can *potentially* provide their own motivation does not mean that they always or necessarily do so. In the first place it is not the possession of capacities per se that is motivating but the anticipation of satisfactions following their exercise. Ordinarily this presupposes a history of previous satisfying use of the capacity in question. Unfortunately, however, we cannot always depend on individuals to exercise all of their capacities spontaneously. They may be unaware of their existence, preoccupied with other competing activities, or discouraged by negative pressures in the environment. They may also be indisposed to attempt their use because of fear of failure or injury, because of reluctance to expend the necessary effort, or because they find it preferable or more expedient not to do so. It is also conceivable that after having put a given capacity to use, the individual finds it either unsatisfying or lacking in sufficient challenge to warrant further exercise. In any event it is difficult to understand why suitable forms of external stimulation or encouragement should be considered incompatible with endogenous motivation unless the latter is regarded as sacrosanct. Second, where the exercise of such mature capacities as responsibility and self-control is involved it is unrealistic to expect spontaneous use habitually in the absence of appropriate social demands and expectations. Not only are there hedonistic advantages in suppressing the exercise of such capacities, but pending complete indoctrination the individual ordinarily learns to govern their expression in accordance with how much is expected of him.

REFERENCES

1. Aldrich, C. A., Sung, C., and Knop, C.: The crying of newly born babies. I. The community phase. *J. Pediat. 26*: 313-326, 1945.
2. ——, ——, and ——: *Ibid.* II. The individual phase. *J. Pediat. 27*: 89-96, 1945.
3. Allport, G. F.: *Personality, a Psychological Interpretation.* New York, Holt, 1937.
4. Ames, L. B.: Motor correlates of infant crying. *J. Genet. Psychol. 59*: 239-247, 1941.
5. Anderson, A.: Some observations on birth weights. *Med. Off. 89*: 15-17, 1953.
6. Ausubel, D. P.: *Ego Development and the Personality Disorders.* New York, Grune and Stratton, 1952.

7. ——: Introduction to a threshold concept of primary drives. *J. Gen. Psychol.* *56*: 209-229, 1956.

8. Bakwin, H., and Bakwin, R. M.: External dimensions of the newborn. *Am. J. Dis. Child. 48*: 1234-1236, 1934.

9. Baumgartner, L., et al.: Weight in relation to fetal and newborn mortality; influence of sex and color. *Pediat. 6*: 329-342, 1950.

10. Beasly, W. C.: Visual pursuit in 109 white and 142 Negro newborn infants. *Child Develop. 4*: 106-120, 1933.

11. Blanton, M. G.: Behavior of the human infant during the first thirty days of life. *Psychol. Rev. 24*: 456-483, 1917.

12. Bridges, K. M. B.: Emotional development in early infancy. *Child Develop. 3*: 324-341, 1932.

13. Bühler, C.: *The First Year of Life*. New York, John Day, 1930.

14. Bundesen, H. N.: Natal day deaths: the long neglected field of infant mortality. *J.A.M.A., 153*: 466-473, 1953.

15. Cates, H. A., and Goodwin, J. C.: The twelve-day-old baby. *Hum. Biol. 8*: 433-450, 1936.

16. Chase, W. P.: Color vision in infants. *J. Exper. Psychol. 20*: 203-222, 1937.

17. Clarke, F. M.: A developmental study of the bodily reaction of infants to an auditory startle stimulus. *J. Genet. Psychol. 55*: 415-427, 1939.

18. *Current Theory and Research in Motivation*. Symposium. Lincoln, University of Nebraska Press, 1953.

19. Dean, R. F. A.: The effect of undernutrition on the size of the baby at birth and on the ability of the mother to lactate. *Proc. Roy. Soc. Med. 43*: 273-274, 1950.

20. Delman, L.: The order of participation of limbs in responses to tactical stimulation of the newborn infant. *Child Develop. 6*: 98-109, 1935.

21. Dennis, W.: A description and classification of the responses of the newborn infant. *Psychol. Bull. 31*: 5-22, 1934.

22. ——: Infant reaction to restraint: an evaluation of Watson's theory. *Tr. N. Y. Acad. Sci. 2*: 202-217, 1940.

23. Disher, D. R.: The reactions of newborn infants to chemical stimuli administered nasally. *Ohio State Univ. Stud. Contr. Psychol.* No. 12, 1934, pp. 1-52.

24. Dollard, J., and Miller, N. E.: *Personality and Psychotherapy*. New York, Mc-Graw-Hill, 1950.

25. Feldman, W.: *The Principles of Ante-natal and Post-natal Child Physiology, Pure and Applied*. New York, Longmans, 1920.

26. Gesell, A.: The ontogenesis of infant behavior. *In* L. Carmichael, Ed. *Manual of Child Psychology*, ed. 2. New York, Wiley, 1954, pp. 335-373.

27. ——, and Ilg, F. L. *Feeding Behavior of Infants: a Pediatric Approach to the Mental Hygiene of Early Life*. Philadelphia, Lippincott, 1937.

28. Gibson, J. R., and McKeown, T. Observations on all births (23,970) in Birmingham 1947. V. Birth weight related to economic circumstances of parents. *Brit. J. Soc. Med. 5*: 259-264, 1951.

29. Halverson, H. M.: Studies of the grasping responses of early infancy (I, II, III). *J. Genet. Psychol. 51*: 371-449, 1937.

30. ——: Mechanisms of early infant feeding. *J. Genet. Psychol. 64*: 185-223, 1944.

31. Hewitt, D., and Stewart, A.: The Oxford child health survey: A study of the influence of social and genetic factors on infant weight. *Hum. Biol. 24*: 309-319, 1952.

32. Hofstaetter, P. R.: The rate of maturation and the cephalization coefficient: a hypothesis. *J. Psychol. 31*: 271-280, 1951.
33. Irwin, O. C.: The amount and nature of activities of newborn infants under constant external stimulating conditions during the first ten days of life. *Genet. Psychol. Monogr. 8*: 1-92, 1930.
34. ———: Infant responses to vertical movements. *Child Develop. 3*: 167-169, 1932.
35. ———: The distribution of the amount of motility in young infants between two nursing periods. *J. Comp. Psychol. 14*: 415-428, 1932.
36. ———, and Curry, T.: Vowel elements in the crying vocalization of infants under ten days of age. *Child Develop. 12*: 99-109, 1941.
37. ———, and Weiss, A. P.: A note on mass activity in newborn infants. *J. Genet. Psychol. 38*: 20-30, 1930.
38. ———, and Weiss, L. A.: The effect of clothing on the general and vocal activity of newborn infants. *Univ. Iowa Stud. Child Welf. 9*: 149-162, 1934.
39. ———, and ———: The effect of darkness on the activity of newborn infants. *Univ. Iowa Stud. Child Welf. 9*: 163-175, 1934.
40. Jensen, K.: Differential reactions to taste and temperature stimuli in newborn infants. *Genet. Psychol. Monogr. 12*: 361-479, 1932.
41. Jersild, A. T.: *Child Psychology*, ed. 4. New York, Prentice-Hall, 1954.
42. Jones, H. E.: The galvanic skin reflex in infancy. *Child Develop. 1*: 106-110, 1930.
43. ———: The galvanic skin reflex as related to overt emotional expression. *Am. J. Psychol. 47*: 241-251, 1935.
44. Jones, M. R., Ed.: *Nebraska Symposium on Motivation, 1954*. Lincoln, University of Nebraska Press, 1954.
45. Kantrow, R. W.: An investigation of conditioned feeding responses and concomitant adaptive behavior in young infants. *Univ. Iowa Stud. Child Welf. 13*: No. 3, 1937.
46. Landis, C., and Hunt, W. A.: *The Startle Pattern*. New York, Rinehart, 1939.
47. Marquis, D. P.: Can conditioned responses be established in the newborn infant? *J. Genet. Psychol. 39*: 479-492, 1931.
48. ———: Learning in the neonate: the modification of behavior under three feeding schedules. *J. Exper. Psychol. 29*: 263-282, 1941.
49. ———: A study of frustration in newborn infants. *J. Exper. Psychol. 32*: 123-138, 1943.
50. Maslow, A. H.: Higher needs and personality. *Dialectica 5*: 257-265, 1951.
51. McGraw, M. B.: *Growth: a Study of Johnny and Jimmy*. New York, Appleton-Century, 1935.
52. ———: Development of the plantar response in healthy infants. *Am. J. Dis. Child. 54*: 240-251, 1937.
53. ———: *The Neuromuscular Maturation of the Human Infant*. New York, Columbia University Press, 1943.
54. Meredith, H. V.: Birth order and body size. II. Neonatal and childhood materials. *Am. J. Phys. Anthrop. 8*: 195-224, 1950.
55. Morgan, C. T., and Stellar, E.: *Physiological Psychology*, ed. 2. New York, McGraw-Hill, 1950.
56. Murphy, G.: *Personality: a Biosocial Approach to Origins and Structure*. New York, Harper, 1947.
57. Pratt, K. C.: The neonate. *In* L. Carmichael, Ed., *Manual of Child Psychology*, ed. 2. New York, Wiley, 1954, pp. 215-291.

58. ——, Nelson, A. K., and Sun, K. H. The behavior of the newborn infant. *Ohio State Univ. Contr. Psychol.* No. 10, 1930.

59. Richards, T. W.: The importance of hunger in the bodily activity of the neonate. *Psych. Bull. 33*: 817-835, 1936.

60. ——, and Irwin, O. C.: Plantar responses of infants and young children: an examination of the literature and reports of new experiments. *Univ. Iowa. Stud. Welf. 2*: No. 1, 1934.

61. Rosenzweig, S.: Babies are taught to cry: a hypothesis. *Ment. Hygiene 38*: 81-84, 1954.

62. Sherman, M.: The differentiation of emotional responses in infants. I. Judgments of emotional responses from motion picture views and from actual observation. *J. Comp. Psychol. 7*: 265-284, 1927.

63. ——: The differentiation of emotional responses in infants. II. The ability of observers to judge the emotional characteristics of the crying of infants and the voice of an adult. *J. Comp. Psychol. 7*: 335-351, 1927.

64. ——: The differentiation of emotional responses in infants. III. A proposed theory of the development of emotional responses in infants. *J. Comp. Psychol. 8*: 385-394, 1928.

65. ——, and Sherman, I. C.: Sensori-motor responses in infants. *J. Comp. Psychol. 5*: 53-68, 1925.

66. ——, ——, and Flory, C.: Infant behavior. *Comp. Psychol. Monogr. 12*: No. 4, 1936.

67. Simsarian, F. P., and McLendon, P. A.: Feeding behavior of an infant during the first twelve weeks of life on a self-demand schedule. *J. Pediat. 20*: 93-103, 1942.

68. ——, and ——: Further records of the self-demand schedule in infant feeding. *J. Pediat. 27*: 109-114, 1945.

69. Smith, J. M.: The relative brightness values of three hues for newborn infants. *Univ. Iowa Stud. Child Welf. 12*: No. 1, 1936.

70. Stewart, A. H., et al.: Excessive infant crying (colic) in relation to parent behavior. *Am. J. Psychiat. 110*: 687-694, 1954.

71. Stubbs, E. M.: The effect of the factors of duration, intensity, and pitch of sound stimuli on the responses of newborn infants. *Univ. Iowa Stud. Child Welf. 9*: No. 4, 1934.

72. Taylor, J. H.: Innate emotional responses in infants. *Ohio State Univ. Stud. Contr. Psychol. 12*: 69-81, 1934.

73. Taylor, R.: Hunger in the infant. *Am. J. Dis. Child. 14*: 233-257, 1917.

74. The hazardous first months of life. *Stat. Bull. Metropolitan Life Ins. Co. 33*: 1-4, 1952.

75. Wagner, I. F.: The establishment of a criterion of depth of sleep in the newborn infant. *J. Genet. Psychol. 51*: 17-59, 1937.

76. Watson, J. B.: *Psychology from the Standpoint of a Behaviorist.* Philadelphia, Lippincott, 1919.

77. Weiss, L. A.: Differential variations in the amount of activity of newborn infants under continuous light and sound stimulation. *Univ. Iowa Stud. Child Welf. 9*: 1-74, 1934.

78. Wenger, M. A.: An investigation of conditioned responses in human infants. *Univ. Iowa Stud. Child Welf. 12*: 9-90, 1936.

79. Wickens, D. D., and Wickens, C.: A study of conditioning in the neonate. *J. Exper. Psychol. 26*: 94-102, 1940.

CHAPTER 8

Infant Care: Problems, Issues and
Implications for Development

ALTHOUGH THIS BOOK is not primarily concerned with practical aspects of child rearing, two important considerations demand that we give serious attention to the theoretical implications of practices and problems of infant care. First, there is the matter of the immediate, normative and cumulative impact of such practices on the child's behavior and development. The stimulation and interpersonal contacts involved in everyday infant care determine a large part of his daily activity and furnish much of the raw experience that contributes to his cognitive, motor, emotional and social development. This experience also leads to the imposition of cultural controls on physiological rhythms and to initial social patterning (socialization) of drives and emotions. In their day-to-day effects on the child's behavior, we may reasonably anticipate that certain practices will be more in accord with his developmental needs and capacities and more conducive to his well-being and contentment than others. Second, there is the issue of whether or not particular practices have *enduring* and *differential* consequences for the structuring of personality. Do these practices, irrespective of specific differences, merely provide a common pool of raw experience that determines in essentially similar ways for most children the sequential landmarks of ego development or do the specific differences have lasting and differential effects that are crucial in accounting for inter-cultural and idiosyncratic differences in personality development?

DOGMA, FADS AND FASHIONS

Still another reason for this chapter is the need for subjecting to critical scrutiny various dogmatic notions and fads about the nature of desirable infant care and about the personality implications of such care. In this field there is perhaps more ex-cathedra dogma than in any other branch of medicine, psychiatry or psychology. It may be referred to as dogma because it consists largely of empirically unvalidated assertions and opinions dispensed with the authority and confidence befitting indisputably proven scientific fact. Actually much of what passes as pediatric or psychological science in the area of infant care has no scientific basis whatsoever. This, of course, does not apply to the diagnosis and treatment of children's

233

diseases and to much genuine knowledge of nutrition and immunization, but to such issues as breast or bottle feeding, self-demand or scheduled feeding, early or late weaning, "rooming-in," mothering, thumbsucking, and the personality consequences of these practices.

Although the violent shifts that have taken place regarding acceptable practices of infant care bear little relationship to scientific evidence, they have followed rather closely "changing theories of education and personality formation."[74] Thus, "one has the feeling that social science theory . . . often moves in cycles like fads or persists like customs, for historical reasons, rather than progressing firmly in one direction because certain truths have been established by objective tests and can be built upon by the exercise of reason."[50] For example:

> The past two decades have witnessed a revolution in child training practices in America which has been tremendous in its scope and far-reaching in its effects. From an era where the mother was taught that the child must have his physical wants cared for and then be left alone, must be fed on a rigid schedule, must learn to cry it out, must be toilet trained early and must not be spoiled by attention, we have come to a time when exactly the opposite advice is advocated. Today the mother is advised to feed the baby when he's hungry, to delay toilet training until he is ready for it, to see that the baby gets a reasonable amount of cuddling and mothering, to let the baby initiate the weaning process. And just as a mother of 1930 was taught that the popular doctrine of 1930 would produce the right kind of child, so the mother of today is assured that if she weans and toilet trains and cuddles in the approved fashion, her child will have a well-adjusted personality."[69]

At this point it might be instructive to inquire "how these ideas can change over a period of three decades to represent polar views and yet be promulgated as the findings of science."[74] Several possible explanations may be offered tentatively. First, because infant care constitutes an important and emotionally loaded segment of any cultural value system, parents and other persons concerned with policy decisions in these matters have a strong need to believe that prevailing practices are the best possible practices. Hence, despite their frequent origin in arbitrary custom or historical accident, they tend to be defended very positively and with much force and heat, as if derived from self-evidently valid rational grounds. Second, many notions of what constitutes desirable infant care are derived deductively from such theoretical systems of personality development and psychotherapy as psychoanalysis and client-centered therapy; and since the adherents of these systems tend to conceive of them as bodies of scientifically established truths rather than as bodies of interrelated hypotheses and opinions, they naturally tend to accept such derived propositions as axiomatically true. Third, even when efforts are made to test hypotheses empirically, the difficulties of isolating single variables and measuring subjective aspects of personality and behavior in infants and young children (see pp. 132 and 273) are so formidable that present prospects of obtaining rigorous and definitive data are discouraging indeed.

Lastly, the requirements and traditions of the clinical situation tend to invest opinions about infant care with an authority and positiveness that they do not intrinsically deserve. Mothers consult a pediatrician when practical and frequently urgent problems of infant management arise. At such times they are not in the mood for hearing opinions or hypotheses. Since they want to be told the *correct* thing to do, they naturally desire to believe that authoritative knowledge is available in all phases of infant care. They are reassured in this belief by extrapolating from other areas within the pediatrician's realm of competency. Surely if the latter knows what to do when the baby has mumps or meningitis, he must certainly be able to answer their simple questions about "crying it out" and thumb-sucking. The pediatrician in turn is under the pressure of having to render a decision calling for action despite the lack of definitive evidence in support of his opinion. To admit the uncertainty he feels, however, would not only completely upset mothers' conceptions of the nature and status of pediatric knowledge, but would probably undermine whatever confidence they have in him, destroy whatever value his advice might have, and inevitably drive them to another physician who can give them the certainty they crave. Thus, at first, the pediatrician is literally coerced into voicing greater confidence and positiveness in giving his opinions about infant care than he realizes is warranted by the facts. With the passage of time, however, as he enacts this role habitually, he tends to forget that the mantle of clinical authority was originally assumed for reasons of therapeutic necessity and comes to believe that it actually reflects the state of knowledge in the field.

Nevertheless, the prospects for a genuine science of infant care are not quite as bleak as have been pictured. Despite changing fads and fashions, much real progress has been achieved. A growing body of empirically grounded principles in child development is presently available from which credible and testable prospositions about infant care may be derived; and even if not directly testable, some such propositions can be accepted tentatively on the basis of face validity or concordance with related data. Other encouraging signs include a tendency away from sentimental and romantic formulations of maternal role,[69] a more cautious and less dogmatic tone in theoretical discussions of infant care,[74] and greater recognition of the need for empirical evidence.

PRACTICAL ISSUES AND PROBLEMS

The modern body of infant care doctrine is exemplified most explicitly in a movement known as the "Cornelian corner" (after Cornelia, the mother of the Gracchi). Founded in 1942 by a group of psychoanalytically oriented psychiatrists and pediatricians, it was expressly dedicated to the relief of unnecessary developmental tensions associated with the feeding, toilet training and discipline of children.[45] It criticized prevailing methods as rigid, excessively concerned with the mother's convenience, and in conflict with the emotional needs of both mother and child. The theoretical cornerstones of the new doctrine are self-regulation, maximal permissiveness, and effusive mothering (from the very moment of birth) in handling the infant. After a brief review of some of the specific issues, we shall attempt a more general appraisal of this point of view (see pp. 258-259).

Rooming-In

The rooming-in plan was devised to enable mothers so inclined to care for their infants during the course of their stay in the lying-in hospital. Its practical advantages over the segregated hospital nursery plan are many. It capitalizes on the initial, hormonally facilitated development of maternal attitudes in the nursing contact situation and relieves the anxiety that mothers often feel about their remotely separated babies. Mothers have an opportunity to adapt gradually to the physiological and developmental characteristics of the newborn, to learn how to interpret and manage his crying, and to practice various routines of infant care when abundant sources of help and advice are available. Thus, as a result of not being suddenly confronted at home with full responsibility for the infant—while feeling confused, apprehensive and inadequate—they tend to be calmer, more relaxed, and more confident in performing their maternal functions. The infant in turn benefits from this situation since tense, erratic, flustered and insecure handling has been shown to increase his crying.[18, 70] The rooming-in plan also brings the father into earlier and closer contact with his child and encourages him to assume a more active and responsible role in its care. He learns first-hand some of the problems and anxieties associated with infant care and (in company with siblings) becomes accustomed early to the fact that henceforth much of the mother's attention will necessarily be focused on the neonate. A final practical advantage is the elimination of epidemics of neonatal diarrhea which sometimes sweep through hospital nurseries with devastating results.

Desirable as these advantages of rooming-in are, there is no reason to believe that when the plan is *not* followed, infants either undergo serious deprivation or suffer lasting personality damage.* Furthermore, it is obvious that this plan is inadvisable when the mother is physically exhausted after prolonged labor or operative delivery, or when she is excessively anxious, tense, immature or ambivalent about her maternal role. In the latter instances, rooming-in increases anxiety and conflict about motherhood and gets both mother and neonate started on the wrong foot.

Breast or Bottle Feeding

No issue of infant care has been debated more persistently or heatedly on the basis of less definitive evidence than the long-standing belief among many pediatricians that "breast feeding is inevitably more advantageous to the child than artificial feeding."[59] The nutritional and immunological advantages of mother's milk are indisputable, and at first glance seem to leave little room for argument. Compared to cow's milk it is richer in most vitamins,† iron and copper, cannot become bacterially contaminated, is less allergenic for human infants, and contains antibodies that are protective against human disease.[26] Most of these advantages, however, are no longer very significant in the light of modern methods of milk handling, the routine use of vitamin supplements, commonly employed practices of immunization against children's diseases, and the availability of "canned" breast milk and synthetic milk substitutes for allergic infants. Thus, bottle fed infants today tend to survive about as well as breast fed infants[16] and to weigh as much or more at the end of the first and second years of life[16, 19, 29]; they also tend less frequently to be hungry and underfed. Finally, there is little unequivocal evidence that they are significantly inferior in terms of general health, resistance to infection, and rate of mental and physical development. Most studies reporting differences in these respects have failed to utilize representative samples of children or to hold constant such crucial variables as socioeconomic status.

Even more controversial are the alleged psychological advantages of breast feeding. Evidence that behavior problems arise more frequently among artificially fed children cannot be interpreted on a cause-and-effect basis because of inadequate control of other relevant variables.[50] Thus in studies holding occupational and social class status constant, no significant relationships are found between type of infant feeding, on the one hand, and later personality traits, adjustment, and oral symptom formation, on

*²The claims that close postnatal contact between mother and infant is necessary to replace the disrupted chemical union formerly provided by the placenta, to alleviate the neonate's overwhelming feelings of anxiety, and to establish his emotional security[57] will be considered under the issue of *mothering* (p. 255).

†This is true for raw cow's milk and even more so when pasteurized or boiled.

the other.[61, 62] When length of breast feeding (in months) is correlated with later qualities of personality and adjustment, significant relationships are either absent[51, 73] or are positive for some durations of breast feeding and negative for others.[50]

It seems fair to conclude, therefore, that although breast feeding may possibly enhance maternal attitudes and constitute an emotionally more satisfying experience to the mother and an *immediately* more gratifying experience to the infant than bottle feeding, available evidence does not support the notion that the personality development of the artificially fed infant is adversely affected by his "unnatural" manner of obtaining his nourishment. It also seems more credible to suppose that if any enduring effects on personality were to result from the feeding situation, they would reflect the attitudes underlying breast or bottle feeding rather than the use of either practice per se* Since is is highly questionable, however, whether young infants can perceive subtleties of maternal attitude, they may only respond to the overtly satisfying or frustrating properties of practices that have implications for immediate behavior but not for later personality structure.

Weaning

According to Freudian doctrine,[20] late and gradual weaning is desirable for future personality development because the infant supposedly has an innate and insatiable need for suckling. Conversely, early and abrupt weaning is said to frustrate and perpetuate (through fixation) this craving, thereby giving rise to a sadistic and pessimistic personality. On a priori grounds, however, no compelling reasons exist for believing that the infant has any innate or insatiable need for obtaining his nourishment from any *particular* external source. Furthermore, hypotheses derived from psychoanalytic conceptions of weaning are not confirmed by studies that relate age and gradualness of weaning to later personality traits, incidence of maladjustment, and oral symptom formation in children and adults.[61, 62, 73]

It would be difficult, of course, to deny that weaning is an unpleasant and possibly traumatic experience, or to dispute the wisdom of conducting it as gradually as possible. The enforced relinquishment of a canalized method of obtaining relief from hunger and of the associated satisfactions of contact and affection is bound to have *immediate* frustrating effects on behavior. It is also conceivable that if weaning occurs in the general context of the infant's ego devaluation (decrease in parental subservience, increase in parental training demands), as it does in many cultures, it con-

*In as much as the incidence and length of breast feeding vary tremendously in accordance with cultural norms, social class membership, family tradition and child rearing ideology, it is unwarranted to assume that the choice and prolonged duration of breast feeding are necessarily indicative of positive maternal attitudes (and vice versa).

tributes to the discontinuous alteration in biosocial status that precipitates this *normative* phase of ego development.

Lasting *differential* effects of weaning on personality development, however, such as would give rise to idiosyncratic personality differences, are another matter. Their occurrence probably depends on whether the attitudinal orientation underlying the practice is representative of a generalized and characteristic parent attitude (e.g., rejection, over-solicitude) and on whether the child is mature enough to perceive the latter. It would seem, therefore, as some evidence indicates, that weaning experiences would be more likely to have lasting personality repercussions in the older than in the younger infant.[77] These effects, however, would not be reflective of the earliness or lateness of terminating breast feeding per se (or of the manner in which it is terminated) but only of the extent to which these factors are characteristic of broader dimensions of parent behavior.

Sucking and Thumbsucking*

We have already considered sucking as a neonatal *response* to tactile stimulation of the lip region which is selectively facilitated (on an unlearned basis) by a state of hunger. The question may now be raised whether sucking is a drive determinant as well as a drive response. Do infants have a need or desire to suck per se (i.e., not merely as a means of obtaining nourishment) in the same sense that they have a need or desire for food? Because of the frequency and universality of non-nutritional sucking, most observers are in agreement that an affirmative answer to this question is warranted. The controversial aspect of the problem has to do with whether or not the need is innate or acquired.

According to the Freudian view the need to suck exists innately by definition. As a central component of libidinal drive characterizing the "oral stage" of psychosexual development it is allegedly prestructured in advance. From our analysis of the nature of primary drives, however (see pp. 223-226), it follows that unless needs (drive determinants) have a demonstrably physiological basis, it is theoretically more parsimonious to conceive of them as acquired rather than as innate.† It is true, of course,

*Since this volume is primarily concerned with theoretical issues and problems of normal development, behavioral disorders will not be considered as such but only insofar as they have implications for the understanding of normative developmental processes. Management of behavior problems will receive no attention whatsoever.

†Ribble[56, 57] has attempted to provide such a physiological basis for a sucking need by asserting that exercise of innate oral drive is necessary and must be encouraged in order to foster both normal functioning of vegetative bodily systems and normal neuromuscular and language development. However, neither convincing theoretical nor empirical reasons exist for believing that sucking per se is physiologically necessary or could *not* be dispensed with completely if it were desirable and feasible to do so.

that inherent in every capacity is a potential need to put it to use; but this need remains potential until it is actualized by satisfying exercise. In the case of sucking, since the response is habitually associated with reduction of hunger, it tends to become gratifying and desired in its own right irrespective of whether it leads to actual relief of the physiological basis of the hunger state.[12]

What little empirical evidence there is also tends to support the conception of sucking as a derived rather than as an innate drive. Breast-fed neonates (who are required to suck more than bottle- or cup-fed babies to obtain their nourishment and who, therefore, do more sucking in a rewarding context) develop "a stronger sucking reflex than either of the other two groups."[12] The cup-fed infants also show no greater evidence of frustration or of spontaneous mouthing in the first ten days of life as one might reasonably expect if the sucking drive were innate.[12] Furthermore, infants who are weaned to the cup *after* two or more weeks of sucking experience, tend to exhibit more signs of weaning frustration and show a suggestively greater tendency toward thumbsucking at two and one-half years of age than do earlier weaned infants who have less opportunity to develop a derived sucking drive.[60]

Once the need to suck per se is established as a result of sufficient satisfying exercise, deprivation of opportunity to do so in the course of ordinary feeding experience leads to non-nutritional finger- or thumbsucking. This latter type of sucking, therefore, tends to increase if larger holes are made in the infant's nipple or if he is switched to cup or spoon feeding relatively soon after a derived need for sucking is established.[40, 41] For similar reasons children who do little sucking during regular feeding tend to do more thumbsucking (both as infants and during later childhood) than do children who have ample opportunity to suck at mealtime[58, 77]; and commensurate with the greater opportunities available for nutritional sucking experience, thumbsucking occurs relatively infrequently among children in primitive societies[50] and less frequently in lower- than in middle-class children.[9]

From the foregoing it is undeniable that a positive relationship prevails between oral deprivation and fingersucking. Nevertheless, the fact that the latter practice also occurs in children who are seldom if ever orally deprived demonstrates unequivocally that other determinants must also be operative. Most children, even satisfied breast-fed infants in our own and primitive societies who are nursed on demand, suck their thumbs at one time or another.[3, 13, 66] Since marked individual differences in amount of thumbsucking still appear in infants when both original degree of reinforcement of the sucking response and subsequent extent of frustration are held constant,[12, 60] it seems reasonable to infer that children possess genically determined predispositions to develop needs of varying strength for feeding satisfaction (e.g., enjoyment of food, eating). If a child develops an exceedingly strong need to suck on this basis it is conceivable that even nutritional sucking on demand will not completely satisfy him; and conversely if the corresponding need is relatively weak he may only rarely resort to finger sucking regardless of the degree of oral deprivation to which he is subjected.

Because of its ready accessibility, thumbsucking (like masturbation) must also be regarded as a nonspecific form of compensatory gratification for frustrations of *any* origin. Perhaps for this reason Negro middle-class children do as much finger sucking as white middle-class children despite the fact that they undergo less oral deprivation. Lastly, on the basis of temperamental and experiential differences, thumbsucking may become the preferred and characteristic technique of adjusting to nonspecific frustrations in some children and only an occasional or adjunctive adjustive technique in others.

Complete assessment of oral behavior during infancy must also take account of the sensory functions of lips, mouth and tongue in exploring the shape, consistency and temperature of newly encountered objects. Although the tendency to use the mouth in a sensory capacity probably stems in part from its prominence in the all-important feeding activities and satisfactions of infancy, it is reasonable to suppose that this form of oral activity eventually becomes functionally autonomous of its origins.

Biting and chewing become part of the repertoire of oral activity slightly before the first tooth emerges. Chewing first appears in the sixth month of life, becomes partially efficient (for ground foods) at ten months and more completely efficient (for unground foods) at 18 months.[7] It is understandable, of course that biting may become an outlet for expressing angry or hostile feelings. Except for crude metaphor, however, no more logical grounds exist for postulating the presence of an innate "oral hostility" drive on the basis of the cutting action of the teeth than for relating an "oral receptive" drive to the inward flow of milk during sucking.

Self-Demand Feeding Schedules

Several consistent findings have emerged thus far from studies of the practice of feeding young infants as much and as frequently as they desire.[66, 68] In all instances the children gain weight satisfactorily and otherwise do well nutritionally. Initially they take more feedings and spend more time nursing than do infants fed on a regular schedule. Gradually, however, despite considerable diurnal variability in total caloric intake, the number of daily feedings tends to decrease and approach a consistent pattern for the individual child.

On practical grounds this method enjoys certain obvious advantages over the rigid practice of feeding infants only at arbitrarily designated intervals. It not only takes account of individual differences among children but also allows for diurnal fluctuations in a given child. Thus it avoids much unnecessary hunger and crying that result from ignoring these elementary considerations. On the other hand, it also presents certain practical difficulties to many mothers and has some serious disadvantages. In the first place, parents are frequently unable to distinguish hunger cries from those of vague or unknown origin. Hence, if they use crying as the principal criterion for nursing there is always danger of over-feeding, particularly in bottle-fed babies. Second, the unpredictability of self-demand feeding tends to disrupt the household, interfere with the mother's other duties and opportunities for rest and recreation, and to generate anxiety in mothers who are compulsive or disorganized about their housework. Lastly, a minority of self-demand babies continue to demand night feedings until two or three years of age and concomitantly become sleeping problems. For these reasons a definite schedule is frequently superior to self-demand feeding provided that the interval between feedings is adjusted to the individual child and that the parent is somewhat flexible about diurnal fluctuations in frequency and amount of feedings.

Claims regarding the developmental and personality benefits of self-demand feeding rest on less solid ground. Evidence that one year old infants raised on this regimen exceed test norms on gross visuomanual coordination[36] is not definitive because of inadequate sampling and control of other variables. The widespread belief that these children grow up to be more secure and less neurotic in their personality make-up is not supported by studies measuring their personality traits, general adjustment and oral symptom formation at ages five and six.[62] On logical grounds also, there is reason to question the assertion that scheduled feeding involves excessive frustration for young infants or gives rise to feelings of rejection. Most children learn to adapt very well to a regular feeding schedule; and by the time they become sufficiently mature to perceive and respond to the attitudinal undertones of parental practices, most of them in our culture are on three meals a day, irrespective of the feeding practice on which they are reared. In any event, even if parent attitudes were perceived as such, it hardly seems likely that a *single* practice would be determinative of feelings of rejection.

Somewhat more credible (although unprovable) are the less extreme claims that the infant on self-demand feedings perceives his social environment as more dependable, benevolent and deferential to his needs,[39] and in the light of these perceptions is better able to tolerate frustration and occasional delay in the gratification of his desires. Also, although he does become habituated to expect compliance with rather than ignoring of his expressed demands for nursing and attention, he does *not* learn that he has to be importunately demanding in order to obtain routine satisfaction of his needs or that the attention he receives is totally unrelated to his appeals for same.

Self-Selected Diets

When young children from post-weaning to preschool age are permitted freely to select their own diets from a wide choice of nutritious foods, the results are just as satisfactory from a health and nutritional standpoint as when infants determine by themselves the quantity and frequency of their feedings. Their spontaneous choices also conform to accepted principles of nutrition in terms of total caloric intake, minimal requirements of vitamins and minerals,* and appropriate redistribution of caloric balance in accordance with age changes in energy output and tissue growth. At first, selections tend to be widely and seemingly randomly distributed, but definite individual preferences soon appear, often involving highly unorthodox choices and combinations of foods. Both prolonged sprees on a single food and unpredictable fluctuations in preference are common. Although diets are frequently unbalanced on a diurnal basis, nutritional balance is achieved over longer intervals of time. In general the data indicate that in spite of individual preferences based on appetitie (taste, smell, consistency), responsiveness to cues of physiological need is a sufficiently salient determinant of spontaneous food choices to make self-selection of diet nutritionally trustworthy.

Self-selection of diet is practically advantageous in that it minimizes a common cause of feeding problems derived from preconceived and arbitrary parental notions regarding amounts, kinds, and combinations of foods required for good health. On the other hand, it tends to be rather expensive when used for a single child and requires considerable knowledge of nutrition, patience, and self-confidence on the part of the mother. It should also be appreciated that after a while, as a consequence of the cumulative inroads of appetite, canalization and enculturation, the child loses his ability to select foods in accordance with his physiological needs. The juvenile diabetic, for example, shows no aversion toward candies and sweets.

*Not only do signs of vitamin deficiency fail to occur among such children, but pre-existing deficiency conditions such as rickets are spontaneously corrected[11]

From a theoretical standpoint, however, the most dangerous implications of these findings arise from the attempt to use them as scientific justification for a program of unbridled permissiveness in child care. If the child can successfully choose his own diet, the argument runs, then he must certainly know what is best for him in all areas of growth. He should, therefore, be permitted to self-select everything—his clothes, toys, curriculum, discipline, etc. Obviously, these conclusions do not follow logically from their premises. Because the individual is sensitive in early childhood to internal cues of physiological need, we cannot conclude that he is similarly sensitive to cues reflective of psychological and other developmental needs; even in the areas of nutrition, self-selection is an unreliable criterion of genuine need in older children. It is also unwarranted to infer from these findings that only endogenous and spontaneously expressed needs are indicative of the child's genuine developmental requirements and that environmentally derived needs are authoritarian in spirit and inevitably fated to thwart the actualization of his developmental potentialities. Actually, unless one assumes that the direction of development is primarily determined from within, endogenously derived needs constitute only a small fraction of the individual's total repertoire of needs. To believe otherwise would require that we deny the crucial role of cultural factors and interpersonal relations in the genesis and patterning of needs.

Feeding Problems*

Serious feeding problems constitute the most important single kind of difficulty encountered in the routine aspects of child care.[33, 59] They are most prominent during infancy and early childhood[33] since situations associated with eating are psychologically more salient for both parent and child at this time than during later childhood. The parent is primarily concerned with providing a nutritionally adequate diet, whereas the child is naturally more concerned with such matters as appetite and palatability. Because of the importance she attaches to nutritional issues, the mother is more disposed to make concessions to achieve her ends in this area than perhaps in any other area of infant care. Hence, the child's resistiveness and self-assertiveness with regard to eating tend to be relatively rewarding and to afford him the most promising means of obtaining some control over her. Another reason for the frequency of feeding problems is that quite apart from matters of nutrition and satisfaction of appetite activities con-

*Feeding problems naturally vary in type and severity. Customarily, however, they refer to prolonged resistiveness on the part of the child to eating those items and quantities of food deemed nutritionally adequate by the parent, accompanied by such emotionally toned parental reactions as coaxing, nagging, badgering, anxiety and irritation.

nected with eating represent the most important occasions for the communication of feelings and attitudes germane to the parent-child relationship.* They symbolize the respective roles of parent and child and thus serve as an admirable index of the quality of interaction between them.

Feeding difficulties, therefore, may either originate within the feeding situation per se or may be symptomatic of a more generally disturbed parent-child relationship. The first category of problem is found frequently in sickly, allergic, or unusually finicky children. It also tends to arise when the parent exaggerates the danger of malnutrition and starvation, fails to appreciate the existence of individual differences and of phasic and diurnal fluctuations in nutritional needs, entertains fixed and narrow notions about the kinds, order and combinations of foods that may properly be eaten, and is unrealistically overdemanding about table manners. Such excessively rigid beliefs and standards on the part of the parent lead inevitably to nagging, badgering and regimentation, to which the child reacts in turn with resistive and assertive behavior of his own, thereby setting up a vicious cycle.

Somewhat more serious in prognosis is the second category of feeding problems that is not indigenous to the feeding situation as such. Here food merely provides a frequently available occasion and battle-ground for the expression of such unfavorable parent attitudes as rejection, hostility and oversolicitude.† These generalized attitudes give rise to the same kind of coercive, inflexible behavior as do rigid notions about nutrition, but are obviously less correctable by educational measures. In the older infant and preschool child who is capable of perceiving the attitudinal implications of parent behavior, feeding activities also provide a major outlet for the expression of reactive hostility and aggression and an unusually successful opportunity for obtaining attention and controlling parents.

The consequences of protracted feeding problems for later development are potentially serious. First, they may extend into and spoil other aspects of the parent-child relationship; or if originating in a generally unsatisfactory parent-child relationship they may easily worsen it. Second, food tends to become a source of repugnance, hostility and friction instead of an occasion for pleasure. Lastly, if the child refuses to eat adequate quantities of nutritious foods because of conflict and unpleasantness associated with eating he may develop such deficiency conditions as nutritional anemia.[54]

*As already pointed out, the child's ability to perceive the attitudinal substrate of parent behavior probably requires more cognitive maturity than is present in early infancy.

†See p. 365 for a discussion of the source of these attitudes.[54]

Table Manners and Self-Help in Eating. Closely related to feeding problems are issues growing out of table manners and self-help in eating. Conformity to the standards of the culture in eating behavior is one of the earliest and most stringent demands that parents impose upon children; but because of the importance attached to such conformity, the expectations of parents in this regard are often unrealistic, thereby generating a long-standing source of friction between them and their children.

The proper use of eating utensils is a complex skill, the attainment of which requires considerable practice as well as neuromuscular maturation. For example, efficient use of the cup for drinking purposes is not required until the child is fifteen months old.[23] Ability to use the spoon develops in the second year of life, but finger feeding both coexists and persists long thereafter. However, parents somehow expect these kinds of abilities to be acquired without providing the child with adequate opportunity for performing such tasks by himself and learning from his mistakes. To be sure, their impatience in these matters is aggravated by the messy consequences of spilling and by the child's frequent insistence on trying his hand before he is ready[32]

Various normative stages in ego development are mirrored in the child's acquisition of table manners and self-help in eating (see pp. 284-300). Between two and one-half and three years of age, in accordance with his grandiose and regal concept of self, he is imperious at the table, resistive to parental demands regarding self-help, and obstreperously demanding of attention.[24] With continued ego devaluation, resistiveness about self-help may be replaced by a belligerent and over-confident insistence on doing everything by himself.

Problems in these areas may obviously be minimized by not setting premature and unrealistic expectations. This does not mean that a laissez-faire approach is indicated. Of course, if the parent makes no demands and sets no limits whatsoever the possibility of conflict is automatically precluded—but at the expense of socialization and ego maturation. And to the argument that table manners after all are merely arbitrary products of culture that enjoy no intrinsic validity, there is the self-evident reply that most customs are arbitrary but nonetheless essential for the perpetuation of culture.

Sleep and Sleeping Problems

In addition to the age changes in sleep already described (p. 215), a gradual reduction occurs in the number of day-time naps taken by infants and young children. The early morning and late afternoon naps drop out first, coalescing with night-time sleep. Afterwards, the late morning nap is given up, leaving just the afternoon nap which is still present in 95 per cent of children at two and one-half years of age. At this age, two-thirds of the children sleep through the night without interruption.[59]

As in the case of self-demand feeding schedules, wide individual differences are noted from one child to another in the amount of sleep required when the principle of self-regulation is followed.[55] Considerable diurnal fluctuation also occurs for a given child, but individual consistency over a longer period of time is the rule. Lost sleep tends to be made up gradually over the course of a few days rather than just on the day immediately following the loss. In the older child self-demand is a less trustworthy criterion of actual sleep requirements since many children are willing to forego sleep for play, entertainment and excitement. For practical reasons also it is desirable that the child's waking hours do not coincide with the time that his parents are normally asleep.

In delineating sleeping problems it is important to exclude at the outset transitory and even longer lasting difficulties that are so common as to constitute normative characteristics of various age groups. Occasional inability to achieve sleep release, especially after excitement, fear or over-fatigue, occurs in all children. Some resistance to going to bed, delaying tactics and bedtime rituals are also practically universal in American children of nursery school age.[24, 59] The child utilizes these devices not only to postpone the moment of sleep but also to obtain special attention and intimate affection from his parents.[32] Coming under the heading of genuine sleeping problems are obstreperous refusal to go to bed at night, insistence upon having companionship until asleep, and awakening habitually for long intervals and demanding admission to the parent's bed or repetition of earlier bedtime routines.

Paralleling the etiology of feeding difficulties, the causes of these more serious sleeping problems may either inhere in the sleeping situation itself (indicating improper management), or may stem from a broader and more fundamental disturbance of the parent-child relationship. The former, relatively more benign category includes the parent's failure to appreciate individual differences in need for sleep, the provision of too long an afternoon nap, and excessive permissiveness in handling the child's bedtime and middle-of-the-night demands. Less amenable to correction are sleeping problems that reflect a high level of chronic anxiety and insecurity in the child or a strong need on his part for the parental attention and affection of which he feels deprived in the daytime. Even if the child's irregular sleeping habits do not elicit sympathetic attention from the parent, they may still prove rewarding by constituting a highly effective outlet for the expression of reactive hostility which can hardly be ignored. Parents find few viccissitudes of life more distressing than habitual loss of sleep.

Sphincter Control

Bowel and bladder control is acquired relatively late because it depends on voluntary regulation of muscles (anal and urethral *external* sphincters) located in the caudal region of the body. Regardless of whether or not the delay is attributable to late maturation of the pyramidal tract in this region, it is a well established fact that cortical (voluntary) control of neuromuscular functioning appears later in caudal than in cephalic bodily segments. Before the external sphincters are brought under voluntary control, elimination of feces and urine is an involuntarily controlled autonomic reflex: in response to afferent stimulation induced by distension of rectum and bladder, the walls of these hollow viscera contract and their internal sphincters relax, resulting in evacuation of accumulated waste substances. The automaticity of this sequence can only be interrupted when the child is able to utilize sensory cues of bowel and bladder accumulation for voluntary contraction of the external sphincters until such time as voiding is desired and permissible. Completion of voluntary control naturally requires ability to relax as well as to contract the external sphincters at the appropriate time.[24]

Exactly when sufficient anatomical and physiological maturation has occurred to make training for voluntary sphincter control practicable is difficult to determine. Extrapolating from normative and experimental findings[9, 13, 23, 39, 42, 59, 76] in our own and other cultures, however, we might place this age at about 18 months*—when the child walks, demonstrates awareness of and interest in his eliminative functions, responds to language, and is able to imitate his elders. Using the method of co-twin control, McGraw found that systematic daily training begun after the first few weeks of life did not result in significantly earlier bladder control than when such training was postponed 14 to 24 months.[42] Under conditions of duress, however, as when in some cultures incontinence in six- and nine-month old infants is severely punished,[76] voluntary sphincter control is apparently achieved very much earlier. In more usual circumstances the achievement of early control is typically involuntary in nature and is much less dependable than voluntary control. It is based primarily upon parental vigilance and anticipation, and sometimes upon the conditioning of reflex evacuation to time and place cues.

Sphincter control is characteristically established between the second and third years of life. Rectal control is achieved before bladder control, probably because defecation is less frequent and more regular, and is associated with more definite anticipatory sensations than is micturition.

---

*Wide individual differences obviously prevail in age of maturational readiness, depending on rate of development and sensitivity to the discomfort of being wet and soiled.

Girls attain bladder control before boys but the reverse tends to be true with regard to bowel training.[59] Until sphincter control is thoroughly consolidated, relapses are not uncommon and may even occur occasionally long after toilet habits are well established. They are associated with situational stresses, transitory negativism, overfatigue, preoccupation with a newly acquired ability such as talking, and disinclination to interrupt absorbing play. Sometimes they are used as an attention-getting device or as a means of competing with a newly arrived sibling for parental attention. Persistent and more serious incontinence in normally intelligent children is indicative of extreme self-assertiveness, of gross errors in toilet training that leave a child panic stricken and confused, or of strongly hostile and aggressive reactive trends in the child that stem from a severely disturbed relationship with his parents.

Since sleep raises the threshold of awareness for all sensory cues, including those of bladder distension, it understandably takes longer to achieve nighttime than daytime urinary control. *Enuresis* refers to habitual nocturnal bedwetting once day control is already established; in older children it more usually refers to a regressive loss of nocturnal control. It may be caused by the same factors listed above as responsible for urinary or fecal incontinence, by genically determined structural defects of the urinary tract[4] and spinal column (spinabifida), and especially by a parent attitude of rejection associated with rigid toilet training.[6] As a vehicle for expressing resentment or hostility toward parents, however, it is more efficacious than daytime wetting and soiling; parents find it more difficult to adopt a punitive attitude since the condition apparently lies beyond the sleeping child's control. The successful response of many cases to conditioned reflex therapy[48] indicates that the more benign type of enuresis may also be attributed to exceptionally sound sleep. Therapy here consists of conditioning the child to awaken to a full bladder by the use of an ingenius apparatus placed in his bed which causes a bell (unconditioned stimulus) to ring after the first few drops of urine are passed.

Implications for Immediate Behavior and Normative Development. Quite apart from any of the alleged personality benefits of delayed toilet training, the practice can be recommended for practical reasons and because of its *immediate* beneficial effects on infant behavior. When delayed until voluntary control can be exercised without undue punitive pressures, the acquisition of sphincter control becomes a relatively effortless and untraumatic process; but when hurried coercively before volitional control is normally possible, toilet training inevitably increases *current* tension and disharmony in the parent-child relationship, and according to one study of "problem children,"[30] increases the child's *immediate* burden of frustration, fear and rage. As we shall see, shortly, however, lasting or differential effects on personality development do not necessarily ensue.

From the standpoint of ego development and socialization, toilet training has approximately the same significance as weaning and the learning of table manners. It constitutes one of the earliest and most stringent set of parental demands imposed upon the child for curbing immediate impulses and gratifications, and for conforming to the expectations of the culture. Hence, in general, it exerts an ego devaluing effect (see p. 288). Also, since parents commonly impart ethical connotations ("good" and "bad") to success and failure in exercising sphincter control, this training represents in a sense the child's first experience in learning behaviors invested with moral significance. Later on, because of attitudes of shame, self-consciousness, concealment and prudishness connected with elimination in our culture, and because of the close cultural and anatomical association between eliminative and sexual functions,* the moral implications of bowel and bladder control are accentuated even further.

Implications for Later Differential Personality Development. According to Freudian doctrine, anal evacuation is a sexually gratifying experience, the need for which exists innately in the form of a libidinal drive. The expression of this drive is supposedly the distinguishing characteristic of a major stage of psychosexual development interposed between oral and genital phases.[21] Thus psychoanalytically oriented theorists conceive of bowel training as basically inhibiting erogenous gratifications. If this training is especially severe the child allegedly adjusts by reaction formation, renouncing all spontaneous hedonistic impulses. He thus tends to develop a character structure marked by such traits as stinginess, perfectionism, self-punitiveness, rigidity and meticulousness. But again, as in the case of oral erogeneity, it is difficult to appreciate why interference with a particular kind of sensuous gratification should have invariable, lasting and widespread characterological effects, unless one assumes that the specific satisfactions involved play an indispensable or crucial role in normal personality development. Since there is no self-evident reason for believing that this is so in the case of anal sensuality, it is more parsimonious to suppose that toilet training affects both normative and differential aspects of personality growth by influencing the child's total life situation, his relationship with his parents, or his biosocial status.

We may hypothesize, therefore, that special toilet training practices contribute to the differential development of personality only insofar as they are reflective of characteristic and pervasive parent attitudes that the child is mature enough to perceive. Because any particular practice

*See p. 254 for a discussion of this relationship

such as coercive toilet training is also determined by many factors totally unrelated to parent attitudes, and because it does *not* have uniform psychological significance for all parents who employ it, we cannot infer that the occurrence of the practice per se is necessarily indicative of a given attitudinal orientation.* This is indicated by findings that the personality traits and adjustment status of five- and six year olds are generally unrelated to earliness of bowel and bladder training and to punishment for toilet accidents.[61] Thus, the characterological consequences of a specific toilet training practice may be expected to *vary* depending on the particular generalized attitude it typifies in a given parent. For example, *one possible* general orientation toward child rearing that *may* be expressed in coercive toilet training is undue emphasis upon conformity, orderliness, self-control and punctiliousness. But even if this is the case the parent undoubtedly inculcates these same values in countless other direct and indirect ways throughout the entire period of childhood. Under these circumstances, it seems more credible to believe that if a school child treats his money, clothes and notebooks with exaggerated care it is because of the cumulative impact of such indoctrination rather than solely because of the rigid toilet training he experienced as an infant.

Infantile "Sexuality"

Genital Play. In the course of bodily exploration the infant inevitably discovers and manipulates his genitals. Upon experiencing the pleasurable effects of this activity he may repeat it in order to re-experience the pleasant sensations involved, or (as in the case of thumbsucking) to obtain a nonspecific type of tension relief following frustration or anxiety of any origin. In some primitive cultures, as a matter of fact, it is common for mothers to stroke the naked genitals of crying, fretful infants as a means of soothing them.[59, 76] The incidence of self-stimulation (at one time or another) in children under three years of age is exceedingly high.[40] Girls reportedly indulge much less frequently than do boys,[38, 40] but this difference may be misleading since the habit is appreciably more difficult to detect in girls. Toward the close of the preschool period, as more and more children become introduced to its pleasurable properties and become aware of its availability as a tension reducing device, the practice tends to become more widespread and persistent, especially in emotionally tense children; and in accordance with the imposition of parental and cultural taboos, indulgence tends to become more furtive.[15] Beginning at this age

*In some relatively homogenous samples, however, a significant relationship may (and does) exist between rejecting parent attitudes and incidence of rigid toilet training practices.[6]

also, curiosity about sexual anatomy and differences may stimulate some children to "peek" and play genitally exhibitionistic and manipulative games with youngsters of the same or opposite sex. Although varying tremendously in extent from one culture or subculture to another (in direct proportion to adult tolerance for such experimentation),[76] these interests and activities are still relatively sporadic and uninsistent in comparison with those of post-pubertal individuals.[34, 43]

The "Oedipus Situation." Subsumed under this designation is the Freudian doctrine that during the "genital phase" of psychosexual development the parent of opposite sex is the child's principal love object. Supposedly inherent in the "phylogenetic unconscious" of the male child is a potent libidinal drive for incestuous sexual union with the mother accompanied by hatred for the father as a sexual rival and desire for his death.*[20, 21] Giving this theory a certain measure of superficial plausibility is the fact (impressionistic to be sure) that among many (but not all) families in our culture the father-son relationship in early childhood appears to be marked by more hostility and less intense emotional attachment than either the mother-son or father-daughter relationships. Other explanations for these phenomena, however, are available that seem far more parsimonious and self-evidently valid.

The young boy's typically more affectionate regard for his mother can be satisfactorily explained on the grounds that in our culture she provides the major source of his emotional support. During early childhood the father tends to play a relatively secondary and less clearly defined role than the mother in the child's upbringing. Thus, the mother's greater importance in the boy's emotional security system rather than her alleged role as a sex object is the crucial factor in determining the greater intensity of his emotional attachment to her. This interpretation is bolstered by the fact that the majority of studies in this area[24, 47, 65] show that the mother is the preferred parent of both boys and girls. Furthermore, no incontrovertible evidence (see p. 444) exists which justifies the inference that the young boy's emotional response to his mother is sexual in nature or ordinarily involves anything more than affection or desire for bodily warmth and personal closeness. In our culture, such overtly affectionate relationships between mother and son (or between daughter and either parent) are regarded as quite appropriate, whereas, even when the underlying feelings are present, expressions of affection between father and son tend to cause embarrassment for both parties. We would conclude, therefore, that if sexual considerations as such do enter into the child's preference of parent,

---

*The oedipus situation in the female child corresponds to that described for the male except that the respective objects of love and hatred are reversed.

it seems more likely that they originate with the parent (whose biological sex role is undoubted) than with child (in whom adult-like sexuality has never been unequivocally demonstrated).

Turning now to the other side of the coin, conflict between father and son can also be attributed more credibly to the former's authority role in our culture and to competition for the mother's *affectional* attention than to the boy's perception of the father as a sexual rival. If fathers have any distinctive role in our culture it is that of disciplinary agent and moral arbiter; and traditionally, in enforcing the disciplinary code, they are sterner and more demanding in relation to sons than to daughters. It is true, of course, that the mother also administers punishment, but her punitive role is not only generally less harsh but is also apparently resented less; because she is concomitantly the child's principal source of emotional security, he probably regards her as more entitled to control his behavior. In support of this view that the father's actual authority role (rather than a phylogenetically determined perception of him as a sexual rival) is the principal cause of whatever hostile feelings the boy manifests toward him are the findings (a) that in father-separated families, the father is perceived both as less aggressive and more affectionate than in father-home families and in approximately the same light as he is received by girls in father-home families[2]; and (b) that in matrilineal societies, where the mother's brothers enforce discipline instead of the father, boys tend to resent their maternal uncles in much the same way as boys do their fathers in our culture.[13]

Finally, mutual rivalry for the mother's affection may play a role in engendering father-son conflict. The child may perceive the father as he would an older sibling—as a competitor for the love and attention of the most important individual in his interpersonal world. The father, in turn, particularly if he is emotionally overdependent on his wife or has good reason to feel supplanted by the child in his wife's affections, may react to him with feelings of hostility which in due time tend to be reciprocated.

Erotic Significance. What is the erotic significance of the several phenomena that psychoanalytic theory groups under the heading of "infantile sexuality"? To what extent is the meaning of the oral, anal and genital activities we have reviewed above qualitatively equivalent to that of adult sexuality? Our position here is that *adult sexuality (true eroticism) can only be conceived of as a form of self-expression in which the individual enacts and experiences himself in a biological sex role.* Prerequisite to such experience, we believe, is (a) either current hormonal facilitation or exposure to such facilitation in the past, and (b) social and self-recognition as a sexually mature person capable of desiring a sexual object as such, and of serving in this capacity himself.[1] Since these conditions cannot possibly be fulfilled prior to puberty, the "erotic" behavior of children cannot be regarded as qualitatively comparable to adult sexuality. It lacks the social significance of adult eroticism, its significance in the total economy of personality organization, its rich feeling tones, its urgency and regularity, and its status as an absorbing interest in its own right separate from other play. Hence despite the not infrequent attempts of children to engage in intercourse,[34, 35, 76] and the occurrence of orgasm experience in female children,[35,] both Kinsey[34] and Malinowski[43] conclude that a qualitative as well as, frequently, a temporal break in continuity occurs between preadolescent and adolescent sex activity.

"Infantile sexuality," therefore, consists chiefly of erogenous *sensuality* that is both indulged in for its own sake and to relieve the tensions of frustration and anxiety. It also includes the elements of exploratory and manipulative activity, of curiosity about the anatomy and physiology of sex and reproduction, and of desire for affectional closeness with the parent, accompanied perhaps by feelings of rivalry for perceived competitors. As we shall see later (p. 444), however, because the child lacks a true biological (erotic) sex role, sex differences are not intrinsically important to him. Their true significance for personality development in childhood inheres in the fact that they constitute one of the principal bases for the differential structuring of social roles and behavior.

The origin of the psychoanalytic confusion between infantile sensuality and adult sexuality is not difficult to locate. First, it is easy to be overimpressed with the obvious fact that the same bodily parts are involved in both phenomena. This superficial resemblance, however, is both irrelevant and misleading: masturbation, for example, does not have the same psychological significance for child and adult simply because both individuals stroke the same organ. Second, in adult life sensuous and sexual pleasure *are* interwoven in erotic experience.[1] Hence, since adults find it extremely difficult to exclude their cumulative experiential perspective in interpreting the behavior of children (adultomorphism), they may confidently attribute erotic significance to the oral and genital play of the latter or "remember" that these same activities had sexual meaning in their own childhood. Even the sensual pleasure connected with anal and bladder evacuation, which ordinarily is not incorporated into adult sexual expression, may be "remembered" as having had erotic significance in early childhood years. This can be explained by the close association between eliminative and genital functions as a result of anatomical proximity, the shame and pleasure that is common to both, and their linkage in folklore and folk language. Thus, by virtue of this prior association, when genital activities are eroticized in adult life retrospective distortion may operate to superimpose some sexual significance on childhood memories of anal-urethral sensuality.

Some neo-Freudians recognize that "infantile" and adult sexuality are not phenomenologically comparable but argue nevertheless that *eroticism* or *sexuality* should be defined broadly enough to encompass both sensuality and expressions of affection as well as sexual behavior in the more literal sense. In the writer's opinion this only results in unnecessary semantic confusion and in a lamentable loss of scientific precision. If three distinguishably different phenomena can be discriminated conceptually, what possible advantage could accrue from subsuming all of them under the same single term that is commonly understood as referring to only one of the three?

The Need for Mothering

Straightforward consideration of the relevant data available should leave little room for controversy regarding the need for adequate mothering in infancy and early childhood. Thus, in discussing "infant deprivation" in the more general context of developmental reversibility (see p. 121), we have already concluded that gross, habitual and unmitigated "emotional" neglect of infants after six months of age leads to high morbidity and mortality rates, acute behavioral syndromes, and often irreversible retardation in motor, cognitive and personality development. The issue has become controversial nevertheless because of unwarranted inferences and extrapolations that have been made far beyond the data, and because of fanciful explanations that have been advanced to account for both the beneficial effects of mothering and the unfortunate consequences of maternal deprivation. The major points under dispute may be categorized under the following headings: (a) what constitutes *adequate* mothering, (b) how early it must be instituted to avoid detrimental effects, and (c) the reasons that have been offered to explain why mothering is necessary.

How Much is Adequate? By adequate mothering, adherents of the Cornelian corner generally mean the provision of plentiful fondling, abundant physical contact, and maximal amounts of succorance, solicitous attention and social stimulation by a single *mother figure*. Several lines of evidence, however, indicate that this prescription is over-generous for the ends it seeks to accomplish, namely, the maintenance of good health and nutrition, adequate developmental progress, normal personality development, and emotional stability. All that seems to be required is a minimally sufficient degree of individualized care, personal attention, and social stimulation from a familiar person (or persons) to give the child a sense of security in the responsiveness and dependability of his interpersonal environment once he is mature enough to perceive his executive incompetence and dependence on others.

In the first place, in all instances in which deleterious effects have been shown to follow inadequate mothering, the children concerned have not just been deprived of the Cornelian corner ideal of adequate care but of the *minimally* adequate level of maternal care as well. High mortality rates, marasmus, and developmental retardation (hospitalism) occur when infants receive practically *no* personalized care or attention, no social stimulation and no regular handling whatsoever from a mother or mother surrogate (see p. 121). The sudden withdrawal of the mother which precipitates anaclitic depression (see p. 121) not only involves loss of fondling and affection but also of the physical presence of the individual who is habitually associated with the infant's sense of security. Hence, at this stage of development there is no evidence that affection for or intrinsic acceptance of the child are essential in order to prevent symptoms of deprivation,* or even that these parent attitudes can be perceived.

Second, more direct and positive evidence regarding the amount of mothering required comes from studies which indicate that normal health and development can be expected during the first year of life under conditions of minimal contact, social stimulation and affectionate handling (see p. 122). No permanent neuromuscular or social retardation is found in Albanian infants who customarily spend most of the first year of life bound to a wooden cradle board placed in a dark corner of the room[8]; and the typical picture of hospitalism can be prevented by the simple expedient of providing brief daily visits by the mother (see p. 122). Thus, while it is quite clear that minimally adequate mothering (as defined above) is necessary to prevent deprivation phenomena, no one has yet succeeded in demonstrating that these phenomena occur in the absence of *lavish* mothering, nor (as in the case of vitamins) that a superfluity of mothering beyond the minimal requirements improve health and development at this stage of maturity.

Third, the need for care by a *single* mother figure has in no sense been unequivocally demonstrated. In all cases in which separation from the accustomed mother is followed by damaging consequences, the infant is previously conditioned to derive his security from her alone. On the other hand, in many primitive cultures characterized by an extended family (e.g., the Hopi), infants seem just as content when placed in the care of maternal aunts or older siblings who habitually share child care duties with the mother.[17]

Lastly, what constitutes adequate mothering is of course relative to the

*Somewhat later, of course, emotional rejection and lack of love (as distinguished from neglect) *do* have serious but different consequences, i.e., inability to satellize and acquire a derived status, etc. (see p. 294).

infant's age and cognitive maturity. Until he is sufficiently mature to have a functional concept of self, to appreciate his executive helplessness and dependence on others, and to comprehend and anticipate threats to his future safety (six to nine months), he is effectively shielded from such psychological trauma as personal inattention, lack of social stimulation and separation from the mother. Hence, the damaging effects of infant deprivation have not been reliably demonstrated in infants under six months of age; most observers place the period of maximum susceptibility between nine months and three years of age (p. 122). With increasing cognitive and social sophistication the child also becomes aware of attitudes of acceptance-rejection and intrinsic-extrinsic valuation which influence subsequent personality development in important ways. These attitudes are discriminably distinct from the variables involved in mothering and have very different effects.

Why Necessary. Adding appreciably to the controversy regarding mothering have been some of the untenable reasons commonly put forth to explain why it is necessary.* The core of Ribble's position on this matter, for example, is that the neonate's general health is extremely delicate because his major organ systems allegedly function precariously close to the minimal level of sufficiency compatible with life.[56, 57] Cardiovascular and respiratory capacity are said to be inadequate for neonatal needs, thereby placing the newborn infant under imminent threat of asphyxiation and circulatory failure. Actually, as already pointed out in part (see p. 198), the physiological margin of safety is comfortably wide in full-term infants, and the shift from prenatal to postnatal mechanisms significantly improves their cardiovascular, respiratory and nutritional status.† It is true that because of lack of prior use gastrointestinal functions tend to be relatively unstable and imperfect shortly after birth; but there are neither logical nor empirical grounds for believing that intensive mothering can impove alimentary dysfunction anymore than it could conceivably correct circulatory or respiratory inadequacy if such existed.

Related to this line of reasoning is an argument used sometimes to rationalize the rooming-in plan. Close physical contact between mother and child is advocated postnatally to compensate for the disruption of "chemical union" that occurs during birth.[56] The termination of placental communication happens to constitute a physiological improvement; and even if it were traumatic it is difficult to appreciate how physical closeness could com-

*It should be appreciated, of course, that the intrinsic value of a practice is not reduced simply because its advocates advance the wrong reasons to account for its effectiveness.

†An excellent review of the relevant evidence is available.[52]

pensate for circulatory separation unless one invokes a purely metaphorical analogy.

A second type of argument employed in defense of effusive mothering is that it is necessary to alleviate the "anxiety to which the infant is allegedly so vulnerable shortly after birth. This contention, however, rests upon the discredited assumptions that the neonate both can make highly differentiated fear responses and is able to perceive the mother as a person. Although it is probably true that the infant's *eventual* need for mothering stems from insecurity feelings associated with awareness of executive dependence, such awareness has not been convincingly demonstrated prior to six to nine months of age.

Finally, exaggerated notions of the infant's intolerance of frustration are frequently used to rationalize prescriptions for extreme mothering in some pediatric circles. However, quite apart from the fact that complete avoidance of frustration is a practical impossibility in any home (regardless of how indulgent the parents may be), the achievement of this goal can hardly be defended as either necessary or desirable. It is unnecessary (a) because even if the infant is relatively intolerant of frustration, he is not that fragile that occasional or brief postponement of need satisfaction is seriously traumatic, especially if the environment is generally benevolent; (b) because unless frustration is habitually excessive its acute emotional effects on behavior are typically transitory in nature; and (c) because frustration tolerance tends to increase with age. And although it is true that scrupulous avoidance of frustration undoubtedly removes much cause for anger and conflict, it simultaneously creates hazards for the attainment of personality maturity (see p. 307).

Evaluation of "Newer" Pediatric Approach

By way of summary and conclusion, the following evaluative points may be made about the newer approach to problems of infant care:

1. Many of the prescribed practices (e.g., self-demand feeding, delayed toilet training, rooming-in) may be recommended because of practical advantages associated with their use in the day-to-day management of infants. They take into account maturational readiness, recognize individual differences among children and diurnal fluctuations within the same child, avoid the imposition of unnecessary frustrations, enhance the child's perception of his environment as generally dependable and benevolent, and encourage parents to develop confidence in their own judgment. Thus, in general, their immediate impact upon child behavior is to eliminate many causes of unnecessary friction between parent and child, to increase the latter's frustration tolerance, and to reduce the incidence of behavior problems associated with infant care.

2. None of the above practices, however, are *invariably* superior to their predecessors, and some of them (e.g., breast-feeding, late weaning) have not been shown to be superior at all to other alternatives. In either case it is clear that when used inflexibly or carried to extremes they create serious new problems of their own.

3. In general it has not been demonstrated that these practices significantly improve health, nutrition, and general development or exert lasting differential effects on personality or adjustment.

4. In addition to dogmatic insistence upon the invariable superiority of particular practices and exaggerated claims made for their long-term effects, the often far-fetched and implausible reasons advanced for their use has tended to accentuate the fad-like characteristics of this movement and hence to endanger the genuine contributions it has made to infant care.

INFANT TRAINING AND ADULT PERSONALITY

In reviewing various infant care practices above, we have already considered empirical evidence bearing on the relationship between these practices and later personality outcomes. This evidence, in general, has not supported the widely-held belief that *specific practices in and of themselves* contribute significantly to enduring psychosocial and idiosyncratic differences in personality development. Our purpose in the present section is to propose possible reasons for this absence of relationship and to suggest how and under what conditions infant and early childhood experience might conceivably influence the development of intracultural (idiosyncratic) differences in personality structure as well as the distinctive (psychosocial) patterning of personality traits in different cultures.

Psychosocial Traits

Since cultures obviously tend to perpetuate themselves, i.e., to produce adult individuals who develop ways of behavior that are consonant with prevailing norms,[28] it is self-evident that cultural values must somehow be woven into the developing fabric of personality structure. In the course of growing up, for example, certain influences must be brought to bear on the Hopi child that reliably produce a Hopi adult who more nearly approximates the Hopi than the American or Japanese idea of adult personality. The issue under discussion here is whether the psychosocial aspects of personality are primarily transmitted (a) via specific infant care practices as such or as representative of broader cultural values, or (b) via more direct and recurrent exposure to implicit and explicit expressions of pervasive cultural norms during the *entire* period of development prior to adult life but subsequent to infancy.

Assuming for the moment that particular infant care practices do not exert any specific invariant influence on personality development simply because they impinge on given erogenous zones,* is it possible nevertheless that such practices consistently reflect basic cultural values and hence give rise to predictable personality outcomes on this basis? On a priori grounds alone this does not appear very likely. Since the realization of the same cultural goals and the expression of the same cultural attitudes can be achieved through different and even antithetical methods,²² the presence or absence of a particular practice cannot possibly have uniform attitudinal significance from one culture to another. In addition, child rearing practices are influenced by such non-attitudinal and non-value factors as customs of marriage and family organization,⁴⁹ economic conditions, and historical accident. Thus, in their cross-cultural survey of child training practices, Whiting and Child found that

> the practices of a society for one system of behavior are almost entirely independent of its practices with respect to another. This . . . suggests that aspects of child training . . . do not grow out of cultural attitudes toward children such as might produce general laxness or general strictness, but rather out of antecedents specific to each system of behavior.⁷⁶

This leaves us with the remaining possibility that cultural attitudes toward children, as well as other pervasive values, might be reflected in the *manner of administering* different practices if not in the mere fact of their presence or absence. Although careful observation would probably confirm this hypothesis, at least in part, it is still unlikely that cultural attitudes expressed in this way play an important role in structuring personality. First, during infancy the individual's contact with the culture is largely indirect and buffered by his family group. In a general way, of course, the family serves as the representative of the culture in dealing with the child. But parents differ considerably in how they interpret cultural norms relative to child rearing and in their need for conforming to such norms; and in any event, they are probably less disposed to follow the cultural prescription slavishly when the child is young and his lapses are excusable than when he is older. Furthermore, the actual flavor of the cultural attitude that is conveyed to the infant is undoubtedly influenced by affective and temperamental dimensions of the parent-child relationship that are intercultural in distribution (e.g., acceptance-rejection, under- or overdomination). Second, even if the cultural attitudes reflected in the manner of administering infant care practices were expressed more proximately and less variably, they could still not be perceived and understood very effectively by the perceptually

*See p. 262 for a discussion of this point.

and cognitively immature infant.* Hence, if this mechanism of transmission does function at all it probably first becomes a significant factor in the postinfantile period. Environmental stimulation is not irrelevant during the first year of life but only plays a supportive role; within a wide range of cultural diversity in child rearing attitudes, developmental outcomes remain essentially constant.

Therefore, in seeking to identify the mechanisms whereby cultures transmit the psychosocial attributes of personality it would seem more fruitful to look beyond the limited field of infant care practices. We would expect that the transmission of values, goals, interpersonal roles, and ways of perceiving and thinking would take place directly, as appropriate occasions for indoctrination arise, rather than obliquely and symbolically in the way parents administer the routines of child care†; that the culture would not limit its major indoctrinating efforts to cognitively immature infants but would exert socializing pressures continuously, recurrently, and in mutually reinforcing situations. Lastly we would expect that psychosocial traits would reflect certain *institutionalized* aspects of handling and timing shifts in children's biosocial status, i.e., the amount and explicitness of recognition accorded different stages of development, the choice of socializing methods and agents, the degree of role and status discontinuity existing between children and adults, the extent to which new demands and expectations are geared to maturational readiness and to individual differences,[44] and the abruptness, duration and anxiety level associated with transitional stages of development.

Idiosyncratic Traits

Similar kinds of questions may be raised about the impact of infantile experience on the development of idiosyncratic traits as were asked in considering the impact of such experience on psychosocial traits. Do idiosyncratic traits develop (a) as consequences of *specific* infant care prac-

*See p. 257 for a more complete discussion of this point.

†This does not mean that all indoctrination is accomplished by means of explicit training procedures. As a matter of fact, the influence of culture is so pervasive that perhaps most indoctrination occurs incidentally and on an implicit basis. Nevertheless incidental learning occurs most effectively in children when it is *not* indirect (inferential from or tangential to immediate experience). As Ralph Piddington observes in his *Introduction to Social Anthropology*, vol. 2, 1957, much indoctrination occurs on an impersonal level and its effects depend as much on its content as on the way in which it is carried out. The actual psychological mechanisms whereby individuals acquire the psychosocial traits that the culture transmits will be discussed in Chapter 13, pp. 423-425).

tices per se, (b) as consequences of *general parent attitudes* expressed in the presence or absence of practices or in the manner in which they are administered, or (c) as consequences of recurrent interpersonal experiences in later childhood and adolescence?

Practices versus Attitudinal Substrate. Two basic assumptions underlie the psychoanalytic doctrine that particular infant care practices in and of themselves exert specific, invariant, point-to-point effects on adult personality structure. First, it is assumed that the excess, sufficiency, or deficiency of "erotic" satisfaction experienced when a given practice impinges on a particular stage of psychosexual development (and its associated libidinal drive and erogenous zone) plays a crucial organizing and directional role in subsequent personality development. Second, it is assumed that the type of nureomuscular activity associated with erogenous experience (contraction or relaxation, sucking or biting) influences in a predetermined way the kind of personality trait that emerges.

It is not at all clear, however, why the satisfactions and frustrations resulting from such experience should have more than *immediate* effects on behavior. No self-evident reasons are apparent why these effects should be lasting, generalized, or involve core aspects of personality. It is true, of course, that since much parent-child interaction occurs in relation to erogenous zones and to the satisfactions, demands and expectations connected therewith this experience acquires wider significance for the child's biosocial status, his sense of security, and his feelings of volitional and executive dependence and independence. But if this is the case the impact of infant care practices on personality development must be attributed to the child's reactions to the variable attitudinal, role, and status implications of these practices and not to the experience of particular erogenous satisfactions and gratifications per se or to any inherent relationships between sucking and passivity, biting and hostility, or anal retention and stinginess.

Acceptance of the orthodox psychoanalytic thesis would also require that we arbitrarily exclude many important sources of variability associated with the meaning of a particular child rearing practice. We would have to assume that the feeling tones and attitudes connected with the administration of a practice and the general psychological context of role and status relationships in which it occurs make no difference; that the child's past experience and present expectations and the attitudinal tenor of other parent practices are irrelevant. Hence, the more credible hypothesis at this point would be that it is the attitudinal substrate of a practice and its implications for biosocial status rather than its immediate hedonistic consequences which influence later personality development.

Underlying parent attitudes, however, cannot be inferred directly from the presence or absence of a practice. In the first place it is quite conceivable that the choice of a particular practice in preference to another may have no attitudinal significance whatsoever. At any rate it rarely has any *exclusive* attitudinal significance that is patently self-evident, varying rather in meaning from one parent to another in accordance with individual differences in personality and experience. Second, it also depends upon many factors completely unrelated to parents' attitudes or personality trends, such as social class membership, family tradition, and child rearing ideology. Thus in a given parent the choice of a particular practice may not have much attitudinal significance or be reflective of characteristic and pervasive general attitudes; and except in extremely homogeneous populations it is unlikely that its attitudinal significance will be similar for different individuals. It is hardly surprising, therefore, that children's personality traits in general are not significantly related to the presence or absence of particular infant care practices in their early upbringing (see pp. 237-251), and that "favorable" techniques in different areas of child rearing are not highly associated with each other.[63] Sewell, Mussen and Harris found low and generally nonsignificant intercorrelations among child rearing practices, even in a quite homogeneous population, and concluded therefrom that parents "may follow what appears to be permissive treatment with respect to one practice or during one period of the child's development but employ restrictive techniques in other aspects of training."[63]

Evidence such as this, however, does not prove that parents do not manifest characteristic, generalized, and pervasive attitudes in their child rearing practices. It merely indicates, for the reasons pointed out above, that lack of generality and individual self-consistency is found with respect to such formal aspects of these practices as presence or absence, duration, and age of initiation and termination. If we were to observe carefully the manner in which different practices were administered it is much more likely, as some preliminary studies[5, 64] suggest, that persistent and pervasive attitudinal constellations characteristic of individual parents' approaches to child rearing could be identified. Such generalized *individual* attitudes reflected in child rearing practices are probably more effective in influencing the development of idiosyncratic traits than *cultural* attitudes are in influencing the development of psychosocial traits. A single parent can be more consistent and less variable in expressing his own personality trends than many different parents can be in interpreting and expressing cultural values. Also, unstandardized temperamental and attitudinal aspects of parent personality are communicable to children more readily and directly, less inferentially, and at an earlier age in the daily routines of child care than the stylized aspects of cultural values which ordinarily require more appropriately structured occasions for effective indoctrination.

Regardless of whether child rearing practices per se or the parent attitudes they reflect are considered as significant in influencing subsequent personality development, it is important to avoid the frequently committed error of confusing antecedence with causality. This is the error of assuming that a particular practice (or the attitudes underlying it) *causes* a later personality trait simply because it precedes the latter chronologically. In the first place, it stands to reason that any generalized parent attitude will be expressed in *many* rather than in only one child rearing practice. Hence, no single practice can ever be crucially determinative by itself. If consistent with a general attitudinal trend, it would merely constitute one of many supportive practices serving the same end; if inconsistent, its influence would be nullified by the cumulative weight of other practices. Second, at the same time that the child is exposed to reflections of parent attitudes and values in child rearing practices he is also exposed to these same attitudes and values in other contexts both within and outside the family circle. Thus it is clear that manner of administering child rearing practices represents only one facet through which parent attitudes may be expressed, and that these attitudes impinge on the child's personality development through other channels (e.g., formal and informal instruction, interpersonal climate within family, observation of parents interacting with other persons) not only simultaneously but also continuously and recurrently throughout the entire period of childhood. Many anthropological generalizations regarding alleged causal relationships between specific infant care practices and various features of adult personality (see p. 150) are suspect both for these reasons and because either (a) they are frequently derived from a sample of only one culture, and hence it is not even possible to ascertain whether the observed concomitance between infant training and adult personality is statistically significant on a cross-cultural basis; or (b) in most cross-cultural comparisons, the cultures are not sufficiently well matched on all other variables (apart from the specific practices under investigation) to warrant the drawing of definitive causal inferences.

Limiting Factors. Even if we grant that the child's personality development may be influenced by broad, pervasive parent attitudes reflected in infant care practices, this statement of relationship must be qualified by three important limiting conditions: parent attitudes cannot be communicated until infants are sufficiently mature to perceive and react to them, the reactions they make are in part a function of constitutional factors, and the effects of early infantile experience on personality may be modified (reinforced, altered, reversed) by subsequent experience in later childhood, adolescence and adult life.

We have good reason to believe that the young infant's perceptual and cognitive immaturity tends to insulate him from the influence of parent attitudes. His relatively slow rate of perceptual-social development, in comparison to that of the young of infrahuman mammals, limits his ability to perceive attitudinal cues and to comprehend their significance, to make subtle discriminations among feeling tones, to generalize and conceptualize his interpersonal experience, or even to remember it for any length of time. Thus, it is difficult to accept the currently fashionable view[72] that infants are aware of the subtlest shadings of parent attitudes by virtue of some special empathic sensitivity to covert cues communicated through bodily tensions and expressive movements. Both the logic and the evidence with respect to perceptual development indicate that children first become aware of gross and overt elements in the cognitive field and only later, as differentiation occurs, do they respond to partial, subtle and covert cues (see p. 551). It is true that infants tend to be quiescent when handled by calm, relaxed and confident mothers and to cry and fuss when handled by tense and flustered mothers who have ambivalent feelings about motherhood.[70] But it is much more parsimonious to suppose that maternal attitudes affect the smoothness and pleasantness of handling procedures and that the infant reacts to the immediate hedonistic and frustrating properties of the handling practices as such than that he perceives and responds to the attitudes underlying them. Hence we would conclude that until he actually perceives the parent attitudes that are reflected in the daily routines of child care they influence his immediate behavior rather than his personality development.

It would be a serious mistake, however, to assume that even *perceived* parent attitudes in late infancy and early childhood exert an irreversible effect on adult personality or that early favorable or unfavorable experience predetermines the outcome of later crucial stages of personality development. Thus, although favorable infantile and early childhood experience undoubtedly does much to insure the development of a well-adjusted adult personality, the damaging impact of serious trauma in late childhood, adolescence, and adult life cannot be discounted. Later rejection by parents, exposure to overprotective and under- or overdominating attitudes, crippling disease, extreme somatic deviations in adolescence, problems of acculturation and culture conflict,* severe economic hardships, etc., all leave their mark in undoing part of the desirable foundation established in childhood. Thus, despite affectionate care and early indulgence in an infant-centered home, adult Hopi life is characterized by marked discord, anxiety, suspicion, distrust and fear of death. Eggan attributes this to abrupt

*A discussion of the variables affecting the impact of acculturation on personality is available.[27]

restriction of aggression and to the inculcation of supernatural fears in middle childhood, to culture conflict and ambivalence about white rule, and to the rigors of exacting a livelihood from a dry rocky terrain.[17] The same situation applies more or less in the case of the Navaho and for very much the same reasons.*

An additional source of trauma affecting later personality development lies in the tremendous contrast that prevails in certain cultures between the permissiveness of early upbringing and the severity of the demands and expectations imposed upon the adult.[25] This consideration is vital in evaluating the suggestion advanced by Moloney[46] and others that we import into our own culture some of the maximally permissive practices employed by some primitive peoples. Thus, prolonged and extreme mothering might be quite appropriate in Okinawa where the culture as a whole is relatively simply organized, undemanding and noncompetitive and might indeed constitute *one* of the reasons for the relatively low incidence of psychosis among the Okinawans. But when the same practices are employed by immigrant Okinawan parents in the highly stratified and competitive Hawaiian culture, the incidence of psychosis is significantly greater than among other ethnic immigrant groups of comparable socioeconomic status.[75]

Evidence regarding the apparently irreversible effects of certain infantile experiences on the later behavior of infrahuman mammals (see p. 120) cannot be applied indiscriminately to human infants. In the first place young infrahuman infants are relatively more mature, perceptually and socially, and hence can be influenced more crucially by early infantile experience. Second, personality development is more complex in human beings: a larger number of component developmental processes is involved; and as the critical phases of the different processes succeed each other, the relative importance of different interpersonal variables keeps shifting. Lastly, the possibilities for reversing the direction of personality development are much enhanced in human beings because of their greater ability to verbalize and generalize their experience, and because of the more important role of the environment in patterning major aspects of their development.

A final consideration affecting the impact of infantile experience is the matter of constitutional differences. The active, self-assertive child, for example, neither perceives nor reacts in the same way to parental rejection or overdomination as does the phlegmatic, submissive child; and this reactive difference in turn differentially affects the perpetuation or modification of the parent attitude in question. Thus, constitutional factors not only

*A summary of evidence regarding the importance of later childhood and adolescent experience for adult personality is available[37, 39, 50, 71] and discussions can be found on pages 36-37[50] and 949.[37]

provide for interindividual variability in response to similar infantile experience, but also account for much intraindividual continuity in personality structure. If a given personality trait remains stable over the years, its persistence need not necessarily be attributed to the indelible influence of infantile experience, but may be explained both by the stability of certain temperamental predispositions and by the recurrence of the same environmental factors.

REFERENCES

1. Ausubel, D. P.: *Ego Development and the Personality Disorders*. New York, Grune & Stratton, 1952.
2. Bach, G. R.: Father-fantasies and father-typing in father-separated children. *Child Develop. 17*: 63-80, 1946.
3. Bakwin, H.: Thumb- and finger-sucking in children. *J. Pediat. 32*: 99-101, 1948.
4. ———: Enuresis. *Pediat. Clin. North America,* August, 819-825, 1955.
5. Baldwin, A. L., Kalhorn, J., and Breese, F. H.: Patterns of parent behavior. *Psychol. Monogr. 58*: No. 3, 1945.
6. Bostock, J.: Enuresis and toilet training. *Med. J. Australia 2*: 110-113, 1951.
7. Bühler, C.: *The First Year of Life*. New York, John Day, 1930.
8. Danzinger, L., and Frankl, L.: Zum Problem der Funktionsreifung. *Z. Kinderforsch. 43*: 219-254, 1934.
9. Davis, A., and Havinghurst, R. J.: Social class and color differences in child-rearing. *Am. Sociol. Rev. 11*: 698-710, 1946.
10. Davis, C. M.: Self-selection of diet by newly weaned infants. *Am. J. Dis. Child. 36*: 651-679, 1928.
11. ———: Results of the self-selection of diets by young children. *Canad. M.A.J., 41*: 257-261, 1939.
12. Davis, H. V., Sears, R. R., Miller, H. C., and Brodbeck, A. J.: Effects of cup, bottle, and breast feeding on oral activities of newborn infants. *Pediat. 2*: 549-558, 1948.
13. Dennis, W.: *The Hopi Child*. New York, Appleton-Century, 1940.
14. ———, and Dennis, M. G.: Does culture appreciably affect patterns of infant behavior? *J. Soc. Psychol. 12*: 305-317, 1940.
15. Dillon, M. S.: Attitudes of children toward their own bodies and those of other children. *Child Develop. 5*: 165-176, 1934.
16. Douglas, J. W. B.: The extent of breast feeding in Great Britain in 1946, with special reference to the health and survival of children. *J. Obst. & Gynaec. Brit. Emp. 57*: 335-361, 1950.
17. Eggan, D.: The general problem of Hopi adjustment. *Am. Anthropol. 47*: 516-539, 1945.
18. Escalona, S. K.: An appraisal of some psychological factors in relation to rooming-in and self-demand schedules. *In* M. J. E. Senn, Ed., *Problems of Early Infancy*, Transactions of First Conference, 1947. New York, Josiah Macy, Jr. Foundation, 1948, pp. 58-62,
19. Faber, H. K., and Sutton, T. L.: A statistical comparison of breast-fed and bottle-fed babies during the first year. *Am. J. Dis. Child. 40*: 1163-1176, 1930.
20. Fenichel, O.: *The Psychoanalytic Theory of Neurosis*. New York, Norton, 1945.

21. Freud, S.: *Three Contributions to the Theory of Sex*. New York, Nervous and mental Disease Pub. Co., 1930.
22. Fromm, E.: Psychoanalytic characterology and its application to the understanding of culture. *In* S. S. Sargent and M. W. Smith, Eds., *Culture and Personality*. New York, Basic Books, 1949, pp. 1-10.
23. Gesell, A., and Ilg, F. L.: *Feeding Behavior of Infants*. Philadelphia, Lippincott, 1937.
24. ——, and ——: *Infant and Child in the Culture of Today*. New York, Harper, 1943.
25. Goldfrank, E.: Socialization, personality, and the structure of Pueblo society. *Am. Anthropol. 47*: 516-539, 1945.
26. Haddy, T. B., and Adams, F. H.: Factors of importance in breast milk. *J. Pediat. 40*: 243-253, 1952.
27. Hallowell, A. I.: The use of projective techniques in the study of the socio-psychological aspects of acculturation. *J. Proj. Tech. 15*: 26-44, 1951.
28. Henry, J., and Bogg, J.: Child rearing, culture, and the natural world. *Psychiatry 15*: 261-271, 1952.
29. Hewitt, D., and Stewart, A.: The Oxford child health survey: a study of the influence of social and genetic factors on infant weight. *Hum. Biol. 24*: 309-319, 1952.
30. Huschka, M.: The child's response to coercive bowel training. *Psychosom. Med. 4*: 301-308, 1942.
31. Jackson, E. B., and Trainham, G.: *Family Centered Maternity and Infant Care*. New York, Josiah Macy, Jr., Foundation, 1950.
32. Jersild, A. T.: *Child Psychology*, ed. 4. New York, Prentice Hall, 1954.
33. ——, Woodyard, E. S., and del Solar, C.: *Joys and Problems of Child Rearing*. New York, Teachers College, Columbia University, 1949.
34. Kinsey, A. C., et al.: *Sexual Behavior in the Human Male*. Philadelphia, Saunders, 1948.
35. ——, ——: *Sexual Behavior in the Human Female*. Philadelphia, Saunders, 1953.
36. Klatskin, E. H.: Intelligence test performance at one year among infants raised with flexible methodology. *J. Clin. Psychol. 8*: 230-237, 1952.
37. Kluckhohn, C.: Culture and behavior. *In* G. Lindzey, Ed., *Handbook of Social Psychology*. Vol. 2. *Special Fields and Applications*. Cambridge, Mass., Addison-Wesley, 1954, pp. 921-976.
38. Koch, H. L.: An analysis of certain forms of so-called "nervous habits" in young children. *J. Genet. Psychol. 46*: 139-170, 1935.
39. Leighton, D., and Kluckhohn, C.: *Children of the People*. Cambridge, Harvard University Press, 1947.
40. Levy, D. M.: Fingersucking and accessory movements in early infancy. *Am. J. Psychiat. 7*: 881-918, 1928.
41. ——: Thumb or fingersucking from the psychiatric angle. *Child Develop. 8*: 99-101, 1937.
42. McGraw, M. B.: Neural maturation as exemplified in achievement of bladder control. *J. Pediat. 16*: 580-590, 1940.
43. Malinowski, B. *Sex and Repression in Savage Society*. New York, Harcourt, Brace, 1927.

44. Mead, M.: On the implications for anthropology of the Gesell-Ilg approach to maturation. *In* D. Haring, Ed., *Personal Character and Cultural Milieu.* Syracuse, Syracuse University Press, 1949, pp. 508-517.
45. Moloney, J. C.: The Cornelian corner. *Psychiat. Quart. 20*: 603-609, 1946.
46. ———: The Cornelian corner and its rationale. *In* M. J. E. Senn, Ed., *Problems of Early Infancy,* Transactions of First Conference, 1947. New York, Josiah Macy, Jr., Foundation, 1948, pp. 17-26.
47. Mott, S. M.: Mother-father preference. *Charact. & Pers. 5*: 302-304, 1937.
48. Mowrer, O. H. and Mowrer, W. M.: Enuresis—a method for its study and treatment. *Am. J. Orthopsychiat. 8*: 436-459, 1938.
49. Murdock, G. P., and Whiting, J. W. M.: Cultural determination of parental attitudes: the relationship between the social structure, particularly family structure and parental behavior. *In* M. J. E. Senn, Ed., *Problems of Infancy and Childhood,* Transactions of Fourth Conference, 1950. New York, Josiah Macy, Jr., Foundation, 1951.
50. Orlansky, H.: Infant care and personality. *Psychol. Bull. 46*: 1-48, 1949.
51. Peterson, C. H., and Spano, F.: Breast feeding, maternal rejection and child personality. *Charact. & Pers. 10*: 62-66, 1941.
52. Pinneau, S. R.: A critique on the articles by Margaret Ribble. *Child Develop. 21*: 203-228, 1950.
53. ———: The infantile disorders of hospitalism and anaclitic depression. *Psychol. Bull. 52*: 429-452, 1955.
54. Pollock, G. H., and Richmond, J. B.: Nutritional anemia in children. *Psychosom. Med. 15*: 477-484, 1953.
55. Reynolds, M. M., and Malley, H.: Sleep of young children. *J. Genet. Psychol. 43*: 322-351, 1933.
56. Ribble, M. A.: *The Rights of Infants.* New York, Columbia University Press, 1943.
57. ———: Infantile experience in relation to personality development. *In* J. McV.. Hunt, Ed., *Personality and the Behavior Disorders,* vol. 2. New York, Ronald Press, 1944.
58. Roberts, E.: Thumb and finger sucking in relation to feeding in early infancy. *Am. J. Dis. Child. 68*: 7-8, 1944.
59. Roberts, K. E., and Schoellkopf, J. A.: Eating, sleeping, and elimination practices of a group of two-and-one-half-year-old children. *Am. J. Dis. Child. 82*: 121-152, 1951.
60. Sears, R. R., and Wise, G. W.: Relation of cup-feeding in infancy to thumb-sucking and the oral drive. *Am. J. Orthopsychiat. 20*: 123-138, 1950.
61. Sewell, W. H.: Infant training and the personality of the child. *Am. J. Sociol. 58*: 150-160, 1952.
62. ———, and Mussen, P. H.: The effects of feeding, weaning, and scheduling procedures on childhood adjustment and the formation of oral symptoms. *Child Develop. 23*: 185-191, 1952.
63. ———, ———, and Harris, C. W.: Relationships among child training practices. *Am. Sociol. Rev. 20*: 137-148, 1955.
64. Shirley, M. M.: Impact of mother's personality on the young child. *Smith Coll. Stud. Soc. Wk. 12*: 15-64, 1941.

65. Simpson, M.: *Parent Preference of Young Children*. New York, Teachers College, Columbia University, 1935.
66. Simsarian, F. P.: Self-demand feeding of infants and young children in family settings. *Ment. Hygiene 32*: 217-225, 1948.
67. ——, and McLendon, P. A.: Feeding behavior of an infant during the first twelve weeks of life on a self-demand schedule. *J. Pediat. 20*: 93-103, 1942.
68. ——, and ——: Further records of the self-demand schedule in infant feeding. *J. Pediat. 27*: 109-114, 1945.
69. Stendler, C. B.: Sixty years of child training practices. *J. Pediat. 36*: 122-134, 1950.
70. Stewart, A. H., et al.: Excessive infant crying (colic) in relation to parent behavior. *Am. J. Psychiat. 110*: 687-694, 1954.
71. Straus, M. A.: Childhood experience and emotional security in the context of Sinhalese social organization. *Soc. Forces 33*: 152-160, 1954.
72. Sullivan, H. S.: Conceptions of modern psychiatry. *Psychiatry 3*: 1-117, 1940.
73. Thurston, J. R., and Mussen, P. H.: Infant feeding gratification and adult personality. *J. Pers. 19*: 449-458, 1951.
74. Vincent, C. E.: Trends in infant care ideas. *Child Develop. 22*: 199-209, 1951.
75. Wedge, B. M.: Occurrence of psychosis among Okinawans in Hawaii. *J. Psychiat. 109*: 255-258, 1952.
76. Whiting, J. W. M., and Child, I. L.: *Child Training and Personality*. New Haven, Yale University Press, 1953.
77. Yarrow, L. J.: The relationship between nutritive sucking experiences in infancy and non-nutritive sucking in childhood. *J. Genet. Psychol. 84*: 149-162, 1954.

PART III

Personality Development

CHAPTER 9

Ego Development*

The investigation of the self-concept in early infancy is obviously fraught with serious scientific hazards. In the absence of verbal reports from the child regarding his perceptions of self and universe, we must have recourse to speculation and inference from the way he is treated, from the demands made upon him, from his reactive capacities, and from a subjective estimate of the degree of cognitive sophistication that determines his perception of these things. In making such inferences, the greatest single source of error is an "adultomorphic" approach which can never be completely avoided (see p. 14). But despite this limitation and the probable impossibility of ever obtaining objectively verifiable data, speculation is still necessary and desirable in order to avoid important gaps in our theory of personality development. Later stages of ego development are naturally dependent in part upon beginning phases in the evolution of a notion of self—even if the infant cannot tell us what they are. Speculative formulations are as allowable here as in other theoretical areas, provided that they possess some plausibility, obey the law of parsimony, are logically reconcilable with related empirical data at a later stage of development, and are uttered with the humility and tentativeness befitting their status as hypotheses rather than as definitively established facts. And in this particular instance there is the additional requirement that they be consistent with the presumed cognitive maturity of infants.

DEFINITION OF CONCEPTS

To avoid confusion later it is necessary to distinguish at the outset between the terms *self, self-concept, ego,* and *personality,* which constitute in the order given an ascending hierarchy of complexity and inclusiveness. The *self* is a constellation of individual perceptions and memories consisting of the visual image of the appearance of one's body, the auditory image of the sound of one's name, images of kinaesthetic sensations and visceral tension, memories of personal events, etc. The *self-concept,* on the other hand, is an abstraction of the essential and distinguishing characteristics of the self that differentiate an individual's "selfhood" from the environment and from other selves. In the course of development, various evaluative

*The material in this chapter is largely a revised and highly abridged version of material presented in earlier publications of the writer [6, 7]

attitudes, values, aspirations, motives and obligations become associated with the self-concept. The organized system of interrelated self-attitudes, self-motives and self-values that results may be called the *ego*. This constellation of ego referents in turn undergoes conceptualization: a least common denominator is abstracted which at any given stage of development constitutes the conceptual essence of the person's notion of himself as a functioning individual endowed with certain attributes related to role and status. Insofar as this abstraction is a discriminable content of awareness characterized by personal identifiability and some continuity over time, it enjoys a measure of psychological substantiveness. Hence, as long as one does not reify it (i.e., attribute corporeality, activity or motivation to it) it is justifiable to refer to the ego as an entity.

Personality is a still more inclusive term than ego. It includes *all* of the behavioral predispositions characteristic of the individual at a given point in his life history. Thus it embraces the more peripheral, transitory and trivial as well as the more central aspects of his behavioral repertoire. This distinction between ego and personality highlights the crucial role of the ego in the individual's personality organization. His psychological world is hierarchically ordered in terms of a gradient of ego-involvement consisting of concentric zones of objects, persons, values and activities varying in distance of affective proximity to self. The more central zones are areas of concern and importance to him. He has a vital stake in them. What happens in these areas is a source of pride or shame, of feelings of success or failure. It is these central ego-implicated constituents of personality which give it continuity, consistency, and generality.

In the present chapter we propose to present a normative overview of ego development, to delineate the changes in ego structure that accompany shifts in the biosocial status of the developing individual. The remaining chapters will consider in greater detail various component aspects (emotions, values and interests) and determinants (relationships with parents, peers, teachers, and the wider culture) of ego development. Still other determinants of ego development (physical and motor capacity, language, and cognition) which also constitute important areas of child development in their own right will be considered in Part IV, *Special Aspects of Development.*

PREDETERMINISTIC APPROACHES TO EGO DEVELOPMENT

According to psychoanalytic doctrine the ego is formed as a characterological precipitate of the id as it comes into contact with reality.[24, 25, 36] It supposedly serves both as a subjugator of socially unacceptable id impulses and as an ally of the id in satisfying its libidinal drives through acceptable means.[24, 25] Thus psychoanalytic theory does not regard the ego as completely preformed but as an experiential derivative of innate drives. Nevertheless it is clear that this theory follows basically predeterministic lines: variability in ego development can only occur within the framework of an innately patterned sequence of prestructured libidinal drives; ego drives do not arise autonomously in the course of changing interpersonal experience but can only be derived (sublimated) from the original source of libidinal energy; since individual and cultural variability in the unfolding of psychosexual drives is made coextensive with ego development the *only* kind of experience that is considered relevant to this development is that which involves frustration and gratification of erogenous drives.*

The psychoanalytic view of ego development also contains elements of preformationism as well as predeterminism. All properties of the ego are not considered to evolve from experiential modification of the id; the existence of a rudimentary ego and of some specific ego attributes is assumed at birth before there is any opportunity for interpersonal experience.[25, 36] Thus the neonate is said to react with anxiety to the "trauma" of placental separation from the mother,[26] to be capable of volition, and to experience feelings of omnipotence[22]; and the male child is presumed to have innate attitudes of both hatred toward and identification with his father.[25] In addition, even though psychoanalysis attributes the genesis of patterned psychosexual drives exclusively to a phylogenetic id, too many core aspects of personality related to the self-concept are implicated in the origins of sexual behavior to exclude it arbitrarily from ego structure. Hence, psychoanalytic concepts of psychosexual drives actually constitute a preformationist approach to an integral component of ego development.

AN INTERACTIONAL APPROACH TO EGO DEVELOPMENT

Ego development may be viewed as the resultant of a process of continuous interaction between current social experience and existing personality structure that is mediated by perceptual responses. According to this interactional view, neither the direction nor the patterning of ego development are predetermined by endogenous genic factors or by the sequential unfolding of psychosexual drives. It is felt instead that a wide range of interpersonal experience (both current and internalized within person-

*Gesell's approach to ego development, as already pointed out (see p. 29), is also predeterministic. It presumes that (just as in the case of early motor development) "the basic order and the general modality if not the specific outline of differentiations are determined by intrinsic factors ['ancestral genes']."[27] Environmental factors allegedly account for only minor variations in ego development, whereas all basic uniformities are attributed to internal "morphogenic" factors.

ality) constitutes the major determinant of inter- and intracultural uniformities in ego development.* Such experience is prerequisite to the genesis of the ego and of ego attributes, including psychosexual drives. Its salient components are not infant care practices that impinge on erogenous zones but significant dimensions of parent attitudes, shifts in role and status, and changes in cultural demands and expectations. From exposure to influences such as these, ego drives are generated autonomously rather than being sublimated from prestructured libidinal drives.

Major Variables Affecting Ego Development

The more important variables that participate in ego development may be classified as social (external) endogenous (internal), and perceptual (mediating). Social variables include all aspects of institutional, intergroup, intra-group, and interpersonal relationships and organization that affect the course of ego development. They not only comprise the current stimulating conditions that help determine the direction of behavior and development at any particular moment, but also, through a process of internalization, contribute significantly to the growing structure of personality. Endogenous (or internal) variables constitute the growth matrix (see p. 52) of ego development. They are a product of all previous relevant interactions between heredity and environment, and selectively predispose or limit the direction of change in response to current experience. Internal variables include personality and temperamental traits, level of motor and cognitive capacity, physiological factors, and, most important, the prevailing state of ego organization itself. Thus, it is clear that most significant personality development is not a simple and immediate function of social experience. Always interposed between the two are both perceptual factors and the ego structure that the individual brings into the social situation.

Perceptual variables play a mediating role in the interactional process underlying ego development. Before social experience (e.g., parent attitudes, cultural norms), various competencies related to self, and different ego needs, motives and attributes can be brought together in the same interactional field, they must first be reacted to perceptually (i.e., give rise to a clear content of awareness). The stimulus world, therefore, whether of internal or external origin is not the proximate antecedent of behavior or development; the perceptual world is.† Thus although a child's role and

---

*Various patterning predispositions and potentialities of genic origin (see table 1, p. 65) also give rise to intercultural uniformities in ego development. These genic factors, however, influence primarily those general features of human behavior that set limits to variability in ego development rather than determine the direction of such development in their own right.

†Perceptual reality considered as a dependent variable is itself an interactional product of stimulus content, cognitive maturity and ego structure.

status in the home and his parents' behavior toward him are objective social events in the real world, they affect his ego development only to the extent and in the form in which they are perceived. This does not imply that the perceived world *is* the real world but that perceptual reality is both psychological reality and the actual (mediating) variable that influences behavior and development.

Insofar as perception itself undergoes systematic developmental changes during the life cycle, level of perceptual maturity must be considered a determining as well as a mediating variable in ego development. We have already seen the extent to which perceptual immaturity insulates the young infant from awareness of environmental threat and from the attitudinal effects of parent practices. This same perceptual immaturity, for example, does not enable the child to appreciate fully his executive dependence and incompetence or the meaning of parental deference to his needs during infancy; it obscures awareness of subtle interpersonal attitudes and of the functional and reciprocal nature of social rules and obligations within the childhood peer group. On the other hand, increasing perceptual maturity makes it possible for the self-concept and the ego to become abstract conceptual entities. Also, many of the more complex constituents of the ego, such as self-esteem, self-critical ability, and the ability to set consistent levels of aspiration could only exist in very rudimentary fashion in the absence of verbal symbols.

How can we explain these evidences of growth in perceptual maturity? One obvious possibility is that perceptual maturity is a function of cognitive capacity and sophistication which, in turn, tend to increase with age and experience. Here we must consider the impact on perception of increased ability to verbalize, to manipulate symbols and abstractions, and to form categorical judgments; to make more subtle differentiations within the stimulus field, to avoid animistic thinking, and to disregard irrelevant instances of concomitance in reaching judgments of causality (see Chapter 17.) Some aspects of perceptual maturation, however, are probably attributable to normative modifications of ego structure itself, e.g., changed perceptions of parents and peers following upon ego devaluation (see pp. 288, 464).

The Nature and Acquisition of Biosocial Status

The term "biosocial status" is a convenient abstraction which makes it possible to refer to the generalized aspects of both role and status pertaining to an individual of given sex and functional age level in a relatively homogeneous cultural setting. Its *culturally standardized* attributes are anchored in the organizational procedures, requirements, values and traditions of social groupings and institutions. Thus infants, as a group in American middle-class culture, have a stereotyped biosocial status recognizably distinct from that of male and female children, adolescents and adults. The role aspects of biosocial status consist of significant interpersonal behavior functionally differentiated in part by adjustment to the demands and expectations of others; the status aspects delineate hierarchical position vis-a-vis others as defined by relative dominance, control, prerogatives, independence, prestige, etc. However, the actual biosocial status that any *individual* enjoys is a *particular* interactional product that is a variant of the cultural stereotype. The latter serves as an external determinant entering into the formation of personal biosocial status by generating (through appropriate representatives) specific demands and expectations to which the individual carriers of the culture react (as they do to any social stimulus) in terms of existing ego structure, idiosyncratic personality traits and perceptual maturity.

But it is not enough to say that individuals in accordance with idiosyncratic personality dispositions and social situations enact and enjoy variants of a perceived cultural stereotype of biosocial status. Because of an all-too-easy tendency to conceive of age level roles in a reified sense, as an ordered sequence of socially stylized masks and robes racked up in a cultural prop room all ready to don as the player moves across the stage of life, it is necessary to insist explicitly on the fact that biosocial status is for the most part an *individual achievement* in an interpersonal setting. Except for hereditary princes, few persons inherit a ready-made status; and except in the relatively rare instances of highly structured social situations, roles require considerable improvisation. Each of us must achieve our own biosocial status within the framework of the culturally standardized stereotype.[14]

This becomes more clear when one inquires how roles are learned. The formal concept of role implies that an individual acquires a role by learning from a model the actions, words, grimaces and gestures appropriate for him in a given situation. But when one actually looks for this model in childhood it turns out to be little more than a reified abstraction. Does a child learn the child's role by attending the children's theatre, by reading books about children, or even by observing friends and siblings? No. In early childhood the cultural model gets into the act as a psychological reality mainly through the influence it exerts on the *parents'* child rearing practices. In much the same manner as the young of other mammalian species,[61] the human infant after highly variable initial contacts with parents, siblings and others enters into increasingly more standardized and stable relationships with them. The upshot of these repeated interactions are roles that he himself and his opposite numbers have *created*. It is only as the child grows older and is exposed more directly to the symbolic values of the culture that preconceived notions and models become important in the initial structuring of interpersonal "transactions" between human beings.

Primary and Derived Status. Whenever social life is characterized by differences in roles and status and by dependence of one person on another or on the group as a whole, one of the more basic kinds of human interaction that arises under such conditions is the reciprocal relationship of identification-acceptance. This type of relationship includes in varying proportions the elements of "dominance-subordination," "leadership-followership," and "care-dependency" described by Scott for different infrahuman mammals.[61] Much confusion results, however, from the failure to distinguish between two essentially different kinds of identification-acceptance, each of which involves a reciprocal relationship between a relatively independent and dominant individual (or group) and a relatively dependent and subordinate individual.[6]

One type of identification which is very common in the canine and simian worlds and very uncommon in the feline world may be called satellization.[6] In a satellizing relationship the subordinate party acknowledges and accepts a subservient and deferential role, and the superordinate party in turn accepts him as an *intrinsically* valuable entity in his personal orbit. The satellizer thereby acquires a vicarious or *derived* biosocial status (a) which is wholly a function of the dependent relationship and independent of his own competence or performance ability, and (b) which is bestowed upon him by the fiat of simple intrinsic valuation by a superordinate individual or group whose authority and power to do so are regarded as unchallengeable.

On the other hand, the two parties to the same "transaction" could relate to each other in quite a different way. The subordinate party could acknowledge his dependency as a temporary, regrettable, and much-to-be remedied fact of life requiring, as a matter of expediency, various *acts* of conformity and deference; but at the same time he does not have to accept a dependent and subservient status as a *person*. In turn, he could either be rejected outright or accorded qualified acceptance, i.e., not for intrinsic reasons (as a person for his own sake), but in terms of his current or potential competence or his usefulness to the superordinate party. The act of identification, if it occurs at all, consists solely in using the latter (superordinate) individual as an emulatory model so that he can learn his skills and methods of operation and thus eventually succeed to his enviable status; and accordingly, the only type of biosocial status that can be engendered in this situation is the *primary* status that reflects his actual functional competence, power, or control. This non-satellizing type of identification occurs for one of two reasons: either the superordinate party will not extend unqualified intrinsic acceptance (e.g., as in the case of the rejecting parent or the parent who values his child for ulterior self-enhancing purposes), or the subordinate party is unwilling to or incapable of satellizing.

The wider significance of primary and derived status for personality structure, as we shall hypothesize in detail later, is that each is associated with distinctive patterns of security (freedom from anticipated threat to physical integrity), adequacy (feelings of self-esteem, worth, importance), and other ego attributes (level of ego aspirations, dependence and independence, etc.) Corresponding to derived status in ego structure are both feelings of *intrinsic* security that inhere in the affectional aspects of a satellizing relationship, and feelings of *intrinsic* adequacy that are relatively immune to the vicissitudes of achievement and position. Corresponding in turn to primary status are (a) feelings of *extrinsic* security that depend upon biosocial competence or the possession of a competent executive arm in the person of an available superordinate figure, and (b) feelings of *extrinsic* adequacy that fluctuate with both absolute level of ego aspirations and the discrepancy between the latter and perceived accomplishment or hierarchical position (see p. 289).

Experienced versus "Objective" Dependency. It is important to realize that feelings of dependence and independence in ego structure do not correspond in point to point fashion to the theoretically expected "realities" of the environmental dependency situation. This is so because more proximate than these latter "realities" in determining dependency feelings are actual attitudes and behaviors of parents and the child's perceptions of same. During early infancy, for example, when the child is most helpless and dependent "in fact," he is treated with most deference by his parents. Thus, despite his actual helplessness to gratify his needs or compel conformity to his wishes, considerable environmental support is given to his perception of self as volitionally independent. Perceptual immaturity adds further to the discrepancy between the child's actual biosocial incompetence and the minimal feelings of dependency he probably does experience (see p. 286).

Executive and Volitional Dependence. At this point it might be helpful to make more explicit the distinction between executive and volitional dependence. Both consist of affectively colored self-perceptions of limited self-sufficiency and freedom of action, but *executive* "refers to the manipulative activity involved in completing a need-satisfaction sequence, whereas *volitional* refers solely to the act of willing the satisfaction of a given need apart from any consideration as to how this is to be consummated."[6] As perceptions also they correspond only *more or less* to their relevant stimulus content. And although these two ego attributes tend to be positively related to each other, marked discrepancies may exist between them at any point in the life cycle, especially during infancy when it is reasonable to suppose that the child conceives of himself as both volitionally independent and executively dependent.*

In addition to constituting perceived ego attributes, volitional and executive dependence (or independence) also constitute ego *needs*. Their strength varies in relation to other ego attributes (such as notions of omnipotence), to needs for primary and derived status, and to parental and cultural demands, reinforcement and punishment. The need for executive dependence is compatible with and reinforced by the exalted (regal) self-concept of infants and with the benevolent, undemanding environment in which they live (see p. 286). The young child is coerced by environmental pressures and by the need for derived status to both surrender much volitional independence and to acquire more executive independence. During adolescence the attainment of executive independence is essential for achieving the volitional independence and primary status necessary for adult personality maturation.

Sources of Psychosocial and Idiosyncratic Differences

Psychosocial differences in ego development reflect both differences in the ways various cultures institutionalize interpersonal relationships on the basis of age, sex, and kinship, and differences in basic values and ideals of personality structure. These factors in turn influence such crucial aspects of ego development as the handling and timing of shifts in bio-social status (e.g., explicitness, abruptness, choice of socializing agents), the amounts and kinds of status that individuals are expected to seek, and the degree of personality maturity considered appropriate for different age levels. In our culture, for example, girls are expected to satellize more than boys, and women are expected to obtain a larger proportion of their current biosocial status than are men from derived rather than from primary sources. Thus, girls more than boys tend to perceive themselves as accepted and intrinsically valued by parents,[10] and "are more apt to be relatively docile, to conform . . . to adult expectations, [and] to be 'good.' "[53] Boys' wishes and emotional responsiveness exceed girls' in the areas of self-aggrandizement, personal achievement, and possessions, and are surpassed by girls' in the direction of social and family relationships, physical appearance, and personal characteristics.[20, 38, 79]

Within the normative schema of ego development to be presented below, numerous opportunities also exist for the elaboration of idiosyncratic differences. First, it might be expected that children who are *temperamentally*

*Failure to make this distinction between volitional and executive dependence is responsible for the unexplained contradictory allegations in psychoanalytic literature that the infant both regards himself as omnipotent and feels overwhelmed by his dependence on parents.

more assertive, "thick-skinned," self-sufficient, energetic, or resistive to stress, would be less dependent on others' approval, more capable of maintaining self-esteem in the face of less primary or derived status, and in general less disposed to satellize than children with the opposite set of temperamental traits; that individuals genically predisposed to develop strong hedonistic needs would tend to be more resistive to pressures directed toward attentuation of these needs during the course of ego maturation; and that children who are accelerated in motor or cognitive development would be subjected to greater parental demands for mature behavior. Second, as will be seen shortly, differences in such basic dimensions of parent attitudes as acceptance-rejection, intrinsic-extrinsic valuation, and over- or under-domination, have important implications for variability in satellization, desatellization, needs for achievement, and mode of assimilating values. A third source of idiosyncratic differences in development lies in variability in perceptual sensitivity. It seems reasonable to suppose, for example, that the perceptually more sensitive child is more vulnerable to the detrimental effects of unfavorable parent attitudes and is more apt to be aware of his own limitations and the realities of the dependency situation. Finally, once differences in such ego attributes as relative propensity to satellize are established they themselves serve as important sources of variability in ego development. Thus we might predict that, everything else being equal, the more intrinsic self-esteem a child enjoys the less need he has to strive for ego aggrandizement and the more realistically he is able to adjust his current aspirational level to prior experience of failure.[10]

NORMATIVE SEQUENCES IN EGO DEVELOPMENT*

In this section we propose to outline normative uniformities in the sequential course of ego development during childhood. Most of the evidence for this analysis comes from materials drawn from our own culture. Nevertheless, it is believed that sufficient intercultural commonality prevails in genic patterning predispositions, behavioral potentialities, and in intrafamilial and social needs, problems and conditions of adaptation (see table 1, p. 65) to make many of the hypothesized general features of ego development applicable to all cultural environments. This assumption, however, can only be verified by extensive cross-cultural investigation.

Differentiation of the Self-Concept

Preverbal Stage. As a unified abstraction of its essential properties, the self-concept is a complex ideational entity that is slow in developing and usually requires the facilitating influence of language. Nevertheless the child

*I wish to emphasize again that the theoretical propositions contained herein are frankly speculative and are offered as *hypotheses* only.

possesses a functional *perception of self*, *i.e.*, of the distinction between that which is within and that which is beyond the borders of his own body, long before he acquires any language. As in the evolution of any new percept, the basic problem is that of defining boundaries between figure and ground. In the case of the self-percept, the boundaries of the self must be delimited from the wider environment of objects and persons with which it is initially fused.[28, 51, 66]

This latter process occurs along multisensory lines as the infant comes into contact with his physical environment. The sense of touch acquaints him with the presence of objects outside himself[28]; kinaesthetic sensations make him aware of his own movements in space; and the sense of pain vividly informs him that transgressions of the self-not-self boundary are unpleasant. The visual *body image* as manifested by self-recognition of a portrait or mirror reflection[78] and by correct identification of own age, size, sex and skin color in a series of pictures[19, 42] first becomes a stable self-percept during the preschool period. Apparently, therefore, in the early years of childhood it serves more as an abstract symbol of self-identity than as a concrete functional datum helping the child to differentiate between himself and the environment.

Self-perception is facilitated further by the infant's reaction to the mother as a person. As early as six weeks he smiles differentially to the sound of the human voice[17] even though it is not associated habitually with care and attention[21]; and in the third month of life he smiles and vocalizes spontaneously in response to the human face.[21, 68] Thus "mother's outline serves as an anchorage point for the slowly accumulating self pattern."[51] It provides a scaffolding for the elaboration of his own self-portrait as a person,* and as we shall see shortly, makes possible a perception of mother as a manipulator of his reality and as a causal agent in the satisfaction of his needs.

Perhaps the most poignant experience leading to the consciousness of self develops as an outgrowth of inevitable delays in the gratification of the infant's organic needs. Here the contrast between inner experience and the outside world is highlighted by the juxtaposition of awareness (a) of painful discomfort and pleasant satisfaction referable to the *body* and (b) of objects and persons in the *environment* that lead to dramatic change in the affective quality of consciousness. Later, when a sense of volition develops, the act of willing (as a directed expression of the self as an entity) and the

---

*Perception of other persons also precedes self-perception in the recognition of body image[78] (as in mirror reflections and photographs) and in the development of language concepts dealing with persons.[28] Perceptual discrimination between self and others is acquired more slowly when others are similar to self, as in pairs of twins.[46]

assistance it invokes from other persons sharpens even more the distinction between self and environment. Further accentuation of the self-environment dichotomy accompanies the appreciation of cause-effect sequences and emerging perceptions of own helplessness, executive dependence, and volitional omnipotence to be described below.

Verbal Stage. The abstraction of a unified concept of self from its component percepts (cutaneous, visceral, visual, volitional, etc.) requires the intervention of language. Two preliminary steps precede the final emergence of the self-concept in its most highly developed verbal expression as the first-person singular: (a) the concept of possession, and (b) third-person reference to self. By the eighth month, "possessive emotions toward toys are manifested . . . Between the tenth and twelfth months . . . a positive sense of property becomes observable."[67] By 21 months* this is conceptualized as "mine," a generalized term that not only includes all *personal* possessions but also excludes the possessions of others. This concept of possession presupposes a sharpening of the distinction between self and others to the point where objects come to "belong" to the person habitually using them.

A slightly more advanced stage in the acquisition of a verbal concept of self is completed at 24 months. At this time, the child becomes aware of himself as an entity in the same sense that he perceives other persons as entities.[28] Before he referred to another child as "baby"; now he uses this same term or his own given name in making third-person reference to himself, his possessions and his activities. The highest degree of nominative abstraction in relation to the self appears at 27 months when the child uses the personal pronoun "I."[28] This "I" constitutes an abstraction of all the separate perceptions of self. It implies a genuine conceptual self-consciousness. In contrast to third-person usage which merely indicates cognizance of himself as a *person like other persons,* the use of the first-person singular means that he designates himself as a special and unique kind of personal entity, *distinct from all other persons.* After this point is reached, a new abstract level of self-reactions becomes possible: identification with persons, goals and values; incorporation of standards; competitive behavior; and finally, self-judgments, guilt feelings, and conscience.[1, 6, 28, 31, 58, 66]

The Omnipotent Phase

The stage of ego development that follows the emergence of a functional self-concept may be designated as the omnipotent phase (roughly, the period

*The Yale norms reported here were obtained from a very specialized and unrepresentative group of children. As used in this chapter they are only intended to convey a rough notion of *mean* age and sequential order of development in an unrepresentative but relatively homogeneous sample of children in our culture. It is not implied that the same designated mean ages or sequences necessarily apply to all children everywhere.

from six months to two and one-half years). It seems paradoxical and contradictory that feelings of omnipotence should coexist with the period of the child's greatest helplessness and dependence on adults. Yet, as we shall see shortly, the paradox is easily resolved if the nonunitary concept of dependence is first broken down into its easily discriminable executive and volitional components; when this is done self-perceptions of volitional independence and executive dependence are seen as quite compatible with each other under the biosocial conditions of infancy. Unlike the psychoanalytic doctrine of infantile omnipotence[22] which assumes the existence of both a preformed ego and of volition at and even prior to birth, the present theory conceives of omnipotent feelings in infants as a naturalistic product of actual interpersonal experience (parental deference) and cognitive immaturity. It is self-evident that the child's perception of his relative omnipotence cannot be demonstrated empirically prior to the advent of language; and even then it can only be inferred from rampant expressions of imperiousness and possessiveness that are so prevalent during the latter portion of this age interval.[1, 28]

Development of Executive Dependence. Although completely helpless and dependent *in fact,* it is highly improbable that the newborn infant appreciates his helplessness and executive dependence. Before he could conceivable recognize his helplessness, he would first have to be capable of deliberately willing the satisfaction of his needs and perceiving in a causal sense his own inability to do so. Similarly, to appreciate that he is dependent on *another* for the execution of his wishes requires that he perceive the latter as a person and the succorant acts of this person as causally related to his need-satisfaction sequences. In the first few months of life, however, crying is not volitional, mother is not perceived as a person, and the child probably has no conception of causality. It is true, of course, that the mother is always present before and during the act of need reduction, and that after the first month of life merely holding the infant without offering him nourishment is sufficient to still his hunger cry. But at this early stage of development it is more credible (for the reasons given above) to suppose that the mother (by virtue of habitual association with need reduction) serves as a signal of imminent need satisfaction and perhaps as a substitutive satisfying object in her own right, than that the infant perceives his helplessness and the *causal* connection between mother's presence and the reduction of his hunger.

From the foregoing analysis it would seem that the development of a sense of volition is a prerequisite first step before a feeling of executive dependence can arise. How this development is brought about, however, must remain forever in the realm of speculation. The most credible hypothesis we can suggest here is that volition is a learned outgrowth of the innately determined pattern of general excitement in response to any intense internal or external stimulus (e.g., hunger). This reactive pattern, particularly crying, has adaptive value in that it frequently evokes maternal succorant activity which reduces the need responsible for the excitement. Eventually, after repeated observation of the efficacy of crying in relieving the tensions of need, it may be supposed that a causal connection is perceived between antecedent and consequent. At this point crying becomes a conscious, deliberately employed (volitional) device rather than an almost reflex response for relieving unpleasant sensations referable to self.

Once volition is acquired, it reciprocally facilitates the perception of causality, since the act of willing constitutes a vivid antecedent in many causal sequences. The child is now in a position to perceive that his expression of will does not lead to need satisfaction through his own manipulative activity (perception of own helplessness) but only through the intervention of an external agency (perception of executive dependence). In this instance ability to perceive the mother as a person facilitates the perception of causality in as much as it is undoubtedly less difficult to conceive of a person than of an object as a causal agent and manipulator of reality.

Environmental and Perceptual Supports of Omnipotence. But all the while that a conception of executive independence is being developed, a notion of *volitional* independence and omnipotence is concomitantly engendered. It is precisely when the child is most helpless that almost invariably in all cultures he is accorded more indulgence and deference by parents than at any other period of childhood.[75] At this time parents tend to be most solicitous and eager to gratify his expressed needs. In general they make few demands upon him and usually accede to his legitimate requests. If training is instituted, it tends to be delayed, gradual and gentle.[43, 75] In this benevolent environment, therefore, much support is provided in external stimulus conditions for a perception of parental subservience to his will. Furthermore, it is unlikely that he is sufficiently mature, cognitively speaking, to appreciate the relatively subtle motivations (i.e., love, duty, altruism) underlying their deference. The immaturity does not inhere in lack of ability to perceive the overt attitudes and behaviors of individuals in his interpersonal world; he does not expect to receive the same degree of deference from older siblings as he does from parents. It is manifested rather at the level of perceiving the more subtle, covert or motivational aspects of attitudes. Thus arises the quite understandable autistic misperception that because of his volitional power the parent is *obliged* to serve him rather than that the subservience is altruistic out of deference to his extreme helplessness.

The infant's appreciation of his *executive* dependence does not detract essentially from his self-concept of relative *volitional* omnipotence and in-dependence. He perceives his helplessness and dependence on others, but nevertheless when he wills the satisfaction of his needs they seem to be satisfied. Hence his perception of dependency is limited to the executive sphere. A volitionally powerful individual has no need for executive compe-tence as long as other competent persons are at his beck and call. In fact it may even enhance the child's notion of his own power that success in need gratification takes place *despite* the manifest handicap of executive incompetence. He might, therefore, legitimately think, "My will must be powerful indeed if a tiny, helpless creature like myself can compel omniscient adults to gratify my desires." At the very most, perceived executive de-pendence qualifies the regal scope of his will by making it subject to the availability of a compliant executive arm. Feelings of executive dependence thus become satisfactorily integrated as a subsidiary aspect of the more in-clusive self-image of volitional omnipotence. And despite objective biosocial incompetency the infant's sense of adequacy (self-esteem) at this point—his feeling of personal worth, importance, and ability to control and manipu-late the environment to his own ends—is predominantly of the *primary* type; that is, it depends upon a misinterpretation of early parental sub-servience to his needs and desires as a result of which he vastly exaggerates his volitional power and independence.

The self-perception of helplessness, however, constitutes a potential threat to the infant's physical safety and integrity. Hence it gives rise to an under-current of insecurity which can only be allayed by the continued availability of the executive arm upon which he is dependent (mother). Thus at this stage of development his sense of security—his level of confidence regard-ing the future benevolence of his interpersonal environment in providing for his basic needs—is closely allied with feelings of executive dependence; and in as much as a need for security exists it generates a parallel need for perpetuating executively dependent relationships. These dependency needs are reinforced both by (a) the perceived efficacy of such relationships in providing security, and in relieving hunger, discomfort and insecurity (reward), and (b) by the undesirable consequences associated with un-availability of mother, i.e., insecurity, hunger, discomfort (frustration), the alleviation of which can only be accomplished through the highly canalized device of the dependency situation. Thus when the dependency needs of infancy are not satisfied because of abrupt separation from the mother, sudden change or ambiguity in the conditions of succorance, or premature demands for executive independence, there is some evidence of residual over-dependence in young children[64, 69] and of overanxiety about dependence in adults.[75]

The Ego Devaluation Crisis

As long as the infant is helpless in fact, parents are content to be indulgent and deferential in treating him, expecting only that he grow and realize the phylogenetic promise of infancy. In part this attitude is indicative of solicitousness and altruism; but it is also the only realistic expectation they could have in the light of his actual incapacity for responding to their direction. They are naturally desirous of being liberated from this subservience as soon as possible and of assuming the volitionally ascendent role that is warranted in the relationship. In addition they begin to feel the social pressure and the responsibility of training the child in the ways of his culture. But typically in all cultures they wait until he attains sufficient motor, cognitive, and social maturity to enable him to conform to their wishes.

The age deemed appropriate for ending the stage of volitional independence and executive dependence varies between two and four in different cultures. In our own middle-class society it is closer to two than four.[75] At this time parents become less deferential and attentive. They comfort the child less and demand more conformity to their own desires and to cultural norms. During this period the child is frequently weaned, is expected to acquire sphincter control, approved habits of eating and cleanliness and to do more things for himself. Parents are less disposed to gratify his demands for immediate gratification, expect more frustration tolerance and responsible behavior, and may even require performance of some household chores. They also become less tolerant toward displays of childish aggression. In short, all of these radical changes in parent behavior tend to undermine environmental supports for infantile self-perceptions of volitional independence and omnipotence.

Increased cognitive sophistication also contributes to ego devaluation by enabling the child to perceive more accurately his relative insignificance and impotence in the household power structure. He begins to appreciate that his parents are free agents who are not obliged to defer to him and only satisfy his needs out of altruism and good will; that he is dependent upon them volitionally as well as executively. Now volitional independence is no longer perceived as compatible with executive dependence. As a consequence of ego devaluation, the situation is precisely reversed: increased *executive* independence is required along with greater *volitional* dependence. From this point on, perceived lack of executive independence is no longer regarded as a regal badge of omnipotence but as a condition necessitating dependence on the will of others.

The Satellizing Solution to Ego Devaluation

The devaluing pressures described above precipitate a crisis in ego-development that is conducive to rapid discontinuous change. They tend to

render the infantile ego structure no longer tenable and to favor reorganization on a satellizing basis, since in no culture can the child compete with
adults on better than marginal terms. The only stable, nonmarginal status
to which he can aspire and still retain a reasonably high level of self-esteem
requires the adoption of a volitionally dependent and subordinate role in
relation to his parents. Since he cannot be omnipotent himself, the next best
thing is to be a satellite of persons who *are*. By so doing he not only acquires a derived status which he enjoys by the fiat of being accepted and
valued as important for himself (i.e., irrespective of his competence and
performance ability), but also by perceiving himself as allied with them[13]
shares vicariously in their omnipotence. His sense of security now becomes
less a function of having competent persons available to satisfy his physical
needs than of maintaining an emotionally and volitionally dependent relationship with stronger, protective and altruistic persons, which implies among
other things the provision of whatever succorance is necessary. He is also
relieved of the burden of justifying his adequacy on the basis of hierarchical
position or actual performance ability, which at the very best could be
marginal and, in any event, are subject to unpredictable fluctuations.

The satellizing solution to the ego devaluation crisis is more stable and
realistic and less traumatic than any alternative solution open to the child
at this time. Since feelings of adequacy (self-esteem) are largely a function of achieving status commensurate with level of ego aspiration, the retention of grandiose aspirations of volitional independence and omnipotence
in the face of a reality which constantly belied these pretensions would obviously make him chronically vulnerable to serious deflation of self-esteem.
On the other hand, there are limits to the degree of ego devaluation that is
consonant with the maintenance of feelings of adequacy. If the child's ego
aspirations had to be lowered to the point necessary to bring them into line
with his *actual* ability to manipulate the environment, the resulting abrupt
and precipitous trauma to self-esteem would probably be even greater than
if the untenable pretensions to omnipotence were retained. Thus, by satellizing he avoids both unfavorable alternatives and maintains the maximal
degree of self-esteem realistically compatible with the cultural status of
children.

Prerequisites for Satellization. From the foregoing it is apparent that
satellization cannot occur in just *any* kind of home environment. Before the
child can accept volitional dependency and seek a derived status he must
first perceive himself as genuinely accepted and valued for himself; for in
the absence of these two parent attitudes, the potential advantages of satellization (i.e., the acquisition of a guaranteed and stable derived status and
the assurance of intrinsic security and adequacy) are vitiated, and the child
has little incentive for relinquishing the aspirations of volitional independ-

ence and becoming subservient to the will of another. Acceptance of volitional dependence on powerful figures is a hazardous venture indeed unless one feels assured in advance of their benevolent intentions. The rejected child also cannot acquire any derived status when his parents, instead of extending emotional support and protection, regard him as an unwanted burden. Rejection is the most extreme method of indicating to the child that the omnipotent and omniscient parents consider him unworthy.

Similarly, the advantages of a derived status cannot accrue if the parent only values the child in terms of his potential eminence.* Sooner or later the child realizes that he is not valued for himself but in terms of his potential capacity for gratifying frustrated parental ambitions. In his case, however, the infantile ego structure is more tenable and less subject to the usual pressures forcing devaluation. The over-valuing parent has no interest in deflating infantile notions of omnipotence and grandiosity. He interprets these characteristics as portentous of future greatness, and continues through indulgence and adulation to provide an environment which helps to maintain for some time the fiction of infantile omnipotence.

Several other variables related to the personality characteristics of parent and child tend to make the process of satellization more or less difficult or prolonged but do not affect ultimate outcome crucially. An unduly submissive or permissive parent who fails to impress the child with the distinction between their respective roles and prerogatives tends to prolong the phase of omnipotence. The child is spared the pressure of parental demands for conformity to their will and standards, and hence exhibits less need for ego devaluation. But if he is truly accepted and valued for his own sake he will eventually perceive his actual biosocial status and choose satellization as the most feasible solution to the problem of maintaining childhood self-esteem in an adult dominated society. Reference has already been made to the effect of temperamental variables in the child on tendency to satellize (see p. 281).

Consequences of Satellization. Satellization has profound consequences for all aspects of ego structure and for the future course of personality development. Part of the satellizing shift in source of biosocial status involves abandonment of notions of volitional omnipotence and independence and

*Evidence from the study of children's perceptions of parent attitudes[10] indicates that it is possible for extrinsically valuing parents to be perceived as accepting (although for ulterior motives). The same evidence, however, supports the logical supposition that the rejecting parent cannot possibly extend intrinsic valuation to his child. In general, acceptance and intrinsic valuation are highly correlated. And since extrinsically valued children are almost invariably overvalued, the latter term alone will be used henceforth in referring to children who are overvalued for ulterior purposes. It is not rare, however, for accepted, intrinsically valued children to be overvalued.

of the centrality of self in the household social economy. But to compensate for this the child acquires a guaranteed source of derived status from which he obtains intrinsic feelings of security and adequacy. Thus children who perceive themselves as more intrinsically valued tend to undergo more ego devaluation: they conceive of their capacities in less omnipotent terms and are less tenacious about maintaining unrealistically high levels of aspiration in a laboratory task after cumulative experience of failure.[10] School children ranked high on acceptance tend to be characterized by "willing obedience" and relative lack of self-sufficiency and ego defensiveness.[59]

Another product of satellization that is related to but distinguishable from its devaluing features (i.e., changes in status, aspiration level, volitional independence) has to do with the *object* or *content* of the child's conformity to parental volitional direction. It encompasses the training goals underlying the new parental demands and expectations to which the child is conforming. These goals may be designated as *ego maturity* goals since (irrespective of later changes in source of status, independence and volitional control) they remain as constant objectives of personality maturation throughout the desatellizing and adult as well as the satellizing period of ego development. Although there is much intercultural variability in the ideals of personality maturity, the needs of individual and cultural survival require that infantile hedonism, executive dependency, and moral irresponsibility be attenuated in all cultures. With respect to all of these components the infant is characteristically at one pole and the mature adult at the other.

Hence, as children increase in age beyond the period of infancy, they are expected to grow in ability to develop nonhedonistic motivations, to plan in terms of larger and more distant goals, and to forego immediate satisfactions in order to gratify more important, long-term aspirations. Second, they are expected to develop more executive independence. Growth in motor capacity for self-help is not always matched by equal *willingness* to carry out the often tedious and time-consuming manipulations necessary in gratifying needs. Parents, however, are unwilling to serve indefinitely as the executive arm of their offspring's will, and demand that children acquire a certain measure of self-sufficiency in the ordinary routines of living. In contrast to younger children, for example, older children are less apt to request a helping hand in walking a plank blindfolded.[40] Lastly, it is expected that children will internalize parental standards, accept the moral obligation to abide by them, and regard themselves as accountable to parents for lapses therefrom.

During the satellizing period the child is motivated to undergo change in these areas of personality development in order to obtain and retain parental approval, since only in this way can he feel sure that the derived status he enjoys will continue. His sense of security and adequacy becomes increasingly dependent upon conformity to parental expectations of more mature behavior. Highly accepted children are judged as willing to exert much "conscientious effort" to hold the approval of "admired authorities"[59]; and children who perceive themselves as intrinsically valued at home are rated by teachers as more executively independent and more able to postpone the need for immediate hedonistic gratification.[10] It has also been shown that task-oriented children (who presumably satellize more and have less need for ego aggrandizement) exhibit more emotional control and make fewer demands on adults.[32]

Finally, satellization has important implications for the mechanisms by which norms and values are assimilated from elders and from membership and reference groups. The essential motivation directing the satellizer's organization of his value system is the need to retain the acceptance and approval of the persons or groups that provide his derived status. Hence he develops a generalized set to perceive the world in the light of the values and expectations he attributes to the latter individuals. Children who perceive themselves as most intrinsically valued by parents are least apt to make value judgments deviating from perceived parent opinions.[10] Later, this orientation is reinforced by the desire to avoid the guilt feelings that are associated with repudiation of parental values. Value assimilation is thus an unconditional act of personal loyalty in which both considerations of expediency and the objective content of what is internalized are largely irrelevant, that is, from a motivational standpoint. The satellizing child identifies uncritically with the moral values and membership groups of his parents even when these are only meaningless symbols. Thus, irrespective of his actual experience with Negro children, the white child of five and six tends to assume his parents' attitudes (favorable or unfavorable) toward Negroes.[41]

Negativistic Reactions to Devaluation. Ego devaluation is not usually brought about smoothly and painlessly. Typically (although not invariably) the child first resists the threatened loss of his infantile ego status by more vigorous and aggressive assertion of its grandiose-imperious features before acknowledging that the advantages of a derived status offer him a more tenable biosocial position.[4] This leads to resistive or negativistic behavior which tends to reach a peak between two and three years of age.[2, 28, 57] The sources of resistance to ego devaluation are many: the inertia of existing personality organization; the insecurity and loss of immediate status involved in any rapid transition; the loss of advantages associated with present status and the disadvantages perceived in the new status; aggression and counteraggression.

The two or three year old has been accustomed for some time to living with the prerogatives and immunities of his omnipotent ego structure.

Hence, he is understandably reluctant to part with an orientation that placed him at the center of his universe and to accept instead the role of dependent satellite. To retain parental approval he must inhibit hedonistic impulses, surrender volitional independence, and conform to parental standards; and until the prospects for satellization are entirely certain he must contend with the marginality and anxiety of transitional status. Rage, however, is a more conspicuous component of the child's response to ego devaluation than anxiety providing that the latter takes place in a generally benevolent and accepting atmosphere. Such an atmosphere mitigates anxiety by providing a pervasive sense of security and opportunity to satellize. Finally, negativism during this period constitutes a form of counteraggression against the often aggressive and interfering behaviors which parents use in pressing their training demands. Thus it tends to be less intense when either parent or child happens to be temperamentally unassertive or submissive.

Issues regarding self-help are frequent excitants of negativism. The child vigorously resists attempts to abolish the executive dependence and "baby ways" which are part of his omnipotent self-concept. On the other hand, denying him the opportunity for self-help is also a common precipitant of resistiveness. We may hypothesize here, however, that the child's ire is aroused not so much because desire for executive independence per se is frustrated but because of interference with his notion of volitional independence, i.e., with his perceived prerogative to do a particular task by himself *if he* so chooses.[4] The birth of a sibling is often such a traumatic event because the dethroning and transfer of indulgent attention to a new child comes at a time when the ego is already bearing the brunt of a violent devaluing process. Thus sibling rivalry tends to be less severe if the younger child is born either before or after (i.e., less than 18 or more than 42 months) the crucial stage of devaluation in the older sibling.[65] Girls apparently manifest less negativism at this age than do boys* for two reasons: First, because they perceive themselves as more accepted and intrinsically valued by parents[10] and have a more available like-sexed person with whom to identify, they can acquire more derived status. Second, they are able to obtain more subsidiary primary status than boys can by participating in female household tasks.[53]

In any particular instance of this kind of negativism specific normative, temperamental, or situational factors are undoubtedly important. Because of volitional immaturity, compliance may be difficult without prior or simultaneous execution of the opposite alternative of refusal.[28] Genuine misunderstanding of requests, disinterest in particular tasks, or requiring the child to exercise control and discrimination beyond his developmental capacity for

*See F. L. Goodenough, Anger in young children. *Inst. Child Welf. Monogr.* No. 9, 1931.

same also instigate negativistic behavior. At any rate children's negativism seems more blatant than adults' since they lack the latter's language reper- toire of polite evasions and circumlocutions when aroused.[57]

The Non-Satellizing Solution to Ego Devaluation

The satellizing solution, for the reasons given above, is hypothesized as the most acceptable and satisfactory, and hence as the most frequently chosen way in which children resolve the crisis of ego devaluation. It pre- supposes that they can acquire a derived status through the medium of a dependent parent-child relationship. In all cultures, however, a variable number of parents are psychologically incapable of or unwilling to extend acceptance and intrinsic valuation to their offspring. Thus, deprived of the self-esteem provided by the fiat of unconditional parental acceptance, such children must continue to seek primary status and feelings of adequacy on the basis of their *own* power to influence and control their environment. There is this important difference however: whereas before a grandiose pimary status could easily be assumed on the basis of a misinterpretation of parental subservience to their desires, increased cognitive maturity no longer makes this possible. Although the environment may continue to pro- vide some support for the notions of volitional independence and omnipo- tence, these notions must be increasingly related to *actual* performance ability (executive competence) and hierarchical position.

If satellization is impossible, two alternatives now remain for resolving the crisis of ego devaluation: ego aspirations can still be maintained at the omnipotent level, or else drastically reduced so as to correspond to actual biosocial competence unenhanced by the derived status afforded by parental acceptance and prestige. In the first instance no devaluation of ego aspira- tions takes place; in the second, devaluation is complete. Although the latter alternative (complete devaluation) is conceivable under certain circum- stances, it is not very probable. In the first place, it involves an overly drastic, abrupt, and traumatic depreciation of self-esteem. To aim high is in itself an enhancement of self-esteem, whereas immediate capitulation to the most unpalatable ego status available implies defeat and degradation. Second, various factors in the parent-child relationship operate against complete devaluation. An individual who fancies himself omnipotent does not react passively but with counter-aggression, bitterness and vengeful fantasies to the hostility, aggression, and humilating depreciation of his self-esteem implied in rejection by parents. By setting his sights on power and prestige, he hopes someday to obtain revenge and negate parental judg- ments regarding his worthlessness. In the case of the extrinsically valued (over-valued) child complete devaluation is also an unlikely outcome. The parent who intends to aggrandize his own ego through the child's future eminence does all in his power to perpetuate the fiction of the latter's infantile omnipotence by maintaining a worshipful and deferential attitude. Thus, only where rejection takes the more passive form of prolonged emotional neglect and deprivation (as in foundling homes) is the child apt to undergo complete devaluation instead of attempting the preservation of omnipotent aspirations (see p. 122). If the neglect is thoroughgoing enough no real need for devaluation exists since omnipotent fancies do not develop in the first place; and in the absence of overt parental aggression the maintenance of grandiose aspirations as a mechanism of counteraggression and revenge is unnecessary.

Consequences of Failure in Ego Devaluation. The child who fails to satellize generally fails also to undergo ego devaluation. The infantile personality structure that is not presented with the prerequisite conditions for reorganization tends to persist despite various shifts in biosocial status. Unable to achieve feelings of security and adequacy on a derived basis, he continues to seek their extrinsic counterparts. Feelings of adequacy continue to reflect primary status, whereas feelings of security remain a function of the parents' availability in providing for his basic needs until he possesses sufficient power, position and prestige to feel unthreatened in facing the future.

Under these conditions the child is not obliged to relinquish aspirations for volitional independence, renunciation of which is implicit in the self-subordination of anyone who satellizes (i.e., who derives his status by the mere fact of dependent relationship to or acceptance by another). It is true that increased capacity to perceive the social environment more realistically compels him to revise somewhat both these aspirations and his self-estimate in a downward direction. But even though a discrepancy between aspirational level and current status is inevitable for some time, his high ego aspirations still tend to persist. In the absence of satellization which guarantees a derived intrinsic status, the acquisition of extrinsic (primary) status becomes a more compelling necessity. Hence, because of this compensatory need for high primary status, exaggeratedly high levels of ego aspiration remain tenaciously resistant to lowering despite their relative untenability in the present. The child hopes to close the gap in the future; and even in the meantime the maintenance of a high aspirational level in and of itself elevates self-esteem. Lending some empirical support to these speculations are the findings (a) that children who perceive themselves as extrinsically valued by parents tend to have more omnipotent conceptions of their capacities and to maintain a tenaciously high level of aspiration on a stylus maze task despite persistent failure[10]; and (b) that low acceptance by parents tends to be associated with high scores on self-sufficiency and ego defensiveness and low scores on "willing obedience" in school children[59] and with high need for achievement in college students.[48]

Although both rejected and overvalued children can enjoy no derived status and fail to undergo substantial devaluation in terms of aspirations for volitional independence and omnipotence, important differences between them are observable during the childhood years. In an austere and hostile home environment the rejected child cannot possibly acquire any primary status or entertain any immediate aspirations for same. Hence, not only is it impossible for him to enjoy any current self-esteem, but also all of his aspirations for power and prestige must either be projected outside the home (e.g., school, peer group) or into the more distant future. The need for survival also compels a humiliating outward acceptance of an authority and control he resents. In such generally insecure surroundings the catastrophic impairment of self-esteem to which he is subjected tends to make him overreact with fear to any new adjustive situation posing a threat to his sense of adequacy.* Nevertheless, hypertrophied ego aspirations are carefully nurtured within and there is no inner yielding of independence and no true subordination of self to others. The environment of the overvalued child, on the other hand, provides abundant satisfaction of both current needs for primary status and immediate aspirations for volitional independence and omnipotence. The child is installed in the home as an absolute monarch and is surrounded by adulation and obeisance. Hence he suffers no impairment of current self-esteem and has no current cause for neurotic anxiety. These eventualities first threaten when the protection offered by his unreal home environment is removed and his hypertrophied ego aspirations are confronted by peers and adults unbiased in his favor.

Satellizers and non-satellizers also differ markedly with respect to motivation for achieving ego maturity goals (i.e., executive independence, attenuation of hedonistic needs, development of moral responsibility). In contrast to the satellizing child who merely assimilates these goals and standards of parental training through a process of value assimilation (see pp. 292, 382), the non-satellizer is primarily motivated in his orientation to values by considerations of expediency and attainment of primary status. He responds to the prestige suggestion of authority figures not because of any need to agree unconditionally with them but because he acknowledges their suitability as emulatory models and stepping stones to power and prestige. Children who perceive themselves as extrinsically valued tend to disagree more with perceived parent opinions,[10] and children who fail to identify emotionally with their parents only assimilate the latter's values superficially.[80]

*This condition corresponds to *neurotic anxiety* discussed on p. 329.

The non-satellizer, therefore, does not accept the unconditional obligation to abide by *all* internalized values but tends to be selective in this regard. The basis of this selectivity is the expediential criterion of potential usefulness for ego enhancement. Thus, the curbing of hedonistic impulses and the acquisition of executive independence are regarded as essential for ego enhancement and, therefore, become invested with moral obligation. Hence, with respect to these attributes of ego maturity, rejected school children tend to be rated just as favorably as their accepted contemporaries[10]; whereas in the light of these same criteria extrinsically valued children (who are under little external pressure from parents to conform to standards of mature behavior) are temporarily retarded,[10] probably until their status depends more on persons outside the home. On the other hand, values such as truthfulness and honesty do not always serve and sometimes oppose the interests of self-aggrandizement. In such instances, as suggested by the higher incidence of delinquency in children who are made to feel rejected, unloved and unwanted (see p. 391), the sense of obligation may selectively fail to operate unless buttressed by either strong convictions of equity or by coercive external sanctions.

The Satellizing Stage

After the negativistic reaction to ego devaluation subsides, the child who finds it possible to satellize is less self-assertive and more anxious to please and conform. He is more responsive to direction and can be bargained with or put off until "later."[28] His appraisal of his own power and position is much depreciated and he feels quite dependent upon parental approval. In their eyes he is a "good boy," that is, relatively docile, obedient and manageable.[28] But progress toward satellization does not proceed in a straight line. Changing capacities engender new self-perceptions with resulting fluctuations in disposition to remain content with a satellizing status.

Early Fluctuations. The four year old is more conscious of his own power and capacity. Marked strides have taken place in intellectual, motor, and social growth and he is much less dependent on his parents. He learns new ways of manipulating persons and social situations and establishes a modicum of independent status for himself outside the home in the world of his peers. With increased self-consciousness of capacity comes a resurgence of infantile ego characteristics; and possessing still but a rudimentary self-critical faculty, he tends to exaggerate his newly acquired abilities. This tendency toward self-overestimation is facilitated by the intoxication accompanying initial success, by exposure to competitive cultural pressures, and by a past history of grandiose thinking only recently abandoned. Apparently there are times when he even believes he is capable enough to regain volitional independence and cast aside satellization in favor of seeking an extrinsic status on the basis of his own competence. Deference to parental authority can become burdensome, especially when it is so obvious to him that he "knows better." Parents are also always interfering with his desires for immediate pleasure.

Thus at four the child becomes expansive, boisterous, obstreperous and less anxious to please, obey, and conform.[28] His behavior shows resistiveness to direction and is typically "out-of-bounds." He is "bigger" than everyone and can do everything.[28] Now for the first time he becomes intensely competitive in his play and desires to excel others.[1, 28, 31, 44] * Everything that he has or can do is compared with the possessions and abilities of others, and the decision regarding relative superiority is invariably made in his favor. He is acutely resentful of the privileges accorded older siblings. His concern with power and prestige is also manifested by his preoccupation with possession, by interference with and teasing of other children and household pets, and by snatching of toys.[52] With the growth of language his resistance assumes more verbal, subtle and symbolic forms. Threats, boasts, contentiousness, deceit, delaying and stalling tactics replace temper tantrums and open aggression.

It is important to distinguish between the negativism current at four from the variety prevailing at two and one-half. The goal of the latter is to perpetuate a highly autistic brand of omnipotence reflecting a very immature grasp of the social reality in which the child lives. The basis of parental subservience is completely misinterpreted and no incompatibility is perceived between executive dependence and volitional omnipotence. At four, however, omnipotent pretensions are given a more legitimate and realistic basis. Executive competence is accepted as prerequisite for volitional independence, but because of an inadequate self-critical faculty a very minimal degree of executive ability is inflated to the point of omniscience. Resistance is provoked when the exuberantly self-confident child tries to capture volitional control from the parent but meets with rebuff. At this age also self-assertion is no longer an end in itself; stimulated by competitive pressures, the child seeks to demonstrate his own superiority and reveal the weaknesses of others. But despite his bold front, the expression of negativism begins to acquire moral implications which were previously absent. This is revealed by a growing tendency to disclaim responsibility for resistive behavior; to ascribe it to accidental causes, to coercive agents operating on him, or to other persons; and to rationalize it as desirable or as a form of self-defense.

*See also J. P. McKee and F. B. Leader, *Child Develop.* 26: 135-142, 1955.

At other times, however, the four year old becomes painfully aware that he is only a child. When his bluff is called, his inescapably dependent bio-social position brings him back to reality with a thud. Thus he is torn between two opposing forces—a longing for volitional independence based on an exaggerated self-estimate of his executive competence, and a fright-ened desire to return to the protection of his dependent status as he stretches his wings too far and falls. This conflict is generally resolved in favor of the need to retain parental approval and derived status (that is, in the case of emotionally accepted, intrinsically valued children). The eventual triumph of satellization is not only aided by the development of a more realistic self-critical faculty but is almost an inevitable product of the child's dependent biosocial status in all cultures. The acceptance of parental control is also facilitated by the growing prestige authority of the parent in the child's unstructured attitudinal field, by the operation of guilt feelings in the child, by the latter's rationalization of compulsory parental demands as elective desires of his own, and by the liberal application of rewards, threats and punishment.

Later Aspects. Five, like three, is also a relatively quiet, well-conforming age that succeeds a period of negativism. As the child's self-critical faculty improves, his self-exuberance diminishes with a resulting loss of confidence in and enthusiasm for his own powers.[29] He is more dependent on adult emotional support, tends to be sympathetic, affectionate and helpful, and is likely to invite supervision.[29] The parents are idealized and appear more omnipotent than ever. The extent to which the child accepts parental value judgments is indicated by his almost tearful sensitivity to approval. A minor threat or mild show of disapproval is remarkably successful in effecting compliance. But until identification with the parent reaches a maximum at about the age of eight,[29, 39] one more major fluctuation in level of satellization still has to occur. It is precipitated by changes in biosocial status occasioned by the child's entrance into school.

The six year old tends to be aggressive, expansive, boastful, and resistive to direction.[29] His negativism follows the same pattern met with at age four: there is much of the same cockiness and blustering self-assurance based on an exaggerated notion of a recent gain in competence. But this time there is more real cause for crowing and ego inflation. For the first time now he is conceded an official status in the culture which is independent of the home; several hours every day he enjoys—at least in part—an extrinsic status which reflects his relative competence in mastering the curriculum. In addition, the authority of his parents is undermined by the termination of their reign as sole dispensers of truth and moral values. At the same time school exerts a sobering influence on the child since it also makes greater demands for mature behavior. Hence there is an improvement in such attributes of ego maturity as independence and reliability.[70] School does not have the same impact on all children. The satellizer tends to react to the teacher as a parent substitute, but the approval he receives from her is less unconditional and more related to performance ability than that which he receives from parents. In the total economy of his personality, also, the primary status he earns at school still plays a relatively peripheral role in comparison to the derived status provided by his home. The rejected child finds in school his first major opportunity to obtain any status whatsoever, whereas the overvalued child almost inevitably suffers a loss in appreciation at the hands of his classmates.

Satellizing and non-satellizing tendencies are not mutually exclusive or all-or-none characteristics. Superimposed on the satellizing child's quest for intrinsic status is a greater or lesser striving for a subsidiary extrinsic status. Similarly, non-satellizers are more or less able to form satellizing-like attachments to non-parent individuals who qualify better for this relationship. In addition to these individual differences, typical normative changes also take place in the balance between satellizing and non-satellizing tendencies. Despite periodic fluctuations, the general trend between three and eight years of age is toward greater satellization. Thereafter, rapid strides in social maturity, the new source of status available in the peer group, resentment over exclusion from the adult world, the impetus of sexual maturation, and changing expectations from adults all play a role in undermining the satellizing attitude. But even in adult life, as already pointed out, satellizing attitudes continue both to provide a subsidiary source of current status and to influence in substrate fashion level of ego aspirations, susceptibility to neurotic anxiety and mode of assimilating new values (see p. 100).

The Ego Maturation Crisis: Desatellization

Before ego development can be complete, one more important maturational step is necessary: emancipation from the home and preparation to assume the role of a volitionally independent adult in society. But before adult personality status can be attained, ego maturation must achieve a new balance between the dichotomous needs for independence and dependence—a balance which is closer to the volitional independence and self-assertiveness of infancy than to the docility and submissiveness of childhood. This involves largely a process of desatellization: the path away from volitional independence trod during early childhood must be largely retraced. Although the consummatory aspects of desatellization must be postponed until late adolescence, important preparatory aspects are accomplished during middle and late childhood.

In terms of the needs arising out of the child's dependent biosocial status, satellization is the most felicitous of all possible solutions to the crisis of ego devaluation. However, beginning in late childhood and extending throughout adolescence, a second major shift in biosocial status precipitates a new crisis in ego development, the maturation crisis, which demands a reorganization of comparable scope and significance. Confronted by changing biosocial conditions and under pressure to become more volitionally independent and acquire more primary status, the satellizing organization of personality becomes just as untenable and unadaptive as the omnipotent organization was at an earlier date. But since the home and parents still continue to function as the major status-giving influences in the child's life until adolescence, the actual crisis phase (transitional disequilibrium, disorientation, marginality and anxiety) is postponed until that time.

Despite much intercultural diversity in the specific content and method of ego maturation, the *general* goals of personality maturation tend to be similar in most cultures (see table 1, p. 67). Ego maturation encompasses two essentially different kinds of personality changes—changes in (a) ego maturity goals, and in (b) ego status goals. *Ego maturity* goals include the attenuation of hedonistic motivation; the acquisition of increased executive independence and frustration tolerance; the development of greater moral responsibility, more realistic levels of aspiration, and more self-critical ability; and the abandonment of special claims on others' indulgence. Beyond infancy there is continuity of cultural expectation regarding these goals for individuals of all ages, the only differences being in the purposes they serve and in the *degree* of development expected. Thus, progress toward ego maturity goals is made during the satellizing as well as the desatellizing period. During the latter period the motivation underlying the attainment of these goals tends to shift from the retention of derived status and parental approval to the fact that such attainment is perceived as prerequisite to the achievement of higher standards of volitional independence and primary status. In deciding whether to assimilate new values the desatellizing child is more prone than the satellizing child to use such criteria as expediency and capacity for enhancing ego aspirations instead of the criterion of blind personal allegiance (satellizing orientation). This new approach to value assimilation (which also characterizes the non-satellizer at *all* ages) will henceforth be referred to as the *incorporative* orientation.

The *status goals* of ego maturation, on the other hand, are discontinuous from early childhood to late childhood, adolescence, and adult life. They include the acquisition of greater volitional independence and primary status; heightened levels of ego aspirations; the placement of moral responsibility on a societal basis; and the assimilation of new values on the basis of their perceived intrinsic validity or their relation to the major goals of the individual. With respect to these goals the child is not expected to be a miniature adult. Volitional independence, for example, is high during infancy, drops to a lower point during middle childhood and starts rising again during late childhood. The child obtains the major portion of his status from derived sources and the adult his from primary sources; and although this reversal is not completed until adolescence, the balance begins to shift during middle and late childhood. Hence, insofar as the realization of ego status goals is concerned, the stage of satellization represents a period of retrogression rather than of progress. But even though desatellization restores many of the ego inflationary features of the infantile period, this doesn't mean that the adolescent is back in the same place which he left at the close of infancy; for supporting this gain in ego enhancement is considerable growth in cognitive sophistication and executive competence, much real accomplishment in the goals of ego maturity, and fundamental changes in social pressures and expectations.

Pressures toward Desatellization. No sooner is the dependency of satellization achieved than new conditions are created which undermine it and alter the shifting balance of dependence-independence. First among the factors impelling change toward personality maturation is the cumulative impact of progress in cognitive and social capacities, which in turn induces modification of parental and societal expectations. During the period of middle childhood there is an unspectacular but steady gain in the child's ability to comprehend abstract relationships, to reason, and to generalize (see pp. 548-554). His level of sophistication in perceiving the attitudes, needs and feelings of others, the relative status positions of various persons (including himself) in the group, and the distinguishing criteria of social class status (see pp. 434-470) is gradually pushed forward. Thus, understanding more thoroughly the nature of the environment in which he lives, he feels less awed by its complexity and more confident to navigate alone and unguided. He feels that he now possesses a sufficient fund of social and intellectual competence to qualify for a more mature and responsible role in the affairs of his culture, to engage in the status-giving activities that he formerly regarded as the exclusive prerogative of adults. Hence he tends to wish more than younger children for such status-conferring attributes as good looks, stature, mental ability and popularity,[20] to prefer difficult tasks which he cannot complete to easier ones which he can,[58] and to be less hedonistic and authority conscious in his emotional responsiveness to different situations.[38] But this time, unlike the situation at four, he really possesses sufficient executive competence to warrant a serious and legitimate quest for more primary status and greater volitional independence.

Neither the parent nor the culture are unaware of the growth in cognitive and social competence that takes place during the preadolescent years. In accordance with practical economic needs and the overall cultural training program, therefore, the child is expected to acquire a source of extrinsic status to supplement his role as dependent satellite in the family configuration.* Depending on the degree of cultural discontinuity prevailing between children's and adult's roles,[12] he either acquires a sub-adult, fringe status in adult society or primary status in peripheral activities (e.g., school, peer group) far removed from the main stream of status-giving operations in the adult world. In most primitive cultures the home serves as both the source of subsidiary extrinsic status and the training institution for developing more mature and responsible behavior. The child is assigned responsible tasks of considerable social and economic importance in agriculture, handicrafts, household arts, looking after younger siblings; and "the tasks that are expected of it are adapted to its capacity."[12]

In complex modern cultures children have little opportunity for exercising independence, responsibility and identification with the world of adult concerns, necessitating a complete separation of the activity and interest systems of child and adult. Such children are given no responsibilities in the workaday world of adult concerns, and evolve a complete set of prestige-giving values of their own. They are obliged to find sources of primary status in peripheral activities and to supplement this with the vicarious status that can be obtained through identification with the glamorous exploits of prominent figures in public life, and with whatever satisfaction can be gained by carrying on covert guerrila warfare with adults and adult standards.

One undesirable consequence of excluding children from *genuine* responsibility in the adult world is that deprived of this necessary role-playing experience, related aspects of ego maturation tend to lag behind. Study of children in grades four through twelve "reveals little evidence [of] . . . marked developmental progress in the child's amount of responsibility"[34] or of any relationship between his sense of responsibility and the number of home duties he assumes.[35] The fact that these relationships hold true for rural as well as urban children suggests that the child in our culture has no *real* opportunity for socially responsible participation. The routine assignments he carries out are so subordinate and expendable that they have little bearing on his primary status or volitional independence.

*Achievement motivation tends to be relatively high in children whose mothers make early demands for and reward independent accomplishment highly.[16] There are also marked intercultural and social class differences in achievement motivation (see pp. 310 and 435).

A second consequence of the displacement of the home as a training center for ego maturation is that the child becomes increasingly dependent on nonparental sources of primary and derived status. In his peer group he is given a chance to obtain the mature role-playing experience from which society excludes him and which his parents are unable to furnish. Identification with this group also provides a substitute source of derived status providing him with ego supports that reduce his dependence upon parental approval. By attributing the prerogatives of volitional independence and moral decision to a group fashioned in his own image he effectively demolishes his exclusive association of these powers with parental figures and thus paves the way for eventually assuming them himself. School serves a very similar function. It provides both a new subsidiary source of primary status based upon academic ability and a fresh source of derived status which challenges the parent's monopoly of this commodity and of omniscience as well.

All of these factors—the availability of other sources of derived status, the possession of subsidiary primary status, the need for going beyond the home for sources of extrinsic status, the child's own greater competence, exposure to a diversity of family and social climates with resulting awareness of alternative standards and ways of doing things,[15] and the emergence of new authorities to challenge his parents' omniscience—tend to break down the child's deified picture of his parents. Thus, beginning with late childhood, glamorous figures such as movie stars and sports heroes, attractive visible adults, and composite portraits of admired adults start to displace parents as emulatory models.[39] As the ties of dependency weaken and the perceived omnipotence of the parent diminishes, the latter's power to confer by fiat an absolute intrinsic value on the child begins to ebb; and as the parents' glory fades, less vicarious status can be reflected to the satellite.

Systematic observation of the eight year old indicates that he is already more outgoing and in greater contact with his environment. "He resents being treated as a child and . . . can't wait to grow up."[29] The nine year old is more independent, responsible, cooperative and dependable. After making a futile attempt to draw the adult into his world,[29] he seems to accept the fact that fusion is impossible. "He becomes very busy with his own concerns and doesn't have time for routines or parents' demands."[29] There is "much planning in great and practical detail."[29] He "may prefer work to play."[29] But these concerns are "now oriented more toward his contemporaries than toward his parents . . . and he verbally expresses indifference to adult commands or adult standards."[29] Thus begins a long period of estrangement between children and adults which persists until the former attain adulthood themselves. Insurmountable barriers to commonality of feeling, to mutual understanding, and to ease of communication are often built up. This alienation is not unaccompanied by resentment and bitterness. Although outright resistance to adult authority is usually withheld until adolescence, there is reason to believe that the preadolescent's apparent conformity is only a veneer which hides the smoldering rebellion from view. This is suggested by the often contemptuous and sneering remarks he makes about adults in his own company; and perhaps were it not for compensatory outlets in movies, comics, and opportunities for fighting with peers and bullying younger children, it would come more into the open.[52] Because girls are able and expected to satellize more and longer than boys (see p. 281) and can also achieve more primary status at home and in school they tend to be more conforming to and less at war with adult standards and values.

Mechanisms of Desatellization. From the foregoing description of the nature and determinants of the desatellizing process it is apparent that three different kinds of mechanisms are involved. The first mechanism may be called *resatellization.* It involves gradual replacement of parents by agemates and others as the essential socializing agents of children and as the individuals in relation to whom the satellizing orientation is maintained. Resatellization follows the same pattern of dependent emotional identification with stronger, prestigeful individuals or groups as did satellization. The identifications are merely transferred in part from parents to teachers, parent surrogates, agemates and others on whom the child is dependent for derived status. Values, goals and attitudes are now acquired from *these* individuals as by-products of personal loyalty. But although resatellization is a prominent feature of desatellization in our culture, it tends not to occur in most primitive cultures.[23, 50] Here the parents remain the chief socializing agents and source of standards and derived status; the older child and adolescent merely acquires greater volitional independence and primary status within the family circle without revolting "against the authority of the head of the household."

Thus, more important in bringing about desatellization than the issue of who (parents or peer group) becomes the object of residual satellizing trends are the child's increased needs for obtaining primary status and the sources from which it is available. The satellizing orientation is abrogated more effectively by the displacement of derived by primary status as the basis of self-esteem than by replacement of parents by peers, teachers and adult leaders as the source of derived status. Hence, the more crucial contribution of these latter individuals to the desatellizing process is the primary status they are able to furnish the preadolescent and adolescent child. At first, the opportunity of gaining parental approbation constitutes the child's chief motivation to acquire the primary status resulting from independent accomplishment; thus in the beginning the acquisition of extrinsic status is largely a modified form of satellization. Later, primary status becomes an end in itself; and accordingly there is a parallel shift in the child's orientation toward value assimilation and in his motivation for achieving the attributes of ego maturity (see p. 301).

A third but relatively minor mechanism through which desatellization is effected depends upon the operation of the *exploratory* orientation to value assimilation. This is a task-oriented approach to the problem of values that stresses such criteria as objective validity, logic, and equity, and de-emphasizes status considerations, both derived and primary, that underlie the satellizing and incorporative orientations respectively (see pp. 292 and 301). The utilization of the exploratory orientation is obviously limited during childhood since it conflicts with basic loyalties to parents and hence precipitates strong guilt feelings. But as subservience to parental values wanes it can be used more freely; and continued use in turn promotes desatellization. Extensive use, however, tends to be precluded by the fact that it also threatens the new sources of primary and derived status that becomes available at this time.

Facilitating and Retarding Factors. Desatellization is a difficult and conflictful phase of ego development. The child is expected to become more independent and self-assertive; and in achieving this goal he has to combat ambivalent tendencies in both himself and his parents. If he is too submissive and dependent he loses face in his own eyes and in the eyes of his peers; if he is too independent and aggressive, he feels guilty for excessive repudiation of his parents. Whether or not and the extent to which ego maturation actually occurs depends on the ways in which various factors of parent behavior, child temperament and cultural expectations facilitate or retard the mechanisms whereby desatellization is effected. Desatellization, for example, is facilitated if the child (in contradistinction to his behavior) is accepted unconditionally, that is, if obedience and conformity are not made the price of acceptance. Similarly, the more impersonal the basis on which obedience and conformity are required the less likely is the desire for independence to be inhibited by feelings of personal loyalty and guilt. The dangers of excessive satellization may also be avoided if the child can find derived status in multiple sources rather than in the parents alone. Under such circumstances the one source is no longer so precious. Fortified by the ego support he receives from friends, grandparents, siblings, teachers, etc., he can afford more easily to assert his volitional and ideational independence.

For children to develop the skill and confidence necessary for competent exercise of volitional independence, they require opportunity for practicing self-direction, making plans and decisions, actually participating in mature role-playing experience, and learning from thir own mistakes. Over-dominated children, although mature in such respects as "conscientious effort" and "orderly production,"[59] tend to be shy, submissive, lacking in self-confidence, and deficient in the volitional aspects of independence.[45, 71] The latter outcome also holds true for overprotected children whose parents withhold the opportunity for independent decision-making lest it lead to injury or frustration.[45, 69,71]

It also seems reasonable to suppose that if children are to develop executive independence and frustration tolerance, learn how to set realistic goals for themselves and make reasonable demands on others, and acquire self-critical ability and capacity for restricting hedonistic urges, they must have first-hand experience in coping with frustration and must be confronted unambiguously with the expectations and limitations defining their biosocial position. The overly permissive parent fails to develop frustration tolerance,* executive independence, and non-hedonistic motivation in the child[45, 71] by both failing to demand independent accomplishment and by yielding excessively to the child's demands for hedonistic gratification and help whenever he encounters difficulty. He fails also to structure realistically the limiting and restrictive aspects of the child's world, thereby making difficult the setting of realistic goals and the accurate perception of self-role and the boundaries of acceptable behavior. The extremely underdominated child, therefore, tends to be aggressive, rebellious, and disobedient; he may develop the notion that he is a very precious and privileged person and that his parents and others *have* to do things for him because he has a special claim on their indulgence.[45, 71] And insofar as the desire to protect the child from all frustration leads to similar kinds of parental behavior, comparable developmental outcomes may be expected in the overprotected child.[45, 69, 71]

Ego maturation in response to parental expectations of more mature behavior may ordinarily be expected to lag initially because of the phenomenon of perceptual constancy in the child. The prepotency of habitual expectations may temporarily force *altered* parent behavior into *familiar* perceptual molds despite manifest changes in stimulus content. The rate of ego maturation is also held back by ambivalent feelings in the child, who is naturally reluctant to part with the protection and security of dependency. This ambivalence is probably greater in children with strong needs for hedonistic gratification (who find long-range striving difficult) and in

*For a study of frustration tolerance in "under-controlling" children, see J. Block and B. Martin, *J. Abnorm. Soc. Psychol. 51*: 281-285, 1955.

sedentary, shy, "thin-skinned" and introverted children to whom self-assertion comes painfully.

Lastly, ego maturation is a function of cultural expectations and of the availability of mature role-playing experience. These latter factors reciprocally influence each other as well as generate pressure and opportunity for personality reorganization on a more mature basis. Largely for these reasons, when ego maturation in our culture is appraised in a cross-cultural context, the acquisition of ego status goals (e.g., volitional independence, primary status) is seen to lag markedly behind the acquisition of ego maturity goals (e.g., executive independence).[75] Parents in our culture expect much executive independence and conformity to adult standards but allow children relatively little opportunity to fend for themselves.[75]

Preparatory and Consummatory Stages. The preparatory changes in ego maturation catalogued above as well as the factors bringing them about are certainly important in the total scheme of personality maturation. Yet the transition to adult personality status cannot be consummated merely by the cumulative impact of these factors. The extrinsic status of childhood—even if achieved in economically significant activities—can constitute only a subsidiary source of status. The sexually immature (prepubescent) individual can nowhere acquire adult personality status; the primary status he enjoys must inevitably play a subordinate role in the larger Gestalt of volitional dependency and derived status which characterize the biosocial position of children the world over. Until adolescence, parents and home continue to function as the major status-giving influences in the child's life. The ego maturity of childhood remains qualitatively different from that of adolescence and adult life until derived and primary sources of status exchange positions as central and peripheral respectively in the total economy of ego organization.

Pubescence, therefore, plays the role of crucial catalytic agent in inaugurating the consummatory aspects of ego maturation. It constitutes a prerequisite condition for reversing social expectations and individual aspirations about the major type of status that the child may appropriately seek. For the pubescent individual the social value of derived status depreciates while the corresponding value of extrinsic status increases; and simultaneously social pressure is put on the parents to withdraw a large portion of the derived status which they had hitherto been extending to him.

Ego Maturation in Non-Satellizers. As already indicated, the non-satellizer never really surrenders his aspirations for volitional independence and exalted primary status. Hence in a sense the ego-status goals of maturation are already accomplished in advance; and since the main function of most ego-maturity goals is the enhancement of primary status, these tend to be acquired with little difficulty. The chief exception here relates to the development of realistic goals which is largely precluded by the non-satellizer's insistent need to maintain high ego aspirations irrespective of the situation or his level of ability. It would also seem reasonable to question under certain conditions the stability of values that were never implicitly internalized on the basis of personal loyalty but solely for purposes of ego enhancement. The obligation to abide by all internalized moral values, for example, is threatened by the fact that many such values are often in conflict with the ends of ego enhancement.

SOME ASPECTS OF EGO FUNCTIONING

Once a verbal concept of self emerges, the stage is set for the development of ego goals, motives, and attitudes, and of subjective ego responses (e.g., self-esteem) to such changes in status as success or failure in goal achievement.

Ego-Involvement

Ego-involvement is not synonymous with ego enhancement. It merely refers to the degree of self-implication in a given task or performance (i.e., whether or not the outcome is a matter of concern or importance to the individual) and does not make explicit the motives for his concern. Thus, non-ego-involved areas in the environment are relatively peripheral and undifferentiated; failure in such areas is easily sloughed off, and success does not inspire elation. As already pointed out, since the magnitude and tenacity of aspirations vary with degree of ego-involvement in a task (see pp. 102 and 157), the generality of aspirational (as well as of other) "trait" behavior depends upon holding ego-involvement constant. Even more than success or failure in performance, degree of ego-involvement also determines the extent to which children find tasks attractive.[60] Failure lowers the attractiveness of a task much less when children perceive themselves as "trying hard" to do well than when they are indifferent about performance.[60]

The *motivation* underlying ego-involvement, however, is quite another matter. In many ego-involved tasks the chief object of the activity is ego enhancement, in which case we speak of *ego orientation*. Here the task is pursued as a source of either derived or primary status. On the other hand, the motivation for some ego-involved activities may be entirely unrelated to ego enhancement, being energized solely by a need to acquire mastery or to discover a valid solution to a problem. Thus human beings may become intensely ego-involved in tasks in which the outcome per se rather than its relation to self-enhancement is the major focus of concern. In such instances the person is *task-oriented*. He experiences feelings of success and failure, but not loss or gain in ego status or self-esteem.

It follows that before ego-involvement can arise developmentally, the child must first possess a functional concept of self in relation to which various objects and activities in his environment are ordered in a hierarchical arrangement. When this occurs he is able to experience success and failure whenever ego-involved goals are either gratified or frustrated. The capacity for ego enhancing motivation, on the other hand, requires in addition that the child be able to set ego aspirations and respond with fluctuations in self-esteem to success and failure affecting these aspirations. This is illustrated by the competitive behavior of children in our culture which first appears at the age of three and becomes increasingly more prominent thereafter [1, 27, 28, 31, 44]; such behavior presupposes comparison of own and others' performance, appreciation of the concept of surpassing others, and desire to excel. It is also illustrated in the practical setting of aspirational levels for self-help in informal situations; in two- to three year olds these aspirations adhere quite closely to level of ability.[3] However, consistent levels of aspiration in more formal laboratory situations are not apparent until about the age of five.[28] For this kind of behavior the child requires a clear notion of the immediate future, some self-critical ability,[31] and acceptance of the cultural value of aspiring to goals that are less accessible[77] or somewhat beyond prior level of performance.[58]

Ego oriented motivation in our culture tends to have a competitive and self-aggrandizing flavor based upon the proposition that "no one can enhance . . . himself without encroaching upon the self-enhancement . . . of others.[51] Children typically work harder in response to prestige incentives than under anonymous conditions,[5] and in response to competitive personal rewards rather than in group contests.[49] But although all ego oriented motivation is directed toward self-enhancement, this does not necessarily imply a desire for ego aggrandizement. Even in our own culture many children will exert themselves tremendously under conditions that at most allow for private satisfaction with achievement.[5] The Navaho child strives little for individual achievement and seeks to avoid "being singled out . . . for superior performance."[43] The essential feature of primary status is that it is gained through an individual's own efforts (rather than vicariously by virtue of a dependent relationship to others) and depends upon the quality of his performance. It does not necessarily mean individual success, prestige, power, or competitive advantage. It may just as well be based upon competence for personal satisfaction, modest security, and approval for group-mindedness. In noncompetitive cultures self-enhancing primary status may be best acquired by renouncing individual ambitions and doing a good job of self-effacing, self-denying cooperative activity directed toward the welfare of others.

Level of Aspiration

Much insight into ego organization and functioning can be gained by observing the extent to which individuals take past performance into account in setting their level of aspiration for future performance. Children with adequate amounts of self-esteem (well-adjusted, academically successful children [33, 62,]) respond to the cultural pressure for achievement by aspiring to performance levels somewhat above the level of prior perfomance. However, since they do not have compensatorily high ego aspirations, they neither aspire beyond the range of present capacity nor cling rigidly to high aspirations after failure experience. In this way they minimize feelings of failure associated with a marked discrepancy between aspiration and performance levels.

Individuals with relatively little self-esteem (e.g., especially unsuccessful non-satellizers), on the other hand, are coerced by their high ego aspirations into maintaining tenaciously high levels of aspiration despite realistic considerations to the contrary. They find surrender of their high aspirations more traumatic than the immediate feelings of failure accompanying performance that is below aspirational level; also, merely in the maintenance of their high levels of aspirations, they find a source of ego enhancement. If they can manage to disinvolve their egos from the task, however, they tend to aspire to unrealistically low performance levels which they can always surpass, and thus at least spare themselves immediate failure experience.[62]

In support of the above interpretation of level of aspiration behavior are the following findings: (a) since boys possess less derived status than do girls (see p. 281), they tend to set higher levels of aspiration;[73] (b) handicapped or socially stigmatized children who presumably have a compensatory need for high extrinsic status, e.g., physically handicapped and asthmatic children,[47, 74] Negro children,[16] individuals of low social and economic status,[30] and children who fail chronically in school,[62] tend more than control groups to aspire unrealistically beyond present level of performance; (c) children or adolescents who perceive themselves as extrinsically valued,[10] who have high prestige needs[9] and unrealistic ambitions,[37, 63] and who manifest high levels of anxiety,[8, 9] all tend to adhere rigidly to high levels of aspiration in the face of persistent failure experience.

Egocentricity, Egoism and Subjectivity

By egocentricity is meant the extent to which the individual's self (in contradistinction to *other* persons, things, and events) is central as an object of attention in his psychological field. At the superficial level of saliency of awareness it merely connotes preoccupation with self and relative indifference to external events.* At a deeper level of value, concern and importance, i.e., as indicative of high degree of ego-involvement in self and of relative inability to relate emotionally to others, it is more appropriate to speak of *egoism*. Although egocentricity and egoism are probably related positively to each other, they are determined by different kinds of factors. Egocentricity-sociocentricity depends upon social maturity, social poise and skill, sociability, introversion-extroversion, etc.; egoism is more a function of magnitude of ego aspirations. Thus, it is conceivable that an outgoing person may be sociocentric but egoistic (superficially interested in others and their affairs, yet not *really* concerned with their welfare), and that a shy, introverted person may be egocentric but capable of genuine concern for and warm attachments to others. In the course of intellectual, social, and personality maturation, both egocentrism and egoism tend to diminish with increasing age. In communicating with others, children gradually increase in ability to perceive, pay sustained attention to, and take into account the feelings and viewpoints of others, to interchange ideas as well as talk to each other.[1, 28, 29, 56] In their play they tend as they grow older to become more aware of the presence and needs of others, more cooperative, considerate and altruistic (see p. 464).

Closely related to but distinguishable from egocentricity is the young child's overly *subjective* approach to the analysis of experience, his perceptual autism, and his lack of reality testing.[54, 55] He is as yet relatively unable "to dissociate what belongs to objective laws from what is bound up with the sum of subjective conditions."[55] As he advances in age he becomes increasingly able to approach questions of equity from a less personal and more detached point of view, and to argue from the standpoint of a hypothetical proposition.[29, 54] His pictorial representations of reality come to resemble more and more the model rather than the artist.[11]

Self-Critical Capacity

A prerequisite condition for the growth of a mature self-critical capacity is the ability to appraise self on the same basis that is used in evaluating others. Of all the subjectivistic proclivities characterizing early childhood, the child finds it most difficult to liberate himself from the tendency to apply selectively preferential standards to his own capacities, productions, and behavior. This development depends on more than possession of sufficient intellectual capacity to make critical judgments, since children are able to perceive deviations from acceptable standards in *others* at a much earlier age than they can in themselves;[28, 55] in fact, prior to five years of age the latter ability is infrequently observed.[28]

*When the self and its attributes are the focus of psychological self-analysis the term *introspection* is applicable.

Self-critical ability, therefore, is obviously important for the implementation of moral obligations. This presupposes that an individual does not selectively exempt himself from the standards he expects in others, and that he can become sufficiently aware of his own wrongdoing to experience feelings of guilt. We have also seen how immaturity of the self-critical capacity contributes to exaggerated notions of volitional power and executive independence, and how development of this capacity helps to promote ego devaluation and satellization. Further growth in self-critical ability is essential for acquiring primary status and for realistic exercise of volitional independence. At the operational level of ego functioning, a harsh self-critical faculty reduces the amount of self-esteem available to the individual, whereas an overly gentle self-critical faculty unwarrantedly enhances feelings of adequacy.

It also seems reasonable to suppose that the prevailing level of self-esteem influences self-critical ability. Although an individual with relatively little self-esteem may tend generally to take a harsh view of his accomplishments, he may at times be extremely reluctant to acknowledge shortcomings and culpability that would further depress his already damaged self-esteem. A person who enjoys adequate self-esteem, on the other hand, is less threatened by confrontation with unflattering aspects of his behavior. Thus, in line with findings for adult subjects, better adjusted children are able to accept significantly more disparaging statements about themselves than less well-adjusted children.[72] On logical grounds one could also expect a more severe self-critical faculty to develop when children are overdominated, overcriticized and underappreciated than when the opposite conditions prevail.[6]

REFERENCES

1. Ames, L. B.: The sense of self of nursery children as manifested by their verbal behavior. *J. Genet. Psychol. 81*: 193-232, 1952.

2. Ammons, C. H., and Ammons, R. B.: Aggression in doll-play: interviews of two- to six-year-old white males. *J. Genet. Psychol. 82*: 205-213, 1953.

3. Anderson, C.: The development of a level of aspiration in young children. Unpublished doctor's dissertation, University of Iowa, 1940.

4. Ausubel, D. P.: Negativism as a phase of ego development. *Am. J. Orthopsychiat. 20*: 796-805, 1950.

5. ——: Prestige motivation of gifted children. *Genet. Psychol. Monogr. 43*: 53-117, 1951.

6. ——: *Ego Development and the Personality Disorders.* New York, Grune & Stratton, 1952.

7. ——: *Theory and Problems of Adolescent Development.* New York, Grune & Stratton, 1954.

8. ——, Schiff, H. M., and Goldman, M.: Qualitative characteristics in the learning process associated with anxiety. *J. Abnorm. Soc. Psychol. 48*: 537-547, 1953.

9. ——, ——, and Zeleny, M. P.: "Real-life" measures of level of academic and vocational aspiration in adolescents: relation to laboratory measures and to adjustment. *Child Develop. 24*: 155-168, 1953.

10. ——, et al.: Perceived parent attitudes as determinants of children's ego structure. *Child Develop. 25*: 173-183, 1954.

11. Belvés, P.: Le portrait d'après nature. *Enfance 3*: 299-301, 1950.

12. Benedict, R.: Continuities and discontinuities in cultural conditioning. *Psychiatry 1*: 161-167, 1938.

13. Bennett, E. M., and Johannsen, D. E.: Some psychodynamic aspects of felt parental alliance in young children. *J. Abnorm. Soc. Psychol. 49*: 463-464, 1954.

14. Blumer, H.: Psychological import of the human group. *In* M. Sherif and M. O. Wilson, Eds., *Group Relations at the Crossroads*. New York, Harper, 1953, pp. 182-202.

15. Bossard, J. H. S.: Process in social weaning: a study of childhood visiting. *Child Develop. 22*: 211-220, 1951.

16. Boyd, G. F.: The levels of aspiration of white and Negro children in a non-segregated elementary school. *J. Soc. Psychol. 36*: 191-196, 1952.

17. Bühler, C.: The social behavior of children. *In* C. Murchison, Ed., *A Handbook of Child Psychology,* ed. 2. Worcester, Clark University Press, 1933, pp. 374-416.

18. Child, I. L.: Socialization. *In* G. Lindzey, Ed., *Handbook of Social Psychology*. Vol. II. *Special Fields and Applications*. Cambridge, Mass., Addison-Wesley, 1954, pp. 655-692.

19. Clark, K. B., and Clark, M. K.: The development of consciousness of self and the emergence of racial identification in Negro preschool children. *J. Psychol. 7*: 91-99, 1939.

20. Cobb, H. V.: Role-wishes and general wishes of children and adolescents. *Child Develop. 25*: 161-171, 1954.

21. Dennis, W.: Infant development under conditions of restricted practice and minimum social stimulation. *Genet. Psychol. Monogr. 23*: 143-189, 1941.

22. Ferenczi, S.: Steps in the development of a sense of reality. In *Sex in Psychoanalysis*. Boston, Badger, 1916.

23. Frank, L. K.: The adolescent and the family. In *Adolescence,* Forty-third Yearbook, Natl. Soc. Stud. Educ. Chicago, University of Chicago Press, 1944.

24. Freud, A.: The mutual influences in the development of the ego and the id: introduction to the discussion. *Psychoanl. Stud. Child 7*: 42-50, 1952.

25. Freud, S.: *The Ego and the Id*. London, Hogarth, 1935.

26. ——: *The Problem of Anxiety*. New York, Norton, 1936.

27. Gesell, A. The ontogenesis of infant behavior. *In* L. Carmichael, Ed., *Manual of Child Psychology,* ed. 2. New York, Wiley, 1954, pp. 335-373.

28. ——, and Ilg, F. L.: *Infant and Child in the Culture of Today*. New York, Harper, 1943.

29. ——, and ——: *The Child from Five to Ten*. New York, Harper, 1946.

30. Gould, R.: Some sociological determinants of goal strivings. *J. Soc. Psychol 13*: 461-473, 1941.

31. Greenberg, P.: Competition in children: an experimental study. *Am. J. Psychol. 44*: 221-248, 1932.

32. Gruber, S.: The concept of task orientation in the analysis of play behavior of children entering kindergarten. *Am. J. Orthopsychiat. 24*: 326-335, 1954.

33. Gruen, E. W.: Level of aspiration in relation to personality factors in adolescence. *Child Develop. 16*: 181-188, 1945.

34. Harris, D. B., Clark, K. E., Rose, A. M., and Valasek, F.: The measurement of responsibility in children. *Child Develop.* 25: 21-28, 1954.

35. ——, ——, —— and ——: The relationship of children's home duties to an attitude of responsibility. *Child Develop.* 25: 29-33, 1954.

36. Hartman, H.: The mutual influences in the development of the ego and the id. *Psychoanal. Stud. Child* 7: 9-30, 1952.

37. Hausmann, M. F.: A test to evaluate some personality traits. *J. Gen. Psychol.* 9: 179-189, 1933.

38. Havighurst, R. J., and MacDonald, D. V.: Events and situations which arouse emotions in New Zealand children. *In* R. J. Havighurst, Ed., *Studies of Children and Society in New Zealand.* Christchurch, N. Z., Canterbury University College, 1954.

39. ——, Robinson, M. Z., and Dorr, M.: The development of the ideal self in childhood and adolescence. *J. Educ. Res.* 40: 241-257, 1946.

40. Heathers, G.: Emotional dependence and independence in a physical threat situation. *Child Develop.* 24: 169-179, 1953.

41. Horowitz, E. L.: The development of attitude toward the Negro. *Arch. Psychol.* No. 194, 1936.

42. Horowitz, R. E.: A pictorial method for study of self-identification in preschool children. *J. Genet. Psychol.* 62: 135-148, 1943.

43. Leighton, D., and Kluckhohn, C.: *Children of the People.* Cambridge, Harvard University Press, 1947.

44. Leuba, C.: An experimental study of rivalry in young children. *J. Comp. Psychol.* 16: 367-378, 1933.

45. Levy, D. M.: *Maternal Overprotection.* New York, Columbia University Press, 1943.

46. Lézine, I.: Recherches sur les étapes de la prise de conscience de soi chez les jeunes jumeaux. *Enfance* 4: 35-49, 1951.

47. Little, S. W., and Cohen, L. D.: Goal setting behavior of asthmatic children and of their mothers for them. *J. Personal* 19: 376-389, 1951.

48. McClelland, D. C., et al.: *The Achievement Motive.* New York, Appleton-Century-Crofts, 1953.

49. Maller, J. B.: *Cooperation and Competition: an Experimental Study in Motivation.* New York, Teachers College, Columbia University, 1929.

50. Mead, M. Social change and cultural surrogates. *J. Educ. Sociol.* 14: 92-100, 1940.

51. Murphy, G.: *Personality: A Biosocial Approach to Its Origins and Structure.* New York, Harper, 1947.

52. Murphy, L. B.: Social factors in child development. *In* T. Newcomb and E. L. Hartlet, Eds., *Readings in Social Psychology.* New York, Holt, 1947.

53. Parsons, T.: Age and sex in the culture of the United States. *Am. Sociol. Rev.* 7: 604-616, 1942.

54. Piaget, J.: *The Child's Conception of the World.* New York, Harcourt, Brace, 1929.

55. ——: *Moral Judgment of the Child.* New York, Harcourt, Brace, 1932.

56. ——: *The Language and Thought of the Child,* ed. 2. New York, Harcourt, Brace, 1932.

57. Reynolds, M. M.: *Negativism of Preschool Children.* New York, Teachers College, Columbia University, 1928.

58. Rosenzweig, S.: Preferences in the repetition of successful and unsuccessful activities as a function of age and personality. *J. Genet. Psychol., 42*: 423-441, 1933.

59. Sanford, R. N., et al.: Physique, personality and scholarship. A cooperative study of school children. *Monogr. Soc. Res. Child Develop. 8*: No. 1, 1943.

60. Schpoont, S. H.: Some relationships between task attractiveness, self-evaluated motivation, and success or failure. Unpublished doctor's dissertation, University of Illinois, 1955.

61. Scott, J. P.: Implications of infra-human social behavior for problems of human relations. *In* M. Sherif and M. O. Wilson, Eds., *Group Relations at the Crossroads*. New York, Harper, 1953, pp. 33-73.

62. Sears, P. S.: Levels of aspiration in academically successful and unsuccessful children. *J. Abnorm. Soc. Psychol. 35*: 498-536, 1940.

63. ———: Level of aspiration in relation to some variables of personality: clinical studies. *J. Soc. Psychol. 14*: 311-336, 1941.

64. Sears, R. R., et al.: Some child-rearing antecedents of aggression and dependency in young children. *Genet. Psychol. Monogr. 47*: 135-234, 1953.

65. Sewall, M.: Two studies in sibling rivalry. I. Some causes of jealousy in young children. *Smith Coll. Stud. Soc. Wk. 1*: 6-22, 1930.

66. Sherif, M., and Cantril, H.: *The Psychology of Ego-Involvements*. New York, Wiley, 1946.

67. Spitz, R. A.: The role of ecological factors in emotional development in infancy. *Child Develop. 20*: 145-154, 1949.

68. ———, and Wolf, K. M.: The smiling response: a contribution to the ontogenesis of social relations. *Genet. Psychol. Monogr. 34*: 57-125, 1946.

69. Stendler, C. B.: Possible causes of overdependency in young children. *Child Develop. 25*: 125-146, 1954.

70. ———, and Young, N.: The impact of beginning first grade upon socialization as reported by mothers. *Child Develop. 21*: 241-260, 1950.

71. Symonds, P. M.: *The Dynamics of Parent-Child Relationships*. New York, Teachers College, Columbia University, 1949.

72. Taylor, C., and Combs, A. W.: Self-acceptance and adjustment. *J. Consult. Psychol. 16*: 89-91, 1952.

73. Walter, L. M., and Marzolf, S. S.: The relation of sex, age and school achievement to levels of aspiration. *J. Educ. Psychol. 42*: 285-292, 1951.

74. Wenar, C.: The effects of a motor handicap on personality. I. The effects on level of aspiration. *Child Develop. 24*: 123-130, 1953.

75. Whiting, J. W. M., and Child, I. L.: *Child Training and Personality: A Cross-Cultural Study*. New Haven, Yale University Press, 1953.

76. Winterbottom, M. R.: The relation of childhood training in independence to achievement motivation. Unpublished doctor's dissertation, University of Michigan, 1953.

77. Wright, H. F.: The influence of barriers upon strength of motivation. *Duke Univ. Series, Contr. Psychol. Theor. 1*: No. 3, 1937.

78. Zazzo, R.: Images du corps et conscience de soi. Materiaux pour l'etude expérimentale de la conscience. *Enfance 1*: 29-43, 1948.

79. Zeligs, R.: Children's wishes. *J. Appl. Psychol. 26*: 231-240, 1942.

80. Zuker, H. J.: Affectional identification and delinquency. *Arch. Psychol. No. 286*, 1943.

CHAPTER 10

Emotional Development

THE NATURE OF EMOTION

EMOTION MAY BE DEFINED as a heightened state of subjective experience accompanied by skeletal-motor and autonomic-humoral responses, and by a selectively generalized state of lowered response thresholds. In this chapter we shall consider both pleasant emotions that the child tries to prolong and unpleasant emotions that he attempts to avoid or terminate, by approaching and withdrawing respectively from relevant stimulating conditions.

The following sequential steps are involved in the instigation of an emotional response: (a) *interpretive* phase—perception or anticipation of an event that is interpreted as threatening or enhancing an ego-involved need, goal, value, or attribute of self; (b) *preparatory reactive* phase consisting of a selectively generalized lowering of the particular response thresholds implicated in a given emotion*; (c) *consummatory reactive* phase with subjective, autonomic-humoral, and skeletal-motor components; and (4) a *reflective reactive* phase involving subjective awareness of the drive state and of visceral and skeletal responses.

Genic and Environmental Determinants

A potentiality for developing patterned emotions is genically inherent in all human beings, although affective reactivity at birth is limited to undifferentiated excitement in response to any intense or prolonged stimulus. In addition, genically determined *patterning* predispositions exist, both with respect to the general categories of stimulation that evoke a particular emotion and with respect to the general ways in which such affect is expressed. Thus, frustration (at least in the early stages of emotional differentiation) primarily inspires rage and less frequently fear; whereas a per-

*This is equivalent to a drive state, and hence increases the magnitude and extensity of the response although decreasing its specificity and accuracy.[6, 16, 63] Such states tend to facilitate adaptive learning by activating performance, and by providing for selective reinforcement (through drive reduction) of successful variants.[63] On the other hand, in novel problem solving situations[6] and in the execution of delicate skills[16] the net effect of intense emotion is disruptive (i.e., promotes maladaptive perseveration and inaccuracy).

317

ceived threat to personal safety more often evokes fear than anger. Smiling appears in the three month old infant as an unlearned response to the human face (see p. 283), and laughter typically accompanies tickling in the six month old.[54]

The hierarchy of responses that may be released in connection with a particular emotional state (i.e., the relative probability of their occurrence in accordance with the selective lowering of response thresholds) is also genically determined in part. Flight and avoidance tend to be associated with fear, and aggression with anger. The appearance of facial expressions in only ten-month-old infants that can be correctly identified (by adult judges) with specific emotional experiences suggests that the "language of [emotional] expressions is . . . built upon a core of native reaction patterns . . . that can hardly be ascribed to training."[29] Similar conclusions are indicated by findings that the facial expressions exhibited by normal and blind-deaf children in experiencing various emotions are highly comparable.[29, 30]

Environmental factors help determine both intercultural uniformities and differences in emotional patterning. Along with genic factors, universal kinds of interpersonal relationships and conditions of adaptation to the personal and social environments (see table 1, p. 65) account for *psychobiological* aspects of emotional behavior. Specific cultural variations in the conditions evoking particular emotions, institutionalized modes of elaborating affective expression, and culturally stylized preferences in type of emotional response deemed appropriate for a given situation are responsible for *psychosocial* differences in emotional patterning.* *Idiosyncratic* differences in emotional expression are determined both by variability in experience and by inter-individual differences in temperamental traits. Children not only differ among each other in the patterning of autonomic responses to emotional stimuli,[7] but also exhibit self-consistency in such patterning over different situations[7, 51] (see p. 320). Consistent individual differences also exist in the extent to which autonomic and visceral components are represented in the total emotional response. Some children respond most vigorously in the motor sphere, others most vigorously in the autonomic sphere, and still others with equal vigor in both spheres.[43]

Because emotions like drives are *multiply determined,* it is impossible, even in a designated cultural context, to predict from the eliciting stimulus alone what the emotional reaction will be. The individual's interpretation of the stimulus is always influenced by his idiosyncratic experience and temperamental make-up, and by such situational factors as current goal,

*Thus, fathers in our culture transmit the general cultural pattern of male aggression to their sons. Mothers transmit their own idiosyncratic pattern of aggression to both sons and daughters. (R. D. Hess and G. Handel, *J. Genet. Psychol. 89*: 199-212, 1956.)

the familiarity of the behavioral setting, and the relationship between instigating agent and reacting person. Lastly, as we shall show in a later section, emotional response is also determined in part by developmental (age level) differences in cognitive and social maturity and in ego structure.

Accessibility and Identifiability

Emotions vary both in the extent to which they are accessible to consciousness and in the degree of precision with which they can be identified. This variability applies to all phases of the emotional sequence. Sometimes it is the excitant (e.g., nature of the threat, cause of anger) that is relatively inaccessible or unidentifiable; at other times the child may be unaware of or unable to identify the area of personality concern to which the excitant refers (e.g., what is threatened). Still another possibility is that he might not be aware of his subjective feelings or of the relationship between these feelings, the excitant and the referent. This would tend to be especially true in the case of emotional situations and responses that are difficult to verbalize.

Because of cultural pressures to suppress certain kinds of emotional responses, the child is most apt to inhibit those aspects of emotional expression that have most social visibility, namely motor and vocal reactions. Subjective components of emotion are more difficult to inhibit; and since they can be hidden from public view, they are only coercible by such internal pressures as shame and guilt. Physiological aspects of emotional response are least inhibitable and under no pressure whatsoever to be inhibited; for this very reason, and when other outlets are blocked, they may constitute the chief channel for affective reactivity. Thus, visceral responsiveness to emotional stimuli (as measured by the galvanic skin reflex) is much greater in older than in younger children; and among adolescents an inverse relationship tends to prevail between autonomic reactivity, on the one hand, and motor activity, talkativeness, animation, and assertiveness, on the other.[43] In the recollection of past emotional experience, inaccessibility may occur at any of these points in the emotional sequence, and inhibition of response may occur for any of the same reasons as occurred in the original arousal.

The notion of "free-floating" emotions, i.e., emotional states that are phenomenologically unrelated to particular excitants and selective patterns of response, is psychologically untenable. The illusion of "free-floatingness" is created by lack of accessibility and identifiability, and by delayed occurrence of the consummatory stage of response, leaving the individual in a prolonged state of readiness or vigilance without tangible awareness of a relevant consummatory excitant.

Autonomic Patterning

Recent experiments[7, 51, 94] have shown that contrary to previous belief each major emotion is associated with a distinctive pattern of autonomic reactivity. This autonomic patterning of the different emotional states is much more complex than the vastly oversimplified differentiation made earlier between "vegetative" (parasympathetic) and "emergency" (sympathetic) reactions. Naturally, much variability prevails from one person to another in the pattern of responses exhibited for a given emotion; intra-individual variance, however, tends to be less than interindividual variance.[7, 51] Although it seems credible to suppose that characteristic differences between the autonomic profiles of the different emotions are largely a reflection of typical interpretive differences in response to the usually perceived excitants of these emotions, we cannot discount the possibility that cognitive repercussions of autonomic differences may contribute to the distinctive feeling tones associated with each emotion.

Emotional and Cognitive Interaction

Emotional and cognitive development are interrelated in many intricate ways. In terms of priority of development it is difficult to dispute the fact that young children exhibit intense and well differentiated feelings long before a capacity for logical thought is prominent; emotions similarly precede reasoning in the phyletic scale. Nevertheless, since the earliness and lateness of emergence respectively of differentiated emotions and logical thought have both been grossly exaggerated, the developmental gap between feelings and thought is probably not nearly as great as was once believed true. Also, although thought undoubtedly tends to be liberated somewhat from autistic and subjectivistic influences with increasing age (see p. 553), abundant evidence indicates that attitudes and wishes continue to distort logical thinking in persons of all ages. And not only do feelings influence thought, but level of cognitive sophistication, as we shall see shortly, also has a profound influence on emotional reactivity. It is the cognitive interpretation of the perceived excitant, after all, rather than the latter per se which determines the nature of the emotional response.

GENERAL TRENDS IN EMOTIONAL DEVELOPMENT

Differentiation of Specific Emotions

One of the earliest features of affective development is the differentiation of specific emotions out of the state of general excitement that limits emotional reactivity at birth.* This development occurs, roughly speaking, between the second half of the first year and the third year; in subsequent sections it will be traced separately for each emotion. By way of general introduction, it will suffice to point out here that the process of differentiation affects excitants, feeling tones, and modes of expression, and depends

*See pages 219-221, for a discussion of emotional experience in the neonate, the evidence against specific emotions, and the probable reasons for lack of differentiation.

for the most part on (a) the development of a self-concept and other ego attributes that provide sufficiently salient personality referents to warrant the instigation of emotional states, and (b) the growth of sufficient cognitive sophistication to make possible the differential interpretation of perceived and anticipated events that enhance or threaten the self. To some extent also, the emergence of new reactive capacities (e.g., volitional aggression and avoidance) and of differential autonomic responses contributes to the distinctive properties of differentiated emotions; but these contributions are only reflective and secondary since the skeletal and visceral reactions accompanying emotional states are themselves determined by interpretive (cognitive) differences in response to excitants with self-reference. According to this view, the hypothalamus is not a primary determinant of emotional quality in its own right, but a coordinating center for the *expression* of emotional reactions already determined at a sophisticated cortical level.

Changes in Excitants

With increasing age, systematic changes occur in the properties of stimuli evoking emotional reactions or in the responsiveness of children to different categories of emotional stimulation. Some of these changes undoubtedly reflect *specific* family and cultural training when and under what conditions the expression of particular emotions is considered appropriate. Many of them, however, are attributable to cumulative increments in cognitive and personality maturity resulting from neural maturation and incidental experience and training in these *other* areas of development. As notions of omnipotence decline and as frustration tolerance increases, children react less vigorously to volitional constraint. As self-esteem and self-criticism become more prominent in the economy of personality organization, children become more susceptible to feelings of anxiety. And with increasing cognitive sophistication, we can expect that the scope of emotional reactivity will be extended to new situations and that some excitants of affective response at earlier stages of development will no longer be effective.

The range of stimuli instigating emotional reactions inevitably broadens in subtlety and complexity as children become more able to perceive, anticipate and imagine potential implications for self in more intricate life situations.* Infants' susceptibility to fear increases as they become suffi-

*Some extension of the range of susceptibility can be explained on the basis of simple conditioning, i.e., contiguous occurrence of adequate and inadequate stimuli with or without resulting expectancies and symbolic equivalence of stimuli.[89] However, conditioning can only account for relatively few and adventitious instances of extension—not for the systematic changes that depend on cognitive and personality maturation. Also, new, formerly inadequate stimuli can become adequate following increased cognitive sophistication *without* being temporally associated with adequate stimuli.

ciently mature to grasp the threatening implications of strangeness and other previously unrecognized hazards.[13, 26, 38, 44] Thus, brighter preschool children become afraid of certain situations at an earlier age than their duller contemporaries.[36] Older children are more responsive than younger children to less tangible and more symbolic excitants of emotion;[38] they react not only to the immediate perceptual properties of an emotional stimulus but also to its long range and deducible implications.[41]

While the scope of emotional responsiveness is being extended to more subtle, abstract and complex excitants, the child is simultaneously desensitized to other kinds of emotional stimuli. By virtue of the same gain in cognitive maturity he is able to discount formerly adequate excitants based on misconceptions, misinformation, inexperience and lack of skill in coping with problems. As he becomes more critical and less suggestible,[1] as he accumulates successful experience in handling various situations,[51] he becomes less aroused emotionally by many previously provocative stimuli. With shifts in ego goals, ego-involvements, and internal endocrine states, as for example during adolescence, he becomes less responsive to some stimuli (e.g., thrills, adventure) and more responsive to others (e.g., heterosexual concerns).[1]

Changes in Expression

Paralleling the age level changes in responsiveness to different kinds of excitants are developmental changes in mode of expression. In general, emotional responses become less diffuse and more specific, directed, and adaptive with increasing age.[28] Instead of reacting indiscriminately and with exaggerated and uniform intensity to all excitants the older child tends to utilize a selective gradation of response intensity appropriate for the situation at hand. At the same time the response becomes more highly differentiated or distinctive in relation to the feeling tones involved. Newly acquired reactive capacities (avoidance, aggression) are superimposed upon a genically determined core pattern of expression. The young infant can only cry and thrash about; the young child can hide, run away, strike out, shout defiance or argue contentiously. Later, culturally directed training further restricts the range of acceptable alternatives and specifies the appropriate type of response and the time, place and conditions under which it may be legitimately made. In our culture lower-class children learn to express their emotions in motor activity; middle-class children, on the other hand, are taught to express their feelings in more abstract and ideational form.[15, 83] In all children a tendency toward more subtle, symbolic and devious affective expression is a regular accompaniment of emotional development. But despite selectively greater utilization of covert expressive components, the correspondence between the two kinds of reactions tends to improve with increasing age (see p. 220), indicating a more integrated type of total organismic response.

Invariably, as children grow older, the culture demands greater suppression of overt emotionality, and accordingly the former gradually learn increased emotional control.[69] An inevitable concomitant of this trend is an increase in the strength of the autonomic component and a corresponding decrease in the strength of the skeletal-motor component of affective behavior—a state of affairs which tends to make emotional response less superficial and more long lasting in its effects. It is illustrated by the gradual decline of crying as a form of emotional expression. For a given age group, however, the incidence of crying varies considerably in accordance with situational factors; it is less at school than at home,[74] when sympathetic observers are absent, and when hurts are accidental rather than deliberately inflicted. The pressure for control also varies from one culture, subculture and family to another in the type of emotional expression that has to be suppressed and in the degree of suppression required. Middle-class children, for example, are under greater pressure than lower-class children to repress the physical components of aggression.[15, 61, 83] Boys are expected more than girls to repress fear and crying, but are permitted greater expression of physical aggression.

FEAR

Fear is in a generic sense a differentiated emotional experience that betokens cognitive awareness of threat to some highly ego-involved aspect of the individual's self-concept such as his physical well-being or his self-esteem. Regardless of how else they may be classified,[33] all excitants of fear embody some such threat to self. Although fear states usually include autonomic-humoral reactions, selective lowering of relevant perceptual and response thresholds, a somewhat variable pattern of motor responses, and the conscious repercussions of these different reactions, the only *essential* component of fear experience is subjective awareness of threat following cognitive interpretation of an adequate excitant. The autonomic-skeletal concomitants of fear, whether induced by direct hypothalamic stimulation, injection of adrenalin, or by abrupt loss of physical support in older children,[72] cannot by themselves (in the absence of perceived threat) generate genuine states of fear. Furthermore, because of cultural pressures, the somatic aspects of fear are either frequently repressed or else constitute highly modified and variable derivatives of original, genically patterned neuromuscular and avoidance responses.

Although the maladaptive effects of intense fear on problem solving and delicate skills (see footnote, p. 317) are not to be underestimated, we should not for this reason discount the important role of fear as a protective, motivating and socializing agent. Fear promotes the prudent avoidance of danger and the exercise of reasonable caution. It alerts the individual to potential threat and mobilizes his reactive capacities. And most important of all, fear of punishment, social censure, failure, guilt, and loss of status are ubiquitous and indispensable factors in the acquisition of socialized and moral behavior and in the realization of ego status and ego maturity goals.

Classification of Fear States

By specifying whether the excitant evoking fear is a current or anticipated threat and whether the individual's physical well-being or self-esteem is being threatened, it is possible to classify generic fear experience into four subcategories (see table 2). *Fear* (in the specific sense) and *anxiety-fear* refer to fear states elicited in response to current threats; whereas *insecurity* and *anxiety* are referable to anticipated threats. Both fear and insecurity involve affective reactions to threats directed at the individual's physical safety or continuance as a biological and psychological entity; whereas in the case of anxiety-fear and anxiety, his self-esteem is perceived as under attack.

TABLE 2.—*Classification of Fear States**

Temporal Position of Perceived Threat	What Is Threatened	
	Physical Well-Being	Self-Esteem
Current	Fear	Anxiety-Fear
Anticipated	Insecurity	Anxiety

Threats vary in their accessibility to consciousness and in their identifiability—both with respect to their source (the origin or nature of the threat) and their object (the aspect of self that is threatened). Repression of awareness (inaccessibility) temporarily reduces fear but is maladaptive in the long run since it does not permit the individual to cope constructively with the threat confronting him. Unidentifiable threats tend to generate more fear than identifiable threats since the threatened individual cannot prepare his defenses adequately when he can specify neither the source nor the target of danger. Thus arises the common mechanism of displacement— giving a vague or unpalatable intrapersonal source of threat concrete external reference and shifting the object of threat from an unspecifiable

*Adapted from D. P. Ausubel, *Ego Development and the Personality Disorders.*[5]

aspect of self-esteem to a more tangible (and manageable) aspect of physical safety. *Phobias* are just such displaced fears.

The persistence of "irrational fears in children", that is, fears of situations that are out of all proportion to the actual probability of their occurrence (fear of wild animals and ghosts[40] and of failing in school[37]) probably represent a form of phobia or displaced fear. Also frequently involved in such fears are intrapersonal sources of threat (e.g., feelings of inadequacy, guilt feelings, aggressive impulses) over and above the objective hazards confronting the individual. In certain instances the seemingly exaggerated fear response to an improbable catastrophe (e.g., failure in school) may not even be irrational if the child is reacting to the imagined calamitous consequences that would ensue if the improbable event actually *did* occur rather than to the statistical probabilities involved.

Development of Fear in Infants

In the first half year of life potentially harmful stimuli are not perceived as threats and hence elicit diffuse excitement or distress rather than fear (see p. 220). Before threat can be perceived as such, the infant must first be able to perceive and discriminate between persons and objects, between the familiar and unfamiliar in his environment; he must possess sufficient cognitive maturity to appreciate that certain persons and situations can threaten his continued existence as an individual. And it goes without saying that threats can have no self-reference (and hence insufficient salience to instigate fear) until a functional notion of identity exists.

Once the prerequisites for experiencing fear are fulfilled, the adequate stimuli initially eliciting this affect are practically coextensive with the factors instigating general excitement (i.e., any intense stimulation), provided that the elements of suddenness, unexpectedness, or unfamiliarity are also present. During early infancy fear is most commonly elicited by unexpected loud noises, rapid or abrupt displacement in space, pain, strange events, and sudden movements.[38] However, such stimuli should not be conceived of as "original" in a reflex-like sense; it appears rather that at this primitive level of cognitive maturity *only such* gross, concrete, and immediate stimuli as these have threatening implications. At the stage when he is first able to distinguish between a smiling and scowling face,[13] the six months old infant first becomes sufficiently mature to appreciate, so to speak, that strange persons with whose intentions he is as yet unfamiliar[38, 80, 82] or confinement in a small pen[26] may be potentially dangerous. Furthermore, the adequate stimuli here are neither specific (in the sense of being restricted to loud noise or loss of support) or invariable (independent of situational determinants). If an infant enters a strange room in the company of his mother, for example, he is less frightened than when entering alone.[3]

Developmental Changes

Altered Responsiveness. Developmental shifts in responsiveness to fear are mirrored in the changing range and properties of fear excitants as children advance in age. Many stimuli that effectively instigate fear during earlier years become less adequate as children gain in experience, understanding, and the ability to cope with trying situations. Many other factors, on the other hand, simultaneously enhance susceptibility to fear. The broadening of the older child's physical and psychological worlds inevitably brings him into contact with a much wider array of potential excitants. Merely through contiguity of occurrence with adequate stimuli[89] and the associated phenomena of expectancy, symbolic equivalence, and stimulus generalization, many formerly inocuous objects and situations acquire fear-arousing properties. More complex ego functioning—the development of self-esteem and self-critical ability, responsiveness to social norms, goal setting, competition with others, ego reactions to failure, the emergence of inadequacy and guilt feelings—create fear of failure, of censure, and of morally unacceptable impulses. It is largely because of this personality growth (which makes children more responsive to ego-social occasions for and to intrapersonal determinants of fear experience) that the source of threat tends to become increasingly less identifiable. This circumstance in turn encourages displacement of threat to more specifiable but elusive sources (e.g., supernatural figures*) that are more admissable and less threatening than fear of failure, ridicule, retribution and loss of status.

The principle cause of altered responsiveness to fear lies in cognitive maturation—the child's increased ability to perceive and anticipate danger in more subtle and remote situations, to remember previous occasions of fear, to imagine dangerous encounters that transcend his own experience, and to infer danger by deduction and generalization. During the preschool period, such tangible sources of fear as loud noises, dogs, high places, falling, and strange places decline in importance and are gradually replaced by more remote, abstract, imaginary, and improbable excitants with which he has relatively little direct experience (darkness, solitude, abandonment, wild animals, storms, criminal characters, supernatural figures, death, occult phenomena) and by fear of school failure, social ridicule and personal inadequacy.[31, 38] This trend continues into and becomes even more pronounced during the elementary school years.[40]

Expressive Characteristics. In accordance with general developmental

---

*Unless these phobic displacements were outside the realm of direct experience they would be easily discounted and extinguished, and hence no longer serviceable.

trends in emotional expression, the expression of fear becomes more subtle, abstract and devious, and less transparent and overt with increasing age. Not only are the gross motor components of fear (crying, trembling, shrinking, clinging, cringing, flight) repressed, but subjective content as well. If subjective repression is impossible, the child may either fail to recognize his feelings as fear or to acknowledge any relationship between them and relevant excitants. In either case the autonomic-humoral component of fear response is enhanced.

The reasons for these trends are rather self-evident. First, since the excitants of fear tend to become more imaginary, symbolic, unidentifiable, and intrapersonal in origin, overt response becomes less possible. Second, since in many cultures the expression of fear is regarded as opprobious and as a confession of weakness or cowardice it is treated with contempt and ridicule: As the child learns to fear ridicule he also learns to fear the expression of his own fears. Internalization of this cultural standard also makes self-acknowledgement of fear sufficient cause for self-contempt, thereby favoring suppression of subjective awareness.

Other Factors Affecting Responsiveness to Fear

Children's responsiveness to fear is affected by cultural influences, by individual differences in personality structure, and by situational factors. The form that fears take is largely molded by cultural stereotypes, that is, by social expectations, by traditional views of what constitutes an adequate stimulus, and by the particular uses adults make of fears in the socializing process. In our culture, in accordance with differential social expectations, girls exceed boys in almost all categories of fear expression;[31] and only oblique but highly suggestive references are made to bogeymen, witches, and goblins as instruments of retribution. In some North American Indian cultures actual enactment of these roles by masked and robed relatives is relied upon as a principal means of disciplining children and exacting conformity to social norms.[87]

Interindividual differences in responsiveness to fear are related to such temperamental traits as timorousness and "toughness of skin," to actual incompetence or feelings of inadequacy, and to the extent that fear is utilized by children (or parents) as a means of obtaining attention and affection or of perpetuating executive dependence. Children are more responsive to fear in an atmosphere of fearfulness, insecurity and hostility, when they are burdened prematurely with adult worries and problems, and when they ae chronically subjected to threat, intimidation, harsh punishment, and demands beyond their capacity. They are also more fearful when parents are overprotective* or set an example of fear, since not only

*See A. L. Baldwin, *Child Develop.* 20: 49-62, 1949.

is fear contagious but in this instance it also deprives them of their main source of support and reassurance. Thus, a high positive correlation prevails between the number of fears children have and the number possessed by their mothers.[31] And lastly, children are more prone to be aroused by fear in unfamiliar physical settings and in unstructured social situations in which standards of acceptable behavior are ambiguous.

ANXIETY

Anxiety is a special variety of fear experience in response to an *anticipated* threat to self-esteem. It always includes the interpretive and preparatory reactive phases of an emotional experience. The consummatory phase, however, with its subjective, autonomic-humoral, and motor components (and their reflective repercussions) may either be experienced as an advance reaction to the anticipated threat, or may be delayed until the threat is current or self-esteem itself actually undergoes impairment. In the latter instances, the response is identical in content with that of *anxiety-fear* except that it is initiated by an anticipatory stimulus and involves a prolonged preparatory phase. Anxiety (and insecurity also) thus include both a currently experienced emotion and a "set" to respond affectively to an anticipated threat; and since these reactions implicate such stable and salient features of ego structure as adequacy and security feelings, they too become conceptualized as ego attributes in relation to the self-concept. Hence, quite apart from the existence of *particular* anticipated threats, an individual tends to conceive of himself as *typically* manifesting a given affective level of anxiety and insecurity.

Except for these designated differences, anxiety and insecurity share all of the properties of fear states described above. They vary in degree of accessibility, identifiability and displacement, both with respect to source and object of threat; and the component aspects of the affective response may also undergo varying degrees of repression. In the writer's opinion, therefore, the many attempts that have been made to differentiate between fear and anxiety (on the grounds that in anxiety states the source of threat is allegedly less accessible, identifiable and exogenous, the object of threat more central, and the response more apt to be both disproportionately great and subjectively inaccessible) are warranted neither by logic nor by empirical data. The current threat to physical safety in fear states is always psychologically salient, is frequently unidentifiable, and may also inhere largely in feelings of inadequacy, guilt and hostility; whereas in many instances of anxiety, the threat is external and specifiable, the individual is completely aware of the feelings it evokes, and the response (except in neurotic anxiety) is wholly commensurate with the objective magnitude of the danger involved.

Varieties of Anxiety

The basic problem in classifying anxiety states is to distinguish between anxiety as a pathologic entity (neurotic anxiety) and as a normal situational or developmental type of fear behavior under certain warranted conditions. Since every affect, neurotic or otherwise, must be instigated by a *subjectively* adequate stimulus, it is only possible to designate as "neurotic" that anxiety in which the exogenous or endogenous threat to self-esteem is not *objectively* adequate to instigate fear but appears *subjectively* adequate to the individual because of existing impairment of self-esteem itself (i.e., of the very target of threat). He over-reacts with fear not because his self-esteem is threatened by objectively adequate hazards, failings, or feelings of guilt and hostility, but because *any* trivial threat to an ego-involved area of self-esteem is *actually* calamitous to an individual whose self-esteem is already impaired and lacks a reasonable margin of safety. Hence, in neurotic anxiety the fear response is disproportionate to the objective degree of threat emanating from sources distinct from the object of threat itself (self-esteem).

It is reasonable to suppose that the degree of impairment of self-esteem predisposing toward neurotic anxiety is characteristically found only in children who have not undergone satellization in the course of development. First, they lack the background of derived status that provides a current or residual core of intrinsic self-esteem irrespective of environmental vicissitudes in the quest for primary status. Second, their extrinsic feelings of adequacy are extremely vulnerable to catastrophic impairment by virtue of chronic rejection, precipitous devaluation outside the home (in the case of overvalued children), and unrealistically high ego aspirations.

Normal *transitional* anxiety arises during periods of crisis in ego development. Its source lies in pressures that are inherent in the very nature of developmental transition (see p. 104). Hence it occurs more or less universally in all individuals and at every age when rapid personality change is required. The relevant factors entering into the threat are new social expectations regarding the abandonment of an established and the gaining of a new biosocial status; the need to accomplish new developmental tasks; an intermediate period of attitudinal disorientation and marginal status; and uncertainty whether the new status will ever be attained—a state of affairs deliberately fostered by the culture to encourage a high and sustained level of motivation regarding the acquisition of new ego maturity and ego status goals.

Because of exposure to certain undesirable parent attitudes it is understandable that transitional anxiety may be more severe in some children than in others. Overprotected and overdominated children are especially threatened by the need to relinquish derived status and to strive for primary

status and volitional independence (see p. 307). During the course of
socialization the underdominated child must cope with the anxiety arising
from the absence of effective internal and external control of his aggressive
impulses. The children of unappreciating and hypercritical parents may
experience serious doubts about their ability to meet the new requirements
and standards of more mature personality status; and in the case of rejected
and overvalued children the excitants of transitional anxiety may furnish
the occasion for either the initial generation of or the release of existing
neurotic anxiety.

Situational anxiety is the normal type of anxiety that arises in relation
to exogenous threats to self-esteem. It is a self-protective reaction which
is limited to the duration of the situation that elicits it and is proportionate
to the objective magnitude of the threat involved. Situational anxiety is
inherent in almost any new ego-involved task or problem that exposes the
individual to the possibility of frustration, failure or loss of self-esteem.
Susceptibility to situational anxiety is increased by any of the situational,
personal, and interpersonal factors enhancing responsiveness to fear (see
p. 327) ; by past experience with such traumatic events as accidents, operations, separations, vivid frights, and sudden privations;[57] and by predisposition to neurotic anxiety. Also influencing general responsiveness to
situational anxiety are such cultural factors as the extent to which society
values the individual for himself or coerces him into competing for hierarchical status, the availability of the extrinsic status for which the culture
motivates its members to strive, and the incidence of cultural crisis and
social disorganization.

Endogenous anxiety is similar to situational anxiety except for the fact
that the threat arises from within the individual rather than from the
environment. Unlike neurotic anxiety the threat is objectively adequate
in relation to the response it evokes, and the source of the threat does not
inhere in impaired self-esteem. A common type of endogenous anxiety is
derived from objective physical, motor, intellectual and social disabilities
which constitute a threat to self-esteem insofar as they expose the individual to ridicule and ostracism, loss of status, and failure in various adjustive situations. Hostility and other socially unacceptable impulses and
attitudes generate anxiety by threatening the individual (if they are expressed) with loss of acceptance from the persons on whom he is dependent
for derived status and with reprisals from authority figures who control
his primary status.* Indirectly, by giving rise to guilt feelings (awareness
of moral culpability, self-reproach), these impulses endanger self-esteem

---

*Fear of physical retaliation and loss of succorance engendered by aggressive im-
pulses is really a form of insecurity.

and induce anxiety. Strength of aggressive tendencies is thus positively related to degree of anxiety which in turn frequently takes the displaced and
projected form of unreasonable fear of other persons and of supernatural
figures.[91]

Development of Anxiety

Insecurity is differentiated out of general excitement several months
later than is fear since it requires the ability to anticipate danger or perceive future threat to safety in current cues. It is first manifested at about
the age of nine months in response to abrupt separation from the customary
mother figure (see p. 121). The infant at this age is aware of his executive
dependency and hence perceives the deprivation of his executive arm as
a threat to his physical well-being. After satellization takes place and the
child identifies his security with parental acceptance, disapproval becomes
a more salient precipitant of insecurity feelings.

Anxiety appears relatively late on the emotional horizon. It presupposes
the child's ability to conceptualize his own biosocial status, to react to
depreciation of such status with lowered feelings of adequacy, and to
anticipate future threats to self-esteem. Anxiety, therefore, can make its
first appearance only after a primitive sense of adequacy emerges which
initially reflects the infant's tendency to perceive himself as volitionally
omnipotent and independent. Serious challenges to this status, as occur
during the period of ego devaluation, threaten self-esteem sufficiently to
instigate transitional anxiety; but since the devaluation is generally carried
out in a setting of benevolence and affection, this anxiety tends to be
overshadowed by negativism (see p. 293). During the preschool and early
elementary school years, anxiety is instigated mostly in relation to parent-
child and peer-child conflicts[22, 85] that threaten the child's derived status.
As cognitive sophistication increases with advancing age and ego functioning becomes more complex, the child becomes responsive to a wider, more
subtle, abstract, remote, and unidentifiable array of situations threatening
his self-esteem. Threats to primary status (school failure, personal inadequacy) become more prominent excitants of anxiety[70, 96] which like fear
are increasingly subjected to repression.

Role in Motivation and Learning

Although much motivation for activity and personality maturation is
derived from more positive sources (see p. 228), culturally instigated anxiety
still constitutes an important factor in promoting the acquisition of mature
and socialized goals and ego attributes. In most children anxiety regarding
failure and loss of status in the group tends to energize performance,
increase effort, and raise aspirational level; and anxiety reduction in adjus-

tive situations reinforces the successful variant. Especially in non-satellizers with impaired self-esteem, a relentless drive for extrinsic adequacy and ego aggrandizement tends to compensate for the absence of intrinsic adequacy and to allay the anxiety associated with the reaction-sensitivity to over-respond with fear to anticipated threat.

The effect of anxiety on learning is most disruptive in novel problem solving or adjustive situations rather than in familiar or routine tasks.*[6, 52] The individual with impaired self-esteem is naturally threatened most by problems with which he has no successful past experience or established pattern of response. He thus finds opportunity for advanced preparation and practice more anxiety reducing and beneficial for learning than do non-anxiety ridden persons,[6] and frequently utilizes it for these purposes. It is postulated, therefore, that neurotic anxiety impairs problem solving because feelings of inadequacy about ability to improvise in unfamiliar situations leads to (a) an habitual and rigid learning set to adhere to stereotyped response patterns; (b) reliance upon such patterns as a learning "crutch" and means of anxiety reduction; and (c) a face-saving attempt to produce any "visible" response when panic associated with initial or cumulative frustration would otherwise result in blocking or utter confusion.

ANGER

Anger is a differentiated emotional experience instigated by threat to an ego-involved aspect of self in which awareness of threat (and its preparatory, autonomic-humoral and motor consequences) is partly or completely replaced by aggressive subjective content and corresponding activity in the autonomic-humoral and motor spheres. Although frequently aroused by threats to physical well-being and self-esteem or by attacks on property and reputation, it is most typically elicited by frustration of volitional desires or by interference with goal-directed volitional activity. But just as anger may be instigated by excitants other than frustration, frustration may also lead to outcomes other than rage or aggression. It is true that aggression is perhaps the earliest acquired differentiated response to volitional frustration. In the course of learning, frustration may become associated with fear, insecurity, and anxiety, with submission, avoidance and dependency,[90] and with nonspecific compensatory satisfactions (see p. 241) and regression.[9]

Anger and fear are closely related. Similar factors are involved in instigating and increasing responsiveness to each, and either emotion may accompany or give rise to the other. An individual's awareness of his own hostility often precipitates fear and, contrariwise, many acts of aggression

*See also Chapter 17.[28]

are prompted by fear. Anger, however, is encountered more frequently in children than is fear[23] because it is aroused more easily, is less avoidable, and is more apt to be effective in gaining goal satisfaction.

Because parental and cultural tolerance for children's aggression almost invariably diminishes as they leave infancy,[91] the expression of anger is subjected to varying degrees of inhibition. More commonly only the motor-verbal components of rage are inhibited; sometimes, however, the subjective component is also repressed. Frequently when the overt motor-verbal expression of aggression is inhibited because of fear of punishment or retaliation, indirect, disguised and covert outlets are utilized, e.g., passive sabotage, exaggerated friendliness, imagining or wishing injury to others. The amount of overt aggression a child displays is a poor indication of the amount he feels. Korner obtained only low positive correlations between real-life and different kinds of fantasy aggression,[48] and Sears found that preschool children highly punished by their mothers for aggression tend to rank low on frequency of aggressive acts in school but high on doll play aggression.[77] Results of other studies support the view that amount of overt and fantasy aggression are positively related in children provided that they do not fear punishment excessively for their aggressive impulses.* [66] Without additional interview data it is impossible to ascertain the extent to which such fantasy aggression is accessible to consciousness and is recognized as such. Subjective repression implicating the excitant and the referent as well as the feeling tones themselves is especially apt to occur when hostility is accompanied by either guilt feelings or intense anxiety. Children may further protect themselves from the consequences of their own hostility by failing to perceive hostile acts directed against themselves.

All of the factors promoting the inhibition of aggression also favor the displacement of the object or person against whom anger is directed. The anger children feel toward parents and other persons in authority is frequently displaced to animals, siblings and classmates,[59] or is expressed in the form of truancy, delinquency, antisocial attitudes, and racial prejudice. Sometimes children turn their anger against themselves and court injury in order to provoke guilt feelings in parents or to involve them in personal and financial difficulties. Krall found that a group of accident-prone children exhibited significantly more aggression in doll play than did a matched group of accident-free children.[50] Children also frequently project their aggressive feelings onto others as a means of both disowning and justifying them.

*Extent of overt and fantasy aggression are highly correlated when both have the same goal object and mode of expression. (J. Kagan, *J. Abnorm. Soc. Psychol.* 52: 390-393, 1956.

Differentiation from Excitement

As in the case of fear, the differentiation of rage from excitement presupposes the development of a functional concept of self and sufficient cognitive maturity to appreciate the significance of threat. In addition, before rage can be evoked in response to volitional frustration, a sense of volition must first exist. Thus restraint as such—even initial strapping to the cradle board—evokes no response whatsoever from neonates[18, 19]; and rough restraint, like any intense stimulus, merely elicits undifferentiated excitement (see p. 220). Later, as the infant becomes more responsive to interference per se as a form of frustration, persistent restraint of motion evokes excitement.[18, 19, 56] If he is accustomed to the cradle board, he does not experience restraint as frustration; in fact he cries and is unable to sleep if he is kept off it.[10]

True rage is not observed until about the tenth month of life,[81] when needs are expressed in volitional form. It is instigated most commonly at first by bodily restraint and delay in the gratification of visceral needs,[28] but the adequate stimulus soon becomes generalized to include any interference with goal-directed activity. The violence of the affective response to volitional frustration is attributable in part to the anticipatory set of compliance associated with the omnipotent self-concept.* Because of its intensity, refractoriness to control, longevity, and self-perpetuating properties, anger easily gets out of hand and continues long after the aroused child has ceased being aware of the exciting cause. Rage also constitutes the core of the negativistic reaction to ego devaluation since the pressures responsible for this shift in ego structure challenge the child's notion of volitional independence and the goal-directed activity predicated upon it.

Developmental Changes

Altered Responsiveness. Many factors operate both to increase and decrease responsiveness to excitants of rage as children advance in age. Thus the relative frequency of anger outbursts at a particular age is a result of these opposing influences. Partly for this reason and partly because the expression of overt anger tends to undergo increasingly greater inhibition with age, evidence regarding age trends is highly equivocal. Goodenough found that outbursts of anger reach maximum frequency at 18 months and then decline regularly in frequency throughout the preschool period[28]; after the age of four, however, the after-effects of anger were found to be more frequent and prolonged than in younger children.[2, 28] These findings are supported by Jersild and Markey's study of social conflicts

---

*Chronically neglected children reared in foundling homes do not develop notions of omnipotence and hence exhibit shallow and superficial emotionality.[27]

in preschool children[39]; but other investigators either fail to obtain a consistent trend with age[61, 75] or report a trend in the opposite direction.[67] Doll play aggression tends to increase somewhat in frequency between three and four years of age but remains relatively constant between the fourth and fifth years.[76]

Cognitive maturation generally broadens the child's range of responsiveness to rage producing stimuli. The widening of his intellectual and social horizons and the emergence of goal strivings in a social context provide many new occasions for the occurrence of frustration and anger. Bodily restraint and training routines thus become less important excitants of rage,[28] whereas conflict with peers and adult authority[28] and perceptions of unfairness and inequity[34] correspondingly gain in importance. Increasing cognitive sophistication and motor competence, on the other hand, enable the child to cope more adequately with difficulties and hence decrease the likelihood of frustration. With increased understanding of his environment and with greater self-critical ability he also becomes less easily inflamed by unintentional injury and better able to set realistic goals.

Normative changes in ego development also affect responsiveness to anger. As pretensions of omnipotence decline and as acceptance of parental authority increases children become less insistent on doing the impossible and more willing to tolerate delay in need-satisfaction, to accept realistic restrictions on their volitional desires, and to bow to the inevitable. Frustration tolerance also increases as the child learns through gradual dosing that denial of his legitimate needs is usually only temporary in a generally benevolent environment, and that initial frustration in problem solving situations can be endured until a successful solution is forthcoming. The older child learns to ignore many frustrating situations or to interpret them in ways less threatening to his volitional goals.

Expressive Characteristics. The earliest expression of rage is typified by the diffuse, explosive, and uninhibited temper tantrum. With increasing age the rage becomes better controlled and tends to be more adaptively directed against the perceived excitant or obstacle. During the preschool period, crying, screaming and physical forms of attack (striking, pushing, kicking) decline in frequency and tend to be replaced by such verbal techniques as threatening, name-calling, scolding, fussing, belittling and teasing.[28, 39, 74] To the extent that cultural tolerance for aggression diminishes as children grow older, direct and overt forms of aggression also give way to more devious manifestations.

Factors Affecting Responsiveness to Anger

Sex and social class are important determinants of the frequency and form of aggression in children. Practically all studies of overt[17, 28, 39, 67] and doll play[8, 76] aggression in preschool children indicate that boys are significantly more aggressive than girls. The fact that these differences are not obtained prior to the age of two suggests that they originate in differential parental expectations,[71] in the different ways that mothers handle aggression in the two sexes,[78] and in the differential availability of derived and extrinsic status and of the mother as an emulatory model (see p. 293). These factors also account for sex differences in the expression of rage after the age of two—the greater decline of physical aggression in girls[32, 39, 67, 76] and of screaming and crying in boys,[17, 39] and the greater utilization of verbal forms of aggression by girls.[17, 32] Probably because of greater parental tolerance of aggression, less parental supervision, and greater material deprivation, lower-class children tend to be physically more aggressive than middle-class children in play situations[2, 14, 39, 61]

Responsiveness to rage is also influenced by situational, endogenous and interpersonal factors. Fatigue, hunger, and transitory disturbances in health[28] as well as such temperamental factors as ascendance and high energy output[25, 56] increase susceptibility to frustration and rage.* Anger is more likely to occur in ambiguous social situations,[28] in physically crowded play areas,[39] when children are exposed to excessively difficult tasks,[46] and when many siblings and adults are present in the home.[28] Habitual and excessive thwarting increases susceptibility to anger whereas training in frustration tolerance through gradual dosing has the opposite effect.[46] Anger outbursts tend to occur more frequently when they are effective in securing gratification of desires and when parents threaten, cajole, or nag children.[28] They also occur more frequently in children with anxious, over-critical, inconsistent or recriminating parents,[28] and in underdominated children who are not required to learn self-control.[55, 84]

Punishment is perhaps the most important and complex antecedent of aggression in children. Its effects are difficult to interpret because (depending in part on the nature of the punishment) it both increases and decreases the strength of aggressive tendencies and, too, it inhibits their overt expression. Even under the best of circumstances children find the authority role of parents restrictive and frustrating. Hence they tend to react with some degree of aggression providing that it actually serves the retaliatory function of paining and annoying parents (as indicated by the latter's angry or punitive responses).[78] Those children who are most severely punished at home exhibit the highest level of latent hostility, as measured by doll play aggression,[35, 77] whereas those children who are subjected to

---

*Children who have high power-dominance needs react more aggressively to frustration (R. B. Otis and B. McCandless, *J. Abnorm. Soc. Psychol.* 50: 349-353, 1955.)

least maternal punishment exhibit the least amount of both real-life and doll play aggression.*[77] In cultures where parents administer much punishment for aggression during early socialization, adults tend to be relatively aggressive and hence to manifest a great deal of anxiety about aggression.[91] If, in particular cases, punishment is also unreasonably harsh, capricious, discriminatory or indicative of rejection, children develop a deep sense of resentment which may find indirect expression in bullying, cruelty to animals, and delinquency.[73] By the same token, insofar as punishment is administered benevolently and is accepted by children as rightful, it tends to stimulate remorse rather than aggression. In such instances the tendency to *acquire* aggressive impulses in response to parental punishment is weakened by fear of further punishment and by the need to avoid the guilt feelings that accompany aggression. Thus, Hopi children resent the formal authority role of the maternal uncle much more than they do that of their parents which is part of a larger affectional relationship.[19]

Punishment also affects aggressive behavior by inhibiting the extent to which a child's latent aggressive tendencies are overtly expressed. Children who are very severely punished for aggression at home[77] or who show considerable fear of punishment for aggression[66] exhibit much fantasy aggression but relatively little overt aggression. Under such circumstances aggressive feelings against parents tend to be displaced to age mates,[78, 92] especially if such behavior is approved of and rewarded by parents.[14] Stringent punishment of aggression during early childhood tends to be associated with adult anxiety about aggression at the hands of figures who are most remotely related to the original punitive agents.[91] If fantasy (e.g., doll play) aggression is also punished it too tends to be inhibited.[35]

JEALOUSY AND ENVY

Jealousy is a composite affective state combining the elements of generic fear and anger in which an individual feels threatened when he perceives *his exclusive* possession of a source of security, status or affection challenged by the needs, aspirations and activities of others. Envy is a related but more complex and later developing emotion in which the threat to self-esteem emanates from a perception that other persons are superior in status, attainments or possessions. As already pointed out, the mere quest for primary or derived status does not necessarily presuppose competition, jealousy, or envy (see p. 310). For jealousy to arise a special kind of competitive situation is required—one in which some restriction prevails in

*Amount of fantasy aggression is positively related in boys to degree of identification with aggressive, punitive fathers (H. Levin and R. R. Sears, *Child Develop.* 27: 135-153, 1956.) .

the availability of a desired object or relationship and in which possession tends to exist on a preclusive basis. Once this situation exists, jealousy develops if the individual desires or claims exclusive entitlement, perceives a challenge to his claim, and feels threatened by this perception. Later, even if he possesses ample exclusive sources of status and security and does not perceive anyone trying directly to share in or deprive him of same, he may still feel threatened by the perceived superior status of others (envy); it is as if his own worth and self-esteem were automatically depreciated by the very existence of competence in other persons and by the recognition accorded them. Thus, envy is predicated on the proposition that "the more and better selfhood a person has, the less is available for others— that no one can enhance or defend himself without encroaching upon the self enhancement and self-defence of others."[64]

The interpersonal and social conditions necessary for the generation of jealousy and envy exist almost universally, but obviously vary greatly in degree and extensity, both inter- and intraculturally. Envy flourishes especially in a cultural milieu in which "the individual can . . . [not] rejoice naively in elementary physical or social selfhood . . . [but] must compare the self continually with a standard set up within or with an objective standard defined by the self-gratification available to others."[64] But even in this type of highly competitive social climate, susceptibility to envy varies in accordance with many temperamental, personality and interpersonal factors.

Sibling Jealousy

Sibling jealousy is the most common and important type of jealousy encountered during childhood. It emanates from the desire for exclusive possession of the parents' nurturant affection and of the source of derived status in the home. Inescapable conditions of family organization render this aspiration universally untenable whenever and wherever it exists— except, of course, in single-child families. Newborn infants require much protective care; and because of their greater helplessness and lesser frustration tolerance, their needs are given priority, and fewer demands are made on them than on their older siblings.* The latter, therefore, must not only share nurturance and affection with the newcomer but must also surrender the lion's share to him. It is no wonder then that sibling jealousy has been observed in a wide variety of cultures.[19, 53, 62] The intensity of the jealousy, however, varies greatly with cultural and familial practices and with the personality make-up of parent and child. Much depends on the abruptness and completeness with which the older child is "dethroned" and on whether other relatives are available (as in the extended family group) to provide

*This situation obviously facilitates the process of ego devaluation (see p. 293).

care and solicitude. The Balinese lap baby, for example, is deliberately taunted and teased at the time of weaning with the fact that his former pre-eminent position is being usurped by a new sibling; and if an actual sibling is not available an infant is borrowed for this purpose.[62]

It should be realized though that not all conflict and discord among siblings is indicative of rivalry over parental affection. Children in the same household invariably get in each other's way and compete for material things, for dominance, and for other forms of primary status. Teasing, tormenting and bullying are also manifestations of exuberance, pecking order behavior, and of the mischievous fun and play found in the young of other primate species;[95] they constitute as well part of an institutionalized pattern of jockeying for position in peer relationships. In any event it is self-evident that the presence of rivalry and jealousy does not preclude the possibility of much genuine friendliness, affection and loyalty in the relationship between siblings.

Expressive Outlets. Sibling jealousy is frequently expressed (especially by younger children) in direct bodily assault[79] or verbally in the form of belittling, teasing and tattling. Sometimes the parent as well as the rival sibling becomes the object of the jealous child's ire. With advancing age, as such behavior is subjected to increasingly greater punishment and disapproval, it tends to be replaced by more devious kinds of aggression. Latent hostility toward a baby sibling may be displaced to older siblings and age mates,[53, 79] or give rise to vengeful fantasies that are enacted in doll play settings.[55, 76] In older children, sibling jealousy often takes the form of extreme competitiveness over prestige and accomplishment; ostensibly no hostile feelings are intended, but secretly each rival may strive more for the other's humiliation than for his own success. Various withdrawal techniques are also frequently utilized—studied indifference, blustering nonchalance, and persistent obliviousness to and even outright denial of the younger sibling's existence.[68, 79] The older child may bid for the parents' attention by regressing to infantile habits of eating, dressing, sleeping and sphincter control,[79] by feigning fear, by resorting to silliness and naughtiness, and by strutting about and showing off.[68] He may try to win his parents' favor by being excessively submissive, obedient, and helpful, and even by showing extreme solicitude for his rival's well-being.

As children develop new interests, affiliations and sources of status outside the home, sibling rivalry over parental affection tends to diminish in intensity. And as they compete more for status and prestige, in school and peer group, siblings are replaced by age mates as objects of jealousy, and jealousy in turn is superseded by envy.

Factors Affecting Susceptibility to Jealousy. It seems reasonable to suppose that children who are genically and experientially predisposed toward dominance, self-sufficiency, and independence (and who therefore are less dependent on derived or primary status for feelings of adequacy) would be less threatened by others' status and by the need to share parental affection than would "thin-skinned," submissive, dependent and timorous children.* Less susceptibility to sibling jealousy might also be anticipated in girls who are predisposed temperamentally or by familial and cultural pressures to adopt maternal attitudes toward infants. On the other hand, children who are insecure or who lack intrinsic feelings of adequacy might be expected to feel especially threatened by loss of exclusive possession of parental nurturance and by the accomplishments of their siblings. Thus, excessive jealousy or envy is frequently only one of many indications of maladjustment in children.[24] The stage of personality development through which the child is passing must also be considered. During the period of ego devaluation, dethronement merely adds insult to injury; whereas during the period of desatellization, when the child is less dependent himself on parental care and affection, he may actually vie with the parent in extending protection to the infant.

Intrafamilial variables are perhaps the most significant factors affecting responsiveness to sibling jealousy. Marital discord, favoritism, discrimination, and inequitable distribution of affection obviously tend to enhance the development of jealous feelings. A rejected child frequently displaces the resentment he feels toward parents onto a sibling, especially if the latter is correspondingly favored. Jealousy is less apt to arise when the age difference between siblings is greater than 42 months.[79] By this age ego devaluation is more or less completed and the child begins to find interests outside the home. Furthermore, the new sibling is so much less competent as to lie outside his competitive range—at least during the phase of early infancy. Less jealousy develops when the age difference is small (less than 18 months), since the older child still requires and receives much protective care. Like twins, such siblings also make more compatible playmates. In large families where children are more accustomed to share parental affection and look after each other, jealous behavior is less pronounced.[79] Under such circumstances, since dethronement is a fate that systematically befalls each new child in turn, his predecessors are less likely to interpret their own experiences in this regard as uniquely personal affronts.

AFFECTION

More systematic attention has been given to the impact of parental affection (or lack of affection) on children's development than to the

---

*Iatmul children, who are trained to be volitionally and executively independent from a very early age,[62] show conspicuous lack of jealousy toward their infant siblings.

development of affection in children. We have already considered the infant's need for "mothering" and the conditions under which gross deprivation of affection tends to be associated with impairment of bodily functioning and of motor, cognitive, and emotional development. (See pp. 121-122 and 255-257). In discussing ego development during early childhood, we have also considered the importance of parental affection as part of a larger pattern of acceptance and intrinsic valuation necessary for satellization and the development of intrinsic feelings of security and adequacy (see p. 289).

Although a potentiality for developing feelings of affection is undoubtedly inherent in all human beings, it is self-evident that the infant is first on the receiving rather than on the giving end of love. Prior to the emergence of a self-concept it is hardly credible to suppose that any perception he might have of other persons could be sufficiently salient to instigate affectionate impulses within him. What Watson mistook for "love" in the neonate was probably nothing more than feelings of satiety reflecting the gratification of visceral needs and the absence of bodily discomfort. Since the mother is customarily present under such circumstances, these feelings tend to be associated with her presence, as they would with any contiguous stimulus. In this way she becomes both a cue for impending gratification and a partial substitute for such gratification, and hence is able to comfort the hungry infant merely by holding him. Later, as the child perceives the mother as a person, he responds to her more actively—with smiling, cooing and gurgling;[20] but neither can these unlearned reactions be equated with affection.

After a functional self-concept emerges and the child appreciates his executive incompetence, the causal role of his parents in gratifying his needs, and his dependence upon them for continued survival, then his sense of security becomes contingent upon their availability. His positive emotional feelings toward them at this time, as individuals who provide security and relief from insecurity, probably constitute the earliest manifestations of affection. But although he will eventually exhibit spontaneous affection toward those who care for him,[20] at this stage he is more apt to return affection than to assume the initiative in offering it. Feelings of affection become more spontaneous and prominent when the child derives his major source of security and adequacy from an affectionate, satellizing relationship (see p. 289). One would hardly anticipate, therefore, that a rejected child would display much affection for his parents. And although overvalued children do receive considerable affection from their parents, the ulterior motives from which it stems neither allow satellization to occur nor inspire affectionate impulses in the child.

Beyond this point, everyday observation and logical inference (in the absence of empirical data) suggest the following developmental changes in affection: First, the conditions evoking affectionate responses broaden from simple receipt of succorance and derived status to include moral obligation, gratitude, loyalty, and helplessness in others. Second, other emotional components are added to the expression of affection. With increasing age the latter becomes coupled with altruistic, compassionate, and protective attitudes, with imitative displays of adult romanticism, and finally (after pubescence) with the enactment of a biological sex role. Third, the objects of affection are gradually expanded in scope. In addition to parents, affection is extended to siblings, other persons, pets and inanimate objects in the household, and later to adults and age mates outside the home. However, the development of such relationships beyond the family circle tends to be restricted if affectionate ties to parents are either lacking or excessively strong. The overprotected child is isolated emotionally from other persons by physical barriers, by induced fears, and by an overwhelming dose of parental love. The rejected child is desirous of entering into affectionate relationships with others but tends to regard himself as unworthy of love; hence he withdraws from emotional involvements in order to avoid further traumatic rebuff. The overvalued child, on the other hand, is so habituated to *receiving* adulatory affection and has such a grandiose self-concept that he develops little capacity for loving others.

JOY AND BOREDOM

Between the second and third months of life, physiological satiety and relief of physical discomfort are accompanied by more positive signs of emotion than mere quiescence or absence of excitement. The smiling, laughter, cooing and gurgling that occur then under these circumstances[11, 13] are the earliest manifestations of pleasure or delight. They constitute primitive hedonic responses to visceral satisfaction that require neither cortical involvement* nor the presence of a self-concept. When conditioned to the presence of other persons they are frequently mistaken for affection.

Following the emergence of the self-concept, pleasure-giving stimuli become more salient and instigate more intense and active signs of elation such as crowing and clapping of hands.[13] The eliciting stimuli are also extended to include exteroceptive and erogenous stimulation and uninhibited motor activity. During early childhood, joy and happiness are largely associated with such hedonic satisfactions and activities as accompany holidays and birthdays.[42] But as children grow older, factors that enhance self-esteem through the acquisition of new capacities and primary status become increasingly more important determinants of elation.[42] An ephemeral type of elation

*Expressions of pleasure can be elicited in decorticate but not in decerebrate animals.

is also encountered more frequently in which self-esteem is enhanced by grandiose daydreaming or by temporary depression of the self-critical faculty.

Boredom is a characteristic affective state induced by absence of challenging stimulation and activity or by oversatiation of a need.[58] As objects and activities satisfy the needs that instigate them, their current attractiveness diminishes, and unless they are temporarily discontinued, oversatiation or boredom results.[58] Repetition or monotony leads to boredom more rapidly in children than in older individuals because of their smaller attention span and frustration tolerance, because of the greater wholeheartedness with which they enter into activities,[58] and because they are less capable of rigidly insulating one experience from another.[49] Thus, Kounin demonstrated that with mental age held constant, the satiation of both the same and related activities occurs more rapidly in younger than in older persons.[49] Children though are less likely than adults to encounter monotony since the vast majority of life's experiences still lies before them.

SYMPATHY

Sympathy refers to sorrow induced by perceived distress in others. Because of the relatively mature capacities it presupposes, it does not appear much before the age of two.[65] Before sympathy can be felt a child must possess sufficient cognitive maturity to appreciate situational cues of distress when he himself is not threatened. If he had never experienced similar difficulties himself, he must be able to extrapolate from related experience and knowledge. Thus, a three year old is not moved to sympathy by black and blue marks, crutches, or funerals, but does respond sympathetically to such evidence of calamity as bandages, falls, confinement, and deprivation of toys, food, and mother.[65] Over and above this cognitive appreciation, susceptibility to sympathy is also a function of sensitivity to the feelings of others (empathy). Although wide interindividual differences undoubtedly prevail at all age levels, empathic ability partly depends on degree of social maturity and experience. Finally, the child must have the capacity for being affected by the perceived predicaments of others. In other words he must be capable of affection or emotional relatedness to others.

With increasing age the child reacts sympathetically to a wider and more subtle range of distress symbols.[65] As he grows in motor competence, verbal facility and social experience, he is also able to respond more actively and helpfully—by comforting, soliciting aid, and removing the cause of distress, rather than by just staring and whimpering.[65] The greater his interest in and responsiveness to others the more sympathy he is apt to display; hence, because socially active children are more intensely involved in interpersonal concerns, they tend to be both more sympathetic and more aggressive than socially phlegmatic children.[65] Disposition toward sympathetic behavior is also affected by whether the child is merely a witness or the effective cause of another's distress. In the latter instance, the need to disclaim responsibility is obviously incompatible with the expression of sympathy.[60] Some children tend to be less responsive to others' distress once their own position in the group is consolidated.[65] In their case, sympathy is largely a projection of anxiety or a bid for favor. Other children who are intrinsically more secure and capable of generosity tend to become more sympathetic as their own status improves.[65]

HUMOR

Humor is a complex state of joy or elation instigated by cognitive appreciation of surprise or incongruity. It neither consists of a single emotional content that is invariably present in all instances nor is its adequate stimulus reducible to any single psychological element. Subjectively there may only be elevation of mood in response to a cognitively amusing situation. Frequently, as when a prestigeful or authority figure is exposed to ridicule, humor enhances self-esteem or constitutes an expressive outlet for hostile feelings.[45, 93] At other times it serves the adjustive purposes of minimizing failure and frustration, of providing release from strain and anxiety, and of expressing socially unacceptable interests.[45, 93]

Laughter has been reported from the fourth month onward in response to surprise stimuli (chirruping sounds, sudden movements, peek-a-boo games) and tickling.[11, 13, 54, 88] It is apparently an unlearned and stereotyped expressive manifestation of humor that is highly contagious at all age levels. During the preschool years, laughter occurs mostly in social situations[21, 47] and frequently in the course of motor activities, particularly when the child is a participant.[21, 45, 47] Also, during this period, socially unacceptable situations and appreciation of incongruity and of relative superiority over others become increasingly important excitants of laughter.[45, 47] The crucial role of cognition in humor is borne out by the fact that brighter children laugh more frequently than children of average intelligence,[47] especially in response to absurd and incongruous situations.[12, 47] During middle and late childhood, adequate stimuli for humor are still predominantly visual and auditory and of the "slapstick" variety.[12] Incongruity, violations of rules and tabooed topics are common instigants of a type of group merriment that is frequently disapproved of by adults.[12] Appreciation of verbal humor, such as puns, requires considerable intellectual sophistication and is a relatively late development.[12, 93] When it does become more prominent at the beginning of the adolescent period, favorite jokes become more subtle and pithy and employ more elaborate disguises for the expression of tabooed ideas.[93]

REFERENCES

1. Anderson, J. E.: Changes in emotional responses with age. *In* M. L. Reymert, Ed., *Feelings and Emotions*. New York, McGraw-Hill, 1950, pp. 418-428.

2. Appel, M. H.: Aggressive behavior of nursery school children and adult procedures in dealing with such behavior. *J. Exper. Educ. 11*: 185-199, 1942.

3. Arsenian, J. M.: Young children in an insecure situation. *J. Abnorm. Soc. Psychol. 38*: 235-249, 1943.

4. Ausubel, D. P.: Prestige motivation of gifted children. *Genet. Psychol. Monogr. 43*: 53-117, 1951.

5. ———: *Ego Development and the Personality Disorders*. New York, Grune & Stratton, 1952.

6. ———, Schiff, H. M., and Goldman, M.: Qualitative characteristics in the learning process associated with anxiety. *J. Abnorm. Soc. Psychol. 48*: 537-547, 1953.

7. Ax, A. F.: The physiological differentiation between fear and anger in humans. *Psychosom. Med. 15*: 433-442, 1953.

8. Bach, G. R.: Young children's play fantasies. *Psychol. Monogr. 59*: No. 2, 1945.

9. Barker, R., Dembo, T., and Lewin, K.: Frustration and regression; an experiment with young children. *Univ. Iowa Stud. Child Welf. 18*: No. 1, 1941.

10. Bateson, G., and Mead, M.: *Balinese Character: A Photographic Analysis*. New York, New York Academy of Sciences, 1942.

11. Bridges, K. M. B.: Emotional development in early infancy. *Child Develop. 3*: 324-341, 1932.

12. Brumbaugh, F. N.: Stimuli which cause laughter in children. Unpublished doctor's dissertation, New York University, 1939.

13. Bühler, C.: *From Birth to Maturity*. London, Routledge & Kegan Paul, Trench Trubner, 1935.

14. Davis, A., and Dollard, J.: *Children of Bondage*. Washington, D.C., American Council on Education, 1940.

15. Davis, A., and Havighurst, R. J.: *Father of the Man*. Boston, Houghton Mifflin, 1947.

16. Davis, D. R.: Increase in strength of a secondary drive as cause of disorganization. *Quart. J. Exper. Psychol. 1*: 22-28, 1948.

17. Dawe, H. C.: An analysis of two hundred quarrels of preschool children. *Child Develop. 5*: 139-156, 1934.

18. Dennis, W.: Infant reaction to restraint. *Tr. N. Y. Acad. Sci. 2*: 202-217, 1940.

19. ———: *The Hopi Child*. New York, Appleton-Century-Crofts, 1940.

20. ———: Infant development under conditions of restricted practice and minimum social stimulation. *Genet. Psychol. Monogr. 23*: 143-189, 1941.

21. Ding, G. F., and Jersild, A. T.: A study of laughing and smiling of preschool children. *J. Genet. Psychol. 40*: 452-472, 1932.

22. Dorkey, M., and Amen, E. W.: A continuation study of anxiety reactions in young children by means of a projective technique. *Genet. Psychol. Monogr. 35*: 139-183, 1947.

23. Felder, J. G.: Some factors determining the nature and frequency of anger and fear outbreaks in preschool children. *J. Juv. Res. 16*: 278-290, 1932.

24. Foster, S.: A study of personality make-up and social setting of fifty jealous children. *Ment. Hygiene 11*: 53-77, 1927.

25. Fries, M. E.: The child's ego development and the training of adults in his environment. *Psychoanal. Stud. Child.* 2: 85-112, 1946.

26. Gesell, A.: The individual in infancy. *In* C. Murchison, Ed., *The Foundations of Experimental Psychology.* Worcester, Mass., Clark University Press, 1929.

27. Goldfarb, W.: Psychological privation in infancy and subsequent adjustment. *Am. J. Orthopsychiat. 15:* 247-255, 1945.

28. Goodenough, F. L.: Anger in young children. *Inst. Child Welf. Monogr.* No. 9, 1931.

29. ——: The expression of the emotions in infancy. *Child Develop.* 2: 96-101, 1931.

30. ——: Expression of the emotions in a blind-deaf child. *J. Abnorm. Soc. Psychol.* 27: 328-333, 1932.

31. Hagman, R. R.: A study of fears of children of preschool age. *J. Exper. Educ. 1:* 110-130, 1932.

32. Hattwick, L.: Sex differences in behavior of nursery school children. *Child Develop. 8:* 343-350, 1937.

33. Hebb, D. O.: *The Organization of Behavior: A Neurophysiological Theory..* New York, Wiley, 1949.

34. Hicks, J. A., and Hayes, M.: Study of the characteristics of 250 junior high school children. *Child Develop. 9:* 219-242, 1938.

35. Hollenberg, E., and Sperry, M.: Some antecedents of aggression and effects of frustration in doll play. *Personality 1:* 32-43, 1951.

36. Holmes, F. B.: An experimental study of the fears of young children. In A. T. Jersild and F. B. Holmes: Children's fears. *Child Develop. Monogr. 20:* 167-296, 1935.

37. Jersild, A. T., Goldman, B., and Loftus, J. J. A comparative study of the worries of children in two school situations. *J. Exper. Educ. 9:* 323-326, 1941.

38. ——, and Holmes, F. B.: Children's fears. *Child Develop. Monogr.* No. 20, 1935.

39. ——, and Markey, F. V.: Conflicts between preschool children. *Child Develop. Monogr.* No. 21, 1935.

40. ——, ——, and Jersild, C. L.: Children's fears, dreams, wishes, daydreams, likes, dislikes, pleasant and unpleasant memories. *Child Develop. Monogr.* No. 12, 1933.

41. ——, and Meigs, M. L.: Children and war. *Psychol. Bull. 40:* 541-573, 1943.

42. ——, and Tasch, R. J.: *Children's Interests.* New York, Teachers College, Columbia University, 1949.

43. Jones, H. E.: The study of patterns of emotional expression. *In* M. L. Reymert, Ed., *Feelings and Emotions.* New York, McGraw-Hill, 1950, pp. 161-168.

44. ——, and Jones, M. C.: Fear. *Childhood Educ. 5:* 136-143, 1928.

45. Justin, F.: A genetic study of laughter provoking stimuli. *Child Develop. 3:* 114-136, 1932.

46. Keister, M. E.: The behavior of young children in failure: an experimental attempt to discover and to modify undesirable responses of preschool children to failure. *Univ. Iowa Stud. Child Welf. 14:* 29-82, 1937.

47. Kenderdine, M.: Laughter in the pre-school child. *Child Develop. 2:* 228-230, 1931.

48. Korner, A. F.: *Some Aspects of Hostility in Young Children.* New York, Grune & Stratton, 1949.

49. Kounin, J. S.: Intellectual development and rigidity. *In* R. G. Barker, J. S. Kounin, and H. F. Wright, Eds., *Child Behavior and Development.* New York, McGraw-Hill, 1943, pp. 179-198.

50. Krall, V.: Personality characteristics of accident repeating children. *J. Abnorm. Soc. Psychol. 48:* 99-107, 1953.

51. Lacey, J. I., and Vanlehn, R.: Differential emphasis in somatic response to stress. *Psychosom. Med. 14:* 71-81, 1952.

52. Lazarus, R. S., et al.: Effects of psychological stress upon performance. *Psychol. Bull. 49:* 293-317, 1952.

53. Leighton, D., and Kluckhohn, C.: *Children of the People.* Cambridge, Harvard University Press, 1947.

54. Leuba, C.: Tickling and laughter: two genetic studies. *J. Genet. Psychol. 58:* 201-209, 1941.

55. Levy, D. M.: Studies in sibling rivalry. *Res. Monogr. Am. Orthopsychiat. Assoc.* No. 2, 1937.

56. ———: On the problem of movement restraint. *Am. J. Orthopsychiat. 14:* 644-671, 1944.

57. ———: On evaluating the "specific event" as a source of anxiety. *In* P. H. Hoch and J. Zubin, Eds., *Anxiety.* New York, Grune & Stratton, 1950.

58. Lewin, K.: Behavior and development as a function of the total situation. *In* L. Carmichael, Ed., *Manual of Child Psychology,* ed. 2. New York, Wiley, 1954, pp. 918-970.

59. ———, Lippitt, R., and White, R. K.: Patterns of aggressive behavior in experimentally created "social climates." *J. Soc. Psychol. 10:* 271-299, 1939.

60. McFarland, M. B.: Relationships between young sisters as revealed in their overt responses. *Child Develop. Monogr.* No. 23, 1938.

61. McKee, J. P., and Leader, F. B.: The relationships of socio-economic status and aggression to the competitive behavior of preschool children. *Child Develop. 26:* 135-142, 1955.

62. Mead, M.: Age patterning in personality development. *Am. J. Orthopsychiat. 17:* 231-240, 1947.

63. Miller, N. E.: Studies of fear as an acquirable drive. I. Fear as motivation and fear-reduction as reinforcement in the learning of new responses. *J. Exper. Psychol. 38:* 89-101, 1948.

64. Murphy, G.: *Personality: A Biosocial Approach to Its Origins and Structure.* New York, Harper, 1947.

65. Murphy, L. B.: *Social Behavior and Child Personality.* New York, Columbia University Press, 1937.

66. Mussen, P. H., and Naylor, H. K.: The relationships between overt and fantasy aggression. *J. Abnorm. Soc. Psychol. 49:* 235-240, 1954.

67. Muste, M. J., and Sharpe, D. F.: Some influential factors in the determination of aggressive behavior in preschool children. *Child Develop. 18:* 11-28, 1947.

68. Neisser, E. G.: *Brothers and Sisters.* New York, Harper, 1951.

69. Paulsen, A. A.: Personality development in the middle childhood years. A ten-year longitudinal study of 30 public school children by means of Rorschach tests and social history. *Microfilm. Abst. 13:* 592-593, 1953.

70. Pintner, R., and Lev, J.: Worries of school children. *J. Genet. Psychol. 56:* 67-76, 1940.

71. Radke, M. J.: The relation of parental authority to children's behavior and attitudes. *Univ. Minnesota Inst. Child Welf. Monogr.* No. 22, 1946.

72. Ray, W. S.: A study of the emotions of children with particular reference to circulatory and respiratory changes. *J. Genet. Psychol. 40*: 100-117, 1932.

73. Redl, F., and Wineman, D.: *Children Who Hate.* Glencoe, Ill., The Free Press, 1951.

74. Ricketts, A. F.: A study of the behavior of young children in anger. *Univer. Iowa Stud. Child Welf. 9*: No. 3, 159-171, 1934.

75. Roff, M., and Roff, L.: An analysis of the variance of conflict behavior in pre-school children. *Child Develop. 11*: 43-60, 1940.

76. Sears, P. S.: Doll play aggression in normal young children: influence of sex, age, sibling status, father's absence. *Psychol. Monogr. 65*: No. 6, 1951.

77. Sears, R. R.: A theoretical framework for personality and social behavior. *Am. Psychol. 6*: 476-483, 1951.

78. ———, Whiting, J. W. M., Nowlis, V. and Sears, P. S.: Some child-rearing antecedents of aggression and dependency in young children. *Genet. Psychol. Monogr. 47*: 135-234, 1953.

79. Sewall, M.: Two studies in sibling rivalry. I. Some causes of jealousy in young children. *Smith Coll. Stud. Soc. Wk. 1*: 6-22, 1930.

80. Shirley, M. M.: *The First Two Years: a Study of Twenty-five Babies.* Vol. 2. *Intellectual Development.* Minneapolis, University of Minnesota Press, 1933.

81. Spitz, R. A.: The role of ecological factors in emotional development in infancy. *Child Develop. 20*: 145-154, 1949.

82. ———: Anxiety in infancy: a study of its manifestations in the first year of life. *Internat. J. Psychoanal. 31*: 138-143, 1950.

83. Swanson, G. E., Miller, D. R., McNeil, E. B., and Allinsmith, W.: *Learning Psychological Defenses.* New York, Holt (in press).

84. Symonds, P. M.: *The Dynamics of Parent-Child Relationships.* New York, Teachers College, Columbia University, 1949.

85. Temple, R., and Amen, E. W.: A study of anxiety reactions in young children by means of a projective technique. *Genet. Psychol. Monogr. 30*: 59-113, 1944.

86. Terman, L. M., and Tyler, L. E.: Psychological sex differences. *In* L. Carmichael, Ed., *Manual of Child Psychology,* ed. 2. New York, Wiley, 1954, pp. 1064-1114.

87. Wallis, R. S.: The overt fears of Dakota Indian children. *Child Develop. 25*: 185-192, 1954.

88. Washburn, R. W.: A study of the smiling and laughing of infants in the first year of life. *Genet. Psychol. Monogr. 6*: 397-537, 1927.

89. Watson, J. B., and Rayner, R.: Conditioned emotional reactions. *J. Exper. Psychol. 3*: 1-14, 1920.

90. Whiting, J. W. M.: The frustration complex in Kwoma society. *Man 44*: 140-144, 1944.

91. ———, and Child, I. L.: *Child Training and Personality.* New Haven, Yale University Press, 1953.

92. Wittenborn, J. R.: A study of adoptive children. *Psychol. Monogr. 70*: No. 1-3, 1956.

93. Wolfenstein, M.: *Children's Humor: A Psychological Analysis.* Glencoe, Ill., Free Press, 1954.

94. Wolf, S., and Wolff, H. G.: *Human Gastric Function. An Experimental Study of a Man and His Stomach.* New York, Oxford, 1947.

95. Yerkes, R. M.: *Chimpanzees.* New Haven, Yale University Press, 1943.

96. Zeligs, R.: Children's worries. *Sociol. Soc. Res. 24*: 22-32, 1939.

CHAPTER 11

Parent-Child Relationships

PARENTAL INFLUENCES are so crucial and pervasive in child development that it is almost impossible to discuss any aspect of this field without considering its relationship to parent attitudes and behavior. We have, for example, already considered the origin of maternal *behavior* during the neonatal period (pp. 190-194), the relationship between child rearing *practices* and the development of psychosocial and idiosyncratic personality traits (Chapter 8), and the impact of specific parent *attitudes* on major phases of ego and emotional development (Chapters 9 and 10). In the present chapter we propose to consider some of the following more *general* aspects of parent-child relationships: the individual and social sources of parent attitudes, and their continuity, consistency and characteristics in relation to sex of the parent and ordinal position of the child; the various dimensions of parent-child interaction; the mechanisms through which parent attitudes shape the personality development of the child and the factors that limit their influence; the impact of socialization in the home on later phases of socialization; and the characteristics of parental discipline and their effects on personality development.

Parent-child relationships deserve such extensive treatment because they constitute perhaps the most important single category of variables impinging on the personality development and socialization of the child. In their capacity as socializing agents and representatives of the culture, parents determine many intercultural uniformities (psychobiological traits) and differences (psychosocial traits) in development; and in their capacity as individuals with unique personalities of their own, parents determine a large part of the personality variance in children within a given culture (idiosyncratic traits). The nuclear family of father, mother and children has evolved as a universal cultural solution to a common core of interpersonal problems, needs and conditions of adaptation to the physical and social environments. Despite the myriad forms it adopts, it performs everywhere the same basic functions of extending physical and emotional succorance to children, taking responsibility for their socialization and enculturation, and providing for mutual sharing of commodities and services in a continuing group structure marked by division of labor and differentiation of roles. The universality of these functions of the nuclear family, of certain of its membership and interactional characteristics, and of various sequential shifts in role and status within its organizational framework (see table 1, p. 67) constitutes a major source of psychobiological traits.

349

Although commonplace today, conceptions of personality development that emphasize the crucial role of the parent-child relationship in its broader aspects have appeared only relatively recently in the history of personality theory. The belated recognition accorded this factor can be attributed largely to the influence of Freud. He and his followers were among the first to stress the importance of early childhood experience and parental treatment for later personality formation. However, they selected out of this experience only those specific child rearing *practices* that impinge on the individual's alleged psychosexual development, and more or less ignored the impact of broader emotional *attitudes* (e.g., rejection, overprotection) on the salient features of ego development traced in Chapter 9. They also exaggerated the communicability of parent attitudes to young infants (see p. 265) and the importance of child rearing *practices* in determining psychosocial traits (see p. 260).

Parenthood involves both satisfactions and burdens for most persons, some of which are anticipated and some of which are not. It is self-evident, however, that the demands of parental role are more compatible with the needs and personality traits of some individuals than they are with those of others (see p. 188); but since the functions of the parent vary in content and emphasis with the age of the child, the congeniality of parental role is subject to change. Many parents enjoy only the early period of cuteness and dependence, and lose interest or feel at a loss when their children become more competent and independent individuals with concerns outside the home. In our culture parents find satisfaction in the affection and companionship of children, in observing the emergence of personality traits and intellectual qualities, and in the routine aspects of child care.[27, 60] On the other hand, unfavorable personality traits, management of troublesome routines, and unsatisfactory sibling relationships constitute some of the major dissatisfactions mentioned by parents.[27]

GENERAL DETERMINANTS OF PARENT ATTITUDES

How do parents come to acquire the attitudes they hold in relation to their children? In general, four categories of determinants may be delineated: the wider culture, the parent's own family and childhood experience, his personality structure, and various situational variables. The first factor accounts for intercultural or subcultural (psychosocial) variability in parent attitudes, and the latter three factors for idiosyncratic variability.

Determinants of Psychosocial Variability in Parent Attitudes

The extent to which parents are disposed to be accepting, protective, dominative, etc. in dealing with their children is obviously determined in part by the prevailing cultural ideology defining appropriate norms of parent-child interaction.* These norms and values are products of custom, tradition, ideological evolution and historical accident; of economic, social, political and religious beliefs and institutions; of institutionalized modes of timing and handling shifts in the biosocial status of the child; and of different ways of ordering marital relationships, family structure and intrafamilial roles.[40] In our culture approved standards of parent behavior tend to evolve in waves of dogmatic fad and fashion (see pp. 233-235) that are related to fluctuations in developmental, psychological and educational theory (Chapter 2). Hence, conformity to currently approved (i.e., permissive, democratic) child rearing fashions is positively related to both degree of formal education[14, 45, 56] and to liberality of political opinion.[51]

The cultural ideology influences parents' child rearing attitudes because it serves as a major, prestigeful frame of reference in the evolution of such attitudes. It has been shown, for example, that parents' expectations of children's level of play are easily manipulated by "expert" opinion.[37] Parents also feel a sense of obligation to rear their children in conformity to prevailing social values, and fear both social censure and feelings of guilt if they deviate too much from what is expected of them. If alternative philosophies of child rearing are available, the parent is naturally more apt to choose one that is consonant with his temperamental preferences. His choice is also characterized respectively by varying degrees of intellectual objectivity or subjective rationalization, of independent thinking or uncritical acceptance of the current vogue, and of emotional or merely verbal identification. Irrespective of the basis on which they are chosen, as long as emotional involvement is present such beliefs have the same impact on parent behavior as do attitudes derived from idiosyncratic personality factors. Purely verbal acceptance of child rearing beliefs is not entirely without effect on parent behavior but obviously leads to less spontaneous impulses as well as impulses that are often negated by underlying attitudes.

Social Class Factors. Present-day investigations of social class differences in parent attitudes suggest that more middle-class than lower-class parents have assimilated the permissive-democratic approach in interacting with children and managing child care routines. Reflecting the greater inroads of the Cornelian corner philosophy on middle-class parents, earlier reported findings[19] indicating greater lower-class permissiveness with respect to breast-

---

*The cultural ideology, as already suggested, helps to perpetuate the distinctive characterology of a given culture by contributing to the determination of psychosocial traits. It does this not so much by the selection of particular infant care practices nor by the manner in which such practices are administered, but by pervasively influencing parent attitudes. These attitudes in turn, reinforced by the child's direct contact with the culture, affect his personality formation recurrently throughout the entire period of development (see pp. 259-261).

feeding, weaning, and feeding schedules are no longer corroborated by more recent investigations,* and are actually reversed in the case of early toilet and sex training.[29, 35] These changed findings are consistent with the previously noted positive correlation between degree of permissiveness and number of years of formal schooling, with the shift toward greater permissiveness in the women's magazines and baby books (see p. 000), read primarily by middle-class mothers, and with the empirical finding that grandmothers are stricter than mothers in all areas of child care.[56] Even more important manifestations of the greater adherence of middle-class parents to the "new" approach in child rearing are the greater evidences of warmth and affection in middle-class homes;[35] of less authoritarian, hierarchical and absolutistic parent attitudes, and of more open communication between parents and children;[34] of greater tolerance for developmental immaturity and for aggressiveness toward the parent;[34, 35] of greater emphasis on fostering wholesome personality development and establishing good rapport than on obedience, respect and the physical aspects of care;[21, 27] of greater reliance on reasoning and inner controls in disciplining the child than on physical punishment and ridicule;[18, 35] and of greater parental concern with and participation in the child's interests.[19, 25]

At the same time, middle-class parents exercise much greater supervisory control and are more restrictive of the child's activities *outside* the home— of his freedom to come and go as he pleases, to attend movies alone and keep late hours, to choose his own associates, and to explore the life of the streets.[19, 25,34] They are also more zealous in inculcating aspirations, values and behaviors that are associated with higher social class status and conformity to adult standards. Thus, they place greater stress on success in school and on good habits of eating, dress, and speech; on the virtues of honesty, respect for property, self-reliance, initiative, and civic responsibility; and on the curbing of physical aggression and socio-sexual expression.[1, 18, 19, 24, 25, 42] These latter social class differences in parental attitudes have presumably been less eroded in recent years than the differentials in income and living standards separating the lower- and middle-classes.

Determinants of Idiosyncratic Variability in Parent Attitudes

Since all aspects of goal and method in child rearing are not culturally standardized, much room remains for the operation of situational factors

---

*Although these social class differences are negligible at the present time, the same practices probably have a different basis in each class. In the lower-class they are more a matter of custom, tradition and folk-lore acquired from parents, relatives and friends. In the middle-class they are more an expression of belief in the formal ideology of child rearing currently approved by the "experts."

and of genically and experientially determined differences in temperament, values, and resourcefulness.* But even in those areas in which cultural prescriptions do exist, idiosyncratic variability in parent attitudes may still occur. First, even in a relatively homogeneous subculture, parents perceive much heterogeneity in child rearing practices[14] and interpret selectively— in accordance with their own preferences—whatever homogeneity does exist. The more heterogeneous the cultural norm is perceived to be, the less coercive is its influence on individual attitudes. Hence, in the absence of any clear-cut normative standard of discipline, mothers tend to rely more on their own experience and predilections than to conform to the perceived modal view.[14] Second, all cultures tolerate a certain degree of deliberate non-conformity from its members which is quite variable from one culture to another. Generally speaking, greater individual latitude is permitted in matters of method than in matters of goal since it is often appreciated that different techniques may yield the same end result. Thus the culture makes fewer demands on parents for conformity during early childhood when the achievement of goals is still distant and when children are largely restricted to their own homes. On the other hand, parents are more inclined to follow their own preferences when their children are older and they (the parents) have acquired a greater backlog of child rearing experience. In any case the extent to which the individual parent is disposed to ignore social guide-posts and expert opinion and follow his own notions is extremely variable,[37] and depends on such traits as self-sufficiency, self-confidence, independence of thought, suggestibility, critical sense and need for public approval.

Idiosyncratic variability in parent attitudes is partly a function of family tradition, of parents' memories of their own childhood, and of their affective reactions to the practices of their own parents (see p. 192). The influence of situational factors (e.g., current economic stresses, marital discord, personality characteristics of the child) on maternal attitudes has already been discussed elsewhere (see pp. 187 and 192). Even more important, in relation to intracultural variation in child rearing, is the fact that parent attitudes are largely a characteristic manifestation of an individual's ego structure (e.g., feelings of adequacy and security, ego aspirations, level of anxiety, volitional and executive independence, moral obligation, self-preoccupation, ability to postpone hedonistic gratification, emotional relatedness to others) and of other personality traits such as ascendence, introversion-extroversion, motherliness, hostility, and acceptance of the female role. Observed parent behavior and measured parent characteristics are substantially related.[46] "In the mother's social interaction with the child as she takes on the

*Parents' degree of acceptance of children was found to be independent of social class factors (G. R. Hawkes, et al., *J. Home Econ.* 48: 195-200, 1956).

maternal role she . . . expresses . . . emotional needs" that are salient in the current economy of her personality organization.[10] The attitudes that are evoked by these needs are sometimes directly adjustive in the sense that they satisfy needs for ego enhancement (as in overvaluation) or reduce anxiety (as in overprotection). On the other hand, they may chiefly give vent to deep seated feelings (e.g., hostility) or insulate the individual from parental obligations that interfere with the satisfaction of more pressing needs (as in rejection attributable to anxiety or narcissism).

CHARACTERISTICS OF PARENT ATTITUDES

Attitudes and Practices

We have already taken the position (see pp. 262-264) that rearing practices in and of themselves can only affect the immediate behavior of the child unless they are reflective of· broad, pervasive, and reasonably self-consistent parent attitudes. Although personality factors are undoubtedly prepotent in fashioning the major content of the more significant parent attitudes, cultural, familial, and situational determinants cannot be ignored (see p. 350). Regardless of their source, all parent attitudes affect child rearing practices. Purely verbal and ego-peripheral beliefs, however, are associated with practices that tend to have a transitory effect on the behavior of the child rather than a more lasting influence on his personality development. Thus it was found in one intensive interdisciplinary study of preschool children that "the child's adjustment to socialization was significantly related to the 'total mother person' and specifically to her character structure, but insignificantly related to the mother's specific rearing techniques."[10] (See also the summary of evidence on the relationship between personality and child care practices on pages 263-267).

Because of other nonattitudinal determinants of practices and because of individual differences in the meaning which identical practices have for different parents it is not possible to infer from the mere presence of a practice in a given parent what its attitudinal significance is. We have to look for the latter in the parent's manner of administering a large number of specific practices in recurrent situations. This very pervasiveness of parent attitudes renders any single practice relatively insignificant as a determining factor in personality development. It is also important to realize that parent attitudes can be communicated to children in other ways than through rearing practices and that such attitudes are both reinforced and counter-acted by other socializing agents (see p. 264).

Consistency and Continuity

Consistency is an important aspect of parent behavior because of its undoubted effect on the behavior and personality development of the child.

Inconsistency generates confusion regarding what is expected, creates momentary conflict,[38] increases susceptibility to fear and anger (Chapter 10), and probably retards ego maturation and socialization. Although parents naturally vary greatly in the consistency of their rearing attitudes,[8, 9] such attitudes (like any other meaningful expression of personality) must necessarily be characterized by considerable intersituational generality. Apart from reasons inherent in the very organization of personality, (see p. 100) a conscious need for self-consistency apparently operates in many persons. This does not preclude inconsistency stemming from situational factors, ambivalent feelings, or particular idiosyncrasies; inconsistency which the parent is unable to recognize; or genuinely high tolerance for self-perceived inconsistency.

Some direct evidence of intersituational consistency in parent attitudes has been found in studies of parent-child interaction.[31, 52] Such consistency can also be inferred from the fact that logically related parent behaviors intercorrelate meaningfully to form more inclusive attitudinal clusters.[8, 9] Apparent evidence of inconsistency, on the other hand, i.e., non-significant intercorrelations among permissiveness scores on different rearing practices,[50] is mostly phenotypic; it reflects the operation of non-attitudinal determinants of these practices and variability in attitudinal meaning associated with a given practice (see p. 263). Although mothers may employ seemingly contradictory practices, the attitudinal content permeating the *manner in which they are administered* may be highly uniform for both mother and child. This supposition is consistent with the finding that high positive correlations may exist between the child's adjustment and the mother's character structure and maternal role even though no significant relationships prevail between adjustment and specific rearing practices.[10]

Continuity. Despite the abundance of clinical impressions,[33, 52, 59] systematic empirical evidence of longitudinal continuity in parent attitudes is extremely sparse. Nevertheless, since a parent's child rearing attitudes might be expected to remain about as stable as his personality it is plausible to suppose that within certain limits of variation a given parent tends to manifest the same general kinds of rearing attitudes throughout his parental tenure. The determinants of longitudinal continuity in personality structure have been discussed in detail elsewhere (see pp. 97-100). In addition to those factors that operate to keep personality functioning relatively stable, numerous cultural expectancies regarding parental role tend to constrict intra- as well as interindividual variability in the expression of parent attitudes.

However, considerable basis also exists for discontinuity in parent attitudes—both in the culture and in the personality functioning of the parent. Apart from the influence of changing fads and fashions, many culturally

standardized modifications and reversals in parent attitudes are expected
with shifts in the biosocial status of the child (Chapter 9); and even if no
basic changes occur in the parent's personality structure, the manifest
behavioral correlates of feelings of security and adequacy, of level of anxiety
and ego aspiration, and of self-preoccupation all tend to vary with vicissitudes in life history. Because of inescapable ambivalence in his feelings, the
parent is also apt to be more impressed at certain times than at others with
either the satisfactions on the burdens of child rearing. As more children
are added to the family he may find one sex or temperament more or less
congenial; he may also either adapt better to the responsibilities of parenthood or find them increasingly intolerable. Finally, as already suggested
(p. 350), because of marked preference or distaste for different age period
aspects of parental role his over-all attitudinal orientation toward the child
may undergo marked change.

Difficulties in Measuring Parent Attitudes

Inasmuch as parents are highly ego-involved in their role, it is extremely
difficult to obtain valid measures of their rearing attitudes. Observational
and self-report techniques are partly contaminated by the parent's natural
hesitancy in revealing information or behavior that would give an unfavorable impression of his adequacy or intentions as a parent. It is especially
difficult to overcome this methodological problem in the case of middle-
class parents, since they are particularly well-informed about the kinds
of attitudes and practices that are currently approved by the "experts."
Partly for this reason and partly because the personality development of
children is influenced more proximately by the attitudes *they* perceive than
by the objective properties of the latter (as reported by parents or observers),
we have advocated that parent attitudes be measured by ascertaining how
they are perceived by children (see p. 156). This can be done either through
direct subjective inquiry or by using projective techniques. Although the
former method is more transparent it enjoys the advantages of greater
denotative specificity and intersituational generality (see p. 161).

Maternal and Paternal Roles

Although maternal and paternal roles overlap to a great extent, they
are clearly differentiated in all cultural settings. This differentiation is
naturally related to the social sex roles, to the concepts of masculinity and
femininity, and to the division of labor prevailing in a given culture. In
our culture it tends to become increasingly more salient as the child advances
in age, since the father participates more fully and in more distinct ways
in the older child's upbringing. During the last decade, however, the experts'
emphasis upon an earlier, more active, and less authoritarian role for the

father[60] has tended to render the contrast between maternal and paternal role less sharp than in previous generations. In general, the mother's role is more highly structured and culturally standardized than the father's; for one thing fathers, unlike mothers, seldom compare notes about their offspring. The father's role is also derived more completely from learned concepts and interpersonal experience; it is reinforced at no time by hormonal factors or by childbearing and lactation.

Child rearing is more of the mother's special function and responsibility in our culture, just as economic support is more characteristic of the father's role. She obviously provides most of the routine nurturant care, emotional succorance,* and discipline and is so perceived by the child;[39, 44] for this reason she is more frequently the preferred parent, especially in times of stress (see p. 252), and occupies the central position in the child's image of the family.[39] She is also perceived by girls as a model to be emulated in growing up.[22] Previously, in the early years of the child's life, the father's role was more passive and adjunctive; he was an amused or bored spectator, occasional nursemaid, baby-sitter, playmate and sibling rival. Now there is some evidence that at least the urban father participates more actively in the daily routine care and discipline of the child and considers it part of his function.[44, 60]

If the father has any special role in the family (apart from economic provider), it is that of chief authority figure, moral arbiter, and disciplinarian. Traditionally his discipline is more arbitrary and severe[44] than the mother's; when mutiny is brewing it is he who "lays down the law." If their reactions to thematic materials are truly reflective of real-life behavior, children adopt more submissive attitudes toward the father than toward the mother.[28] This situation probably still prevails despite the trend toward a more equalitarian type of father-child relationship.†[44, 60] In addition as far as their limited time permits, fathers consciously play the roles of guide, teacher, companion and affectionate rearer,[60] influence the mother's practices, and help establish the value structure of the home. Extremely important in structuring the father-child relationship is the mother's attitude toward her husband and his parental role. As the major socializing influence in his life, the child takes his cue from her in responding to his father, especially when the latter is separated from the home.[4]

*Mothers tend to be more accepting than fathers in their attitudes toward children (G. R. Hawkes, et al., *J. Home Econ. 48*: 195-200, 1956.

†Mothers actually give more coercive responses than fathers to hypothetical problem situations because they bear the greater share of the responsibility in managing children's misbehavior. However, to act consistently with cultural expectations of femininity they tend more to sugar-coat their aggressiveness. (P. W. Jackson, *Child Develop. 27*: 339-349, 1956).

The father's role is also somewhat differentiated for the two sexes.* He helps the girl define her biological and social sex roles by treating her endearingly as a little woman. She in turn tends to find his personality more congenial than the mother's.[22] In relation to the boy, although not consciously recognizing it,[60] the father serves as a model of masculinity and of the male sex role, including acceptable forms of exhibiting male aggression.[22, 49] He also subjects his son to more rigorous disciplinary control than his daughter and is much less affectionate toward him; boys accordingly tend to regard the mother's disposition as more genial.[22] These inferences regarding the father's special role relative to his son are supported by measured differences between the doll play of boys in father-separated and father-present homes. The former exhibit less aggression toward the father and child dolls, show less awareness of maleness and femaleness, and tend to resemble girls in their fantasy productions.[4, 47, 49] Absence of the father has relatively little effect of the doll play of girls.[4, 47, 49]

Ordinal Position in the Family

Parent attitudes toward and treatment of the child vary to some extent with the latter's ordinal position in the family constellation. Partly because of such differences in parent attitudes and expectations and partly because of differences in roles, responsibilities and experiences associated with the child's position in the birth order, birth rank tends to be consistently related to certain personality traits within a given culture. The youngest child, for example, is ordinarily never "dethroned"; and only the next-to-the-youngest is "dethroned" without seeing his successor subjected to the same treatment. In a large family "each sibling . . . develops his specialized role on the basis of, and in relation to the roles which have already been established. No sibling wishes to be the exact counterpart of another."[13]

The positions of the oldest, youngest, and only child are most highly differentiated. With the first child, parents tend to be less relaxed and warm, and more restrictive, demanding and coercive.[32] They are less permissive with respect to feeding and weaning, more worrisome about sickness and danger, and more nurturant at bedtime.[48] The oldest child is often given responsibility for the other siblings and is expected to "set a good example";[13, 36] hence in doll play he exhibits less physically violent aggression[47] despite the fact that he is apt to be more jealous and vengeful,[19, 30] to resent both his responsibilities and the attention given the other children,[36] and to show more anger and teasing and less frustration tolerance than second-born children.[30] Only and youngest children tend to receive an excess

*See page 252 for a discussion of the so-called "Oedipus" complex. Differential parental treatment of boys and girls in relation to sex typing is discussed on page 450.

of attention and supervision, and thus display the most infantile home relationships.[61] The youngest is also most frequently the "spoiled one" in the family,[13] is most given to peculation,[61] and exhibits attention-seeking behavior,[36] school difficulty and intersibling conflict.[61]

IMPACT OF PARENT ATTITUDES ON PERSONALITY DEVELOPMENT

Basis of Impact

On what grounds is it postulated that during early childhood parent attitudes exert extremely important determining effects on later personality development? First, the parent is associated from the very beginning in a benevolent and altruistic light with the satisfaction of the child's visceral needs, biological survival and emotional security; and throughout the entire period of childhood he continues to wield tremendous power in regulating the child's motivations, satisfactions and standards, and in influencing the course and outcome of various stages of ego development (Chapter 9). Since perception of persons and emotional response to their presence and absence antedate similar awareness of and reaction to inanimate objects,[55] the sense of self emerges and grows in an interpersonal context.

Second, early experience has a disproportionate effect on development because it enjoys the benefits of *primacy*. In the unstructured attitudinal field of children, from which most competing influences are excluded, the specific behavioral differentiations and value systems of parents soon become relatively pre-emptive in their patterning effects. These effects tend to perpetuate themselves by making the individual selectively reaction-sensitive to the conditions that bring them about; and once consolidation occurs, reorganization is resisted because of "perceptual constancy," the tendency to utilize existing orientations and habits before acquiring new ones, and the stability of ego-involved components of personality (see p. 97-100). Further enhancing the effects of primacy is the fact that childhood embraces many critical periods of development in which maximum susceptibility to environmental influences prevails. During these periods when development is still not committed in a particular direction, the individual is extremely flexible; afterwards, the very fact that commitment has already occurred makes for rigidity.

Less crucial contributory factors accounting for the tremendous impact of parent attitudes include the following: (a) increased susceptibility to trauma because of immature interpretive and adjustive capacities; (b) the insusceptibility of preverbal learning to counteractive verbal influences;[17] (c) the resistance of inconsistently reinforced learning to extinction;[17] and

(d) the transferability of attitudes and habits acquired in early family life to later behavior as spouse and parent.[17]

Factors Limiting the Impact of Parent Attitudes

The above statement regarding the impact of parent attitudes on personality development requires many serious qualifications. The effects of parent attitudes are dependent on their communicability to children; vary with normative and individual differences in cognitive capacity and perceptual acuity, with the particular developmental needs that are dominant at a given stage of personality growth, and with the temperamental characteristics of the child; and are modifiable for better or worse by concurrent or subsequent experience outside the home. Thus, since parent attitudes are not the sole determinants of personality development and are frequently not even communicable to children, the widespread tendency to blame parents for *all* behavior problems is not only unwarranted, but leads to unwholesome self-recriminatory and apologetic attitudes toward children.

We have already emphasized repeatedly that the infant's cognitive immaturity insulates him from all but the most overt and obvious manifestations of interpersonal attitudes. Hence, the impact of the parent's attitudinal substrate first begins to overshadow the influence of his grosser feelings and actions when the child enters the postinfantile stage. But even later it is highly questionable whether many covert and adequately screened attitudes that are only uncovered in the course of psychotherapy (e.g., hostility underlying apparent over-solicitude) are ever perceived (even "unconsciously") by many children; much depends here on individual differences in perceptual sensitivity or empathic ability. Cognitive and verbal immaturity also limit the child's ability to make fine distinctions among feeling tones, to conceptualize and generalize his impressions, and to retain his experiences over long periods of time. Furthermore, when he is mature enough to form categorical judgments he tends to dismiss the manifest content of immediately perceived experience (unless it is too obtrusive to be ignored) and to infer from a culturally standardized proposition (i.e., all parents are *supposed* to love and protect their children) that his parents must obviously love him.

Constitutional factors also limit and modify the influence of parent attitudes. Because of variable, genically determined temperamental predispositions in children, the *same* parent attitude may have very different effects. Apathetic and submissive children tend to become passively dependent in response to overprotection, whereas self-assertive and ascendent children are more apt to react aggressively.[33] Depending on their strength such predispositions may prove very tenacious—even in the face of opposing environmental pressures.[52] They not only *evoke* different kinds of behaviors in the parent, but may also modify the latter's child rearing attitudes.

Apart from changes in the parent's needs, personality traits, insights and current level of adjustment, other influences both within and outside the home modify and counteract the impact of early parent attitudes on the child's personality development. Balancing forces are usually at hand to soften extreme attitudes and practices. The deviant parent must first contend with the objections of his spouse, and later with the opposition of relatives, neighbors, and friends. As the child grows older he is increasingly exposed to the direct influence of persons other than parents—to siblings, age mates, relatives, teachers, and other adults. Some children, who never manage to identify with their parents, find an almost satisfactory substitute in a relative, teacher, or parent of a playmate. By the same token, the beneficial influence of favorable intrafamilial experience in early childhood may be partly undone by detrimental parent attitudes in later childhood, or by crippling disease, delayed pubescence, economic hardship, racial discrimination, etc. (see p. 265).

Unfavorable parent attitudes are also limited in their effects when they are not operative during the particular critical periods of developmental need or maximal growth for which they are especially relevant. In the presatellizing period all that is required for adequate personality development is a certain amount of succorance, personal attention and overt affection (see p. 119). The other major dimensions of the parent-child relationship that are so crucial for later stages of ego development seem relatively unimportant for the essential developmental tasks of infancy. Overdominating and overprotecting parents, parents who value their children for ulterior motives, and parents who are basically rejecting despite a veneer of affection, all seem to provide an adequate enough environment for the development of the omnipotent ego structure. During the second and third years of life, however, genuine emotional acceptance and intrinsic valuation of the child are essential for satellization; and the child accordingly becomes selectively sensitized in perceiving these aspects of parent attitude. Hence it no longer suffices for a parent to exhibit the outward manifestations of affection; evidence of an intrinsically accepting attitude in the smaller and more subtle aspects of feeling and action is required. It is at this time therefore that rejection has the most damaging effects on personality development. At a later age the child's more versatile and mature ego structure and his well-established set of defenses protect him somewhat from the trauma of rejection; at this time also there is more opportunity of forming satellizing and satellizing-like relationships to other adults and to the peer group. Finally, the dominative, protective, motivating, and critical aspects of parent attitude are most crucial during the period of desatellization. Unless the parent sets appropriate expectations, standards, and limits, applies necessary coercive pressures, allows sufficient freedom for exploration, goal setting and decision making, and shows appreciation of the child's progress in these directions, the ego status and ego maturity aspects of desatellization may be retarded (see p. 301).

A final limiting factor that should be considered is the *wide margin of safety* that applies to parent attitudes as to most regulatory conditions affecting human development. If the attitudes of parents are generally wholesome in relation to their children, considerable deviancy from the theoretical optimum and occasional "mistakes" are still compatible with normal personality development. In view of this fact and the probable non-communicability of many attitudes, merciless self-recrimination about the underlying motivations and the possible irrevocable consequences of minor deviations from "accepted" practices is not only unnecessary but also robs parenthood of much joy and spontaneity.

DIMENSIONS OF PARENT ATTITUDES

The preceding discussion of the impact of parent attitudes on personality development points up the importance for theoretical and research purposes of identifying and defining clearly as many significant variables as possible that are encompassed by the parent-child relationship. In no other way will it be possible to determine unambiguously the antecedents and consequences of various parent attitudes. Much of the difficulty in the past can be ascribed to confusion between popular and scientific usage, overlapping of terms, and lack of clarity in defining the precise aspects of the parent-child relationship to which these terms refer. In the popular literature about child care, for example, "spoiled," "indulged," "over-protected," "underdominated" and "overvalued" are used almost interchangeably.

Early attempts at a more precise categorization of parent attitudes tended to oversimplify matters by using unidimensional (acceptance) or bi-dimensional (acceptance-domination) scales. At the other extreme of explicitness, the multiple scale approach, illustrated by the Fels Parent Behavior Rating Scales,[16] is much too unwieldly and atomistic in orientation to be useful in elucidating developmental sequences. Even when reduced in size by factor analysis,[46] or when inter-related variables are grouped meaningfully into naturally occurring 'syndromes,'[9] these scales still leave much to be desired from the standpoint of making significant predictions from parent-child relationships to child behavior or adult personality. Without differential weighting in terms of relationship to and significance for successive developmental tasks, they do not help us to understand how children in general progress from one sequential stage of personality to another or why a particular child acquires or fails to acquire the major attributes of ego structure characteristic of his age level. Similar parent attitudes may have quite different outcomes depending on whether the individual is or is not a satellizer. Overprotection, overdomination and rejection have very different effects in infancy, early childhood and preadolescence. Phenotypically different attitudes such as rejection and extrinsic valuation are both associated with the same outcome of non-satellization. Without some conceptual scheme for systematizing the data one ends up with a bewildering maze of discrete and uninterpretable correlations.

Another source of confusion has arisen from the widespread tendency to subsume the dominative aspects of parent behavior under overprotection, i.e., to consider over- and underdomination as subtypes of overprotection.[33] Although such combinations of attitudes are frequently encountered, they are by no means inevitable. Many overprotective parents are able to maintain a proper balance of domination; contrariwise, over- or underdominated children are not necessarily overprotected. The dimension of protectiveness refers to extent of parental care and solicitude. The overprotecting parent unduly prolongs infantile care, provides excessive personal contact and supervision, and seeks to furnish an environment for his child which is free of hurt, disappointment, failure, frustration, and exposure to the harsher realities of life. Its basis lies in projected anxiety: the parent mitigates his own unidentifiable anxiety by projecting threat onto the child and giving it more concrete reference. The dimension of dominance, on the other hand, refers to the relative balance of volitional self-assertiveness and deference between parent and child and is not related in origin to parent anxiety (see p. 368). Thus the confounding of the protective and the dominative aspects of parental attitudes is extremely unfortunate since each refers to clearly different roles and functions of parenthood. Only conceptual confusion can result when two discriminably different variables are treated as if they were coextensive. The confusion is even more regrettable when the entirely different origins and consequences of the two kinds of attitudes are considered.

It is true that overprotection and underdomination have an important point in common—great reluctance in frustrating the child. In the overprotecting parent, however, it is part of the larger anxiety reducing goal of sparing the child psychological and physical trauma rather than a manifestation of unassertiveness; if deferring to the child's will exposes the latter to physical or social danger, the overprotective parent would sooner frustrate the child's volitional independence. Thus, although the underdominating parent tends to be consistently deferential, the overprotecting parent can be yielding only in situations which either increase the child's infantile dependency or which do not contain threats of illness, injury or failure.

It would seem more fruitful and economical of effort, therefore, to start with a theoretical structure hypothesizing various stages of personality development with their component attributes and developmental tasks. By defining and categorizing parent-child relationships in terms of dimensions compatible with this structure, one could then test various hypotheses regarding the intrafamilial antecedents of various developmental outcomes by relating measurements of these dimensions to personality variables in children and adults. The dimensions of the parent-child relationship designated in table 3 were formulated with this end in view. They are not the only dimensions that could possibly be identified but they encompass the major aspects of this relationship that have relevance for the developmental tasks and processes described in Chapter 9.

TABLE 3.—*Dimensions of the Parent-Child Relationship**

Dimension (Parent Attitude or Behavior)	Child's Position on Scale	
	Upper Extreme	Lower Extreme
1. Emotional acceptance	Accepted	Rejected
2. Valuation of child for self or in terms of parent's ego needs	Intrinsically valued	Extrinsically valued
3. Magnitude of valuation of child's importance	Overvalued	Undervalued
4. Protectiveness (care, solicitude)	Overprotected	Underprotected
5. Dominance (self-assertiveness or deference to child's will)	Overdominated	Underdominated
6. Level of aspiration for child	Overmotivated	Undermotivated
7. Criticism of child (overt or implied)	Overcriticized	Undercriticized
8. Appreciation (recognition of child's competence)	Overappreciated	Underappreciated

Although the above dimensions are separate variables, permitting in theory an almost infinite number of combinations and permutations, the actual number of important combinations occurring in practice is sharply limited by hierarchical factors and psychological compatibility. Most important is the patterning influence of the key attitudes leading to satellization and

*Adapted from D. P. Ausubel, *Ego Development and the Personality Disorders.*[2]

non-satellization respectively. Satellizers are all both emotionally accepted and intrinsically valued, whereas non-satellizers are either rejected and extrinsically valued or accepted and extrinsically valued. The rejected group of non-satellizers is usually underprotected, overdominated, underappreciated, over-criticized and undervalued. The extrinsically valued group of non-satellizers is almost invariably overvalued, underdominated, overmotivated, undercriticized and overappreciated. For all practical purposes it is most convenient to refer to these two groups of non-satellizers as "rejected" and "overvalued" respectively. Greater variability in patterning prevails among parents of satellizing children. Except for the uniformity provided by the two prerequisite conditions, almost any combination of the remaining parent attitudes is possible.

ORIGIN OF SPECIFIC PARENT ATTITUDES

The attitudes which an adult displays as a parent go back in large part to his own childhood and the kind of relationship he enjoyed with his own parents. They reflect both the impact of the parent-child relationship on personality development and the influence which parents exert as models of parental role and function.

Rejection and Overvaluation

Both clinical experience and developmental logic suggest that non-satellizing children tend to have parents who themselves were non-satellizers. It is by no means true, however, that *all* non-satellizers have non-satellizing children. A history of rejection or extrinsic valuation in the parent's childhood predisposes him toward high ego aspirations and neurotic anxiety; and in such an individual, immersed in his own ambitions and harassed by constant threat to self-esteem, self-preoccupation is easily understandable. In the case of women it leads to reluctance to accept the feminine role in life and the compromises in prosecuting a career that motherhood necessarily entails. Under these circumstances, responsibility for the protective care and emotional succorance of a child may seem like such a formidable and burdensome duty that rejection becomes a very likely alternative. Other equally possible alternatives are attempts to achieve vicarious ego enhancement through projection of omnipotent ego aspirations onto the child (overvaluation) and efforts directed toward anxiety reduction through the mechanism of displacement, i.e., perceiving the child as the object of threat (overprotection). The tendency toward self-preoccupation is also enhanced by narcissism and the inability to relate emotionally to others that so frequently characterize non-satellizers. These traits are more pronounced in overvalued than in rejected persons, since they proceed more from habituation to a one-way flow of affection and interest than from dread of emotional involvement for fear of repeating an experience of rejection. In some instances the hostile attitudes of a rejecting parent seem to stem at least in part from an unresolved residue of hostility toward his own parents or siblings which in turn resulted from a situation of rejection or favoritism. By identifying with the role of his own rejecting parent he vicariously gives vent to these feelings.

Given all of these personality predispositions toward becoming an over-valuing or rejecting parent, it does not necessarily follow that the non-satellizing individual will actually become one. Much depends on other personality traits as well as on various situational factors. His level of anxiety, for example, can be kept under better control if he is an able, enterprising, organized and socially perceptive person. The more self-indulgent and viscertonic he is, the more resentful he is of any responsibilities toward others which interfere with the gratification of his own hedonistic needs. If he has a strong sense of moral obligation he may endeavor to inhibit much of his hostility or even become oversolicitous in order to avoid guilt feelings. The unhampered expression of rejecting tendencies is also limited by the individual's sensitivity to prevailing cultural norms and to social censure. If he is concerned with appearances he can usually find "reputable excuses for hating a child"[59]; and only too frequently, the same narcissistic preoccupation with himself that causes him to neglect his child provides him with a thick skin in the face of public or private criticism.

The prevailing level of anxiety or hostility that becomes manifest from underlying personality trends is also affected by numerous situational factors. Latent residual hostility toward a parent is often reactivated by an unhappy marital relationship and then displaced onto the child. This is more likely to occur if the parent feels that he is being rejected by his spouse in favor of the child. Thus, a moderately positive correlation prevails between marital adjustment and the acceptance of children.[43] The entrance of an infant into the household, especially if he is ill or if his parents are confronted by vocational or financial difficulties, frequently exacerbates chronic anxiety. In any event the child's chances of being rejected are obviously increased if his sex, physique or temperament are at variance with the parent's preferences. A docile child's reaction to rejection usually encourages a hostile or narcissistic parent to continue this treatment since the parent is not even required to placate his nuisance value. An irritable, self-assertive and rebellious child, on the other hand, may destroy the equilibrium of an anxiety-torn parent who then utilizes the child's behavior as justification for the original rejection and the subsequent counter-aggression.

The probability of developing *consistently* rejecting parent attitudes is determined in part by the individual's capacity for relating himself emotionally to others. In rejected persons this capacity, which is ever latent but inhibited by fear of rejection, has an excellent opportunity for overt expression in the form of warm, accepting parent attitudes since little threat of rejection can be anticipated from a child. Self-preoccupation here is largely a function of anxiety and can be mitigated if other personality traits and situational factors are favorable for keeping the level of anxiety under control. In overvalued individuals, on the other hand, self-preoccupation seems to be more a reflection of narcissism and incapacity for relating emotionally to others, and hence is less apt to be favorably influenced by benign environmental conditions. For similar reasons, the overvalued parent is also more disposed than the rejected parent to extend a more *passive* kind of rejection to his children. Lack of concern for the needs of others stemming from narcissism leads to neglect and indifference which arouse little guilt feelings since they reflect an habitual orientation in interpersonal relations. If current exacerbations of anxiety were to induce self-preoccupation in rejected parents, passive neglect and avoidance of parental responsibility would more likely engender guilt feelings. Thus the rejected parent tends more to continue to care for and interact with the child but resentfully and with evident hostility which he tries to rationalize as a form of counter-aggression made necessary by the latter's perverseness.

A final problem has to do with the basis of choice between rejecting and overvaluing attitudes. What differences might we anticipate between two parents, both non-satellizers with grandiose ego aspirations, one of whom finds the child a cumbersome and unwanted burden, while the other is able to utilize him as a principal vehicle for ego aggrandizement? Much seems to depend on the parent's capacity to perceive the dependent child as an extension of himself rather than as entity in his own right, and to react to his triumphs as if they were his own achievements. This capacity probably reflects in part some degree of pessimism in the parent's appraisal of his chances for ego aggrandizement through his own efforts. Also, everything else being equal, the parent faced with the choice of either rejecting or overvaluing his child is more likely to choose the latter alternative as he is less hostile, embittered and withdrawn, and is more extroverted, sociocentric and better able to relate to others.

Overprotection

We have already suggested that the principal basis of overprotecting attitudes is a form of parental anxiety in which the object of threat is displaced from parent to child. The parent is anxious, insecure, fearful of impending disaster, and feels inadequate to cope with the ordinary adjustive problems of life. By projecting the object of threat onto the child he is able to mitigate his own anxiety in two ways: (a) some of the perceived threat to himself is reflected, thereby making the environment look less foreboding, and (b) he is better able to cope with the threats confronting the child than those besetting himself. He can isolate the child from painful experiences by using himself as a shield, since the frustrations facing a child are relatively concrete and avoidable; whereas he cannot insulate himself from the world and still maintain his own intense strivings. But the success he enjoys in protecting his child from danger and frustration is transferable to his own situation. Since the anxiety-ridden personality is also predisposed toward rejecting and overvaluing attitudes, overprotection may be regarded as an alternative to the latter orientations. Sometimes it occurs as a reaction-formation for covert rejecting tendencies or as a form of expiation for overt rejecting behavior. In some instances the predisposing anxiety is reinforced by such contributory factors as marital unhappiness, a long history of sterility or miscarriages, severe illness or injury in the child, and death of a previous child or close relative.[33, 57]

Under- and Overdomination

The simplest explanation of the origin of under- and overdominating attitudes is that they reflect a temperamental disparity in self-assertiveness between parent and child. A combination of mild, self-effacing parent and aggressive, ascendant child (or vice versa) is not a statistical rarity. Frequently, however, the explanation is not as simple. A truly ascendant and self-reliant parent may have little need to assert himself with his children,[11] whereas (as some evidence suggests) the submissive, ineffective parent who lacks self-assurance[11] may use his relationship with the child as a means of compensating for lack of status, prestige, or authority vocationally or in the eyes of his spouse. The overdominating or underdominating parent may sometimes pattern his behavior after his recollections of his own parents' way of dealing with him. On the other hand, if he believes that his parents' practices were undesirable, he may make a deliberate effort to veer to the opposite extreme. In some cases underdomination is a manifestation of passive rejection; the parent is only too happy to leave the child to his own devices as long as he himself is not bothered. Actively rejected children, however, are usually overdominated. In overvaluing parents underdomination is generally a projection of exaggerated ego aspirations. Since the parent hopes for vicarious ego enhancement through the accomplishments of a volitionally omnipotent child, he can hardly afford to frustrate the latter's will. Either orientation (but especially under-domination) may also represent adherence to a current philosophy of child rearing.

In terms of both source and expression, parental overdomination is largely the antithesis of underdomination. But although the general consequences of both attitudes are quite similar in their impact on ego maturation, much greater possibility for heterogeneity in the child's response exists in the case of the former. This heterogeneity results from variations (a) in the brusqueness or kindliness with which the overdomination is administered, and (b) in the self-assertiveness of the child. The first variable governs the acceptability of the overdomination to the child. The second variable determines the type of resistance that will be offered if over-domination is unacceptable, i.e., active (rebellion) or passive (sabotage).

EARLY SOCIAL DEVELOPMENT IN THE FAMILY

Parents as Cultural Representatives

Especially during the early years, the child is not exposed directly to a representative sample of the culture at large but to a restricted, family-biased version of it. The parent is under obligation both to interpret the culture to the child and to serve as its official representative in dealing with him. He is under pressure to produce and deliver an individual who is a reasonable facsimile of the prevailing cultural pattern. If he himself—within acceptable limits of deviancy—has assimilated the values and expectations of his culture with respect to the goals of child rearing, relatively little difficulty ensues in playing the role of cultural representative. If, however, his personal values and attitudes are at variance with cultural norms he is often resentful and ambivalent about this role, sometimes showing open defiance, but more often conforming verbally while covertly following his own inclinations.

In what ways does the child's indirect exposure to the culture through his parents differ from the more direct kind of exposure that he later receives at the hands of other socializing agents? First, the family presents a highly idiosyncratic picture of the culture to the child. Parents are always selective in the cultural alternatives they choose to transmit and in their perceptions of cultural norms. Furthermore, they not only deviate deliberately in varying degrees from cultural prescriptions, but also improvise their own prescriptions in the more unstandardized aspects of parent-child relationships. In any event, salient features of their own idiosyncratic personality traits are always expressed in their dealings with the child. Second, the *specific* models of behavior presented by the parents differ qualitatively from *other* specific models the child perceives in the wider community. The idiosyncratic features of the latter tend to lose their individual identity in the composite role portraits that eventually emerge; but because of their primacy, the models provided by mother and father retain their idiosyncratic properties. Their particular specificity constitutes in itself and becomes equivalent to other general categories or abstractions in which only commonalities are retained while nondistinguishing specificities are discarded. Finally, the home "environment is not only a social one but . . . is also intensely personal and intimate. Rewards and punishments come with simple directness from persons, never from abstract symbols."[15] Home, therefore, can never be more than a rough preview of what the child can anticipate from the wider culture. He can only predict that it (the culture) will treat him more objectively, casually and impersonally[16]; he can expect no special privileges, no special concern with his welfare and no favored treatment. But apart from these negative forecasts, he is much more at a loss regarding the kinds of behavior he may anticipate from others since he is confronted on the outside by a much larger array of persons about whose attitudes he knows substantially less.

Initial Social Behavior in the Home

The child's first social behavior occurs within the family circle in relation to adults rather than to other children. Considering his immaturity in other spheres—perceptual, cognitive, language, and motor—it is unusually well developed. This precocity reflects the operation of potent, genically determined capacities for social responsiveness, including specific predispositions for such stereotyped expressive characteristics as smiling, cooing and gurgling in response to the human voice and face (see p. 283). Sensitization to the social environment is shown by earlier recognition and differentiation of and emotional responsiveness to persons than to inanimate objects.[55]

The child's social responsiveness is also facilitated by his dependency, which requires that his needs be satisfied from the very beginning in an interpersonal context. He becomes accustomed and responsive to the behavior and communicative acts of others in the course of having his needs satisfied by them. Initially, however, until the child becomes *psychologically* dependent (see p. 285), the objective dependency situation primarily influences the *parent's* social behavior. It is conceivable, nevertheless, that even before he appreciates the mother's causal relationship to the satisfaction of his needs, her status as substitutive reward and signal of imminent gratification (see p. 285) facilitates his social responsiveness to and recognition of her. Once he perceives his helplessness and dependence on her availability for his continued physical survival his very sense of security acquires social reference. He now initiates social interaction with adults, responds affectively to their presence and absence, discriminates between friendly and angry expressions, and shows fear when a stranger approaches. During this time he also acquires needs for the affection and stimulation that parents provide; and during the satellizing period he becomes dependent on their acceptance and approval for security and adequacy feelings. It is little wonder then that social relationships with persons—through which all other needs are satisfied—should become important needs in their own right.

Impact of Intrafamilial Experience on Later Social Development

One of the most important consequences of early parent-child relationships is the pronounced tendency for the child's later interpersonal relations with peers and other adults to reflect the influence of social attitudes, expectancies and adjustive techniques experienced in dealings with his first socializers, his parents.* To the child the world of interpersonal relations is completely unstructured at first; and for the first few years of life most of the differentiation of this unstructured field occurs in the home. Hence, in the absence of any other frame of reference for basing his expectations of what people in the outside world are like and for reacting to them, it is most natural for him to use the model provided by his parents and to employ adaptive techniques previously utilized in the home situation. Moreover, habituation to *particular* satisfying features of the parent-child relationship creates needs for them in the child, needs which can only be satisfied by conditions analagous to those which produced them in the first place.

The child's capacity for forming wholesome interpersonal relationships outside the home, therefore, is influenced by the following aspects of the intrafamilial situation: (a) whether on the basis of friendly relations with parents he is led in advance to expect the best from people unless given cause to feel otherwise; (b) the extent to which his parents do not create unique or unrealistic needs and expectations in him which only they are willing and able to satisfy, or encourage the development of special adjustive techniques to the exclusion of the more usual and adaptive abilities necessary for most social situations; (c) the availability (neither insufficient nor excessive) of family support, assurance and guidance should he encounter difficulties with others; (d) the absence of home attachments that

*See pages 120 and 121 for a discussion of the structuring effect of early experience (in the "critical period") on the social development of animals and its relevance for the social development of humans.

are so strong as to be pre-emptive; (e) not acquiring personality traits or adjustive habits from the parent-child relationship that other children find offensive; and (f) not being predisposed by home training to withdraw from extrafamilial social experience to the point where the learning of realistic social roles becomes impossible.

The child's social behavior is also profoundly affected by whether or not he has undergone satellization, which in turn is an outcome of the parent-child relationship. To the satellizing child, group membership provides derived status and constitutes an intrinsic ego support. He experiences a certain spontaneous joy and enthusiasm in group activity which follows from the "we-feeling" associated with group relatedness. To the non-satellizer, on the other hand, the field of interpersonal relations is just another arena in which he contends for extrinsic status and ego aggrandizement. There is no identification with or self-subordination to group interests, and no possibility of deriving spontaneous satisfaction out of gregarious activity. A similar type of dichotomy prevails in the relationships satellizers and non-satellizers respectively establish with teachers and other adults.

The rejected individual has strong needs for volitional autonomy but finds it difficult to assert himself effectively in interpersonal relationships. Not only has he failed to master customary roles and techniques necessary for adult self-assertion but he also *feels* incapable of playing these roles convincingly. This is partly a direct carry-over from his feeling of helplessness as a child in coping with the ruthless domination of parents; but in part it also reflects feelings of unworthiness attributable to his parents' negative valuation of him, lack of intrinsic self-esteem, and chronic anxiety. Because he doesn't appear adequate to protect his own interests and avoid being taken advantage of he invites aggression from others; but in view of his genuine needs for volitional independence he resents any subservience to which he is subjected and may eventually react explosively. More typically he withdraws from conflictful social situations and intellectualizes his aggression; and if he can overcome his haunting fear of further rejection he may even try to establish satellizing-like relationships with non-threatening persons.

During childhood, rejected individuals are alternately described as shy and submissive on the one hand, and as aggressive, quarrelsome, noncompliant and resistive to adult guidance on the other hand.[8, 44] Without a secure home base to which they can return they tend to adjust less successfully than accepted children to novel and stressful social situations.[26, 53] Juvenile delinquency is significantly more frequent in homes characterized by lack of parent warmth.[23] Where rejection is prolonged but passive (e.g., as in foundling homes), children tend to establish emotionally shallow interpersonal relationships (see p. 122) and to display social immaturity.[12, 54]

The underdominated child is encouraged to assert himself, but at the same time no demands are made on him to develop the mature personality traits necessary for realistic implementation of volitional independence (see p. 307). Because he has little direct experience with the restrictive features of reality and is not required to learn the limits of acceptable conduct, he cannot easily choose realistic roles and goals. As a result of being conditioned to a relationship in which all of the yielding is done by the other party, he comes to think of himself as a unique person to whom others just naturally defer. In his relations with other children and adults, he tends to be domineering, aggressive, disobedient, petulant, and capricious.[33] He is unwilling to defer to the judgment and interests of others, always demanding his own way upon threat of unleashing unrestrained fits of temper.[33] But despite his conspicuous lack of social success outside the home, he still tends to persist in this type of domineering behavior, partly because he is so thoroughly overtrained in it and partly because of the imperious need to dominate which he has acquired from the parent-child relationship.[15, 33] The overvalued child for very similar reasons develops the same type of social behavior, but has stronger needs for volitional independence and ego aggrandizement (see p. 296). Hence, although he never basically abandons his grandiose aspirations and desire for deference he is more highly motivated to modify the strategy of his interpersonal behavior in order to establish the overtly satisfactory social relationships he recognizes as important in the quest for status and power.

Because of constrictive and dominative home environments respectively, both overprotected and overdominated children fail to learn the social skills necessary for adequate self-assertion and self-defense. Unable to defend their rights successfully, they are continually fearful of being duped and exploited by others. Since the peer group is unwilling to satisfy their special needs for protection and direction, they tend to withdraw from peer relationships and to seek the company of parents and adults who can play the roles their needs demand. Overprotected children are generally submissive, shy, anxious[33, 44] and inadequate in meeting stressful situations.[53] They are extremely dependent on their mothers and experience great difficulty in making friends.[33] Overdominated children exhibit the same traits and in addition tend to be dependable, polite and self-conscious.[5, 44, 59] Autocratic, harsh and capricious overdomination, however, may not be accepted by the child, and hence may lead to active rebellion in ascendent, extroverted children and to passive sabotage in docile, introverted children. These latter two groups probably account for the reported frequency of quarrelsome, uncooperative, uninhibited, and inconsiderate behavior in children from autocratic homes.[44, 59] Children from "democratic homes" tend to be active, competitive and socially outgoing, both in friendly and in aggressive and domineering ways, and to enjoy high acceptance from their age mates. In contrast to overdominated children, they show originality, intellectual curiosity and constructiveness in school activities.[6]

DISCIPLINE*

The Need for Discipline

Although much cultural diversity prevails in the severity and techniques of discipline, the phenomenon itself is encountered in all cultural settings. We have already (see p. 307) elaborated on the reasons for believing that every noteworthy advance in personality maturation is accompanied by some change in the expectations of significant persons in the child's environment which is enforced in part by some coercive form of pressure. On both counts parents occupy a strategic position. Not only do their own expectations change as a result of altered needs and new perceptions of the child's behavioral capacity but also channeled through them are changing cultural expectations of appropriately mature behavior at different age levels. In either case the parent is one of the most appropriate agents for applying whatever coercive measures are necessary for effecting conformity of the child's behavior to changed patterns of expectations. Direct experience with limiting and restrictive factors in the environment is necessary for learning a reasonable degree of conformity to social norms of acceptable behavior, for the learning of realistic roles and goals, for learning to make reasonable demands on others, and for the acquisition of responsibility, self-control, and the capacity for deferring need satisfaction. Since these aspects of socialization are not written into the genes, they would not be acquired spontaneously. To be sure, the removal of all pressures for conformity would undoubtedly eliminate most interpersonal conflict and negativism, but it still has to be demonstrated that normal personality maturation would also occur under these conditions.

Discipline is also necessary from the standpoint of the child's emotional security. Without unambiguous standards of social reality in relation to which he can orient his behavior and control his impulses, he feels confused and insecure. The absence of external standards places too great a burden on his limited degree of self-control and attitudinal sophistication. In a completely permissive environment, he is afraid of the consequences of his own uninhibited behavior—of both the retribution and the guilt; and

*As used in this section, *discipline* refers to the imposition of standards and controls by others on the child's behavior. The relative absence of discipline is equivalent to maximal permissiveness (underdomination) in the handling of children.

in the absence of punishment there is also very little opportunity for reducing guilt feelings.

Ambiguous control also cannot be avoided unless discipline consists of punishment as well as reward. It is unrealistic to expect that in the early and middle years of childhood approval for acceptable behavior automatically endows its logical opposite with negative valence. The child does not make inferences so easily and does not typically operate at the level of logical consistency that this approach assumes. Especially during the early years the positive valence of an attractive but forbidden activity is not effectively reduced until such time as explicit evidences of reproof are administered.

Democratic Discipline

Proponents of extreme permissiveness frequently equate their philosophy with democratic discipline and assert that other forms of discipline are synonymous with authoritarianism. The arguments and evidence used in this latter connection (see p. 441) only discredit autocratic types of control (overdomination)—*not* all types of non-permissive discipline. This evidence merely supports the need for democratic methods of control rather than for maximally permissive (laissez-faire) methods (underdomination), the effects of which are no more desirable than those of overdomination (see p. 441). There is also no rational basis for believing that the parent's authority role is necessarily incompatible with a relaxed and cordial parent-child relationship. Most children recognize their parents' right to impose controls and do not question the legitimacy of disciplinary measures.[44] A democratic approach to discipline does not require the parent to renounce his prerogative of making final decisions or to refrain from imposing "external" standards and restraints on the child. Although it is true that the only effective and durable kind of discipline we can hope to establish is a self-discipline based upon internalization of external standards, the latter can never be completely abandoned. Before anything can be internalized it is self-evident that especially in the beginning it must first exist in external form. Furthermore, internalization occurs only gradually and is never complete. Even when a genuinely wholesome conscience is operative, adults as well as children need the support of external sanctions to avoid succumbing occasionally to temptation.

Characteristics. Democratic discipline disavows tyrannical, harsh, vengeful and discriminatory methods of control, does not seek obedience as an end in itself, avoids any attempt to intimidate the child, and repudiates the use of punishment as an outlet for parental aggression. It does not propose to eradicate the distinction between parental and filial roles. The parent is recognized as the more mature and dominant party in the relationship; his judgments are given more weight and his demands more authority. Nevertheless, no exaggerated emphasis is placed on status differences, and all artificial barriers preventing free communication are removed. Respect is always a two-way proposition: the child's rights, opinions, and especially his dignity as a human being are never disregarded. The child is encouraged to participate in the determination of goals and standards whenever he is qualified to do so, and maximal reliance is placed on inner controls. Verbal exhortations are reinforced by personal example.

Democratic discipline is also as rational and as unarbitrary as possible. The parent provides explanations for decisions and permits the child to present his point of view; and even when the latter is too young to understand reasons, he (the parent) tries to use a reasonable tone of voice. For many reasons, however, a wholly rational approach is unfeasible since (a) cognitive limitations make it impossible to render many explanations intelligible to the child; (b) many parental requests cannot be justified on the basis of reason but must nevertheless be heeded on the grounds of either necessary conformity to cultural tradition or of superior experience and judgment; and (c) many emergency situations in childhood require complete, immediate, and unquestioning obedience.

Other Aspects of Parental Discipline

Methods of parental control must obviously be adapted to meet changing conditions of personality organization and maturity. In the presatellizing period parents are largely dependent on physical restraint, reward, and punishment. During the satellizing stage they can rely more upon approval and disapproval, prestige suggestion, personal loyalty, and moral restraints of conscience and guilt feelings. Later, in the desatellizing period, the child is less disposed to conform on the basis of personal allegiance and desire for approval; considerations of expediency and ego enhancement become more salient at this time. With increasing age, therefore, effective discipline becomes more rational and less authoritarian. It is more acceptable to the older child if the parent acts as an impersonal agent of the culture in interpreting and enforcing social norms than if he continues to serve as a personal source of authority and to demand obedience as an axiomatic right. Parents also instigate less resistance if wherever possible they bring children into line by letting age mates apply "lateral sanctions" than by applying hierarchial sanctions themselves.

As already suggested discipline is most effective when it is unambiguous, consistent and relevant to the misbehavior to which it is applied. Arbitrary and inconsistent rules tend to be cognitively unclear,[7] and hence are learned with great difficulty. Rules are also inevitably ambiguous if the parent fails to define the limits of acceptable behavior, does not differentiate clearly between filial and parental prerogatives, and handles every situation as a special case according to the demands of expediency. The ambiguity surrounding the limits of unacceptable behavior is further enhanced by an habitual tendency to avoid issues by distracting the child. Two other favorite techniques of the ineffectual parent are self-insulation (pretending unawareness) and empty verbalism when an occasion for discipline arises. Half-hearted verbal reproof that is not accompanied by effective disciplinary action actually reinforces misbehavior by guaranteeing to the child that he can expect no *real* interference from the parent.

REFERENCES

1. Aberle, D. F., and Naegele, K. D.: Middle-class fathers' occupational role and attitudes toward children. *Am. J. Orthopsychiat. 22*: 366-378, 1952.
2. Ausubel, D. P.: *Ego Development and the Personality Disorders.* New York, Grune & Stratton, 1952.
3. ——, et al.: Perceived parent attitudes as determinants of children's ego structure. *Child Develop. 25*: 173-183, 1954.
4. Bach, G. R.: Father-fantasies and father-typing in father-separated children. *Child Develop. 17*: 63-80, 1946.
5. Baldwin, A. L.: Socialization and the parent-child relationship. *Child Develop. 19*: 127-136, 1948.
6. ——: The effect of home environment on nursery school behavior. *Child Develop. 20*: 49-62, 1949.
7. ——: *Behavior and Development in Childhood.* New York, Dryden, 1955.
8. ——, Kalhorn, J., and Breese, F. H.: Patterns of parent behavior. *Psychol. Monogr. 58*: No. 268, 1945.
9. ——, ——, and ——: The appraisal of parent behavior. *Psychol. Monogr. 63*: No. 299, 1949.
10. Behrens, M. L.: Child rearing and the character structure of the mother. *Child Develop. 25*: 225-238, 1954.
11. Block, J.: Personality characteristics associated with fathers' attitudes toward child-rearing. *Child Develop. 26*: 41-48, 1955.
12. Bodman, F.: The social adaptation of institution children. *Ment. Health. London 9*: 68-69, 1950.
13. Bossard, J. H. S., and Boll, E. S.: Personality roles in the large family. *Child Develop. 26*: 71-78, 1955.
14. Brodbeck, A. J., Nogee, P., and DeMascio, A.: Two kinds of conformity: a study of the Riesman typology applied to standards of parental discipline. *J. Psychol. 41*: 23-45, 1956.
15. Cameron, N.: *The Psychology of Behavior Disorders: A Biosocial Interpretation.* Boston, Houghton Mifflin, 1947.
16. Champney, H.: The variables of parent behavior. *J. Abnorm. Soc. Psychol. 36*: 525-542, 1941.
17. Child, I. L.: Socialization. *In* G. Lindzey, Ed., *Handbook of Social Psychology.* Vol. II. *Special Fields and Applications.* Cambridge, Mass., Addison-Wesley, 1954, pp. 655-692.

18. Davis, A., and Dollard, J.: *Children of Bondage*. Washington, D. C., American Council on Education, 1940.

19. ———, and Havighurst, R. J.: Social class and color differences in child-rearing. *Am. Sociol. Rev. 11*: 698-710, 1946.

20. Deutsch, H.: *The Psychology of Women*. New York, Grune & Stratton, 1944.

21. Duvall, E. M.: Conceptions of parenthood. *Am. J. Sociol. 52*: 193-203, 1946.

22. Gardner, L. P.: An analysis of children's attitudes toward fathers. *J. Genet. Psychol. 70*: 3-28, 1947.

23. Glueck, S., and Glueck, E.: *Unraveling Juvenile Delinquency*. New York, Commonwealth Fund, 1950.

24. Griffiths, W.: *Behavior Difficulties of Children as Judged by Parents, Teachers, and Children Themselves*. Minneapolis, University of Minnesota Press, 1952.

25. Havighurst, R. J., and Taba, H.: *Adolescent Character and Personality*. New York, Wiley, 1949.

26. Heathers, G.: The adjustment of two-year-olds in a novel social situation. *Child Develop. 25*: 147-158, 1954.

27. Jersild, A. T., Woodyard, E. S., and del Solar, C.: *Joys and Problems of Child Rearing*. New York, Teachers College, Columbia University, 1949.

28. Kates, S. L.: Suggestibility, submission to parents and peers, and extrapunitiveness, intropunitiveness, and impunitiveness in children. *J. Psychol. 31*: 233-241, 1951.

29. Klatskin, E. H.: Shifts in child care practices in three social classes under an infant care program of flexible methodology. *Am. J. Orthopsychiat. 22*: 52-61, 1952.

30. Koch, H. L.: Some personality correlates of sex, sibling position, and sex of sibling among five- and six-year-old children. *Genet. Psychol. Monogr. 52*: 3-51, 1955.

31. Lafore, G. G.: Practices of parents in dealing with preschool children. *Child Develop. Monogr.* No. 31, 1945.

32. Lasko, J. K.: Parent behavior toward first and second children. *Genet. Psychol. Monogr. 49*: 97-137, 1954.

33. Levy, D. M.: *Maternal Overprotection*. New York, Columbia University Press, 1943.

34. Maas, H. S.: Some social class differences in the family systems and group relations of pre- and early adolescents. *Child Develop. 22*: 145-152, 1951.

35. Maccoby, E. E., Gibbs, P. K., et al.: Methods of child-rearing in two social classes. *In* W. E. Martin and C. B. Stendler, Eds., *Readings in Child Development*. New York, Harcourt, Brace, 1954, pp. 380-396.

36. Mauco, G., and Rambaud, P.: Le rang de l'enfant dans la famille. *Rev. franc. Psychanal. 15*: 253-260, 1951.

37. Merrill, B.: A measurement of mother-child interaction. *J. Abnorm. Soc. Psychol. 41*: 37-49, 1946.

38. Meyers, C. E.: The effect of conflicting authority on the child. *Univ. Iowa Stud. Child Welf. 20*: 31-98, 1944.

39. Mott, S. M.: Concept of mother—a study of four- and five-year-old children. *Child Develop. 25*: 99-106, 1954.

40. Murdock, G. P., and Whiting, J. W. M.: Cultural determination of parental attitudes: the relationship between the social structure, particularly family struc-

ture and parental behavior. *In* M. J. E. Senn, Ed., *Problem of Infancy and Childhood*. Tr. Fourth Conference, 1950. New York, Josiah Macy, Jr. Foundation, 1951, pp. 13-34.

41. Parsons, T., and Bales, R. F.: *Family, Socialization and Interaction Process*. Glencoe, Ill., Free Press, 1955.

42. Pope, B.: Socio-economic contrasts in children's peer culture prestige values. *Genet. Psychol. Monogr. 48*: 157-220, 1953.

43. Porter, B. M.: The relationship between marital adjustment and parental acceptance of childen. *J. Home Econ. 47*: 157-164, 1955.

44. Radke, M. J.: The relation of parental authority to children's behavior and attitudes. *Univ. Minnesota Inst. Child Welf. Monogr.* No. 22, 1946.

45. Remmers, H. H., and Drucker, A. J.: Teen-ager's attitudes toward problems of child management. *J. Educ. Psychol. 42*: 105-113, 1951.

46. Roff, M.: A factorial study of the Fels Parent Behavior Scales. *Child Develop. 20*: 29-45, 1949.

47. Sears, P. S.: Doll play aggression in normal young children: influence of sex, age, sibling status, father's absence. *Psychol. Monogr. 65*: No. 6 (Whole No. 323), 1951.

48. Sears, R. R.: Ordinal position in the family as a psychological variable. *Am. Sociol. Rev. 15*: 397-401, 1950.

49. ——, Pintler, M. H., and Sears, P. S.: Effect of father separation on preschool children's doll play aggression. *Child Develop. 17*: 219-243, 1946.

50. Sewell, W. H., Mussen, P. H., and Harris, C. W.: Relationships among child rearing practices. *Am. Sociol. Rev. 20*: 137-148, 1955.

51. Shapiro, M. B.: Some correlates of opinions on the upbringing of children. *Brit. J. Psychol. 43*: 141-149, 1952.

52. Shirley, M. M.: Impact of mother's personality on the young child. *Smith Coll. Stud. Soc. Wk. 12*: 15-64, 1941.

53. ——: Children's adjustments to a strange situation. *J. Abnorm. Soc. Psychol. 37*: 201-217, 1942.

54. Skeels, H. M., Updegraff, R., Wellman, B. L., and William, H. M.: A study of environmental stimulation: an orphanage preschool project. *Univ. Iowa Stud. Child Welf.* No. 4, 1938.

55. Spitz, R.: The role of ecological factors in emotional development in infancy. *Child Develop. 20*: 145-154, 1949.

56. Staples, R., and Smith, J. W.: Attitudes of grandmothers and mothers toward child rearing practices. *Child Develop. 25*: 91-97, 1954.

57. Staver, N.: The child's learning difficulty as related to the emotional problem of the mother. *Am. J. Orthopsychiat. 23*: 131-141, 1953.

58. Stolz, L. M., et al.: *Father Relations of War-born Children*. Stanford, Calif. Stanford University Press, 1954.

59. Symonds, P. M.: *The Dynamics of Parent-Child Relationships*. New York, Teachers College, Columbia University Press, 1949.

60. Tasch, R. J.: The role of the father in the family. *J. Exper. Educ. 20*: 319-361, 1952.

61. Wile, I. S., and Davis, R.: The relation of birth to behavior. *Am. J. Orthopsychiat. 11*: 320-334, 1941.

CHAPTER 12

Values, Interests, Fantasy Life and Moral Development

VALUES REFER TO WAYS of striving, believing, and doing whenever purpose and direction are involved or choice and judgment are exercised. Values are implied in the relative importance an individual attaches to different objectives and activities, in his moral, social and religious beliefs, and in his aesthetic preferences. They underlie sanctioned ways of behaving and interacting with people in a given culture and the kinds of personality traits that are idealized. Values therefore are important factors in determining goals and goal seeking behavior, standards of conduct, and feelings of obligation to conform to such standards and to inhibit behavior at variance with them. They help order the world of the child differentially in terms of degree of ego-involvement (i.e., determine his interests), orient him to his cultural milieu, influence the content of his perceptions, and selectively sensitize him to perceive certain classes of objects and relationships (see p. 425).

THE TRANSMISSION OF VALUES

Three component problems are involved in the intracultural transmission of values. First we must consider the external patterning factors to which the child is exposed and which influence him selectively to interiorize certain values in preference to others. Second, we must identify the mechanisms through which the external standards are interiorized. Third, we must reckon with the sanctions (both internal and external) that maintain values in relatively stable form once they are internalized.

External Patterning Factors

The young child's world of value judgments is largely unstructured for lack of a relevant experiential frame of reference and, hence, is very susceptible to the influence of prestige suggestion from significant figures in his environment (see p. 359). First through his parents and later through other socializing agents, he is exposed to both explicit and implicit indoctrination. The latter occurs insidiously through recurrent and unobtrusive exposure to the underlying value assumptions of family and culture. Thus, young children tend to identify with the value symbols of their parents' membership and reference groups long before they are sufficiently mature to comprehend the meaning of these symbols. Preschool and early school age children, for example, assimilate the racial and religious prejudices of their parents quite independently of any actual contact with the groups concerned (see p. 428), and identify with parental religious and political attitudes without any rational understanding of the issues involved.[43]

Several studies have provided experimental evidence of children's susceptibility to prestige suggestion. Direct person-to-person influence has been shown to modify their food[20] and art[5] preferences and judgments of line length.[10] Duncker was also successful in making preschool children prefer a previously disliked food merely by reading a story in which the food was represented as the hero's favorite.[20] Prestige suggestion is more effective (a) when the authority's opinion is rationalized rather than arbitrary, and (b) in ambiguous judgmental situations where the child has little past experience, an indefinite and unformed evaluative frame of reference, and no incontrovertible sensory evidence before him.[5] The child's peers are more apt to induce judgmental shifts than are adults when children have reason to suspect that adults have ulterior motives in expressing preferences or supposedly authoritative opinions.[10, 20] Children naturally vary greatly in their susceptibility to prestige suggestion; but it is still unsettled whether suggestibility can be considered a general personality trait. Evidence from studies with adults indicates that degree of susceptibility is inversely related to self-sufficiency, self-assertiveness and relative indifference to others' approval. In accordance with their social sex role of being more docile, conforming, and submissive to adult authority, girls tend to be more responsive than boys to prestige suggestion.[5, 10, 20, 65]

Mechanism of Interiorization

On the basis of the degree of motivation involved, we may distinguish between two essentially different ways of interiorizing the values of other persons or of groups. Simply through *habituation* to a given set of norms their underlying values may acquire an aura of axiomatic rightness and be accepted as self-evidently valid. Here no particular needs of the individual are satisfied. A simple, mechanical type of *imitation* belongs in the same category: the expressed values of one person serve as a stimulus instigating acceptance of comparable values by another. This process is facilitated in group situations and is very similar to behavioral "contagion" (see p. 485). However, whenever such imitation involves a more active *need* to be like other persons or to conform to their expectations (apart from fear of punishment), it is more proper to speak of motivated interiorization or identification. Identification, therefore, is a motivated form of imitation in which the *interpersonal relationship* (direct or fantasied) between imitator and imitatee as well as the imitated act itself is highly significant for the learning that ensues.

Although identification implies an underlying motive in one person's acceptance of another's values, the term itself without further qualification does not specify the type of motivation that is operative. In order to designate more precisely the individual's motivational orientation to value assimilation we have used the terms, *satellizing* and *incorporative* (non-satellizing). In each case the child responds to prestige suggestion* but for different reasons (see p. 301). The non-satellizer (in contrast to the satellizer) does not accept prestige authority blindly and uncritically from a person or group out of personal loyalty or desire for derived status, but because the authority of the suggester is respected as relevantly influencing the outcome of his quest for primary status. The purpose of his hero worship is not to be a loyal and devoted camp follower but to emulate and displace the hero, to use him as a guide and stepping stone to ego enhancement. Conformity to group norms in his case is more a matter of expediency, of obtaining the status advantages of group reference or membership than a reflection of a need for self-subservient belongingness or "we-feeling." The *exploratory* orientation to value assimilation (see p. 306), on the other hand, is a more task-oriented, objective, problem solving approach that ignores considerations of primary and derived status and places major emphasis on objective evidence, logical validity, and equity in determining the acceptability of different value positions.

External and Internal Sanctions

After the child is exposed to and assimilates values from significant persons in his environment, both external and internal sanctions operate to keep them relatively stable and to insure (in the case of moral values) that behavior is kept compatible with them. At the disposal of parents, teachers and peer group are such forms of control as reward and punishment, approval and disapproval, ridicule, withdrawal of love and respect, depreciation of status in the group, and ostracism. From within, a parallel set of controls is operative. The child feels apprehensive about the consequences of deviation from his internalized values, e.g., possible loss of present staus and the threat of not attaining future status goals. He learns gradually to respond with feelings of shame to the negative evaluation of himself by others, acquires a feeling of *obligation* about inhibiting behavior that is at variance with his value structure, and feels guilty when he fails to do so. The need to avoid these highly unpleasant guilt feelings and to retain

*No difference in responsiveness to prestige suggestion was obtained between children displaying satellizing and non-satellizing orientations respectively.[5]

feelings of belongingness in and acceptance by the group eventually becomes one of the most effective of all behavioral sanctions. In the case of satellizing children, personal loyalty is also an important factor in preventing deviancy from internalized standards.

DEVELOPMENTAL TRENDS IN VALUE ASSIMILATION

Since socialization is a gradual and cumulative process, it is hardly surprising that with increasing age children show progressively closer approximation to adult moral, social,[22, 59, 70] and aesthetic[78, 81] norms, and correspondingly greater agreement among themselves.[22, 70] A parallel trend is a gradual increase in the conformity aspects of personality as measured by Rorschach responses.[82] This greater conformity to adult standards naturally depends in part upon increased ability to perceive what is expected and to discriminate between finer shadings of behavioral standards. Progressive improvement occurs in ability to perceive own and others' sociometric status (see p. 470) and to discriminate between the behaviors that teachers approve and disapprove of[93] and between different degrees of seriousness of offense against property.[22] Children also become progressively more aware that they are expected to conform to adult roles and to inhibit aggressive, socially deviant behavior.[31] Another consequence of growth in cognitive capacity is the fact that values tend to be organized on a more abstract basis, thereby permitting greater generality and consistency from situation to situation.[36]

Although much interindividual variability prevails at any given age level, the growing importance of attaining primary status during the desatellizing period increasingly tends to favor a shift from the satellizing to the incorporative and exploratory motivational orientations in value assimilation. In interiorizing new values and goals, therefore, such considerations as ego enhancement, expediency, social recognition, and status in the group become more relevant than adult approval or personal loyalty; and satisfaction of these considerations demands much more critical examination of values prior to internalization. Accordingly, the evidence shows that suggestibility in children decreases as a function of age.[65, 71] The adoption of the exploratory orientation is also greatly facilitated during the desatellizing stage by the opportunity of following objective evidence and principles of equity to their logical conclusions without incurring such heavy burdens of guilt and disloyalty and without being so concerned about the possible loss of derived status.

Reflective of this shift in value assimilation is the increasing sensitivity of children to the disapproval of such authority figures outside the home as the school superintendent,[7] the decreasing importance of the parents as emulatory models,[87] and the replacement of the latter by glamorous, historical and public figures.[37, 42] As shown by the steadily diminishing correlations from the age of 10 to 16 between children's reputations for various traits and the closeness of affectional ties in the family,[13] parents become increasingly less influential than other socializing agents in determining children's values. Values acquire a wider social base as increased exposure to new social environments, coupled with less subservience to parental views, enables the older child to perceive the standards of his home as merely special variants of subcultural norms. Hence, with increasing age, his values tend to become more typical of the culture at large and less typical of his own family.

With increasing age children also tend to adopt a less subjectivistic approach to values. They consider them from a less personal and more detached point of view, show greater ability to argue from the standpoint of a hypothetical premise, and think more in terms that transcend their own immediate experience (see p. 553). A corresponding trend in value assimilation is a decline in egoism and an increase in altruism.[87, 97] Children become more aware of the needs, feelings and interests of others and more able to consider a situation from another's point of view. For example, the reason offered for the unacceptability of stealing tends to shift from fear of apprehension and punishment to the perceived injury it causes others.[22]

MORAL DEVELOPMENT

Morals constitute that part of our cultural and personal value systems concerned with the proper ends of man's activities and strivings, with questions of good and evil, and with responsibility or accountability for behavior. Thus, the learning of moral values is only a component aspect of ego development and obeys all of the principles regulating the assimilation of any ego related value. From a developmental standpoint, we can see no theoretical advantage in divorcing moral development from ego development or in postulating the existence of a separate layer of personality such as the Freudian superego. Hence, in our analysis of the development of conscience, we shall be concerned with the same type of variables that determine the outcome of other aspects of ego development (see p. 276).

Importance for Child Development

During the past three decades or more, psychology—the science of behavior—has attempted to evade coming to terms with ethics, the science of ends, norms, good, right and choice. The focus of psychological concern has been on adjustment as an end in itself, the contention being that moral values are subjective and unverifiable. According to this view moral judgments are matters of arbitrary preference and opinion beyond the pale of science; no objective psychological criterion is possible. Behavior may be appraised as constructive or antisocial, but never as good or evil. The purpose of psychology is to explain conduct, not to judge it; questions of accountability are held to be irrelevant in the light of psychological determinism, and hence the proper concern of only jurists and philosophers.

In reply to this line of argument, we would say first that to ignore ethical considerations is to overlook one of the most significant components of human conduct. Whether the psychologist chooses to recognize it or not, most purposeful behavior in human beings has a moral aspect the psychological reality of which cannot be ignored. The goals of human development, insofar as they are determined by man and culture are always predicated upon certain moral assumptions. Thus, the development of the individual is invariably influenced by coercive exposure to the particular set of assumptions which his culture espouses and which he himself eventually assimilates. Second, empirically validatable ethical propositions *can* be discovered once we accept certain basic *philosophical* value judgments regarding the proper ends of development which themselves are phenomenologically unverifiable. If, for example, we were to grant that self-realization were the highest goal toward which man could strive, it would be possible to establish which behavioral alternatives are most compatible with this goal and hence most ethical. But even if the primary value judgments are not empirically verifiable, they must still be predicated upon empirically determined human capacities for the kind of norms that are advocated. It is futile to speak of life goals that are motivationally unsupportable or of standards of maturity that only angels could reach. The same criterion obviously applies also to principles of accountability which must be grounded on attainable norms of moral development. Finally, moral behavior is of interest to the child development specialist because it has a developmental history. It undergoes orderly and systematic age level changes and manifests psychobiological uniformities and psychosocial as well as idiosyncratic variability. In terms of the underlying psychological processes involved in conscience development, we deal with genically determined potentialities. However, the actual acquisition of moral behavior, the normative sequences, and the variability in development are largely determined by experiential and sociocultural factors.

By means of a developmental and cross-cultural approach, it becomes possible (a) to determine the limits that define man's capacity for acquiring moral behavior and the sequential steps involved in moral growth; (b) to predict the various types of delinquent behavior that may arise as a consequence of aberrant moral development; and (c) to determine under what conditions individuals may be held morally accountable for their misdeeds.

*Importance for Socializing Process**

Moral obligation is one of the most important psychological mechanisms through which an individual becomes socialized in the ways of his culture. It is also an important instrument for cultural survival since it constitutes a most efficient watchdog within each individual serving to keep his behavior compatible with the moral values of the society in which he lives. Without the aid it renders, child rearing would be a difficult matter indeed. If children felt no sense of accountability to curb their hedonistic and irresponsible impulses, to conform to accepted social norms, or to acquire self-control, the socializing process would be slow, arduous and incomplete. Sheer physical force, threat of pain, deprivation and punishment, or withholding of love and approval would be the only available methods— combined with constant surveillance—to exact conformity to cultural standards of acceptable behavior. And since it is plainly evident that the maintenance of perpetual vigilance is impractical, that fear alone is never an effective deterrent again antisocial behavior, and that the interests of personal expediency are not always in agreement with prescribed ethical norms, a social order unbuttressed by a sense of moral obligation in its members would enjoy precious little stability.

The cultural basis of conscience development in the individual may be found in the potent need of both parents and society to inculcate a sense of responsibility in the child. Not only the physical survival of its members, but also the perpetuation of its selective way of life is contingent upon the culture's degree of success in this undertaking. Thus, the attenuation of infantile irresponsibility might be considered part of the necessary process of ego devaluation and maturation that presumably characterizes personality development in all cultures. Socialization demands the learning of self-control and self-discipline, the subordination of personal desires to the needs and wishes of others, the acquisition of skills and self-sufficiency, the curbing of hedonistic and aggressive impulses, and the assimilation of culturally sanctioned patterns of behavior. It seems highly unlikely that any of these propensities could become thoroughly stable before conscience is firmly established.

Psychological Components of Conscience

The term *conscience* is an abstraction referring to the cognitive-emotional organization of an individual's moral values, to the feeling of obligation to abide by these values, and to other psychological processes in-

*This section is adapted from Ausubel, D. P., Relationships between shame and guilt in the socializing process, in *Psychol. Rev.* 62: 378-390, 1955, with permission of the publishers.

volved in keeping conduct compatible with internalized moral standards. It presupposes, first, that he is able to assimilate certain external standards of right and wrong or good and evil and accept them as his *own* (see pp. 381-382). The assimilation of moral values does not necessarily mean that these values will influence conduct in any stable and systematic fashion until a sense of *obligation* evolves to conform to them in his own *personal* behavior and to feel accountable for lapses therefrom. The sense of obligation is itself a moral value and must undergo internationalization; developmentally, however, this step occurs *after* the interiorization of other ethical values. That is, the child believes that certain actions are good or bad and applies these designations to *other* persons' conduct before he feels that he ought or ought not do them himself. But unlike other values, moral obligation has the regulatory function of compelling adherence to internalized norms of behavior. Hence, it is the core value of his moral system which not only makes possible the implementation of other values but also welds them together into an organized system of behavior. It gives generality and genotypic consistency to moral conduct by entering into every moral decision he makes. For example, the disposition to refrain from commiting an act of dishonesty depends on more than the strength of honesty in a given context. The *total* inhibitory control that can be exercised in this situation is rather the strength of the particular moral value (honesty) weighted by a general factor represented by the strength of the moral obligation to abide by *all* internalized values.

The operation of conscience also presupposes the capacity to *anticipate* the consequences of actions in advance of their execution and to exercise volitional and inhibitory control in order to bring these anticipated consequences into line with perceived obligation. The acquisition of such inhibitory self-control is naturally a very gradual process that parallels the growth of ability to endure postponement of immediate hedonistic gratification. A final psychological process involved in the operation of conscience is the *self-critical* faculty. Without this capacity for objectively appraising one's own intentions and behavior in the light of internalized moral principles, it is neither possible to inhibit immoral actions nor to experience guilt after they are committed. The importance of the self-critical faculty in the development of conscience can be seen in the fact that the latter remains in a rudimentary state until the former is reasonably well advanced. When self-criticism can be employed, guilt feelings become possible since these are a reaction to the perception of a discrepancy between one's own behavior and the moral standards in relation to which a sense of obligation exists.

Guilt is a special kind of negative *self-evaluation* that occurs when an individual acknowledges that his behavior is at variance with a given moral value to which he feels obligated to conform. It always includes feelings of shame in perceiving or imagining the negative evaluation of himself *by others* for violating a moral obligation. It also involves other *self-reactions* that are at least partially independent of the actual or presumed censure of others, namely, self-reproach, self-disgust, self-contempt, remorse, lowered self-esteem, and various characteristic and subjectively identifiable visceral and vasomotor responses. Through the processes of retrospective association and anticipation, guilt tends to be incorporated into the behavioral system of conscience; and since it is an extremely uncomfortable, self-punishing and anxiety producing phenomenon, the need to avoid it becomes a strong motivating force to keep behavior consistent with moral obligation. Behavior leading to guilt evokes the anticipation that retribution will be inevitable either through the suffering inherent in guilt feelings, the seeking out of social punishment as a means of guilt reduction, or through the medium of a supernatural agency. The perceived inevitability of punishment, therefore, is one of the characteristic properties of conscience reactions.

It is evident from the foregoing that conscience embodies several component psychological processes and is in no sense a single reified entity. It does, however, enjoy an apparent measure of psychological substantiveness reflective of (a) generalized inhibitory potential (based on the strength of particular moral values and general feelings of obligation) which lowers the probability of occurrence of acts perceived as incompatible with internalized standards; and (b) anticipation of highly identifiable guilt reactions if such behavior should nevertheless occur. It only confuses the issue to postulate that a separate layer of personality (i.e., the superego) embodies in reified fashion the properties associated with conscience reactions and arises in an inevitably predetermined manner (apart from actual interpersonal experience) in relation to a single aspect of psychosexual development. The Freudian superego is not coextensive at all with the developmental concept of conscience described above. It restricts the genesis of conscience *solely* to the child's supposed identification with the moral values of the like-sexed parent as a means of repressing both sexual rivalry toward the latter and libidinal (Oedipal) desires for the parent of opposite sex,* and assumes that this identification is facilitated by its postulated occurrence in the "prehistory [phylogenetic unconscious] of every person."[26] Furthermore, it asserts that the moral values assimilated in this context are qualitatively different from other interiorized social norms, and

*The Freudian theory of conscience naturally assumes the reality of the so-called Oedipus complex. See the critique on pages 252-253.

makes no provision for the fact that the underlying bases of value assimilation and moral obligation undergo marked developmental changes (see pp. 383-384).

Normative Changes in Conscience Development

Although none of the conditions necessary for the emergence of conscience can ever be satisfied at birth, all human beings are potentially capable of acquiring conscience behavior under minimally favorable circumstances. Culture may make a difference in the form which this behavior takes and in the specific kinds of stimuli which instigate it, but the capacity itself is so basically human and so fundamental to the sanctions by which social norms are maintained and transmitted to the young in *any* culture that differences among individuals within a culture would probably be as great as or greater than differences among cultures.* Thus, despite the probable existence of many important culturally conditioned differences in children's acquisition of guilt behavior, there are presumptive grounds for believing that considerable communality prevails in the general patterning of sequential development. Such communality would be a product of various uniformities regarding (a) basic conditions of the parent-child relationship, (b) minimal cultural needs for socialization of the child, and (c) certain gross trends in cognitive and personality growth from one culture to the next.†

Normative shifts in conscience development reflect both gains in cognitive maturity and age level changes in personality organization. Significant personality factors include alterations in dependency relationships, ego status needs, and mode of assimilating values. Significant cognitive factors include increased capacity for perceiving social expectations and the attributes of social roles, and increased ability to discriminate, generalize, formulate abstractions, and take multiple perspectives. Growth in self-critical ability and capacity for a less egocentric and more objective approach to values belong in both categories. Interaction between these cognitive and personality variables is responsible for most developmental changes in the basis of moral obligation and in notions of moral law, justice and culpability; because of the many psychological components of conscience, however, it is entirely conceivable that some aspects of moral development are influenced more by one type of factor than by another. McRae, for example, found that children's disapproval of moral transgressions was positively related to measures of

---

*It is theoretically possible, of course, that in certain extreme cases a culture may be so anarchic in terms of the obligations it engenders in its members that the potentiality for conscience behavior is never realized as, for example, among the Dobu.[8]

†Adapted from *Psychol. Rev.* 62: 378-390, 1955, with permission of the publishers.

parental authority, whereas conceptions of equity and culpability were not.[62] In general, cognitive capacities seem more important as prerequisites for reaching certain normative levels of moral functioning than as determinants of interindividual differences (see p. 397).

Age level changes in the development of conscience are primarily reflective of qualitative shifts in the basis of moral obligation and in conceptions of moral law rather than of quantitative improvement in moral conduct. After conscience is stabilized by the development of an adequate self-critical faculty, total character (e.g., helpfulness, truthfulness) scores do not improve consistently[36]; in fact, during this age period of 10 to 13, older children are significantly more deceitful than younger children.[36] Improvement is shown only in those aspects of conduct that depend on knowledge of societal moral standards and in motivational traits that are necessary for the acquisition of greater primary status.[36, 60] This situation is probably reflective in part of the characteristic moral confusion and expediency of our culture (see p. 399). Children gradually learn that honesty is preached more than it is practiced and that detection of dishonesty is not inevitable.

Presatellizing Stage. Presatellizing "conscience," for the most part, involves little more than the development of inhibitory control on the basis of learning to anticipate and avoid punishment. Previous experience with a given type of unacceptable behavior leads the child to expect pain, deprivation, isolation or disapproval if such behavior is repeated, and leads to feelings of insecurity in contemplating same. Inhibition of such behavior, therefore, is rewarding since it reduces insecurity. During this stage children obey prohibitory commands but do not consistently honor unenforced positive requests. Such conduct is devoid of any moral implications since it only indicates submission to authority rather than genuine acceptance of it.

Satellizing Stage. As the child perceives his dependence upon parents for volitional direction and decides to accept a satellizing role in relation to them, he gradually acquires a need to assimilate their values. Acceptance of parental standards of rightness and wrongness depends upon this satellizing relationship to parents,[56, 69] and is facilitated by prestige suggestion and by the parent's altrusistic role. "But acceptance of these values does not obligate him—in the absence of a still undeveloped sense of moral responsibility—to regulate his own behavior accordingly."[4] Hitting, for example, is perceived as "bad" when *other* persons do it but not when gratification of his *own* aggressive impulses is involved.[23]

"Behavior can first be regarded as manifesting moral properties when a sense of obligation is acquired."[4] The child's need to retain his derived status makes him acquiesce to the proposition that disobedience is evil, disloyal, and hurtful to his parents. At this point guilt reactions become possible, and the child becomes motivated to conform to parental standards in order to avoid the negative self-evaluation, anxiety and remorse associated with guilt. This development only takes place in children who are accepted and intrinsically valued. Parents of delinquents are typically less accepting, affectionate, and solicitous than parents of nondelinquents.[29, 94, 98] During this stage, children's ideas of right and wrong correlate more with those of their parents' than with the ideas of friends, club leaders, teachers and Sunday school teachers, and more with the mother's ideas than with the father's.[36] Moral identification is facilitated in a democratic home atmosphere of marital harmony and of firm, consistent, and love-oriented discipline.[13, 29, 73] Cross-cultural study also shows that the strength of guilt feelings in adults tends to be correlated with love-oriented techniques of punishment.[90] The child's acceptance of parental restrictions is correlated with overt manifestations of maternal affection,[73, 92] and his disposition toward responsible behavior is related to common participation with and trust and confidence in the parent.[33]

The development of feelings of moral obligation is a gradual and tortuous process. It is not only hampered by negativistic trends (see p. 292), but also by the slow growth of the self-critical faculty and of the ability to generalize principles of right and wrong beyond specific situations. It does not arise spontaneously, but under the pressure of the parents' new authority role and training demands, correlating positively with earliness of socialization.[90] Furthermore, it is reinforced by the parents' physical presence and prestige suggestion, by the continued application of external sanctions (reward and punishment, threat, and ridicule), by the withdrawal of love and approval, and by the child's continued dependence on the parent for physical survival. The early stages of satellizing conscience represent a compromise between aggressive negativism and an unstable sense of moral responsibility. The preschool child strenuously attempts to rationalize his misdeeds by attributing them to accident, forgetting, real or imaginary playmates, sensory deficiency, involuntary movements, and misunderstanding.

Stabilization of the sense of moral obligation occurs primarily as a result of gains in self-critical ability. Once the child is able to appraise himself and his situation realistically enough to accept the dependent biosocial status that is inevitably his in any culture, he can finally acknowledge parental authority as unquestionably and unconditionally valid. Improved self-critical ability also enables him to perceive his own wrongdoing. There is a marked increase during the fifth year of life in sensitivity to reproof and in the intensity and duration of remorse reactions.[28] Conscience to a large extent becomes its own taskmaster and functions largely in the absence of external coercive agents. The child appears concerned with the spirit as well as the letter of moral duty, and threats of reprisal for punishment are less frequently uttered. Reinforcement of the sense of moral obligation is provided by feelings of guilt which become more anxiety-producing than external punitive agents. In the first place, the remorse of guilt is more recriminating than pain or deprivation. Second, it is more inevitable since self-detection is less avoidable than discovery by others. Lastly, unlike punishment by parents the punishment dispensed by a guilty conscience does not reduce guilt or confer absolution.

Because of the child's social inexperience, satellizing orientation to value assimilation, and cognitive inability to appreciate the functional basis of moral law, the organization of conscience during early and middle childhood is necessarily authoritarian and absolutistic. Moral obligation hinges on implicit acceptance of parental values, personal loyalty, and dependence on derived status. Rules are highly specific and possess an axiomatic, "sacred" and self-evident rightness that tolerates no exception regardless of what extenuating circumstances may exist.[56, 69] Hence, infractions of rules (consequences per se) are perceived as inherently evil irrespective of the intentions of the wrongdoer, and punishment is conceived as automatic and as inherent in the external world as the consequences of physical antecedents.[69]

Desatellizing Stage. During the desatellizing period the basis of moral obligation and conceptions of moral law undergo significant change. Feelings of moral accountability are placed on a societal basis instead of remaining a function of the parent-child relationship, and are referred to more abstract principles of justice and responsibility. The notion of unilateral obligation and respect for the adult gives way to a concept of reciprocal obligations based on voluntary cooperation and mutuality of consent.[69] The child becomes extremely concerned about equalitarian fairness predicated upon identical rights and punishments for all;[28, 69] only later does he accept the idea that these should be related to the varying needs, abilities, and maturity of the individual.[69] This situation naturally creates great discord among parents and siblings.

The child's conceptions of rules and punishment also become less absolutistic. He interprets them more as man-made functional contrivances based on mutual consent that are designed to facilitate social interaction than as axiomatic and unmodifiable givens emanating from an external authority.[69] When the rules per se are perceived as less sacrosanct, he can place more weight on intentions than on consequences and can recognize the necessity for sometimes departing from the letter of the law in order to preserve the spirit. The number of things "thought wrong"[70] as well as unequivocal condemnation of lying and stealing tend to decline with increasing age.[74, 76, 86]

Not only is more account taken of extenuating circumstances, but concessions are also made to prevailing standards of moral laxness and expediency, e.g., willingness to steal from corporations or as long as there is no possibility of apprehension.[76] Finally, during this stage, concepts of good and bad that were formerly confined to discrete situations become organized on a more abstract basis and hence acquire greater consistency and generality.[28, 36]

The above changes are instigated by modification in the parent-child relationship, shifts in the child's needs for and source of status, alterations in his group experience, and maturation of his perceptual and cognitive capacities. As he begins to lose his volitional dependence upon parents and to become more concerned with acquiring primary status, the child's satellizing orientation to value assimilation becomes increasingly less serviceable for the satisfaction of his ego needs (see p. 383). Since the inherent sacredness of moral standards also depends in part upon a perception of parents as infallible and omniscient beings, it begins to break down as the child enters the school and community and discovers that there are other authorities, various moral alternatives, and different versions of the truth. The more he comes into contact with the variable moral beliefs of the culture at large, the more his parents' early monopoly on moral authority is challenged and the less axiomatic their values become.

The changing nature and organization of peer group experience also promotes developmental changes in moral behavior. A primary function of the early peer group is to provide a supplementary source of derived status; and the child accepts its authority on the same unilateral and absolutistic basis as he does the parents'. Prior to the age of eight he also operates in small, isolated and informally organized groups in which roles are poorly differentiated and a lack of functional division of labor exists. Later, groups become larger, less isolated, and more stable. Children experience membership in several different groups exhibiting a variety of rules, practices and values, and begin to improvise their own rules to meet new situations. As individual roles are differentiated the need for cooperation and mutual obligations increases. The older the child becomes the more he looks to the group as a source of primary status and the more the group tends to supplant parents as the source of moral authority.

However, it is mostly in heterogeneous urban cultures that values (during preadolescence and especially adolescence) tend to acquire a wider social base and peers tend to replace parents as interpreters and enforcers of the moral code. But neither phenomenon is indispensable for the maturational changes in moral organization that occur at this time. Repudiation of parental authority and of filial ties is *not* necessary for the acquisition of mature conceptions of moral responsibility and culpability based on intention, interpersonal needs, and reciprocal obligations. All that is required from a personality standpoint is a change in status and dependency needs and sufficient social experience to appreciate the functional basis of existing authority relationships. In the first place, in a population of boys from 5 to 14 in our own culture, it was found that neither the extent of parental control nor the internalization of parental requirements decrease with age.[62] Second, there is impressive evidence of the development of mature and rational conceptions of moral law both in a particular American Indian culture where only a single moral standard prevails[66] and in a Chinese-American community where traditional emphasis is placed on filial piety.[58] Thus, when parental authority continues in undiminished force during pre-adolescence, adolescence and adult life, its underlying basis evidently changes: the parent becomes less of a personal authority figure and more of a symbol of the moral authority of society.

Acting conjunctively with personality factors in bringing about desatellizing changes in moral development are various facets of cognitive maturation. Increased ability to generalize and to think in more logical and abstract terms makes possible a more objective and integrated approach to moral issues. Much normative change in moral conduct can also be attributed to the fact that with increasing age, as he becomes more able to "take multiple perspectives extensively, flexibly and abstractly,"[77] the child's perceptions of social roles become more accurate;[57, 77] for "built into role conceptions are the justifications of motivations for behavior appropriate or inappropriate to enactment of roles."[77] In this way he gradually acquires realistic knowledge of societal moral standards—of what is expected, of allowable exceptions, and of conventionally accepted *reasons* for prevailing practices. The impact on moral development of such factors as increased self-critical faculty (p. 313) and use of the exploratory orientation (p. 306), and of decreased egocentricity (p. 311) and subjectivism (p. 312), which depend on both cognitive and personality factors, has already been considered under developmental trends in value assimilation (see pp. 383-384).

Several studies[19, 34, 57, 62] have found a positive relationship between lower social class status in children and more absolutistic, rigid and authoritarian conceptions of moral law and more punitive and retaliatory notions of discipline. This situation is undoubtedly reflective in part of the authoritarian lower-class parent-child relationship (see p. 352), and of inconsistent training in the "official" moral ideology* (see p. 401); since the latter is accepted only half-heartedly and is inconsistently enforced, it must be adhered to rigidly if it is to be maintained at all. This cannot be the entire

---

*Both honesty[36] and truthfulness[74] are positively correlated with socioeconomic status.

explanation since we have already seen that authoritarian parent-child relationships are not incompatible with mature concepts of moral law. Lower-class children are also less aware of socially accepted (middle-class) standards and undergo development less rapidly in cognitive aspects of moral growth.[62]

Individual Differences in Moral Development

In the foregoing sketch of age level changes in moral development we attempted to trace sequential stages that can presumably be found in all cultural settings. Still to be considered are psychosocial aspects of moral development, and personality and cognitive factors that account for interindividual (idiosyncratic) differences within a culture.

Personality Considerations. Evidence pointing to an integral relationship between accepting parent attitudes and the satellizing stage of conscience development has already been presented (see p. 391). The *non-satellizer* obviously fails to undergo the various changes in conscience development associated with satellization, and is similarly spared the changes resulting from desatellization. His moral development is less discontinuous than that of the satellizer. During early and middle childhood the non-satellizer continues to conform to parental standards for the same expediential reasons as during infancy; he fails to develop a sense of obligation in relation to a general attitude of subservience, loyalty, and need for approval and retention of derived status. Fear of deprivation and loss of succorance rather than guilt avoidance keep him in line and check the overt expression of his hostility. Moral obligations are assimilated on a selective basis only, that is, if they are perceived as leading to ego enhancement.

During late childhood the non-satellizer becomes capable of internalizing moral values and obligations on the basis of the exploratory orientation. Unhampered by satellizing loyalties he finds it easier to grasp functional concepts of moral law based on equity and reciprocal obligations. In this way he too acquires the prerequisites for a guilt-governed conscience. But the stability of moral obligations that circumvent a preliminary history of satellization is highly precarious because (a) infantile irresponsibility has never been attenuated by strong, emotionally charged feelings of obligation toward significant figures in his interpersonal world, and (b) powerful needs for ego enhancement are often in conflict with the content and goals of ethical norms.

Under such conditions moral obligations are seldom repudiated outright; this would require direct and inexpedient conflict with cultural sanctions. However, two less drastic alternatives are available: (1) indirect evasion of the demands of conscience and the punishment of guilt when the needs of ego aggrandizement are too strong to be denied; and (2) buttressing conscience by the mechanism of reaction-formation when moral obligations are too solidly entrenched to be circumvented.

Moral obligation may be evaded either (a) by selectively inhibiting the self-critical faculty so that, when expedient, even glaring discrepancies between precept and practice cannot be perceived, or (b) by claiming superior status so that one is *above* the law for *ordinary* people. Reaction-formation rigidly suppresses motives that are at variance with internalized moral obligations and substitutes more acceptable motives in their place. Nevertheless, many loopholes for surreptitious circumvention are still present. Antisocial trends can often be expressed under the guise of lofty ideals. At the very best, the moral behavior of the non-satellizer becomes unspontaneous, stereotyped and unduly circumscribed. Awareness of the underlying strength of unacceptable motives encourages the erection of exaggerated defenses.

The overvalued child who has never felt much pressure to conform to parental standards frequently regards himself as exempt from ordinary moral obligations. The rejected child, on the other hand, is not likely to claim such unique exemptions since he has been subjected to rigorous discipline. In most instances he will acquire a strong rational conscience buttressed by reaction-formation and permitting occasional moral lapses through impairment of the self-critical faculty. However, the concomitance of harsh rejection by parents and extreme self-assertiveness in the child may result in the child repudiating the entire fabric of parental moral values; this type of delinquency is known as aggressive, antisocial psychopathy. When rejection is expressed in parental neglect and self-love, the child displaces the hostility he feels for his parents onto others. Such behavior is reinforced by the parents' tendency to condone it as long as they themselves are not disturbed. On the positive side, the rejected child possesses a latent capacity for forming satellizing-like relationships which enable him to experience the type of guilt feelings that occur in satellizing children.

Among *satellizers*, aberrations in conscience development are generally less severe. The more serious problem is presented by the underdominated child who has great difficulty acquiring a sense of moral obligation. To begin with, he is not required to inhibit hedonistic motivations or to curb aggressive impulses. The limits of unacceptable behavior are poorly defined and inadequately or inconsistently enforced. Second, like the overvalued child, he is treated as a specially privileged person exempt from usual responsibilities toward others, and is not encouraged to develop a realistic self-critical faculty. Capricious and inconsistent parental discipline is associated with lack of self-discipline in children[73] and is more characteristic of delinquents than of nondelinquents.[29] Fortunately the motivation for immoral behavior is more likely to lie in hedonistic self-indulgence than in unprincipled ego aggrandizement at the expense of others. The chief difficulty in moral development for overprotected and overdominated children lies in transferring feelings of moral obligations from parents to society and in arriving at independent value judgments. This situation leads to no serious consequences as long as the parent is alive and does not subscribe to antisocial attitudes. However, if the parent is a moral deviant, uncritical loyalty on the part of the child can lead to delinquent behavior; whereas the death or removal of the parent can create a vacuum in moral responsibility.

Ascendence and viscerotonia are probably the most important of the temperamental variables influencing the course of conscience development. The more self-assertive a child is the more likely will he be to resist the imposition of parental standards upon his behavior. Similarly, the greater his need for hedonistic satisfactions, the more reluctant he will be to accept the obligation of conforming to rules aimed at minimizing these satisfactions. Dishonest children tend to be impulsive, emotionally unstable and suggestible.[36, 74] Delinquents may also be more prone for temperamental reasons to utilize aggression as a defense or status-gaining mechanism.[39] In contrast to nondelinquents they have been described as more restless, active, impulsive and danger-loving.[29, 39]

Cognitive Factors. Since values and moral behavior obviously have a cognitive aspect, we could reasonably anticipate that they would be influenced by both intelligence and moral knowledge. A minimal degree of intelligence is required for acquiring abstract principles of moral value, for perceiving the moral expectations of the culture, for anticipating the consequences of behavior, and for appreciating the advantages of conforming to social norms. Moral conduct also presupposes moral knowledge. However, it seems that these two variables are only significantly related to moral behavior when they fall below a certain critical level. Beyond this point, personality and motivational variables are the crucial determining factors.

It is true that intellectually gifted children surpass their "average" contemporaries in such traits as conscientiousness, perseverance, prudence and truthfulness.[80] Their superiority, however, prevails mostly in moral traits that either depend on moral knowledge or are important for achieving individual success rather than in traits reflective of socially mature or altruistic attitudes;[36, 49, 80] correlations between intelligence and helpfulness are extremely low.[36, 48] The following factors probably contribute to the positive relationship between intelligence and certain kinds of moral traits. (1) Brighter children are better able to perceive the expectations of their culture and to learn appropriate forms of conduct. They can also perceive more accurately which character traits are required for success. (2) The personality traits that correlate most highly with intelligence are also most highly prized by middle-class homes; and as will be pointed out later (see p. 602), intelligence test scores are positively related to social class status. (3) Highly motivated children tend to be persistent, stable and responsible, and to make the most of their intellectual endowment by continually exercising their cognitive capacities and by performing maximally on intelligence tests.

The moderately positive relationship between intelligence and honesty[36, 48] can be largely attributed to such extrinsic considerations as less reason to cheat in order to do well in school work and shrewdness in avoiding detection or inadvisable opportunities for cheating. This interpretation is supported by the fact that intelligence correlates more highly with moral conduct than does moral knowledge.[36] Evidently then, intelligence affects such conduct less by influencing moral knowledge than in some extraneous fashion. Mental deficiency occurs more frequently among delinquents than nondelinquents,[40] and the mean I.Q. of the former is also somewhat lower;[68] but I.Q.'s are *generally* lower in the urban slum areas in which juvenile delinquency breeds, as shown by the negligible difference in mental test performance between delinquents and nondelinquent siblings.[40] Scores on moral knowledge are not highly correlated with moral conduct,[36] and fail to differentiate between delinquents and nondelinquents. Thus, low I.Q. per se cannot be an important etiological factor in delinquency, but may constitute one of the larger constellation of variables associated with depressed socioeconomic conditions that contributes to the development of delinquent behavior. Intellectual deficit, for example, increases suggestibility, the tendency to take unwise chances, and the probability of apprehension.

*Moral Beliefs and Character.** The *true* moral beliefs of an individual are an excellent reflection of his character and are more significantly related to it than is his overt behavior. The widespread opinion that belief and character are unrelated springs from (a) confusion between moral *belief* and moral *knowledge;* (b) confusion between *expressed* and *true* belief; and (c) confusion between deliberate insincerity and unavoidable lack of discriminative ability as determinants of the discrepancy between belief and conduct. As already indicated, moral knowledge only involves one cognitive aspect of moral belief and is a relatively minor factor in the total configuration of variables determining its development.

For various reasons either expressed belief or overt behavior may be at

Character, here, is used synonymously with the moral aspects of personality. It refers to the totality of enduring, relatively stable behavioral predispositions in an individual that are influenced by feelings of moral obligation. A *true moral belief* is an accurate self-report of such predispositions.

variance with true moral belief. For example, a child who wishes to make a good impression may state insincere beliefs which naturally are inconsistent with his actual behavior; but here, although expressed belief is inconsistent with both conduct and true belief, it is quite probable that behavior is consonant with *true* belief. In other instances, for reasons of legitimate expediency or conformity to social norms, both expressed belief and behavior may be incongruent with true belief. Under these conditions the discrepancy between true belief and conduct is not a reflection of inconsistency or weakness of character but of coercive factors preventing the translation of belief into congruent behavior. In still other instances, where the disparity between true belief and conduct cannot be attributed to legitimate expediency, the true belief actually exists but is negated by competing behavioral tendencies which at a particular moment happen to undergo disinhibition or are situationally more potent.

Lastly, conduct may be inconsistent with true belief not because of any insincerity or deliberate attempt at dissimulation but (a) because of cognitive limitations in logic, insufficient generalization of moral values, or inability to apply general principles to real-life problems; and (b) because of institutionalized inconsistencies in cultural values that the individual is either unable to perceive or obliged to accept.

Cultural Factors Influencing Moral Development

Cultural and social class variables affect the development of conscience and account for intercultural differences (or intracultural uniformities) by influencing (a) the particular moral values that are assimilated (see p. 420) and their mode of transmission (see p. 380), (b) the kinds of internal and external sanctions that are imposed (see p. 382), and (c) the ways in which guilt feelings are instigated and expressed (see p. 403). The effects of both types of variables are exceedingly pervasive but differ in that individuals are typically influenced by the norms of other social classes but only rarely by the standards of other cultures.

A general problem arises in the impact of culture on conscience development when serious discrepancies or inconsistencies exist between the professed (official) moral ideology and the ideology that is really believed and actually practiced. This situation is illustrated in our culture by the formal endorsement of humility, kindliness, helpfulness, and fair play, and the simultaneous overvaluation of aggressiveness, prestige, and success at any price. It is symptomatic of both a rate of social and economic change that has by far outstripped its ideological substrate and of widespread moral disintegration and confusion. In the struggle for material success concern for moral values and traditional moral restraints are being swept aside. The form rather than the content and intention of behavior is becoming the chief criterion of moral judgment in our society. What it means for a child to grow up in such a moral climate is something that still requires considerable investigation. We can only predict on logical and historical grounds that it will encourage expediential lack of principle and cynical acceptance of moral depravity. We can expect children to grow up hypocritical, deceitful, unconcerned with human values and the welfare of others, indifferent to injustice, and sold on the principle of getting the most out of people and valuing them solely on the basis of their market price.

At the very best this situation leads to ethical confusion and inconsistency and a potentially heavy burden of guilt. However, because of the prestige suggestion inherent in the operation of social norms and because of extremely high tolerance for moral ambiguity, inconsistent values may be assimilated in such a way that their incompatibility is never perceived. It is presumed by the perceiver that inconsistency in cultural values is inconceivable; hence, an advance "set" exists to perceive such values as consistent regardless of manifest content—even if logic-tight compartments must be constructed. If perceived, awareness of moral inconsistency and culpability may be subsequently repressed or disowned. More direct forms of guilt reduction include confession, expiation and reaction-formation. Various culturally stereotyped types of guilt reduction are also available, such as verbal magic, pseudo-remorse, and hypocritical religious observance. It is not necessary to believe, however, that all guilt feelings are intolerable and must somehow be repressed, disowned, rationalized, expiated for, etc. Man's portrait of himself need not be free of all moral blemishes. Hence, a good deal of guilt can be tolerated on a conscious level without any efforts made toward guilt reduction. In other instances, true guilt feelings may fail to develop because no *real* internalization of moral obligation has taken place, or because self-criticism is inhibited to the point where no discrepancy can be perceived between behavior and obligation.

Thus, many children may fail to perceive that any problem of moral inconsistency exists, others may be acutely disillusioned, and still others may perceive the problem but fail to be disturbed by it. This type of moral climate is in a sense made to order for the ego needs of the non-satellizer, except when he happens to have a strong rational conscience. On the other hand, the satellizer who perceives what is going on is unable to make the required adaptations without experiencing feelings of conflict, guilt, and resentment toward a culture that requires such moral compromises for the sake of survival and legitimate ego enhancement.

Other culturally derived sources of moral confusion and inconsistency also exist. First, the values of a particular social class may be at variance with the prevailing values of the culture at large. The parents of lower-class children, for example, do not consistently enforce middle-class standards despite verbal affirmation of same.[38] Second, the various socializing agencies may set up norms that are at odds with each other. Lower-class children and the children of immigrants or recently urbanized farmers are especially subjected to conflicts between the standards of home, school and peer groups. When grandparents live with the family still another opportunity for value conflict arises. Third, children experience difficulty in appreciating that conduct which is phenotypically discrepant but genotypically compatible with certain generalized norms (e.g., a "white lie") is *really* different from other situations in which specific practice (e.g., intolerance toward a particular minority group) conflicts with general preachments regarding tolerance. Lastly, because they are unable to evaluate clearly the issues involved when adults are sometimes coerced by conditions beyond their control into making moral compromises, children are apt to emulate and internalize the undesirable conduct instead of regarding it as a temporary and unavoidable expedient.

Culturally determined differences in social sex role (see p. 449) also make for corresponding sex differences in moral behavior. Girls are more sensitive to social situations and expectations[93] and hence make higher scores on tests of moral knowledge and self-control,[36] lie more for conventionally social reasons,[36, 86] and tend to be somewhat more cooperative and socially generous.[36] The greater aggressiveness of boys (see p. 336) is similarly associated with a higher incidence and more aggressive type of juvenile delinquency. Boys tend to do less cheating than girls on tests of deceit,[36] but girls tend to be more variable in this respect.[1, 36]

Peer Group. The child's peer group, apart from the wider adult culture, exerts a significant influence on his moral development. It provides a context in which he can learn the rules of the game, principles of equity, and self-subordination to group goals. Hence, it is hardly surprising that children who are members of character-building clubs exceed nonclub members in such traits as cooperativeness, but that in more general moral traits, such as honesty, which are less dependent on structured group experience, no significant difference prevails.[36] This evidence supports the logical inference that the peer group does not constitute in itself an important source of moral values during childhood. Its values tend to mirror those of significant adults (parents, teachers, clergy, etc.) in the subculture in which it is embedded. The influence of the peer group is more important in providing a *situational climate* that affects the child's inhibitory control in *particular* instances in which relevant moral obligations are not thoroughly interiorized. Thus the correlation of .23 between "best friends" on deception scores increases to .66 when they are members of the same class and can influence each other's behavior more directly.[36] Significant differences between different classes in the same school and between "progressive" and traditional schools also point to the influence of group morale.[1, 36] This situational influence is especially important in the instigation of delinquent activity. Bolstered by group suggestion and moral sanction the individual child will sometimes participate in aggressive antisocial behavior that he would never think of doing on his own. In such participation he also responds to implied threats of ostracism and to genuine feelings of loyalty to either intimate associates or to the group as a whole. Hence, most juvenile delinquency is committed by groups of children rather than by individuals.[39]

Mass Media. Despite their unofficial status in our culture, the various mass media probably exert more influence on moral development than some of the more traditional socializing agencies charged with this responsibility such as school and church. Their efficacy in this regard can be attributed to the fact that in addition to presenting a more dramatic version of life to children they are also not bound by reality restraints. Because they provide unmatched opportunities for vicarious ego enhancement and satellizing hero worship they may influence the kinds of values that children interiorize, the inhibitory potential of moral obligation, and the development of guilt feelings.

The first type of effect is illustrated by the manipulation of children's ethical standards through the showing of selected motion pictures.[48, 84] The second type of effect is illustrated by scattered findings that motion pictures,[11] crime magazines,[39] and comic books[44] may be contributory factors in causing juvenile delinquency. By suggesting that cleverly executed wrongdoing may go unpunished, stories of successful aggression may release the inhibitory restraints of conscience without (as Brodbeck's data show) necessarily affecting moral values or associated guilt feelings.[12] Other relevant factors in the influence of mass media on delinquency are (a) identification with glamorous or prestigeful figures who portray violence and ruthlessness in a laudable light, and (b) the suggestive presentation of detailed information necessary for the execution of criminal acts. In opposition to this line of reasoning, it has been argued that mass media do not create but only release existing delinquent trends and also provide a harmless outlet in fantasy for aggressive tendencies that might otherwise be expressed in real life. In most instances, furthermore, right is pictured as triumphing in the end. Thus it is conceivable that depending on the way themes of violence are handled and on the particular circumstances and individuals involved, mass media may have either an inhibitory or facilitating effect on delinquent behavior.

Generality of Moral Conduct

This controversial issue has already been considered at great length in a more general context (see pp. 101-103). We have concluded that although many factors indigenous to personality organization in children make their moral conduct unusually susceptible to the influence of situational variables, much of the apparent lack of generality is a function of such measurement difficulties as variability in ego-involvement, different phenotypic expressions of the same genotypic tendency, and the masking effect of normative uniformities on individual differences. In support of this view is (a) evidence showing the close relationship between ego-involvement and scores on objective measures of character and personality (see p. 102); (b) the tendency for the generality coefficients of moral traits to be higher in older children and adolescents than in young children;[36, 38] and (c) evidence from several studies of moral conduct in children that show greater generality of function than was reported by Hartshorne and May (see p. 101).

Shame and Guilt

Within recent years, various cultural anthropologists[9, 55, 64] have advanced the paradoxically ethnocentric view that guilt is not universally present or prominent as a sanction in mediating and sustaining the culture. They contend that in some cultures "sensitivity to shame . . . largely takes the place that remorse and self-punishment have in preventing anti-social conduct" in Western civilization.[55] Instead of acknowledging that guilt behavior can occur whenever and wherever an individual internalizes moral obligations and can exercise sufficient self-critical ability to perceive his own wrongdoing, they lay down three indispensable criteria for the development of guilt behavior. First, the child must accept the parent as omniscient and as the source of all moral authority. Second, genuine guilt feelings can only exist when shame and other external sanctions are not operative. Third, guilt must be characterized by conviction of sin and need for atonement. Behavior that does not conform to these requirements is categorized as shame.

If we accepted the first criterion, there could be no guilt behavior in the numerous cultures in which children do not regard parents as omniscient and in which the authority for moral sanctions is derived laterally or from the group as a whole. However, actual examination of the moral behavior of children and adults in such cultures (e.g., Navaho) does not confirm this proposition. The same criterion would also deny the observed occurrence of guilt among adolescents and adults in our own culture who accept the peer group and society (rather than parents) as the source of moral authority, and among non-satellizers who never accept the moral authority of parents, but who nevertheless interiorize moral obligations on the basis of abstract principles of equity.[4] The second criterion ignores the fact (a) that guilt (a negative *self*-judgment for violating moral obligations) is invariably accompanied by shame (a self-deprecatory reaction to the actual or presumed judgments of *others*), and (b) that at all stages of development internal sanctions are reinforced by external sanctions. Hence, although shame and guilt are distinguishable from each other, they are neither dichotomous nor mutually exclusive.[4] The third criterion is peculiarly specific to certain religious doctrines and beliefs about the original nature of man that prevail in cultures adhering to the Judaic-Christian tradition,[4] and hardly applies to peoples like the Japanese who nevertheless show striking evidences of both guilt and shame in their moral behavior.

Moral Accountability

Although a philosophical discussion of moral accountability and "free will" versus determinism is obviously out of place in this volume,* it should be noted that acceptance of the psychological schema of conscience organization and development presented above implies a belief in moral accountability. If we accept the fact that an individual has the power to inhibit immoral impulses and prevent the occurrence of wrongdoing, we can accept the notion of accountability for failure to do so without necessarily denying psychological determinism or asserting the existence of "free will." The *explanation* of his moral lapses on the basis of antecedent genic and environmental factors in his developmental history is a matter of psychological determinism; since he has no control over many of these factors no one can claim that he is a free agent in regulating his development. But the issue of whether or not he is morally accountable is an entirely different matter: it refers to something which *is* under his control, namely, the power to regulate present behavior in accordance with perceived moral obligations. Thus, regardless of events beyond his control that once transpired, if he is *presently* capable of complying with moral obligations but fails to do so, he is accountable for his misdeeds. The vast majority of immoral and delinquent acts are committed under conditions where there is clear awareness of a moral issue and reasonable opportunity for exercising adequate inhibitory control.

This issue would hardly concern us except for the fact that liability to punishment for morally culpable behavior is an integral rather than an arbitrary component of the notion of moral obligation which children interiorize in the course of moral development. Hence, if we followed the prevailing opinion of social scientists and only instituted therapy for

*For a full discussion of the writer's views on this subject see pages 465-471.[2]

immorality, immoral behavior would be indistinguishable from other behavior disorders and the very basis of conscience would be jeopardized.

Significance of Religion in Moral Development

Because religion is inextricably bound up with other environmental factors, it is difficult to isolate its impact on the development of children. Church membership and religious observance are intimately related to social class status and affect the social standing and character reputation of the child and his family.[38] It is also virtually impossible to separate religious from moral values in most cultures. Even if a child receives no formal religious instruction he is still influenced indirectly by religious precepts in his home training, secular schooling, peer group experience, and exposure to mass media. Partly for this reason and partly because of problems of measurement it is extremely difficult to assess the effect of religion on children's moral conduct and development. This becomes immediately apparent if we attempt to use extent of religious instruction or observance as our measure of the independent variable in the latter relationship. For some children religious observance is perfunctory and religious doctrine is almost completely divorced from everyday life; to other children religion is an important consideration in determining moral choice and regulating interpersonal relationships. Thus, the fact that children who attend Sunday school are only negligibly more honest and helpful than children who do not[36] only tells us that religious *observance* is not highly correlated with moral conduct— not that religious *belief* and moral behavior are unrelated. In fact, just the opposite is indicated by findings that Mennonite children ascribe religious values to more life situations and more moral authority to the church than non-Mennonite children,[50] and that adolescents in a particular closely-knit Lutheran community have very high reputations for honesty and reliability despite relatively low social status.[38]

We have little direct evidence regarding developmental changes in children's religious beliefs. Extrapolating from comparable trends in their value and moral development and from trends in adolescent religious development[3] however, it would be reasonable to suppose that with increasing age such beliefs become less concrete, literal, dogmatic and ritualistic, and more abstract, tolerant, and concerned with intentions as opposed to practices.

FANTASY LIFE

The fantasy life of the child provides an excellent behavioral mirror of the trends that are central in his personality organization. Partly uninhibited by conventional considerations and by the stylized restraints of reality, it reveals his basic needs, feelings, attitudes and aspirations. Under the inclusive heading of fantasy we shall consider the child's own imaginary productions and make-believe as well as his response to the structured presentations of vicarious experience that he encounters in cultural art forms and in the various mass media. Culturally generated fantasy obviously has close ties to reality since it must be intelligible to a large number of persons with diverse experiential backgrounds. Individual fantasy productions, on the other hand, may be quite private and unshared and, hence, more completely in the realm of irreality. Although common observation indicates that children possess the rudiments of fantasy life prior to the advent of language, the latter development coincides with an abrupt spurt in imaginative activity.[63]

Significance of Fantasy in Development

The role of fantasy in the economy of children's personality development may be summarized under the following seven functions: First, by identifying with glamorous, historical and public figures (hero worship), or by daydreaming about their own imaginary exploits, children have a readily available source of either derived or primary status (see p. 303). A substantial percentage of the daydreams of children between the ages of five and twelve deal with the general theme of self-glorification.[46] Second, fantasy constitutes an inexhaustible source of vicarious experience that immeasurably extends in time and space the child's sphere of interaction with persons, objects and events. Mass media, for example, bring him into contact with the standards and interpersonal behaviors of the wider community at an age when he would ordinarily be limited to the home and immediate neighborhood. Hence, fantasy plays a significant role in increasing the child's level of social sophistication, in desatellization, and in the devaluation of parents (see p. 402). Third, as already pointed out, mass media influence the kinds of values that are interiorized and the inhibitory potential of moral obligation; and insofar as they broaden the base of moral values, they counteract moral absolutism and facilitate the transfer of moral authority to the wider community (see p. 402).

Fourth, and perhaps most important, the different media of fantasy available in a culture serve as a device for socializing children. They communicate approved values and ways of behaving in interpersonal situations, indicate when rewards and punishments may be anticipated, and familiarize children with the various age, sex and status roles they will encounter in others as well as the ones they are expected to learn themselves. Content analysis of children's textbooks, for example, shows that they perform all of the latter functions.[15] In a more active sense, spontaneously generated fantasy also provides much of the raw material for children's play and affords opportunity for learning necessary techniques of social interaction. In such play situations children acquire practice in exercising self-control, in accepting socially imposed restrictions, and in learning the social amenities. By shifting roles rapidly they improve their understanding of others' points of view, of reciprocal obligations, and of the rules of the game.

Fantasy also has adaptive, problem solving, and adjustive functions.[12] It provides the child with an opportunity for formulating and articulating his personal problems in a nonthreatening setting, and allows him to experiment with and perfect different kinds of solutions before he is required to commit himself to a course of action in real life. The mass media are also helpful in this regard. They suggest different adaptive possibilities and, by offering vivid contrasts between reality and irreality, help him to differentiate between them. To the extent that they are unrealistically sanguine,[15] however, they may also generate confusion and false expectations. In the area of adjustment, fantasy makes possible compensatory gratification of frustrated needs[46] and vicarious expression of repressed hostility, thereby reducing the total load of frustration in everyday life. Through this medium the child can embroider the drab and distasteful aspects of his real world or even escape completely from them for a while. He can overcome his fears by desensitizing himself to them in imaginary play and can reduce anxiety by pretesting solutions to anticipated threats to his self-esteem. By the same token he may also magnify groundless sources of apprehension by rehearsing unsuccessful solutions.

Finally, through the experience gained in fantasy behavior the child advances in intellectual and motor development. The practice he acquires this way in motor skills and in the manipulation of language and ideas is no less efficacious in promoting development because it is vicarious rather than real. As a matter of fact most of this vicarious experience would be unavailable to him in real life because of limitations in status, ability and opportunity.

Fantasy and Reality

Although it is undoubtedly true that reality and fantasy are less well differentiated by young children than by older individuals,[69] the former by no means confuse the two states as readily as is commonly believed or as seems evident at first glance. In *play* settings, for example, they will "eat" small cardboard squares with as much relish as genuine candy;[75] but this does not mean that they *really* think the cardboard *is* candy. When invited in *serious* situations to eat the cardboard represented as candy, 50 per cent of three year olds rejected it completely, 40 per cent accepted it on a trial basis and then rejected it, and 10 per cent played with it "according to its own nature."[75] Older preschool children were even more emphatic in this situation: 70 per cent rejected it completely and 30 per cent treated it as a toy; none attempted to eat it.

At all ages the play of children is primarily concerned with portrayal of and participation in real life situations. They use their imaginations less to create an unreal world than to play at enacting real roles, to simulate reality, and to fill in gaps for objects and capacities they lack. During the elementary school period children generally prefer reading materials that treat the natural world factually and objectively to sentimentalized accounts that abound in whimsy and personification.[91] The effects of mass media fantasies on children's behavior are greatest when the latter feel that the stories have actually occurred in real life, are less intense when they only feel that the stories *could* occur, and are least intense when they believe the stories could not happen at all.[12]

"Adult Discount"

The term, "adult discount," has been used to characterize the diminished responsiveness of older children to dramatic situations that are exciting to their younger contemporaries.[12, 21, 24] This development may be attributed in part to more mature aesthetic standards and to greater social sophistication, in the light of which juvenile drama appears implausible and unconvincing.[12] These two factors are not unrelated since children who show greater maturity of aesthetic taste are also more critical in judging the reality reference of dramatic material.[12] They are less willing to accept the characterization of persons in blacks and whites, the use of exaggerated plots, and the epitomization of complex feelings in simple symbols.* Ability to predict what will happen also enters into "adult discount." Repeated exposure to the same dramatic situation results in progressively less intense physiological responses that are indicative of emotional excitement.[21] Similarly the typical cowboy thriller exerts most emotional impact on young, unsophisticated children[12, 18, 24] who are least familiar with the stereotyped pattern of action sequences. However, when the script is edited and provided with a novel ending, even the behavior of older children seems to be affected.[12] Familiarity and reality reference are partially interdependent factors. To seem plausible a drama must be somewhat familiar; but after a certain point of stereotypy is reached it may seem implausible no matter how real it is. On the other hand, a real life story that is completely unfamiliar is also apt to appear unreal and unconvincing.[12]

Two additional developmental factors must be considered in explaining "adult discount."[24] First, older children respond less to separate incidents

*The symbols that children use in their own fantasy productions also neither have uniform psychological significance for all individuals nor retain a constant meaning for the same child from one developmental stage to another. Hence, Freudian systems of fantasy interpretation[17] that rely on a table of universal and fixed symbolic equivalents to decipher the meaning of children's play, dreams, or artwork tend to lack logical validity.

in a dramatic presentation than to the plot as a whole.[18] This greater "ability to encompass a plot as a unified whole" also enables them to predict more accurately the ensuing course of action.[24] Second, older children adopt a more detached attitude to dramatic situations. They are more able to objectify a narrative and to react to it as entertainment rather than as something happening to themselves—to perceive it as a representation of reality rather than as reality itself.[18]

Age level differences in mass media interests generally illustrate the above developmental trends in fantasy life. Older children gradually acquire reading tastes for adult fiction and drama, history, science and biography[30, 60] as their fascination for adventure, mystery, sports, animals, and home life wanes.[53] The same trends also hold true for radio and movie interests.[60] However, sex differences in reading interests are greater than age differences and differences between the bright and dull.[67, 83] Boys are much more interested in themes of adventure and mystery, whereas girls prefer emotional fiction dealing with home and school life;[60, 79] similar sex differences are found in radio and movie interests.[60]

In recent years television viewing has largely supplanted interest in movies, books, comics and the radio,[61] but has interfered less with other recreational interests such as scouting, dancing, music, dramatics, and athletics.[16] It has tended to increase the amount of shared recreation in the home, but in a passive and parallel rather than in an interactive direction.[61] Although it has been accepted as a wholesome influence by the vast majority of parents, its effects are apparently regarded less critically by lower-class groups.[16] In general it has caused greatest change in the recreational patterns of children from low-income homes.[16]

Other Trends in Aesthetic Development

Paralleling the enculturative trend in the development of other values (see p. 383), the aesthetic standards of children gradually approach adult norms. In many instances, of course, such as preference for differently proportioned rectangles[81] and for facial proportions,[78] the basis for choice is purely arbitrary and represents the cumulative effects of repeated incidental exposure to and familiarity with socially approved standards.[81] In the case of artistic[25, 32] and literacy preferences,[30, 96] changes in taste are partly a matter of "adult discount" and partly a reflection of more deliberate indoctrination. Aesthetic standards in children can be improved by a guided series of experiences combining objective exercises and explanation.[89]

Color and familiarity of content are the most important determinants of children's artistic preferences during the preschool period.[41] During the elementary school years, however, subject matter and trueness to life become more important considerations.[52, 72] Children in the latter age group also prefer traditional to abstract paintings.[5, 51] This preference is positively correlated with chronological age, I.Q., and socioeconomic status,[51] but is modifiable in part by exposure to expert opinion.[5] As might easily be predicted, maturity of aesthetic judgment is related to verbal intelligence in both art[85] and literature.[14]

INTERESTS

Interests are highly significant organizers of the psychological field. As already pointed out (see p. 309), the psychological field of any individual may be divided into different concentric zones reflective of varying degrees of intensity of ego-involvement. The more central zones are areas of concern and importance to him. He has a vital stake in them. What happens in these areas is a source of feeling pride or shame, success or failure. He becomes perceptually and cognitively sensitized to these segments of the environment. Hence, in contrast to peripheral zones, they tend to become highly differentiated. It is important to realize, however, that this map only identifies areas of concern (interests) and does not make explicit the motives for concern (see p. 309). It is also important to avoid confusing frequency of mention with saliency, an error that is commonly made in questionnaire studies (see p. 154).

Factors accounting for developmental changes in interests may be either psychobiological or psychosocial in nature. The first category includes determinants that are intercultural in distribution, i.e., various aspects of cognitive, motor, social and aesthetic development that bring about universal normative shifts in interest patterns. On a priori grounds, for example, one might reasonably suppose that the developmental changes associated with "adult discount" are not restricted to our own culture. In the second category belong factors that are more specific to a given social environment and account for differences among cultures, subcultures and social classes. Sex differences in interest patterns, for example, are probably more reflective of institutionalized concepts of social sex role than of differences in physical strength, motor skills and temperamental predispositions. Since changes in mass media interests have been discussed elsewhere (see p. 409), we shall only consider play and school interests here.

During infancy and early childhood, as Jersild[45] points out, what a child does and is interested in doing are almost completely a reflection of what he is *able* to do. Later, opportunity, stimulation, and differential reward become increasingly important. Thus the older child exercises only *some* of his potential capacities, and his *expressed* interests can no longer be considered coextensive with the potential range of interests he is capable of developing with appropriate stimulation. For these reasons, the current widespread tendency to regard only the expressed and "endogenously derived" needs of the child as genuine and representative of his "true" needs and capacities is hardly defensible on logical grounds.

With increasing age children indulge less in crude make-believe games such as dolls and cowboys and develop a greater taste for sedentary as well as active games.[54, 88] Solitary games increase in popularity.[54] The total number of activities engaged in decreases, since many gross muscular skills which younger children pursue as ends in themselves (e.g., running, jumping, dodging) become incorporated into more complex team sports such as baseball.[54] At all ages marked sex differences prevail. Boys' games are more strenuous, organized, competitive and variable (football, shooting, building, wrestling); girls' games are more sedentary, conservative, and concerned with persons rather than things (dolls, "house," dressing up, cooking, knitting.[79] Despite the increasing segregation of the sexes during middle childhood a certain amount of overlapping occurs. The overlapping more frequently involves an invasion of boys' interests by girls[53, 54] (girls' interest in baseball, rough games and boys' books) than vice versa. For both sexes there is a marked decline in liking for academic school subjects during the elementary and junior high school years with a concomitant increase in preference for the social, athletic, and prevocational (e.g., mechanical and industrial arts) aspects of school life.[47]

The influence of gross social and cultural factors on the development of interests is self-evident. Differences in the physical environment, in the availability of recreational materials and participants and, most important, in the prevailing values, conventions, and expectations of the cultural group impose many specific characteristics on the general developmental picture. Rural children, for example, participate more in solitary, out-of-doors, and collecting activities and are required by the low density of population to play less organized and less formal games embracing a wider age range of participants. Social class and racial differences in interest patterns reflect discrepancies in purchasing power as well as broader differences in values. *Interindividual* differences in interest patterns are related to variability in abilities, in those aspects of personality determining selectivity in tastes, and in the types of activities that are encouraged and rewarded by significant persons in each child's familial, school and peer group environment. Original proclivities for certain activities perpetuate themselves by leading to successful and satisfying experiences, frequent practice, and hence to greater enhancement of the relevant ability or trait. Hence, through canalization, perceptual sensitization, and progressive differentiation of the psychological field, increasing selectivity in the organization of interests becomes a characteristic feature of psychological development. Through the gradual acquisition of dislikes, on the basis of what is incompatible with central values, interest patterns also become more self-consistent* (see p. 101).

Interest and I.Q. are reciprocally related. A certain minimal degree of intelligence is obviously required to pursue various intellectual activities successfully and enjoyably. Bright children, for example, engage in more intellectual hobbies, do more extracurricular reading, and have more mature reading interests than their duller contemporaries.[54, 67, 80, 83] Other things being equal, children tend to develop those interests that they can prosecute most successfully. The interests of a child, in turn, play an important role in the later differentiation of his cognitive abilities, i.e., in determining the particular areas that will be maximally or minimally developed (see p. 590).

REFERENCES

1. Ausubel, D. P.: Prestige motivation of gifted children. *Genet. Psychol. Monogr.* 43: 53-117, 1951.

2. ———: *Ego Development and the Personality Disorders.* New York, Grune & Stratton, 1952.

3. ———: *Theory and Problems of Adolescent Development.* New York, Grune & Stratton, 1954.

4. ———: Relationships between shame and guilt in the socializing process. *Psychol. Rev.* 62: 378-390, 1955.

5. ———, DeWit, F., Golden, B., and Schpoont, S. H.: Prestige suggestion in children's art preferences. *J. Genet. Psychol.* 89: 85-93, 1956.

6. Bartlett, E. R., and Harris, D. B.: Personality factors in delinquency. *School & Soc.* 43: 653-656, 1936.

7. Bavelas, A.: A method for investigating individual and group ideology. *Sociometry* 5: 371-377, 1942.

8. Benedict, R.: *Patterns of Culture.* Boston, Houghton Mifflin, 1934.

9. ———: *The Chrysanthemum and the Sword.* Boston, Houghton Mifflin, 1946.

10. Berenda, R. W.: *The Influence of the Group on the Judgments of Children.* New York, King's Crown Press, 1950.

11. Blumer, H., and Hauser, P. M.: *Movies, Delinquency and Crime.* New York, Macmillan, 1934.

12. Brodbeck, A. J.: The mass-media as a socializing agency. Paper read at *Am. Psychol. Assoc.,* San Francisco, September 1955.

13. Brown, A. W., Morrison, J., and Couch, G. B.: Influence of affectional family relationships on character development. *J. Abnorm. Soc. Psychol.* 42: 422-428, 1947.

14. Burton, D. L.: The relationship of literary appreciation to certain measurable factors. *J. Educ. Psychol.* 43: 436-439, 1952.

15. Child, I. L., Potter, E. H., and Levine, E. M.: Children's textbooks and personality development; an exploration in the social psychology of education. *Psychol. Monogr.* 60: No. 3, 1946.

*See L. E. Tyler, *J. Genet. Psychol. 86*: 33-44, 1955.

16. Coffin, T. E.: Television's impact on society. *Am. Psychologist 10*: 630-641, 1955.

17. Davidson, A., and Fay, J.: *Phantasy in Childhood.* New York, Philosophical Library, 1953.

18. DeBoer, J. J.: The emotional responses of children to radio drama. Unpublished doctor's dissertation, Univ. of Chicago, 1938.

19. Dolger, L., and Ginandes, J.: Children's attitude toward discipline as related to socioeconomic status. *J. Exper. Educ. 15*: 161-165, 1946.

20. Duncker, K.: Modification of children's food preferences through social suggestion. *J. Abnorm. Soc. Psychol. 33*: 487-507, 1938.

21. Dysinger, W., and Ruckmick, C. A.: *The Emotional Responses of Children to the Motion Picture Situation.* New York, Macmillan, 1933.

22. Eberhart, J. C.: Attitudes toward property: a genetic study by the paired-comparisons rating of offenses. *J. Genet. Psychol. 60*: 3-35, 1942.

23. Fite, M. D.: Aggressive behavior in young children and children's attitudes toward aggression. *Genet. Psychol. Monogr. 22*: 151-319, 1940.

24. Freidson, E.: Adult discount: an aspect of children's changing taste. *Child Develop. 24*: 39-49, 1953.

25. French, J. E.: Children's preferences for pictures of varied complexity of pictorial pattern. *Elem. Sch. J. 53*: 90-95, 1952.

26. Freud, S.: *The Ego and the Id.* London, Hogarth, 1935.

27. Fromm, E.: *Man for Himself.* New York, Rinehart, 1947.

28. Gesell, A., and Ilg, F. L.: *The Child from Five to Ten.* New York, Harper, 1946.

29. Glueck, S., and Glueck, E.: *Unravelling Juvenile Delinquency.* New York, Commonwealth Fund, 1950.

30. Gray, W. S.: Reading. In *Child Development and the Curriculum,* 38th Yearbook, Natl. Soc. Stud. Educ. Chicago, University of Chicago Press, 1939.

31. Griffiths, W.: *Behavior Difficulties of Children as Perceived and Judged by Parents, Teachers and Children Themselves.* Minneapolis, University of Minnesota Press, 1952.

32. Gunthorp, J. M.: Aesthetic maturity. *J. Genet. Psychol. 57*: 207-210, 1940.

33. Harris, D. B., Rose, A. M., Clark, K. E., and Valasek, F.: Personality differences between responsible and less responsible children. *J. Genet. Psychol. 87*: 103-109, 1955.

34. Harrower, M. R.: Social status and the moral development of the child. *Brit. J. Educ. Psychol. 4*: 75-95, 1934.

35. Hartley, R. E., Frank, L. K., and Goldenson, R. M.: *Understanding Children's Play.* New York, Columbia University Press, 1952.

36. Hartshorne, H., May, M. A., et al: Studies in the nature of character. I. *Studies in Deceit.* II. *Studies in Self-control.* III. *Studies in the Organization of Character.* New York, Macmillan, 1930.

37. Havighurst, R. J., Robinson, M. Z., and Dorr, M.: The development of the ideal self in childhood and adolescence. *J. Educ. Res. 40*: 241-257, 1946.

38. ———, and Taba, H.: *Adolescent Character and Personality.* New York, Wiley, 1949.

39. Healey, W., and Bronner, A. F.: *New Light on Delinquency and Its Treatment.* New Haven, Yale University Press, 1936.

40. ———, and ———: What makes a child delinquent? In *Juvenile Delinquency and the Schools,* 47th Yearbook, Natl. Soc. Stud. Educ. Chicago, University of Chicago Press, 1948, part 1.

41. Hildreth, G. H.: Color and picture choices of young children. *J. Genet. Psychol.* *49*: 427-435, 1936.

42. Hill, D. S.: Personification of ideals by urban children. *J. Soc. Psychol. 1*: 379-393, 1930.

43. Hirschberg, G., and Gilliland, A. I.: Parent-child relationships in attitude. *J. Abnorm. Soc. Psychol. 37*: 125-130, 1942.

44. Hoult, T. F.: Comic books and juvenile delinquency. *Sociol. Soc. Res. 33*: 279-284, 1949.

45. Jersild, A. T.: *Child Psychology,* ed. 3. New York, Prentice-Hall, 1947.

46. ———, Markey, F. V., and Jersild, C. L.: Children's fears, dreams, wishes, day-dreams, likes, dislikes, pleasant and unpleasant memories. *Child Develop. Monogr.* No. 12, 1933.

47. ———, and Tasch, R.: *Children's Interests.* New York, Teachers College. Columbia University, 1949.

48. Jones, V.: *Character and Citizenship Gaining in the Public School.* Chicago, University of Chicago Press, 1936.

49. ———: Character development in children—an objective approach. *In* L. Carmichael, Ed., *Manual of Child Psychology,* ed. 2. New York, Wiley, 1954, pp. 781-832.

50. Kalhorn, J.: Values and sources of authority among rural children. *Univ. Iowa Stud. Child Welf. 20*: 99-151, 1944.

51. Katz, E.: *Children's Preferences for Traditional and Modern Paintings.* New York, Teachers College, Columbia University, 1944.

52. Lark-Horovitz, B.: On art appreciation of children. I. Preference of picture subjects in general. *J. Educ. Res. 31*: 118-137, 1937-1938.

53. Lazar, M.: *Reading Interests, Activities and Opportunities of Bright, Average, and Dull Children.* New York, Teachers College, Columbia University, 1937.

54. Lehman, H. C., and Witty, P. A.: A study of play in relation to pubescence. *J. Soc. Psychol. 1*: 510-523, 1930.

55. Leighton, D., and Kluckhohn, C.: *Children of the People.* Cambridge, Mass., Harvard University Press, 1947.

56. Lerner, E.: *Constraint Areas and the Moral Judgment of Children.* Menasha, Wis., Banta, 1937.

57. ———: The problem of perspective in moral reasoning. *Am. J. Sociol. 43*: 249-269, 1937.

58. Liu, C. H.: The influence of cultural background on the moral judgment of children. Unpublished doctor's dissertation, Columbia University, 1950.

59. Lockhard, E. G.: The attitude of children toward certain laws. *Relig. Educ. 25*: 144-149, 1930.

60. Lyness, P. I.: Patterns in the mass communication tastes of young audience. *J. Educ. Psychol. 42*: 449-467, 1951.

61. Maccoby, E. E.: Television: its impact on school children. *Publ. Opin. Quart. 15*: 421-444, 1951.

62. MacRae, D.: A test of Piaget's theories of moral development. *J. Abnorm. Soc. Psychol. 49*: 14-18, 1954.

63. Markey, F. V.: Imaginative behavior in preschool children. *Child Develop. Monogr.* No. 18, 1935.

64. Mead, M.: Some anthropological considerations concerning guilt. *In* M. L. Reymert, Ed., *Feelings and Emotions.* New York, McGraw-Hill, 1950, pp. 362-373.

65. Messerschmidt, R.: The suggestibility of boys and girls between the ages of six and sixteen years. *J. Genet. Psychol. 43*: 422-437, 1933.

66. Nichols, C. A.: *Moral Education Among North American Indians.* New York, Teachers College, Columbia University, 1930.

67. Norvell, G. W.: *The Reading Interests of Young People.* Boston, Heath, 1950.

68. Owen, M. B.: The intelligence of the institutionalized juvenile delinquent. *J. Juv. Res. 21*: 199-206, 1937.

69. Piaget, J.: *The Moral Judgment of the Child.* New York, Harcourt, Brace, 1932.

70. Pressey, S. L., and Robinson, F. P.: *Psychology and the New Education.* New York, Harper, 1944.

71. Reymert, M. L., and Kohn, H. A.: An objective investigation of suggestibility. *Char. & Pers. 9*: 44-48, 1940.

72. Rudisill, M.: Children's preferences for color versus other qualities in illustrations. *Elem. Sch. J. 52*: 444-451, 1952.

73. Sanford, R. N., et al.: Physique, personality and scholarship. A Cooperative study of school children. *Monogr. Soc. Res. Child Develop. 8*: No. 1, 1943.

74. Slaght, W. E.: Untruthfulness in children: its conditioning factors and its setting in child nature. *Univ. Iowa Stud. Charact. 1*: No. 4, 1928.

75. Sliosberg, S.: A contribution to the dynamics of substitution in serious and play situations. *Psychol. Forsch. 19*: 122-181, 1934.

76. Stendler, C. B.: A study of some socio-moral judgments of junior high school students. *Child Develop. 20*: 15-29, 1949.

77. Strauss, A. L.: The development of conceptions of rules in children. *Child Develop. 25*: 193-204, 1954.

78. Taylor, C., and Thompson, G. G.: Age trends in preferences for certain facial proportions. *Child Develop. 26*: 97-102, 1955.

79. Terman, L. M., and Tyler, L. E.: Psychological sex differences. *In* L. Carmichael, Ed., *Manual of Child Psychology,* ed. 2. New York, Wiley, 1954, pp. 1064-1114.

80. Terman, L. M., et al.: *Mental and Physical Traits of a Thousand Gifted Children.* Stanford, Calif., Stanford University Press, 1925.

81. Thompson, G. G.: The effect of chronological age on aesthetic preferences for rectangles of different proportions. *J. Exper. Psychol. 36*: 50-58, 1946.

82. Thetford, W. N., Molish, H. B., and Beck, S. J.: Developmental aspects of personality structure in normal children. *J. Proj. Tech. 15*: 58-78, 1951.

83. Thorndike, R. L.: *Comparative Study of Children's Reading Interests.* New York, Teachers College, Columbia University, 1941.

84. Thurstone, L. L.: Influence of motion pictures on children's attitudes. *J. Soc. Psychol. 2*: 291-305, 1931.

85. Tiebout, C., and Meier, N. C.: Artistic ability and general intelligence. *Psychol. Monogr. 48*: 95-125, 1936.

86. Tudor-Hart, B. E.: Are there cases in which lies are necessary? *Ped. Sem. 33*: 586-641, 1926.

87. Ugurel-Semin, R.: Moral behavior and moral judgment of children. *J. Abnorm. Soc. Psychol 47*: 463-474, 1952.

88. Van Alstyne, D.: *Play Behavior and Choice of Play Materials of Preschool Children.* Chicago, University of Chicago Press, 1932.

89. Voss, M. D.: A study of conditions affecting the functioning of the art appreciation process at the child level. *Psychol. Monogr. 48*: 1-39, 1936.

90. Whiting, J. W. M., and Child, I. L.: *Child Training and Personality.* New Haven, Yale University Press, 1953.

91. Williams, A. M.: Children's choices in science books. *Child Develop. Monogr.* No. 27, 1939.

92. Winterbottom, M. R.: The relation of childhood training in independence to achievement motivation. Unpublished doctor's dissertation, Univ. of Michigan, 1953.

93. Witryol, S. L.: Age trends in children's evaluation of teacher-approved and teacher-disapproved behavior. *Genet. Psychol. Monogr. 41*: 271-326, 1950.

94. Wittman, M. P., and Huffman, A. V.: A comparative study of developmental, adjustive, and personality characteristics of psychotic, psychoneurotic, delinquent, and normally-adjusted teen-age youths. *J. Genet. Psychol. 66*: 167-182, 1945.

95. Witty, P. A.: Two studies of children's interest in TV. *Elem. Engl. 29*: 251-257, 1952.

96. ——, Coomer, A., and McBean, D.: Children's choices of favorite books: a study conducted in ten elementary schools. *J. Educ. Psychol. 37*: 266-278, 1946.

97. Wright, B. A.: Altruism in children and the perceived conduct of others. *J. Abnorm. Soc. Psychol. 37*: 218-233, 1942.

98. Zucker, H. J.: Affectional identification and delinquency. *Arch. Psychol.* No. 286, 1943.

CHAPTER 13

Psychosocial Aspects of
Personality Development

We have used the term "psychosocial" to refer to certain relatively plastic, socially determined aspects of development that are *approximately* uniform for all individuals sharing a common cultural tradition and are different for individuals coming from diverse cultural environments. Acceptance of such intracultural uniformities (or intercultural differences), however, does not imply endorsement of the extreme relativistic view that personality development is *completely* unique in every culture (that no intercultural uniformities exist), or that it is *completely* uniform for all individuals within a given culture. Nevertheless, differences among even primitive cultures in relevant factors affecting personality development are very widely dispersed[88]; and because of meaningful and self-consistent relationships among component facets of a "custom complex,"[127] such differences also tend to be distributed in systematic fashion.[88]

Insistence on the only *approximately* uniform nature of psychosocial traits rests on more than the fact that each individual experiences a somewhat idiosyncratic version of cultural reality (see pp. 73 and 79). Few customs or institutions apply without exception to all members of a culture; and in complex cultures such as our own, the social environment is differentiated into a number of partially self-contained subcultures on the basis of caste, social class and ethnic origin, each defining in distinctive and semi-restrictive ways both value alternatives and the determining conditions of personality development. Thus, for example, the concept of "national character" is valid only as long as (a) one appreciates that in addition to uniformities referable to a common heritage of customs, traditions, and social institutions, there is also much intranational subcultural variability, and (b) one does not assume in the absence of adequate control data that a specific item or constellation of childhood experiences is *causally* related to distinctive features of adult personality.

Our task in this chapter will be to consider: (1) certain general problems of psychosocial personality development (i.e., mediation of cultural influences; determinants and mechanisms of transmitting psychosocial traits); (2) the impact of specific socializing agencies and conditions other than family (Chapter 11) and peer group (Chapter 14) on the personality development of children, i.e., caste, social class, school; and (3) psychosocial aspects of biological and social sex role. Much of this material, of course, has already been discussed in detail in other contexts, and need only be referred to or summarized here in relation to these three issues. Generally speaking, we shall use our own American culture to illustrate development of psychosocial traits, since this culture is most familiar to the majority of readers.* Wherever necessary, for purposes of contrast, brief reference will be made to other cultures.

INDIRECT MEDIATION OF CULTURAL INFLUENCES

The relationship between social experience and personality development is seldom immediate or direct. Social variables exert their influence indirectly by implicating ego values and aspirations and by modifying ego structure. It is true, of course, that either social or physiological stimuli can instigate behavior directly without involving ego structure; but these effects merely constitute peripheral, transitory and situational fluctuations in the diurnal stream of behavior. Long-lasting normative change in personality development only results when ego structure undergoes substantial modification or reorganization; and typically such reorganization becomes necessary following significant shifts in biosocial status.

Perception, as already pointed out (see p. 276), also acts as a mediating mechanism interposed between social stimulus content and the ultimate content of awareness that actually influences behavior and development. Cognitive maturity is one of the most crucial components of this perceptual process since it determines the child's capacity to respond to social stimuli of varying degrees of sophistication. Cognitive immaturity either insulates him from a large portion of the social world that has relatively uniform perceptual significance for older individuals in his culture, or makes him misperceive it in ways that are congruent with his ego structure and existing level of sophistication (see p. 277). With advancing age and perceptual maturity, however, he is brought into more direct and realistic contact with the social environment. His empathic ability in interpreting interpersonal feelings[36] and expressions of emotion[45, 122] improves, as well as his ability to verbalize and discriminate traits he likes and dislikes in others,[4, 66] to forecast his own and others' sociometric status (see p. 470), and to recognize the relevant symbols of social class status.[112].

The influence of cultural variables on personality development may also

*The same procedure has been and will continue to be followed in considering psychobiological problems. Universally distributed aspects of emotional, ego, moral, cognitive, and motor development can be rendered most comprehensible to the typical reader of this book by considering their manifestations in the contemporary American child.

be considered indirect in the sense that especially in his early formative years, when much socialization takes place, the child's exposure to his culture is largely buffered by the nuclear family group. Partly for this reason, but mostly because of perceptual immaturity and the centrality of psychobiological aspects of development, few differential effects of cultural influence are observable during the first year of life. But as the child is gradually introduced to play group, school, and mass media, he tends to break out of the limiting confines of the family circle and its biased interpretation of the culture. Through increased, broadened, and more direct contact with the wider community, he acquires more first-hand and sophisticated knowledge of social institutions and of caste and class differences in our mosaic-like culture. Acclimitization to the wider community takes place earlier and with greater ease and continuity in cultures where the child visits frequently and is warmly received in other households (e.g., Arapesh, Samoan), and in cultures characterized by an extended family group (e.g., Navaho).

SOURCES OF PSYCHOSOCIAL TRAITS

Two basic problems pervade the study of personality-in-culture. First, how is variability in cultural values, customs, and institutions related to significant intercultural variability in personality structure? What aspects of cultural diversity are related in what ways to characteristic intercultural differences in behavioral orientation? Second, what developmental mechanisms account for the *transmission* of such differences? Through what media do distinctive cultural factors operate to influence personality development differentially so that the child eventually becomes a reasonable facsimile of the modal adult in his culture? We are, in other words, inquiring into (a) the sources or determinants of psychosocial traits, and (b) the vehicles through which such traits are transmitted in the process of enculturation.* In a very real sense these two problems are interrelated. Differential child rearing practices, for example, may simultaneously serve as a source and as a means of transmitting intercultural variability in personality structure. For purposes of analysis, however, it is helpful to consider each problem separately. Since the limiting determinants of psychosocial variability are rather self-evident (see p. 73), the present discussion of the first problem will be restricted to patterning sources.

The culture patterns or differentiates both emotions and primary drives

Enculturation refers to the processes whereby a child acquires the distinctive (psychosocial) behavior patterns of his culture. *Socialization* is a more inclusive term encompassing the effects of *all* social variables on personality development. Hence it includes the acquisition of culturally conditioned traits that are distributed universally (psychobiological) as well as of psychosocial traits. Herskovits[59] uses the two terms to distinguish between adaptation to culture and society respectively.

(i.e., drives in which physiological instigators are especially salient). It helps determine the excitants and the typical occasions under which such drives and emotions are aroused, the particular goal objects or activities that gratify drives, the characteristic kinds of drive reducing responses that are made, the specific ways in which emotions are expressed, the opportunities available for gratification or expression, and the need for repression and deferred or disguised expression. As already pointed out, it is drive determinants and drive responses that are learned in the course of socialization rather than drives per se (see p. 226). In quite similar fashion the culture also patterns sensory and aesthetic preferences and preferred modes of adjustment to difficult situations.

The differential value system of a culture is a basic source of psychosocial traits and of modal personality structure. It determines in part such culturally conditioned aspects of motivation as level and object of striving; relative need for primary as against derived status; desire for ego aggrandizement, hierarchical status and volitional independence; goal frustration tolerance; and level of anxiety referable to ego enhancement. Cultures vary greatly with respect to the kinds of personality traits that are idealized and encouraged and the severity of expectations regarding criteria of adult maturity, i.e., expected degree of executive independence, responsibility, self-critical ability, and ability to postpone hedonistic gratification. They also define the characteristic role attributes of age, sex, kinship, status, and occupation, and such generalized dimensions of interpersonal relationships as cooperativeness-competitiveness, egocentricity-sociocentricity, egoism-altruism, individualism-group mindedness, introversion-extroversion, directness-indirectness, and straightforwardness-duplicity. Such culturally distinctive role stereotypes constitute the available models that children and adolescents use in fashioning their individual role behavior and thus participate in the transmission of psychosocial traits. Lastly, stemming directly or indirectly from the cultural value system is a general *Weltanschauung* or orientation to life. This includes such items as primary life goals or interests (mercantile, spiritual, aesthetic, military, etc.), criteria for evaluating the worth of a person, general attitudes toward children, moral values and sanctions, responsiveness to time and conformity pressures, degree of reality testing, optimistic or pessimistic and casual or somber views of life.

In addition to the pervasive modeling influence of its distinctive value system, each culture exerts a characteristic *experiential* impact on the socialization of its members by virtue of the unique ways in which it institutionalizes basic interpersonal relationships. Since children actually acquire primary and derived status and feelings of security and adequacy as products of such relationships, the "transactions" associated with the individual acquisition of biosocial status are probably a more important source and vehicle of transmitting psychosocial traits than is the observation of cultural role models (see p. 278). Both factors, however—satisfying role experience and the interiorization of cultural goals and values—account for the learning of new, socially conditioned needs or drive determinants ("secondary" drives). The paradigm of the rat learning to fear a white box associated with electric shock, and being motivated by this fear to escape from it,[91] satisfactorily explains how a laboratory animal may acquire a particular fear through conditioning and how the latter may operate as a drive determinant for the learning of avoidance responses. But as a model of how children acquire the characteristic goal structure of their culture it is so alien to the actual conditions and processes underlying the acquisition of culturally derived drives (see pp. 423-425) as to lack relevance and face plausibility.*

Differential institutionalization of interpersonal experience leads to characteristic intercultural and subcultural differences in ego development. Caste and class membership and reference groups furnish an important basis for inflation or deflation of feelings of adequacy. It also makes much difference whether the young child acquires his derived status primarily from the parents as in our culture or from satellizing relationships to siblings and agemates as among the Maori[9]; whether sources of primary status are available to the child at home or only in school and peer group (see p. 303) ; whether parents or agemates are the chief socializing agents in late childhood and adolescence (see p. 304); whether resatellization and devaluation are important aspects of desatellization and value assimilation during the latter periods (see p. 305) ; whether sanctions are applied laterally or by parents. Depending on various institutionalized aspects of handling and timing shifts in children's biosocial status, much or little discontinuity in role and status may prevail between age and sex groups, and transitional periods of development may either be abrupt, prolonged, and anxiety-ridden or gradual, brief, and relatively untraumatic.

*It is true, for example, that the infant acquires conditioned feelings of insecurity when separated from the mother and that these feelings operate as a drive determinant to approach her, a response that is reinforced by the reduction of insecurity and by the satisfactions associated with her presence.[35] Avoidance of anxiety also accounts in part for the learning of other drive determinants and responses (see p. 331). Much positive motivation, however, is unrelated to anxiety avoidance (see p. 228). Furthermore, although the simple paradigm of conditioning via temporal contiguity can explain early separation anxiety from and approach responses to the mother, such complex personality phenomena as are involved in the acquisition of psychosocial drive patterns (satellization, interiorization, feelings of obligation, loyalty, and guilt) cannot be subsumed under it.

Cultures also presumably differ in the characteristic degree of parental acceptance-rejection extended to children; because of much intracultural personality variability among parents the mode of expression rather than content of this parent attitude is more likely to be successfully institutionalized.

At any particular stage in the historical development of a given culture, current political, economic and social vicissitudes exert considerable qualifying influence on the traditional pattern of psychosocial traits transmitted to the growing generation. War, depression, famine, social disorganization, acculturation pressures, technological advances and rapid social change are only some of the more striking current factors that account for historical variation in culture patterns, in the prevailing level of frustration and anxiety, and in the quality of interpersonal relations.

We have already taken pains to indicate that the influence of culturally distinctive child rearing practices as a source and a vehicle of transmitting psychosocial traits has been greatly overrated. Such practices, to begin with, could only have lasting and generalized effects on core aspects of personality if they were reflective of pervasive cultural values—not because they happened to impinge on the gratification of alleged libidinal drives (see p. 262). It is very unlikely, however, that the selection of specific child rearing techniques would consistently have the same psychological significance or reflect the same social values from one culture to another. Many overtly dissimilar practices are compatible with the realization of the same aims of upbringing, and many specific aspects of child rearing are arbitrary products of custom or historical accident and hence have little or no attitudinal significance. It is entirely possible, of course, that the general manner of administering child care (if not the presence or absence of specific practices) in a particular culture is indicative of pervasive cultural attitudes toward children; but the interpretation of such attitudes underlying the cultural prescription undoubtedly varies greatly from parent to parent and in any case is considerably modified in practice by the personality trends of individual parents. Hence, since it is extremely difficult to institutionalize cultural values through the medium of subtle culture-wide common denominators of child handling, and since it is improbable that infants and young children would be sufficiently mature cognitively to perceive their significance even if they were uniformly expressed, general features of child rearing probably constitute a more important source of idiosyncratic than of psychosocial variability.

Parent attitudes, insofar as they are reflective of cultural values, do play an important role in transmitting psychosocial traits, especially during the early years when the child's direct contact with the wider culture is minimal. But it is more credible to suppose that they do so directly through recurrent explicit and implicit indoctrination (training, precept, example, incidental exposure), reinforced by appropriate external and internal sanctions and by later experience with other socializing agents, during the entire period of childhood and adolescence, than indirectly and inferentially through the tenor of child rearing practices during infancy and early childhood.

TRANSMISSION OF PSYCHOSOCIAL TRAITS

We have already considered in another context the intracultural transmission of values in terms of external patterning factors, interiorization, and external and internal sanctions (see pp. 380-383). In general the same explanatory principles apply to the transmission of psychosocial traits since the latter are inclusive of values. The present section is intended as an addendum to the previous discussion. In a broad sense, of course, the acquisition of particular cultural patterns (socially acquired needs, drive determinants, drive responses) constitutes a relatively permanent incremental modification of behavior and hence can be considered a form of learning. Broadly conceived it involves cues, incentives, drives, responses, rewards and punishments. But since this kind of social learning is more complex and implicates more core aspects of personality than the learning of mazes, motor skills, or school information it would greatly oversimplify matters to abandon the specialized frame of reference previously adopted for this type of learning and revert to a more primitive type of analysis.

The first step in the transmission of psychosocial traits involves differential exposure to a restricted learning environment. Children in diverse cultures develop into different kinds of adults because of the cumulative effects of (a) recurrent exposure to different value systems and role models and (b) participation in different kinds of role and status experience. Interiorization and reinforcement by internal and external sanctions, as previously described (see pp. 381-383), and the action of various self-perpetuating mechanisms complete the process of transmission. In the absence of appropriate role experience, however, a child cannot possibly acquire the distinguishing personality attributes of a given cultural or sub-cultural group. On an intercultural level, restriction of experience is usually a function of simple unawareness of the existence of alternatives available in other cultures; where such awareness is not lacking, the selective interiorization of our cultural values is favored by greater primacy, frequency, reward, and saliency, and by the prestige suggestion exercised by personally significant representatives of the individual's particular reference and membership groups. Intraculturally, where the availability of role experience is restricted to particular classes of persons on an institutionalized basis, not only is the necessary experience unavailable to other persons, but the latter also do not perceive it as within their grasp and fail to develop the motivation to obtain it.

> Such status differentiations as these have the effect of defining and limiting the developmental environment of the child. Within each of these participation levels with their cultural environments, a child learns characteristic behavior and values concerning family members, sexual and aggressive acts, work, education and a career . . . These restricted learning environments are maintained by powerful and firmly established taboos upon participation outside of one's status level, . . . [by pressures] exerted not only by those above . . . but also by persons below . . . and by those in one's particular class.[28]

Appropriate age, sex, status and kinship roles are learned both experientially and by observation of culturally stereotyped role models. The influence of the latter, however, first becomes important after a minimal level of cognitive maturity is achieved. It also tends to be vitiated whenever considerable heterogeneity in perceived social norms is present (see p. 353). With increasing age, despite growing ability to generalize from one situation to another, roles tend to become more specific and more rigidly defined. This trend reflects progressively greater differentiation of role behavior as well as the cultural tendency to compartmentalize roles and ignore contradictions between them. Hence the child is conditioned not to perceive role inconsistencies emanating from contradictory values of the different reference groups from which they are derived. Each role merely reigns supreme in its separate domain. If attempts at reconciliation are made, one role may be selected and the others repressed or rejected, or several conflicting roles may be subsumed under a more inclusive loyalty.[55]

> The transmission of differential class levels of aspiration* is achieved by the maintenance [in] the individual of a certain level of anxiety with regard to the attainment of the required behavior for *his status*. This socialized anxiety plays a major role in propelling him along that culture route prescribed by his family, school, and later by adult society at his cultural level . . . Anxiety leads to striving because only thus can anxiety be reduced to a tolerable level . . . The anxiety which middle-status [children] learn is effective, first, because it involves the threat of loss of present status [and the severe social penalties associated therewith], and, second, because it leads as the individual may plainly see in 'successful persons' to the rewards of power [and] . . . social prestige[28] . . . The class goals in education, occupation, and status are made to appear real, valuable, and certain to him because he actually begins to experience in his school, clique, and family life some of the prestige responses. The lower-class child, however, learns by *not* being rewarded in these prestige relationships that the middle-class goals and gains are neither likely nor desirable for one in his position.[25]

*Interiorization and other internal and external sanctions also operate similarly here as in the transmission of values (see pp. 381-383).

Finally, once established, psychosocial traits tend to be perpetuated by the same mechanisms that account for the long-range stability of idiosyncratic traits, i.e., continued exposure to the same environment, inertia, perceptual sensitization, "perceptual constancy," "categorical perception," symbolization, and the organizing effects of central dimensions of personality (see pp. 97-100). Individuals in a particular culture become selectively sensitized to perceive only a restricted sphere of their physical and social environments, and because of a common set of values, beliefs and attitudes toward life tend to "develop a characteristic way of perceiving reality"[117] and to structure the world along perceptually uniform lines.[51, 117] Part of this perceptual standardization is a function of common symbolical and conceptual categories into which raw sensory experience is fitted by cultural convention.[51] These self-perpetuating mechanisms do more than just endow psychosocial traits with longitudinal consistency within individual members of the culture. Since the latter are carriers and transmitters of the cultural pattern as well, they also help in the perpetuation of the culture from one generation to the next.

IMPACT OF SOCIAL STRATIFICATION AND SOCIALIZING AGENCIES

In our heterogeneous society there is no such thing as a uniform social environment determining in the same way the developmental careers of all children. It seems rather that

> the conditions under which persons have access to fundamental biological and social goals are defined by a system of privilege . . . a system of socially ranked groups with varying degrees of social movement existing between them.[28]
> This is a type of hierarchy which ranks people in defined subordinate-superordinate relationships without regard for their age, sex or kinship roles. Listed in order of increasing degrees of in-marriage, the status groups of this . . . type include (1) social classes, (2) minority ethnic groups, and (3) castes.[25]

These status categories, of course, are not mutually exclusive. Negro children, for example, grow up under predominantly lower-class conditions. Broken homes are even more common than among white families in the same social stratum. Because the father is often absent or unreliable, the mother is the chief source of emotional security and the primary authority figure in the Negro home. Negro mothers and grandmothers commonly show preference for girls, and thereby indirectly encourage effeminism on the part of boys.[24] Negro parents of the same social class tend to be more permissive than white parents about feeding and weaning practices and less permissive about toilet training; and more middle-class Negro than white children masturbate and suck their thumbs.[30] In general, class differences are more striking than caste differences, and the "same type of differences exist between middle- and lower-class Negroes as between middle- and lower-class whites."[30]

Racial, Religious and Ethnic Attitudes

Developmental Trends. Awareness of racial differences occurs relatively early. By the age of three, Hawaiian children clearly perceive the difference between Orientals and non-Orientals,[110] and American children are aware of and correctly identify racial differences between whites and Negroes.[19, 47, 74] Awareness of ethnic and religious differences develops at a later age because the differences in question are more difficult to perceive in terms of both stimulus content and degree of social emphasis placed upon them. Ethnic self-recognition precedes ethnic recognition of others[56, 57]; and, as might be reasonably anticipated, membership in an ethnic minority increases the saliency of this social datum and facilitates early development of ethnic awareness.[56, 57] Jewish children in the early elementary school grades are more highly aware of and strongly identified with their own membership group than are Catholic or Protestant children.[103]

Despite the evidence of awareness of racial and ethnic differences during the preschool period, children's concepts of racial and religious membership are understandably vague and confused at this time.[56, 57, 74] With increasing age not only does extent of awareness increase,[47, 74] but also the relevance, abstractness and subtlety of the differentiating criteria. Children first distinguish between different religious groups in terms of conspicuous concrete symbols and only later identify with evaluative statements made about *people* of different religions.[103] The use of racial and ethnic designations (e.g., Negro, Jew) gradually replaces reference to specific persons[56, 57] and to such gross characteristics as skin color.[19]

Racial *self-identification* is a somewhat different matter than awareness of racial differences since it also involves knowledge of the favorable and unfavorable implications of racial membership. Thus, between the ages of three and seven, 66 per cent of Negro children in one experimental sample identified themselves with a white rather than with a brown doll.[19] This choice was not completely autistic or a function of expediential considerations; reality pressures also entered the picture. Significantly more Southern and dark-skinned Negro children identified with the colored doll than did Northern and light-skinned Negro children. Also, with increasing age (except between four and five), the percentage of identification with the colored doll increased.[19]

Except for Negro children, who in general tend to show preference for white skin color,[19, 47, 74] racial *self-preference* is well-established in white and Oriental preschool children.[47, 67, 74, 110] The majority of children in this age range, both Negro and white, are aware of the social significance of racial membership and value people differentially in terms of their color.[47] Even at the age of three, Negro children have learned "that skin color is important, that white is to be desired, dark to be regretted."[74] During the ego-expansive period of three to five (see p. 297), identification with the prestige of the culturally dominant caste seems to be especially important, and the preference of Negro children for white skin color accordingly increases. During the next two years, as identification with parents and age-mates increases, expressed preference for white dolls and white skin color decreases.[19] In contrast to lower-class white and Negro children, white upper-class children react more cognitively and less affectively to skin color. They are more accurate in matching skin colors and show no preference for one color over another.[74]

Behavioral or sociometric cleavage between the races occurs later than attitudinal cleavage. Despite marked verbally expressed preferences, there is little actual hostility; and cross-racial sociometric choices occur relatively frequently during the preschool and early elementary school years.[22, 47, 71] From kindergarten to the twelfth grade, however, racial self-preference, as indicated by sociometric measures, continues to increase[22, 71] and crossing of color lines practically ceases after the tenth grade.[71] At all grade levels until the tenth, white children show more racial self-preference than Negroes.[22, 71] Until the sixth grade, as a matter of fact, the latter choose white children as often as children of their own race.[71] This racial difference is consistent with the preschool trend. It indicates that Negro children are much more desirous of being assimilated by the culturally more prestigeful group than white children are willing to let them. On the other hand, a sociometric study of school children in Hawaii, where Caucasians constitute a minority group, indicates that racial self-preference is greater in Oriental than in white children and diminishes for cross-sex choices and as the size of the minority nationality in the classroom decreases.[111] During the early elementary school years, children also exhibit preferential attitudes toward members of their own religious group.[103]

In accordance with general trends in value assimilation (see p. 383), the racial and ethnic attitudes of children become increasingly more homogeneous and gradually approach the prevailing adult norms in their community.[14, 128, 129] Their stereotypes become more sophisticated and discriminating as shown by the more highly rationalized arguments given for intolerant attitudes[63] and by the attribution of some favorable traits to unfavored minorities.[14] Intraindividually also, prejudice gradually becomes a more highly generalized and self-consistent trait.[63] Consistent with existing cultural contradictions between verbal ideals of democratic tolerance and ac-

.. standards of discriminatory behavior, the affective intensity of children's prejudicial *attitudes* toward minority groups tends to remain relatively constant, [14, 63, 93] whereas desire to exclude them from social participation increases sharply.[22, 71, 63, 93] Thus, in interacting socially with members of these groups, older children and adolescents are guided more by prevailing standards of behavioral segregation and less by affective attitudes toward the group as a whole or by the personal characteristics of individual members.

Determinants. The first step in the acquisition of racial and ethnic attitudes begins in the home. Through explicit or implicit indoctrination by parents, or merely through recurrent exposure to and identification with parental attitudes, children acquire strong feelings about minority groups before they have any first-hand experience with them.[63, 101, 102, 103] Thus, Horowitz found that anti-Negro attitudes in white children were independent of degree of contact with Negro children and were about as marked in New York City as in the South; but in particular instances where parents were favorably disposed toward Negroes on doctrinal grounds, their children were substantially free of anti-Negro bias.[63]

As children approach pubescence and the game of life is conceived as being played more "for keeps," adult indulgence toward spontaneous manifestations of "childish" tolerance decreases. Parental admonitions about associating with the "wrong type" of children become more pointed, and (especially in girls) are reflected in increased attitudinal intolerance toward Negroes.[12] In the meantime, the attitudes learned at home are reinforced by exposure to the prevailing climate of opinion in the wider community[63, 101, 103, 119, 128, 129] and to such officially sanctioned and institutionalized symbols of discrimination as segregated neighborhoods, schools, and churches. Current racial stereotypes as reflected in folklore, jokes, mass-media, and everyday gossip are easily assimilated when attitudinal conformity is habitually rewarded with social approval and nonconformity is punished with scorn and ridicule. Even if no explicit social approval is forthcoming, the belittlement of other persons is rewarding because it leads to ego enhancement.

In the light of these highly ingrained attitudes, actual contact with members of minority groups, even if favorable, probably does more to bolster than to counteract existing prejudices. The prejudiced child tends to force every aspect of minority group behavior into preconceived judgmental molds; hence, the resulting perceptual products all fit the same stereotype, irrespective of actual stimulus content.[102] He is sensitized to notice the bad, to ignore the good, and to misinterpret the inocuous as maliciously intended. Undesirable behavior or traits of particular out-group members, which would be overlooked or regarded as idiosyncratic in members of the in-group, are generalized as indigenous to the basic personality structure of the former group. The small "kernel of truth" in every stereotype is inevitably encountered and provides dramatic and irrefutable confirmation of the validity of his views. Pleasant social contacts, on the other hand, are regarded as exceptions to the general rule and seldom alter the prevailing stereotype.[103] It is small wonder, therefore, that racial and ethnic attitudes constitute logic-tight compartments that are practically unassailable by ordinary experience and by the commonly accepted rules of evidence.

All of these mechanisms are naturally intensified under conditions of chronic inter-group tension or competition for status. The prejudiced child does not perceive his out-group competitor as just another individual with conflicting prestige needs but as a scheming and unscrupulous representative of his malevolent race. He justifies his aggressive impulses toward the latter by projecting his hostility. His aggressive actions provoke counter-aggression and provide in turn further justification for the original prejudice. Frequently the biased attitudes of in-group members are reinforced by the competitive advantage that accrues when discriminatory practices are applied to their out-group rivals. Direct competition, however, is not necessary to evoke hostile feelings toward members of minority groups. The latter represent convenient and constantly available scapegoats on whom aggression may be displaced and to whom misfortunes may be attributed when frustration from *any* source arises, especially if there is a prior history of inter-group tension. Miller and Bugelski demonstrated this mechanism experimentally in a *Northeastern* summer camp for boys by showing that the prejudice of the campers toward Mexicans and Japanese increased markedly following the imposition of frustrating conditions by the camp management.[92]

Although the foregoing considerations apply generally to the development of biased attitudes toward minority group members, all children are not equally prone to acquire such attitudes under comparable circumstances. Consistently high intercorrelations among different forms of ethnic and racial prejudice in older children[43, 48, 63] suggest that prejudice is in part an expression of personality structure. Since expressions of prejudice provide an ample source of ego enhancement and a relatively safe outlet for aggressive impulses, it is hardly surprising that they are more intense among children who are psychologically insecure, hostile, suspicious, punitive, and distrustful of others.[5, 42, 48, 82, 97, 103] Related ways of perceiving, thinking, and ordering knowledge in these children also predispose them toward racial bias. They are relatively incapable of tolerating ambiguity and suspending judgment,[41, 78] tend to perceive social roles in excessively discontinuous, authoritarian, and hierarchical terms,[41, 42, 82] and conform rigidly to conventional values.[42] Direct interracial contact increases racial prejudice in such individuals whereas it reduces bias in children who are unaggressive and who hold favorable attitudes toward parents and agemates.[97] Strong racial and ethnic prejudice is also characteristic of "authoritarian personalities," i.e., adults who typically were rigidly disciplined as children by highly status conscious parents, repressed their resentments, and later expressed them in the form of extreme ethnocentrism.[3] Consistent with these findings is the fact that mothers of highly prejudiced children lean toward authoritarian, punitive methods of control and lack tolerance for annoying aspects of children's behavior.[53, 82] Thus, parents not only transmit racial and ethnic biases directly, but also predispose children toward acquiring such biases by the kind of interpersonal relationships they maintain with them.

Effects on Personality Development. Racial and ethnic bias affects the personality development of both the prejudiced child and the victim of prejudice. Indirectly, the latter is influenced by the impact of discriminatory practices on his parents' child rearing attitudes and goals. It is not unreasonable to suppose that racially victimized parents in our culture are more highly prone than nonvictimized parents either to (a) perpetuate through overvaluation the omnipotent phase of ego development and place undue stress on ego aggrandizement, or (b) so preoccupy themselves with their own frustrations as to reject their children. Other parents who are discriminated against may encourage attitudes of violent counter-aggression, passive sabotage, obsequious submission, or strident counter-chauvinism.

More directly, children who are victims of prejudice soon perceive that they are objects of disparagement and ridicule, and correspondingly experience deflation of self-esteem, shame, humiliation, and embarrassment.* Both the Clarks[19] and Goodman[47] found evidence of extreme emotionality in the responses of preschool Negro children who were tested for racial self-identification; and this anxiety and sensitivity about minority group membership tends to increase with age.[104] As previously noted, one of the earliest reactions of Negro children to awareness of prejudice is acceptance of the negative evaluation that our society places on their skin color, accompanied by disavowal of their own membership group and preference for and identification with the favored group. Behaviorally, minority group children react to perceived prejudice with hyperactivity,[47] aggressiveness,[47, 52] compensatory striving for symbols of prestige, lethargy, submission and passive

---

*These reactions are more acute in Negro girls than boys,[46, 120] perhaps because this treatment contrasts more sharply with their more favored and sheltered position in the home. In completely segregated neighborhoods, however, the reverse appears to be true.[38]

sabotage. Not infrequently, racial or ethnic prejudice is employed as an all-inclusive rationalization for personal shortcomings or incompetence. Negro children, especially, tend to perceive themselves as hopelessly stigmatized for what they are and not for what they do[125]; and since the stigma bears the ethical stamp of the state, it leads to doubts about the legitimacy of the moral authority of society.[125] Sooner or later all minority group children in the United States are confronted in varying degrees with the proposition that they must go through life with the primary status available to them subject to systematic discount on the basis of their racial or ethnic membership.

Much interindividual variability naturally prevails in the reaction of children to minority group membership. Fortunately, sufficient time is available for establishing stable feelings of intrinsic adequacy within the home before the impact of caste, class and ethnic stratification exerts a catastrophically destructive effect on ego development. Depending on whether this foundation of intrinsic self-esteem is built in childhood, the psychological consequences of identification with a stigmatized reference group can assume either central or relatively peripheral significance in ego structure. Thus it was found that Negro children who are most self-accepting also tend to exhibit more positive attitudes toward other Negro and white children.[120] Presumably, then, the more intrinsic self-esteem a child enjoys the less traumatized he is by prejudice and the less need he has for counter-aggression.

The prejudiced child's personality development is also influenced directly by his own attitudes, feelings, and behavior, and indirectly by the interpersonal climate of his home which fosters prejudice (see p. 430). He exhibits snobbishness, denies human values, ignores the feelings of other human beings, behaves cruelly and unfairly and is consumed by hostility, suspicion and jealousy. The opportunity for aggression and ego enhancement that prejudice provides diverts him from constructive solutions to his life problems. In yielding abjectly to social pressures and considerations of expediency he has little opportunity to develop moral courage and is deprived of many potentially worthwhile relationships. Finally, he is burdened with a heavy load of irrationality and inconsistency between his actual behavior and professed ideals of democratic tolerance. To preserve the latter as well as his prejudices, he is driven to tortuous rationalization, self-deception, and the erection of logic-tight ideational compartments.

Social Class Environment

"Social classes may be tentatively described as psycho-social groupings of the population of persons whose socio-economic positions are objectively similar in the main and whose politico-economic interests tend to coincide."[16]

Each class has its own ideology, characteristic patterns of overt behavior, and typical ways of rearing children. Thus within a given social class environment, not only are there distinctive educational and vocational aspirations and accepted forms of social participation for children but also characteristic moral values relating to sex, aggression, honesty, responsibility, etc.[58] In addition, social class membership affects such practical matters as amount of play space and materials available to children and the degree of attention and supervision parents can afford to devote to them. It is important to realize, however, that although home, neighborhood and peer group environments are reasonably well differentiated on the basis of social class, the official socializing institutions of our society—school, church, courts and social agencies—are middle-class in outlook. Their influence impinges on children of all social strata, reinforcing the teachings of middle-class parents and conflicting in part with the standards that lower-class children learn from parents and neighborhood associates.

Despite considerable objective evidence of the functioning of different social class environments in contemporary American society, many persons heatedly deny their existence. The notion of a stratified social system is alien to American democratic traditions and, if accepted at all, is regarded as peculiar to city life or to the remnants of plantation society in the South. When pressed to indicate their class membership, most persons prefer to be identified with the middle-class.[83] Upper-class individuals, who benefit most from the class system, naturally try to persuade others that no class differences prevail in the United States; and regardless of their actual feelings in the matter, they carefully instruct their children to avoid any open show of superiority or snobbishness that would offend the sensibilities of their social "inferiors."

Sociologists generally agree that there are three major social classes in our society with two subclasses in each. Social class differences cut across color, ethnic and religious lines and although less rigid than the latter demarcations are probably more crucial in determining major values and behavior patterns.[30] Considerable variability also prevails within each class with respect to income, occupation, educational status, social participation, political beliefs, and aspirations for social mobility. Social stratification is greater in certain regions of the country than in others, in older and urban communities, and in areas characterized by marked racial or ethnic heterogeneity.

Since the criteria of social class membership are necessarily multiple, perfect agreement among the various criteria does not always occur. Hence, considerable difficulty may be encountered in placing particular individuals. In practice, however, this situation arises relatively rarely. Because of the obliteration and even reversal in recent years of the wage differential between manual and white collar labor, family income is often a misleading criterion; greater stress must be placed on such factors as occupation, neighborhood, education, participation in community affairs, social aspirations, and value structure. Perception of social structure also varies with class membership, being more highly differentiated at the upper end of the continuum.[28] Members of a given class tend to think of themselves as a discriminable group, to maximize differences from and oppose the mobility of groups beneath them, and to minimize distinctions and resent exclusion from groups immediately above them.[28] The latter tendency is presumably reflective of aspirations for higher social status.[28]

Interaction between Social Classes. Social classes are not closed systems. The differentiation of values and behavior on the basis of social class membership does not imply complete homogeneity within a given class. Personal interaction between members of different classes, intercommunication of norms, the development of cross-class loyalties, and upward and downward mobility are commonplace phenomena. At the same time these evidences of overlapping and diffusion do not negate the existence of marked *mean* differences in ideology between classes.

Promoting the downward diffusion of middle-class ideology is the prolonged exposure of all children to school, church, mass media and youth organizations. Lower-class parents also officially profess middle-class values even though they do not enforce them consistently.[58] Social mobility is enhanced by the continuing trend toward higher working-class incomes and a wider dispersion of secondary school and college education. The preservation of class identities, on the other hand, is maintained through the medium of "restricted learning environments."[28] Purely on a physical basis, social distance between upper and lower classes is enforced by neighborhood segregation, large estates, nurses, governesses, private boarding schools, and chauffeured automobiles. Interaction is also discouraged by parental pressures and admonitions and by the gradual acquisition of class loyalties. "Taboos upon participation outside of one's status level" undoubtedly originate from above downwards but soon become retaliatory and reciprocal. They are reinforced by snobbishness and condescension from above and by resentment from persons at or below one's class level.[28]

As segregation of children by social class is prolonged, its effects become increasingly irreversible. The longer a lower-class child is deprived of *intimate* contact with middle-class children the less opportunity he has of acquiring their values and sanctioned patterns of behavior. To rise above his class he must associate consistently with his "betters" and endure their patronizing ways as well as the outspoken resentment of his social peers.

Younger children from lower-class homes who have pleasing personalities and are willing to conform to middle-class standards may often find a measure of peripheral acceptance in middle-class groups. With the approach of adolescence, as class lines are accentuated under the impact of increasing parental and peer group pressures, this type of idiosyncratic social mobility becomes increasingly more difficult.

Perception of Social Class Differences. Development of the ability to perceive social class differences illustrates the general process of perceptual learning or cognitive maturation (see pp. 547-548) as applied to interpersonal and social phenomena. It involves growth in the capacity for abstraction and generalization, increased familiarity and differentiation of the perceptual field, and greater objectivity and less autism in the operation of judgment. Children gradually learn the more relevant symbols of social class status and become more precise and discriminating in their awareness of their own and others' class membership. First-graders tend both to perceive themselves as rich and to overestimate the opulence of their classmates. Fourth-graders are somewhat less euphoric in this regard, and sixth- and eighth-graders are still more conservative.[112] Paralleling the trend among adults, both poor and wealthy children tend to identify with the middle-class; the poor overrate their parents' financial status and the rich underrate it.[112] Although awareness of poverty is generally greater among lower- than among middle-class children, what is physically proximal to the child (e.g., squalor, overcrowding) has not always been found to be psychologically salient. With increasing age, as pressures from adults mount to maintain greater social class distance, awareness of class distinctions concomitantly increases.[89]

*Class Differences in Training, Personality and Behavior.** Although middle-class parents have shifted recently to more permissive practices of infant care and more democratic methods of discipline, they still require more responsibility and self-reliance in the home,[37] and higher standards of table manners, cleanliness, neatness, dress, speech, and punctuality[37] than do lower-class parents (see p. 351). Middle-class mothers are less frequently employed, have fewer children, and supervise and restrict more stringently the child's activities outside the home.[26, 27, 30, 58] Lower-class parents, on the other hand, resort more to authoritarian methods of control and to severe corporal punishment; the latter, however, tends to be relatively ineffective because of inconsistency, the long time lag between its administration and the occurrence of misbehavior, and the frequently poor example

*Reference has already been made to social class differences in the rearing of children (p. 351), in moral behavior (p. 401), in interests and activities (p. 411), in artistic preferences (p. 410), in emotional expression (p. 323), in physical aggression (p. 336), and in thumbsucking (p. 240).

set by parents in matters of responsibility and control of aggressive and sexual impulses.[27] According to one writer,[84] the greater pressures and restrictions on social exploration imposed upon middle-class children are compensated for in part by the opportunity for more open, spontaneous, and flexible psychological communication with peers and adults. In contrast, the interpersonal relationships of lower-class children are characterized as hierarchical, absolutistic, rigidly structured, and marked by dependent attitudes toward contemporaries and psychological distance from adults.

Middle-class parents place greater stress than lower-class parents on the maintenance of high aspirations for primary status and the achievement of high levels of academic and vocational success, financial independence and social recognition.[1, 27, 37, 58, 105, 107] To insure the attainment of these ego enhancement goals, they encourage the development of supportive personality traits. These include (a) habits of initiative and responsibility[1]; (b) the "deferred gratification pattern" of hard work, self-denial, long-range planning, high frustration tolerance, relentless self-criticism, thrift, and prolonged education, vocational training, and economic dependence on parents;[27, 58, 105, 107] (c) emphasis on punctuality, orderliness, honesty, respect for property, good manners, religious observance, and participation in civic affairs;[26, 27, 30, 58] (d) a "business" socio-political ideology;[107] (e) inhibition of physical aggression and premarital sexual expression;[27, 49, 70, 85, 99, 107] and (f) respect (rather than fear) of adult authority and conformity to conventional standards of behavior.[49, 70, 99, 107] Since the majority of these traits are coextensive with the attributes of ego maturity in our culture, it seems plausible to hypothesize that maturational failure would be less common in middle- than in lower-class individuals. The latter should achieve earlier desatellization and volitional independence, should obtain a larger portion of their derived status from age mates, and should bear a lighter burden of impulse frustration and anxiety.

Middle-class children are willing to internalize these ego status goals and to acquire the necessary supportive traits because they perceive the eventual rewards of striving and self-denial as real and attainable for persons of their status. They can both observe the achievement of these rewards by their own parents and experience an early taste of them in their own family, neighborhood, and school life.[27] Their efforts are encouraged by parental example, reinforced by the standards of school, church and peer group, and sustained by the anxiety of forfeiting the advantages of present and future status should they fail in completing these tasks. In the case of lower-class children all of these considerations operate in the opposite direction (see p. 440).

Lower-class children are both more competitive[85] and more aggressive physically[49, 85, 99] than middle-class children in play situations. In contrast to the latter who are strongly admonished about the moral and physical dangers of fighting and are instructed to hit only in self-defense, the former are actually rewarded by parents and peers for fighting prowess and are punished for failing to respond aggressively in conflict situations. They find physical aggression rewarding insofar as it provides an outlet for rage and resentment; and from parental example and their own experience they learn to discount the physical hazards involved.[27] These same factors are also operative in conditioning characteristic class differences in sexual behavior. Sexual exploration is not only discouraged by constant parental supervision but is also fraught with considerable anxiety in middle-class children.[27] Lacking first-hand experience with the "facts of life" they are kept in line by fear of sin, guilt and moral censure, by vague forebodings of pregnancy and venereal disease, and by the promised rewards of virtuous restraint. Lower-class children, on the other hand, are relatively sophisticated in sexual matters and observe frequent instances of unpenalized promiscuity in their family and neighborhood circles. Sexual experimentation is neither punished, tainted with sin, nor inhibited by close supervision or distorted fears of pregnancy and venereal disease.[27]

Urban-Rural Differences

Rural life differs from urban life in many ways that affect the personality development of the child. It should not be imagined, however, that modern rural society is in any way comparable to preliterate cultures. In fact, many of the differences that have existed until relatively recently are being quickly eroded under the impact of the automobile, motion pictures, radio, television, etc.

The rural mother tends to be more casual and permissive than the urban mother in her infant care routines and to place less emphasis on orderliness and cleanliness.[77, 80] The pressure of farm work does not enable her to devote herself as single-mindedly to the care of her children. On the other hand, older farm children share more in the care of babies, and the father is a more constant and integral member of the household.[77] Because of fewer environmental hazards, parents need not issue as many or as arbitrary prohibitory commands.[77] The wider spaces and the lesser density of population affects the play patterns of the rural child in various self-evident ways (see p. 411) and fosters greater communion with nature. Exposed less to mass media and other children, his imaginative productions are necessarily structured more from within.

The rural home plays a more prominent and exclusive role than the urban home in socializing children, in interpreting the culture to them,

and in enforcing the moral code. Rural parents are displaced more gradually as the principal source of their childen's values and are devalued less
rapidly than urban parents. Their children presumably desatellize more
slowly and less prominently through the mechanism of resatellization to
peers and parent surrogates (see p. 305). In general rural children live
in a world of less rapid social change and are able to relate to a more stable
and orthodox set of moral and religious values.[77]

The opportunity for rural children to participate in adult tasks and
to make a more responsible contribution to the economy creates somewhat
less discontinuity between their interest and activity concerns and those of
adults than is typical of urban communities. Thus, the rural child is less
dependent on school and peer group for his primary status than is the
urban child. The significance of this difference, however, should not be
overestimated. Many of the tasks he performs are highly routine and subordinate chores that contribute little to any real sense of responsibility or
volitional independence (see p. 303). Furthermore, for both rural and
urban children, derived status constitutes a much more central component
of self-esteem than does primary status, and in both instances is chiefly
available from parents.

Impact of the School on Personality Development

In addition to its special function of imparting knowledge and intellectual
skills, the school in our society shares in many of the socializing and
enculturative responsibilities exclusively exercised by the family in other
cultures. It not only participates in the transmission of our particular
cultural ideology and psychosocial traits, but also plays an important role
in the development of ego status and ego maturity goals and in the acquisition of acceptable standards of social behavior. For all of these functions
it is admirably suited by virtue of the prolonged and intensive contact it
maintains with children during the formative years of their development.

School constitutes the first major source of primary status available to
the majority of children in our culture. As a result of initial school attendance they acquire heretofore unrealized feelings of bigness and importance.[114]
Academic success not only reinforces objective learnings but also leads to
ego enhancement and increased self-confidence. Chronic school failure,
with its associated emotional trauma and social rejection induces profound
ego deflation.[106] The opportunity for acquiring primary status in school is
somewhat greater for girls than for boys because of their superior verbal
ability and greater conformity to adult authority, and because school success
is less ambivalently prized by their peer group. "In our culture where
the educational system is divided into a [hierarchical] sequence of schools

. . . the child has a sequence of inflating experiences in being among the oldest in each group, which are followed by deflation as he becomes one of the youngest in the next school."[96]

In the school environment the child is inescapably thrust into competition for the solitary kind of primary status (academic proficiency) available in the classroom. He is coerced by prevailing social pressures for high achievement to aspire to at least the class mean of academic performance. This is especially true for the middle-class child since his parents regard academic success as unqualifiedly essential. Thus the objective failure of the low achiever is intensified subjectively by the forced maintenance of unrealistically high levels of aspiration and is only mitigated by the compensatory value of aiming high and conforming to the motivational norm. The only other alternative is ego disinvolvement from the competitive school situation and the setting of aspirational levels that are sufficiently low to guarantee empty feelings of success (see pp. 311 and 439). Hence, early in his school career anxiety becomes an important motivational spur to learning; and both goal tenacity and the affective properties of subject matter become less dependent on objective performance than on degree of ego-involvement (see p. 309) and semester grades.[86]

School attendance facilitates desatellization by providing both a major source of primary status and suitable adults (teachers) in relation to whom resatellization can occur (see p. 300). Under these circumstances the home source of derived status becomes less precious. Furthermore, parents become devalued and lose part of their halo of omniscience in the eyes of many children as teachers take over a substantial portion of the parental role of propounding truth and moral values.[114] Counteracting the current fetish of permissiveness in middle-class homes, the school's greater demands for conformity to adult authority and for more mature behavior has two kinds of effects. It de-emphasizes volitional independence, initiative and spontaneity in children,[6] but brings about improvement in such aspects of ego maturity as executive independence and responsibility.[114]

School does not affect the personality development of all children in the same way. Although the new emphasis on primary status and the devaluation of parents induce greater change in the satellizer's than in the non-satellizer's ego structure, two factors tend to limit the significance of this change. First, the primary status available in school plays only a relatively subsidiary role in relation to the derived status he obtains at home. Second, even though the teacher's valuation of the child is more contingent than the parent's upon satisfactory performance the satellizer still attempts in part to establish an emotionally dependent, satellizing relationship to her. Her approval confers derived as well as primary status. The non-satellizer merely transfers his quest for primary status from home to school, and reacts to the teacher as an emulatory model and as the person to be propitiated if such status is to be won. Hence subservience to her is regarded more as expedientially necessary than as desirable, and her approval becomes important mostly as a symbol of academic success. Because his self-esteem is more completely dependent than the satellizer's on acquiring primary status, he is more anxious about his school progress and is less free to lower his level of aspiration in the face of failure. For reasons designated elsewhere (see p. 300), entrance into school significantly increases the self-esteem of many rejected children but almost invariably has an ego deflationary effect on overvalued children.

Social Class Differences. Since the school reinforces middle-class values and often comes into opposition with lower-class values, it is commonly a source of ego enhancement for middle-class children and of failure, conflict and ego deflation for lower-class children.[27, 58, 61, 123] The distribution of the rewards the school has to offer—good grades, honors, teachers' approval and attention, extracurricular activities—is highly related to pupils' social class status.[2, 61, 123] However, teachers accord preferential treatment to upper status children for many reasons other than favoritism based on class membership per se. The middle-class background and ethnocentric bias of teachers predispose them in favor of children with the same value system and behavioral norms. Middle-class children behave in accordance with their expectations, accept their authority, do homework conscientiously, and strive for good marks.[23, 29] Hence, much of the teacher's preference for children of this class is simply a function of the fact that they tend to be high achievers.[60] Lower-class children frequently display aggressive attitudes toward teachers, ignore their homework, have low academic aspirations, and are ashamed of school success.[23, 29] They cause teachers most annoyance because the latter tend to be especially disturbed by behavior that violates "their personal standards" and challenges "their roles as leaders, disciplinarians and instructors."[68] In addition to their natural inclinations to reward conformity to middle-class ideology, teachers are influenced by implicit and explicit pressures in giving preferential treatment to pupils whose parents are prominent in civic affairs, members of school boards, and leaders in parent-teacher associations.

Middle-class parents are "great believers in education" as an instrument of social progress and as a vehicle of vocational advancement and upward mobility.[58] This attitude is transmitted to their children by encouraging preschool attendance, by teaching them to read and write before they enter first grade, by attaching much importance to the report card,[113] and by stimulating abstract thinking, intellectual curiosity and verbal expression;

it is sustained by peer group and neighborhood sanctions and by appropriate levels of induced motivation and anxiety. It also seems plausible that motivations and attitudes such as these selectively influence the differentiation of general intelligence along verbal lines and effect greater actualization of genically determined endowment in verbal intelligence (see p. 603). In large part they determine the middle-class pupil's greater tendency to perceive the teacher as a "stepping stone" rather than as a friend.[23] In the light of the actual probabilities of entering college and acquiring professional status, passing courses and achieving good grades are real rewards with current as well as stepping stone value. To lower-class children, whose social milieu places no great value on education and who gradually learn that professional status is beyond their grasp, these rewards are unreal and valueless. Furthermore they "remain unmotivated because they are humiliated and punished too severely for having the lower-class culture which their own mothers, fathers, and siblings approve," and because (for reasons of low achievement and discriminatory treatment) they are denied the current status rewards available to middle-class school children.[27]

Teacher-Pupil Interaction. Because the school provides a large percentage of the occasions in which children interact with each other and with adults, it plays an important role in the socialization of interpersonal behavior. It constitutes the major locus of operation for peer group activities under adult supervision. Under its auspices children learn much of their social skills; age, sex, class, and status roles; and adult sanctioned norms of aggression, competition, cooperation, and fair play. The teacher also serves as a role model for the learning of interpersonal attitudes. Children, for example, quickly assimilate her attitudes toward racial and ethnic groups. In one experiment they even mimicked her prejudicial behavior toward an artificially created underprivileged subgroup.[118]

An equally significant outcome of school experience is the learning of a typical pattern of volitional dependence on extrafamilial adults and of conformity to their authority. For purposes of optimal ego maturation in our culture, it is important to achieve a proper balance between realistic acknowledgment of children's biosocial dependence and need for external direction, on the one hand, and their actual capacity for exercising initiative, responsibility, and self-discipline, on the other. The prevailing educational milieu still leans too far toward the traditional "adult rule-child obedience" pattern[6, 23] in which obedience and conformity are perceived by both pupils and teachers as ends in themselves.[11] This type of atmosphere stifles initiative, spontaneity and freedom of reality testing sufficiently to impair the development of volitional independence[6] and of critical, independent thinking (see p. 374). Experimental studies of authoritarian social climates in children's recreational groups also point to the following undesirable effects on group morale and solidarity: generalized apathy; aggressive and dominative behavior toward peers; displaced aggression in the form of scapegoating; submissive, placatory, and attention-demanding behavior toward the adult leader; less "we-feeling," frustration tolerance, and task-oriented behavior; and the break-down of discipline when adult supervision is removed.[79]

Studies such as these only suggest that excessively autocratic methods of handling children's groups in our culture have less beneficial effects on group morale than do more democratic procedures. They give no support to maximally permissive (laissez-faire) approaches that advocate freedom from discipline as an end in itself and removal of all externally imposed direction and restraints. Democracy is no more coextensive with laissez-faire methods than the realistic employment of necessary teacher controls is synonymous with autocracy. The need for discipline is no less urgent in the school than in the home (see p. 374). As a matter of fact, observation of laissez-faire school climates shows that they lead to "confusion, insecurity and keen competition for power among group members"; aggressive pupils become ruthless and retiring pupils become even more withdrawn.[23] Children fail to learn the normative demands of society and how to operate within the limits these set, do not succeed in learning how to deal effectively with adults, and develop unrealistic perceptions of adult social structure. Other unfavorable effects of excessive permissiveness (underdomination) have been discussed elsewhere (see pp. 307 and 373).

The characteristics of democratic discipline that are appropriate in the home (see pp. 375-376) are also applicable to the school situation. A democratic climate of teacher-pupil interaction has been achieved in the classroom by emphasizing respect for the dignity and feelings of pupils as persons, by avoiding techniques of ridicule and intimidation, and by employing various devices that enable children to share in the planning and management of the curriculum and in the regulation of pupil activities and discipline. These procedures do not necessarily ignore the cumulative impact of prior conditioning to anxiety reduction and other extrinsic motivations in the learning situation, and do not seek unrealistically to predicate all learning activity upon inherent desire for knowledge. When properly paced and geared to actual capacities for self-determination such procedures have been successful in improving group morale and in facilitating the development of mature, responsible, and realistically grounded volitional independence.[29, 79] They have also resulted in more "we-feeling" and constructive work products, in greater self-discipline and acceptance of adult authority, and in less overt or displaced hostility.[79, 95]

Teachers' perceptions of and reactions to pupils depend both on their own personality traits and on the characteristics of particular children. The extent to which they are generally tolerant of the annoying qualities of pupils' behavior varies inversely with their tendency to be authoritarian.[17] The highly inequitable but consistent manner in which they distribute approval,[31] indicates that they react differentially to various aspects of children's personality and behavior. For the most part, pupils who receive much teacher approval tend to rank highly on intelligence, academic achievement, and personality adjustment.[31] Teachers vary considerably in their ability accurately to perceive the sociometric status of their pupils.[44, 50] In general, however, their perceptions, which are reasonably accurate in the middle grades,[8, 15, 44, 50] become increasingly less accurate as the latter progress through the grades[8, 94]; and as might be expected they tend to overrate the popularity of children they prefer and vice versa.[15, 50] In perceiving the motivations and academic strivings of pupils,[7] and their personal problems,[44] teachers' predictions of pupil responses either do not or barely exceed chance accuracy.

How pupils perceive and react to teachers also depends on the respective personality traits of the interacting parties. These perceptions define and limit the kinds of interpersonal relationships that can be established in the school. In general teachers are seen as playing three major kinds of roles—friends, opponents, and manipulators of status in learning situations.[23] As friends they are "older and wiser" persons, helpful counselors, heroes, givers of security, and occasionally "pals." As opponents they are cast as "kill-joys" who arbitrarily interfere with legitimate pleasures, as "enemies" to be "fought" and "outwitted," and as demons of power to be feared, respected and placated. In the learning aspects of the school situation they are perceived as "necessary evils" in the acquisition of knowledge, efficient organizers in the direction of work projects, "stepping stones" to future status rewards, dispensers of approval and disapproval, and as moral arbiters who can absolve from guilt as well as point the accusing finger.[23]

The affective reactions of pupils to teachers are as much a function of the personality characteristics of the latter as of their teaching skills. Pupils not only admire clarity, task-orientation, good classroom control and enthusiasm in their teachers, but also such traits as fairness, impartiality, patience, consistency, friendliness and sympathetic understanding.[54, 65, 75] They like teachers who are helpful, kindly and considerate of their feelings, and dislike teachers who are cross, bossy, fussy, talkative, and give too much homework.[54, 75] Although there is considerable overlapping between teachers liked best as persons and teachers thought most effective,[54] the preferences of a particular pupil in this instance depend on whether he is primarily concerned with obtaining help in achieving intellectual tasks or in meeting his emotional-social needs.[32] In general, teachers who like pupils tend in turn to be liked by them.[75]

THE SIGNIFICANCE OF SEX IN CHILD DEVELOPMENT

Although sex membership is ultimately predicted upon anatomic sex criteria, the datum of organic sex differences is not of *intrinsic* psychological importance to the child. This does not mean that he would ordinarily ignore such differences or fail to be curious about them. However, were it not for the fact that they receive special social emphasis from the moment of birth as a principal basis for the differential structuring of role and status behavior in all cultures, he would be relatively indifferent to them. Anatomic sex differences, in other words, are chiefly important to the child because they are significant determinants of the erotic and social behavior of adults, and hence affect both his emulatory behavior and the expectations and socializing procedures of the latter in their dealings with him. For analagous reasons he pays particular attention to skin color differences when these receive comparable emphasis as determinants of role and status in a given culture; and if his culture correspondingly used eye color as a basis for special stratification, the difference between brown and blue eyes would similarly acquire special saliency in his psychological field. That anatomic sex differences are primarily important to children for purposes of social categorization is further suggested by the fact that even preschool children who are well aware of them tend to place greater stress on hair-do and dress as the essential distinguishing criteria of sex membership.[34]

Sex organs, in addition to furnishing a more functional and universal basis for the patterning of social behavior than skin or eye color are also objects of somewhat greater interest in their own right (see p. 251). Nevertheless, they still lack critical importance to children because the prerequisite conditions for enacting a genuine biological (erotic) sex role (see p. 253) are absent in their case. Under these circumstances their "sex behavior" only has peripheral significance in the total economy of personality organization, and concern with the ultimate objects of adult sex striving is correspondingly not very insistent.* But although the child's

---

*These considerations, of course, would be so self-evident as hardly to require mentioning were it not for widespread acceptance (despite the absence of any convincing empirical evidence) of the psychoanalytic doctrine that the sexual behavior of children is qualitatively equivalent to that of adults.

identification with his own sex group carries none of the implications of membership in a biological sex clan, there is no gainsaying the intensity of his sex loyalties and their significance for his social groupings, play interests, values, and aspirations. With some exceptions the social sex roles of boys and girls are miniature editions and precursors of the respective sex roles of men and women.

"Sex Behavior" in Childhood

In our discussion of "infantile sexuality" (see p. 251), we have already presented evidence and reasons for believing that the prerequisite conditions for enacting a true biological sex role are absent in childhood, and hence that adult and childhood sexuality are qualitatively discontinuous from each other.* Generally speaking, "sex behavior" in middle childhood and preadolescence is similar to and has much the same significance as in infancy and early childhood (see p. 253). Abundant evidence from our own (see p. 251) and other cultures[40, 127] indicates that children continue to manifest the following kinds of "sexuality" during the elementary school years: (a) hedonistic sensuality (masturbation) as an end in itself or as a nonspecific form of tension reducing behavior; (b) curiosity about sexual anatomy and the physiology of reproduction (peeking, "creepitis," "show games," mutual genital manipulation, questions about procreation, interest in pornographic art and literature); and (c) desire for non-erotic bodily contacts as expressions of affectional closeness to parents. Particularly characteristic of "sex behavior" during this period is experimentation with the biological sex roles of adults, varying from attempted intercourse to crude imitations of romanticism. It includes flirtation with parents and age mates of the opposite sex, boy-girl "crushes," chasing and kissing, and the furtive passing of "I love you" notes in the classroom. Although the extent of such activity varies greatly both between and within cultures, the near universality of its occurrence provides little support for the psychoanalytic doctrine of a "latency" period in psychosexual development. Nevertheless, it is an assumption of quite another order to equate such behavior with adult sexuality when it lacks all of the distinguishing properties of the latter phenomenon (see p. 253). Pointing to its relatively peripheral status in the total economy of childhood personality organization is the fact that atypical sex behavior in children is not related to personality maladjustment[10] or marital unhappiness[115] in adult life.

Cross-cultural comparisons[40, 127] indicate that the participation of children in overt sex play is largely a function of cultural tolerance for such

---

*See page 254 for an analysis of the origins of psychoanalytic confusion between childhood and adult sexuality.

experimentation, but that surreptitious expression often occurs even when strong cultural taboos are operative.[40] This suggests some degree of genic determination. The *differential* patterning of male and female biological sex roles by genic factors, on the other hand, does not occur prior to pubescence, and in any case is considerably modified by cultural norms of masculinity and femininity. In sexually mature individuals, genic factors either differentially influence perceptual and behavioral thresholds of sexual reactivity through some presently unknown mediating mechanisms or through the differential effects of androgens and estrogens on the nervous system (see p. 77).

In addition to regulating the child's overt sex activity, the culture also influences his general attitudes about sex and his degree of sophistication about sexual matters (see p. 436). The child assimilates much of the cultural folklore (four-letter words, "dirty" stories, etc.) and moral values about sex: that sex is ugly or beautiful, that it is a necessary evil or a saving grace, that it is equally desirable for both sexes or intended primarily for men. He elaborates in fantasy many unshared misperceptions and half-truths which frequently are not subject to social validation for many years. Finally, in our culture, he derives from sex a source of shame, guilt, conflict and anxiety, and a weapon with which to shock adult sensibilities and express defiance of adult authority.

Development of Sex Awareness and Identification

During the preschool and elementary school period sex role differentiation is an important aspect of ego development. Relatively early in their social careers, children learn to think of themselves as male or female. This awareness is absent in most two year olds but is present in many three year olds.[34, 100] However, even when children are familiar with anatomic sex differences they frequently regard the latter as less basic differentiating criteria than hair style or clothing.* Discovery of genital differences is accepted matter-of-factly by most children; actual observation of their reactions[20] gives no support to psychoanalytic assertions that this experience is productive of profound disillusionment, anxiety, hostility, or "penis-envy."

The acquisition of sex awareness and appropriate sex behavior is facilitated by the pervasive and recurrent exposure of boys and girls to differential experience, treatment, expectations, and norms of conduct. Some of these differences in handling are obvious: distinctive clothing and hair style;

*A. Katcher (*J. Genet. Psychol. 87*: 131-143, 1955) reports similar findings. Among hermaphrodites sex role identification is a function of sex of rearing rather than of predominant chromosomal, anatomic, or hormonal factors (J. Money, *Johns Hopkins Hosp. Bull. 96*: 253-263, 1956).

separate toilets, games, toys, books, and interests. Other differences—in valuation by parents, in discipline, and in expectations regarding achievement, conformity, deportment, and emotional expression—are more subtle but no less real. Pressures for learning an appropriate sex role originate in the home and are reinforced by identification with the like-sex parent* and older siblings. Later, school, peer group, and mass media contribute greatly to the learning process by encouraging segregation of and rivalry between the sexes and by providing appropriate emulatory models. Boys and girls in our culture have many reasons for estrangement and mutual antagonism. First, gross differences in play interests necessitate the formation of unisexual play groups. Second, because girls are more docile, obedient, and conforming to adult direction at home and in school, they tend to receive preferential treatment. This provides an endless source of rivalry, discord, resentment, aggression, and counter-aggression. Third, boys become indoctrinated with prevailing notions of male chauvinism and incite girls to retaliate in kind. Fourth, group competitions in school are traditionally staged as contests between the sexes. All of these factors promote strong feelings of intra-sex solidarity and the utilization of the opposite sex as a convenient object for the displacement of hostile feelings of any origin.

Lower-class children become more clearly aware of sex differences and of appropriate sex role behavior at an earlier age than do middle-class children.[100, 124] They are exposed to more sharply and narrowly defined standards of masculinity and femininity and their conformity to such standards is more rigorously enforced. Working-class fathers tend to spend more time at home and actively induct their sons into masculine pursuits. Middle-class fathers, in contrast, are not only home less but the nature of their work is also less concrete; hence their sons find it more difficult to identify with them, especially since they are surrounded by female models at home and in school. Furthermore, middle-class parents define and enforce sex appropriate behavior less rigidly.[100]

Boys seem to be more clearly aware of their social sex roles than girls[100] despite the fact that the latter have greater opportunities for identification with sex appropriate models and activities at home and in school.[98] This apparent paradox is largely a function of the fact that although the sex role of girls is more available and visible than that of boys it is less clearly defined. Boys are taught to view feminine pursuits with disdain and are severely ridiculed if they step out of line. The female sex role tends to be more ambiguous both in childhood and in adult life. It is more inclusive

---

*Five-year-olds both prefer sex-appropriate play activities and perceive their parents as exhibiting the same preference. (L. B. Fauls and W. D. Smith, *J. Genet. Psychol. 89:* 105-117, 1956).

of masculine interests than the male role is inclusive of feminine interests. Thus, the participation of girls in cross-sex activities is regarded more tolerantly and is less subject to prohibition and reproof.

Childhood Differences in Social Sex Role

In contrast to biological sex role which refers to feeling tones, behavior, and impulses (functionally or historically dependent upon gonadal stimulation and social recognition as a sexually mature person), social sex role refers to the differential functions, status and personality traits characterizing the two sexes in a particular cultural setting. Since all cultures provide differential training for boys and girls that will enable them to assume their appropriate roles as men and women,[83, 87, 126] childhood social sex roles tend to mirror and foreshadow their adult counterparts. Because of varying degrees of cultural discontinuity, however, a point to point correlation never exists. Athletic prowess, for example, which is an important determinant of boys' prestige status in their peer group (see p. 478), is a negligible factor in determining the social standing of the adult male. Three component and interrelated aspects of social sex role may be considered here: (a) the hierarchical ordering of relations between the sexes in terms of the relative values placed by the culture on maleness and femaleness respectively and the degree of access each sex has to positions of social power and privilege; (b) social and vocational differences reflective of the division of labor along sex lines; and (c) norms of masculinity and femininity.

Since girls perceive themselves as more highly accepted and intrinsically valued than boys (see p. 281) and have a more available emulatory model in the mother,[98] they tend to satellize more and longer. In addition to enjoying more derived status at home, they can also acquire more primary status from household activities[98] and from school achievement (see p. 437). Nevertheless, although girls enjoy more *current primary* status during childhood, boys have higher *ultimate* aspirations for primary status; their aspirational levels both for laboratory tasks (see p. 311) and for possessions and achievement (see p. 281) are higher. At all socioeconomic levels in our society* girls are subjected to less social pressure to achieve primary status through vocational success. Whereas the middle-class boy fully anticipates that he will be expected to create through his own vocational efforts and achievements the social status of his future family, few girls in the same social class expect as married women to compete with men in their own fields or at occupational levels of equivalent social prestige.[98] Girls are not *really* driven by the culture as are boys to prove their adequacy

*An exception to this generalization has been reported for Negro girls in segregated New York City neighborhoods in what is essentially a matriarchal society.[33]

and maintain their self-esteem by their accomplishments. Their fathers are satisfied if they are pretty, sweet, affectionate, and well-liked.[1] They expect to fall heir to a derived status dependent upon their husbands' station in life, and to acquire primary status in the roles of mother, housewife and supplementary wage earner, augmented perhaps by participation in cultural and community welfare activities.[98] Largely for this reason perhaps— because their status is more attributed than earned—girls and women tend to be more conscious and jealous of status distinctions than boys and men.

The superordinate position of men in our society (and the accompanying male chauvinism) is also reflected in childhood social sex roles. From an early age boys learn to be contemptuous of girls and their activities; and although girls retaliate in kind by finding reasons for deprecating the male sex, they tend to accept in part the prevailing view of their inferiority.[69] Whereas boys express scorn for girls' tasks, games, and future role in life, and seldom if ever desire to change sex,* girls not infrequently wish they were boys.[126] The male equivalent of a "tomboy," who reads girls' books, plays "hopscotch" and relishes housework and sewing is indeed a rarity (see p. 411).

In some ways the acquisition of social sex role is more difficult for boys, but in other ways it is more difficult for girls. Sex appropriate emulatory models and activities are less available to boys, and fewer of the sex-typed activities they learn in childhood can be carried over into adult life (e.g., athletic skills versus housekeeping skills). To acquire the male social sex role boys are also required to undergo greater personality change during late childhood and adolescence than girls undergo in acquiring their social sex role. The implications of de-satellization—volitional independence, self-reliance, striving for primary status—are applied more thoroughly in their case; whereas to a very large degree, women (as wives) can retain many of the dependent and passive attributes of derived status. The female sex role is more ambiguous and inclusive, more productive of conflicting choices, and is changing more rapidly. Girls are understandably more confused than boys about the extent to which they can remain content with a derived status or must struggle for achievement in their own right.

Sex differences in play (see p. 411) and mass media (see p. 409) interests reflect both prevailing norms of masculinity and femininity as well as anticipated cleavage along vocational lines. The sex typing of games is

---

*D. G. Brown has found that elementary school girls show less preference for the feminine role than boys show for the masculine role (Paper read at Am. Psychol. Ass., Chicago, September 1956).

well established during the preschool period.[21, 100] During the elementary school years boys excel in mechanical and athletic skills, in spatial and quantitative abilities, and in science and mathematics; girls excel in verbal fluency, language achievement and clerical aptitude.[116] Sex differences in vocational choice are evident by the age of ten and seem to be patterned by the gradual acquisition of dislike for occupations incongruous with sex role.[121]

Norms of Masculinity and Femininity. In addition to the sex differences in status and interest-ability patterns listed above, boys and girls in our culture typically differ in certain temperamental traits, emotional expression and conformity to social controls. Boys tend to be more active, energetic and versatile in their play activities[62, 72] (see p. 411), more fearless,[109] and more overt in the expression of aggression, rebellion, and friendliness[116] (see p. 336). Girls are more affectionate,[73] suspicious,[109] fanciful,[109] and uninhibited in the expression of fear and hurt feelings[116] (see p. 323). The greatest contrast between boys and girls lies in the area of aggressiveness-compliance. Boys are more aggressive (see p. 336), expressive of anger,[72] rebellious,[72] and negativistic,[72, 73] (see p. 293); more dominant, boastful, exhibitionistic and insistent on their rights[72, 109]; more revengeful, extrapunitive, and alibi-building[72]; more quarrelsome, given to teasing, and uncooperative with peers and teachers[72] (see p. 473). Girls are more obedient and amenable to social controls,[72, 73, 109] more responsible,[72] friendlier to teachers, and more responsive to their approval[72, 73] They are more responsive to prestige suggestion (see p. 381), more sensitive to social expectations, more cooperative, and more discriminative of socially approved and disapproved behavior (see p. 401).

Genic and Environmental Determinants. Two separate though related issues are involved in the determination of social sex role. First we may ask how the modal social sex role comes to be what it is in a particular culture. Second, how do the developing individuals in that culture come to acquire it? The first issue is a problem in the development of culture, the second is a problem in individual psychological development. In both instances we wish to assess the relative influence of genic and environmental determinants.

Tremendous variability in social sex role from one culture to another[87] despite the operation of nearly identical genic variables in all cultures strongly suggests that modal differences in behavior between the sexes is predominantly determined by environmental (cultural) factors (e.g., social, political and economic organization, value system, religion, custom complexes, historical accident). However, since certain behavioral and trait differences between the sexes seem to be differentially influenced by hormones* or sex-linked on a genic basis (and at least partially independent of differential experience) we cannot rule out the possibility of partial panhuman genic determination. Nevertheless, since behavioral differences conditioned by genic factors would not prevail unless they were supported by cultural variables operating in the same direction, and since the latter cultural influences are apparently able to reverse and even negate the presumed effects of genic determinants, they must be accounted the prepotent factors in determining the cultural stereotype of social sex role. The same general division of relative influence prevails in the acquisition of social sex role by individual members of a culture. In the case of children hormonal factors are not operative since differential estrogenic-androgenic ratios do not appear prior to pubescence. Social sex role development in children, therefore, is only influenced by hormones to the extent that the latter contribute to the development of cultural norms of masculinity-femininity.

The component aspects of social sex role are transmitted experientially in much the same manner as any psychosocial trait. First, boys and girls are exposed to and identify with the sex appropriate role models provided by parents, older siblings, age mates, teachers, and mass media stereotypes. If appropriate sex role models are lacking, as in father-absent homes, boys tend to be retarded in the acquisition of male patterns of aggressive behavior (see p. 358). Boys with an older sister also tend to be more sissyish than first-born males with a younger sister or brother.[72] Second, vastly different patterns of standards and expectations impinge on the two sexes in the areas of achievement, emotional expression, conformity, interests, etc. Third, boys and girls are treated much differently by parents and other socializing agents. Girls are more accepted and intrinsically valued by parents (see p. 281) and are protected more from contact with other social classes.[126] Boys are more severely disciplined by their fathers (see p. 358), are allowed more freedom in physical activity, rough play, hitting, getting dirty, swearing, roaming the neighborhood, sex experimentation, and bodily exposure, and less freedom in expressing sentiment, tenderness, fear, weakness, and hurt feelings. It is small wonder, therefore, that boys and girls have different conceptions of maternal and paternal roles.[39] Still other determinants of social sex role—preferential parent attitudes toward the child of opposite sex, differential availability of primary status at home and school, differences in the extent to which boys and girls identify which the mother—are less deliberately planned by socializing agents.

*See page 77 for reference to the effects of androgens, estrogens, and prolactin on behavior. Androgens have been shown to increase social aggression in boys[13] and dominance in a male chimpanzee.[18]

Genic determinants, mediated through hormones (after pubescence), and other presently unknown mechanisms probably have most effect on the temperamental aspects of social sex role.* Prior to pubescence sex differences in activity and output of energy[62, 72] (see page 411) are possibly determined in part by genic variables; wide intercultural variability and overlapping within cultures, however, rules out any prepotent influence. Except for girls' superiority in verbal fluency and lesser susceptibility to related disorders (stuttering, alexia), most sex differences in special cognitive abilities do not appear at early age levels and are probably culturally determined.[116] As already indicated, there is no evidence supporting the psychoanalytic view that social sex differences in children reflect the possession of different sex organs (or reactions to same) or innate differences in libidinal drives.

The interaction of these various determinants of social sex role may be illustrated in the sex typing of aggression-conformity, interests, and achievement. The greater conformity of girls and aggressiveness of boys reflect differential cultural expectations regarding masculinity-femininity, identification with like-sex role models, the more severe disciplinary treatment of boys by fathers, higher activity levels in boys, and the greater derived and primary status available to girls at home and in school. Since girls identify more than boys with the mother, they probably experience as more drastic an equivalent amount of moderate maternal punishment, and hence react less aggressively.[108] The greater friendliness of girls to adults is most marked when they have an older male sibling, suggesting in part that this is a compensatory device for overcoming maternal preferences for their brothers.[72] Sex differences in interests reflect prevocational influences, identification with adult role models, differential norms regarding status achievement and masculinity-femininity, and to a lesser extent differences in physical strength, motor skills and temperamental predispositions. The determination of differential sex patterns with respect to current and ultimate achievement has been discussed elsewhere (see pp. 281 and 447).

REFERENCES

1. Aberle, D. F., and Naegele, K. D.: Middle-class fathers' occupational role and attitudes toward children. *Am. J. Orthopsychiat.* 22: 366-378, 1952.

2. Abrahamson, S.: School rewards and social-class status. *Educ. Res. Bull. 31:* 8-15, 1952.

---

*Physical and motor differences between the sexes (see pp. 502 and 516) are beyond the scope of the present discussion. Sex-linked genic factors are largely responsible for differential rates of conception, viability, mortality, incidence of infectious diseases, sexual and skeletal maturation, and in part for differences in strength and in vital and cardiac capacity.

3. Adorno, T. W., Frenkel-Brunswik, E., Levinson, D. J., and Sanford, R. N.: *The Authoritarian Personality.* New York, Harper, 1950.

4. Amatora, S. M.: Can elementary school children discriminate certain traits in their teachers? *Child Develop. 23:* 76-80, 1952.

5. Ammons, R. B.: Reactions in a projective doll-play interview of white males two to six years of age to differences in skin color and facial features. *J. Genet. Psychol. 76:* 323-341, 1950.

6. Anderson, H. H., and Brewer, J. E.: Effects of teachers' dominative and integrative contacts on children's classroom behavior. *Appl. Psychol. Monogr.* No. 8, 1946.

7. Ausubel, D. P.: Prestige motivation of gifted children. *Genet. Psychol. Monogr. 43:* 53-117, 1951.

8. ———, Schiff, H. M., and Gasser, E. B.: A preliminary study of developmental trends in sociempathy: accuracy of perception of own and others' sociometric status. *Child Develop. 23:* 111-128, 1952.

9. Beaglehole, E., and Beaglehole, P.: *Some Modern Maoris.* Wellington, N. Z., New Zealand Council for Educational Research, 1946.

10. Bender, L., and Grugett, A. E., Jr.,: A follow-up report on children who had atypical sexual experience. *Am. J. Orthopsychiat. 22:* 825-837, 1952.

11. Biber, B., and Lewis, C.: An experimental study of what young children expect from their teachers. *Genet. Psychol. Monogr. 40:* 3-97, 1949.

12. Bird, C., Monachesi, E. D., and Burdick, H.: Studies of group tensions: III. The effect of parental discouragement of play attitudes upon the attitudes of white children toward Negroes. *Child Develop. 23:* 295-306, 1952.

13. Bize, P. R., and Moricard, R.: Psychic changes following injection of testosterone in young boys. *Bull. Soc. Pediat. 35:* 38, 1938.

14. Blake, R., and Dennis, W.: The development of stereotypes concerning the Negro. *J. Abnorm. Soc. Psychol. 38:* 525-531, 1943.

15. Bonney, M. E.: Sociometric study of agreement between teacher judgments and student choices. *Sociometry. 10:* 133-146, 1947.

16. Centers, R.: The American class structure: a psychological analysis. *In* T. M. Newcomb and E. L. Hartley, Eds., *Readings in Social Psychology.* New York, Holt, 1947, pp. 481-493.

17. Clark, E. J.: The relationship between personality traits of elementary school teachers and their evaluation of objectionable pupil behavior. *J. Educ. Res. 45:* 61-66, 1951.

18. Clark, G., and Birch, H. G.: Hormonal modifications of social behavior. I. The effect of sex hormone administration on the social status of a male castrate chimpanzee. *Psychosom. Med. 7:* 321-329, 1945.

19. Clark, K. B., and Clark, M. P.: Racial identification and preference in Negro children. *In* T. M. Newcomb and E. L. Hartley, Eds., *Readings in Social Psychology.* New York, Holt, 1947, pp. 169-178.

20. Conn., J. H.: Children's reactions to the discovery of genital differences. *Amer. J. Orthopsychiat. 10:* 747-755, 1940.

21. ———: Children's awareness of sex differences. II. Play attitudes and game preferences. *J. Child Psychiat. 2:* 82-99, 1951.

22. Crisswell, J. H.: A. sociometric study of race cleavage in the classroom. *Arch. Psychol. 33:* No. 235, 1939.

23. Cunningham, R., et al.: *Understanding Group Behavior of Boys and Girls.* New York, Teachers College, Columbia University, 1951.

24. Dai, B.: Some problems of personality development among Negro children. *In* C. Kluckhohn and H. A. Murray, Eds., *Personality in Nature, Society, and Culture*. New York, Knopf, 1949, pp. 437-458.

25. Davis, A.: American status systems and the socialization of the child. *Am. Sociol. Rev. 6*: 345-354, 1941.

26. ———: *Deep South: A Social Anthropological Study of Caste and Class*. Chicago, University of Chicago Press, 1941.

27. ———: Child training and social class. *In* R. G. Barker, J. S. Kounin, and H. F. Wright, Eds., *Child Behavior and Development*. New York, McGraw-Hill, 1943, pp. 607-620.

28. ———: Socialization and adolescent personality. In *Adolescence*, 43rd Yearbook, Natl. Soc. Stud. Educ. Chicago, University of Chicago Press, 1944, part 1.

29. ———: *Social-Class Influences upon Learning*. Cambridge, Harvard University Press, 1949.

30. ———, and Havighurst, R. J.: Social class and color differences in child rearing. *Am. Sociol. Rev. 11*: 698-710, 1946.

31. de Groat, A. F., and Thompson, G. G.: A study of the distribution of teacher approval and disapproval among sixth-grade children. *J. Exper. Educ. 18*: 57-75, 1949.

32. Della Piana, G. M.: Cognitive-affective values of pupils and teacher-pupil relationships. Unpublished master's thesis, Univ. of Illinois, 1953.

33. Deutsch, M.: Some social and personality factors in scholastic performance of minority group children. Paper read at Am. Psychol. Ass., Chicago, September, 1956.

34. Dillon, M. S.: Attitudes of children toward their own bodies and those of other children. *Child Develop. 5*: 165-176, 1934.

35. Dollard, J., and Miller, N. E.: *Personality and Psychotherapy*. New York, McGraw-Hill, 1950.

36. Dymond, R. F., Hughes, A. S., and Raabe, V. L.: Measurable changes in empathy with age. *J. Consult. Psychol. 16*: 202-206, 1952.

37. Ericson, M. C.: Social status and child-rearing practices. *In* T. M. Newcomb and E. L. Hartley, Eds., *Readings in Social Psychology*. New York, Holt, 1947, pp. 494-550.

38. Estvan, F. J.: The relationship of social status, intelligence, and sex of ten- and eleven-year-old children to awareness of poverty. *Genet. Psychol. Monogr. 46*: 3-60, 1952.

39. Finch, H. M.: Young children's concepts of parent roles. *J. Home Econ. 47*: 99-103, 1955.

40. Ford, C. S., and Beach, F. A.: *Patterns of Sexual Behavior*. New York, Harper Hoeber, 1951.

41. Frenkel-Brunswik, E.: A study of prejudice in children. *Hum. Relat. 1*: 295-306, 1948.

42. ———: Pattern of social and cognitive outlooks in children and parents. *Am. J. Orthopsychiat. 21*: 543-558, 1951.

43. ———, and Havel, J.: Prejudice in the interviews of children: I. Attitudes toward minority groups. *J. Genet. Psychol. 82*: 91-136, 1953.

44. Gage, N. L., Leavitt, G. S., and Stone, G. C.: Teachers' understanding of their pupils and pupils' ratings of their teachers. *Psychol. Monogr. 69*: No. 21, 1955.

45. Gates, G. S.: An experimental study of the growth of social perception. *J. Educ. Psychol. 14*: 449-462, 1923.

46. Goff, R. M.: *Problems and Emotional Difficulties of Negro Children.* New York, Teachers College, Columbia University, 1949.

47. Goodman, M. E.: *Race Awareness in Young Children.* Cambridge, Mass., Addison-Wesley, 1952.

48. Gough, H. G., Harris, D. B., Martin, W. E., and Edwards, M.: Children's ethnic attitudes: I. Relationship to certain personality factors. *Child Develop. 21*: 83-91, 1950.

49. Griffiths, W.: *Behavior Difficulties of Children as Perceived and Judged by Parents, Teachers and Children Themselves.* Minneapolis, University of Minnesota Press, 1952.

50. Gronlund, N. E.: The accuracy of teachers' judgments concerning the sociometric status of sixth-grade pupils. *Sociometry 13*: 197-225, 329-357, 1950.

51. Hallowell, A. I.: Culture, personality and society. *In* A. L. Kroeber, Ed., *Anthropology Today.* Chicago, University of Chicago Press, 1953, pp. 507-523.

52. Hammer, E. F.: Frustration-aggression hypothesis extended to socio-racial areas: comparison of Negro and white children's H-T-P's. *Psychiat. Quart. 27*: 596-607, 1953.

53. Harris, D. B., Gough, H. G., and Martin, W. E.: Children's ethnic attitudes: II. Relationship to parental beliefs concerning child training. *Child Develop. 21*: 169-181, 1950.

54. Hart, F. W.: *Teachers and Teaching.* New York, Macmillan, 1934.

55. Hartley, E. L.: Psychological problems of multiple group membership. *In* J. H. Rohrer and M. Sherif, Eds., *Social Psychology at the Crossroads.* New York, Harper, 1951, pp. 371-387.

56. ——, Rosenbaum, M., and Schwartz, S.: Children's use of ethnic frames of reference: an exploratory study of children's conceptualization of multiple ethnic membership. *J. Psychol. 26*: 367-386, 1948.

57. ——, ——, and ——: Children's perception of ethnic group membership. *J. Psychol.* 387-398, 1948.

58. Havighurst, R. J., and Taba, H.: *Adolescent Character and Personality.* New York, Wiley, 1949.

59. Herskovits, M. J.: On cultural and psychological reality. *In* J. H. Rohrer and M. Sherif, Eds., *Social Psychology at the Crossroads.* New York, Harper, 1951, pp. 145-163.

60. Hoehn, A. J.: A study of social class differentiation in the classroom behavior of nineteen third-grade teachers. *J. Soc. Psychol. 39*: 269-292, 1954.

61. Hollingshead, A. B.: *Elmtown's Youth: The Impact of Social Classes on Youth.* New York, Wiley, 1949.

62. Honzik, M. P.: Sex differences in the occurrence of materials in the play constructions of preadolescents. *Child Develop. 22*: 15-35, 1951.

63. Horowitz, E. L.: The development of attitude toward the Negro. *Arch. Psychol. 28*: No. 194, 1936.

64. Horowitz, R. E.: Racial aspects of self-identification in nursery school children. *J. Psychol. 7*: 91-99, 1939.

65. Jersild, A. T.: Characteristics of teachers who are "liked best" and "disliked most." *J. Exper. Educ. 8*: 164-165, 1939.

66. ——, Markey, F. V., and Jersild, C. L.: Children's fears, dreams, wishes, daydreams, likes, dislikes, pleasant and unpleasant memories. *Child Develop. Monogr.* No. 12, 1933.

67. Johnson, Granville, B., Jr.: The origin and development of the Spanish attitude toward the Anglo and the Anglo attitude toward the Spanish. *J. Educ. Psychol. 41*: 428-439, 1950.

68. Kaplan, L.: The annoyances of elementary school teachers. *J. Educ. Res. 45*: 137-144, 1951.

69. Kitay, P. M.: A comparison of the sexes in their attitudes and beliefs about women: a study of prestige groups. *Sociometry 3*: 399-407, 1940.

70. Kluckhohn, C., and Kluckhohn, F. R.: American culture: generalized orientations and class patterns. *In* L. Bryson, L. Finkelstein, and R. M. Mac Iver, Eds., *Conflicts of Power in Modern Culture.* New York, Harper, 1947.

71. Koch, H. L.: The social distance between certain racial, nationality, and skin-pigmentation groups in selected populations of American school children. *J. Genet. Psychol. 68*: 63-95, 1946.

72. ——: Some personality correlates of sex, sibling position, and sex of sibling among five- and six-year-old children. *Genet. Psychol. Monogr. 52*: 3-51, 1955.

73. ——: The relation of certain family constellation characteristics and attitudes of children toward adults. *Child Develop. 26*: 13-40, 1955.

74. Landreth, C., and Johnson, B. C.: Young children's responses to a picture and inset test designed to reveal reactions to persons of different skin color. *Child Develop. 24*: 63-79, 1953.

75. Leeds, C. H., and Cook, W. W.: The construction and differential value of a scale for determining teacher-pupil attitudes. *J. Exper. Educ. 16*: 149-159, 1947.

76. Leevy, J. R.: Contrasts in urban and rural family life. *Am. Sociol. Rev. 5*: 948-953, 1940.

77. Levinger, L. and Murphy, L. B.: Implications of the social scene for the education of young children. *Yearb. Natl. Soc. Stud. Educ. 46*: 15-43, 1947, part 2.

78. Levitt, E. E.: Studies in intolerance of ambiguity: I. The Decision-Location Test with grade school children. *Child Develop. 24*: 263-268, 1953.

79. Lewin, K., Lippitt, R., and White, R. K.: Patterns of aggressive behavior in experimentally created "social climates." *J. Soc. Psychol. 10*: 271-299, 1939.

80. Lewis, C.: *Children of the Cumberland.* New York, Columbia University Press, 1946.

81. Lewis, O.: *Life in a Mexican Village.* Urbana, University of Illinois Press, 1951.

82. Lyle, W. H., Jr., and Levitt, E. E.: Punitiveness, authoritarianism, and parental discipline of grade school children. *J. Abnorm. Soc. Psychol. 51*: 42-46, 1955.

83. Lynd, R. S., and Lynd, H. M.: *Middletown in Transition.* New York, Harcourt, Brace, 1937.

84. Maas, H.: Some social class differences in the family systems and group relations of pre- and early adolescents. *Child Develop. 22*: 145-152, 1951.

85. McKee, J. P., and Leader, F. B.: The relationships of socio-economic status and aggression to the competitive behavior of preschool children. *Child Develop. 26*: 135-142, 1955.

86. Malpass, L. F.: Some relationships between students' perceptions of school and their achievement. *J. Educ. Psychol.* 44: 475-482, 1953.

87. Mead, M. *Male and Female: A Study of the Sexes in a Changing World.* New York, William Morrow, 1949.

88. ———: Research on primitive children. *In* L. Carmichael, Ed., *Manual of Child Psychology,* ed. 2. New York, Wiley, 1954, pp. 735-780.

89. Meek, L. H.: *Personal-Social Development of Boys and Girls with Implications for Secondary Education.* New York, Progressive Education Association, 1940.

90. Meltzer, H.: The development of children's nationality preferences, concepts and attitudes. *J. Psychol.* 11: 343-358, 1941.

91. Miller, N. E.: Studies of fear as an acquirable drive: I. Fear as motivation and fear-reduction as reinforcement in the learning of new responses. *J. Exper. Psychol.* 38: 89-101, 1948.

92. ———, and Bugelski, R.: Minor studies in aggression: the influence of frustrations imposed by the in-group on attitudes expressed toward out-groups. *J. Psychol.* 25: 437-442, 1948.

93. Minard, R. D.: Race attitudes of Iowa children. *Univ. Iowa Stud. Charact.* 4: No. 2, 1931.

94. Moreno, J. L. *Who Shall Survive?* Washington, D. C., Nerv. & Ment. Dis. Pub. Co., 1934.

95. Mowrer, O. H.: Authoritarianism vs. "self government" in the management of children's aggressive (anti-social) reactions as a preparation for citizenship in a democracy. *J. Soc. Psychol.* 10: 121-126, 1939.

96. Murphy, L. B.: Childhood experience in relation to personality development. *In* J. McV. Hunt, Ed., *Personality and the Behavior Disorders,* vol. 2. New York, Ronald Press, 1944, pp. 652-690.

97. Mussen, P. H.: Some personality and social factors related to changes in children's attitudes toward Negroes. *J. Abnorm. Soc. Psychol.* 45: 423-441, 1950.

98. Parsons, T.: Age and sex in the social structure of the United States. *Am. Sociol. Rev.* 7: 604-616, 1942.

99. Pope, B.: Socio-economic contrasts in children's peer culture prestige values. *Genet. Psychol. Monogr.* 48: 157-220, 1953.

100. Rabban, M.: Sex-role identification in young children in two diverse social groups. *Genet. Psychol. Monogr.* 42: 81-158, 1950.

101. Radke, M., and Sutherland, J.: Children's concepts and attitudes about minority and majority American groups. *J. Educ. Psychol.* 40: 449-468, 1949.

102. ———, ———, and Rosenberg, P.: Racial attitudes of children. *Sociometry 13*: 154-171, 1950.

103. ———, Trager, H. G., and Davis, H.: Social perceptions and attitudes of children. *Genet. Psychol. Monogr.* 40: 327-447, 1949.

104. Radke-Yarrow, M.: Developmental changes in the meaning of minority group membership. *J. Educ. Psychol.* 44: 82-101, 1953.

105. Remmers, H. H., Horton, R. E., and Lysgaard, S.: Teen-age personality in our culture. Report of poll No. 32. *Purdue Opinion Panel,* 1952.

106. Sandin, A. A.: Social and emotional adjustments of regularly promoted and non-promoted pupils. *Child Develop. Monogr.* No. 32, 1944.

107. Schneider, L., and Lysgaard, S.: The deferred gratification pattern: a preliminary study. *Am. Sociol. Rev. 18*: 142-149, 1953.
108. Sears, R. R., Whiting, J. W. M., Nowlis, V., and Sears, P. S.: Some child-rearing attecedents of aggression and dependency in young children. *Genet. Psychol. Monogr. 47*: 135-234, 1953.
109. Sheehy, L. M.: *A Study of Preadolescents By Means of a Personality Inventory.* Washington, D. C., Catholic University Press, 1938.
110. Springer, D. V.: Awareness of racial differences by preschool children in Hawaii. *Genet. Psychol. Monogr. 41*: 215-270, 1950.
111. ——: National-racial preferences of fifth-grade children in Hawaii. *J. Genet. Psychol. 83*: 121-136, 1953.
112. Stendler, C. B.: *Children of Brasstown.* Urbana, University of Illinois Press, 1949.
113. ——: Social class differences in parental attitude toward school at grade I level. *Child Develop. 22*: 37-46, 1951.
114. ——, and Young, N.: The impact of beginning first-grade upon socialization as reported by mothers. *Child Develop. 21*: 241-260, 1950.
115. Terman, L. M.: *Psychological Factors in Marital Happiness.* New York, McGraw-Hill, 1938.
116. ——, and Tyler, L. E.: Psychological sex differences. *In* L. Carmichael, Ed., *Manual of Child Psychology,* ed. 2. New York, Wiley, 1954, pp. 1064-1114.
117. Thompson, L.: Perception patterns in three Indian tribes. *Psychiatry 14*: 255-263, 1951.
118. Thompson, M. M.: The effect of discriminatory leadership on the relations between the more and less privileged subgroups. Unpublished doctor's dissertation, Univ. of Iowa, 1940.
119. Trager, H. G., and Yarrow, M. R.: *They Learn What They Live: Prejudice in Young Children.* New York, Harper, 1952.
120. Trent, R.: An analysis of expressed self-acceptance among Negro children. Unpublished doctor's dissertation, Teachers College, Columbia University, 1953.
121. Tyler, L. E.: The development of "vocational interests": I. The organization of likes and dislikes in ten-year-old children. *J. Genet. Psychol. 86*: 33-44, 1955.
122. Walton, W. E.: Empathic responses in children. *Psychol. Monogr. 48*: 40-67, 1936.
123. Warner, W. L., Havighurst, R. J., and Loeb, M. B.: *Who Shall Be Educated?* New York, Harper, 1944.
124. Weider, A., and Noller, P. A.: Objective studies of children's drawings of human figures. I. Sex awareness and socioeconomic level. *J. Clin. Psychol. 6*: 319-325, 1950.
125. Wertham, F.: Psychological effects of school segregation. *Am. J. Psychotherap. 6*: 94-103, 1952.
126. West, J.: *Plainville, U. S. A.* New York, Columbia University Press, 1945.
127. Whiting, J. W. M., and Child, I. L.: *Child Training and Personality.* New Haven, Yale University Press, 1953.
128. Zeligs, R.: Tracing racial attitudes through adolescence. *Sociol. Soc. Res. 23*: 45-54, 1938.
129. ——: Children's intergroup attitudes. *J. Genet. Psychol. 72*: 101-110, 1948.

CHAPTER 14

Relationships With Peers

ORIGINS OF THE PEER GROUP

IN MANY CULTURES, both primitive and complex, "wherever children and youth are together for any length of time and free to pursue their own purposes," a subculture of peers is operative.[129] Apart from cultural tradition and parental expectations that they join such groups, many other factors facilitate the formation of peer groupings. As a social being man cannot fully experience, develop, or express his own individuality or enjoy a biosocial status except through a system of relationships to constituted groups. The family, it is true, provides such a social identity for the child; and if it includes several siblings it even affords the opportunity for companionship with children approximately his own age. The same applies to the school. Nevertheless, neither one of these institutions can ever satisfy his need for an identity with persons of equal status. In the shadow of superordinate adults he cannot gain recognition, play differentiated roles, practice social skills, or interact with others except as a dependent and subordinate figure. The peer group, of course, could also provide neither primary nor derived status unless it were a superordinate body; but in contrast to parents, teachers, and the adult community its authority reflects a superordination by equals rather than by superiors.

At the very best children can enjoy no more than a marginal, subadult status even in primitive and rural cultures. In complex, urban cultures, extreme discontinuity between child and adult roles does not permit them even this degree of fringe participation. Denied functional and equal membership in the adult community that dispenses status roles in the central stratum of social interaction, they must create a substitutive though peripheral status-giving instrumentality of their own. Hence, out of necessity as well as inclination they "turn to the closer company of age mates . . . to secure . . . a social identity . . . in an adverse, adult-made world in which they are marginal in varying degrees."[112] At first, prolonged discontinuity and exclusion from the wider community, and the accompanying resentment, bitterness, and estrangement, help to solidify the peer group. Later, as children become more firmly anchored in the distinctive goals, values, and loyalties of their own subculture, its very separateness as a world apart serves to perpetuate its existence.

Individual Differences in Orientation to Group Experience

We have been saying that children in their peer group behavior seek to establish a social identity in relation to equals. But the acquisition of biosocial status, differentiated on the basis of age level and sex, does not exhaust the child's needs in this matter. He is also concerned with achieving self-actualization, self-expression, and spontaneity in as benevolent an environment as possible.[70] Hence he also seeks a highly *personal identity* in the group, an identity that is most congruent with his fundamental personality trends and temperamental predispositions, that is particularized with respect to breadth of social responsiveness, motivational orientation to group participation, level of activity, introversion-extroversion, leadership-followership, etc. This is suggested by the marked variability in children's degree and quality of social responsiveness[60] and by the stability of their choice behavior and sociometric status.[21, 22,69, 81]

Much interindividual variability in approach to peer group experience reflects the impact of early socializing experience within the family circle. Partly as a result of this experience the child is predisposed to welcome or avoid contact with his peers, to expect the best or worst from them, and to make realistic or unrealistic demands on them (see p. 371). His reaction to his peers is influenced by early upbringing in a foundling home (see pp. 122 and 255), by ordinal position and sex of siblings (see p. 358), and by such parental attitudes as overprotection, rejection, overvaluation, and over- and underdomination (see pp. 372-374). Even the extent to which he is traumatized by racial or ethnic discrimination is influenced in part by the amount of self-acceptance he can acquire from interaction with his parents (see p. 431).

We have also hypothesized that the pervasive difference between satellizers and non-satellizers in over-all orientation to interpersonal relations generalizes from home to peer group (see p. 372). The satellizing child expects to be accepted for himself by his peers. The group is more than a source of primary status to him. It also provides derived status in much the same way as the parent except that the status-giving authority resides in a corporate body of equals of which he himself is part. By relating to it he obtains the same spontaneous "we-feeling" that he experiences in the family group. The non-satellizer, on the other hand, is not accustomed to assuming an internalized attitude of self-subserviency in relation to the group. To compensate for his lack of intrinsic self-esteem, he has greater need for recognition and applause from his peers. The field of intra-group relations like the home is no place for spontaneous "we-feeling"; it is just another arena in which he contends for prestige, power, and self-aggrandizement. If he is a rejected child, his chances of acquiring primary status in the group are much better than at home; if he is overvalued by his parents, the reverse is true. The non-satellizer is quite capable, of course, of obtaining vicarious status from identification with prestigeful membership or reference groups; but since no subservence of self is involved, it bears little resemblance to the derived status of satellizers.

DEVELOPMENTAL FUNCTIONS OF THE PEER GROUP

An overview of the impact of the peer group on children's personality development can be accomplished most simply by listing briefly the various normative functions it performs:

1. Depending on the prevailing degree of cultural discontinuity between child and adult roles, the peer group furnishes a little to a goodly portion of the child's primary status. In any case it is the only cultural institution in which his position is not marginal, in which he is offered primary status and a social identity among a group of equals, and in which his own activities and concerns reign supreme. As a result his self-concept undergoes expansion and differentiation in terms other than as a child of his parents.

2. The peer group is also a subsidiary source of derived status for the satellizer during childhood.* By achieving acceptance in the group, by subordinating himself to group interests, and by making himself dependent on group approval, the child gains a measure of intrinsic self-esteem that is independent of his achievement or relative status in the group. This "we-feeling" furnishes security and belongingness and is a powerful ego support and basis of loyalty to group norms.

3. By providing primary and derived status, a new source of values and standards, and experience in behaving as a sovereign person, the peer group devalues parents, transfers part of the child's loyalties from them to itself (resatellization), and hence promotes desatellization. As a result of the support the child receives from his peer group, he gains the courage to weaken the bonds of emotional anchorage to parents. By vesting in his peers the authority to set standards, he affirms his *own* right to self-determination since he is patently no different from them. No longer need he implicitly subscribe to the belief that only parents and adults can determine what is right. The peer group also serves as "a bulwark of strength in combating authority . . . By pooling their resistance in groups and throwing up barriers of one kind and another against adult authority and interference," children manage to exclude adults and protect themselves from ". . . the

*In some cultures, where the parent provides little emotional succorance after infancy (see p. 421), the peer group may constitute the chief source of derived status.

coercions that [the latter] are prone to use."[129] By creating precedents and then appealing to the prevailing group standards, the peer culture operates as a pressure group, obtains important concessions for individual members with restrictive parents, and emancipates itself from adult and institutional controls.

4. Like home and school, the peer group is an important socializing, enculturative and training institution. It is here that children learn much of their poise in dealing with persons outside the intimate family circle, acquire approved techniques of sociability, self-assertion, competition and cooperation, and develop sensitivity to cues indicative of group expectations, censure, and approval. By interacting with their peers they learn the functional and reciprocal basis of rules and obligations, how to play differentiated roles, and how to subordinate their own interests to group goals (see p. 393). As previously pointed out, however, the peer group influences moral development more by enforcing or discouraging conformity to values, norms, and goals originating in the particular adult community from which it stems than by generating moral values of its own* Only the peer group can furnish suitable models and occasions for children to observe and practice the social skills and behaviors they must know in order to enact their appropriate age and sex roles both in their own subculture and in the wider community. It constitutes a proving-ground where they can test the workability of techniques they observe elsewhere. Hence, such experience serves as a form of apprenticeship for adult social life. Through the peer group children also pick up much knowledge, misinformation and folklore regarding science, sex, sports, religion, etc.

5. Finally, the peer group provides a *particularized* social identity for the child insofar as it permits him to play roles that are most compatible with his personality orientation toward group experience. For many children it also serves as a corrective influence counteracting the undesirable social effects of such extreme parental attitudes as under- or overdomination and providing a substitutive source of derived and primary status for rejected children.

Differential Impact of Peer Relationships on Later Personality Development

Just as particular kinds of socializing experience in the home determine individual differences in children's initial orientation to the peer group,

---

*This statement is less true of adolescent peer groups and conditions of rapid social change and marked parent-youth conflict. Also, among lower-class children in our culture, the importance of the peer group as a socializing agency (as well as a desatellizing influence and source of primary and derived status) is considerably greater than among middle-class and rural children (see pp. 435 and 437).

the type of interpersonal relationships they characteristically establish in their early experiences with peers differentially conditions their later personality development. The child's early pattern of peer relationships— breadth of social responsiveness, sociometric status, leadership-followership— tends to be remarkably stable from middle childhood through adolescence (see pp. 467 and 485). Similarly, on the basis of early acceptance or rejection by peers, he either acquires enhanced feelings of self-esteem and confidence about being intrinsically accepted by others, or suffers ego deflation and regards social acceptance as something to be won by impressing associates or buying their favor. If peer group experience tends to be habitually unsatisfying or downright threatening, it encourages introversion, retreat into the home, and withdrawal from participation in group life; and if the opportunity for social experience is sufficiently curtailed, it interferes with the acquisition of necessary skills of communication, self-assertion, and self-defense and with the enactment of realistic and effective interpersonal roles during adolescence and adulthood.

Longitudinal consistency in the child's peer group status may be attributed to several factors. First, we may assume some degree of continuity in the personality traits that make him attractive or unattractive to others and more or less capable of satisfying their interpersonal needs. Second, there is presumably some continuity in the relative degree of social skill he possesses and in his individual orientation to group experience. Third, even though he may shift his membership from one peer group to another, not only does the child tend to carry his reputation with him, but much generality over groups also prevails in the criteria determining social acceptability. The group's total impression of him is acquired in the early grades and is extremely difficult to change.[117] In reacting to his rejection by others, he either withdraws further from group activities or develops obnoxiously aggressive traits, thereby increasing his unlikableness and social ineffectiveness. Such alterations in sociometric status as do occur reflect changes in the membership and purposes of the peer group, ego-inflating or deflating experiences outside the peer group, early or late pubescence, increasing sensitivity to social class membership, age level changes in the bases of peer status, and increased ability or incentive to conceal objectionable traits or curry favor with others.

Relationship of Peer Group to Home and Wider Community

In a very real sense the peer group may be considered a buffering medium between home and the wider community. As the child emerges from the sheltered confines of the home, he enjoys relatively little direct contact with the culture at large. He is inducted instead into two special training institutions—school and peer group. In the latter he becomes immersed in a peripheral subculture of his own making which pursues activities and establishes criteria for prestige that bear little resemblance to their counterparts in the adult community. Nevertheless such peer groups still reflect in a larger sense the major values, aspirations, developmental goals, and ethical norms of the social milieu in which they are formed.[112] In addition, many forms of peer group activity in our society (e.g., school clubs, scouts) do not arise spontaneously but are conceived and directed by adults.

In assessing the relative importance of the peer group for personality development in our culture, it would be fair to say that it generally plays only a subsidiary role to the family as a socializing and enculturative agency and as a source of values and derived status, but that it shares with the school the major responsibility of providing the child's primary status. As already pointed out this situation varies interculturally and with social class and urban-rural status within our culture. Also, in a rapidly changing and unstable culture the peer group becomes a more important source of values since family and school are preoccupied with transmitting the established cultural heritage and are less strategically placed for transmitting what is changing. Under any circumstances, the peer group is a less important source of values and derived status during childhood than during adolescence. And since primary status (unlike the situation at adolescence) constitutes only a relatively minor factor in the total economy of the child's ego organization, the derived status he obtains within the family circle must still be accounted the principal interpersonal influence impinging on his personality development.

DEVELOPMENTAL TRENDS IN PEER RELATIONSHIPS

As previously indicated, the dependency of the human infant facilitates the relatively precocious emergence of social behavior and explains why in the first two years of life it is largely restricted to adults (see p. 370). With increasing age, however, a shift occurs in nursery school children from *passive dependence* on adults to attention- and approval-seeking dependence on peers.* In the strictest sense of the term, peer group behavior begins when the child, unmonitored by adults, is permitted to interact freely with his fellows. Initially, a substantial proportion of his contacts with peers are rather closely supervised; and even later when he is largely left on his own, much peer activity still occurs under the over-all supervision of adults.

Trends in Early Childhood

Limiting Factors in Early Peer Relationships. Apart from the pre-emptive influence of initial socialization in relation to adults, many other factors

*See G. Heathers, *J. Genet. Psychol. 86*: 275-279, 1955.

tend to retard the early development of peer relationships. First, motor incompetence restricts the child's ability to participate manually in many joint play activities. Second, because of cognitive immaturity he lacks adequate awareness of others' needs and feelings and experiences difficulty in perceiving group goals and expectations, in sharing common perspectives, and in assuming differentiated roles. Third, difficulties in communication hamper effective group interaction. Even after he acquires sufficient language skills to express his ideas, the young child fails to communicate clearly because he is preoccupied with his own point of view and because he tends to assume that his listeners have access to his thoughts and hence do not require explanatory information.[108] Fourth, a low span of attention limits his ability to engage in group enterprises requiring continuity and sustained concentration. Fifth, ignorance of techniques of sharing, of property rights and of the "rules of the game" precipitates much unnecessary conflict and prematurely terminates many interpersonal transactions.

Just as important perhaps as the foregoing limiting factors is an attitude of egocentricity that is not reflective of developmental immaturity but of the prevailing state of ego organization.* During the omnipotent and negativistic phases of ego development the child is preoccupied with his own needs and activities. "He wants everything to come in to him. His chief interpersonal relation with other children is the acquisition of objects and the protection of any object which he is using, has used, or might use."[3] With satellization, the child's impulses are directed more "outward toward others," and he is "able to demand less for [himself] and to adapt to the needs of others . . . He no longer seems to need to embellish self with many possessions. There is less domineering, less violence, and fewer threats of violence in his relations with other children. He can share, take turns, and make polite requests of others. He begins to say 'We' . . . and 'Me, too.' "[3] The out-of-bounds, expansive four year old, on the other hand, is a quarrelsome, boastful, and self-assertive playmate.[3, 49] At five, more realistic self-appraisal makes him more cooperative, considerate and sympathetic, and less prone to interfere with the liberties of others.[32, 49] Much of children's early egocentricity in peer relationships reflects their early socialization with parents. Accustomed to being on the receiving end of a nurturant relationship, to being favored and given special consideration, they are naturally reluctant to surrender their privileged positions or consider the needs of others. Under atypical conditions, where children become emotionally dependent on each other instead of on adults, egocentricity

*The decline in egocentricity with advancing age is also attributable to various aspects of perceptual, cognitive, moral, and social development (see pp. 311-312 and 553).

is less marked. Thus, in the case of six young orphans reared togther with little succorant attention from adults, ordinary sibling rivalry was absent and the children were spontaneously considerate and solicitous of each other's welfare.[45]

Initial Responses to Other Children. The infant's early responses to other children are primarily egocentric. During the first two years of life, "the majority of his reactions are to himself and his own activities."[3] Although there are "some social relations, largely self-initiated, . . . the child largely ignores other children"[3] or treats them impersonally as objects or play materials.[3, 32, 91] Many of his initial responses are negative and involve conflicts over possessions; but the aggression engendered in such situations also tends to be impersonal. He appears to react to the interfering child as though the latter were a frustrating agent rather than a hostile individual.[3, 91] Toward the close of this period, however, positive social responses toward children increase and become both more personal and more integrated with play materials.[3, 91]

Social Participation in the Preschool Period. Both the quantity and the quality of social participation continue to improve during the preschool years as the inhibitory influence of the aforementioned limiting factors gradually declines. Although sharply demarcated stages cannot be drawn, certain types of social participation are clearly more characteristic of younger preschool children, whereas other types are found more frequently among older children of this age group. Observational studies of nursery school children support the generalization that peer group behavior proceeds from a "solitary" or "onlooker" stage to a stage of "associative" and "cooperative" play, with "parallel" play constituting an intermediate step. Quality of social participation is highly correlated with chronological age,[3, 50, 62, 107] but is unrelated to extent of nursery school experience.[107]

The young nursery school child is still preoccupied with his own activities. Self-initiated approaches to other children are less frequent than responses to the teacher.[3] Consistent with his hoarding proclivities and inability to share is the predominance of either solitary play (that goes on adjacent to but completely without reference to the activities of others) or of a passive type of onlooking.[3, 42, 107] As peer relations increase in frequency and sharing and taking turns become more common, "parallel" play predominates. Here the child pursues the same activities or uses similar toys as his playmates, but plays "beside" rather than with them.[107] Finally, he participates more in a collaborative type of play which at first is mostly associative and later involves "division of labor, group censorship, centralization of control, and the subordination of individual desires" to some group purpose and to a sense of belongingness in the group[107] With increasing age, he tends to play with a larger group of children[53] and to become less emotionally upset upon exposure to a novel social situation.[63]

Although "self-initiated reactions predominate" in the preschool period, the child gradually becomes more responsive to the approaches of other children.[3] Children of this age "are more interested in themselves and their own relationships with other children but have a growing awareness of the playmate choices, likes and dislikes of their fellows."[60] They are particularly aware of attention-getting and nonconforming behavior and of the activities of friends and popular children.[60] During the nursery school period, the degree of social awareness is related neither to chronological age nor to extent of group experience.[60]

As relationships with contemporaries become less impersonal, the preschool child begins to react to "other children as individual persons with special individual characteristics. One child is no longer equally good as another as a playmate."[3] Thus mutually congenial children begin to pair off and the group tends to exclude children with overly aggressive, passive, or otherwise objectionable traits.[3, 119]

Leadership behavior also increases during the preschool years. The independent pursuit of activities is first replaced by following behavior, then by shared leadership, and finally by directing behavior.[107] Degree of leadership is highly correlated with chronological age but not with amount of nursery school experience; it is practically coextensive with degree of social participation.[107] The desire for social attention and applause and for bossing other children evidently becomes greater with increasing age.[62] Parten distinguishes between "artful" and "brute force" leaders in the nursery school and notes that "the technique of leadership is sometimes learned, perhaps, through following a forceful leader."[107] It has also been suggested that the fabrication of imaginary playmates reflects a need to control playmates more completely than is possible in real life.[3] Although the presence of rival leaders often has a disruptive influence on intra-group relationships, quarrels at this age tend to be self-terminating.[119] Situational factors also have an important bearing on leadership. A child may be a leader in one group or type of activity and a follower in another. In breaking into new groups he also tends to revert to more primitive types of leadership and social participation.[119]

Marked variability prevails in degree, quality and breadth of social participation, social responsiveness and leadership "among children of approximately the same social and educational status."[60, 107] Children even show consistent individual differences from day to day in amount of upset to a novel social situation, the less socially adequate children reacting more violently.[63] Intelligence is correlated only slightly with leadership and degree of social participation[107] and not at all with social responsiveness.[60]

Some individual differences in social behavior remain quite stable from early to late childhood. Such characteristics as degree of social participation, leadership, cooperativeness, sensitivity to the feelings of others, respect for property rights, negativism, and flexibility show considerable consistency from nursery to elementary school.[133] After finding his proper role in the group "cumulative experience in these positions enables each child to hold his place as leader or follower thereafter with a minimum of effort and resistance from others."[106] Even 16 to 27 years after being referred as children to a child guidance clinic for shy, withdrawn behavior, a group of 54 adults were still quiet and retiring and showed a preference for sheltered, noncompetitive jobs.[97] In the light of the exaggerated prognostic significance currently placed on such behavior, it is worth noting that two-thirds of these adults were satisfactorily adjusted and only two were mentally ill.[97]

Effect of Nursery School Experience. Attendance in nursery school obviously facilitates the development of peer relations by providing unusually good opportunities for child interaction, social participation, and the learning of necessary techniques of self-assertion, cooperation, and adjustment. In the absence of such or equivalent experience it could be reasonably anticipated that developmental changes in peer group behavior would be somewhat retarded. But although relevant experience is a necessary growth factor in this instance and influences the *rate* of development, it does not seem to account for either the particular direction (sequence of changes) that development takes or for enduring individual differences in peer relations. Thus, as already pointed out, after all children in the group have had a certain minimal amount of social experience, duration of nursery school attendance is *not* related to degree or quality of social participation, leadership, or social responsiveness.[60, 107] Children with prior nursery school experience are initially more socially active than children lacking this experience, but the latter tend to "catch up" rapidly.[71]

In comparing groups of children who do and do not attend nursery school certain predictable differences in social poise, facility, and adjustment almost always appear. The former are more spontaneous and highly socialized,[134] show more initiative, self-reliance, and independence from adults,[62, 71, 76, 134] and are more self-assertive and aggressive.[33, 44, 134] They are less shy and withdrawn in the presence of strangers and show more mature and persistent reactions when faced with frustrating tasks.[61, 133] Such differences are all consistent with the presumed effects of initial deprivation in necessary social experience, but may also be related to differences in parent attitudes that determine whether or not a child attends nursery school. On the other hand, no differences have been found between the two groups in such traits and behaviors as social adaptability,[55] oversensitivity to criticism,[7] fears,[61] temper tantrums,[7, 61] crying, and thumbsucking.[61] The beneficial effects of nursery school attendance are also dependent in part upon the quality of adult supervision, i.e., the warmth, friendliness and personal involvement of the teachers.[124]

Trends in Later Childhood

The previously indicated trends in peer relations, begun during the preschool years, tend to undergo completion during middle childhood and preadolescence. Peer groups continue to grow in size, complexity of organization, and freedom from adult supervision. Children become capable of sustained, spontaneously organized, and highly structured enterprises of their own.[32, 47] Their play interests also reflect the trend toward greater social sensitivity and responsiveness.[82] Play activities involve increasingly greater division of labor, differentiation of roles and status, teamwork, loyalty to a larger group, and breadth of leadership. Highly characteristic is the emergence of strict and formal sets of rules in connection with competitive games. At first these "rules of the game" tend to be conceived as arbitrarily valid, "sacred," and immutable; later they are regarded more as functional contrivances reached through mutual agreement that facilitate the orderly and equitable regulation of play (see p. 392). When willingness to abide by the rules develops children are first able to think of "winning" and "losing" competitive activities in accordance with duly constituted law. They insist on strict compliance with and equalitarian application of the rules and are extremely punitive in dealing with infractions thereof.[98] Only later when their equalitarianism is tempered by considerations of equity (see p. 392) are they willing to be more flexible.

Underlying these changes in the child's peer relations are gradual gains in span of attention and ability to communicate, improved social techniques, a decline in egocentricity, and the experience of satisfactions associated with conformity to the demands of peer group membership. Even more important, perhaps, is unspectacular but steady improvement in cognitive sophistication enabling him to understand complex rules, appreciate subtle group expectations, and perceive the relative hierarchical status of the various group members including his own. Complex group structure first becomes possible when individuals are able to perceive the attitudes of others toward themselves and feel confident enough of their perceptions to hazard both predictions regarding their implications for future dealings and adaptive responses based on such predictions. The individual's adjustment to his peer group, therefore, is partly a function of how well he is able to perceive his own and others' hierarchical positions. Insofar as these perceptions are accurate, a more realistic basis for interpersonal relations is provided; for the child's aspirations with respect to assuming various roles in group activities, his expectations of the roles others might be induced to play, the demands he might legitimately make no others, and the attitudes he might adopt in dealing with them are more or less appropriate in accordance with the validity of his estimates of own and others' sociometric status. When role behavior becomes more formalized, it is true that accurate perception of others' intentions becomes a less relevant determinant of the individual's social behavior.[121] But highly stylized role behavior is hardly characteristic of children's groups; and in any case the perception of hierarchical status is still important, even in a relatively impersonal group setting.

During the preadolescent period children are more interested in joining formal and highly structured groups, both adult sponsored organizations such as scouts,[73] and spontaneously organized gangs* Gang activities at this age (unlike adolescence) are not necessarily indicative of a lower-class environment, social maladjustment or pre-delinquency. They reflect the older child's alienation from the wider community, an anti-adult orientation, and an aggressive bid for primary status through defiance of adult authority. By establishing their own distinctive norms gang members increase group cohesiveness, test adult limits, and enhance the identity of the in-group. Except in urban-slum areas gangs tend to be replaced in adolescence by more intimate and less predatory bisexual crowds and cliques. Decreasing identification with the gang is associated with increased identification with the adult male pattern.†

The preadolescent gang is a closely-knit, unisexual action group with a high degree of role and status differentiation and much intra-group solidarity. It maintains a hostile, rebellious and conspiratorial attitude toward adult society and frequently participates in socially disapproved activity. Great emphasis is placed on excitement and adventure, and on such formal trappings of organizational secrecy as special names, cryptic codes and signals, special meeting places, and unique initiation ceremonies. More so than in other preadolescent groups, leadership in gangs tends to be despotically wielded and based on toughness, daring, and fighting ability.

PERCEPTION OF PEER ATTITUDES AND RELATIONSHIPS

We have already suggested that growing sensitivity to interpersonal attitudes and relationships underlies much developmental progress in the dif-

---

*In somewhat attenuated form, these preadolescent gangs share many of the structural properties of adolescent gangs.[38, 127, 136, 141]

†See A. R. Crane, *J. Genet. Psychol.* 86: 275-279, 1955.

ferentiation of peer interactions. Although empirical evidence bearing on the development of interpersonal perception is sparse, it does seem clear that with increasing age children improve in the ability to interpret expressions of emotion (see p. 418), to discriminate and verbalize traits they like and dislike in others (see p. 418), and to perceive the extent to which fellow group members accept them and other children.[13, 43] Even though this growth in social perceptual capacity presumably cuts across many different areas of interpersonal relations, there is no reason to believe that social sensitivity itself is a unitary personality trait. The child's accuracy in perceiving how others react to him, for example, is not related to his accuracy in perceiving their attitudes toward or relationships with persons other than himself (e.g., their sociometric status or feelings about associates).[12, 43] During late childhood children also become much more discriminating both in their own interpersonal preferences and in their perception of others' interpersonal attitudes. They tend to make less disproportionate use of the upper (favorable) portion of the rating and prediction scales in expressing and predicting sociometric choices.[13]

Children's interpersonal perceptions are influenced by their feelings and attitudinal biases, especially when the objects of perception are relatively ambiguous. On unstructured tasks and particularly in highly stable and cohesive groups they tend to overestimate the performance of associates enjoying high status in the group and to underestimate the performance of age mates with low status.[114] The need to have something in common with individuals they like also makes children perceive group members they prefer most as more similar to themselves than they actually are and as more similar than group members they prefer least.[40] Reflecting their bias in favor of their own sex group, children perceive the latter as possessing more favorable personality traits[2] and as playing more positive social roles[16] than members of the opposite sex.

On purely theoretical grounds, we have argued that more accurate perception of the interpersonal attitudes and status of others leads to more realistic social behavior, and hence facilitates both group interaction and the social adjustment of the individual (see p. 468). What little evidence there is on this issue is highly equivocal however. Children[43] and adolescent girls[12] who are more accurate in predicting the sociometric ratings they receive from classmates also tend to enjoy high sociometric status in the group; but since most children tend to overestimate their own sociometric status, the children who *actually* enjoy high status obtain artifactually more

*In one study at the high school level,[12] it was found that pupils overestimated both the sociometric status of and the sociometric ratings they received from classmates they preferred most. The converse was also true.

accurate prediction scores. Also, when the perceptual task lacks self-reference, as in predicting the feelings[43] or sociometric status[12] of others, the positive relationship between empathic ability and sociometric status no longer prevails.* It is still conceivable that accurate interpersonal perception promotes the child's social effectiveness and adjustment in more subtle ways than by enhancing his sociometric status. The extent to which he is able, for example, to stimulate behavioral contagion in the group (see p. 485) depends in part upon his ability accurately to perceive his own sociometric status.[109]

AGGRESSION AND CONFLICT

Conflicts and quarrels occur frequently among preschool children. In one observational study, the average rate of conflict reported was one per child every five minutes.[72] Characteristically they are brief[41, 72] (about thirty seconds in duration), self-terminating,[119] and resolved without lingering resentment or vindictiveness.[41, 72] Moreover, despite their apparent frequency, they are greatly exceeded in number by friendly, cooperative contacts.[4, 5, 6, 72, 95] For reasons given elsewhere (see pp. 336 and 435), lower-class children tend to be physically more aggressive than middle-class children and to be involved more frequently in conflict with their peers both during the preschool period and during later childhood. We have also discussed elsewhere sex differences in the frequency and techniques of aggression and possible explanations for same (see pp. 336 and 451).

Age Trends

During the preschool period conflicts tend to decrease in frequency† but last longer[41, 72] and have more prolonged after-effects.[8] The substitution of teasing and bullying and of generally more verbal, covert and devious techniques for screaming, crying and overt physical attack has already been discussed (see p. 335). These trends are attributable both to cultural pressures against the direct expression of hostility and to gains in cognitive, personality and social maturity. The cognitively more mature child is more able to cope with difficulties, to appreciate that many hurts are inflicted unintentionally, to disguise his hostility, to avoid misunderstandings, and to use language as both an outlet for aggression and as a means of circumventing conflict. Such concurrent manifestations of personality

---

*In a study of high school seniors, however, a positive relationship was found between sociometric status and accuracy in predicting others' responses on an interest inventory.[48]

†For conflicting evidence on this point see p. 334. Initially as social participation increases in preschool children, the frequency of conflict also increases.[41, 52, 72]

growth as decreased egocentricity, increased frustration tolerance, and greater ability to accept inevitable delays and restrictions in the gratification of his needs also serve to reduce tensions leading to conflict. Finally the older child is more reconciled to the fact that he cannot take his privileged position in the home with him to the peer group. He has learned to share, to take turns, and to accept group norms. He has a better understanding of property rights, of the needs of others, of what is expected of him, of his relative status in the group, of what he can legitimately demand from others and of what they will tolerate from him, and of the retaliatory consequences of aggression. There is less need for grabbing, pushing, and outshouting others when he can appeal to a set of mutually accepted rules.

Yet increased exposure to and awareness of the wider community also creates new instigations for frustration and aggression. As the child enters the more competing atmosphere of the school and participates in competitive activities, new incitements to and outlets for aggressive behavior are provided. Fighting ability also becomes an important determinant of the "pecking order" in boys' groups. Ordinarily this order is established by common agreement after very few actual battles. Thereafter it remains relatively stable without recourse to violence unless marked changes occur in the relative status or physical prowess of the group members.

Determinants of Aggression

The occurrence of conflict in the peer group is influenced by a large variety of precipitating, situational, and intra-group factors. In addition, as is apparent from the wide range of individual differences in frequency of involvement in conflict,[67, 72] such variables as temperament, personality and family environment are important determinants of aggression in the peer group. The significance of the latter factors is highlighted by the fact that individual differences in aggressiveness are extremely stable over a 12 month period.[72]

The major precipitating causes of aggression during the preschool years are disputes over material possessions and interference by one child with another's freedom of movement.[8, 41, 53, 72] Many quarrels are also precipitated by children working at cross-purposes or misunderstanding each other's motives and intentions, and by the discord engendered when a child tries to force his way into a group or activity where he is unwanted.[8] Sometimes a child seems to provoke aggression for no other reason than to test the limits of a situation.

Conflict is more apt to occur between children of the same sex but different ages[41] and in crowded play areas.[72] It is aggravated by ambiguity in the social situation and by hunger, fatigue and physical indispositions (see p. 336). The presence of permissive adults may increase the incidence of aggression since under these circumstances children rely more on the latter and less on their own internalized controls for keeping the peace.[116] Prior experience in solving their own conflicts without adult interference decreases the frequency of quarrels in the long run, even though such interference may prevent the outbreak of conflict at the moment.[72]

Since the opportunities for conflict are obviously enhanced by the frequency of peer interactions, children who are energetic, socially active and friendly tend to be involved in more disputes than phlegmatic and socially unresponsive children.[8, 72] It is not surprising, therefore, that close friends quarrel more with each other than with other children.[52] Degree of temperamental self-assertiveness is also an important predisposing factor. Anderson[4-6] distinguishes between two varieties of ascendant tendencies in children—a tendency to be rigid and inflexible, to work against others and satisfy needs at their expense (dominative behavior), and a tendency to be flexible and receptive to change, to work with others toward improved understanding, mutually satisfying goals, and resolution of conflict (integrative behavior). The effect of each type of behavior, according to Anderson, is to evoke like behavior in others.

Acquired personality trends also influence frequency of involvement in conflict. Aggressiveness in children is often a manifestation of insecurity, impaired self-esteem or jealousy. Sometimes, especially in a previously insecure child, it is indicative of increased self-confidence. The effects of different parent attitudes (see pp. 333, 336) and of varying degrees of punishment (see pp. 336-337) on the generation and expression of aggression have been considered elsewhere. Relatively nonascendant children can be made more ascendant through appropriate training that increases their self-confidence[67, 99, 104] whereas training in social perception and in techniques of cooperation can decrease the incidence of objectionable ascendance in overly dominative children.[37]

COMPETITION AND COOPERATION

Competition is an ego-oriented, self-aggrandizing activity in which the individual vies with others for hierarchical pre-eminence. Cooperation is a group-oriented activity in which the individual collaborates with others to attain some common goal. Nevertheless, neither developmentally nor in terms of psychological content are these two activities wholly antithetical to each other: both imply a considerable degree of interaction within the group as opposed to individual behavior that is carried on with little reference to the activities of others. The child pursues a solitary course with his peers before he is either cooperative or competitive (see p. 465); both types of behavior increase as individualism subsides. Which becomes more prominent (as well as the extent to which individualism is superseded) varies greatly with cultural environment.[92] Our own culture values both kinds of behavior, often inconsistently, and hence fosters much moral confusion (see p. 399). In general, ego-oriented motivation has a self-aggrandizing (competitive) flavor in our culture* (see p. 310), which varies from one social class to another. Although lower-class preschool children tend to be more competitive than middle-class children in play situations,[89] the latter eventually internalize higher aspirations for academic and vocational prestige (see p. 435). According to L. B. Murphy's observations lower-class preschool children also express more affection, are more helpful, and assume more responsibility for others in their peer behavior.[100] Boys are consistently more competitive than girls in our culture during both early[89] and later childhood (see p. 449).

Many activities in the peer group evoke cooperative and competitive behavior either simultaneously or alternately. Team games are competitive contests between two cooperatively organized groups. However, members of the same team may compete against each other while striving jointly for a distinctive team goal, or several teams may compete against each other in furthering a cause common to all. Some children are competitive under cooperative conditions, others are cooperative under competitive conditions,[122] and still others are task-oriented under any conditions.[10] Thus, despite the purportedly cooperative or competitive conditions characterizing a particular enterprise, the extent to which a given child is ego-oriented, task-oriented, or group-oriented can only be ascertained by individual motivational analysis.

Although aggressiveness may be expressed in many ways other than competitiveness, one would ordinarily anticipate a high relationship between the two traits since competition is the most acceptable outlet for aggression in our culture and almost inevitably involves some frustration, hostility or jealousy. In preschool children the relationship is negligible.[89] Evidently then it takes some time for young children first responding to the cultural pressures of competition to learn "to be angry when they are unsuccessful."[89]

Age Trends

Although younger children exhibit impersonal rivalry over possessions

---

*The quest for primary status does not necessarily involve competitive self-aggrandizement (see p. 310). "The Navaho [for example] is completely unaccustomed to an explicitly stated hierarchical ranking of persons . . . Being singled out from [his] fellows for superior performance is embarrassing or actively disturbing rather than rewarding."[83] The same cultural attitude toward competition among the Hopi is associated with a much lower incidence of peer group conflicts.[42]

and more personal rivalry over the affection and attention of adults, true competition in the sense of a performance contest first appears between the ages of three and four.[54, 65, 84] Thereafter, as children gradually internalize a desire to excel from the competitive norms of our culture, competitiveness becomes an increasingly more characteristic feature of their response to peer activities.[49, 54, 84, 89] Such behavior presupposes the ability to become ego-involved in performance, to set levels of aspiration, and to experience fluctuations in self-esteem upon encountering success and failure. Preschool and kindergarten children display competitiveness by grabbing materials from others, cornering a supply, making favorable comments about their own work, withholding assistance, increasing their work output, and showing greater perseverance.[54, 84, 139] As they acquire increasing appreciation of the concept of excelling others according to the rules of the game, and gain in ability realistically to compare their own performance with that of others, competition takes place on a more sophisticated plane. Children of elementary school age work harder under competitive conditions than when working anonymously,[10] and for individual rewards than for group prizes.[90] Even so they are highly responsive to such natural group competitive situations as contests between boys and girls, teams, and classrooms.[90]

Cooperation requires greater cognitive and personality maturity than competition. Rudimentary forms of cooperative play (see p. 465) and of mutual aid in the solution of problems requiring collaborative efforts[140] appear in older preschool children. In one study spontaneous understanding (on a conceptual level) of the nature of cooperative group work was not found prior to the age of six.[65] Cooperation presupposes considerable social responsiveness and capacity for self-subordinating and differentiated role behavior. The child must be able to perceive the possibilities for and advantages of cooperative action in enterprises where individual efforts are inadequate, and must be capable of communicating effectively with his fellows.[140] The development of cooperative behavior, therefore, is related to the growth of sympathy, affection, social sensitivity, language and altruism.* In human beings it is greatly facilitated by the interdependency of social living and by genic capacities for emotional identification with persons and groups.

Determinants

Tendencies toward competitive and cooperative-sympathetic behavior are influenced by numerous situational and personality variables and also show a wide range of individual differences.[10, 54, 90, 100] Relatively low intersitu-

*Altruistic behavior increases between the ages of five and eight (see p. 312) but has not been found to increase between nine and sixteen[132] (see p. 384). The altruism of eight year olds is largely tied to their perceptions of other children's generosity.[142]

ational generality has been reported by Hartshorne and May for such traits as helpfulness (see p. 157). As previously indicated, however, much of this apparent lack of generality is a function of the child's varying degree of ego-involvement in different activities. The extent to which he is competitive in an arithmetic contest, for example, varies directly with his liking for and desire to do well in that subject.[10] Moreover, despite the operation of such situational factors as the child's relationship to the person in distress and to the cause of his suffering (see p. 344), L. B. Murphy found considerable individual consistency in the expression of sympathetic behavior.[100] It is evident, nevertheless, that children's disposition to be cooperative or sympathetic (rather than competitive) in a given situation is greater if their companions are (a) considerably younger than themselves;[100] (b) strangers instead of established friends,* and (c) if the general social atmosphere is cordial.[65]

Temperamental and personality variables are presumably important determinants of cooperativeness and competitiveness but have received little systematic attention in developmental studies. Because socially active and responsive children have relatively much commerce with their peers, they tend to be both more aggressive and more sympathetic than less active children.[100] Children from democratic homes tend to be more outgoing and competitive than children from authoritarian homes (see p. 374); I.Q., however, is only slightly related to sympathy and cooperativeness.[90, 100] Turning to more central personality traits, one might hypothesize that since non-satellizers enjoy little intrinsic self-esteem and have high, tenacious ego aspirations (see p. 311), they would ordinarily be extremely competitive; whatever initial sympathetic and cooperative behavior they might manifest would reflect feelings of insecurity and inadequacy or an expedient bid for favor (rather than genuine "we feeling"), and would be superseded by competitiveness as their status in the group improved. Satellizers, on the other hand, feeling intrinsically more adequate, might be expected to be more group-minded, especially once their own positions in the group were secure.

Effects of Competition on Personality Development

Competition has both desirable and undesirable effects on personality development. On the credit side, it stimulates individual efforts and productivity, promotes higher standards and aspirations, and narrows the gap between capacity and performance. By enabling the individual to obtain a more realistic estimate of his own capacities in relation to those of others, it exerts a salutary effect on the self-critical faculty. Under the stimulus

*This was only true of eight year olds. The opposite tendency was found in a group of five year olds.[142]

of competition the child is better able to discover both his own limitations as well as hitherto unrealized capacities and is motivated to overcome objectionable personality traits. Competition makes group games more interesting and everyday tasks less monotonous.

On the debit side, when carried to unwholesome extremes, competition fosters feelings of inadequacy in less able children and unduly depresses their status in the group. It may lead to a tense, hostile, vindictive, and negative group climate[122] in which ruthlessness, unfairness, and dishonesty are condoned in the interests of emerging victorious. In such an atmosphere the demonstration of superiority per se becomes the primary goal, whereas the intrinsic value of the activity and the enjoyment of participation are deemphasized. When excessive value is placed on superior achievement, children become obsessed with the notion of self-aggrandizement and lose sight of human values. Prestigeful attainment becomes the sole criterion of human worth and source of self-esteem; and the perceived accomplishments of others constitute a threat and a competitive challenge to the individual's sense of adequacy which must be bested or denied.

ACCEPTANCE AND REJECTION

Sociometric techniques provide the most objective and conveniently determined indices of the individual's status in or acceptance by the group. Although fairly good correspondence exists between such different methods of determining sociometric status as the traditional three-choice technique, the paired-comparison method, and the rank-order method,[17] a somewhat different picture emerges when social acceptability is measured by averaging the ratings of acceptance-rejection given an individual by *all* of the group members; when the latter scores are correlated with the more traditional measures of sociometric status, the resulting correlations are relatively low except at the third-grade level.[13, 17] Hence it means one thing to achieve high popularity on the basis of being chosen frequently as a *preferred* associate for various activities and quite a different thing to achieve a high level of acceptance based on ratings from *all* members of a group. The latter method takes *negative* as well as positive feelings into account, discriminates between attitudes of rejection and indifference, is more representative of *total* group acceptance of the individual, and reflects more deep-seated emotional currents in interpersonal relations. The traditional method is more reflective of group structure and of actual functional relationships.

Sociometric status scores show much generality both over different choice situations[17, 56, 69] (e.g., work, play, seating arrangements) and over the ratings of the different persons from whom the scores are derived.[13] Stability (test-retest reliability) is also high over a period of several weeks;[69, 102, 126] it is highest for the paired-comparison method, next highest for the rating scale method and lowest for the partial rank-order (choice) method.[126, 137] For reasons already indicated (see p. 462), social acceptability scores tend to remain quite stable over periods of months and years.[17, 21, 22, 57, 77, 81] Between the ages of seven and ten they are almost as stable as intelligence and achievement test scores.[22] Cross-sex choices, however, are very unstable.[57] The validity of sociometric status scores is demonstrated by their high degree of correpondence with actual behavior choices, even among preschool children.[15]

Correlates of High Peer Group Status

The following traits are for self-evident reasons positively and unequivocally related to high sociometric status in the peer group: (a) *personality traits:* alert, outgoing personality,[23, 103, 130] cheerfulness,[23, 24, 81] emotional stability and dependability,[26,] and honesty;[17] (b) *physical traits:* athletic ability,[17, 88, 130] good looks and tidiness;[23, 24, 81, 130] (c) *social traits:* friendliness,[20, 22, 24, 81, 130] cooperativeness and helpfulness,[26, 28] social conformity,[26, 28, 78] social adaptability,[26, 87] positive social aggressiveness[20, 22, 24, 130] (leadership, daring, enthusiasm), good sportsmanship,[130] and respect for others' property.[78] The weight of the evidence points to a low to moderate relationship between I.Q. and sociometric status.[14, 17, 20, 22, 123] The probable mediating factor here is the greater frequency of scholastic failure, non-promotion, truancy, and inarticulateness among intellectually dull children. All of these conditions also tend to increase emotional instability which, in turn, has detrimental effects on both learning capacity and interpersonal relationships. Children who are above average scholastically and either regularly promoted or under-age for their grade level tend to enjoy a higher sociometric status than low achievers and over-age (non-promoted) pupils.[17, 31, 51, 123] Bonney [19, 20, 22, 24] found consistently high relationships between sociometric status and social class status.* Lower-class membership apparently affects social acceptability adversely insofar as it is associated with untidiness, poor clothing, negative social aggressiveness and low school achievement.

Age, Sex and Social Class Differences. During the elementary school years girls generally enjoy higher sociometric status than boys,[19, 20, 23] and their group structure is more definite and closely-knit.[19] Among boys the pattern of traits associated with high peer group status is less ambiguous.[130] Boys value more active and aggressive traits such as athletic skill, daring, leadership, and good sportsmanship, whereas girls value docility, unassertiveness, and sedateness.[130] These among other factors (girls' greater dependence on derived status and isolation from other social classes) explain why socio-

* These findings are not supported by Laughlin's data.[81]

metric status is more highly correlated with social class status among girls than among boys.[30]

Several noteworthy changes in the determination of peer group status occur with increasing age. From the first to the twelfth grades, restlessness, talkativeness, bossiness and quarrelsomeness become less negatively associated with popularity.[80, 130] During the same period, being prim, docile and lady-like gradually becomes a less important determinant of sociometric status among girls.[130] Especially with the onset of adolescence "many of the criteria for the idealized boy such as extroversion, activity and good sportsmanship are highly acceptable for the girl."[128] Among boys there is more continuity from ages 12 to 15 in the pattern of traits associated with social prestige. Physical skill, aggressiveness and daring are still important, but overt defiance of adult standards is regarded as immature.[128] The factors associated with high peer group status also vary from one social class to another. Self-assertiveness and aggressiveness are more highly valued by lower-class children, whereas middle-class children place a higher value on conformity to adult standards and conventional rules of conduct.[110]

Characteristics of Socially Rejected Children

Four main clusters of socially unacceptable personality traits have been found in children who are rejected by their peer group. First are traits associated with the obnoxiously overbearing, aggressive, and egocentric child who frequently gives a history of being underdominated or overvalued by his parents. Such children are described by their associates or by teachers as noisy, attention-seeking, demanding, rebellious, querulous, arrogant, and boastful.[69, 78, 103, 119] The second group of socially unacceptable traits is typified by apathetic children with few expressive interests. They are listless, lacking in physical vigor, slow-moving, and generally disinterested in their surroundings.[77, 103] The third cluster of seriously unacceptable personality traits reflects a degree of introversion sufficiently disabling to interfere with spontaneous and uninhibited participation in group activities. Included in this group are such characteristics as shyness, timidity, and withdrawing behavior.[78, 103] These children are individualistic, frequently play alone, and ignore or refuse the requests of other children.[26, 78, 119] Many of the latter traits also characterize the overdominated, overprotected or rejected child who fails to learn the give-and-take techniques of peer group play and to develop social poise, skills, and effective methods of self-assertion and self-defense (see p. 372). Others regard him as excessively overdependent, fearful of being misunderstood, abused or taken advantage of, and given to whining, nagging and complaining.[69]

In addition to children who, by virtue of inappropriate group personality traits, motor, intellectual or social incompetence, are rejected *by* the group, we must also consider two other categories of children who enjoy little peer group status: (a) children who reject group experience because they find it traumatic or unrewarding as a result of their personality make-up or social incompetence; and (b) children who neither reject nor are rejected by the group but who are willing to accept ostracism, if need be, to satisfy other needs or pursue other interests. Included in the latter category are opportunists who flaunt group standards to gain adult approval, children who are too individualistic to conform to group expectations, and children with all-consuming interests in esoteric activities. In practice all three categories of low peer status are often found in the same person. For example, the overprotected child who tends to withdraw from group experience because he finds it traumatic may be rejected by his peers for reasons of excessive timidity and overdependence, and may develop strong non-social interests as a compensation for his social isolation.

Interpretation of Peer Acceptance and Rejection

The psychological significance of sociometric status scores is subject to several important qualifications. First, acceptance or rejection is seldom completely unanimous in any sizeable group,[39] or even as unequivocal as appears at first glance. Because of the operation of halo effects, the status of "stars" is perceived as higher than it actually is, whereas the status of "isolates" tends to be underestimated.[11] Second, popularity is not coextensive with adequate social adjustment. An ostensibly popular child may be little more than a "stranger in his group" in terms of the depth of his attachments,[138] or may be popular because he is docile, conforming, and willing to be directed and "used" by others.[1] Contrariwise, the child who is unpopular because of temperamental shyness or strong personal interests is not necessarily socially maladjusted or inevitably fated to become so.[97] Overinfluenced by the modern cult of the out-going personality, many mental hygienists presently fail to appreciate the wide range of variability in introversion-extroversion compatible with normal personality development.

The effects of rejection also depend on many factors that do not inhere in a child's objectively low sociometric status. Such status leads to feelings of inadequacy only to the extent that he is ego-involved in the group and aspires to greater acceptance than he enjoys. Since his acceptance of the group and the group's acceptance of him tend to be unrelated,[39] the mere fact of rejection tells us nothing about his desire to be accepted. Many children rejected by their peers concomitantly reject the latter or *pretend* that their isolation is voluntary or admirable. Thus, in evaluating the significance of rejection, it is important to know the extent to which the individual desires to be accepted by the group and, if he does not, whether his expressed disdain for acceptance is genuine or rationalized. It should be appreciated, however, that even though unconcern with status in the group may (in rejection) be associated with relatively little deflation of self-esteem, it may be symptomatic of much graver defects in personality structure than the rejection of a socially ineffective child who craves acceptance by his age mates.

Further appraisal of the seriousness of an individual case of rejection requires knowledge of (a) how widely shared the attitude of rejection is in the group, (b) whether it reflects active dislike of or passive indifference toward the person involved, (c) the modifiability of the factors on which the rejection is based, and (d) the availability of other compensatory attachments or interests. Finally much depends on whether the child perceives that he is being rejected. Rejection is not as self-evidently obvious as it may seem. Although many overrejected children perceive their low status in the group,[17] others who are just as seriously rejected seem to be unaware of the fact.

FRIENDSHIPS

Friendships represent the ultimate step in the selective differentiation of interpersonal relations along a social distance scale. They satisfy the need for particularized social relationships most compatible with a given child's dominant personality traits. Under the best of circumstances where choice can be exercised, children select friends whose qualities furnish a basis for mutual satisfaction of interpersonal needs. Ordinarily this means that the friends they choose either resemble or complement them in ways most conducive to congeniality. Often however they are obliged to settle for whoever is available. The expression of preference in the choice of playmates is already evident by the preschool period.[36, 53, 105] Indices of friendship increase during these years, first in the number of individuals the child plays with, and later (as he gradually learns that certain relationships are more satisfying than others) in the selective strengthening of particular attachments.[53]

Selective factors in the determination of children's friendships can be inferred from two related lines of evidence: (a) from the extent to which pairs of friends are similar, and (b) from the statements of children about the qualities they seek in friends. Unfortunately, the measuring devices currently available for ascertaining resemblances between friends are too gross to give adequate insight into the subtle factors that generate mutual attraction between individuals. At any rate the evidence we have indicates that friends are more similar than dissimilar to each other.[18, 22, 102]

First, friends are similar in those characteristics necessary for adequate and equitable interaction between persons: in chronological age,[36, 46, 68, 135] I.Q.,[20, 25, 46, 135] socioeconomic status,[20, 25, 68, 101] school grade,[68] and height.[46] Preference for children of the same sex appears during the preschool years[36, 105] and becomes more pronounced with increasing age.[131] Most friends live in the same neighborhod or are in the same class in school*.[9, 46] Similarities in interests and tastes are frequent[9, 25] but are not absolutely essential since considerable dissimilarity in these areas are compatible with strong mutual friendship.[18, 25] Most important perhaps for children's friendships is similarity in orientation toward and competence in social relationships as judged by measures of social participation,[36] social adjustment,[25] social maturity,[46] sociality,[25, 46] and leadership ability.[25] Verbal statements by elementary and junior high school children of the qualities desired in friends stress similarity of interests and tastes,[9, 64, 68] friendliness and cheerfulness,[9, 43] tidiness,[43] good manners,[43] and generosity.[9, 43] With increasing age, as children become more physically mobile and aware of the wider community, propinquity becomes less of a limiting condition in the choice of friends.[46, 75] Other outstanding age level changes in children's friendships include increasing stability[66, 125] and the increased importance of socioeconomic status (especially for girls) and degree of physical maturity.[75]

Consistent with their greater social orientation and interest in persons (see p. 281), girls are more socially active than boys during the preschool years, play with a large number of children, make higher friendship scores, and show greater mutuality of friendship.[36, 52, 105] Their sociometric choices are also more stable at this time.[120] Girls continue to be more sociable than boys during the elementary school period[20] and to establish more intimate and confidential relationships with each other. These differences can also be inferred from the greater frequency of clique formation among girls,[35] the greater mutuality of friendships,[20] and the greater amount of time they spend with their friends. In choosing friends, girls pay more attention than boys to social class standing.[30]

Children's friendships are relatively unstable even over such short periods of time as two weeks. Sixty per cent of sixth-grade pupils change at least one of their three "best friends" during this interval.[9] This suggests that the chief purpose of childhood friendships is to satisfy the need for a congenial companion in the prosecution of mutual interests rather than to obtain intimate interpersonal experience and mutual understanding. At any rate,

*Intra-neighborhood homogeneity in social class membership and social class uniformities in values and social behavior probably account for obtained similarities in socioeconomic status and I.Q.[20, 25, 101] between friends.

unlike preadolescents who are intensely eager for a large number of friends,[64] adolescents desire to form fewer but deeper, more intimate friendships.[94] Principal reasons given by children for terminating friendships include quarrels, changes in interests, lack of recent contact, incompatibility, and charges of conceit, bossiness, disloyalty, and quarrelsomeness.[9] As previously indicated, the stability of friendships increases with age in both sexes[66, 125] beginning earlier in girls.[66]

LEADERSHIP

In contrast to friendship and popularity, which represent the outcome of the *feelings* (like-dislike, acceptance-rejection) that group members develop toward each other, leadership is more closely related to the *functional* properties of groups. This does not mean that the leader's personality and the group members' feelings toward him are irrelevant to the achievement and maintenance of leadership. It means rather that those aspects of the leader's personality that affect the functional effectiveness of the group and those particular feelings of group members toward the leader that are related to his functional efficacy are most relevant to these problems. As groups become more highly structured in terms of role differentiation, leadership refers more to an effect on activities and working relationships than to an influence on persons. Thus in "sociogroups," where the emphasis is on the functional roles of persons in groups, popularity (high sociometric status) is tantamount to leadership; whereas in informal "psychogroups," popularity is more akin to friendship.[70]

The leader may be best described as the person who "moves the group to action."[39] Leadership, therefore, is bestowed by the group on that individual who in its judgment has the personality attributes, experience, and skills to organize, mobilize, and represent the group best in achieving its paramount needs and goals. In "sociogroups" the correlates of high sociometric status have great prestige value and hence are closely related to leadership. In "psychogroups" affectional attitudes toward others are important in their own right. Thus, an easygoing, ineffectual person may be popular by virtue of these very qualities, without necessarily possessing any of the prestige-giving characteristics associated with high sociometric status. And by the same token, although sustained unpopularity is seldom compatible with successful leadership, leaders are not obliged to be the most popular persons in the group or to have many close friends.

How Leadership is Achieved and Maintained

In accordance with its functional nature, "leadership is conferred by the group."[39] The popularly held belief that gangs are creatures of dynamic leaders is seldom true. Quite the contrary, "the gang forms and the leader emerges as the result of interaction."[127] The "group-given nature of leadership is evident from the fact that the leader cannot successfully disregard the established traditions of the group or the common purposes that he is chosen to advance.[127] He cannot wield his power capriciously or abusively.[127] Nor can adult authorities impose a leader on the group by choosing a promising candidate and "training" him for leadership. If this is done, actual leadership power is withdrawn by the group and the adult-imposed individual retains at best a nominal status out of deference to his sponsors.[39] The partly situational nature of leadership also points to its group-given origins. To a certain extent the prestige of leadership ability in one area carries over without any objective justification to an entirely unrelated area ("halo effect"). But the more sophisticated children become in group activities, the more they choose leaders on the basis of situational requirements, and the less they confuse the criteria for leadership with popularity or personal loyalty.[39]

Leadership is acquired in many different ways. Among young children, one can observe both the aggressive, dominative and coercive "bully" and the more integrative and task-oriented "diplomat," who through perceptiveness, social skill and a gift for compromise welds the group into a congenial, smoothly functioning unit.[4, 5, 6, 106] Usually, however, the young leader is a mixture of both stereotypes. But even at the kindergarten age, children express preference for the latter kind of leader;[59] and from related evidence regarding (a) the effects of authoritarian and democratic social climates (see p. 440), (b) the correlates of sociometric status (see p. 478), and (c) the trend with increasing age toward more reciprocal and equalitarian notions of obligation (see p. 392), one can infer that older children increasingly favor the more integrative type of leadership.

In children's "sociogroups," most of the correlates of popularity are also qualities that are highly valued by the group, and hence are determinants of both prestige and leadership. These prestige factors generally include among boys, superior height,[54] strength,[109, 127] and athletic prowess;[54, 86, 109, 127] better than average intelligence;[54] and such group-relevant aspects of personality as independence of adults and social pressure, sex sophistication, and "having ideas for fun."[109] Children with high attributed prestige in the group are more likely than low prestige children to attempt the more direct influencing of others and to be more successful in the attempt. Their approval is solicited by average group members;[86] and since they are also more resistive to direct influence, others tend to approach them indirectly.[109] Children on their way to leadership can usually be identified by their tendency to seek out persons who are already leaders.[69]

Once attained, leadership is maintained in various ways. Control through fear of physical prowess is a significant factor in some groups, especially in lower-class gangs.[127, 136] More important, however, is the leader's ability to give or withdraw belongingness, to help the group achieve its aims by his special skills or general cleverness, and to influence the group to place high value on the activities in which he excels.[39] Leadership fluctuates with changes in the needs of the group as determined both by social maturation and by situational factors. Nevertheless, because of considerable constancy in the personality traits associated with leadership and in the factors making for prestige, a good deal of stability prevails, particularly if leadership is acquired gradually rather than suddenly.[69] The leader's awareness of his high prestige position enables him to use it deliberately in influencing others; and success in this endeavor reinforces the very qualities responsible for his prestige as well as consolidates his position in the group.[109] Leadership in nursery school is prognostic of later leadership in elementary school.[133] Between elementary school and junior high school, however, because of behavioral changes associated with the onset of pubescence, much of this continuity is lost and not regained until adolescence.[85]

"Behavioral Contagion"

"Behavioral contagion" may be defined as "an event in which a person's behavior is changed to resemble that of another person" without any overt intention on the latter's part.[86,109] It involves an act of social imitation or responsiveness to prestige suggestion in which the initiator's behavior serves as a stimulus triggering off comparable behavior in the imitator. Unlike leadership, no direct or deliberate attempt is made to influence another's decisions. As customarily used, the term does not imply an act of identification motivated by either satellizing or incorporative (non-satellizing) considerations (see p. 382). Presumably the initiator's actions structure the field differently for the imitator and provide direction and sanction for his behavior.

The capacity for initiating behavioral contagion is primarily a function of possessing a very high prestige position in the group and of accurately perceiving that position.[86, 109] Apparently, awareness of his high status in the group provides the child with sufficient sense of security to act in the spontaneous manner that is necessary for generating contagion. The same freedom to act spontaneously also makes him more susceptible to contagion initiated by others.[86] In situations of common frustration, however, the child's impulsiveness rather than his prestige position is a more important determinant of his ability to initiate contagion.[109] Contagion is facilitated if the suggested act is visualized as a satisfying means of escaping from a frustrating, conflictful or ambiguous situation[58]; if the restraining influence exercised by anticipation of disapproval or fear of reprisal is reduced;[58] and if the behavior of the initiator is congruent with the goals, value system, and characteristic expressive techniques of the group.[109, 111]

SEX CLEAVAGE

Characteristic of our culture is a progressive trend toward segregation of the sexes during the course of childhood. Although preschool boys and girls show some preference for their own sex in choosing favorite play-mates,[36, 79, 86, 105] considerable cross-sex friendship and overlapping of activities still prevail. Even in the primary grades, a single boy will play unembarrassedly with a group of girls (or vice versa).[35] Preference for like-sex companions increases markedly during the years of middle childhood and preadolescence. This is shown by the rarity of cross-sex sociometric choices,[79, 86] self-consciousness about and avoidance of physical contact with members of the opposite sex,[35] extreme sex-typing of games and activi-ties, sex-biased perceptions of the personality traits and social roles of the sexes,[2, 16] and numerous expressions of indifference, dislike, and rivalry.* Sociometric preference for individuals of the same sex is present even in high school, but declines rapidly[35, 79] (earlier and more prominently in girls). After the kindergarten period and until adolescence girls tend to show more preference for their own sex than boys do.[2, 79, 96] Nevertheless, during the same period, as boys' opinions of their own sex gradually improve, their opinions of the opposite sex correspondingly worsen, with the reverse trends holding true for girls.[118]

As previously indicated, this segregation of the sexes during childhood is neither a manifestation of genic tendencies nor of a predetermined stage of psychosexual development such as the so-called "latency period" (see pp. 444 and 446). It is encouraged by such conditions as the sex-typing of peer interests and activities, the preferential status of girls in the school, and the school's emphasis on separation of and competition between the sexes. Hence, much variability is found in degree of segregation between different cultures[93] and social classes,[27] and also when these conditions differ from one community to another.[27] Sex cleavage obviously makes the transition to adolescent heterosexual behavior more difficult; after years of antagonism frank and open expression of interest in the opposite sex is hardly possible at first. Hence young adolescents resort to such transitional patterns as pseudo-disapproval, simulated hostility, and "crushes" on peers of the same sex or on older persons of the opposite sex.

*This hostility, however, is not wholly incompatible with stylized expressions of romantic interest (see p. 444).

CONFORMITY BEHAVIOR

For two important reasons the peer group demands a certain minimal degree of conformity from its members. First, no institution, especially if it has status-giving functions, can exist for any length of time without due regard by its members for uniform, regular, and predictable adherence to a set of avowed rules and traditions. Hence, in its efforts to establish a new and distinctive subculture and to evolve a unique set of criteria for the determination of status and prestige, the peer society must do everything in its power to set itself off as recognizably distinct and separate from the adult society which refuses it membership. If this distinctiveness is to be actually attained, widespread nonconformity obviously cannot be tolerated. Second, conformity is also required to maintain the group solidarity that is necessary to offer effective and organized resistance to the encroachments of adult authority (see p. 460).

The peer group is in an excellent position to demand conformity from the child as the price of its acceptance. No other institution can offer him a satisfactory social identity in relation to his equals; and to the extent that he enjoys a marginal position in the culture and is alienated from adult society, he is also beholden to the group for much of his primary and derived status. Thus, from middle childhood through adolescence, as the child's dependence on and stake in the effectiveness of the peer group increases, the latter's power to exact conformity is concomitantly enhanced. Conforming tendencies are also reinforced by the fact that group approval brings a welcome reprieve from anxiety and that obligations to abide by group standards are internalized out of feelings of loyalty, belongingness and gratitude. If these implicit group pressures and internalized restraints of the individual are insufficient to keep him in line, explicit sanctions are imposed. Depending on the seriousness of the offense and the nature and functions of the group, the punishment may vary from ridicule, censure, and rebuff to physical chastisement and complete ostracism.

In general, because of the present-day intolerance for deviancy in the wider culture and because of an exaggerated perception of the degree of conformity required for peer group acceptance,* children tend to be over-impressed with the need for conforming to group standards. Some evidence[102] also points to the conclusion that apparent disregard for the group's approval tends to enhance the individual's sociometric status by making him appear above the need for currying favor with others. Hence many perfectly "safe" opportunities are lost for expressing individuality compatible with over-all group standards. In any case marked individual differences

*This misperception can be inferred from the widespread tendency to underestimate the sociometric status of deviant or low prestige individuals.[11]

are evident in the need to conform. The highly self-assertive child, for example, can only restrain his individuality to a point, and the extreme introvert draws a line beyond which he refuses to participate in boisterous activities. The child who has a highly developed set of moral or religious activities may refuse to condone the practices of his group. Other individuals may have overwhelming interests that are regarded with scorn by their age mates. Finally, the non-satellizer's need for ego aggrandizement and his lack of loyalty and "we-feeling" may cause him to betray group interests for personal advantage.

IMPACT OF SOCIAL STRATIFICATION

In various other contexts we have pointed out that as children grow older social stratification in the wider culture has progressively greater influence on peer relationships. Children become increasingly more aware of the symbols of social class status (see p. 434) and pay more attention to racial, social class, and ethnic requirements for membership in particular cliques. The parental and cultural pressures that draw caste and social class lines more sharply with increasing age and make children's racial and class attitudes gradually approximate those of their elders have already been described in detail (see pp. 427, 428, and 433). We have also considered various reasons why girls are more status-conscious than boys (see pp. 448 and 478).

INTER-GROUP BEHAVIOR

As members of particular *in*-groups, children also interact both individually and collectively with members of other groups (*out*-groups). In these instances they react less as individuals in their own right than in terms of their in-group identifications, the prevailing degree of social distance between their respective groups, and various situational factors affecting inter-group relations.[113] In other words, they manifest *inter-group* behavior. Such behavior naturally presupposes a high degree of intra-group solidarity and of role and status differentiation, and hence cannot be expected much before middle childhood or preadolescence. Once such cohesive in-groups are formed, it is possible under experimentally controlled conditions of competition and reciprocal frustration to produce negative group attitudes, unfavorable, stereotype perceptions, and hostile actions in relation to the out-group.[113, 115] These manifestations of hostility toward the out-group are accompanied (after some initial in-group bickering, scapegoating and changes in leadership) by an enhancement of in-group solidarity and friendships, and of favorable perceptions of in-group behavior.[113, 115] However, when groups in this induced state of tension are brought together in a situaation where the attainment of commonly desired, "superordinate" goals exceeds the energies and resources of a single group, inter-group cooperation results, with a concomitant reduction of hostility and negative stereotypes.[115]

REFERENCES

1. Alexander, T., and Alexander, M.: A study of personality and social status. *Child Develop. 23*: 207-213, 1952.

2. Amatora, S. M.: Contrasts in boys' and girls' judgments in personality. *Child Develop. 25*: 51-62, 1954.

3. Ames, L. B.: The sense of self of nursery school children as manifested by their verbal behavior. *J. Genet. Psychol. 81*: 193-232, 1952.

4. Anderson, H. H.: An experimental study of dominative and integrative behavior in children of preschool age. *J. Soc. Psychol. 8*: 335-345, 1937.

5. ———: Domination and integration in the social behavior of young children in an experimental play situation. *Genet. Psychol. Monogr. 19*: 343-408, 1937.

6. ———: Domination and social integration in the behavior of kindergarten children in an experimental play situation. *J. Exper. Educ. 8*: 123-131, 1939.

7. Andrus, R., and Horowitz, E. L.: The effect of nursery school training: insecurity feeling. *Child Develop. 9*: 169-174, 1938.

8. Appel, M. H.: Aggressive behavior of nursery school children and adult procedures in dealing with such behavior. *J. Exper. Educ. 11*: 185-199, 1942.

9. Austin, M. C., and Thompson, G. G.: Children's friendships: a study of the bases on which children select and reject their best friends. *J. Educ. Psychol. 39*: 101-116, 1948.

10. Ausubel, D. P.: Prestige motivation of gifted children. *Genet. Psychol. Monogr. 43*: 53-116, 1951.

11. ———: Socioempathy as a function of sociometric status in an adolescent group. *Hum. Relat. 8*: 75-84, 1955.

12. ———, and Schiff, H. M.: Some intrapersonal and interpersonal determinants of individual differences in sociempathic ability among adolescents. *J. Soc. Psychol. 41*: 39-56, 1955.

13. ———, ———, and Gasser, E. B.: A preliminary study of developmental trends in socioempathy: accuracy of perception of own and others' status. *Child Develop. 23*: 111-128, 1952.

14. Barbe, W. B.: Peer relationships of children of different intelligence levels. *School & Soc. 80*: 60-62, 1954.

15. Biehler, R. F.: Companion choice behavior in the kindergarden. *Child Develop. 25*: 45-51, 1954.

16. Bjerstedt, A.: A double-directed analysis of preference motivations and other pal-description statements: studies in socio-perceptual selectivity. *Acta Psychol. 11*: 257-268, 1955.

17. ———: The interpretation of sociometric scores in the classroom. *Acta Psychol. 12*: 1-14, 1956.

18. Bogardus, R., and Otto, P.: Social psychology of chums. *Sociol. & Soc. Res. 20*: 260-270, 1936.

19. Bonney, M. E.: A study of social status on the second grade level. *J. Genet. Psychol. 60*: 271-305, 1942.

20. ———: A study of the relation of intelligence, family size, and sex differences

with mutual friendships in the primary grades. *Child Develop.* *13*: 79-100, 1942.

21. ——: The constancy of sociometric scores and their relationship to teacher judgments of social success and to personality self-ratings. *Sociometry 6*: 409-424, 1943.

22. ——: The relative stability of social, intellectual and academic status in grades II to IV, and the interrelationships between these various forms of growth. *J. Educ. Psychol. 34*: 88-102, 1943.

23. ——: Relationships between social success, family size, socioeconomic background, and intelligence among school children in grades III to V. *Sociometry 7*: 26-39, 1944.

24. ——: Sex differences in social success and personality traits. *Child Develop. 15*: 63-79, 1944.

25. ——: A sociometric study of the relationship of some factors to mutual friendships in the elementary, secondary, and college levels. *Sociometry 7*: 26-39, 1946.

26. ——: Popular and unpopular children, a sociometric study. *Sociomet. Monogr.* No. 9, 1947.

27. ——: Choosing between the sexes on a sociometric measurement. *J. Soc. Psychol. 39*: 99-114, 1954.

28. ——, and Powell, J.: Differences in social behavior between sociometrically high and sociometrically low children. *J. Educ. Res. 46*: 481-495, 1953.

29. Bridges, K. M. B.: *The School and Emotional Development of the Preschool Child.* London, Kegan Paul, 1931.

30. Brown, W. H., and Bond, L. B.: Social stratification in a sixth-grade class. *J. Educ. Res. 48*: 539-543, 1955.

31. Buswell, M. M.: The relationship between the social structure of the classroom and the academic success of the pupils. *J. Exper. Educ. 22*: 37-52, 1953.

32. Bühler, C.: The social behavior of children. *In* C. Murchison, Ed., *A Handbook of Child Psychology,* ed. 2. Worcester, Mass., Clark University Press, 1933, pp. 374-416.

33. Caille, R. K.: Resistant behavior of preschool children. *Child Develop. Monogr.* No. 13, 1933.

34. Caldwell, O. W., and Wellman, B.: Characteristics of school leaders. *J. Educ. Res. 14*: 1-15, 1926.

35. Campbell, E. H.: The social-sex development of children. *Genet. Psychol. Monogr. 21*: 461-552, 1939.

36. Challman, R. C.: Factors influencing friendship among preschool children. *Child Develop. 3*: 146-158, 1932.

37. Chittenden, G. E.: An experimental study in measuring and modifying assertive behavior in young children. *Monogr. Soc. Res. Child Develop. 7*: No. 1, 1942.

38. Crane, A. R.: Pre-adolescent gangs: a topological interpretation. *J. Genet. Psychol. 81*: 113-122, 1952.

39. Cunningham, R.: *Understanding Group Behavior of Boys and Girls.* New York, Teachers College, Columbia University, 1951.

40. Davitz, J. R.: Social perception and sociometric choice of children. *J. Abnorm. Soc. Psychol. 50*: 173-176, 1955.

41. Dawe, H. C.: An analysis of two hundred quarrels of preschool children. *Child Develop. 5*: 139-156, 1934.

42. Dennis, W.: *The Hopi Child.* New York, Appleton-Century, 1940.
43. Dymond, R. F., Hughes, A. S., and Raabe, V. L.: Measurable changes in empathy with age. *J. Consult. Psychol. 16*: 202-206, 1952.
44. Ezekiel, L. F.: Changes in egocentricity of young children. *Child Develop. 2*: 74-75, 1931.
45. Freud, A., and Dann, S.: An experiment in group up-bringing. *Psychoanal. Stud. Child. 6*: 127-168, 1951.
46. Furfey, P. H.: Some factors influencing the selection of boys' chums. *J. Appl. Psychol. 11*: 47-51, 1927.
47. ——: *The Growing Boy.* New York, Macmillan, 1930.
48. Gage, N. L.: Judging interests from expressive behavior. *Psychol. Monogr. 66*: No. 18, (Whole No. 350), 1952.
49. Gesell, A., and Ilg, F. L.: *Infant and Child in the Culture of Today.* New York, Harper, 1943.
50. Goodenough, F. L.: Inter-relationships in the behavior of young children. *Child Develop. 1*: 29-47, 1930.
51. Goodlad, J. I.: Some effects of promotion and non-promotion upon the social and personal adjustment of children. *J. Exper. Educ. 22*: 301-328, 1954.
52. Green, E. H.: Friendships and quarrels among preschool children. *Child Develop. 4*: 237-252, 1933.
53. ——: Group play and quarreling among preschool children. *Child Develop. 4*: 302-307, 1933.
54. Greenberg, P. J.: Competition in children: an experimental study. *Am. J. Psychol. 44*: 221-248, 1932.
55. Greene, K. B.: Relations between kindergarten and nursery school. *Childh. Educ. 7*: 352-355, 1930-1931.
56. Gronlund, N. E.: Generality of sociometric status over criteria in measurement of social acceptability. *Elem. Sch. J. 56*: 173-176, 1955,
57. ——: The relative stability of classroom social status with unweighted and weighted sociometric choices. *J. Educ. Psychol. 46*: 345-354, 1955.
58. Grosser, D., Polansky, N., and Lippitt, R.: A laboratory study of behavioral contagion. *Hum. Relat. 4*: 115-142, 1951.
59. Hanfmann, E.: Social structure of a group of kindergarten children. *Am. J. Orthopsychiat. 5*: 407-410. 1935.
60. Harris, E. K.: The responsiveness of kindergarten children to the behavior of their fellows. *Monogr. Soc. Res. Child Develop. 11*: No. 2, 1946.
61. Hattwick, B. W.: The influence of nursery school attendance upon the behavior and personality of the preschool child. *J. Exper. Educ. 5*: 180-190, 1936.
62. Hattwick, L. A., and Sanders, M. K.: Age differences in behavior at the nursery school level. *Child Develop. 9*: 27-47, 1938.
63. Heathers, G.: The adjustment of two-year-olds in a novel social situation. *Child Develop. 25*: 147-148, 1954.
64. Hicks, J. A., and Hayes, M.: Study of the characteristics of 250 junior-high school children. *Child Develop. 9*: 219-242, 1938.
65. Hirota, K.: Experimental studies of competition. *Jap. J. Psychol. 21*: 70-81, 1951.
66. Horrocks, J. E., and Buker, M. E.: A study of the friendship fluctuations of preadolescents. *J. Genet. Psychol. 78*: 131-144, 1951.
67. Jack, L. M.: An experimental study of ascendant behavior in preschool children. *Univ. Iowa Stud. Child Welf. 9*: No. 3, 1939.

68. Jenkins, G. G.: Factors involved in children's friendships. *J. Educ. Psychol.* 22: 440-448, 1931.

69. Jennings, H. H.: *Leadership and Isolation.* New York, Longmans, Green, 1943.

70. Jennings, H. S.: Sociometric structure in personality and group formation. *In* M. Sherif and M. O. Wilson, Eds., *Group Relations at the Crossroads.* New York, Harper, 1953, pp. 332-365.

71. Jersild, A. T., and Fite, M. D.: The influence of nursery school experience on children's social adjustments. *Child Develop. Monogr.* No. 25, 1939.

72. ——, and Markey, F. V.: Conflicts between preschool children. *Child Develop. Monogr.* No. 21, 1935.

73. ——, and Tasch, R. J.: *Children's Interests and What They Suggest for Education.* New York, Teachers College, Columbia University, 1949.

74. Joel, W.: The influence of nursery school education upon behavior maturity. *J. Exper. Educ. 8:* 164-165, 1939.

75. Jones, M. C.: Adolescent friendships. *Am. Psychologist 3:* 352, 1943.

76. Kawin, E., and Hoefer, C.: *A Comparative Study of a Nursery School vs. a Non-Nursery School Group.* Chicago, University of Chicago Press, 1931.

77. Kerstetter, L.: Exploring the environment in a classroom situation. *Sociometry 9:* 149-150, 1946.

78. Koch, H. L.: Popularity in school children: some related factors and a technique for its measurement. *Child Develop. 5:* 164-175, 1933.

79. ——: A study of some factors conditioning the social distance between the sexes. *J. Soc. Psychol. 20:* 79-107, 1944.

80. Kuhlen, R. G., and Lee, B. J.: Personality characteristics and social acceptability in adolescence. *J. Educ. Psychol. 34:* 321-340, 1943.

81. Laughlin, F.: *The Peer Status of Sixth and Seventh Grade Children.* New York: Teachers College, Columbia University, 1954.

82. Lehman, H. C., and Witty, P. A.: *The Psychology of Play Activities.* New York, A. S. Barnes, 1927.

83. Leighton, D., and Kluckhohn, C.: *Children of the People: The Navaho Individual and His Development.* Cambridge, Mass., Harvard University Press, 1947.

84. Leuba, C.: An experimental study of rivalry in young children. *J. Comp. Psychol. 16:* 367-378, 1933.

85. Levi, I. J.: Student leadership in elementary and junior high school and its transfer into senior high school. *J. Educ. Res. 22:* 135-139, 1930.

86. Lippitt, R., Polansky, N., and Rosen, S.: The dynamics of power: a field study of social influence in groups of children. *Hum. Relat. 5:* 37-64, 1952.

87. ——: Popularity among preschool children. *Child Develop. 12:* 305-322, 1941.

88. McCraw, L. W., and Tolbert, J. W.: Sociometric status and athletic ability of junior high school boys. *Res. Quart. Am. Assoc. Health & Phys. Educ. 24:* 72-80, 1953.

89. McKee, J. P., and Leader, F. B.: The relationships of socio-economic status and aggression to the competitive behavior of preschool children. *Child Develop. 26:* 135-142, 1955.

90. Maller, J. B.: *Cooperation and Competition: An Experimental Study in Motivation.* New York, Teachers College, Columbia University, 1929.

91. Maudry, M., and Nekula, M.: Social relations between children of the same age during the first two years of life. *J. Genet. Psychol. 54:* 193-215, 1939.

92. Mead, M., Ed.: *Cooperation and Competition Among Primitive Peoples*. New York, McGraw-Hill, 1937.

93. ———: *Male and Female: A Study of the Sexes in a Changing World*. New York, William Morrow, 1949.

94. Meek, L. H.: *The Personal-Social Development of Boys and Girls with Implications for Secondary Education*. New York, Progressive Education Assoc., 1940.

95. Mengert, I. G.: A preliminary study of the reactions of two-year-old children to each other when paired in a semi-controlled situation. *J. Genet. Psychol. 39*: 393-398, 1939.

96. Moreno, J. L.: *Who Shall Survive?* Washington, D. C., Nerv. & Ment. Dis. Pub. Co., 1934.

97. Morris, D. P., Soroker, E., and Burruss, G.: Follow-up studies of shy, withdrawn children. I. Evaluation of later adjustment. *Am. J. Orthopsychiat. 24*: 743-754, 1954.

98. Mowrer, O. H.: Authoritarianism vs. "self-government" in the management of children's aggressive (anti-social) reactions as a preparation for citizenship in a democracy. *J. Soc. Psychol. 10*: 121-126, 1939.

99. Mummery, D. V.: An analytical study of ascendant behavior of preschool children. *Child Develop. 18*: 40-81, 1947.

100. Murphy, L. B.: *Social Behavior and Child Personality; An Exploratory Study of Some Roots of Sympathy*. New York, Columbia University Press, 1937.

101. Neugarten, B. L.: Social class and friendship among school children. *Am. J. Sociol. 51*: 305-313, 1946.

102. Newstetter, W. J., Feldstein, M. J., and Newcomb, T. M.: *Group Adjustment: A Study in Experimental Sociology*. Cleveland, Western Reserve University, 1938.

103. Northway, M. L.: Outsiders: a study of the personality patterns of children least acceptable to their age mates. *Sociometry 7*: 10-25, 1944.

104. Page, M. L.: The modification of ascendant behavior in preschool children. *Univ. Iowa Stud. Child Welf. 11*: No. 3, 1936.

105. Parten, M. B.: Social play among preschool children. *J. Abnorm. Soc. Psychol. 28*: 136-147, 1933.

106. ———: Leadership among preschool children. *J. Abnorm. Soc. Psychol. 28*: 430-440, 1933.

107. Parten, M., and Newhall, S.: Social behavior of preschool children. *In* R. G. Barker, J. S. Kounin, and H. F. Wright, Eds., *Child Behavior and Development*. New York, McGraw-Hill, 1943, pp. 509-525.

108. Piaget, J.: *Language and Thought of the Child*. London, Routledge & Kegan Paul, 1926.

109. Polansky, N., Lippitt, R., and Redl, F.: An investigation of behavior contagion in groups. *Hum. Relat. 3*: 319-348, 1950.

110. Pope, B.: Socio-economic contrasts in children's peer culture prestige values. *Genet. Psychol. Monogr. 48*: 157-220, 1953.

111. Redl, F.: The phenomenon of contagion and shock effect in group therapy. *In* K. R. Eissler, Ed., *Searchlight on Delinquency*. New York, International Universities Press, 1949.

112. Sherif, M., and Cantril, H.: *The Psychology of Ego-Involvements*. New York, Wiley, 1947.

113. ——, and Sherif, C. W.: *Groups in Harmony and Tension.* New York, Harper, 1953.

114. ——, White, B. J., and Harvey, O. J.: Status in experimentally produced groups. *Am. J. Sociol. 60*: 370-379, 1955.

115. ——, et al.: *Experimental Study of Positive and Negative Inter-Group Attitudes between Experimentally Produced Groups. Robbers Cave Study.* Norman, University of Oklahoma, 1954.

116. Siegel, A. E.: Session differences in aggression in children's play in the absence of an adult. Paper read at Am. Psychol. Assoc., Chicago, September 1956.

117. Singer, H., Jr.: Certain aspects of personality and their relation to certain group modes, and constancy of friendship choices. *J. Educ. Res. 45*: 33-42, 1951.

118. Smith, S.: Age and sex differences in children's opinion concerning sex differences. *J. Genet. Psychol. 54*: 17-25, 1939.

119. Sorokin, P. A., and Gove, D. S.: Notes on the friendly and antagonistic behavior of nursery school children. *In* P. A. Sorokin, Ed., *Explorations in Altruistic Love and Behavior.* Boston, Beacon Press, 1950.

120. Speroff, B. J.: The stability of sociometric choice among kindergarten children. *Sociometry 18*: 129-131, 1955.

121. Steiner, I. D.: Interpersonal behavior as influenced by accuracy of social perception. *Psychol. Rev. 62*: 268-274, 1955.

122. Stendler, C. B., Damrin, D., and Haines, A. C.: Studies in cooperation and competition: I. The effect of working for group and individual rewards on the social climate of children's groups. *J. Genet. Psychol. 79*: 173-197, 1951.

123. Taylor, E. A.: Some factors relating to social acceptance in eighth-grade classrooms. *J. Educ. Psychol. 43*: 257-272, 1952.

124. Thompson, G. G.: The social and emotional development of preschool children under two types of educational programs. *Psychol. Monogr. 56*: No. 5, 1944.

125. ——, and Horrocks, J. E.: A study of the friendship fluctuations of urban boys and girls. *J. Genet. Psychol. 70*: 53-63, 1947.

126. ——, and Powell, M.: An investigation of the rating scale approach to the measurement of social status. *Educ. Psychol. Meas. 11*: 440-455, 1951.

127. Thrasher, F. M.: *The Gang.* Chicago, University of Chicago Press, 1927.

128. Tryon, C. M.: Evaluations of adolescent personality by adolescents. *Monogr. Soc. Res. Child Develop. 4*: No. 4, 1939.

129. ——: The adolescent peer culture. In *Adolescence,* 43rd Yearbook, Nat. Soc. Stud. Educ. Chicago, University of Chicago Press, 1944, part 1.

130. Tuddenham, R. D.: Studies in reputation. III. Correlates of popularity among elementary school children. *J. Educ. Psychol. 42*: 257-276, 1951.

131. ——: Studies in reputation. I. Sex and grade differences in school children's evaluation of their peers. *Psychol. Monogr. 66*: No. 1 (Whole No. 333), 1952.

132. Turner, W. D.: Altruism and its measurement in children. *J. Abnorm. Soc. Psychol. 43*: 502-516, 1948.

133. Van Alstyne, D., and Hattwick, L. A.: A follow-up study of the behavior of nursery school children. *Child Develop. 19*: 43-72, 1939.

134. Walsh, M. E.: The relation of nursery school training to the development of certain personality traits. *Child Develop. 2*: 72-73, 1931.

135. Wellman, B.: The school child's choice of companions. *J. Educ. Res. 14*: 126-132, 1926.
136. Whyte, W. F.: *Street Corner Society*. Chicago, University of Chicago Press, 1943.
137. Witryol, S. L., and Thompson, G. G.: A critical review of the stability of social acceptability scores obtained with the partial-rank-order and the paired-comparison scales. *Genet. Psychol. Monogr. 48*: 221-260, 1953.
138. Wittenberg, R. M., and Berg. J.: The stranger in the group. *Am. J. Orthopsychiat. 22*: 89-97, 1952.
139. Wolf, T. H.: *The Effect of Praise and Competition on the Persisting Behavior of Kindergarten Children*. Minneapolis, University of Minnesota Press, 1938.
140. Wolfle, D. L., and Wolfle, H. M.: The development of cooperative behavior in monkeys and young children. *J. Genet. Psychol. 55*: 137-175, 1939.
141. Wolman, B.: Spontaneous groups of children and adolescents in Israel. *J. Soc. Psychol. 34*: 171-182, 1951.
142. Wright, B. A.: Altruism in children and the perceived conduct of others. *J. Abnorm. Soc. Psychol. 37*: 218-233, 1942.

PART IV

Special Aspects

of Development

CHAPTER 15

Physical Growth and Motor Development

PHYSICAL GROWTH IN CHILDHOOD

SINCE THIS BOOK is primarily concerned with problems of psychological development we cannot undertake a definitive discussion of physical growth.*

Yet for several reasons it is important that we at least consider some major theoretical issues and developmental trends. First, physical growth is one of the more overt and impressive indications of children's development. Thus, a well-rounded view of the child and how he develops requires some discussion of normative growth changes and of the interpretation of individual physical status. Second, physical growth clearly illustrates many of the general principles of development discussed in Chapters 3 and 4. Finally, physical growth has an important impact on motor and other aspects of development.

Normative treatment of physical growth data reveals many age level uniformities as well as the orderliness of growth in the form of predictable age level changes in various quantitative, qualitative and sequential aspects of development. Such data are also extremely useful as a standard for evaluating the current status of a given child and for ascertaining whether he maintains his relative position in his age group from one year to the next. When used for this purpose it is obviously necessary to consider the range of variability around the mean. Furthermore, since longitudinal studies show many individual patterns of growth,[8] it is also useful to have an *individual* standard for evaluating the child's current progress and for prognosticating physical development. Generally speaking, for reasons indicated elsewhere (see p. 504), the child's rate of growth in relation to that of his fellows tends to remain relatively constant until adolescence.[10, 75, 83] Although deviations from a predictable growth pattern are hardly rare in physical development,[26] they tend to be normally distributed in magnitude.† (see p. 115).

In appraising the physical growth status of a particular child, therefore,

*A more complete treatment of this topic is available.[6, 39, 51, 58, 77, 81, 83] Problems of children's health, nutrition and diseases are also beyond the scope of this book.

†See page 115 for a discussion of factors responsible for fluctuations in the child's relative status in the group.

two mutually complementary methods are available. We can either compare him to the mean child of his own age and sex or we can use him as his own unique yardstick by relating his currently attained status to his own terminal (adult) status. Obviously, employment of the latter method must await the determination of adult status; thus, while useful for longitudinal analysis of *completed* growth cycles, it cannot be used for current evaluation of a growing child. On the other hand, it is often quite misleading to use simple age-sex norms in judging a child's growth status. For example, a tall, stocky, rapidly maturing, or pubescent child should presumably weigh more than a short, slender, slowly maturing or prepubescent child. Hence, we would also want to consider such factors as height, skeletal maturity, pubescent status, and such indices of physique as could be calculated by relating height to various transverse dimensions of the body (chest circumference, shoulder width, hip width, calf girth).[53, 58, 83] If we wanted to be even more precise we could ascertain the respective contributions of fat, water, muscle, bone, and subcutaneous tissues to a given child's weight.[53]

Since it would be extremely cumbersome to consider all of the above factors in appraising individual growth progress, such modern techniques as the Wetzel Grid and the Massler Nomograms (see p. 504) identify the most significant variables affecting status in a particular function, divide children into various subgroups on the basis of their standing relative to these latter variables, and appraise a particular child's growth sequentially in terms of the subgroup to which he belongs. This approach represents a compromise between the gross normative and the multiple differential methods of individual appraisal. It also effects a compromise between the normative and individual yardsticks since it makes possible a comparison between the child's current status and the adult level achieved by his subgroup.

Dimensions of Growth

In addition to considering quantitative increments in height and weight, an overview of physical development must also include changes in such other dimensions of bodily growth as separate organ systems, qualitative aspects of the skeletal system, body proportions, and physiological maturity. Since rates of growth of different body parts are not highly intercorrelated, it is unlikely that any theoretical growth curve will be generally applicable over long periods of time.[77]

Separate Organ Systems. "The body does not grow as a whole and in all directions at once."[77] In comparing the relative growth of the various organ systems, Scammon's grouping of their growth trends in four main categories (neural, lymphoid, general [skeletal and visceral], and genital) is useful.[39] After following parallel paths in the prenatal period, these four kinds of growth diverge markedly after birth. Neural growth is most rapid; 80 per cent complete by the age of four, it tapers off greatly thereafter. Growth of lymphoid tissues (e.g., thymus, lymph nodes) reaches the adult level at age six, more than doubles the adult level by age 12, and then declines until maturity. Genital growth is negligible between birth and pubescence because of the absence of functional levels of sex hormone stimulation. Growth of the skeletal system is marked by two spurts, one during infancy and the other beginning before pubescence; each spurt is followed by a period of decelerating growth. Growth of the respiratory and vascular organs tends to keep pace with growth in bone and muscle tissue,[57] thereby obviating the possibility of physiological imbalance in meeting the enhanced nutritive needs of an expanding body frame. Throughout childhood, and especially during adolescence, the heart grows more rapidly than the arterial system; as a result, relative cardiac competency increases, heart rate decreasing and blood pressure increasing.

Qualitative Changes in the Skeletal System. Important qualitative changes take place in the bones during the course of skeletal development. First, with increasing age, osseous tissue gradually replaces both connective tissue in the bones of the face and cranium and cartilagenous tissue in the other bones of the skeleton. The process of ossification is then completed by the deposition of calcium salts. Vitamin C is necessary for the first step and vitamin D is required for the latter step. As the percentage of calcium in the bones increases and of water and soft tissues decreases, they become harder, less pliable, and more brittle. Many new centers of ossification also appear in an orderly, predictable fashion.* By the end of childhood the diaphyses (shafts) and epiphyses (expanded terminal portions) of the long bones are completely ossified except for a strip of cartilage at their junction. Thereafter, all longitudinal growth takes place in these epiphysial cartilages until complete ossification at the end of adolescence results in fusion and forever terminates the possibility of increase in stature.

Since ossification of the hand and wrist parallels general skeletal growth, it furnishes a convenient index of a child's skeletal maturity.† A number of age level standards have been prepared by various investigators for determining skeletal age.[24, 35, 78] Degree of skeletal maturity is affected by hereditary factors[24] and is positively related to social class status.[78] Girls

---

*Ossification also follows a cephalo-caudal trend. Since the bones undergoing ossification most rapidly are most affected by nutritional deficiencies, the principal site of rickets during the first year of life is in the cranium. During the second year the site shifts to the thorax, and during the third year to the extremities.

†Degree of calcification of the mandibular third molar is highly related to skeletal age (A. Demesch and P. Wartmann, *Child Develop.* 27: 459-473, 1956).

are consistently more mature than boys in their skeletal development, the sex difference tending to increase with age. [24, 35, 78] Muscular growth parallels general body and skeletal growth throughout childhood and also shows a marked spurt at pubescence. The fat-bone ratio decreases with age in boys and increases with age in girls.[70]

Body Proportions. Because of the cephalo-caudal and proximo-distal trends in physical growth during the fetal period, the head and trunk are disproportionately large and the extremities are disproportionately short at birth. Thereafter, since the head grows most slowly, the proportion of its length to total body length progressively diminishes. The legs grow more rapidly than the trunk throughout childhood and especially during preadolescence; beginning with adolescence, however, the reverse trend sets in.[8] During childhood the face also grows much more rapidly than the rest of the cranium.

The neonate is slender except for his head. He broadens out during the first year of life and then becomes progressively more slender until the age of seven or eight.[8] A broadening trend then begins as the child approaches pubescence, being concentrated in the shoulder girdle among boys and in the hip region among girls.

The foregoing changes in children's body proportions reflect age level shifts in the relative dominance of the different factors regulating skeletal growth[8] (see p. 503). Ordinarily, broad-built children tend to be physically accelerated and slender-built children physically retarded. The former also tend to progress through these sequential changes in body proportions more rapidly.[8]

Anatomical and Physiological Maturity. In general, degree of anatomical and physiological maturity is represented by the extent to which attained status in a given structure or function approaches the adult level. Although not perfectly intercorrelated, different measures of physical maturity tend to be substantially related to each other.[64] Hence, degree of physical maturity may be expressed in terms of pubescent status,[33] skeletal maturity,[33] and percentage of adult height[64] or developmental growth level[83] achieved at a given age. Other functions that advance or decline regularly from birth to adulthood, such as increments in blood pressure, vital capacity, and dental age and decrements in body temperature, pulse, respiratory, and basal metabolic rates,[44, 77] are less useful indices of maturity because they are more variable and less highly intercorrelated.

Skeletal age is an extremely useful general index of physical maturity since it is highly correlated with all measures of pubescent status.[33, 64] It indicates whether the child's skeletal development is proceeding at an average, accelerated or retarded rate. Although reasonably independent of sheer bodily size,[33] in the sense that acceleration or retardation (unless very extreme) does not materially affect terminal stature,[8] it does indicate how close the child has already progressed toward adult status.[8] Hence, from measures of present height and skeletal age it is possible to predict a child's adult stature with a reasonable degree of accuracy,[10] providing that pubescence does not occur abnormally early or late (see p. 504).

Growth in Height

Growth in height is not evenly distributed over the approximately twenty year period in which it occurs. After an interval of rapid growth during the first two years, yearly increments in stature are small and relatively constant until the second growth spurt in pre- and early adolescence.[51, 81] Boys are slightly taller than girls until the age of 11 when the earlier occurrence of the preadolescent gowth spurt in the latter puts them ahead temporarily.[51, 81] However, since this second spurt is more intense and longer lasting in boys, they regain their superiority at about the age of 15.

Height is a typical example of a normally distributed, polygenically determined ontogenetic trait (see p. 57) in which genic influences account for the greater portion of phenotypic variability.* Where genotypes are identical, as among monozygotic twins, environmental differences give rise to relatively small differences in ultimate height (see p. 62). The degree of resemblance between siblings and between parents and children, although substantial,[39] is appreciably less because of greater genotypic diversity. The influence of genic factors is undoubtedly mediated through the secretion of differential amounts of growth hormone (anterior pituitary), thyroxin, and sex hormones, and through the differential responsiveness of skeletal tissues to their stimulation. Growth hormone and thyroxin stimulate skeletal growth from the prenatal period to maturity. The adolescent growth spurt is largely attributable to the early proliferative effect of sex hormones on the epiphysial cartilages. Final ossification of the epiphyses (and the termination of growth) is caused by the later ossifying action of high concentrations of these hormones.[4]

Since height is a polygenically determined trait it is somewhat susceptible to the influence of environmental factors. The adequacy of nutrition—especially the intake of protein, calcium, and vitamin D—plays an important role in determining whether the individual attains the maximum height that is possible within his genic limitations.[22] This is the most plausible

*It is true, of course, that the *range* in which human stature occurs is a species characteristic. Consistent differences are also found between the mean heights of children of different racial stocks growing up in the same environment, e.g., Chinese, Japanese, South European, and North European on the islands of Hawaii.[85] However, much overlapping occurs between groups.

explanation we have for the mean increase in stature of about three inches that has occurred in Britain over the past 70 years,[19] and for the substantial increases in height among children of American immigrants after only a single generation.[14] Nutritional factors also account for the positive relationship between height and social class status[11, 60] and for decrements and increments in the mean height of children coincident with periods of war and prosperity.[43] Greulich et al.[34] have shown that excessive exposure to atomic radiation has adverse effects on the height and skeletal maturity of children (especially of boys).

Because the influence of genic factors on skeletal growth operates with considerable uniformity throughout the growth span, a child who is tall or short at birth also tends to be similarly tall or short at ages six and nineteen. Hence, from his present height and rate of growth (as indicated by skeletal maturity) it is possible to predict his adult stature.[10] His relative position in his age group may be temporarily displaced during adolescence since the age at which the pubertal growth spurt takes place depends on the age of pubescence; ordinarily this displacement does not occur since tall children also tend to become pubescent early and hence have an early growth spurt (the reverse holding true for short children). In any case, the predictable relationship between childhood and *terminal* height is not disturbed by the age of the pubertal growth spurt unless a child matures extremely early or extremely late. In precocious puberty the epiphyses are ossified prematurely and the individual, although tall for his age during late childhood and early adolescence, becomes a short adult. In retarded puberty the epiphyses remain open for an unusually long time and the individual becomes a tall, long-legged adult.

Body Weight and Nutritional Status

Weight is an important correlate of growth and index of nutritional status. Optimal weight depends on age, sex, physique, and pubescent status; it can be calculated most conveniently from the Massler Nomograms which utilize a prediction formula based on the relationship of weight to height and calf girth[58] The general shape of the growth curve for weight (including spurts, plateaus, and sex differences) closely parallels that for height, but the rate of gain is much more rapid. Thus, a child ordinarily doubles his birth weight in six months or less, but requires four years to double his height. Like the corresponding spurt in height, the adolescent spurt in weight occurs earlier in children who mature early, and tends to precede other signs of sexual maturation. The heavier child, like the taller child, also tends to become pubescent earlier. Characteristic sex differences in the distribution of fat do not appear prior to pubescence.

Weight is also a normally distributed polygenically determined trait, but genic factors are much less prepotent than in the case of height (see p. 503). Mediating mechanisms include a polyglandular system of control (thyroid, anterior pituitary, adrenal cortex and gonads) as well as differential tissue responsiveness to hormonal stimulation. Genic factors related to body build are also significant determinants of weight. Ectomorphic children, for example, tend to be skinny despite the fact that their daily caloric intake greatly exceeds that of endomorphs.[69] Weight, however, is much more influenced than height by such environmental variables as exercise, disease, socio-emotional adjustment, and nutrition. The latter factor accounts for weight lag in undernourished children,[22] for the long-term increase in the mean weight of children over the past seven decades,[19] for fluctuations in mean weight during war and prosperity,[43] and for the positive relationship between weight and socioeconomic status.[11, 60] Weight lag has also been noted as a concomitant of disease, operations, and emotional stress.[13, 25]

The Wetzel Grid[83] is a useful technique for appraising the adequacy of a child's growth in weight relative to his height and physique. It indicates rate and consistency of growth, degree of maturity status currently attained, and deviations (lag and lead) from the expected pattern. Ordinarily a child's growth parallels, within rather narrowly defined limits of variation, the growth curve formed by plotting successive age level increments in weight and height of children in his own physique group. Nonpathological deviations from this "channelwise" progression, however, are less uncommon than Wetzel believed, especially among early and late maturing girls and children with unique body builds.[26] Furthermore, although the Wetzel Grid is an excellent clinical tool for revealing pathological aberrations in growth due to disease, malnutrition, or emotional stress, it neither indicates per se the cause of the disturbance nor the relative contributions of fat, bone, muscle, and subcutaneous tissue to an increment in weight. Hence, adequate interpretation of irregularity in a child's growth pattern also presupposes knowledge of his pubescent status, optimal weight, health, nutrition, and socioemotional history.

The Body Image

The body image is the mental picture that each individual has of his own appearance in space. It includes such factors as height, weight, body build, and facial appearance. Ordinarily, during most periods of life (e.g., from childhood to preadolescence), the body image changes imperceptibly because the body itself changes in this way. The small changes in appearance and quantitative increments in height and weight are easily absorbed in the prevailing image the child has of his own body; no radical revisions are necessary. During adolescence, however, conscious and wholesale restructuring of the body image is necessary to account for drastic changes in size, body proportions, primary and secondary sex characteristics, and facial appearance.

As a salient component of the ego, the body image usually has positive or negative rather than neutral affective valence. Whether it contributes positively or negatively to self-esteem depends on the social valuation of particular physical traits, deviations and disabilities, i.e., whether the latter give rise to approval or disapproval, admiration or ridicule. Individuals are usually regarded as ugly or attractive insofar as they conform to or deviate from the idealized anatomic measurements of their own sex group. In our culture shortness and puniness in boys and obesity in either sex tend to detract from a child's status in his peer group. It should be noted, however, that somatic defects and deviations have a less disastrous effect on children's than on adolescents' self-concepts. Among the latter, physical attractiveness is a more crucial determinant of sociometric status and is also important for heterosexual effectiveness. Furthermore, during childhood the individual is less dependent on the peer group for status and approval. He can still retain a flattering self-image if he is intrinsically valued by his parents.

Psychological Effects of Somatic Defects and Deviations

Physical defects and deviations constitute first of all an *objective* handicap in adapting to the social environment. Shortness, ectomorphy, obesity, and retarted pubescent development place a boy at a serious competitive disadvantage in athletic activities. Mesomorphic (muscular) boys enjoy the reputation among their fellows of being "real boys," daring, leaders, good at games, and grown-up, whereas ectomorphic boys have the reputation of being bashful, submissive, and unhappy.[38] Cardiac and orthopedic disabilities limit participation in physical and social activities, and visual and auditory defects restrict the range of sensitivity and responsiveness to important intellectual and social stimuli. When unsuspected and uncorrected they make school learning difficult and simulate mental deficiency; indirectly, they may lead to failure in school by placing too great a strain on the individual's capacity for attentiveness. Chronic strain, pain, fatigue, and hormonal imbalance associated with many physical and sensory defects may also give rise to behavioral disturbance by lowering the general threshold of reactivity. When this happens the affected child manifests undue irritability, restlessness and distractibility, and responds to trifling stimuli with exaggerated, undirected, inappropriate, and frequently aggressive responses.[55]

More important than the objective handicap inherent in physical defects is the *social* disadvantage at which they place the deviant individual. Significant deviancy from group physical norms tends to elicit a negative response from his peers and almost guarantees that he will be treated differently from his fellows. The least common denominators of this differential treatment are devaluation, avoidance, rejection, and accordance of a lower status. Physically accelerated children, on the other hand, are "accepted and treated by adults and other children as more mature."[47] Although they may sometimes be the victims of excessive adult expectations, "they appear to have relatively little need to strive for status. From their ranks come the outstanding student body leaders . . . In contrast, . . . because others tend to treat them as the little boys they appear to be, . . . physically retarded boys exhibit many forms of relatively immature behavior."[47]

The individual's ego response to his own physical disability is largely a reflection of the social reaction it elicits. If the latter is negative, therefore, he responds with feelings of self-depreciation, guilt, hypersensitivity, self-consciousness, and anxiety in facing new or competitive situations.[17, 20, 61] Many children seek to compensate for their physical disadvantage with excessive activity and attention-getting behavior[47]; others become demanding and egocentric or exhibit regressive behavior. The most serious reaction to the ego deflating implications of somatic defect is self-protective withdrawal from social situations. Persistent avoidance of interpersonal relations may lead to irreversible retardation in the socialization process.

It need not be imagined, however, that self-depreciation is an inevitable accompaniment of organic defect. Much depends on the seriousness of the disability or the extent of the deviation, both from the norm of the peer group and from the child's ideal; on its probable duration and its obviousness to others; on its relation to other physical defects and to problems of adjustment arising from nonsomatic sources; and on the availability of other compensatory and status-giving traits.[54] Most important, perhaps, is the attitude of the child's parents toward the condition.[54] If they are rejecting, overprotective, embarrassed, or have unrealistic expectations, ego damage is unavoidable. If they handle the situation realistically, take it in stride, and extend unqualified acceptance, the worst features of impaired self-esteem may be largely circumvented.[17]

Impact of Physical Growth on Motor Development

Skeletal and muscular development self-evidently provide the anatomic substrate for the development of strength and motor skill. Increment in muscle mass tends to precede growth in strength and skill since the latter not only presupposes the structural wherewithall but also the neurophysiological maturity and experience necessary for functional utilization and motor coordination. It is understandable, therefore, why ability in gross motor skills is positively related to such factors as mesomorphy,[73] skeletal maturity,[71] and development of the abdominal musculature.[79] Motor learning of a more complex sort depends on sensori-motor intelligence and is unrelated to gross motor skills and physical ability.[55]

Contrary to popular belief, individual differences in the emergence of locomotor abilities are not determined by weight or body build but by genic factors concerned with their development and by such temperamental characteristics as eagerness, venturesomeness, persistence and curiosity.[68] Children who sit, stand, and walk late tend to be heavier and taller than individuals more advanced in these respects simply because they are older; they are not heavier or taller *for their age* than the latter.[68] Also, under uniform conditions of pediatric and home care, the age at which these functions appear is not affected by general health status.[67]

MOTOR DEVELOPMENT IN INFANCY AND EARLY CHILDHOOD

The motor ability of a child constitutes an important component of his feeling of competence in coping with the environment. It enables him to feel either executively independent and capable of looking after his own needs or relatively dependent on the physical assistance of others. It also constitutes an important source of primary status in the home, school and peer group as well as a basic perequisite for ultimately attaining *volitional* independence. The precise effects on personality development of a gain in motor competence, however, depend on the prevailing state of ego organization. During the stage of omnipotence, the child feels volitionally independent *despite* and possibly even because of his executive dependence (see p. 286). Increased executive independence at this time may therefore result in further feelings of self-enhancement but is certainly not basic to current notions of volitional power; as a matter of fact since it leads to greater parental demands on the child, it tends to be associated with increased volitional dependence, ego devaluation, and satellization. This situation also prevails during the satellizing period since the attained level of motor competence is still insufficient to instigate demands for greater volitional independence.* Beginning with middle childhood enhanced motor competence becomes a major source of primary status and instrument of desatellization. The executively independent child is more free to explore the wider community with some feelings of assurance. Children with motor

---

*Misperceptions of executive competence between the ages of four and five do commonly instigate expansive, out-of-bounds behavior reflective of such demands (see p. 297).

handicaps not only feel more timorous in this respect but also find it difficult to maintain a realistic level of aspiration when faced with motor tasks.[82]

Motor activity is an important outlet for emotional expression (fear, flight, rage, aggression) and source of basic satisfactions and self-expression. Increased motor competence helps reduce frustrations in childhood that are occasioned by inability to manipulate objects and play materials as desired. The way in which a child expresses himself in motor performance is also an excellent reflection of such temperamental and personality characteristics as venturesomeness, energy level, aggressiveness, sociality, and self-confidence.

Not the least important aspect of motor development is its implications for social participation and adjustment. We have already indicated how early participation in cooperative peer activities is limited by motor incompetence (see p. 464), the extent to which athletic prowess determines a boy's prestige and leadership status in his peer group (see p. 478), and how socially ascendant behavior may be increased by improving a child's motor skills (se p. 473). Strength and motor skill are integral components of the body image that impinge on self-esteem since they and their reciprocals are socially admired and disparaged in much the same way as tallness and shortness, mesomorphy and obesity. Retardation in motor competence forms the beginning of a vicious cycle in social maladjustment that is difficult to break. Boys with poor physical abilities tend to enjoy low social prestige in the group. Hence they have reason to shun both motor activities and group participation, because both are associated with failure. Their reluctance to participate, in turn, not only increases their poor reputation but also through lack of practice further depresses their relative standing in these very motor abilities that are so crucial for group status. The upshot may be a compensatory absorption in nonsocial activities that results in social isolation and failure to acquire the skills necessary for successful interpersonal relationships.

Organizational Trends

The principal organizational trends in the development of early motor behavior have already been discussed in Chapter 7 (see p. 205). Particularly striking as the child passes through the various, relatively uniform developmental sequences in the acquisition of postural, locomotor, and prehensile functions is the influence of the cephalo-caudal and proximo-distal trends. Also, as might be reasonably anticipated, "postural control of a given part always precedes controlled movements of that part"[72]; and since the acquisition of upright posture requires dominance of muscles with an antigravity function, the balance between flexor and extensor tonus gradually shifts in favor of the latter.[72] To some extent what has often been referred to as the "large to small muscle" and the "mass to specific" trends is in part a reflection of the proximo-distal trend since smaller muscles and the muscles involved in more specific functions tend to be distally located. The "mass to specific" trend also reflects a general tendency, already evident in the neonatal period, toward the elimination of generalized, superfluous and exaggerated movements irrelevant to the execution of a particular task.

Consistent with the trend toward minimal muscular involvement and economy of effort, bilateral performance of many motor activities is gradually superseded by consistent preference for a single hand.[31, 49, 52] During infancy and childhood, however, unilateral preference tends to be relatively unstable and to alternate with bilateral proclivities.[31] One early manifestation of asymmetrical unilaterality is the tonic neck reflex (rotation of the head to one side when the infant lies in the supine position) which commonly persists for the first three months of life.[29] Various forms of "reciprocal interweaving" also characterize integration of the four extremities during the course of postural and locomotor development. These include ipsilateral and contralateral coordination of synergetic muscle groups, reciprocal opposition of antagonists, and diagonal alternation.[29]

Postural-Locomotor Development*

Postural-locomotor development is characterized by a sequence of stages which are relatively uniform for all children despite individual differences in age of occurrence. Occasionally some steps are omitted by individual children or even by most children in a particular culture (see p. 59). The following is a brief timetable of the more salient landmarks and their median age of emergence[72]: lifting the chin from the prone position (three weeks); raising the head and chest from the prone position (nine weeks); sitting alone for one minute (31 weeks); crawling (37 weeks); standing, holding (42 weeks); creeping (44 weeks); standing alone (62 weeks); walking alone (64 weeks).† These stages encompass non-reflex motor activities that are functionally discontinuous with subcortically regulated locomotor reflexes elicitable in the first few months of life (see p. 211).

Ames[1] has identified fourteen successive stages of prone progression which coalesce and coexist before replacing each other in turn. The three most important precursors of walking are *crawling* (moving with abdomen in

*More detailed accounts of postural-locomotor development are available.[1, 7, 15, 30, 56, 72]

†Bayley[7] reports the same sequence of steps with slightly different age norms.

contact with floor), *creeping* (moving on hands and knees with abdomen parallel to floor), and *hitching* (locomotion in a sitting position).[15] Beginning walkers tend to flex their knees, take short, wide steps, and keep their arms elevated.[15]

Development of Prehension

Prehensile development may be illustrated by successive age level changes in the infant's efforts to reach and grasp a cube placed before him on a table.[37] At 16 weeks he attempts to reach it but generally fails to make contact. At 20 weeks he makes contact but either pushes the cube out of reach or at best manages a "primitive squeeze." The 24 week old infant uses a corralling and scooping approach with his palm and fingers. At 28 weeks he begins to oppose his thumb to his palm and other fingers. Finally, at 36 weeks coordinated grasping occurs between the tips of the thumb and forefinger. This developmental sequence, which is functionally discontinuous from the grasp reflex (see p. 210) is marked by the following noteworthy features: progressive improvement in aim, precision and smoothness of execution; decreasing bilateral involvement and use of shoulder and elbow movements; increasing rotation of the wrist and opposition of the thumb; and gradual replacement of the gross palmar-digital and palmar-thumb approaches by the more localized tip of thumb and forefinger technique.

Handedness

We have already referred to the tendency for bilaterality in motor functioning to be gradually replaced by unilaterality during infancy and early childhood (see p. 510). Consistent preference for a *particular* hand, however, develops slowly. It is not evident at all during the first six months of life, and is quite unstable at the end of the first year.[42, 52] By the end of the second year about 85 per cent of all children are predominantly right-handed.[42] Stability of preference, however, is not established until the age of six, at which time the percentage of left-handedness (7 per cent) roughly approximates that found in the adult population.[42] Hand preference seems to be part of a general lateral dominance, but intraindividual discrepancies with respect to different body parts and even with respect to different activities performed by a single part (e.g., writing throwing, batting) are not uncommon.[23]

Left-handedness is somewhat of a motor handicap since most tools are designed for right-handed persons, and because the latter find it relatively difficult to demonstrate motor skills to left-handed individuals. More important perhaps is the fact that left-handed children are frequently made to feel self-conscious about their condition and are often subjected to strong pressures to shift hand preference. However, there is little evidence to indicate that changing handedness per se contributes to stuttering. Most stutterers give no history of changing handedness, and most children who do shift handedness do not subsequently develop this speech defect.

The determination of handedness is still largely a matter of conjecture. The bimodal distribution of unimanuality[65] suggests that genic predispositions toward lateral dominance probably exist; and since there are only a few left-handed cultures, one might infer that the typical genic predisposition among human beings is toward right-handedness. Genic predispositions are seldom strong enough to be determinative or to offer effective resistance to potent cultural pressures. Right-handed predispositions are presumably reinforced by the culture, and left-handed predispositions are converted to right except in those rare instances when they are extremely tenacious. The most important determinants of handedness, therefore, are deliberate training measures and the cumulative impact of innumerable environmental cues. Occasional cases of left-handedness are attributable to strong genic predispositions, absence of or resistance to training, unresponsiveness to environmental cues, and direct teaching by or imitation of left-handed parents or teachers.

There is little doubt that cerebral and lateral dominance are associated. Even the motor speech area is located in the same cerebral hemisphere that controls the preferred hand. It is more logical to suppose, however, that cerebral dominance is a consequence rather than a cause of handedness. Anatomically it is well established that each cerebral hemisphere controls the voluntary musculature on the opposite side of the body. If, because of genic predispositions and cultural pressures most motor skills are performed by the right hand, it stands to reason that the neuroanatomical and neurophysiological substrate (stimulus-response connections) of these skills will be located in the same hemisphere (left) that regulates voluntary motion in the right hand. On the other hand, if cerebral dominance were innately determined and caused handedness, it would be difficult to explain the not infrequent occurrence of differential, eye, hand, and foot preference.

Preschool Motor Development

After rudimentary locomotion and prehension are established, the child gradually acquires a repertoire of other motor skills. During late infancy and the preschool years he learns to walk backwards and upstairs, jump, hop, climb, skip, operate a tricycle, and throw, catch and bounce a ball.[7, 36] He acquires such skills[28] as drinking from a cup (18 months), pouring from a pitcher (36 months) and eating with a spoon (15-36 months). Two- and three year olds button and unbutton and begin undressing themselves, and a year later they are capable of dressing themselves.[80] A characteristic sequence is followed in the use of wheel toys.[48] Between 21 and 24 months the child merely pushes and pulls them repetitively. Shortly thereafter he concentrates on separate parts and acquires greater muscular control. Between 26 and 36 months more complex skills are practiced and integrated into larger wholes. At 48 months the skills themselves are subordinated to various imaginative and social activities in which they are embedded. Writing skills are also developed during the preschool period, beginning with crude marks and scribbles at the age of two.[41] During the third and fourth years the child adds some horizontal and systematic vertical lines to his repertoire and later some discrete symbols. At five and six he is able to form recognizable letters.

Motor skills involved in such artistic activities as drawing and block building also develop at this time. The youthful artist only makes random and exploratory strokes. After he acquires greater control he is able to manage simple designs, and finally, at about the age of four, crude figures and objects.[12] A typical developmental sequence is seen in the use of blocks.[46] Before he is two, the child merely carries them about and arranges them in amorphous piles. The two- and three year old makes simple structures such as rows and towers, and the three- and four year old more complex structures (e.g., bridges, enclosures). Between four and five, blocks are used more in dramatic play to represent objects such as trains and ships, and the five- and six year year old uses them to reproduce actual structures.

Maturation and Learning

The relative importance of maturation and learning in the acquisition of motor skills is largely a function of whether the latter are phylogenetic or ontogenetic in nature (see p. 212). Phylogenetic skills develop "autogenously" in orderly, uniform sequence despite marked cultural differences in child rearing practices. Their development is not influenced at all by specific practice and is only slightly influenced by opportunities for incidental or nonspecific experience. Environmental stimulation does not accelerate and deprivation of use (within limits) does not retard their rate of development (see pp. 57, 84, 212). The most important factor determining the emergence of a given phylogenetic skill is the adequacy of its neuroanatomical and neurophysiological substrate as determined by genic influences. Hence, the *overt* appearance of earlier stages in a particular locomotor or prehensile sequence is not prerequisite for the development of later stages and may be omitted if opportunities for expression are curtailed under conditions of cradling or cultural taboo (see pp. 57 and 212). Individual differences in rate of development are largely determined by genic factors; intra-pair differences in the acquisition of phylogenetic skills, for example, are much smaller among monozygotic than among dizygotic twins.[74] As previously indicated, temperamental factors may affect age of emergence of these skills (see p. 508), but socioeconomic variables generally play no role (see p. 57). Only extreme emotional deprivation has been found to retard the rate of early (phylogenetic) motor development (see p. 59).

In the case of ontogenetic motor skills, particularly those which are psychosocial or specialized in nature, rate and extent of development are largely dependent on opportunities for practice and on motive-incentive conditions. Advanced stages in the development of ontogenetic skills pre-suppose the prior achievement of lower levels of performance. Much of the deceleration in rate of motor development that sets in about the age of three in our culture is attributable to the lack of challenging environmenal stimulation and to stereotyped playground equipment.[36, 48] Manus children, in contrast, reach a much higher mean level of motor accomplishment in response to an environment which is much more demanding in terms of manual dexterity.[59] The effects of practice are naturally more evident in relatively complex and specific activities such as maze learning, ball throw-ing and roller skating than in skills that would ordinarily be learned in the course of incidental experience, e.g., jumping (see p. 86). Guided practice or coaching also takes maximal advantage of whatever motor readiness is available.[21] In the case of certain skills (e.g., roller skating as against tricycling), however, the effects of practice are not carried over from one age period to another (in the absence of intervening practice), because original patterns of neuromuscular coordination are disrupted by marked changes in size, strength, and body proportions (see p. 87). When an older child is deprived of early experience in a particular skill commonly available to younger children he generally begins at the same primitive level as the latter but progresses more rapidly through the intervening stages.[46]

Maturation also plays an important role in the learning of ontogenetic skills. The child cannot profit from practice in a given activity if his over-all level of neuromuscular ability is not equal to the task. Hence, practice that is postponed until he is ready is much more efficacious than premature practice (se p. 84). The age of motor readiness, however, is quite specific and cannot be predicted on a priori grounds. At 18 months, for example, he is ready to learn roller skating but not tricycling (see p. 86).

Individual differences in the acquisition of ontogenetic motor skills are determined by genic factors, by motivational, emotional, and personality variables, and by opportunities for practice. Although differences between identical twins tend to be less marked than corresponding differences between fraternal twins,[74] environmental variability is associated with greater pheno-typic variability than in the case of phylogenetic traits (see p. 62). Such motivational factors as material incentives[18] and differential cultural expectations relating to sex membership (see p. 449) have an important effect on the acquisition of various motor skills. In general, little or no relationship exists between socioeconomic status and rate of development of gross or fine motor skills[9] (see p. 110); evidently the upper socioeconomic group does not have the same experiential advantage here that it has in the development of intellectual skills.

MOTOR DEVELOPMENT IN LATER CHILDHOOD

During the elementary school years the child learns many new motor skills and also improves on those previously acquired. Changes are generally in the direction of increased strength, speed, versatility, precision and smoothness of execution. Single skills tend to be incorporated into more complex and highly structured team sports. Progressive gains are registered in speed of running, accuracy and distance of throwing, height and distance of jumping, etc.[45, 71] A two-fold increase in strength occurs between the ages of six and eleven[6] as well as an impressive increase in speed of eye-hand coordination[62] and decrease in motor reaction time.[32]

Fine motor skills and sensori-motor learning, as illustrated by maze[63] and rotary pursuit performance,[3] also improve during this period, but "percentage of improvement resulting from given amounts of practice do not appear to change in any consistent way as a function of age."[63] Continued improvement occurs in the writing of letters, numbers and words, and tends to follow an orderly developmental sequence.[2] In general, adult expectations regarding writing skills are out of line with prevailing developmental progress. Children cannot be expected to write with good slant, alignment and proportion before the age of nine. Current emphasis on manuscript writing in the primary grades is in accord with the finding that children are not ready for cursive writing until the age of eight or nine.[2]

Generality of Motor Skills

Positive but low intercorrelations among different gross motor skills[7, 27, 40] suggest that motor ability tends to be relatively specific in nature. Factor analysis[16] also shows that speed and strength are relatively independent factors. Thus, although various tests of strength (or speed) tend to be moderately intercorrelated, correlations between the two factors (or between abilities involving both factors) are relatively low. Furthermore, intercorrelations among various motor abilities tend to decrease wtih increasing age.[7] Hence, either little actual generality of motor ability exists or great variability prevails in opportunity for practicing different motor skills. Some of the existing generality of function must also be attributed to the self-confidence which success in one activity contributes to success in another activity.

Sex Differences

Boys are stronger than girls at all ages but the difference in strength first becomes significant for practical purposes during adolescence.[6] At this time the growth curves which were hitherto parallel begin to diverge. Throughout childhood boys are also superior to girls in most gross motor skills such as climbing, jumping, sliding, skipping, ball throwing, and ball kicking.[21, 36, 45] However, preschool girls are superior to boys in tricycling, hopping, and bouncing and catching a ball.[36, 45] During adolescence the divergence in gross motor skills becomes even greater than that in strength.[4] Under conditions of relatively equal opportunity for practice, sex differences in fine motor skills and sensori-motor learning tend to be small, statistically unreliable, and inconsistent in direction for most laboratory tasks.[32, 63] In everyday mechanical skills relative superiority is almost completely a function of differential opportunities for practice.

Sex differences in strength and gross motor skills during childhood reflect cultural expectations and the sex typing of games. Even the slight advantage that boys have in muscle mass and vital capacity is attributable to the influence of greater physical exertion. During adolescence a more substantial physical basis exists for these sex differences. Muscular hypertrophy caused by androgenic stimulation is much greater in boys, and their superior height, weight, limb length and shoulder breadth give them the advantage of greater leverage.[4] In addition, differences in vital and cardiac capacity, although partly a reflection of differential participation in athletic activities, become sufficiently great to account for marked differences in tolerance for physical exertion.[4] After pubescence, therefore, competitive athletic contests between the sexes are hardly feasible. During childhood, however, sex typing of games and segregation between the sexes in athletic activities cannot be defended on physical grounds.

Effect of Intellectual, Emotional and Personality Factors

The extent to which a child develops his genic potentialities for motor skills obviously depends somewhat on such temperamental and personality factors as energy level, venturesomeness, aggressiveness, and persistence. Since motor skills are primarily developed in a peer group context, much also depends on his sociality and eagerness for group participation and competition. Home environment is also important. Children from over-protecting homes tend to be physically apprehensive and relatively retarded in gross motor development.[5, 48] Williams and Scott [84] attribute the acceleration of Negro children in motor abilities[50] to the permissive child rearing practices which are particularly evident in lower-class Negro homes. High levels of personality anxiety have been found to inhibit trial-and-error learning in children.[66]

Relationships between motor and intellectual ability during childhood have already been discussed in detail in another context (see pp. 108-111). It might be added in passing that a thorough review of research in this area indicates that sensori-motor learning in young children "is unrelated to scores on intelligence tests."[63]

REFERENCES

1. Ames, L. B.: The sequential patterning of prone progression in the human infant. *Genet. Psychol. Monogr. 19*: 409-460, 1937.

2. ——, and Ilg, F. L.: Developmental trends in writing behavior. *J. Genet. Psychol. 79*: 29-46, 1951.

3. Ammons, R. B., Alprin, S. I., and Ammons, C. H.: Rotary pursuit performance as related to sex and age of pre-adult subjects. *J. Exper. Psychol. 49*: 127-133, 1955.

4. Ausubel, D. P.: *Theory and Problems of Adolescent Development.* New York, Grune & Stratton, 1954.

5. Baldwin, A. L.: The effect of home environment on nursery school behavior. *Child Develop. 20*: 49-62, 1949.

6. Baldwin, B. T.: The physical growth of children from birth to maturity. *Univ. Iowa Stud. Child Welf.* No. 1, 1921.

7. Bayley, N.: The development of motor abilities during the first three years. *Monogr. Soc. Res. Child Develop.* No. 1, 1935.

8. ——: Individual patterns of development. *Child Develop. 27*: 45-74, 1956.

9. ——, and Jones, H. E.: Environmental correlates of mental and motor development. *Child Develop. 8*: 329-341, 1937.

10. ——, and Pinneau, S. R.: Tables for predicting adult height from skeletal age. Revised for use with the Greulich-Pyle hand standards. *J. Pediat. 40*: 423-44, 1952.

11. Berry, W. T. C., and Cowin, P. J.: Conditions associated with the growth of boys, 1950-1951. *Brit. M. J. 1*: 847-851, 1954.

12. Biber, B.: *Children's Drawings; from Lines to Pictures.* New York, Bureau of Educational Experiments, 1934.

13. Binning, G.: Peace be on thy house. *Health,* March-April, 1948, p. 6.

14. Boas, F.: *Changes in Bodily Form of Descendants of Immigrants.* Washington, D. C., U. S. Government Printing Office, 1911.

15. Burnside, L. H.: Coordination in the locomotion of infants. *Genet. Psychol. Monogr. 2*: 281- 372, 1927.

16. Carpenter, A: The differential measurement of speed in primary school children. *Child Develop. 12*: 1-7, 1941.

17. Carter, V. E., and Chess, S.: Factors influencing the adaptations of organically handicapped children. *Am. J. Orthopsychiat. 21*: 827-837, 1951.

18. Chase, L.: Motivation of young children: an experimental study of the influence of certain types of external incentives upon the performance of a task. *Univ. Iowa Stud. Child Welf. 5*: No. 3, 1932.

19. Clements, E. M. B.: Changes in the mean stature and weight of British children over the past seventy years. *Brit. M. J. 2*: 897-902, 1953.

20. Cruickshank, W. M.: The relation of physical disability to fear and guilt feelings. *Child Develop. 22*: 291-298, 1951.

21. Dusenberry, L.: A study of the effects of training on ball throwing by children ages three to seven. *Res. Quart. Am. Assoc. Health 23*: 9-14, 1952.

22. Dreizen, S. C., et al.: The effect of nutritive failure on the growth patterns of white children in Alabama. *Child Develop. 24*: 189-202, 1953.

23. Eyre, M. B., and Schmeeckle, M. M.: A study of handedness, eyedness, and footedness. *Child Develop. 4*: 73-78, 1933.

24. Flory, C. D.: Osseous development in the hand as an index of skeletal development. *Monogr. Soc. Res. Child Develop. 1*: No. 3, 1936.

25. Fried, R. I., and Mayer, M. F.: Socio-emotional factors accounting for growth failure in children living in an institution. *J. Pediat. 33*: 444-456, 1948.

26. Garn, S. M.: Individual and group deviations from "channelwise" grid progression in girls. *Child Develop. 23*: 193-206, 1952.

27. Gates, A. I. and Scott, A. W.: Characteristics and relations of motor speed and dexterity among young children. *J. Genet. Psychol. 39*: 423-454, 1931.

28. Gesell, A.: *The First Five Years of Life.* New York, Harper, 1940.

29. ——: The ontogenesis of infant behavior. *In* L. Carmichael, Ed., *Manual of Child Psychology*, ed. 2. New York, Wiley, 1954, pp. 335-373.

30. ——, and Amatruda, C. S.: *Developmental Diagnosis: Normal and Abnormal Child Development.* New York, Hoeber, 1947.

31. ——, and Ames, L. B.: The development of handedness. *J. Genet. Psychol. 70*: 155-175, 1947.

32. Goodenough, F. L.: The development of the reactive process from early childhood to maturity. *J. Exper. Psychol. 18*: 431-450, 1935.

33. Greulich, W. W.: The rationale of assessing the developmental status of children from roentgenograms of the hand and wrist. *Child Develop. 21*: 33-44, 1950.

34. ——, Crimson, C. S., and Turner, M. L.: The physical growth and development of children who survived the atomic bombing of Hiroshima and Nagasaki. *J. Pediat. 43*: 121-145, 1953.

35. ——, and Pyle, S. I.: *Radiographic Atlas of Skeletal Development of the Wrist and Hand.* Stanford, Calif., Stanford University Press, 1950.

36. Gutteridge, M. V.: A study of motor achievements of young children. *Arch. Psychol.* No. 244, 1939.

37. Halverson, H. M.: An experimental study of prehension in infants by means of systematic cinema records. *Genet. Psychol. Monogr. 10*: 110-286, 1931.

38. Hanley, C.: Physique and reputation of junior high school boys. *Child Develop. 22*: 247-260, 1951.

39. Harris, J. A., Jackson, C. M., Paterson, D. G., and Scammon, R. F.: *The Measurement of Man.* Minneapolis, University of Minnesota Press, 1930.

40. Hartman, D. M.: The hurdle jump as a measure of the motor proficiency of young children. *Child Develop. 14*: 201-211, 1943.

41. Hildreth, G.: Developmental sequences in name writing. *Child Develop. 7*: 291-303, 1936.

42. ——: The development and training of hand dominance: II. Developmental tendencies in handedness. *J. Genet. Psychol. 75*: 221-254, 1949.

43. Howe, P. E., and Schiller, M.: Growth responses of the school child to changes in diet and environmental factors. *J. Appl. Physiol. 5*: 51-61, 1952.

44. Iliff, A., and Lee, V. A.: Pulse rate, respiratory rate, and body temperature of children between two months and eighteen years of age. *Child Develop. 23*: 238-245, 1952.

45. Jenkins, L. M.: *A Comparative Study of Motor Achievements of Children at Five, Six, and Seven Years of Age.* New York, Teachers College, Columbia University, 1930.

46. Johnson, H. M.: *The Art of Block Building.* New York, John Day, 1933.

47. Jones, M. C., and Bayley, N.: Physical maturity among boys as related to behavior. *J. Educ. Psychol. 41*: 129-148, 1950.

48. Jones, T. D.: The development of certain motor skills and play activities in young children. *Child Develop. Monogr.* No. 6, 1939.

49. Karr, M.: Development of motor control in young children; coordinated movements of the fingers. *Child Develop. 5*: 381-387, 1934.

50. Knobloch, H., and Pasamanick, B.: Further observations on the behavioral development of Negro children. *J. Genet. Psychol. 83*: 137-157, 1953.

51. Krogman, W. M.: A handbook of the measurement and interpretation of height and weight in the growing child. *Monogr. Soc. Res. Child Develop. 13*: No. 3 (Whole No. 48), 1943.

52. Lederer, R. K.: An exploratory investigation of handed status in the first two years of life. *Univ. Iowa Stud. Child Welf. 16*: 5-103, 1939.

53. McCloy, C. H.: Appraising physical status: methods and norms. *Univ. Iowa Stud. Child Welf. 15*: 1-260, 1938.

54. MacFarlane, J.: The guidance study. *Sociometry 2*: 1-23, 1939.

55. McGraw, L. W.: A factor analysis of motor learning. *Res. Quart. Am. Ass. Health 20*: 316-335, 1949.

56. McGraw, M. B.: Development of neuromuscular mechanisms as reflected in the crawling and creeping behavior of the human infant. *J. Genet. Psychol. 58*: 83-111, 1941.

57. Maresh, M. M.: Growth of the heart related to bodily growth during childhold and adolescence. *Pediatrics 2*: 382-404, 1948.

58. Massler, M., and Suher, T.: Calculation of "normal" weight in children. *Child Develop. 22*: 75-94, 1951.

59. Mead, M.: *From the South Seas.* New York, William Morrow, 1939.

60. Meredith, H. V.: Relation between socioeconomic status and body size in boys seven to ten years of age. *Am. J. Dis. Child. 82*: 702-709, 1951.

61. Mohr, G. J.: Psychosomatic problems in childhood. *Child Develop. 19*: 137-147, 1948.

62. Moore, J. E.: A test of eye-hand coordination. *J. Appl. Psychol. 21*: 668-672, 1937.

63. Munn, N. L.: Learning in children. *In* L. Carmichael, Ed., *Manual of Child Psychology*, ed. 2. New York, Wiley, 1954, pp. 374-458.

64. Nicholson, A. B., and Hanley, C.: Indices of physiological maturity: deviation and interrelationships. *Child Develop. 24*: 3-38, 1953.

65. Ojemann, R. H.: Studies in handedness: I. A technique for testing unimanual handedness. *J. Educ. Psychol. 21*: 597-611, 1930.

66. Palermo, D. S., Castenada, A., and McCandless, B. R.: The relationship of anxiety in children to performance in a complex learning task. *Child Develop. 27*: 333-337, 1956.

67. Peatman, J. G., and Higgins, R. A.: Development of sitting, standing and walking of children reared with optimum pediatric care. *Am. J. Orthopsychiat. 10*: 88-110, 1940.

68. Peatman, J. G., and Higgins, R. A.: Relation of infants' weight and body build to locomotor development. *Am. J. Orthopsychiat.* 12: 234-240, 1942.
69. Peckos, P. S.: Caloric intake in relation to physique in children. *Science 117*: 631-633, 1953.
70. Reynolds, E. L.: The fat/bone index as a sex differentiating character in man. *Hum. Biol. 21*: 199-204, 1949.
71. Seils, L. G.: The relationship between measures of physical growth and gross motor performance of primary-grade school children. *Res. Quart. Am. Assoc. Health 22*: 244-260, 1951.
72. Shirley, M. M.: *The First Two Years: A Study of Twenty-five Babies.* Vol. I. *Postural and Locomotor Development.* Minneapolis, University of Minnesota Press, 1931.
73. Sills, F. D.: A factor analysis of somatotypes and of their relationship to achievement in motor skills. *Res. Quart. Am. Assoc. Health 21*: 424-437, 1950.
74. Stern, C.: *Principles of Human Genetics.* San Francisco, Freeman, 1949.
75. Stuart, H. C., and Meredith, H. V.: Use of body measurements in the school health program. *Am. J. Publ. Health 36*: 1365-1381, 1946.
76. Terman, L. M., and Tyler, L. E.: Psychological sex differences. *In* L. Carmichael, Ed., *Manual of Child Psychology,* ed. 2. New York, Wiley, 1954, pp. 1064-1114.
77. Thompson, H.: Physical growth. *In* L. Carmichael, Ed., *Manual of Child Psychology,* ed. 2. New York, Wiley, 1954, pp. 292-334.
78. Todd, T. W.: *Atlas of Skeletal Maturation.* St. Louis, Mosby, 1937.
79. Vickers, V. S., Poyntz, L., and Baum, M. P.: The Brace Scale used with young children. *Res. Quart. Am. Assoc. Health 13*: 299-308, 1942.
80. Wagoner, L. C., and Armstrong, E. M.: The motor control of children as involved in the dressing process. *J. Genet. Psychol. 35*: 84-97, 1928.
81. Watson, E. H., and Lowrey, G. H.: *Growth and Development of Children.* Chicago, Year Book Publishers, 1951.
82. Wenar, C.: The effects of a motor handicap on personality: I. The effects on level of aspiration. *Child Develop. 24*: 123-130, 1953.
83. Wetzel, W. C.: Physical fitness in terms of physique, development and basal metabolism. *J. A. M. A. 116*: 1187-1195, 1941.
84. Williams, J. R., and Scott, R. B.: Growth and development of Negro infants: IV. Motor development and its relationship to child rearing practices in two groups of Negro infants. *Child Develop. 24*: 103-121, 1953.
85. Wissler, C.: Growth of children in Hawaii based on observations of Louis R. Sullivan. *Memoirs of the Bernice P. Bishop Museum 11*: 109-257, 1930.

CHAPTER 16

Development of Language

DISTINCTIVE ROLE OF LANGUAGE
IN HUMAN DEVELOPMENT

THE CAPACITY FOR INVENTING and acquiring language is one of the most distinctive features of human development. It is undoubtedly both a prerequisite for the original development of culture and a necessary condition for the subsequent acquisition by the individual of the complex cognitive, social and moral products of the culture in which he lives. Without language the development and transmission of shared meanings, values and traditions would be impossible. People would be unable to communicate with each other except in face-to-face situations, individual relatedness to and interaction between groups could not take place in the absence of physical proximity, and all of the countless intellectual, interpersonal and institutional manifestations of cultural existence that depend on verbal conceptualization would be inconceivable.

Language may also be thought of as both a product or reflection of culture and as a patterning or limiting factor in the cognitive development of the individual carriers of the culture. It reflects the particular kinds of psychosocial standardization of word-object and word-idea relationships as well as the characteristic attitudes, values, and ways of thinking that prevail in a given culture. Once constituted, the structure of a language and the conceptual categories it contains definitely influence the perceptual and cognitive processes of the developing individual. He learns to perceive selectively in terms of the classificatory schemes available to him in his mother tongue; if the latter fails to recognize certain conceptual distinctions he is greatly handicapped in making them himself. Thus, characteristic patterns of thought in a particular culture affect the nature of the language that evolves, and the language in turn patterns and limits the type of thinking in which individual members of the culture engage.

Human versus Infrahuman Speech*

In many respects the speech behavior of infrahuman organisms resembles that of children in the early stages of language development. Thus untutored animals vocalize spontaneously, mimic sounds in their environment and

*Discussions of infrahuman speech behavior are available.[9, 51, 52, 56, 58, 60]

521

communicate effectively with each other. Many animals can also be trained to react differentially to different verbal cues, to mimic human words and to make the latter responses to appropriate situations. Representational symbolism (see p. 523) is only rudimentary in animals, however, and is restricted to relatively concrete and immediate situations. Verbal conceptualization and the use of symbols to represent ideas that transcend concrete experience are undoubtedly nonexistent at the infrahuman level. Furthermore, only humans can be said to possess a true language, the import of which is socially rather than genically determined, which possesses an organized structure, and which can communicate meaning without face-to-face contact.

Why only human beings have developed a true language is attributable to several factors. First, they possess an elaborate vocalizing mechanism capable of great versatility in sound production, tend to babble spontaneously as infants, and are relatively proficient at mimicry. Much more important is their immeasurably greater capacity for repesentational symbolism, for verbal conceptualization, and for handling abstract ideas. Lastly, because they live in *cultural* aggregations they are able to standardize and perpetuate shared meanings for the verbal symbols they invent.

PSYCHOLOGICAL COMPONENTS OF LANGUAGE

It will be helpful for the later delineation of the various stages in language development if we indicate first the different psychological components involved in language behavior. These may be grouped under the following five headings: vocalization, mimicry, representational symbolism, concept acquisition, and the motivation underlying speech. With respect to the first two categories, it will suffice now merely to point out that vocalization or sound production constitutes the raw material of speech, and that mimicry, a prerequisite for social language, involves auditory discrimination, learning, kinaesthetic imagery, and motor control.

The basic characteristic of a representational symbol is the fact that it signifies something which it itself is not. This is the very essence of symbolical meaning in a psychological sense. It implies more than the ability of a symbol to evoke the same response from an individual that the signified object does. Simply by virtue of contiguity, a symbol (conditioned stimulus) that is frequently and concomitantly presented with the adequate (unconditioned) stimulus for a particular response acquires the same power to evoke the response as the original unconditioned stimulus. Similarly, by making use of the principles of contiguity, frequency, and reinforcement, it is possible to train an animal or an infant to emit a verbal symbol in response to an appropriate stimulus or situation. In neither case do we have an example of true representational symbolism. In the first instance the symbol does not really *represent* something which it itself is not. It itself has simply become an adequate stimulus *in its own right;* it is reacted to as if it itself *were* the original stimulus rather than a sign designating the latter. In the second instance, the verbal response also does not represent the stimulus or situation to which it refers; it is merely evoked by the stimulus. *A symbol acquires representational properties only when it evokes an image or other ideational content in the reacting subject that is cognitively equivalent to that evoked by the designated object or situation itself.* Mere adequacy as a stimulus or appropriateness as a response does not guarantee that a verbal cue or utterance has meaning as a symbol to the *reacting individual,* even though, in a strictly logical or mathematical sense, it *functions* effectively as a symbol, i.e., as a sign that from the standpoint of the *observer* has the same effect as the stimulus it designates.

When symbols are used in a representational sense it is self-evident that their meanings are not determined by their own stimulus properties. Elementary school children, for example, categorize pictures, three-dimensional models, and word names in much the same way.[66]

It is important to distinguish here between *meaning* in the sense of representational symbolism and *meaningfulness* in the sense of behavioral significance. The cries of a hungry infant are not representational symbols that have meaning but are behaviorally significant (meaningful), i.e., indicative of a state of excitement. The responses of a dog who jumps at the command, "jump," or sits at the command, "sit," are similarly meaningful since they indicate the existence of acquired stimulus-response connections that have a particular training history; they do not necessarily indicate that the commands, "jump" and "sit," evoke images of jumping and sitting or of stimuli that customarily instigate such images. In most instances it is more parsimonious to suppose that the animal is simply reacting to the verbal commands as adequate stimuli in their own right.

A fourth psychological component involved in language behavior is formal concept acquisition or the developmental process whereby a verbal symbol with particular culturally accepted meaning comes to represent a definite conceptual content for the developing individual. Gradually, during the course of experience, the meaning of the symbol undergoes revisions that parallel the changes that occur in the concept to which it refers. At first, the meanings the child attributes to words are more or less at variance with their commonly accepted meanings; words may be used either over- or under-inclusively. Then, as the essential properties of concepts are abstracted from diverse contexts, the symbols that designate them are applied more precisely. Their application is both generalized to include appropriate situations not previously encompassed and restricted to exclude inappropriate situations previously included. In general, developmental changes in symbol-concept relationships are in the direction of closer approximation to corresponding relationships holding for adult members of the community. Much conceptualization at the human level, of course, involves purely verbal changes in meaning in which no concrete imagery whatsoever is implicated.

The final psychological component of language behavior requiring consideration is its motivational aspects. An important motivational condition influencing mimicry in talking birds and infants is the association of the human voice with pleasant experiences.[51, 52] Since the mother's voice is customarily associated with need gratification and the alleviation of insecurity, the child can generate some substitutive satisfaction and security of his own simply by making sounds that resemble hers. Thus children babble in part because "words sound good to them."[51] One probable reason why deaf children do not babble is because the human voice (their own or their mothers') cannot possibly provide any secondary reinforcement. A related incentive for the use of speech in the same general context of parental succorance is the fact that it serves as an effective volitional instrument in summoning aid and gratifying needs. In foundling homes where vocalization is not successful in securing succorance and where children receive little individualized attention (accompanied or unaccompanied by the human voice), the acquisition of language is typically retarded (see pp. 122 and 529).

Infant speech, however, is not wholly dependent upon these motivational factors. Much of it occurs in response to internal and external stimulation or is seemingly spontaneous and partly self-perpetuating (see p. 525). Furthermore, as the Dennises report in their longitudinal study of a pair of fraternal twins, the latter spontaneously began to greet them vocally and with a smile at 15 weeks of age despite the fact that they scrupulously refrained from fondling, smiling and talking to the infants (see pp. 226 and 283). Other motivational factors are also operative in stimulating the development of language in the older child: its role in facilitating social interaction, its efficacy in satisfying his needs if he communicates comprehensibly, the approval he gains from adults for expressing himself correctly, and his desire to resemble adults for satellizing or non-satellizing reasons.

GENERAL STAGES IN LANGUAGE DEVELOPMENT

Now that the psychological components of language behavior have been identified, we are in a better position to order hierarchically the various stages of language development in terms of their underlying mechanisms. A more detailed sequential analysis will be presented later (see pp. 531-539).

Despite the inevitable overlapping of stages and categories that characterizes any developmental schema, it is helpful to make two general distinctions in categorizing the speech of children, namely, (a) between linguistic and pre-linguistic speech, and (b) between representational and prerepresentational speech. The latter pair of terms has already been defined. Prelinguistic speech refers to utterances that are not identifiable with the word-meaning units comprising the constituted language of the culture in which the child lives. It includes crying, syllabic babbling, affectional interjection, and the use of "private" words and gestures. The general trend of development is toward linguistic and representational forms of speech, but during early stages in the development of these more advanced forms they coexist with their precursors. Since the use of representational symbols commonly ante-dates the appearance of linguistic speech, four sequential stages of language development can be designated: (a) prerepresentational, prelinguistic, (b) representational, prelinguistic, (c) prerepresentational, linguistic, and (d) representational, linguistic.

During the prerepresentational stage of prelinguistic speech, utterances are commonly indicative of either general excitement or of more differen-tiated bodily states such as hunger, discomfort, pain, satiety, or anticipated satisfaction. Since they convey meaningful information to the persons caring for the infant and thereby facilitate the gratification of his needs, they can be said to serve an adaptive function; but as long as they are not employed *intentionally* to communicate need states or desires, they can hardly be con-sidered representational. During this stage also, much infant speech either occurs in response to adult speech or other external stimulation or is apparently spontaneous. Apart from the secondary reinforcement it provides, babbling tends to perpetuate itself in the manner of a circular reflex: the sound of his own voice, which is temporally contiguous with the motor response of speech and its original adequate stimulus, becomes an effective conditioned stimulus itself. Prelinguistic speech first becomes representa-tional when it is employed deliberately (volitionally) to describe or com-municate particular need states or desires. Utterances and gestures at this point consistently evoke the same ideational content as the states of affairs to which they refer. Rudimentary concept formation also takes place at the prelinguistic level but is limited to relatively concrete situations. The process of generalization is naturally facilitated if a concept can be subsumed under a verbal symbol,[62] even a prelinguistic symbol, since the latter is much more manipulable than either the object or the mental content it signifies.

The linguistic stage of language development begins when the child uses culturally standardized verbal symbols. Two early types of linguistic speech, however, are prerepresentational. First, differential response to words can occur on the basis of simple conditioning: a particular word associated with an adequate stimulus for a given response eventually becomes and is reacted to as an adequate stimulus in its own right. Second, by virtue of his ability to mimic, the infant learns to repeat sounds and words that others make. Since the words that evoke his imitative verbal responses are heard in relation to particular objects and situations, the responses become appropriately conditioned to the latter objects and situations. Much of the child's early naming and labeling activities illustrate this mechanism. But in as much as he is already capable of using private verbal symbols in a representational sense, he soon grasps the notion that words are socially standardized symbols that can be used in the same way, namely, as substitutes for particular objects and their ideational equivalents. This stage of development first becomes evident when the child uses or reacts appropriately to words even though the objects or situations to which they refer are physically absent. Once words acquire representational meaning much of subsequent language development consists of acquiring a larger repertoire of word-idea relationships, consolidating those already acquired, resolving confusion between similar pairs of these relationships, and restricting and generalizing the application of words in accordance with changes in their conceptual content.

FACTORS INFLUENCING LANGUAGE DEVELOPMENT

The development of language exemplifies the operation of both maturation and learning. Genically determined capacities, neurophysiological growth, incidental experience, environmental stimulation, motivational factors, and deliberate training measures interact in complex ways in accounting for both normative changes and individual differences among children. We have already shown that early coaching in vocabulary prior to readiness for linguistic speech is ineffective (see p. 84). Readiness for different phases of language development is not only a function of genic determinants and neurophysiological growth but also of all the environmental variables enumerated above.

Initial Acquisition of Language

What does it mean when a child begins to talk unusually early or unusually late? From the previous analysis of the psychological components of language behavior (see pp. 522-524), it is clear that variability in mimicry, motivation, and the capacity for representational symbolism and verbal conceptualization (i.e., intelligence) must underlie precocity and retardation in the initial acquisition of language.

Intelligence is perhaps the most important determinant of precocity in speech since it affects both the ability to mimic and to understand the meaning of verbal symbols. Earliness of onset of speech is positively correlated with I.Q.[1] and is one of the most striking developmental characteristics of intellectually gifted children.[77] Even in the first two years of life a small but reliably positive relationship prevails between attained level of infant speech and both current and later measures of intelligence.[10, 73] This is hardly surprising since the comprehension, use, and manipulation of verbal symbols are conspicuous components of the capacities measured by intelligence tests. But although the ability to mimic words is partly dependent upon intelligence level,[63] it is presumably influenced more by such factors as auditory discrimination[39] and kinaesthetic imagery. In any case, mimicry of speech is a less valid indicator of intelligence than is comprehension of language. Many precocious talkers are merely successful mimics who are able to parrot speech accurately without necessarily understanding it. Precocity in talking is a highly over-rated criterion of superior intelligence. In some instances, "only" and overvalued children begin talking at an early age because of the surfeit of adult attention, affection, and stimulation they receive and because of the increased availability of adult speech models.[16] Early acquisition of speech in children is also stimulated sometimes by the competitive example and urging of older siblings. The earlier they learn to communicate verbally the more opportunities they gain for participation in inter-sibling play.

Variability in the same factors, but at the opposite end of the distribution, account for initial retardation in language development. Mimicry may be impaired by such gross defects in the vocalizing apparatus as dysarthria and cleft palate[50]; by hearing disability[28, 39, 50, 63]; and by either the endogenous, familial variety of intellectual deficit[28, 50] or the organic type associated with such conditions as paranatal asphyxia and birth trauma.[5, 63] Low intelligence is also a major handicap in acquiring the meaningful and conceptual aspects of language. But whereas precocity in talking is almost always indicative of at least average intelligence, delayed speech is not necessarily a sign of below average intelligence. It is true that feebleminded children are invariably retarded in language development; on the other hand, many normally intelligent and even intellectually gifted children are late talkers for reasons unconnected with either hearing disability or speech organ pathology.[77]

Some bright children simply have poor auditory discrimination or kinaesthetic imagery. Others either rebel at parroting words until their meanings are clear or prefer to defer speech until their verbal ability catches up with their relatively advanced ideational processes. Environmental impoverishment, inadequate motivation, and personality deviation must also be considered. Delayed speech is more common among institutionalized and isolated children[5, 6] (see p. 529), among children from lower socioeconomic levels,[5] and among twins (see p. 530). It is fostered by highly overprotective parental attitudes and by child rearing practices that anticipate all of the child's needs.[5, 45, 48] Mutism is frequently a negativistic response to parental rejection and coerciveness.[45, 48] It is also characteristic of seclusive children who prefer to play alone[5] and of schizoid and autistic personality trends.[21] In all of these instances of delayed speech, less unwarranted concern would be manifested about the possibility of feeblemindedness if more attention were paid to evidence of language *comprehension* than to indications of verbal facility.

Determinants of Individual Differences

Intelligence. The high positive correlations generally reported between measured intelligence and language proficiency throughout the entire period of childhood[48] are somewhat difficult to interpret. To some extent highly verbal children have a marked advantage and verbally retarded children a serious disadvantage in taking the typical verbal test of intelligence. Bilingual children make a relatively much better showing on nonverbal than on verbal intelligence tests.[12, 37, 38] Part of the obtained correlation also reflects overlapping of content between tests of language and intelligence (e.g., vocabulary, opposites, dissected sentences). On both theoretical and empirical grounds it seems highly improbable that these artifacts can account for *all* of the relationship between language and intelligence. First, factorial analyses of intelligence indicate both that non-language abilities are represented and that the latter are positively correlated with language components (see p. 590). Second, correlations between tests of vocabulary and intelligence are much too high[22] to be explained simply on the basis of overlapping and test advantage. It seems likely that the ability to acquire and utilize language is both a highly representative manifestation of general aspects of intelligence in children and is directly or indirectly implicated in many of the operations of problem solving.

Sex. In the vast majority of studies reviewed by McCarthy,[48] where boys and girls were reasonably well matched with respect to I.Q. and socioeconomic status, girls proved to be superior on almost every conceivable criterion of language proficiency. As early as 10 months of age a sex difference in favor of girls is apparent in number of phoneme types.[33] School achievement tests also show that girls excel boys in language skills but that their superiority is relatively much greater in speed of reading and verbal fluency than in vocabulary and verbal comprehension.[76] These normative findings are duplicated in studies of twins,[20] "only" children,[16] premature children,[30] intellectually gifted children,[77] and children with all kinds of speech and language disabilities.[48, 63, 76]

Partial genic determination of these sex differences is suggested by their consistency and relatively early emergence and by the organic basis of some of the language disorders (e.g., alexia). On the other hand, all of the sex differences in language are consistent with differential cultural expectations, sex-typing of games, and prevailing conceptions of masculinity and femininity; with the greater availability to girls of emulatory models and of primary and derived status in home and school; and with differences in handling by parents and in alienation from adult standards (see pp. 447-451). The fact that sex differences in language abilities are more pronounced in lower than in upper socioeconomic groups also points to their environmental origin. In conclusion, it seems that even if genic factors do contribute to female superiority in language development, their effects are greatly enhanced by environmental variables in our culture.

Environmental Stimulation. The degree of contact that children have with adults is a crucial determinant of their language development. Adults not only provide motivational reinforcement for speech (see p. 524), but are also important sources of intellectual stimulation and models of correct language usage. Hence, children who enjoy increased contact with adults tend to be accelerated in their language development.[44] Generally speaking, children who make high scores on language tests receive more affection from and engage in more conversation with their parents.[49] Anastasi and de Jesus attribute the relative language superiority of Puerto Rican nursery school children over comparable white and Negro children in New York City slum areas—in the face of more severe socioeconomic handicaps—to the fact that they enjoy more contact with adults in the home.[3] A high positive correlation also prevails between the scores of children and parents on language usage tests.[53] Even on a purely situational basis, children tend to use more mature patterns of speech when conversing with adults than when communicating among themselves.

At the opposite pole of the continuum is the retarded language development of institutionalized children which becomes apparent as early as the second month of life in the variety and frequency of phonemes emitted.[6] Differences between institutionalized and noninstitutionalized children in these respects are greater by far than corresponding differences between social class groups, and hence cannot be explained simply on the basis of socioeconomic selectivity in the institutional population.[6] Goldfarb's longitudinal study of children who were and were not institutionalized during the first three years of life (see p. 122) points to the continued language retardation of the institutionalized group throughout childhood and even adolescence. The language development of institutionalized children also lags behind other aspects of intellectual development. Their scores on vocabulary tests, for example, are consistently inferior to those of noninstitutionalized children matched on either mental age or I.Q.[43, 81] Some of this retardation can be offset by providing a special program of enriched language experience.[19]

The development of twins and "only" children furnish neat illustrations of the influence of adult contact on the acquisition of language. Between the ages of two and five, twins become increasingly retarded in all phases of language proficiency.[15, 20] This is not only a reflection of relatively less attention from parents and of being less exposed to adult speech, but also attests to the adequacy of gestures and "private" language for purposes of communication between two children who are almost constantly in contact with each other. Kindergarten attendance leads to a marked spurt in social speech, but twins do not overcome their language handicap until they are almost 10 years of age, and then only if they come from middle- and upper-class homes.[15] Quite the opposite conditions encourage precocious language development in "only" children, more so in the case of girls than of boys.[15, 16]

Language development shows the same positive correlation with social class status that is customarily found with I.Q. Social class differences in language proficiency are evident in the preschool period,[15, 20, 44] tend to increase with age, and are quite marked by elementary school years.[53] These differences reflect the influence of an enriched verbal environment, of greater parent-child contact, of superior language models in the home, and of higher parental expectations regarding verbal accomplishment. Not only do middle-class children have more positive incentives for mastering the verbal components of the school curriculum (see p. 439), but lower-class and minority group children also frequently manifest negativistic or apathetic attitudes toward verbal skills.[2] They exhibit an understandable tendency to reject the accepted model of speech that is symbolic of superordinate status in a social order which accords them second-class membership. Insofar as (a) individual capacity for acquiring language is at least in part a genically determined trait,[54] and (b) the attainment of higher educational and occupational status is in part a reflection of superior native endowment in verbal intelligence, children from homes in the upper occupational strata also start with a genic advantage in the learning of language skills.

Bilingualism. The weight of available evidence indicates that bilingualism in children is predominantly a retarding factor in language development.[3, 37, 69, 70] A bilingual environment apparently has litle effect on the initial acquisition of language,[69] but does lead to later confusion in idea-word relationships and in language structure and to less mature use of language.[69, 70] Bilingual Hawaiian children are retarded about three years at the time of school entrance and speak a type of pidgin English.[70] Much of this language retardation reflects a loss of vocabulary in the first language that is not fully compensated for by a corresponding gain in the second language.[41] Thus, bilingual children possess below average vocabularies in both languages; and even their combined vocabulary is generally inferior to the vocabulary of their monolingual counterparts.[71]

Although bilingualism clearly does not inhibit the development of nonverbal intelligence,[12, 37, 38] it does have an adverse effect on the growth of functional intelligence as measured by verbal tests. Some of this influence can undoubtedly be attributed to language handicap and to the socio-economic factors described above. Nevertheless, the fact that much of the superiority of monolingual children in verbal tests of intelligence is retained even when the latter are matched with bilingual children on the basis of social class status,[12] nonverbal I.Q., and English reading ability[38] suggests that bilingual children suffer an actual *loss* in ability to function verbally that cannot be explained by test disadvantage or social class membership. In view of major gaps in our knowledge, however, these conclusions regarding the effects of bilingualism on the development of language and intelligence can only be accepted on a highly tentative basis. Investigators have thus far failed to study systematically the effects of such important variables as concomitant or successive exposure to two languages, their relative dominance, and the influence of pride and shame, approval and ridicule associated with the use of a minority group language.

PRELINGUISTIC SPEECH

Prelinguistic speech includes (a) crying and other primarily affective utterances, and (b) phonemic utterances that are either spontaneous or responsive, and which may or may not have expressive significance. For the most part, except for volitional crying, gestures, and "private" words, prelinguistic speech is prerepresentational. Non-crying utterances are relatively rare during the neonatal period; and crying itself is phonemically simple, consisting mainly of four "front" vowels and of occasional "back" vowels and consonants.[34, 35] Crying is part of an undifferentiated pattern of mass activity accompanying generalized excitement. During the first month of postnatal life, observers cannot reliably distinguish between cries on the basis of their instigating stimuli (e.g., hunger, pain, and discomfort, see p. 213). By the end of this period, however, according to one observer, such differentiation can be made.[25] Insofar as crying is employed deliberately (volitionally) to express needs and desires it possesses representational properties.

Trends in Phoneme Production

Phonemes refer to the basic sound elements of language that are produced by the vocalizing apparatus. From a developmental standpoint it is important to remember that the organs used in speech are also implicated in the biologically more urgent functions of eating and breathing. Hence, practically no non-crying utterances are heard until breathing and feeding are well established.[34] The relative frequency of the "h" sound in the early months of life is probably indicative of the fact that as an aspirate, its emission is related to the infant's gasping for breath.[46] Conversely, the relatively late appearance of dental and nasal sounds reflects respectively the delayed emergence of the deciduous teeth and the partial blockage of the nasal passages that exists before the infant is able to sit.[46]

As the grosser and less delicately executed elements in vocalization, vowels appear before consonants and dominate phoneme production during the greater part of infancy.[46] The child is one year old before he utters as many consonant as vowel types and is 30 months old before his total production of consonants equals his total production of vowels.[11, 34, 42, 64] Illustrating the cephalocaudal trend in the development of neuromuscular coordination, "front" vowels (made in the anterior portion of the mouth) precede "back" vowels (made in the posterior portion of the mouth).[48] Contrary to popular belief, labials (e.g., *m, b, p*) are not the first consonants to appear. The development of consonants proceeds from back to front,[31] following the proximo-distal trend.[46] Thus, the early-appearing consonants are velars, glottals, and aspirates (associated with the feeding and breathing situations), and the late-appearing consonants are labials, dentals, and postdentals.[31, 34, 46] Plosives and fricatives are prominent during early infancy; afterwards the latter are largely displaced in frequency by nasal glides and semivowels.[32]

One month old infants produce about half of the vowels heard in adult speech but very few consonants. By six months almost all of the vowels are produced and about half of the consonants. The child's consonant pattern at 30 months approaches the adult's in manner and site of articulation, but approximately one-third of the full complement of consonants found in adult speech has yet to appear.[32, 34] Phoneme development includes a process of both expansion and contraction. New sounds emerge spontaneously in the course of maturation and are selectively reinforced and perfected as the child hears them in his environment. However, many spontaneously emitted sounds that are not part of the language of the culture in which the child lives are gradually sloughed off and cannot be produced afterwards without special practice.

Behavioral Significance. Although particular phoneme patterns are not necessarily expressive of particular affective states, they are often (especially in early infancy) consistently and differentially associated with conditions of comfort, discomfort, and anticipation. In this sense they have behavioral significance in contradistinction to meaning (see p. 523). Innate patterns of oral contraction associated with hunger and satiety respectively give rise to characteristic types of phonemes accompanying these states.[42] Oblong contraction of the mouth and nasalization, for example, are characteristic of discomfort and favor the emission of a special group of nasalized vowels and semiconsonants; whereas velar and glottal back consonants associated with swallowing and belching are vocal accompaniments of satiety.[42] At about 10 months of age the labial and dental sounds that precede feeding are probably audible manifestations of anticipatory sucking movements; these sounds, however, presuppose considerable experience in the feeding situation.[42]

Other Prelinguistic Utterances

In addition to crying the infant makes many other expressive utterances of affective significance. Most primitive are his cooing and gurgling sounds accompanying satiety and pleasure between three and six months of age.[4, 26, 48] He also squeals with delight and eagerness and grunts with pain. In the last quarter of the first year various intonations and interjectional responses appear. These are prelinguistic in form but mimic faithfully the expressive content of adult speech.

Babbling and Reactions to Speech

The infant responds vocally to the sound of the human voice between the second and fourth months of life (see p. 283). At six to seven months he babbles either spontaneously or in response to language. Babbling is frequently perseverative because the sound of the infant's own voice soon becomes a conditioned stimulus for the vocal response or otherwise facilitates it. The reflex circle can also be perpetuated if an adult utters a real word approximating that made spontaneously by the infant. Deliberate attempts at imitating adult sounds have been variously reported between six and eleven months of age.[48]

Representational Aspects

The consistent and exclusive use of a particular combination of sounds ("private" word) to convey a particular meaning is a frequent precursor of linguistic speech that ordinarily persists long after the appearance of the conventional "first word." A parallel kind of nonvocal communication that also meets all of the criteria of representational symbolism is the use of expressive gestures. Children generally understand and employ such gestures before they understand and use conventional language. This does not mean, however, that they respond to gestures before they comprehend the affective and intonational content of adult speech.[8, 42] Gestures are most adequate for concrete and pictorial representation of signified objects, actions, and intentions, e.g., pointing, accepting, rejecting, questioning, commanding. They are frequently combined with intonations and interjections.

EARLY LINGUISTIC SPEECH

There is no sharp developmental boundary between prelinguistic and linguistic speech. Long after the child first begins using conventional language, he continues to babble and employ incomprehensible and private words. The transition between prerepresentational and representational linguistic speech is also difficult to locate. Most observers agree that children understand conventional language in a representational sense before they use it themselves[48]; one must be careful, however, not to confuse this with differential response to words on the basis of conditioning (see p. 522). When the child first begins to use conventional language, it is similarly important to distinguish between sheer mimicry and conditioned verbal responses, on the one hand, and the representational use of language, on the other (see p. 522).

Growth of Vocabulary

Because of methodological ambiguities, most of the normative data on the appearance of the "first word" are almost impossible to interpret. Much depends, naturally, on the stringency of the criteria laid down for this phenomenon: whether the word is used meaningfully and consistently; whether its use is appropriately restricted; whether it is conventional or private, intelligible or unintelligible; whether the judge is fond mother or unbiased observer. Thus, although mothers report an average vocabulary for their children of two to three words at one year, observers place the mean appearance of the first comprehensible words at sixty weeks.[64] The commonest of such words are duplicated monosyllables.[42, 64] Their meanings, however, are neither simple nor invariable. Depending on the situation and the accompanying gestures and intonation, a single word may convey the import of an entire sentence as well as a large variety of meanings.[42, 64]

After the "first word" is uttered, vocabulary grows slowly for the next six months as the child seems preoccupied with the mastery of locomotor skills.[64] Between the ages of eighteen months and six years, however, growth is extremely rapid. The new oral vocabulary is built on an existing foundation of concrete concepts and prelinguistic symbols. The problem is one of fitting conventional symbols with standardized meanings to individual conceptual experience until symbol-concept relationships for the individual come to approximate corresponding relationships holding for the culture at large. Initially when a new word is learned it is applied both too inclusively and not inclusively enough. Generalization or extension of use occurs on the basis of the objective, affective, or functional similarity of a new object or situation to the object or situation originally designated by the word in question.[42] After the distinguishing properties of a class of concepts are properly abstracted, overinclusive applications are appropriately restricted and underinclusive applications are appropriately extended.

Methodological ambiguities also becloud interpretation of the normative findings regarding vocabulary growth. Different investigators have employed different methods of counting separate words and different criteria for crediting a child with knowledge of a given word. Some investigators have sampled spoken vocabulary, others have tested ability to define words verbally, and still others have required children to point to one of a group of pictures designated by a stimulus word or to say correctly the word represented by a given picture. In one widely quoted study in which a combination of picture and question techniques were used, the following estimates of total vocabulary were obtained: at 12 months—3 words; at 15 months— 19 words; at 18 months—22 words; at 2 years—272 words; at 3 years—896 words; at 4 years—1540 words; at 5 years—2072 words; and at 6 years— 2562 words.[67] Nouns appear first, followed by action verbs, adjectives, adverbs, and finally pronouns.[44, 64] Connectives (prepositions, conjunctions) are the last parts of speech to appear and are rarely heard before the age of two since they presuppose some appreciation of relationship between ideas.[44] After three and one half, the relative frequencies of the various parts of speech remain virtually unchanged. Concepts of mother, father, home, siblings, pets, food, and furniture loom large in the vocabulary of preschool children, and the most frequently used words either have affective implications or spring from the common needs of children.[65]

Comprehensibility

Much of the child's early linguistic speech, of course, is incomprehensible except perhaps to his parents and intimate associates. Not only does he have difficulty in articulating some individual sounds such as *s, t,* and *th,* but he also tends to contract polysyllabic words by dropping initial or final syllables and to make many mistakes in pronounciation, grammer, syntax, and diction. Although deliberate training measures have little effect at this stage, spontaneous correction occurs gradually in most instances if he is exposed to a reasonably good model of speech and is not encouraged in emotional infantilism. The correction of some mistakes in pronounciation must, of course, await the emergence and mastery of new sounds. Other errors in diction and syntax (e.g., "baby talk") are persistent simply because the form in which they are used is perfectly adequate for purposes of communication even if grammatically and conventionally incorrect. Largely through habituation also, many words continue to be used inappropriately although the original conceptual confusion underlying the error no longer exists. On the other hand, numerous factors made for effective revision of infantile language habits. The child hears the correct pronounciation of words in the environment more frequently than he does his own mistakes. He also finds that more intelligible speech elicits more approval and is more efficacious in communicating his needs. Clarity of speech, however, is not highly correlated with understanding of language or extent of vocabulary.

Normative studies show a steady improvement with increasing age both in the correctness of articulation[75, 79] and in the over-all comprehensibility of children's utterances.[44] By the time they enter school they are able to articulate most sounds correctly and only rarely experience difficulty in making themselves understood. Differences in favor of children from upper socioeconomic levels are apparent in the preschool period, but sex differences (in favor of girls) are not significant before the age of seven.[75]

Loquacity and Fluency

Even more conspicuous than the increase in vocabulary that occurs during the early preschool period is the corresponding gain in loquacity.[36, 67] Individual differences in loquacity are much greater than differences between age groups.[55] Girls also tend to be more loquacious than boys.[36, 55] The increase in loquacity reflects an attempt both to practice speech and to employ it as a technique for establishing and maintaining social contact. Children's questions, for example, are employed as much as an opening wedge in difficult social situations as for informational purposes.

Although preschool children talk very rapidly,[55] their speech is quite disconnected and repetitious. Linguistic fluency requires an oral vocabulary that is adequate for the expression of ideas as well as functional knowledge of connecting devices and language structure. Thus fluency is more highly related to mental age than to chronological age and is substantially correlated with measures of vocabulary.[27] One manifestation of the child's early inability to produce connected and fluid speech is the frequency with which he repeats syllables, words, and phrases (approximately one repetition in every four words). Such repetitions are common enough to be considered typical of early linguistic development rather than indicative of stuttering.[14] They are more frequent among boys than girls, tend to decrease in frequency with advancing age, and to occur especially under conditions of emotional excitement.[14]

Sentences and Syntax[48]

As children gradually become aware of the structure of language and of the rules for combining words into connected utterances, their verbal responses increase in length, become more complex, and adhere more closely to conventional grammatical usage. Girls tend to use longer sentences than boys and bright children similarly surpass their duller agemates.

Short phrases and sentences first appear at about the age of two. Prior to this time a single word accompanied by varied gestures and intonations serves much the same purpose. The early sentence is short, grammatically incomplete, and consists predominantly of nouns. It becomes progressively longer, structurally more complete, and gradually includes the use of inflections, tenses, conjunctions, prepositions, and auxiliary and copulative verbs. Other signs of growing linguistic maturity are the increasing frequency of compound and complex sentences and the decreasing frequency of grammatical errors.

Relation to Other Aspects of Development

We have already discussed in some detail the role of early language incompetence as a limiting factor in peer relationships (see p. 464), the influence of intelligence on language development (see p. 528), and the lag in vocabulary growth that accompanies the early spurt in locomotor development (see p. 534). Even more crucial is the impact of language on ego development. Language is necessary for the abstraction, consolidation, and differentiation of the self-concept, and for such complex aspects of ego functioning as self-criticism, ego-involvement, the setting of levels of aspiration, competition, assimilation of values, and identification with reference groups (see p. 284). It provides a medium for the expression of self-assertion, defiance, and negativism that becomes progressively more subtle, indirect, and circumlocutious with increasing age (see p. 292).

The language of the child also furnishes a window for observing changes in his feelings, self-concepts, ways of thinking, and *Weltanschauung*. As his interpersonal relationships become more stabilized and the expression of his feelings more restrained, the emotional tone of his language becomes less intense.[48, 65] As the sphere of his interests and activities widens, the proper nouns in his conversation make increasingly greater reference to persons and places remote from home and the immediate neighborhood.[13] As he becomes progressively less cocksure of his opinions during the elementary school years, he uses more and more expressions that are indicative of uncertainty.[40]

Somewhat more controversial is the extent to which the child's language may be considered "egocentric" or "socialized." In terms of the sheer frequency of ego reference[24] and the use of "I",[36, 67] there seems to be little question that he has a subjectivistic approach to experience. It is hardly surprising that his own activities are central in his psychological field, that he makes little reference to the experience of others, and that he fails to distinguish adequately between his own impressions and the objective properties of situations. Furthermore, unlike adults and older children, he has not yet learned to suppress the more obnoxious features of self-preoccupation or to confine his subjectivism to unvocalized thought.[78] Much more debatable is Piaget's assertion that the child's speech prior to the age of seven or eight is egocentric in the sense of being a monologue that disregards the point of view of the hearer and is not directed toward a genuine interchange of ideas.[57] It has been pointed out that practically all other investigators repeating Piaget's work have obtained a much smaller percentage of egocentric responses,[44, 48] that adults are also frequently guilty of egocentric speech,[29] and that there is no definite age at which egocentric speech is replaced by socialized speech. Nevertheless, even if children's speech is not as egocentric and the transition to socialized speech not as abrupt as Piaget claimed, it is difficult to dismiss other independently obtained evidence which indicates that with increasing age children become more aware of the needs, feelings and viewpoints of others and more able to consider situations from the standpoint of another person (see pp. 312, 384, and 553). That overlapping occurs between age groups does not in any way vitiate the reality of mean differences between these groups or render impossible the designation of stages of development (see p. 96).

LATER LINGUISTIC DEVELOPMENT

Throughout the elementary school years the vocabulary of children, particularly reading recognition vocabulary, continues to grow at a rapid rate.[59, 72] In defining words, older children tend to employ explanations and synonyms whereas younger children typically offer descriptions, illustrations, and uses.[23] Older children also respond more to the abstract and categorical as opposed to the concrete properties of words.[23] There are many indications that in the primary grades children do not really understand many of the abstractions they read and use in their school subjects unless they have a rich background of relatively concrete information in those particular areas.[61] Individual differences in the comprehension of verbal abstractions are, of course, highly related to intelligence level.[61]

Werner and Kaplan[80] have conducted an important developmental study of the ability to derive word meanings from their contextual reference. They not only found both gradual and saltatory improvement in this ability with advancing age, but also obtained interesting qualitative differences between older and younger children (age range 8.5 to 13.5). The attribution of meaning to words involves a process of "signification" in which the "interdependence of word and sentence meaning" must be perceived.

> In order for the child to signify adequately he has to comprehend that a word has a relatively stable and self-contained meaning and that it is placed in a sentence which itself has a stable structure. He must further understand that the word and sentence, by being specifically related, form a meaningful whole.[80]

The younger child, more often than his older contemporary, fails to appreciate that a word possesses a circumscribed and differentiated meaning "relatively independent of the sentence context in which it appears." He is also more rigid in postulating contextual meaning, is less aware of his semantic inadequacies, and "rather than apprehending the sound pattern as an artificial or conventional symbol for an object . . . identifies sound and meaning."[80]

In addition to learning many new words, the elementary school child learns new meanings and more subtle connotations for old words. The meanings he attributes to words increasingly approximate the meanings they evoke in the culture at large. The progressive trend toward the conventionalization of language is reflected in the decreasing variability of meanings ascribed to words that occurs as a function of increasing age.[80] Meanings also tend to become more precise and less ambiguous. Misconceptions based on similarities between the sound and appearance of semantically unrelated words and on lack of background experience necessary for the comprehension of particular abstractions are gradually cleared up.

During this period the child is also expected to master many new linguistic skills in school such as reading, writing, spelling, punctuation, grammar and composition. Readiness for the acquisition of these skills, as already pointed out, is not simply a matter of "internal ripening" or genic determination, but depends to a large extent on intelligence level and on the background of language experience and motivation of a given child in a particular family, social class, and cultural milieu (see p. 529). Readiness is also relative to the method of instruction employed, the level of abstraction involved, and the specific skill the child is required to learn (see p. 88). Many of the language skills, such as articulation of speech sounds, word usage, length of sentence, and grammatical completeness and complexity of sentence structure are highly intercorrelated.[48] Vocabulary, however, is not substantially related to these latter criteria of language proficiency.[48] Situational context is also important since such characteristic feaures of individual language functioning as loquacity, egocentricity and emotional tone are not very consistent from one situation to another.[48] In general, the mean number of words per sentence in written compositions increases[74] and the mean number of inflectional errors decreases[18] during the elementary school years.

REFERENCES

1. Abt, I. A., Adler, H. M., and Bartelme, P.: The relationship between the onset of speech and intelligence. *J. A. M. A. 93*: 1351-1355, 1929.

2. Anastasi, A., and Cordova, F. A., Some effects of bilingualism upon the intelligence test performance of Puerto Rican children in New York City. *J. Educ. Psychol. 44*: 1-19, 1953.

3. ——, and de Jesus, C.: Language development and non-verbal IQ of Puerto Rican preschool children in New York City. *J. Abnorm. Soc. Psychol. 48*: 357-366, 1953.

4. Bayley, N.: Mental growth during the first three years. *Genet. Psychol. Monogr. 14*: No. 1, 1933.

5. Beckey, R. E.: A study of certain factors related to retardation of speech. *J. Speech Disorders 7*: 223-249, 1942.

6. Brodbeck, A. J., and Irwin, O. C.: The speech behavior of infants without families. *Child Develop. 17*: 145-156, 1946.

7. Bühler, C.: *The First Year of Life.* New York, Day, 1930.

8. ——, and Hetzer, H.: *Testing Children's Development from Birth to School Age.* New York, Farrar & Rinehart, 1935.

9. Carpenter, C. R.: A field study of the behavior and social relations of howling monkeys. *Comp. Psychol. Monogr. 10*: No. 2, 1934.

10. Catalona, F. L., and McCarthy, D.: Infant speech as a possible predictor of later intelligence. *J. Psychol. 38*: 203-209, 1954.

11. Chen, H. P., and Irwin, O. C.: Infant speech: vowel and consonant types. *J. Speech Disorders 11*: 27-29, 1946.

12. Darcy, N. T.: The effect of bilingualism upon the measurement of the intelligence of children of preschool age. *J. Educ. Psychol. 37*: 21-44, 1946.

13. Davis, D. M.: Development in the use of proper names. *Child Develop. 8*: 270-272, 1937.

14. ——: The relation of repetitions in the speech of young children to certain measures of language maturity and situational factors. Part I. *J. Speech Disorders 5*: 235-246, 1940.

15. Davis, E. A.: *The Development of Linguistic Skill in Twins, Singletons with Siblings, and Only Children from Age 5 to 10 years.* Minneapolis, University of Minnesota Press, 1937.

16. ——: The mental and linguistic superiority of only girls. *Child Develop. 8*: 139-142, 1937.

17. ——: Developmental changes in the distribution of parts of speech. *Child Develop. 9*: 309-317, 1938.

18. ——: Accuracy versus error as a criterion in children's speech. *J. Educ. Psychol. 30*: 365-371, 1939.

19. Dawe, H. C.: A study of the effect of an educational program upon language development and related mental functions in young children. *J. Exper. Educ. 11*: 200-209, 1942.

20. Day, E. J.: The development of language in twins. *Child Develop. 3*: 179-199, 1932.

21. Despert, J. L.: Schizophrenia in children. *Psychiat. Quart. 12*: 366-371, 1938.

22. Dunsdon, M. I., and Roberts, J. A. F.: The relation of the Terman-Merrill vocabulary test to mental age in a sample of English children. *Brit. J. Stat. Psychol. 6*: 61-70, 1953.

23. Feifel, H., and Lorge, I.: Qualitative differences in the vocabulary responses of children. *J. Educ. Psychol. 41*: 1-18, 1950.

24. Fisher, M. S.: Language patterns of preschool children. *Child Develop. Monogr.* No. 15, 1934.

25. Gesell, A.: *Infancy and Human Growth.* New York, Macmillan, 1928.

26. ——, and Thompson, H.: *Infant Behavior: Its Genesis and Growth.* New York, McGraw-Hill, 1934.

27. Gewirtz, J. L.: Studies in word-fluency: I. Its relation to vocabulary and mental age in young children. *J. Genet. Psychol. 72*: 165-176, 1948.

28. Goldenberg, S.: An exploratory study of some aspects of idiopathic language retardation. *J. Speech & Hearing Disorders 15*: 221-223, 1950.

29. Henle, M., and Hubbell, M. B.: "Egocentricity" in adult conversation. *J. Soc. Psychol. 9*: 227-234, 1938.

30. Hess, J. H., Mohr, G. J., and Bartelme, P. F.: *The Physical and Mental Growth of Prematurely Born Children.* Chicago, University of Chicago Press, 1934.

31. Irwin, O. C.: Infant speech: consonantal sounds according to place of articulation. *J. Speech Disorders 12*: 397-401, 1947.

32. ———: Infant speech: consonant sounds according to manner of articulation. *J. Speech Disorders 12*: 402-404, 1947.

33. ———, and Chen, H. P.: Development of speech during infancy: curve of phonemic types. *J. Exper. Psychol. 36*: 431-436, 1946.

34. ———, and ———: Infant speech: vowel and consonant frequency. *J. Speech Disorders 11*: 123-125, 1946.

35. ———, and Curry, T.: Vowel elements in the crying vocalization of infants under ten days of age. *Child Develop. 12*: 99-109, 1941.

36. Jersild, A. T., and Ritzman, R.: Aspects of language development: I. The growth of loquacity and vocabulary. *Child Develop. 9*: 243-259, 1938.

37. Johnson, G. B., Jr.: Bilingualism as measured by a reaction-time technique and the relationship between a language and a non-language intelligence quotient. *J. Genet. Psychol. 82*: 3-9, 1953.

38. Jones, W. R.: The influence of reading ability in English on the intelligence test scores of Welsh speaking children. *Brit. J. Educ. Psychol. 23*: 114-120, 1953.

39. Kronvall, E., and Diehl, C.: The relationship of auditory discrimination to articulatory defect of children with no known organic impairment. *J. Speech & Hearing Disorders 19*: 335-338, 1954.

40. L'Abate, L.: Sanford's uncertainty hypothesis in children. Paper read at Am. Psychol. Assoc., Chicago, September 1956.

41. Leopold, W. F.: Speech development of a bilingual child: a linguist's record: I. Vocabulary growth in the first two years. *Northwestern Univ. Stud. Human.* No. 6, 1939.

42. Lewis, M. M.: *Infant Speech: A Study of Beginnings of Language,* ed. 2. London, Routledge & Kegan Paul, 1951.

43. Little, M. F., and Williams, H. M.: An analytical scale of language achievement. *Univ. Iowa Stud. Child Welf. 13*: No. 2, 49-94, 1937.

44. McCarthy, D.: *The Language Development of the Preschool Child.* Minneapolis, University of Minnesota Press, 1930.

45. ———: Language and personality disorder. *Reading Teacher 6*: 28-36, 1952.

46. ———: Organismic interpretation of infant vocalization. *Child Develop. 23*: 273-280, 1952.

47. ———: Some possible explanations of sex differences in language development and disorders. *J. Psychol. 35*: 155-160, 1953.

48. ———: Language development in children. *In* L. Carmichael, Ed., *Manual of Child Psychology,* ed. 2. New York, Wiley, 1954, pp. 492-630.

49. Milner, E.: A study of the relationships between reading readiness in grade one school children and patterns of parent-child interaction. *Child Develop. 22*: 95-112, 1951.

50. Morley, M., Court, D., and Miller, H.: Childhood speech disorders and the family doctor. *Brit. M. J. 4653*: 574-578, 1950.

51. Mowrer, O. H.: *Learning Theory and Personality Dynamics.* New York, Ronald Press, 1950.

52. ———: Speech development in the young child: I. The autism theory of speech

development and some clinical applications. *J. Speech & Hearing Disorders 17*: 263-268, 1952.

53. Noel, D. I.: A comparative study of the relationship between the quality of the child's language usage and the quality and types of language used in the home. *J. Educ. Res. 47*: 161-167, 1953.

54. Ohira, K.: A study of the degree of physical maturity, intelligence, and proficiency in the Japanese language in twins. *Jap. J. Psychol. 24*: 218-225, 1953.

55. Olson, W. C., and Koetzle, V. S.: Amount and rate of talking in young children. *J. Exper. Educ. 5*: 175-179, 1936.

56. Osgood, C. E.: *Method and Theory in Experimental Psychology.* New York, Oxford University Press, 1953.

57. Piaget, J.: *The Language and Thought of the Child.* New York, Harcourt, Brace, 1926.

58. Revesz, G.: The language of animals. *J. Gen. Psychol. 30*: 117-147, 1944.

59. Russell, D. H.: The dimensions of children's meaning vocabularies in grades four through twelve. *Univ. Calif. Publ. Educ. 11*: 315-414, 1954.

60. Schneirla, T. C.: Problems in the biopsychology of social organization. *J. Abnorm. Soc. Psychol. 41*: 385-402, 1946.

61. Serra, M. C.: A study of fourth grade children's comprehension of certain verbal abstractions. *J. Exper. Educ. 22*: 103-118, 1953.

62. Shepard, W. O.: The effect of verbal training on initial generalization tendencies. *Child Develop. 27*: 312-316, 1956.

63. Sheridan, M. D.: *The Child's Hearing for Speech.* London, Methuen, 1948.

64. Shirley, M. M.: *The First Two Years: A Study of Twenty-five Babies.* Vol. II. *Intellectual Development.* Minneapolis, University of Minnesota Press, 1933.

65. ———: Common content in the speech of preschool children. *Child Develop. 9*: 333-346, 1938.

66. Sigel, I. E.: The dominance of meaning. *J. Genet. Psychol. 85*: 201-207, 1954.

67. Smith, M. E.: An investigation of the development of the sentence and the extent of vocabulary in young children. *Univ. Iowa Stud. Child Welf. 3*: No. 5, 1926.

68. ———: A study of some factors influencing the development of the sentence in preschool children. *J. Genet. Psychol. 46*: 182-212, 1935.

69. ———: A study of the speech of eight bilingual children of the same family. *Child Develop. 6*: 19-25, 1935.

70. ———: Some light on the problem of bilingualism as found from a study of the progress in mastery of English among preschool children of non-American ancestry in Hawaii. *Genet. Psychol. Monogr. 21*: 119-284, 1939.

71. ———: Measurement of vocabularies of young bilingual children in both the languages used. *J. Genet. Psychol. 74*: 305-315, 1949.

72. Smith, M. K.: Measurement of the size of general English vocabulary through the elementary grades and high school. *Genet. Psychol. Monogr. 24*: 311-345, 1941.

73. Spiker, C. C., and Irwin, O. C.: The relationship between I.Q. and indices of infant speech sound development. *J. Speech & Hearing Disorders 14*: 335-343, 1949.

74. Stormzand, M. J., and O'Shea, M. V.: *How Much English Grammar?* Baltimore, Warwick & York, 1924.

75. Templin, M. C.: Norms on a screening test of articulation for ages three through eight. *J. Speech & Hearing Disorders 18*: 323-330, 1953.
76. Terman, L. M., and Tyler, L. E.: Psychological sex differences. *In* L. Carmichael, Ed., *Manual of Child Psychology*, ed. 2. New York, Wiley, 1954, pp. 1064-1114.
77. ——, et al.: *Genetic Studies of Genius:* Vol. I. *Mental and Physical Traits of a Thousand Gifted Children.* Stanford, Stanford University Press, 1925.
78. Vigotsky, L. S.: Thought and speech. *Psychiatry 2*: 29-54, 1939.
79. Wellman, B. L., et. al.: Speech sounds of young children. *Univ. Iowa Stud. Child Welf.* No. 2, 1931.
80. Werner, H., and Kaplan, E.: The acquisition of word meanings: a developmental study. *Monogr. Soc. Res. Child Develop. 15*: No. 1 (Whole No. 51), 1950.
81. Williams, H. M., and McFarland, M. L.: A revision of the Smith vocabulary test for preschool children. Part III. Development of language and vocabulary in young children. *Univ. Iowa Stud. Child. Welf. 13*: No. 2, 35-46, 1937.

CHAPTER 17

Perceptual and Cognitive Development

IN THIS CHAPTER we shall consider such component aspects of perceptual and cognitive development as perceptual learning, memory, concept formation, problem solving and thinking. Our concern here will be with growth trends and distinctive features of these processes during childhood rather than with theoretical issues and descriptive data bearing on perception and cognition as "contemporaneous" phenomena (see p. 3).

INTERPRETING THE INFANT'S COGNITIVE EXPERIENCE
Before the infant is capable of giving verbal introspective reports we can only speculate on the nature of his cognitive experience. Such speculation must rest on inferences from behavior, on logical plausibility, and on estimates of prevailing cognitive sophistication, and is obviously subject to all of the errors of "adultomorphism" (see p. 273). Since all perceptual and cognitive phenomena deal by definition with the *contents and processes of awareness** they cannot always be inferred from overt behavior. Behavior, for example, frequently reflects the organism's capacity for experiencing differentially the differential properties of stimuli. Nevertheless, since *all* differential psychological experience preceding or accompanying behavior does *not* necessarily involve a content or process of awareness, we cannot always consider it perceptual or cognitive in nature. Several examples may help to elucidate this distinction.

We have previously shown that a young infant will follow a patch of color moving across a multicolored background (see p. 217), will cease crying when he hears his mother's footsteps (see p. 221), and will respond differentially to various verbal commands (see p. 522). Conditioning experiments during infancy also show that the child is able to "discriminate" between different sizes, colors, and shapes of objects and between different pitches of sound (see p. 566). Does this constitute evidence of genuine perception, memory, discrimination, and understanding of representational symbols? In all of these instances we know that differential reverberations in the nervous system associated with differential stimulation are sufficiently distinctive to eventuate in differential responses. Such reverberations constitute psychological experience of a kind; but in no case do we have un-

---

*Cognition, of course, also includes processes involving the traces of experiences that at one time impinged on awareness.

equivocal evidence of clear awareness of the properties of objects and situations, of imaginal traces of such awareness, or of interaction between the contents and traces of awareness. Hence it is unwarranted to assume that we are dealing here with psychological processes qualitatively similar to perception and cognition in the older individual.

Bearing this qualification in mind it is reasonable to suppose that much of the sensory experience impinging on the infant is too diffuse, disorganized, and uninterpretable to constitute the raw material of perception and cognition, despite evidence of differential response to stimulation. Clear and meaningful contents of awareness presuppose some minimal interpretation of incoming sensory data in the light of an existing ideational framework. In the first few months of life not only is the experiential basis for this framework lacking, but the necessary neuroanatomic and neurophysiologic substrate for cortical functioning is also absent (see p. 85). In due time simple and relatively undifferentiated perceptions appear, followed by images, concrete and functional concepts, symbolization, perceptual discrimination and crude notions of causality. These trends are illustrated in part by the early development of the self-concept, the differentiation between self and the environment, and the emergence of differentiated emotions and of notions of executive dependence and volitional omnipotence (see pp. 282-287, 320-321). Following the acquisition of language, more complex features of cognitive development (see p. 549), concept formation (see p. 559), problem solving (see p. 566), and reasoning (see p. 570) become evident.

PERCEPTUAL DEVELOPMENT

We have already considered perception as a process mediating the interaction of social and endogenous factors in ego development (see p. 276). Level of perceptual maturity, on the other hand, has been regarded throughout as a crucial determining factor in ego (see p. 277), emotional (see p. 320), moral (see p. 389), and social (see p. 469) development. In this section we propose to consider perceptual development itself, that is, the factors that bring about age level changes in maturity of perceptual functioning. Before turning to this task, however, it may be worthwhile to indicate briefly the various factors that determine the nature of any given perception.

A particular perceptual experience always reflects interaction between internal and external determinants. *External* determinants include such structural characteristics of the physical stimulus situation as figure-ground relationships, proximity, similarity, continuity, etc., as well as various contextual factors. *Internal* determinants include: (a) "contemporareous" variables, such as the nature of receptor and central processes involved in sensation, (b) transitory states of the organism that influence perceptual thresholds (e.g., needs, values, expectancies, and sets), and (c) developmental factors. The *developmental* category of internal determinants refers to variables whose effect varies with the maturity level and experience of the child. It includes: (1) structural and functional maturation of the cerebral cortex during the first few months of life, which provides the neural substrate necessary for true perception[50]; (2) progressive enculturation and language development, resulting in the child's gradual acquisition of the perceptual sensitivities and patterning proclivities typical of the adult members of the culture (see pp. 99 and 425); (3) changes in personality organization (e.g., ego devaluation, decreased hedonism) that are responsible in part for such perceptual trends as the decline in autism and egocentricity (see Chapter 9); and (4) progressive cognitive sophistication, both in a general sense and in particular areas of experience.

We are primarily concerned in this chapter with those determinants of perception that change as a function of increasing age. Of these, the only one still requiring extensive discussion is cognitive sophistication. One non-developmental problem that will first receive some brief attention, however, is the way in which transitory need states influence perception. This exception is made in order to link perceptual to other behavioral responses in our theory of drive states (see pp. 223-226), and because of the apparent decline with advancing age in the effect of needs and desires on perceptual outcomes.

Effects of Transitory Need States on Perception

Despite some methodological ambiguities in experimental design,[18, 27, 39, 121] there seems to be little doubt but that transitory motivational states affect perceptual responses. This effect is illustrated by such phenomena as accentuation, sensitization, and the increased tendency to perceive desired objects in ambiguous stimulus configurations under conditions of extreme need. Poor children, for example, are more prone than rich children to overestimate the size of coins when making their judgments from memory.[27] It is obvious that the influence of such motivational determinants is proportional to the ambiguity of the external (stimulus) determinants.[27] In fact it is doubtful whether motivational variables would ever influence perceptual experience appreciably if the stimulus properties were completely clear.

Unfortunately, the relevant experiments have not been conducted in such a way as to permit a clear choice between the types of mechanisms mediating the effects of motivational factors. Does motivation influence perception directly, or does its effects reflect the operation of such principles of associative learning as frequency, recency, and reinforcement? Postman[121] believes that the latter possibility alone can account for all of the empirical findings in this area. These two views, however, are not necessarily mutually exclusive. If perceptual responses are regarded as analagous to behavioral responses, it follows that drive determinants could similarly induce a *transitory* and selectively generalized lowering of perceptual response thresholds (see p. 224). This does not in any way exclude the possibility that the more *permanent strength* of a given perceptual response disposition is governed by general principles of learning.

Perceptual Learning

Implicit in the notion that perception is a multi-determined phenomenon is a rejection of the nativistic view that the nature of a percept is inherent in the coercive organizational properties of the stimulus field and in the predeterminedly parallel organization of the neural traces of that field. This is not to deny that structural and functional properties of receptors influence perception or that perceptual patterning predispositions exist in much the same way that some responses are inherently more relevant or elicitable than others under specified conditions of need and stimulation. Nevertheless, if what is perceived represents the outcome of interaction between sensory input and an experientially acquired and constantly developing cognitive and personality structure, it is impossible to escape the conclusion that percepts are largely learned. Perceptual learning occurs in the sense that older children perceive the stimulus world differently than do younger children because a more sophisticated cognitive structure participates as the major internal variable in the interactional process determining perception. Learning in this sense does *not* imply that perceptual development proceeds from a *tabula rasa* basis, that inherent perceptual capacities are nonexistent, or that one type of percept is as likely to occur as another irrespective of stimulus content, receptor and neural organization, or genically determined patterning predispositions.

Normal growth in perceptual capacity depends on progressive cognitive sophistication derived from cumulative experience with a wide range of stimulation. If such experience is unduly restricted, cognitive sophistication and hence perceptual learning fail to take place. This is demonstrated in dramatic fashion by the perceptual immaturity and the extremely slow development of discriminative abilities in individuals who first acquire vision in adult life as a result of successful operations on congenital cataracts. A preliminary period of orientation is necessary before they can organize visual experience, make even simple discriminations between geometrical figures, and recognize the same objects in different contexts.[65] Similar evidence has been presented for chimpanzees reared in darkness (see p. 84). Furthermore, repeated exposure to particular kinds of perceptual discrimina-

tion problems greatly enhances educability. Initially, learning occurs tor-
tuously on a trial-and-error basis. As a consequence of interproblem learning and the formation of learning sets, discriminations are made rapidly
and proficiently.[62] The animal "learns to learn," or, in this case, learns
to perceive.

It is clear that in order to delineate developmental trends in perception
(or progressive stages in perceptual learning) we must indicate what kinds
of changes occur during the course of cognitive sophistication. This, naturally, will not explain *how* perceptual learning actually occurs. It will
merely identify component determinants of perceptual development and
correlative age level changes in the nature of perception. The precise mechanisms mediating the effects of these determinants can only be uncovered
by focusing research efforts on this particular aspect of perceptual learning.

In considering the nature of cognitive sophistication it is also necessary
to distinguish between (a) *general* attributes that reflect the cumulative
impact of *all* kinds of experience as well as more advanced levels of ideational organization and functioning, and (b) cognitive sophistication in
particular areas of experience. Thus, with increasing age, the child's cognitive structure becomes generally more sophisticated irrespective of the
specific nature of his experience, and this increased sophistication affects
in a general way the maturity level of any percept. On the other hand, his
actual perceptual dispositions with respect to particular kinds or properties
of stimulation mirror most directly the specific types of sophistication acquired in corresponding areas of experience.

GENERAL TRENDS IN COGNITIVE SOPHISTICATION

In this section we propose to specify the characteristics of cognitive
sophistication during infancy and childhood.* These characteristics not only
have relevance for developmental trends in perception, but also have an
important bearing on age level changes in such other aspects of cognitive
functioning as memory, concept formation, and problem solving. Since
higher levels of cognitive sophistication typify both the adult (as compared
to the child) and the more advanced (as compared to the more primitive)
stages in the development of a culture, the child's cognitive development
recapitulates in a rough way various historical stages in the intellectual
development of his culture (see p. 36).

Widening and Complexity of Cognitive Field. Kindergarten and first-

*Since the appropriate distinction will always be self-evident from the context
in which cognitive sophistication influences an ideational process, it will not be necessary to designate explicitly in a given instance which attributes of sophistication
are general and which are reflective of particular experience.

grade children tend to be relatively oblivious of events in the environment which have no personal or immediate significance for them.[122] During the elementary school years, however, the world of time and space is gradually extended beyond the confines of home, neighborhood, personal concern, and the immediate present to include the wider community, the globe, the historical past, and the historical future. An entirely new perceptual vista involving complex and subtle shades of meaning and relationship is opened to view as children become responsive to written symbols and abstractions. Their heroes tend to be drawn less from their immediate surroundings and more from historical, fictional, and public characters[69]; and in free discussion periods they make increasingly greater reference to national and international news in contradistinction to events which they witness or are involved in personally.[11] Widening of the temporal field also makes possible more long-range planning and anticipation of future consequences. Finally, as their cognitive structure becomes progressively more elaborate, systematic, and flexible,[129] they become capable of interpreting increasingly more complex patterns of stimulation.

Increased Familiarity of Psychological World. One of the most important consequences of repeated encounters with the same array of stimulation is an increase in the familiarity or recognizability of the stimuli in question.[52] This seems to be a necessary preliminary step before differentiation of the stimulus field is possible.[65] Much of the facilitation of perceptual discrimination that occurs as a result of the formation of "learning sets"[62] can undoubtedly be attributed to the acquisition of a general background of familiarity. Since the entire stimulus world is unfamiliar to the infant, perceptual discrimination proceeds very slowly at first in all areas, and also periodically whenever he is introduced to a brand new array of stimulation.

Decreased Dependence of Perception on the Stimulus Field. As the child's cognitive structure becomes increasingly more elaborate and systematized, the stimulus field correspondingly tends to become a decreasingly important determinant of perception. Percepts become less stimulus-bound and less dependent on sensory information. Another way of conceptualizing this development is to say that the laws of field organization are much less compelling to older than to younger children.[12] Three kinds of consequences are evident from this shift in the relative significance of stimulus conditions and cognitive organization in the determination of perception:

First, older children are better able to form complete percepts from only partial and indirectly relevant sensory data. Ability to recognize only partially complete representations of objects increases with advancing age.[55] By utilizing information from contextual and auxiliary cues, older children are able to make perceptual inferences that go beyond the information given in the immediate stimulus situation. This tendency accounts in part for certain types of illusions, e.g., the "size-weight" illusion.

Second, new stimulus information tends, if at all possible, to be subsumed under appropriate, already existing categories of objects and phenomena in the individual's cognitive organization. The formation of such "categorical judgments" (see pp. 99 and 360) often requires that pertinent first-hand information be distorted or disregarded. Thus, in reading ambiguous controversial material, children are prone to perceive meanings that are compatible with their own attitudinal biases[96]; and in reproducing unfamiliar and meaningless designs they alter them in ways that increase their familiarity and meaningfulness.[68] Expectancies established on the basis of past experience also tend to force stimulus properties into preconceived perceptual molds even if the actual stimuli are partly incongruous with the anticipated percepts.

Lastly, as a consequence of his more organized conceptual structure, the older child is better able to interrelate new experiences with each other and with ideational traces of previous experience. Thus, cross-sectional study of Rorschach responses reveals progressively greater ability to organize meaningful relationships.[146]

Acquisition of Object Permanence and Constancy. An important aspect of cognitive sophistication is learning that objects and symbols have permanent properties despite fluctuations in sensory data and meaning respectively that are reflective of shifting contexts[118, 160] (see p. 538). In order to perceive accurately the permanent properties of objects, the child must learn to discount contextual sensory information that would otherwise modify their essential identifying characteristics. If he thus learns to perceive the permanent external world as it actually exists rather than as it appears from the images it projects on his receptors, he acquires a significant advantage in adapting to physical reality. Although some evidence of visual size constancy has been obtained in six months old infants,[32] with advancing age objects tend increasingly to be perceived as possessing a constant size, form and color despite the fact that actual retinal images vary in accordance with changing conditions of distance, orientation and illumination.* Still another manifestation of the acquistion of object permanence is the emergence at about the age of one year of behavior (e.g., persistent searching) that presupposes a belief in the continuing existence of objects even when partially or wholly removed from view.[118]

We have already alluded to another type of perceptual constancy reflec-

*A review of the literature on the development on perceptual constancy is available.[12, 19, 32] With increasing age children's percepts of form become more independent of spatial orientation (V. D. Hinton, *J. Genet. Psychol.* 86: 281-288, 1955).

tive of anticipatory "sets" and established categorical propositions. This tendency enables the child to maintain a relatively constant view of significant persons in his psychological world in the face of transitory, nonrepresentative fluctuations in their behavior. If carried too far, however, it interferes with the perception of actual (more permanent) changes in the demands and expectations of his social environment. Baldwin[12] also speaks of "value constancy" by which he means the child's growing capacity to perceive the intrinsic value of a goal or incentive irrespective of such essentially irrelevant considerations as remoteness. However, the ability to strive for long-range goals also depends upon widening of the temporal field, possessing a sufficient backlog of experience as a basis for anticipation, facility in verbal pre-testing of alternatives, and interiorization of parental and cultural standards of maturity (see p. 381).

Increased Differentiation and Specificity of Cognition. Perceptual differentiation refers to the increasing tendency upon repeated exposure to a given array of stimulation to perceive distinctions, separate regions, and detailed structure in what originally appears to be a global and homogeneous field.[52] As a result, stimuli that at first seem to be functionally identical gradually begin to acquire distinctiveness. We have already referred to the young child's difficulty in discriminating between a smiling and scowling face, between subject and object, reality and fantasy, the self and the not-self. With increasing age he not only learns to make these distinctions, but also shows gradual improvement in his ability to make finer discriminations in such areas as form perception[13] and judgments of relevance in causal relationships.[10] Rorschach records also reveal progress over the preschool and elementary school years in elaboration and specification of detail.[6, 97] Lastly, as children grow in cognitive sophistication they tend less to use only the extreme categories of a judgmental scale, e.g., to perceive themselves and their friends both as all rich (see p. 434) and as highly accepted by their classmates (see p. 470).

Two other more indirect manifestations of increasing differentiation might be mentioned briefly. First, older children are better able to distinguish boundaries between figure and ground and are less distracted by obtrusive background factors from perceiving the essential features of a configuration. Hence, ability to isolate geometric and meaningful figures embedded in a complex background tends to improve with advancing age.[161] Second, as Baldwin[12] points out, some part of children's proclivity for animistic thinking must be attributed to their difficulty in discriminating between the origin and mediation of action, between what is truly alive and what only apparently possesses some of the attributes of living organisms.

An important by-product of cognitive differentiation is an increase in the precision and specificity and a decrease in the diffuseness of perception[6, 97] after successive exposures to a designated stimulus field. A given pattern of stimulation tends to evoke just one instead of several percepts, and a given percept tends to be instigated by only a particular instead of by many patterns of stimulation.[52]

Concrete to Abstract. Cognitive development during childhood is characterized by an increasing ability to comprehend and manipulate verbal symbols and to employ abstract, classificatory schemata. This trend has several major, self-evident implications for perceptual and cognitive functioning. First, as already indicated, the anticipation of consequences and the pretesting of alternatives are facilitated. Second, the child becomes more responsive to abstract features of his environment and, in turn, apprehends the world in more abstract and categorical terms than in terms of tangible, time-bound and particularized contexts. It is only toward the close of the elementary school period that abstract concepts of government, interpersonal relationships, characterology, science, etc. acquire any real meaning for him. At this time cartoons are first interpreted at an abstract level rather than literally and pictorially.[131] Third, perception, imagery and ideation all become less dependent on the physical presence of objects. The older child is better equipped than his younger contemporary to comprehend relationships without having directly to manipulate the objects involved.[116, 118] Thinking becomes concurrently more independent of concrete imagery,[144] even in such relatively tangible areas as spatial relationships.[102] Finally, the child is able with the aid of verbal symbols and abstractions to handle much more complex problems of logic and reasoning and to generalize much more efficiently.

Specific to General. With advancing age children tend to perceive, think and organize their cognitive worlds in increasingly more general terms.[15] They show greater understanding of general propositions and are less situation-bound in formulating wishes,[78] rules and moral judgments (see p. 393). Another expression of this tendency is shown in the growing trend to attribute properties to objects and situations on the basis of inference (generalization) rather than on the basis of direct experience. Such attribution is mediated through generalizations of equivalence and distinctiveness predicated respectively on common and differential categorical membership* At the more complex level of generalizing from categorical propositions to specific instances and vice versa (i.e., in deductive and inductive reasoning) the same cognitive processes are involved and follow similar developmental trends.[20]

Largely accounting for this trend toward increased generalization of

*A review of the experimental literature on the "acquired distinctiveness and equivalence of cues" in children is available.[139]

cognitive phenomena is the older child's greater ability to use verbal symbols and abstract forms of categorization. The availability of verbal symbols facilitates generalization (see p. 570) because such symbols are more manipulable and have less particularized connotations than objects or concrete images and because they simplify the process of labeling or identifying a given situation; whereas abstract categorization facilitates generalization by making the latter process less dependent on *tangibly* perceived similarities and differences. Hence, more remote degrees of transposition can be effected by older and more intelligent children and in instances where the distinctive properties of a situation can be characterized by a categorical symbol.[139]

Selective Schematization. After repeated exposure to a given array of stimulation, perception tends to become increasingly more schematic.[52] Accordingly, every possible property of the stimulus field is not included in the percept but only those aspects that are selectively relevant for the particular motivational context currently dominating the individual's attention. This suggests that with advancing age children learn to structure their percepts along less literal lines. The omission of irrelevant detail results in a synopsized and diagrammatic representation of the stimulus field that is functionally more manipulable for the purposes of the moment.

Decline in Egocentricity and Subjectivity. An integral aspect of cognitive sophistication is the decreasing prominence of egocentricity and subjectivity in the child's approach to experience. The older child makes fewer references to himself and his own experiences,[11] is more aware of the thoughts and feelings of others,[112] is more capable of viewing situations from the standpoint of other persons,[113] and effects a more genuine interchange of ideas in his discussions.[11, 112, 114] Unlike his younger contemporary he is quite aware of and better able to communicate the workings of his thought processes,[113] and can transcend in his thinking the limits of his own experience.[113, 114, 115] Hence, he tends less to argue from the premise of particular, isolated cases and is more able, for purposes of discussion, both to argue from the perspective of another person and to assume the validity of a hypothetical proposition.[113, 114]

There are also many indications that with advancing age children are capable of adopting a more objective and detached approach to problem solving situations.[113, 114] The older child distinguishes more between object and subject in his drawings (see p. 312), engages more in reality testing,[114] and feels more bound by logical necessity and the need for verification.[113] On the Rorschach Test he is more influenced by the objective properties of the stimulus field and makes fewer arbitrary and confabulatory responses.[6, 97] Although internal (cognitive) factors play a more determinative role in perception, perceptual autism itself becomes less flagrant, i.e., objective sensory data are less distorted by conditions of need and desire.[113]

Piaget relates this decline in subjectivity to a corresponding decrease with advancing age in animistic and magical thinking, "nominal realism," and "moral absolutism." Involved in part in animistic and anthropomorphic thinking is a subjectivistic attribution of the child's own characteristics to inanimate objects and nonhumans. Subjectivity (ethnocentrism) similarly enters into "nominal realism"[114] and "moral absolutism" (see p. 392) insofar as the child assumes that the names of objects and the content of moral law in *his* particular culture are inherently and axiomatically given rather than arbitrarily designated or chosen by mutual agreement. Magical thinking, on the other hand, is predicated on the austitic supposition that, by means of occult verbal formulas, will and desire can be successfully interposed between naturalistically related antecedents and consequences.

Increased Attention Span. Gradual growth in the ability to concentrate and to sustain attention is a significant component of cognitive development during childhood. Generally speaking "staying power" (interest span, attention span) with a given task increases during the preschool period.[59, 150] However, not only is there considerable overlapping between age groups, but much intra-group variability also prevails, reflecting the influence of situational, task, personality, and motivational variables. Furthermore, since some tasks are more appropriate for some age levels, than for others, mean attention spans do not necessarily increase in regular fashion from one level to the next.[103]

DEVELOPMENTAL TRENDS IN MEMORY

In accounting for the continuing representation of prior conscious experience in present cognitive structure it is necessary to assume the existence of some hypothetical construct such as the memory trace—even if the neurophysiological basis of the trace is currently unidentifiable. Cognitive functioning and organization may then be conceptualized in terms of various interrelationships between existing trace systems and between the latter and ongoing perceptual processes. *Memory* does not refer to all of the possible dimensions and interactions of memory traces, but only to their relative availability as measured by recognition, recall, or the facilitation of relearning. It does *not* include behavioral evidence of the residual neural effects of noncognitive experience, such as most instances of conditioning.

It seems reasonable to suppose that cognitive structure is hierarchically organized in terms of highly stable and inclusive conceptual clusters under which are subsumed less stable and less inclusive illustrative materials. As new perceptual and ideational data are experienced, they too are appropriately "catalogued" under relevant conceptual foci, since this is the most orderly and efficient way of organizing large quantities of information for ready availability. At first, for a variable period of time, the recently catalogued materials can be dissociated from their subsuming concepts and are reproducible as individually identifiable entities. Because it is most economical and least burdensome to subsume as much material under as inclusive categories as possible, the import of many specific illustrative items is assimilated by the generalized meaning of the more established and highly conceptualized subsuming foci. When this happens these items are no longer dissociable or identifiable as entities in their own right and are said to be "forgotten." Hence, barring repetition or some other special reason (e.g., primacy, uniqueness, affective content) for the perpetuation of dissociability strength, specific items of experience that are supportive of an existing conceptual entity tend to be irreversibly assimilated by the generality of the latter. This process is very similar to the abstraction of particular experiences by virtue of which the concept itself is originally formed (see p. 559).

Early Signs and Development of Memory

Once the infant experiences genuine percepts, crude forms of memory undoubtedly exist but are difficult to demonstrate convincingly. Early signs include unequivocal evidence that he recognizes his mother (see p. 283) and persistent searching activity for objects hidden or removed from view (see p. 550). More objective evidence has been obtained through the use of the delayed reaction experiment.[104] Here the child is first taught to respond differentially to a particular situation. After being isolated from it for varying intervals of time, he is re-exposed and tested for retention of the appropriate response. With advancing age the delayed reaction occurs after increasingly greater intervals between original learning and subsequent re-exposure. The maximum period for the one year old varies between 30 and 60 seconds. During the preschool period it is often as long as one month.

Two principal factors account for the relative instability of memory in early childhood. First, in the absence of an organized and differentiated cognitive structure percepts tend both to be vague and unclear and to have no stable, relevant conceptual foci under which they may be catalogued. Second, in the absence of an adequate vocabulary much of early experience remains unspecifiable and dependent on concrete imagery for its continuing cognitive representation. "Possession of verbal names for . . . stimuli [on the other hand] permits [the] subject to produce a representation of the absent stimuli during the delay period" and hence facilitates retention in the delayed reaction experiment.* Once a minimal cognitive structure is established, forgetting also reflects the operation of irreversible subsumption. Because of their uniqueness and psychological salience, novel emotional experiences stand the best chance both of resisting this subsumption and of being retained in a relatively impoverished, undifferentiated, and nonverbal cognitive field. By disorganizing perception and being more susceptible to "repression," the more intense and disruptive of these experiences may later become less available to consciousness than more neutrally-toned experiences.

Memory in early childhood, however, is not nearly as unstable as might be inferred from the paucity of adult recollections referable to the third and fourth years of life. Because a college student cannot recall a particularly striking event that occurred when he was two and one-half does not mean that he was similarly unable to do so when he was three years old. One might also question at this point how much he will remember of his college days after a comparable lapse of time. Furthermore, many early memories are not totally lost but are simply below the threshold of recall and could be demonstrated by using recognition and relearning methods or the techniques of hypnosis and free association. Burtt showed that an eight year old child required fewer repetitions to learn Greek passages that had been read repeatedly to him when he was only 15 months old than to learn comparable passages to which he had never been exposed.[21] By the age of 18, no residual effects of childhood learning were apparent.[22]

With the growth of language and the establishment of a more adequate cognitive structure, memory gradually becomes more stable. Children become capable of remembering more difficult and larger quantities of material over longer periods of time.[76, 104] Both immediate memory span after a single exposure and ability to memorize poems, narratives and nonsense syllables increase with advancing age.[104] Recall in older children also tends to become more spontaneous, that is, to be instigated ideationally rather than by external stimuli.

Adult Recall of Childhood Events

Adult recollections of childhood events throw some light on the nature of early memory but must be interpreted cautiously because they are subject to all of the errors of retrospective distortion (see p. 133). It should also be borne in mind that even if specific events cannot be recalled, a developmental precipitate of all past experience is represented in current cognitive and personality structure and in the prevailing level of cognitive sophistication.

*See C. C. Spiker, *J. Exper. Psychol. 52*: 107-111, 1956.

The "earliest memory" of college students typically dates back to the third or fourth year of life,[37, 38] is visual in content, and has a pleasant (joy) or unpleasant (fear) rather than a neutral affective tone.[37, 38, 136] It more often involves a pleasant than an unpleasant and a novel than a repetitive experience.[37, 38, 136] The earliness and number of childhood memories vary positively with success in formal education and with precocity in talking.[136] For the latter reason, perhaps, women tend to have more and earlier childhood memories than men.[37, 38, 136] The actual nature of childhood and current experience is also a determining factor. Older children (age 10 to 14) who are better adjusted and who have been reared in favorable surroundings respectively report more pleasant memories than do poorly adjusted children and children reared in unfavorable surroundings.[110] The particular earliest event that happens to be remembered by a given adult also depends on its importance for his life history, the kind of personality structure he had when it first occurred, and its relevance for current personality trends.

Factors Influencing the Rate of Forgetting

In the absence of overlearning, children and adults forget memorized material very rapidly at first and then progressively more slowly.[104] It has been found, however, that when children (or adults) only partially learn highly conceptualized material such as poetry, more is recalled after an interval of several days than immediately afterwards. This phenomenon of reminiscence[104] is probably attributable to the fact that the dissociability of newly assimilated materials is at a minimal level immediately after the initial shock of interaction with their subsuming concepts, and tends to improve spontaneously for a limited time thereafter as confusion gradually dissipates. The relatively prolonged period of temporary inhibition and disinhibition of availability responsible for reminiscence under these conditions is only present in the case of meaningful "substance" items. When meaningless, rote material is memorized, the duration of inhibition and reminiscence (and the very longevity of retention itself) is only measured in terms of minutes.[154]

Many factors influence the rate of forgetting in children.* The facilitating effect of stable and relevant conceptual foci on retention has already been mentioned. Meaningful and highly conceptualized materials ("substance" items, explanations, generalizations) are more resistant to irretrievable subsumption and, hence, are retained longer than "verbatim" items and specific information.[42, 153] Repetition with intention to learn is the time-honored method of minimizing proactive inhibition and irreversible subsumption. It is most efficacious when distributed rather than massed, when recitation

*A more complete discussion of this topic, which can only receive brief mention here, is available.[104]

and passive reading are judiciously combined, and when the choice of whole or part methods is adapted to the nature and difficulty of the material. Most studies show a moderate to high relationship between memory and I.Q.[104]

Longevity of retention is also affected by various subjective factors. Pleasant words[26] and interrupted tasks[164] respectively tend to be remembered better than unpleasant words and completed tasks. Other things being equal, children tend selectively to recall value-laden items that are consistent with rather than in opposition to their own attitudinal biases.[96, 145]

Some attention has been devoted to systematic changes in the *content* of what children remember. By means of selective omission and invention, their recollections of narratives tend to be reformulated in terms and settings that are more congruent with prior experience.[107] These tendencies diminish with increasing age since less is unfamiliar to the older child and reality considerations are more paramount. Drawings reproduced from memory tend to be simpler and more symmetrical than the originals,[3] and show the organizing influence of the objects they resemble.[60] All of these effects suggest that with the passage of time what is remembered conforms less and less to the original percept and more and more to the subsuming concept.

INTELLECTUAL CURIOSITY

Intellectual curiosity, especially during the preschool years, is reflected in the number and kinds of questions that children ask. The frequency of questions naturally increases concomitantly with the spurt in language development between the second and third years of life; thereafter they constitute about 10 to 15 per cent of all linguistic utterances.[44] Early questions reflect an interest in learning the names of objects and persons in the environment. *Why* and *how* inquiries are a somewhat later development. The vast majority of questions are instigated by current rather than by remote happenings and are largely concerned with human actions and intentions.[135] More questions are asked of adults than of peers and about novel than about familiar occurrences.[33] Consistent with previously mentioned findings, girls ask more questions than boys about interpersonal relations, whereas the latter make more inquiries about causal relationships.[33] The positive correlation between socioeconomic status and number of questions asked[95] reflects social class differences in language proficiency, the amount of time parents spend with children, the value placed on intellectual achievement, and the probability of parents providing satisfactory answers.

Children's questions are motivated by more than intellectual curiosity and desire for information. Just as frequently they are utilized as a technique for establishing and maintaining social contact. The child can feel more confident that he is holding his parents' attention when they are pre-occupied with answering his questions. Sometimes, also, he is less interested in obtaining information than in confirming his preconceptions, receiving sanction for his views, and in being reassured that his apprehensions are groundless. Under certain conditions persistent questioning may be used as an attention-getting device or as a delaying tactic.

CONCEPT FORMATION

Although it is conceivable that infrahuman primates can acquire rudimentary concepts, their conceptual learnings, even compared to those of two year old children, are faltering, limited to simple, concrete representations, and are not very transferable to analagous situations.[49] It is largely because of their superior ability to formulate abstract concepts (which both makes possible and is dependent on language symbols) that human beings are singularly capable of solving complex relational problems without coming into direct contact with the objects and phenomena involved.

Concept formation consists of a process of abstracting the essential common features of a class of objects out of a series of situations in which they vary contextually, in unessential details, or along dimensions other than the particular ones under scrutiny. These "common features" are not discrete elements shared by a number of stimulus patterns but are comparable configurations or sets of relationships. Component psychological processes involved in the most highly developed form of concept formation include the following in the sequence given: (a) discriminative analysis of different stimulus patterns; (b) the formulation of various hypotheses regarding common elements; (c) subsequent testing of these hypotheses in specific situations; (d) selective designation from among them of one general category under which all of the variants can be successfully subsumed; and (e) representation of this categorical content by a language symbol that is congruent with conventional usage. The last-mentioned linguistic aspect of conceptual learning has already been discussed (see p. 523); ordinarily it constitutes the final step in concept formation. In certain instances where the verbal symbol is learned by rote in the absence of the preceding steps, it has no ideational referents and does not represent a genuine concept.

General Developmental Trends

The most significant developmental trends in conceptualization consist of a gradual shift from a precategorical to a categorical basis of classifying experience and from a concrete to an abstract basis of categorization. In the precategorical stage, conceptualization does not proceed beyond the step of discriminative analysis.[133, 159] Experiences are classified in terms of their immediately perceived properties rather than in terms of their class membership. Thus, younger children are apt to classify objects on the basis of nonessential, incidental features, spatial and temporal contiguity, or similarity of action and location.[124, 133, 152] At a somewhat later stage, similarity of structure or function becomes a more important classificatory criterion.[133] With advancing age, however, *categorical* classification tends to become the dominant mode of organizing experience. At first concrete images are employed to represent a general class of objects; but these are gradually replaced by more abstract representational symbols detached from the stimulus properties they signify.[99, 116, 118, 159] Various dimensional properties (e.g., size, form, color) also tend at first to be restricted to the particular objects in relation to which they are initially experienced. With increasing age they become conceptualized and attain independent status in their own right. They can then be applied to any relevant object or situation. Concomitantly, new and more inclusive higher-order abstractions tend to be formed out of existing first-order concepts.[116, 156]

It is clear therefore that concepts are cumulative precipitates of cognitive experience and that "later meanings are not only built upon but absorb earlier and simpler ones."[143] Conceptual development involves a continuous series of reorganizations in which existing concepts are modified as they interact with new perceptions, ideational process, affective states and value systems.[143] Increasing cognitive sophistication also leaves its mark on conceptualization. Concepts become more elaborate, systematic and flexible[129, 151] and less diffuse, syncretistic and subjectivistic.[137, 151] Older children, for example, are less disposed to regard conceptual opposites (e.g., ugliness and beauty) as reified entities[137] than as opposite ends of a conceptual continuum.

Determinants

By virtue of the very way in which concepts are generally formed, it is inevitable that the acquisition of particular concepts is dependent on a rich background of relevant experience.[130] Concepts in early and middle childhood especially, reflect the cumulative impact of first-hand, concrete experience over extended periods of time. Hence, there tends to be a higher relationship between degree of experience (as indicated by school grade and chronological age) and scores on concept tests than between the latter scores and I.Q.[36, 151] For this reason also genuine understanding of such concepts as are involved in the appreciation of temporal and sociological relationships cannot be materially increased by exposing children to special periods of essentially second-hand, verbal practice in school.[40, 120] When abstractions are introduced prematurely, some children become quite adept at mouthing them and at the same time concealing their lack of true understanding. This obviously becomes a fertile source for misconceptions and uncritical acceptance of ideas.

Although superior mental age, in the absence of corresponding life experience (chronological age), provides little advantage in comprehending abstractions, such comprehension is definitely related to I.Q. *within* a grade level.[130] The correlation between concept scores and either vocabulary or verbal intelligence is higher than the correlation between these scores and nonverbal intelligence.[36, 71] Cultural or social class environment does not have much effect on ability to conceptualize,[36] but does sensitize the individual to particular areas of conceptual experience.

Development of Some Specific Concepts

Form and Color. Form and color are among the earliest conceptual acquisitions of the child and typify in parallel fashion the development of first-order abstractions from concrete sensory experience. *Precategorical* perceptual discrimination occurs in relation to both form[90] and color[99] stimuli within the first six months of life, especially under conditions where the latter have differential significance for a need-satisfaction sequence. *Categorical* concepts of form (first at a concrete and then at a prelinguistic level) appear between 15 and 24 months of age and are used functionally in problems requiring discrimination and transfer.[49, 134, 151] Color matching similarly antedates color naming.[31] In the early linguistic stage of conceptualization, a single color is often named correctly for a long time while other color names are confused.[99] With advancing age knowledge of color names is gradually consolidated and is substantially complete by the end of the preschool period.[31] Children under three years of age predominantly use form in preference to color as the basis for classifying objects. Between the ages of three and six there is a gradual shift to color; but after the age of six form becomes dominant again.[17, 157] Apparently both the very young and the older child prefer a functional to a descriptive basis of classification once fascination with vivid descriptive categories declines.

Space and Position. An individual's conceptualization of space is in a sense coextensive with his cognitive representation of the external world. Using Piaget's scheme of analysis,[118] Baldwin[12] has identified the following developmental acquisitions as necessary for minimally mature and objective cognition of the spatial environment: (a) appreciation of the permanence of objects; (b) distinction between the permanent properties of objects and their transitory spatial relations; (c) realization that movements are reversible and that the location of an object is independent of the path taken to reach it; (d) distinction between own and external movements; (e) ability to locate the self in the spatial field; (f) perception of the spatial field as consisting of more than the objects relevant to the satisfaction of own needs; (g) the unification of information from different sensory modalities; and (h) ideational representation of absent objects. All of these steps are characteristically completed during the first 18 months of life.[118]

Evidence of positional memory has already been referred to in connection with the delayed reaction experiment (see p. 555). Children remember the position of an object best when it can be related to such salient anchoring points in the spatial field as the ends of lines or the apices of triangles.[85] In determining directional relationships, elementary school children typically use concrete ideational schemata.[94] For example, in working out relationships between distant places they tend to project the problem on an image of a conventional geographical map; and in orienting themselves locally they use familiar landmarks (e.g., main streets) to represent the four points of the compass.[94] With advancing age comprehension of abstract concepts of position (e.g., "middleness") increases[57] and spatial relationships are represented in increasingly more abstract terms.[102]

Magnitude, Quantity and Number. Nonverbal but functional concepts of magnitude and quantity emerge quite early in the child's cognitive development, antedating the appearance both of corresponding verbal concepts and of formal number concepts.[77, 117] Concepts of "biggest" and "littlest," for example, are evident at about the age of 14 months, and comprehension of "middle-sizedness" is present in most three year olds.[148, 155] Concepts of quantity require somewhat greater cognitive sophistication since they presuppose appreciation of the fact that only like elements are additive and that the spatial dispersion of objects (bunching or spreading out) does not affect their quantity.[117] With increasing age, children become progressively more aware of the quantitative features of visual stimulus patterns,[100] acquire a more versatile vocabulary of quantitative expressions,[100] and show finer discrimination in their handling of quantitative differences.[91, 100] Spontaneous responsiveness to quantitative aspects of the environment is only negligibly related to I.Q. and to formal number ability.[100] Unlike the latter ability it is also more highly developed in boys than in girls during the preschool and early elementary school years.[100]

Concepts of ordinal and cardinal numbers are abstracted out of more diffuse quantitative concepts. According to Piaget,[117] ordination and cardination first occur at a global level and are dominated by immediate perceptual experience. After passing through an intermediate "intuitive" stage characterized by limited analysis and a trial-and-error approach, they gradually become more ideational, flexible and predicated on insightful analysis. Only in the latter stage does the child comprehend the reversible relationship between cardinal value and ordinal position.[117] Counting, however, is often learned on a rote basis prior to the acquisition of functional number concepts and under such conditions cannot be considered a product of conceptual development. Ilg and Ames have prepared elaborate normative inventories of arithmetical abilities.[77] Their data support the generally obtained finding that boys of school age are superior to girls in arithmetical reasoning.

Time. The development of time concepts illustrates many age level trends in conceptualization, i.e., concrete to abstract, specific to general, current to remote, precategorical to categorical, subjective to objective. The child first acquires a practical (precategorical) appreciation of time relations in coordinating his own movements sequentially, but at this stage of the game has no concept of duration per se.[118] He later conceptualizes in concrete terms a notion of before-and-after relationships and of durational intervals between a series of ongoing, external events.[118] Finally, he is able to deal with concrete images of future and past events and eventually to represent them symbolically.[118]

Similar trends characterize the acquisition of verbal time concepts. The child responds to time words before he uses them himself.[5] He is able to localize the time of his own daily activities before he can tell time by a clock or answer questions about time relations.[5, 140] The word, "today," appears at 24 months, "tomorrow" at 30 months, and "yesterday" at 36 months. At four the child distinguishes between "morning" and "afternoon," and at five he knows the days of the week. The seven year old is cognizant of the time of day, the month, and the season; and the eight year old usually knows the day of the month and is able to name all of the months of the year. However vagueness in comprehending the conventional time system, especially in regard to historical time and sequence, is very common until at least the sixth grade.[45, 108] As already pointed out, the acquisition of time concepts is mostly a cumulative product of incidental experience[140] and is not materially benefited by special instruction.[120]

Death. Age level changes in children's theories of death illustrate the interaction that occurs among cognitive, emotional and personality factors in the development of concepts that have more than an ordinary degree of ego reference. Prior to the age of five, according to Nagy's normative data, the child categorically denies the reality and irreversibility of death.[105] Between the ages of five and nine he is only willing to accept death in a figurative sense; death is depicted as a person or spirit. The nine and ten year old, on the other hand, reluctantly acknowledge death as an inevitable process and as the cessation of coporeal existence.

From a purely cognitive standpoint the idea of death is undoubtedly enigmatic and perplexing. Moreover, it is shunned, euphemized, and rationalized by adults, and shrouded in mystery and superstition. Nevertheless, it is difficult to discount completely the suggestion that underlying the child's resistance to the notion of death must be more than just the objective complexity of the concept itself and the usual degree of animism and personification characterizing thought at this level of cognitive sophistication. The idea of death seems at least in part to be rejected so strenuously because it constitutes a grave and unpalatable threat to ego identity. When the child can no longer deny the inevitability of death he manages to forestall the insecurity feelings it would otherwise engender by repressing thoughts of it below the threshold of consciousness, by giving it third-person reference, and by relegating its occurrence to the vague and unforeseeable future. This repression can be successfully maintained as long as he possesses a certain minimal level of self-esteem. Morbid preoccupation with and fear of death, therefore, probably reflect impaired self-esteem and acute deep-seated anxiety.

Misconceptions

The commonness of misconceptions during childhood may be attributed to several factors. First, children do not have the cognitive sophistication and the cumulative background of experience necessary for the complete development of many concepts. The pressure on children to mouthe inadequately understood concepts and at the same time to conceal their lack of understanding further encourages the development and perpetuation of misconceptions. Some children, who have inordinate "intolerance for ambiguity," are predisposed toward acquiring misconceptions since they are prone to reduce the threat and discomfort of tentativeness by resorting to premature conceptual closure.[86] Second, many of children's misconceptions are derived from erroneous and incomplete information and from misinterpretation or uncritical acceptance of what they read or are told. This is especially true in a socially taboo area such as sex which has both a rich folklore and a special mythology for children. Such misconceptions are highly resistive to extinction since they tend to be insulated from the corrective influences of social verification. Still another group of childhood misconceptions can be traced to confusion between words with different meanings that either look or sound alike.

Since there is often a time lag between the correction of misconceptions and the revision of language usage it cannot be assumed that conceptual confusion necessarily exists in all instances where words are used inappropriately. On the other hand, some instances of incorrect diction that seem to be largely linguistic in origin may have a conceptual basis. The common tendency for children to use "tell" instead of "ask," for example, may indicate lack of cognitive appreciation of the distinction involved. It may also indicate that although some ego-expansive children appreciate the distinction they conceive of themselves as "telling" in situations where others would be "asking."

OTHER DEVELOPMENTAL ASPECTS OF LEARNING

In the most general sense of the term, learning includes *any* relatively permanent alteration in the responsiveness of an organism attributable to practice. This definition excludes momentary fluctuations in the availability of a response due to drive as well as effects of incidental experience (maturation). It encompasses both *cognitive* learning involving volitional responses and/or products and contents of awareness, and *noncognitive* learning at the conditioned response level. Cognitive learning in turn includes (a) such relatively quantitative aspects of ideational processes as their stability, longevity, cohesiveness and identifiability in the course of interacting with other perceptual and trace systems (memory), and (b) the emergence of new concepts, meanings, and insights. Memory, concept formation, motor learning and neonatal conditioning have already been considered. Hence, in rounding out our treatment of learning we have yet to consider age level changes in problem solving, reasoning, conditioning, and the motivational conditions of learning. Inclusion of conditioning in this chapter, however, does not imply that this process is regarded as cognitive in nature.

It is universally accepted that with increasing age children are able to learn more quickly and efficiently and to solve more complex problems. Compared to their older contemporaries, young children are relatively refractory to conditioning (see pp. 222 and 566), acquire complex motor skills slowly (see p. 515), can solve less difficult problems (see p. 570), and are more prone to use a trial-and-error approach in problem solving (see p. 902). More controversial is the issue of whether learning in children is qualitatively different from learning in adults. Our position here is essentially similar to Munn's, i.e., that the learning *process* is fundamentally the same in children and adults, that no sudden transition in learning *ability* occurs at any age, and that most differences between children and adults in learning process and ability are differences in degree attributable to disparity in previous experience, motivation and neuromuscular coordination.[104] This does not mean that there are no qualitative differences whatsoever in *other* dimensions of learning. As we shall point out later (see p. 571), numerous qualitative differences in problem solving and thinking follow inevitably from the consequences of functioning at different levels of cognitive sophistication.

Conditioning of Older Infants and Children[104]

Following the neonatal period (see p. 222) conditioned responses are established more readily and tend to be more stable. Spontaneous recovery is more evident and can even be demonstrated after a lapse of several months between series of trials. Generalization of fear conditioning to previously neutral stimuli is also demonstrable in relation to startle, avoidance, and galvanic skin responses. Of greatest developmental significance is the possibility of establishing, in the first few months of life, conditioned responses to a differential range of auditory and visual stimulation. This suggests the very early emergence of discriminability within a given exteroceptive modality at a primitive cortical level of functioning. Nevertheless, despite this behavioral evidence of cortical discrimination, it is unwarranted to assume that the infant necessarily "perceives" such distinctions in a cognitive sense.

During the preschool period the ease of establishing and experimentally extinguishing conditioned responses tends to be positively correlated with chronological age and brightness level. In children of school age, however, these relationships are either zero[54] or negative.[104] Higher-order conditioning has been demonstrated in children 15 months to 15 years of age, and in older children differential words have been used successfully as conditioned stimuli. Although partial reinforcement renders a conditioned response less vulnerable to experimental extinction than does continuous reinforcement,[43] the latter condition is more effective in generalizing a conditioned response to other stimulus situations.[138]

DEVELOPMENTAL TRENDS IN PROBLEM SOLVING

Problem solving refers to any activity in which the cognitive representation of prior experience is utilized in reorganizing the components of a current situation in order to achieve a designated objective. Such activity may consist of more or less trial-and-error variation of available alternatives or of a deliberate effort to formulate a principle or discover a system of relations underlying the solution of a problem (insight). When the activity is limited to the manipulation of images, symbols, and symbolically formulated propositions and does not involve overt manipulation of objects it is conventional to use the term *reasoning*. It is clear, however, that depending on the approach taken reasoning may either employ the method of insight or may merely be an implicit variety of the trial-and-error procedure. Whether insight or trial-and-error learning is employed in the solution of a particular problem is a function of both the kind of problem involved and the age, prior experience, and intelligence of the subject.

The developmental relationship between language and thought is still a controversial and unsolved "chicken-or-egg" type of problem. Although simpler kinds of reasoning depend on relatively concrete perceptual and imaginal operations—and are evident in action prior to the emergence of propositional thought—the ability to think in abstract terms obviously requires the use of abstract symbols.[119] At the same time these symbols could neither be invented nor utilized in the absence of cognitive capacity for propositional thinking. It seems that language and thought are mutually interdependent and that language is a necessary rather than a sufficient condition for the development of thought.[119]

The Problem of Stages

Piaget's assertion of qualitatively distinct stages in the development of children's thinking.[112-115] has been a powerful stimulus to research in this area as well as a perennial source of theoretical controversy. For several reasons however the issue remains unresolved. Some of these reasons are inherent in Piaget's unstandardized methods of investigation; the subjectivity and adultomorphism of his interpretations; his disregard for statistical analysis and problems of sampling and reliability; the arbitrariness and over-elaborateness of his classifications; his indifference to differences among individual children and to differences emanating from particular content areas of problem solving; his assumption that the sequential development of thought in children necessarily parallels the order in which logicians would hierarchically rank a graded series of logical operations; and his implied endorsement of Gesell's view that stages of development are inevitably determined by internal "maturational" factors. More important, however, has been the failure of investigators on both sides of this controversy (a) to reach some agreement as to what is meant by the designation of a "stage" of development, and (b) to specify the particular dimensions of problem solving in which qualitative differences between successive phases of development are or are not discernible. If the issue is no longer approached from the standpoint of an all-or-none proposition, much truth can be found on both sides: Some dimensions of problem solving are characterized by qualitative age level differences, others are not; and stripped of its gratuitous connotations the problem of "stages" can be resolved within the framework of available empirical data.

A "stage" of development is merely a sequential phase in an orderly progression that is *qualitatively* different from adjacent phases and generally characteristic of most members of a broadly defined age range. It does not presuppose abrupt shift in attainment, absence of overlapping between age groups, "internal ripening," or complete generality of function over all components of a trait. Although some qualitative changes in development emerge abruptly others arise through a process of cumulative quantitative accretion (see pp. 93-96). Some overlapping and specificity are inevitable whenever considerable variability prevails with respect to the multiple factors determining a trait; and, as in any growth process where experiential factors are crucial, age per se is less important than degree of relevant experience.

Considered in this light the evidence regarding "stages" becomes less contradictory. In support of Piaget's view, children do seem to pass through gross qualitative stages of causal thinking[34, 35, 58, 127] and rarely appreciate antecedent-consequent relationships in the adult sense of the term prior to the age of eight to ten.[30, 83] Even Piaget's severest critics concede that there is gradual improvement with increasing age in the quality of children's causal explanations.[36, 109] On the other hand, much overlapping prevails between age groups. All kinds of causal explanations are found at all age levels[36, 58, 109 127]; some adolescents and adults even give responses characteristic of young children.[35, 64, 109] Furthermore, changes tend to occur gradually and the quality of causal thinking shows much specificity and dependence on particular relevant experience[34, 36, 109] None of these facts, however, are incompatible with the existence of stages in children's thinking as defined above.

In talking about "stages" it is equally important to designate the particular *dimensions* of problem solving that are characterized by qualitative age level changes. The evidence (see below) clearly indicates that older children's superior *ability* to solve problems reflects changes in degree rather than in kind. Similarly, the evidence[20, 92, 93, 158] points unmistakably to the conclusion that the same kinds of thought processes, logical operations, and problem solving techniques are employed at all age levels, differing principally in degree or complexity. Both trial-and-error and relational (insightful) learning are found in preschool children, children of school age, adolescents, and adults (see below). The only developmental changes in problem solving that are striking enough to be designated as qualitative in nature reflect the cumulative impact of the various components of cognitive sophistication discussed above*; and since cognitive sophistication is a gradual product of relevant experience we could hardly anticipate that its effects on problem solving would be saltatory, devoid of overlapping between age groups, or completely homogeneous within a given individual.

Approaches to Problem Solving

In terms of approach, two principal kinds of problem solving may be distinguished, both of which occur at all age levels. (1) The *trial-and-error* approach consists of random or systematic variation, approximation, and

*See pages 548-554 for a discussion of cognitive sophistication. Qualitative changes in problem solving are considered on page 571.

correction of responses until a successful variant emerges. (2) The *insightful* approach, on the other hand, implies a "set" that is oriented toward discovery of a meaningful means-end relationship underlying the solution of a problem. It may involve the transposition of a previously learned relational principle to an analogous new situation, or cognitive restructuring and integration of prior and current experience to fit the demands of a designated objective. Characteristically, insightful solutions emerge suddenly or discontinuously and are invariably accompanied by some subjective appreciation of the relational principle involved even if it cannot be successfully verbalized. This understanding is demonstrated functionally in being immediately reproducible upon subsequent exposure to the same problem and in being transferable to related problems. Hence, not only is insightful solution of problems frequently a reflection of transfer or application of a previously learned principle, but transferability itself is perhaps the most important criterion of insight. Genuine understanding of a general relational principle greatly facilitates (through transfer) the solution of particular problems based upon it.[80]

The utilization of hypotheses, while characteristic of insightful learning does not, in and of itself, guarantee that an insightful approach is being employed in problem solving. Unless hypotheses incorporate means-ends relationships they may merely represent systematic trial-and-error elimination of available alternatives. The absence of overt trial-and-error also does not necessarily imply insightful learning; trial-and-error manipulation in this instance may simply be covert or implicit in thought. On the other hand, insightful solutions are not always complete, perfect or immediate. They often follow an initial period of random search and fumbling overt manipulation.

Trial-and-error learning is more or less inevitable in problems where no meaningful pattern of relationships exists or is discernible. Hence, it is generally characteristic of the motor learning described in Chapter 15 and of the solution of most mazes and complex puzzle box problems.[104] It occurs most efficiently when the subject is aware of the direction and extent of his deviations from the desired solution and is permitted to *execute* the necessary correction and approximation by himself. Copying is a much more successful way of learning to write than is tracing.[47] This does not necessarily mean that *verbal* coaching (i.e., explicit pointing out of errors, suggesting more effective techniques) and drill aimed at specific disabilities[84] are not efficacious in the learning of motor skills. The occurrence of positive transfer in maze learning[104] is not attributable to the application of relevant relational principles but to such factors as general familiarity with and orientation to the type of approach necessary and to elimination of initial "warm-up" time.

Age Level Trends in Problem Solving Ability

The increasing ability of children to solve more complex problems with advancing age has been demonstrated for both trial-and-error learning[104] and for such tests of insightful learning as the double alternation,[48, 70] transposition[2] and other relational[67, 126] problems, inductive and eliminative reasoning,[20] and various tool utilization problems.[101] Younger children profit less from hints[158] and are less able to generalize or transpose solutions to more abstract and remote situations.[139, 142, 158] They have more difficulty with problems at higher levels of abstraction,[20, 158] with more complex kinds of reasoning operations,[92, 93] and with problems demanding the integration of two isolated experiences.[98] Much of the superiority of older children in these latter instances inheres in the advantages that ability to use verbal symbols provides for the process of generalization (see p. 553). The facilitating effect of "naming" in problem solving has received most extensive confirmation in studies of discrimination learning and the transposition problem.[2, 23, 132, 139]

Age Level Trends in Problem Solving Approach

With advancing age, as might readily be anticipated, the frequency of overt trial-and-error approaches to problem solving declines.[61, 104, 106] Hypothesis oriented approaches become more evident[61] and insightful solutions become more complete.[4, 125] These trends obviously reflect in part increasing ability to generalize and to manipulate abstract symbols. As Lewin points out they also reflect the widening and greater differentiation of the child's "life space."[87] In the "detour" problem, for example, older children focus less exclusively on the obtrusively obvious barrier and are better able to appreciate that the most direct route to the goal is not necessarily the shortest.[87]

Older children are more aware than younger children of the existence of a problem when exposed to one.[67] Their plan of attack is more systematic and their solutions tend to be less stereotyped and perseverative.[61, 89, 98] Since their knowledge tends to be organized in terms of more highly systematized, inclusive, and self-consistent categories, they adopt a less fragmented approach to problem solving; and because they are better able to bring prior experience to bear on a current problem,[93] they profit more from past mistakes.[89] Younger children, on the other hand, are limited by their inability to focus on more than one aspect of a problem at a time,[117] by the diffuseness of their thinking,[119] by their low frustration tolerance, and by their reluctance to accept the immutable givens of a problem. They are more situation-bound and less able to generalize beyond a particular context.[116, 119] Their formulations are more dependent on concrete imagery and the physical presence of objects and derive less benefit from the use of abstract symbols, higher-order concepts, and categorical propositions.[119, 158] Finally, after solving a problem they are less capable of verbalizing (and hence transfering) the underlying principles.[67, 119, 126]

Age Level Trends in Quality of Problem Solving

The developmental decline in egocentricity and subjectivism (see p. 553) is the principal aspect of cognitive sophistication accounting for age level changes in the quality of problem solving. The growing child becomes more aware of his own thought processes and better able to distinguish between external reality and his own experience, between "the sign and the thing signified," and between thought and the object thought about.[113, 114] Logical inference becomes less a matter of subjective preference and less tied to autistic premises.[66, 113] The more important of these trends can be illustrated by considering changes in subjectivism associated with the child's development of notions of causality.

Externalization and objectification are relatively early steps in the development of ideas of causality.[118] The infant must learn to distinguish between independent systems of cause-and-effect in the external world and effects attributable to his own volition and action.[118] He begins to do this when he appreciates that mere volitional wishing does not satisfy his needs, that parents are mediators of need satisfaction, and that he is executively dependent on them (see pp. 285-286); but although magical thinking tends to decline with increasing age,[34, 35, 115, 127] it by no means disappears, even in adults.[35, 64, 109] It does become less naive and more highly formalized; that is, magical properties and powers are attributed more to special words, objects, rituals, and beings and less to wishing per se. Concomitantly, mechanical and naturalistic interpretations of causality increase and animistic and "artificialistic" interpretations decrease in frequency.*

By animism Piaget means the "tendency to regard objects as living and endowed with will."[114] The related concept of *artificialism* refers to a type of personification in which creative activity in nature is attributed to some human agency rather than to naturalistic phenomena.[114] At first, according to Piaget, the child regards everything that is active, whole, and useful as alive. Later, life is only attributed to *moving* objects. The still more sophisticated child applies the criterion of *spontaneous* movement. Finally, only plants and animals or only animals are considered to be alive.[114] Other investigators[73, 81] have shown that when a child states that something is "alive," he mostly means that it is active and does not necessarily attribute

*See page 568 for a discussion of age level trends in casual thinking.

to it the anthropomorphic characteristics of feeling, seeing, knowing, think-ing, wanting, breathing, etc. Animistic tendencies are also not restricted to children but are manifested even by educated adults in our culture when required to explain events completely beyond their sphere of experience and competence.[64, 109] This suggests that the crucial factor in causal think-ing is making a judgment of relevance between antecedent and consequent.[10] For the unsophisticated child (or adult) antecedence per se, as well as animistic, magical and artificialistic connections between antecedent and consequent seem to be sufficient criteria of relevance.[115] Given the benefit of increased incidental experience and instruction, however, he learns to avoid attributing causal significance to irrelevant and purely temporal antecedents of consequences and to avoid generalizing the expectation of similar conse-quences in all situations superficially similar to a particular cause-effect sequence.[10]

Determinants

I.Q. is positively related to both trial-and-error[104, 106] and insightful[48, 104] problem solving. For those kinds of problem solving that depend on cumula-tive incidental experience, e.g., causal thinking[36] and applications of the lever principle,[111] school grade is a more significant correlate of success than either I.Q. or socioeconomic status. Brightness level also affects approach to prob-lem solving. When mental age is held constant in a categorization problem, older (and duller) children adopt a more concrete and less self-consistent approach, use more categories, and are more "immedite-minded." They also find it more difficult to shift from one basis of categorization to an-other.[82] Sex differences in verbal problem solving[104] and causal thinking[127] are not significant, but boys tend to surpass girls in mechanical puzzle prob-lems[104] and in arithmetical reasoning (see p. 563). Such temperamental and personality characteristics as high kinetic level, venturesomeness, self-con-fidence, persistence, and frustration tolerance self-evidently facilitate prob-lem solving.[4] Excessive emotionality, on the other hand, narrows the cogni-tive field and promotes rigidity and perseveration.[61] The role of anxiety in problem solving has been discussed elsewhere (see p. 332). Compared to low scoring children on a measure of anxiety, high anxiety children tend to show inferior performance on the difficult, and superior performance on the easier components of a task.[28]

MOTIVATIONAL FACTORS IN LEARNING

Few theoretical issues in psychology provoke more heated controversy than the role of motivation in learning. Positions vary all the way from the assertion that no learning whatsoever takes place without motivation to a complete denial that motivation is a significant variable in the learning process. Much of this controversy bears on the nature of learning as a "contemporaneous" phenomenon and hence cannot properly receive any systematic consideration in a book on developmental psychology. We can only be concerned here with the distinctive role of motivation in the learning of children and with age level changes in this relationship.

Although motivation is a highly significant factor in and greatly facilitates children's learning it is by no means an indispensable condition. Considerable evidence indicates that much learning is apparently "unenergized" by motivation and occurs without any motivational reinforcement or drive reduction. Respondent conditioning, for example, merely depends on temporal continguity of the conditioned and unconditioned stimuli. A good deal of learning also occurs incidentally without any explicit intention to learn. Children acquire much specific information about objects irrelevant* to the solution of particular incentive-motivated problems[141] and, without any obvious motivation for so doing, effectively retain over long periods of time information presented in motion pitcures.[72] Appreciation of a means-end relationship is commonly acquired and selectively retained either through insight or trial-and-error variation of responses even if unaccompanied by the original existence and later reduction of a drive state. This statement does not preclude the possibility that if a drive state were operative problem solving might be greatly expedited and the responses reducing the drive more highly reinforced.

In addition, as Tolman[149] points out, motivation may facilitate learning in ways other than by reinforcing the successful variant through drive reduction. It also exerts a purely cognitive effect in highlighting or emphasizing what is to be learned. This is particularly evident in discrimination learning problems where correct responses are reinforced and incorrect responses are not.[24] Reinforcement here primarily helps make the discrimination cognitively more salient.

Even where motivation is clearly operative in children's learning, it is misleading to extrapolate the familiar paradigm of homeostatic drive reduction that is characteristically used to explain animal learning.[63] Such drives are quickly satiated and when accompanied by intense affect disrupt learning.[63] Hence, hunger, thirst, pain, and the like rarely motivate children's learning; and although material rewards are often effective, intrinsic (task-oriented) and ego-oriented motives tend increasingly to dominate the

---

*It is true, however, that the amount of such "superfluous" learning increases with degree of spatial relevance to the goal. It also increases as a function of advancing age.[141]

motivational picture with advancing age* Material rewards also tend to become less ends in themselves than symbols of derived and primary status and sources of self-esteem and self-confidence. Both in infrahuman primates[63] and in children much learning is motivated by curiosity, urge to explore and manipulate, and desire to know. Thus, responses that satisfy these urges are drive reducing and hence are selectively reinforced. It is hardly surprising, therefore, that in many learning situations the provision of explicit rewards makes relatively little[1] or no[7] difference in speed of learning or in performance level. Because so much learning attributable to task-oriented or ego-oriented motives has already occurred, the later injection of material rewards into the learning situation does not dramatically accelerate the rate of learning as it does in comparable animal ("latent learning") experiments.[1]

This point of view, of course, is not in conflict with findings that in comparison with neutral motivational conditions, material[1, 29] and prestige[9] incentives, as well as group rivalry,[16, 75] have a facilitating effect on learning. Material rewards tend to be more efficacious than verbal praise[1, 46]; the effectiveness of the latter deteriorates rapidly during the course of learning.[1] Partial motivational reinforcement is more effective than continuous reinforcement,[88] and material rewards administered over the last half of a series of trials are just as effective as when administered throughout.[1] Although praise is generally considered a more efficacious motivational agent than reproof,[29 ,74] some investigators have obtained equivocal findings on this point.[128, 147] Much depends on the personality of the child[56, 147] (e.g., introversion-extroversion) and on the personality of the administering individual.[128] The motivational effectiveness of cooperation and competition as well as individual and situational differences in response to these factors have been considered in another context (see pp. 473-477). Other individual differences in motivational orientation to learning will be considered below.

Age Level Trends in Motivational Orientation to Learning

Since little or no systematic research has been conducted on age level changes in children's motivational orientation to learning or on the relative efficacy of different kinds of incentives among different age groups, we must resort to logical inferences from general principles of personality development (Chapter 9). We have already suggested that with increasing age material reward and punishment motivate learning less in their own right than as symbols of approval and disapproval, of enhanced and depreciated self-esteem, and of derived and primary status. Second, as part of the trend

---

*We have also insisted that in most instances the origins of these so-called "secondary" drives are historically or functionally independent of any connection with homeostatic drives (see p. 227). Secondary derivatives of homeostatic drives are also rapidly extinguished without reinforcement.[63]

toward desatellization values tend to be assimilated more on an *incorporative* and exploratory than on a satellizing basis (see pp. 305 and 383), and the need to excel in school or other performance becomes motivated more by the desire for personal prestige than for parental approbation (see p. 305). During this period, therefore, children become more responsive to the stimulus of competition (see pp. 310 and 475). Third, as a reflection of their quest for greater volitional independence and primary status children become more critical and resistive to prestige suggestion, particularly to the kind predicated on personal loyalty (see pp. 301 and 383). They are more resistive to training and less willing docilely to learn rote skills and arbitrarily presented information merely because an authority figure thinks them important. The mouthing of meaningless phrases is also more of an affront to minds that have a greater capacity to understand abstract ideas. Finally, as a result of their anti-adult orientation (see pp. 305 and 460), they are predisposed in advance to reject many of the learning goals advocated by adult society. This accounts among other reasons for the gradual deterioration of their school morale and their increasing degree of dissatisfaction with school as they climb the educational ladder.[79]

Individual Differences in Motivational Orientation

Coexistent with and probably exceeding age level differences in motivational orientation to learning are individual differences in the extent to which satellizing, incorporative and exploratory orientations are employed.* Depending upon individual differences in personality development, different motivational orientations toward learning receive varying emphasis over and above the influence exerted by general developmental trends. They not only affect the mode of assimilating goals and values but also the acquisition of academic skills and knowledge.

Although the incorporative and exploratory orientations generally become more conspicuous with increasing age they are only dominant in non-satellizers. Satellizers chiefly manifest a satellizing motivational orientation, at least until adolescence. In varying degrees, however, all three orientations are usually present in most individuals. Not infrequently, as a result of continued successful experience, motivations that are originally absent in a given learning activity are developed retroactively. A socially rejected child, for example, may seek originally to achieve competence in some academic field solely for compensatory ego enhancement. Eventually, however, he may develop genuine task-oriented interests that are functionally autonomous of his original motivation.

When ideas are accepted on a satellizing basis, resistance to new learning proceeds largely from conflicting ideological trends in the new set of values,

*The principal features of these different orientations are described in detail on pages 292, 297, and 306.

which can only be accepted at the cost of repudiating prior loyalties and assuming the associated burden of guilt. Nevertheless, this must take place for resatellization to occur. The satellizer feels secure in his derived status only as long as approval is forthcoming. He finds disapproval threatening and, when incurred through disloyalty, productive of guilt feelings. In the case of the non-satellizer, new ideas are resisted because they constitute a potential threat to self-esteem by challenging (a) the existing system of values organized on an ego prestige basis, and (b) various presumptions of independence, originality, infallibility and omniscience. Because he lacks "sufficient confidence in the ultimate outcome of the learning process he is naturally reluctant to undertake new learning which could end in failure, or at any rate constitute a threat to his security while still incomplete and tentative."[8] Resistance is usually overcome when "the possibility of future ego aggrandizement by incorporation of the new value" is perceived.[8]

Since non-satellizers are more likely to suffer from impaired self-esteem and from anxiety (see p. 329), they are more likely to feel inadequate in new learning situations, to over-respond with fear, and to avoid improvisation (see p. 332). Disapproval does not threaten a relationship from which vicarious status is derived or provoke feelings of guilt; it serves rather as an objective index of failure with attendant consequences to self-esteem. The motivation for learning is generally higher than in satellizers because self-esteem is dependent solely upon extrinsic considerations and is largely a function of superior accomplishment.

The Relationship of Needs and Active Learning to Meaningfulness

For meaningful learning to occur, subject matter must be related to felt needs. Inability to see any need for a subject is the reason students mention most frequently for losing interest in high school studies.[163] Doing without being interested in what one is doing results in relatively little learning[25] since only that material which is relevant to areas of concern in the psychological field of the individual can be meaningfully assimilated. It is unrealistic to expect that school subjects can be effectively learned until pupils develop a felt need to acquire knowledge as an end in itself—since much school knowledge can never be rationalized as necessary for meeting the demands of daily living. Once such a need is developed, learning naturally becomes more meaningful; but it is difficult to stimulate the development of such needs until subject matter can be presented meaningfully in the first place.

We have already referred to the mistaken notion in some educational circles of regarding expressed needs as the only possible basis on which to organize a curriculum, as endogenously derived and axiomatically reflective of what is "truly best" for the individual (see p. 244). The choices that individuals make themselves are not invariably as appropriate as teleological theorists would have us believe. In fact one of the primary functions of education is to stimulate the development of potentially worthwhile needs. Recognition of the role of needs in learning means that teachers should try to develop needs in pupils for the subject matter they wish to present as well as take cognizance of existing concerns. It does not mean that the curriculum should be restricted to the specific interests that happen to be present in a group of children growing up under particular conditions of intellectual and socioeconomic stimulation.

Since meaningfulness is largely a personal phenomenon, it can be achieved only if the individual is willing to expend the *active* effort required to integrate new conceptual material into his unique frame of reference. This means translating and rephrasing new ideas into his own terms and relating them to his own experience, personal history, and system of values.[25]

If learning is to be active, ultimate responsibility for its accomplishment must lie with the pupil. Pupils, not teachers, need to ask more of the questions and to be more concerned with formulating perceived problems than with learning answers to questions where problems are not perceived.[25] The teacher cannot learn for the pupil nor navigate intellectually for him. He can only present ideas as meaningfully as possible—and more from a psychological than from a logical criterion of meaningfulness. The actual job of articulating new ideas into a personal frame of reference can only be performed by the learner. It follows that ideas that are forcibly imposed upon pupils or passively and uncritically accepted by them cannot possibly be meaningful in the true sense of the term.

When the results of "activity" programs and joint teacher-pupil planning are compared to those of more traditional methods of instruction,[123, 162] it is typically found that children under the newer regimen learn about the same amount of subject matter but show more initiative, cooperation and leadership. More sensitive measuring instruments than are currently employed would be necessary to demonstrate differences in quality of thinking and approach to problem solving.[123]

REFERENCES

1. Abel, L. B.: The effects of shift in motivation upon the learning of a sensori-motor task. *Arch. Psychol. 29*: No. 205, 1936.

2. Alberts, C. A., and Ehrenfreund, D.: Transposition in children as a function of age. *J. Exper. Psychol. 41*: 30-38, 1951.

3. Allport, G. W.: Change and decay in the visual memory image. *Brit. J. Psychol. 21*: 133-148, 1930.

4. Alpert, A.: *The Solving of Problem Situations by Preschool Children.* New York, Teachers College, Columbia University, 1928.

5. Ames, L. B.: The development of the sense of time in young children. *J. Genet. Psychol.* *68*: 97-125, 1946.

6. ——, Learned, J., Metraux, R., and Walker, R.: Development of perception in the young child as observed in responses to the Rorschach test blots. *J. Genet. Psychol.* *82*: 183-204, 1953.

7. Auble, D., and Mech, E. V.: Partial verbal reinforcement related to distributed practice in a classroom situation. *J. Psychol.* *36*: 165-186, 1953.

8. Ausubel, D. P.: Ego development and the learning process. *Child Develop.* *20*: 173-190, 1949.

9. ——: Prestige motivation of gifted children. *Genet. Psychol. Monogr.* *43*: 53-117, 1951.

10. ——, and Schiff, H. M.: The effect of incidental and experimentally induced experience in the learning of relevant and irrelevant causal relationships by children. *J. Genet. Psychol.* *84*: 109-123, 1954.

11. Baker, H. V.: Children's contributions in elementary school general discussion. *Child Develop. Monogr.* No. 29, 1942.

12. Baldwin, A. L.: *Behavior and Development in Childhood.* New York, Dryden, 1955.

13. Baldwin, B. T., and Wellman, B. L.: The pegboard as a means of analyzing form perception and motor control in young children. *J. Genet. Psychol.* *35*: 387-414, 1928.

14. Bayley, N.: Mental growth during the first three years. *Genet. Psychol. Monogr.* *14*: 7-92, 1933.

15. Biber, B., Murphy, L. B., Woodcock, L. P., and Black, I. S.: *Child Life in School.* New York, Dutton, 1942.

16. Bouchard, J. B.: An exploratory investigation of the effect of certain selected factors upon sixth-grade children in arithmetic. *J. Exper. Educ.* *20*: 105-112, 1951.

17. Brian, C. R., and Goodenough, F. L.: The relative potency of color and form perception at various ages. *J. Exper. Psychol.* *12*: 197-213, 1929.

18. Bruner, J. S., and Goodman, C. C.: Value and need as organizing factors in perception. *J. Abnorm. Soc. Psychol.* *42*: 33-44, 1947.

19. Brunswik, E.: *Systematic and Representative Design of Psychological Experiments.* Berkeley, University of California Press, 1947.

20. Burt, C.: The development of reasoning in children. *J. Exper. Pedag.* *5*: 68-77, 1919.

21. Burtt, H. E.: An experimental study of early childhood memory. *J. Genet. Psychol.* *40*: 287-295, 1932.

22. ——: An experimental study of early childhood memory: final report. *J. Genet. Psychol.* *58*: 435-439, 1941.

23. Cantor, G. N.: Effects of three types of pretraining on discrimination learning in preschool children. *J, Exper. Psychol.* *49*: 339-342, 1955.

24. ——, and Spiker, C. C.: Effects of nonreinforced trials on discrimination learning in preschool children. *J. Exper. Psychol.* *47*: 256-258, 1954.

25. Cantor, N.: *The Teaching-Learning Process: A Study in Interpersonal Relations.* New York, Dryden, 1953.

26. Carter, H. D.: Effects of emotional factors upon recall. *J. Psychol.* *1*: 49-59, 1935.

27. Carter, L. F., and Schooler, K.: Value, need and other factors in perception. *Psychol. Rev.* *56*: 200-208, 1949.

28. Castenada, A., Palermo, D. S., and McCandless, B. R.: Complex learning and performance as a function of anxiety in children and task difficulty. *Child Develop. 27*: 327-332, 1956.

29. Chase, L.: Motivation of young children: an experimental study of the influence of certain types of external incentives upon the performance of a task. *Univ. Iowa Stud. Child Welf. 5*: No. 3, 1932.

30. Cohen, J., and Hansel, C. E. M.: The idea of independence. *Brit. J. Psychol. 46*: 178-190, 1955.

31. Cook, W. M.: Ability of children in color discrimination. *Child Develop. 2*: 303-320, 1931.

32. Cruikshank, R. M.: The development of visual size constancy in early infancy. *J. Genet. Psychol. 58*: 327-351, 1941.

33. Davis, E. A.: The form and function of children's questions. *Child Develop. 3*: 57-74, 1932.

34. Dennis, W.: Piaget's questions applied to a child of known environment. *J. Genet. Psychol. 60*: 307-320, 1942.

35. ———: Animism and related tendencies in Hopi children. *J. Abnorm. Soc. Psychol. 38*: 21-36, 1943.

36. Deutsche, J. M.: *The Development of Children's Concepts of Causal Relationships.* Minneapolis, University of Minnesota Press, 1937.

37. Dudycha, G. J., and Dudycha, M. M.: Adolescents' memories of preschool experiences. *J. Genet. Psychol. 42*: 468-480, 1933.

38. Dudycha. G. J., and Dudycha, M. M.: Childhood memories: a review of the literature. *Psychol. Bull. 38*: 669-681, 1941.

39. Dukes, W. F.: Psychological studies of values. *Psychol. Bull. 52*: 24-50, 1955.

40. Eaton, M. T.: *A Survey of the Achievement in Social Studies of 10,220 Sixth Grade Pupils in 464 Schools in Indiana.* Bloomington, University of Indiana, 1944.

41. English, H. B., and Edwards, A. L.: Reminiscence, substance learning and initial difficulty—a methodological study. *Psychol. Rev. 46*: 253-263, 1939.

42. ———, Welborn, E. L., and Kilian, C. D.: Studies in substance memorization. *J. Gen. Psychol. 11*: 233-260, 1934.

43. Fattu, N. A., Mech, E. V., and Auble, D.: Partial reinforcement related to "free" responding in extinction with pre-school children. *J. Exper. Educ. 23*: 365-368, 1955.

44. Fisher, M. S.: Language patterns of preschool children. *Child Develop. Monogr.* No. 15, 1934.

45. Friedman, K. C.: Time concepts of elementary-school children. *Elem. Sch. J. 44*: 337-342, 1944.

46. Garmezy, N., and Harris, G., Jr.,: Motor performance of cerebral palsied children as a function of their success or failure in achieving material rewards. *Child Develop. 24*: 287-300, 1953.

47. Gates, A. I., and Taylor, G. A.: The acquisition of motor control in writing by preschool children. *Teach. Coll. Rec. 24*: 459-468, 1923.

48. Gellerman, L. W.: The double alternation problem: II. The behavior of children and human adults in a double alternation temporal maze. *J. Genet. Psychol. 39*: 197-226, 1931.

49. ———: Form discrimination in chimpanzees and two-year-old children. I. Form (triangularity) per se. *J. Genet. Psychol. 42*: 3-27, 193

50. Gesell, A., Ilg, F., and Bullis, G. E.: *Vision: Its Development in Infant and Child.* New York, Hoeber, 1949.

51. Gibson, E. J.: Improvement in perceptual judgments as a function of controlled practice or training. *Psychol. Bull. 50*: 401-431, 1953.

52. Gibson, J. J.: Social psychology and the psychology of perceptual learning. *In* M. Sherif and M. O. Wilson, Eds., *Group Relations at the Crossroads.* New York, Harper, 1953, pp. 120-138.

53. ———, and Gibson, E. J.: Perceptual learning: differentiation or enrichment? *Psychol. Rev. 62*: 32-41, 1955.

54. Goldstein, R., Polito-Castro, S. B., and Daniels, J. T.: Difficulty in conditioning electrodermal responses to tone in normally hearing children. *J. Speech & Hearing Disorders 20*: 26-34, 1955.

55. Gollin, E. S.: Some research problems for developmental psychology. *Child Develop. 27*: 223-235, 1956.

56. Grace, G. L.: The relation of personality characteristics and response to verbal approval in a learning task. *Genet. Psychol. Monogr. 37*: 73-103, 1948.

57. Graham, V., Jackson, T. A., Long, L., and Welch, L.: Generalization of the concept of middleness. *J. Genet. Psychol. 65*: 227-237, 1944.

58. Grigsby, O. J.: An experimental study of the development of concepts of relationship in preschool children as evidenced by their expressive ability. *J. Exper. Educ. 1*: 144-162, 1932.

59. Gutteridge, M. V.: *The Duration of Attention in Young Children.* Melbourne, Australia, University of Melbourne Press, 1935.

60. Hall, V.: The Effect of a Time Interval on Recall. *Brit. J. Psychol. 27*: 41-50, 1936.

61. Hamilton, G. V. N.: A study of perseverance reactions in primates and rodents. *Behavior Monogr. 3*: No. 2, 1916.

62. Harlow, H. F.: The formation of learning sets. *Psychol. Rev. 56*: 51-65, 1949.

63. ———: Motivation as a factor in the acquisition of new responses. In *Current Theory and Research in Motivation.* Lincoln, University of Nebraska Press, 1953, pp. 24-49.

64. Hazlitt, V.: Children's thinking. *Brit. J. Psychol. 20*: 354-361, 1930.

65. Hebb, D. O.: *The Organization of Behavior.* New York, Wiley, 1949.

66. Heidbreder, E. F.: Reasons used in solving problems. *J. Exper. Psychol. 10*: 397-414, 1927.

67. ———: Problem solving in children and adults. *J. Genet. Psychol. 35*: 522-545, 1928.

68. Hildreth, G.: The difficulty reduction tendency in perception and problem solving. *J. Educ. Psychol. 32*: 305-313, 1941.

69. Hill, D. S.: Personification of ideals by urban children. *J. Soc. Psychol. 1*: 379-392, 1930.

70. Hodges, A.: A developmental study of symbolic behavior. *Child Develop. 25*: 277-280, 1954.

71. Hoffman, H. N.: A study in an aspect of concept formation, with subnormal average and superior adolescents. *Genet. Psychol. Monogr. 52*: 191-239, 1955.

72. Holaday, P. W., and Stoddard, G. D.: Getting ideas from movies. *In* W. W. Charters, P. W. Holaday, and G. D. Stoddard, Eds., *Motion Pictures and Youth.* New York, Macmillan, 1933.

73. Huang, I., and Lee, H. W.: Experimental analysis of child animism. *J. Genet. Psychol. 66*: 69-74, 1945.

74. Hurlock, E. B.: The value of praise and reproof as incentives for children. *Arch. Psychol. 11*: No. 71, 1924.
75. ———: The use of group rivalry as an incentive. *J. Abnorm. Soc. Psychol. 22*: 278-290, 1927.
76. ———, and Schwartz, R.: Biographical records of memory in preschool children. *Child Develop. 3*: 230-239, 1932.
77. Ilg, F., and Ames, L. B.: Developmental trends in arithmetic. *J. Genet. Psychol. 79*: 3-28, 1951.
78. Jersild, A. T., Markey, F. V., and Jersild, C. L.: Children's fears, dreams, wishes, daydreams, likes, dislikes, pleasant and unpleasant memories. *Child Develop. Monogr.* No. 12, 1933.
79. ———, and Tasch, R. J.: *Children's Interests and What They Suggest for Education.* New York, Teachers College, Columbia University, 1949.
80. Judd, C. H.: The relation of special training to general intelligence. *Educ. Rev. 36*: 28-42, 1908.
81. Klingensmith, S. W.: Child animism: what the child means by "alive." *Child Develop. 24*: 51-61, 1953.
82. Kounin, J. S.: Intellectual development and rigidity. *In* R. G. Barker, J. S. Kounin, and H. F. Wright, Eds., *Child Behavior and Development.* New York, McGraw-Hill, 1943, pp. 179-198.
83. Lacey, J. I., and Dallenbach, K. M.: Acquisition by children of the cause-effect relationship. *Am. J. Psychol. 53*: 575-578, 1940.
84. Lehman, H., and Cole, L.: The effectiveness of drill in handwriting to remove specific illegibilities. *School & Soc. 27*: 546-548, 1928.
85. Leuba, C.: Children's reactions to elements of simple geometric patterns. *Am. J. Psychol. 53*: 575-578, 1940.
86. Levitt, E. E.: Studies in intolerance of ambiguity. I. The decision-location test with children. *Child Develop. 24*: 263-268, 1953.
87. Lewin, K.: Behavior and development as a function of the total situation. *In* L. Carmichael, Ed., *Manual of Child Psychology*, ed. 2. New York, Wiley, 1954, pp. 918-970.
88. Lewis, D. J.: Partial reinforcement in a gambling situation. *J. Exper. Psychol 43*: 447-450, 1952.
89. Lindley, E. H.: A study of puzzles with special reference to the psychology of mental adaptation. *Am. J. Psychol. 8*: 431-493, 1897.
90. Ling, B. C.: Form discrimination as a learning cue in infants. *Comp. Psychol. Monogr. 17*: No. 2, 1941.
91. Long, L., and Welch, L.: The development of the ability to discriminate and match numbers. *J. Genet. Psychol. 59*: 377-387, 1941.
92. ———, and ———: Reasoning ability in young children. *J. Psychol. 12*: 21-44, 1941.
93. ———, and ———: Influence of level of abstractness on reasoning ability. *J. Psychol. 13*: 41-59, 1942.
94. Lord, F. E.: A study of spatial orientation of children. *J. Educ. Res. 34*: 481-505, 1941.
95. McCarthy, D.: *The Language Development of the Preschool Child.* Minneapolis, University of Minnesota Press, 1930.
96. McKillop, A. S.: *The Relationship Between the Reader's Attitude and Certain Types of Reading Response.* New York, Teachers College, Columbia University, 1952.

97. McLeod, H.: A Rorschach study with preschool children. *J. Proj. Tech. 14:* 453-463, 1950.
98. Maier, N. R. F.: Reasoning in children. *J. Comp. Psychol. 21:* 357-366, 1936.
99. Malrieu, P.: Some problems of color vision in children. *J. de Psychol. et norm. path. 52:* 222-231, 1955.
100. Martin, W. E.: Quantitative expression in young children. *Genet. Psychol. Monogr. 44:* 147-219, 1951.
101. Matheson, E.: A study of problem solving behavior in pre-school children. *Child Develop. 2:* 242-262, 1931.
102. Michaud, S.: The child's interpretation of geometrical figures. *J. de Psychol. et norm. path. 42:* 295-308, 1949.
103. Moyer, K. E., and Gilmer, B. V.: Attention spans of children for experimentally designed toys. *J. Genet. Psychol. 87:* 187-201, 1955.
104. Munn, N. L.: Learning in children. *In* L. Carmichael, Ed., *Manual of Child Psychology,* ed. 2. New York, Wiley, 1954, pp. 374-458.
105. Nagy, M.: The child's theories concerning death. *J. Genet. Psychol. 73:* 3-27, 1948.
106. Nelson, V. L.: An analytical study of child learning. *Child Develop. 7:* 95-114, 1936.
107. Northway, M. L.: The influence of age and social group on children's remembering. *Brit. J. Psychol. 27:* 11-29, 1936.
108. Oakden, E. C., and Sturt, M.: Development of the knowledge of time in children. *Brit. J. Psychol. 12:* 309-336, 1922.
109. Oakes, M. E.: *Children's Explanations of Natural Phenomena.* New York, Teachers College, Columbia University, 1946.
110. Pattie, F. A., and Cornett, S.: Unpleasantness of early memories and maladjustment of children. *J. Personal. 20:* 315-321, 1952.
111. Peterson, G. M.: An empirical study of the ability to generalize. *J. Gen. Psychol. 6:* 90-114, 1932.
112. Piaget, J.: *Language and Thought of the Child.* London, Routledge & Kegan Paul, 1926.
113. ———: *Judgment and Reasoning in the Child.* New York, Harcourt, Brace, 1928.
114. ———: *The Child's Conception of the World.* London, Routledge & Kegan Paul, 1929.
115. ———: *The Child's Conception of Physical Causality.* New York, Harcourt, Brace, 1932.
116. ———: *The Psychology of Intelligence.* New York, Harcourt, Brace, 1950.
117. ———: *The Child's Conception of Number.* New York, Humanities Press, 1952.
118. ———: *The Construction of Reality in the Child.* New York, Basic Books, 1954.
119. ———: Language and thought from the genetic point of view. *Acta Psychol. 10:* 51-60, 1954.
120. Pistor, F.: How time concepts are acquired by children. *Educ. Meth. 20:* 107-112, 1940.
121. Postman, L.: Experimental analysis of motivational factors in perception. *In Current Theory and Research in Motivation.* Lincoln, University of Nebraska Press, 1953, pp. 59-108.
122. Probst, C. A.: A general information test for kindergarten children. *Child Develop. 2:* 81-95, 1931.

123. Rehage, K. J.: A comparison of pupil-teacher planning and teacher-directed procedures in eighth grade social studies classes. *J. Educ. Res. 45*: 111-115, 1951.

124. Reichard, S., Schneider, M., and Rapaport, D.: The development of concept formation in children. *Am. J. Orthopsychiat. 14*: 156-162, 1944.

125. Richardson, H. M.: The growth of adaptive behavior in infants: an experimental study of seven age levels. *Genet. Psychol. Monogr. 12*: 195-359, 1932.

126. Roberts, K. E.: The ability of preschool children to solve problems in which a simple principle of relationship is kept constant. *J. Genet. Psychol. 40*: 118-135, 1932.

127. Russell, R. W.: Studies in animism. II. The development of animism. *J. Genet. Psychol. 56*: 353-366, 1940.

128. Schmidt, H. O.: The effects of praise and blame as incentives to learning. *Psychol. Monogr. 53*: No. 3, 1941.

129. Schuessler, K., and Strauss, A.: A study of concept learning by scale analysis. *Am. Sociol. Rev. 15*: 752-762, 1950.

130. Serra, M. C.: A study of fourth grade children's comprehension of certain verbal abstractions. *J. Exper. Educ. 22*: 103-118, 1953.

131. Shaffer, L. F.: *Children's Interpretation of Cartoons.* New York, Teachers College, Columbia University, 1930.

132. Shepard, W. O., and Shaeffer, M.: The effect of concept knowledge on discrimination learning. *Child Develop. 27*: 173-178, 1956.

133. Sigel, I. E.: Developmental trends in the abstraction ability of children. *Child Develop. 24*: 131-144, 1953.

134. Skeels, H. M.: A study of some factors influencing form board accomplishments of two- and three-year-old children. *J. Genet. Psychol. 40*: 375-395, 1932.

135. Smith, M. E.: The influence of age, sex, and situation on the frequency, form and function of questions asked by preschool children. *Child Develop. 4*: 201-213, 1933.

136. ———: Childhood memories compared with those of adult life. *J. Genet. Psychol. 80*: 151-182, 1952.

137. Spiegel, L. H.: The child's concept of beauty: a study in concept formation. *J. Genet. Psychol. 77*: 11-23, 1950.

138. Spiker, C. C.: The effects of number of reinforcements on the strength of a generalized instrumental response. *Child Develop. 27*: 37-44, 1956.

139. ———: Experiments with children on the hypotheses of acquired distinctiveness and equivalence of cues. *Child Develop. 27*: 253-263, 1956.

140. Springer, D.: Development in young children of an understanding of time and the clock. *J. Genet. Psychol. 80*: 83-96, 1952.

141. Stevenson, H. W.: Latent learning in children. *J. Exper. Psychol. 47*: 17-21, 1954.

142. ———, and Bitterman, M. E.: The distance-effect in the transposition of intermediate size of children. *Am. J. Psychol. 68*: 274-279, 1955.

143. Strauss, A.: The development and transformation of monetary meaning in the child. *Am. Sociol. Rev. 17*: 275-286, 1952.

144. Szuman, S.: Comparison, abstraction, and analytic thought in the child. *Enfance 4*: 189-216, 1951.

145. Taft, R.: Selective recall and memory distortion of favorable and unfavorable material. *J. Abnorm. Soc. Psychol. 49*: 23-28, 1954.

146. Thetford, W. N., Molish, H. B., and Beck, S. J.: Developmental aspects of personality structure in normal children. *J. Proj. Tech. 15*: 58-78, 1951.

147. Thompson, G. G., and Hunnicutt, C. W.: The effect of repeated praise or blame on the work achievement of "introverts" and "extroverts." *J. Educ. Psychol. 35*: 257-266, 1944.

148. Thrum, M. E.: The development of concepts of magnitude. *Child Develop. 6*: 120-140, 1935.

149. Tolman, E. C., Hall, C. S., and Bretnall, E. P.: A disproof of the law of effect and a substitution of the laws of emphasis, motivation, and disruption. *J. Exper. Psychol. 15*: 601-614, 1932.

150. Van Alstyne, D.: *Play Behavior and Choice of Play Materials of Preschool Children.* Chicago, University of Chicago Press, 1932.

151. Vinacke, W. E.: The investigation of concept formation. *Psychol. Bull. 48*: 1-32, 1951.

152. Wallon, H.: Pre-categorical thinking in the child. *Enfance 5*: 97-101, 1952.

153. Ward, A. H., and Davis, R. A.: Individual differences in retention of general science subject matter in the case of three measurable objectives. *J. Exper. Educ. 7*: 24-30, 1938.

154. Ward, L. B.: Reminiscence and rote learning. *Psychol. Monogr. 49*: No. 220, 1937.

155. Welch, L.: The development of size discrimination between the ages of 12 and 40 months. *J. Genet. Psychol. 55*: 243-268, 1939.

156. ——: The genetic development of the associational structures of abstract thinking. *J. Psychol. 10*: 211-220, 1940.

157. ——: A preliminary investigation of some aspects of the hierarchical development of concepts. *J. Gen. Psychol. 22*: 359-378, 1940.

158. ——, and Long, L.: Comparison of the reasoning ability of two age groups. *J. Genet. Psychol. 62*: 63-76, 1943.

159. Werner, H.: *Comparative Psychology of Mental Development.* Chicago, Follett, 1948.

160. ——, and Kaplan, B.: The developmental approach to cognition: its relevance to the psychological interpretation of anthropological and ethnolinguistic data. *Am. Anthropologist 58*: 866-880, 1956.

161. Witkin, H. A., et al.: *Personality Through Perception: An Experimental and Clinical Study.* New York, Harper, 1954.

162. Wrightstone, J. W.: *Appraisal of Newer Elementary School Practices.* New York, Teachers College, Columbia University, 1938.

163. Young, F. M.: Causes for loss of interest in high-school subjects as reported by 631 college students. *J. Educ. Res. 25*: 110-115, 1932.

164. Zeigarnik, B.: Über das Behalten von erledigten und unerledigten Handlungen. *Psychol. Forsch 9*: 1-85, 1927.

CHAPTER 18

The Growth of Intelligence

IN THIS CHAPTER we propose to discuss the growth of intelligence considered as a *measurement construct designating level of cognitive functioning*. Developmental changes in the actual psychological capacities and processes involved in cognitive functioning, namely, symbolization, language use, concept formation, memory, and problem solving, have already been considered in Chapters 16 and 17. When level of ability in performing these functions is measured by a graded series of tasks and regarded as representative of a general capacity for utilizing abstract symbols in the solution of abstract problems, the construct designating this measured capacity may be referred to as intelligence.

In the sense that the construct of intelligence is derived from a particular set of measurement operations, it is obviously an abstraction that has no phenomenological existence apart from these constituent operations. It is also an abstraction in the sense that a *general* level of cognitive functioning has no phenomenological reality apart from the particular kinds of cognitive functioning represented in an intelligence test. Nevertheless, insofar as the construct is logically tenable, related to naturalistic data, and derived from relevant and technically appropriate operations it is by no means merely an arbitrary and fictitious invention of psychologists. It is definitely related to an existing state of affairs in the real world (i.e., cognitive capacity) and has much heuristic value in explaining cognitive and other aspects of behavioral development and in predicting the cognitive level at which individuals function.

The concept of intelligence by definition clearly excludes level of functioning in all noncognitive areas of behavior. This definition renders largely irrelevant the commonly voiced criticism that the I.Q. is misleading because it does not indicate an individual's capacity for coping with nonverbal, concrete, mechanical or interpersonal problems. The I.Q. is not intended to represent these latter capacities and no claim is made that it does. In fact, if the intelligence test were modified so that it could perform these functions it would automatically lose whatever effectiveness it possesses as a measure of cognitive ability. The argument here is not that indices of maturity level in other noncognitive areas are theoretically or practically unimportant, but that it is utterly naive to expect a single instrument adequately to measure several largely unrelated kinds of abilities. Also

585

irrelevant in much the same sense is the criticism that the I.Q. does not indicate cognitive strengths and failings or typical ways of attacking problems. No single summary score could possibly do so. If such information is desired it is available in the detailed test protocol from which the I.Q. is derived and in the qualitative observations of the examiner.

Much futile controversy rages over the issue of whether or not the intelligence test measures native (genically determined) cognitive endowment. Although an effort is made to maximize the influence of genic factors by using test items that only presuppose very generally available kinds of experience, it is obviously impossible to rule out the differential effects of exposure to different types of cognitive experience, to different levels of cognitive stimulation, and to different personality and motivational variables. Hence, intelligence can only be regarded as a multiply determined functional capacity the level of which in a given individual reflects the relative potency of these various factors as they exist and interact in his particular case.

Another equally pointless controversy is the argument over whether the intelligence test score is a measure of performance or capacity. Obviously capacity cannot be measured directly and must be inferred from performance; but if the I.Q. were only an index of how adequately an individual utilizes his cognitive capacity (i.e., performs) rather than an index of existing capacity per se, its theoretical and practical usefulness would be strictly limited. Hence, the more meaningful and relevant question here is whether capacity can be validly inferred from performance or whether test performance provides a fair estimate of capacity. An affirmative answer to this question is indicated if (a) the test includes a representative sample of cognitive functions, (b) the specific items on the test are related to equally available experience, and (c) the individual is motivated to perform as well as he can. If the latter two conditions are not met, performance is an underestimate of capacity; improvement in score that is attributable to correction of test disadvantage or inadequate test motivation is reflective of a gain in performance rather than a gain in capacity. All increments in I.Q. do not necessarily fall in this category of more efficient utilization or fairer opportunity of displaying unchanged capacity. If the change is brought about through significant alterations in level of cognitive stimulation or in personality structure it is reflective of a genuine change in capacity, since cognitive capacity (according to the definition of intelligence adopted above) refers to a multiply determined phenotype (actualized genic endowment) rather than to genic potentiality.

In this book we can only be concerned with *developmental issues* bearing on intelligence as a construct designating an individual's general level of cognitive functioning—either in absolute terms, as a developmental age (mental age), or relative to his agemates, i.e., as a developmental quotient (I.Q. or brightness level) (see p. 113). These issues include (a) quantitative and qualitative changes in intelligence with increasing age; (b) the constancy of individual rates of growth; and (c) the nature-nurture problem— the relative contributions of heredity and environment to the development of intelligence and the extent to which intelligence is modifiable. We cannot devote any attention to the construction and standardization of intelligence tests, to problems of scoring, reliability, validity, and interpretation of results, to a description of the various kinds of tests that are available, to problems of retardation and acceleration in cognitive growth, or to educational and clinical applications. These latter issues are customarily considered in textbooks on psychological testing, clinical psychology and educational psychology.

Intelligence is related in two principal ways to other aspects of development that have already been considered in previous chapters and need only be referred to briefly here. First, since intelligence is a general manifestation of cognitive ability it is obviously related to various measures of particular kinds of cognitive functioning. We have already discussed the relationship of intelligence to age of talking (pp. 526-527), language ability (p. 528), bilingualism (p. 531), verbal fluency (p. 536), memory (p. 558), concept formation (pp. 527 and 560), and problem solving (p. 572). Second, intelligence functions as a determinant and source of individual differences with respect to fear (p. 322), laughter (p. 344), moral behavior (p. 397), interests (p. 412), sociometric status (p. 478), leadership (pp. 467 and 484), friendship (p. 482), and sensori-motor learning (p. 508). The problem of cognitive-physical relationships has also been considered in detail (pp. 108-109, 109-110) in relation to the wider issue of parallelism and divergence among component aspects of development.

DEVELOPMENTAL CHANGES IN INTELLIGENCE

The measurement of age level changes in intelligence is beset by many complicating factors. First, growth curves vary simply because of differences in the respective content, measurement units, discriminating power, and ceiling of different intelligence scales. This difficulty is compounded by the fact that separate scales are commonly employed to measure the intelligence of infants, preschool children and children of school age. Thus, before a continuous curve can be legitimately plotted from such data it is necessary to transpose scores into comparable units.[10] Second, even when a single scale is employed throughout the entire age range different types and combinations of sub-tests must be used to test intelligence at the various age levels. This procedure is defensible only if the changing composition of the test is truly reflective of actual developmental changes in the organization of intelligence. Only if this condition is met can we assume that different batteries of sub-tests, although patently dissimilar, are equally representative of general intelligence at their respective age levels. A third difficulty is the problem of constructing units of measurement that are equivalent at all points on the scale. It cannot bè assumed, for example, that a mental age increment of three months at three years is equivalent to the same increment at six years and at twelve years; for one thing, intra-age group variability tends to increase with increasing age.[11] Thurstone[88] and others have attempted by various statistical procedures (e.g., comparison of overlapping frequency distributions at adjacent age levels) to devise approximately equal mental growth units at different levels of maturity.

Still other factors complicate the task of arriving at a valid growth curve of intelligence. Using the same raw data, two investigators may come up with strikingly different growth curves simply on the basis of differences in the statistical procedures used in treating the scores and plotting the curves. Sampling discrepancies, particularly in cross-sectional studies are also important causes both of differences in the appearance of different growth curves and of distortions within a single curve. Finally, it should be realized that any growth curve of intelligence is based on averaged composite scores. Not only does every individual exhibit his own unique pattern of intellectual growth (see p. 596), but each component cognitive function also grows at a different rate. Vocabulary, general information, and arithmetical ability reach their peak of development at a later age than does rote memory[22, 33]; and during preadolescence and adolescence vocabulary and ability to dissect sentences grow at a more rapid rate than reasoning ability.[22]

Growth Curve of Intelligence

Most investigators agree that cognitive growth is most rapid in infancy and early childhood and tends to increase thereafter at a progressively decreasing rate. This is in accord with everyday experience and with the fact that overlapping between distributions of adjacent age groups increases with advancing age.[7] A linear curve of growth, as already pointed out, is simply an artifactual outcome of plotting mental age in terms of units that are deliberately calibrated so that one year of intellectual growth is on the average achieved during the course of a calendar year (see p. 134). In general, the growth curve of general intelligence is negatively accelerated when based either on raw scores,[30] on absolutely scaled scores, or on scaled scores transformed into percentages of adult attainment (see p. 134). Some investigators report positive acceleration in the early months[10] or years[88] of life and a slight reversal in the rate of negative acceleration during the preadolescent period.[30, 88, 92] On the basis of scaled CAVD test scores, Thorndike et al. postulated a parabolic growth curve according to which about half of mature intellectual status is attained by the age of three. Growth begins to taper off in middle adolescence and continues very slowly thereafter until ultimate capacity is achieved.[9, 30, 88]

Since the tapering off process is so gradual it is difficult to tell when growth actually ceases. The widely accepted finding of Terman and Merrill[80] that mental age does not increase after the age of fifteen is now attributed to the limited ceiling of the 1937 revision of the Stanford-Binet test. The best estimates, based on testing a wide age sample of a relatively homogeneous population[43, 91] or on retesting the same population at suitable intervals[10, 30, 43, 84, 85] places the age of terminal growth at 18 to 20 and even beyond. Gains in intelligence test scores have been reported at age 25 on the Wechsler Bellevue test[10] and at age 50 on the Army Alpha[62] and Concept Maturity tests.[13] The age of terminal growth obviously varies for different individuals and for different kinds of cognitive processes.[43]

Organizational Changes

Since there is much disagreement regarding the way in which intelligence is organized it is obviously impossible to make any definitive statement about developmental changes in its organization. The weight of the evidence, however, points to: (a) an initial stage (infancy and the early preschool period) in which the abilities measured by intelligence tests are predominantly perceptual and sensori-motor in nature and are largely unrelated both to each other and to later manifestations of abstract intelligence; (b) an intermediate stage (from approximately the late preschool period to preadolescence) in which abstract intelligence is highly general in nature, i.e., cognitive abilities are highly intercorrelated; and (c) a later stage (preadolescence and beyond) marked by increasing differentiation of intellectual abilities.

Factor analysis of infant intelligence scales demonstrates a high degree of specificity for the cognitive abilities measured by these scales.[10] The only distinct factors that are isolatable during the first four years are such global entities as "motor ability," "sensory motor alertness," and "persistence." Thereafter the much different factor of "abstract symbol manipulation" predominates and its constituent cognitive functions are more highly interrelated. Before the age of two years composite scores on intelligence scales, as well as particular sub-scale scores, have relatively little predictive value for later performance on corresponding scales intended for school-age children. Between the ages of two and four some sub-tests have moderate predictive value, but solely on an empirical basis; the items that are predictive have very little in common with respect to the kinds of abilities they measure. It appears therefore (a) that "intelligence . . . [is] a dynamic succession of developing functions, with the advanced and more complex functions in the hierarchy depending on the prior maturing of earlier simpler ones"[10]; and (b) that abstract cognitive ability as manifested in the older individual has not yet emerged in the younger child and cannot possibly be measured by infant intelligence scales. This does not mean that the more complex functions develop independently of their precursors but that new determining factors are implicated at the higher levels which attenuate the predictive value of earlier for later performance.

At the age of five the organizational picture is quite different. Abstract abilities are much in evidence and are so highly intercorrelated that it is relatively difficult to isolate independent factors. In contrast to the eight "primary abilities" that he was able to identify in a population of adolescents and young adults, Thurstone was only able to isolate five comparable abilities among five- and six year olds.[87, 89] As children grow older, particularly during the preadolescent period and beyond, there is evidence from factor analysis* of increasing differentiation of intellectual ability[32, 33] (see p. 110 for additional evidence). By the time an individual reaches adolescence differential factors of interest, relative ability, specialization of training, motivation, success and failure experience, and cultural expectation operate selectively to develop certain original abilities and to leave others relatively undeveloped. However, inasmuch as considerable interrelatedness among different cognitive functions still remains,[87] evidence of increasing differentiation at the older age levels does not render the concept of general intelligence completely untenable. Furthermore, relatively high correlations between intelligence test scores obtained in the primary grades and retest scores obtained during adolescence (see p. 595) indicate that there is much overlapping between the factors determining early level of general cognitive ability and later level of differentiated cognitive ability.

For practical purposes an intelligence test score has less utility after preadolescence than during the early elementary school years. The older child's standing in one ability has relatively little predictive value for his standing in another ability; and composite scores on intelligence tests are not very useful for predicting performance in a given school subject. Much more meaningful than a total score is a profile showing the relative standing of an individual on a wide variety of basic intellectual abilities. Thurstone's tests of "primary mental abilities" provides such a profile. By expressing intelligence in terms of the smallest number of relatively "pure" and independent factors it gives a much more definitive, convenient, and quantifiable qualitative analysis of cognitive ability than could be obtained from examination of the protocol of the more traditional Binet type of scale

*Using other kinds of tests, Vernon[90] failed to obtain consistent evidence of increasing differentiation.

composed of batteries of heterogeneous sub-tests. However, any given factor ("primary ability") is solely a measurement construct derived by a purely empirical procedure from a specific table of intercorrelations. Hence, it cannot be assumed that simply because the measured abilities from which the factor is abstracted are highly and selectively intercorrelated they are necessarily manifestations of the *same* underlying cognitive function.

Sex Differences

Sex differences in general intelligence tend to be negligible in magnitude and inconsistent in direction.[82] Most of the obtained differences can be attributed to differential weighting of the particular tests used with various component aspects of intelligence in which boys and girls differ in opposite directions, i.e., vocabulary, verbal fluency, rote memory, spatial and numerical abilities.[82] Evidence regarding sex differences in variability also tends to be inconsistent and equivocal. These differences, when found, are most marked at the extremes of the distribution; but the operation of variables other than genic factors makes interpretation difficult. Although the incidence of intellectual eminence is indisputably higher among males than among females, differential conditions of cultural expectation, motivation, and opportunity cannot be ignored. Lending support to this interpretation are Terman's findings that in a population of intellectually gifted children boys more frequently than girls retain their high status as they advance in age.[81]

Other complicating factors raise similar questions of interpretation regarding the preponderance of boys in classes for mentally retarded children and in institutions for the feebleminded. Not only does paranatal brain injury occur more frequently among male infants,[48] but mental deficiency is also a socially more conspicuous and disabling handicap in the case of boys. Furthermore, parents are less reluctant to commit sons than daughters to institutions. We must conclude, therefore, that until more definitive evidence is available it is impossible to decide to what extent obtained sex differences in variability are attributable to such genuine determinants as genic and relevant environmental factors, on the one hand, and to purely extraneous considerations, on the other hand.

Differences between the sexes on particular cognitive abilities tend to be larger and more significant than on tests of general intelligence. When boys and girls are compared on "primary mental abilities," clear differences in favor of girls are found in word fluency, rote memory, and reasoning.[37, 38] In other areas findings are more equivocal. Most investigators[37, 38, 52] agree that boys are superior in spatial ability, but Koch[44] failed to find a significant sex difference at the ages of five and six. No sex difference[44] and a difference in favor of girls[37] have been reported for numerical ability. The situation with respect to vocabulary is even more confusing. Some investigators[30, 38, 44] report a difference in favor of boys, some[22, 33] report a difference in favor of girls, and still others[37] find no difference. In view of the fact that, with the exception of verbal fluency, most sex differences in cognitive abilities are not evident at the younger age levels, [82] it seems reasonable to suppose that they are for the most part culturally determined (see p. 451).

Differences Among Ability Levels

Available evidence indicates that bright, dull and average children grow intellectually at different rates and differ with respect to organization and qualitative pattern of cognitive abilities. Although the terminal age of intellectual growth is the same for all three groups, dull children attain a disproportionately large percentage of their ultimate intellectual status during the early years[11] and tend to grow step-wise in spurts and pauses.[23] Normal children exhibit a more constant rate of growth,[30] whereas bright children "show an accelerated rate of growth in later childhood"[30] that slows down somewhat in middle and late adolescence.[23, 30] The net effect of these differences is that the bright tend to "grow away" from the dull.[22, 88] Duller individuals (as could reasonably be anticipated from their greater chronological age) also show greater differentiation of intelligence than do brighter younger children of the same mental age.[83] Greater differentiation concomitantly makes for decreased plasticity or increased rigidity (see p. 118). When chronological age is held constant, however, differentiation of cognitive traits[70] is more marked among bright children (higher mental age *and* higher I.Q.).

There are also good reasons for believing that normal (mean) cognitive functioning at a given maturity level is qualitatively different from the performance of accelerated younger or retarded older individuals at the same mental age level. First, sub-scale analysis of the Stanford-Binet test shows significant differences between old-dull and young-bright individuals of comparable mental age in the types of items handled successfully.[41, 46, 57] Second, bright and dull children tend to exhibit more "scatter" (i.e., spread of successes and failures on component sub-tests over a wider range of difficulty) on this test than do average children. Third, bright and dull children of equivalent mental age excel in different kinds of cognitive abilities. The bright are generally superior in tests demanding comprehension and use of language, reasoning, abstraction, and generalization[1, 24, 65, 66]; the dull are superior in spatial ability,[66] word fluency[66] and manipulation of concrete materials.[1] Kolstoe[45] however, found very few significant differences between such children on the various sub-tests of the Wechsler Intelligence Scale for Children. Fourth, normal children do better than mentally retarded children of the same mental age in such school skills as arithmetic reasoning,[26] spelling,[26] reading comprehension,[14, 26, 57] ability to profit from contextual cues,[26] memory for factual details,[14] and understanding of ideational relationships.[14] No significant differences were found in the simpler and more mechanical reading skills[14] and in arithmetic fundamentals.[26] Finally, bright and dull children of the same mental age show characteristic differences in approach to problem solving (see p. 572).

CONSTANCY OF INDIVIDUAL RATES OF GROWTH

Quite apart from normative fluctuations in the rate of intellectual development (see p. 588), it is important to ascertain whether children tend to retain the same *relative* status in their age group as they grow older. To the extent that this type of constancy prevails, the child's developmental quotient (I.Q.) will fluctuate little from one age level to another and his score at an earlier stage of development will not only be indicative of his relative status at that age level but will also have predictive value for his relative status at later stages of development. The constancy of the I.Q. (or its predictive value) may be expressed either in terms of its probable error or in terms of the coefficient of correlation between the intelligence test scores of a group of children determined on two separate occasions (the coefficient of stability).

Generally speaking, once the I.Q. approaches stability it tends to remain relatively constant and existing degrees of inconstancy tend to be normally distributed. At the age of nine, for example, the probable error of an I.Q.[80] is about five points* (varying with brightness level) and the coefficient of stability (with an interval of three years between tests) is approximately .85.[39] The predictive value of the I.Q. is greatly influenced by the age of the child at the time of initial testing and by the length of the interval between test and retest. The older the child when first tested and the shorter the interval between tests the greater will be the predictive accuracy of the initial test.[3, 4, 9, 39] Intelligence test scores gradually become more stable with advancing age and first acquire sufficient stability to be practically useful for predictive purposes when the child reaches school age.[9] In this section we shall consider age level changes in the stability of the I.Q. as well as various measurement, genic and environmental factors that account for both consistency and fluctuations in individual rates of growth.

Age Level Changes in the Stability of the I.Q.

The scores children make on infant intelligence scales have very little predictive value for their later intellectual status. Prior to the age of six

*This means that one-half of the I.Q. tested persons do not deviate more than five points on retesting.

months these scores tend to be negatively correlated with intelligence test scores determined at the age of four; and between seven and nine months the correlation with six-year-old scores is generally about zero.[8] Stability increases gradually. At 12 months the correlation with test scores subsequently determined at age five is .085, and the corresponding correlations at 18 and 24 months are .23 and .52 respectively.[4] Scores at 21 months, however, have little or no predictive implications for terminal intellectual status; the correlation between these scores and I.Q. at 18 years[39] is only .08. The items on infant scales that have most predictive value also show no particular overlap with those items that are most satisfactory for measuring current intellectual status.[56]

Reasons for the instability of infant intelligence scores as well as for the increasing stability of test scores with advancing age are not difficult to find. First, because of the very rapid rate of growth and the exceedingly narrow range of individual differences during infancy, temporary acceleration or retardation in rate of growth results in much larger fluctuations in test scores than when the rate of growth is slower and greater interindividual variability prevails. Second, relatively much less overlap in test content exists between successive age levels during infancy than during later childhood. "Infant tests, as presently constituted measure very little if at all the function which is called intelligence at later ages."[3] Third, errors of measurement are maximal during infancy because of difficulties in communication and rapport, misinterpretation of responses, fluctuations in attention and motivation, negativistic reactions, etc. (see p. 596). Fourth, subabilities measured by infant scales are very specific (not highly intercorrelated). Hence they have very little predictive significance for any general ability that transcends the particular functions they measure. Finally, infant scales have not been validated as have the later tests against ratings of brightness, academic achievement, or criteria of internal consistency.[3] The only criterion generally employed has been increase in score with advancing age.[3] This is a necessary but not a sufficient criterion, especially since items that satisfy it are not necessarily the same items that have the most predictive value.

Although most of the shortcomings of infant scales are inherent in the task of measuring, under extremely difficult conditions, an ability that for the most part has yet to emerge, some steps can be taken to increase their predictive accuracy. MacRae has shown that infant tests have more predictive value if ratings on a five point scale (mentally defective, below average, average, above average, and superior) rather than specific scores are correlated with intellectual status at age nine.[55] This is especially true if such ratings are based on more than one test and are supplemented by independent clinical observations and by a judgment as to whether "optimal functioning is elicited from the child."[3, 28, 34] Another approach has been to employ the criterion of correlation with terminal intellectual status in selecting items. This method, however, has thus far enjoyed only very limited success and only in children beyond the age of two (see p. 589).

Preschool intelligence tests measure a larger portion of abstract intellectual ability and hence have greater predictive value than infant scales. After the age of two, scores on preschool tests show a moderate (.46 to .66) and progressively increasing correlation with scores determined at the age of seven [3, 39]; but it is not until the age of school entrance that scores on intelligence tests are reasonably well correlated with terminal intellectual status.[9, 39] If preschool tests are administered accurately and on more than one occasion, school age status can be predicted with a degree of error that rarely exceeds one category on a five point scale. During the later elementary school years I.Q. remains relatively stable, both on a year-to-year basis and over a period of three or more years.[9, 39] Although some fluctuations in test scores do occur, most children tend to retain the same relative position in their age group.

Determinants of Constancy and Fluctuation

Much of the constancy of the I.Q. can undoubtedly be attributed to genic factors. To the extent that the development of intelligence is determined by polygenic influences (see p. 597), some measure of constancy is inherent in the fact that the genotype of an individual remains invariable throughout his lifetime. The environment also accounts for some constancy, since for any particular individual it tends within limits to remain relatively stable.* The relative contributions of heredity and environment to the constancy of the I.Q. would, of course, be proportionate to their respective weights in determining cognitive development. A third factor making for constancy is the phenomenon of developmental irreversibility or the limiting influence of current developmental status on potentialities for future growth. New growth always proceeds from the existing phenotype rather than from potentialities inherent in the genotype. If as a result of a consistently poor environment during the early formative years superior genic endowment is not actualized, the attained level of functional capacity (although incommensurate with genic potentiality) significantly limits the extent to which later environmental improvement can increase the rate of cognitive growth. An individual's prior success in developing his intellectual potentialities, in other words, tends to keep his future rate of growth relatively constant despite fluctuations in relevant environmental variables.

*Because of the relatively small range of intraindividual variability in environment, the stability of the I.Q. cannot be interpreted to mean that environmental factors are not significant determinants of level of cognitive functioning. This proposition can only be tested by relating variability in intellectual status to a wide range of environmental variability.

Fluctuations in I.Q. are caused by measurement, genic and environmental factors. Included under the first heading are: (a) errors of measurement inherent in the selection and placement of test items and in the use of items that are not equally representative of generally available experience, thereby leading to variable amounts of test disadvantage at different points in the life cycle and for different groups of children; (b) errors of test administration and scoring, especially during infancy and early childhood when difficulties of communication are maximal; (c) situational variability in such factors affecting test performance as personality of the test administrator, rapport,[63] fatigue, physical well-being, general attitude, motivation, attention span, frustration tolerance, self-confidence, level of aspiration, emotional stability, level of anxiety, reaction to failure, venturesomeness, and negativism[68]; (d) variation in the standardization sample over the age range; (e) variation among age groups in test ceiling and in degree of variability of test scores; and (f) variable exposure to practice and coaching on intelligence tests[95] and to test experience generally.

The most important measurement factor making for instability of the I.Q. are age level changes in the composition of intelligence tests and in the degree of overlap of test content between adjacent age groups.[3, 10] Because infant intelligence scales measure a largely unrelated type of sensorimotor ability instead of the cognitive ability tested at later age levels, a child with high genic endowment for abstract intelligence tends to score much closer to the mean on earlier than on later tests. Hence he makes a spuriously low score on the initial test and registers a spurious gain on the second test; the reverse holds true for the child deficient in abstract intelligence.[3] Dissimilarity in test content, on the other hand, is necessary and desirable in instances where genuine developmental change occurs in the organization of intelligence (see p. 587). For example, intelligence tests should be more highly differentiated at age fifteen than at age five.

Just because the genotype remains constant, we cannot assume on a priori grounds that its effects on development lead to individual constancy in relative rate of growth. Since genic factors determine normative fluctuations in rate of cognitive development over the life span (see p. 588) they may also give rise to intraindividual variability in rate of growth. Longitudinal analyses of individual growth curves of intelligence by Bayley (see p. 116) and Cornell and Armstrong[23] are consistent with this interpretation. The latter investigators were able to classify most growth curves under three main patterns—a continuous growth curve from age five to eighteen, a step-like curve consisting of alternate spurts and pauses, and a discontinuous curve breaking at puberty and showing either a steeper or more gradual slope thereafter.

Environmental factors contribute in two ways to fluctuations in the I.Q. First, physical and emotional vicissitudes of a transitory nature (e.g., illness, emotional trauma, separation from parents, rejection by peers) may impair a child's intelligence test performance without basically affecting his cognitive capacity. This issue is discussed on page 115. Second, radical and sustained changes in cognitive stimulation or motivation may modify actual level of intellectual functioning. However, as will be pointed out below, significant alterations in I.Q. of such origin can only be anticipated in young children who are removed from a markedly impoverished to a normally adequate or enriched environment.

NATURE AND NURTURE

Various methods have been used in attempting to arrive at a quantitative estimate of the relative influence of heredity and environment on the development of a given trait (see p. 60). Applying these methods to the study of twins,[58] foster children,[15, 47] and relationships between intelligence, schooling, and reasoning ability[17] different investigators have reached quite different conclusions regarding the proportional contributions of nature and nurture to measured differences in phenotypic intelligence. However, because of the many uncontrollable sources of error involved in making precise quantitative estimates (see p. 60), as well as the questionable validity of the assumptions underlying the statistical procedures employed,[51] it seems preferable in the present state of our knowledge merely to examine the various kinds of evidence bearing on the heredity-environment issue and to essay a *rough* approximation of their relative effects on inter- and intragroup variability in intelligence test scores.

Heredity imposes absolute limits on level of cognitive attainment in the individual, influences the rate and pattern of his intellectual growth, and affects the differentiation of his intellectual abilities. Except for such relatively rare conditions as phenyl-pyruvic amentia, cerebral agenesis, and cretinism (see p. 77), the mechanisms mediating genic influences on intellectual development are not presently understood. As in the determination of any ontogenetic trait, *environment* also plays a limiting and patterning role in the development of intelligence. Even if it could be held constant it would still play this active regulatory role rather than merely constitute a passive field for the unfolding of a trait completely determined by genic factors; its effects under such conditions would simply operate in a uniform way for all individuals. However, since it does vary in important ways that affect the development of intelligence it also contributes to inter- and intracultural variability, both in the patterning and in the realization of genic potentialities. It determines the extent to which existing genic endowment can be converted into phenotypic functional capacity and helps determine which particular components will be selectively emphasized as the latter undergoes differentiation with advancing age.

Culture, social class and family have many ways of influencing attained level of cognitive development. By providing more or less opportunity for training and experience, by offering more or less encouragement and stimulation, and by selectively valuing and rewarding intellectual attainment, the operation of these factors leads to substantial differences in ultimate outcome among individuals with comparable genic potentiality. Personality variables of temperamental and environmental origin play a similar role. Especially important in this connection are (a) such determinants of task-oriented motivation as intellectual curiosity, activity level, and venturesomeness; (b) intensity and area of ego-involvement; (c) such correlates of ego-oriented motivation as need for primary status, competitiveness, responsiveness to prestige incentives, level of ego aspiration, goal tenacity, frustration tolerance, and anxiety level; and (d) need for volitional and executive independence.* Intellectually gifted children tend to excel in most of these traits.[49, 81] Although some of the relationship between motivational and intellectual superiority may be attributed to common association with high socioeconomic status or to better ability to perceive the characterological ingredients of success (see p. 397), it is entirely conceivable that level of motivation directly influences extent of actualization of genic endowment.

The Problem of Modifiability

Once we grant that the I.Q. represents a multiply determined functional capacity in the development of which experiential and motivational factors play an important regulatory role, it is superfluous to inquire whether it can be modified by significant changes in such factors. The more relevant questions at this point are the extent of modification that is possible and the conditions under which it occurs. The most important limiting factors are: (a) irreversible loss in attainable capacity following prolonged failure to actualize genic potentiality (see p. 595); (b) diminished plasticity in older children (see p. 118); and (c) the crucial role of genic influences in setting absolute as well as relative restrictions on the amount of change that can occur. From these considerations it is apparent that significant environmental modification can only be anticipated in early childhood and after correction of serious deprivation. It is hardly likely that discriminable

---

*When overprotecting parents try to keep their children emotionally dependent or when the latter attempt to retain an infantile, dependent status, failure to develop intellectual competence admirably serves both purposes.[79] See also L. W. Sontag, et al., *Am. J. Orthopsychiat.* 25: 555-562, 1955. Children from homes characterized by warmth, freedom of exploration, and "acceleratory pressure" make the largest gains in I.Q.[6]

changes in I.Q. will be found following improvement in an environment that is already reasonably adequate from the standpoint of intellectual stimulation and motivation.

Before changes in I.Q. can be validly interpreted as evidence of environmental modification of cognitive capacity it should be obvious that such changes must be reliably greater than fluctuations attributable to measurement factors alone. Failure to take this consideration into account has led to many unwarranted and exaggerated claims regarding the modifiability of the I.Q. Hence, before we review studies of the effects of such factors as foster home placement, continued institutionalization, or nursery school attendance on level of intellectual functioning we would do well to consider various nonenvironmental sources of change.

First, because of very large errors of measurement in infancy and early childhood (see pp. 594 and 596), infant and preschool scales are not even very reliable measures of current "intellectual" status. Many of these errors of measurement lead to underestimation of a given child's actual intelligence; in other instances intelligence is overestimated. In either case there is a tendency toward regression to the mean upon subsequent testing. Relatively large changes in measured I.Q. reflective of test unreliability occur irrespective of any concomitant alteration in environment. Instability of such origin should certainly not be confused with evidence of genuine plasticity.[3]

Second, because of their emphasis on neuromuscular and sensori-motor functions infant scales do not really measure abstract verbal ability and, therefore, have very little predictive value for later intellectual status (see p. 594). Scores on infant scales constitute neither an adequate baseline from which to measure subsequent gains or losses in relative intellectual standing nor an adequate criterion in terms of which infant or preschool subjects may be matched for relative intellectual ability.[3] Simply on the basis of actual genotypic capacity for abstract cognitive functioning that is *not* measured by the initial test, large spurious increments and decrements in intelligence are registered in later years (see p. 596). For example, quite apart from any environmental influence progressive decline in I.Q. may be anticipated from poorly endowed orphanage children because of their spuriously high scores on infant scales. Selective factors that operate in the adoption of orphanage children (e.g., greater likelihood of placing brighter, better endowed children) may account in part for the retention or even improvement of initial status. In evaluating the gains associated with a "good" foster home or nursery school environment it is important to realize that test disadvantage (relative unfamiliarity with specific test material or indifferent test motivation) is more apt to occur in an impoverished than in a reasonably adequate environment.

Finally, in appraising studies of attempted modification of the I.Q., attention should be paid to the principle of filial regression and to the possibility of genically determined intraindividual variation in rate of growth. Independent of any errors of measurement or change in the environment, the children of intellectually dull individuals tend to score higher than their parents on intelligence tests, and many children show considerable fluctuation in relative status during their growth careers.

Parent-Child Resemblance

Correlations between parent and child I.Q. are initially about zero[42, 75] but increase gradually with advancing age as amount of overlap between the abilities measured by intelligence tests at the respective age levels increases. By school age parent-child correlations are in the neighborhood of .50.[15, 21, 47] However, since the existing degree of relationship could reflect the influence of either heredity or environment, these data shed little light on the nature-nurture problem. Nevertheless, two clues point to the greater weight of heredity. If environment were a highly significant factor we would expect (a) that since mothers bear the major burden of child rearing in our society the I.Q. of children would be more highly correlated with mothers' than with fathers' I.Q., and (b) that since siblings share a more uniform developmental environment with each other than with their parents, inter-sibling resemblance would be greater than parent-child resemblance. As available data[21] confirm neither hypothesis the environmentalist position is accordingly weakened.

More crucial evidence on the nature-nurture problem is provided by comparison of foster parent-foster child and true parent-true child resemblances in I.Q. Foster children share only their parents' environment whereas true children share both heredity and environment with their parents. In the foster home situation, where the genic basis of resemblance is removed, parent-child correlations[15, 47] are considerably lower* (approximately .20) than in the natural home situation (approximately .50). Similarly, intra-pair differences between children whose *own* fathers are at opposite extremes of the occupational hierarchy are markedly higher than intra-pair differences between children whose *foster* fathers are in comparable positions.[16] It seems, therefore, that the greater part of the variance in children's I.Q.'s is attributable to genic rather than to environmental factors. This conclusion is consistent with findings[75, 76] that whereas the I.Q. of foster children is only negligibly related to their foster parents' educational status, it is moderately correlated at school age with true mothers' educational

---

*Some of the resemblance between children and foster parents may also reflect the influence of selective adoption, i.e., the tendency to match foster and true parents in terms of I.Q. and occupational background.[31, 47]

status (.35) and I.Q. (.40). The latter correlation is almost as high as that between children and true parents who are domiciled together.

Sibling and Twin Resemblance*

We have already noted that the absence of significant difference between parent-child and inter-sibling correlations in I.Q. lends support to the hereditarian position. Other related findings point in the same direction: (a) the resemblance between true siblings reared in the same home is substantially greater than the resemblance between foster siblings[31]; (b) similarity with respect to age and sex does not increase inter-sibling resemblance in I.Q. as one might expect if environmental factors exercised considerable weight[42]; (c) resemblances between foster siblings are no greater than foster parent-foster child resemblances despite greater similarity in environment[15, 31, 47]; (d) separation of siblings does not lower inter-sibling correlations[42]; and (e) when *interfamilial* environmental variability is eliminated, as in the orphanage situation, neither the resemblance between sibling pairs nor the degree of variability in I.Q. scores is correspondingly reduced.[42]

Comparative studies of identical and fraternal twins shed more light on the nature-nurture problem inasmuch as identical twins have approximately identical genotypes whereas fraternal twins are genically no more similar than ordinary siblings. Here, too, the findings give little comfort to environmentalists. Identical twins are markedly more similar in I.Q. than fraternal twins (correlations of .80 to .90 as against .50 to .60); and even when identical twins are separated, differences in I.Q. are generally smaller than among fraternal twins reared together.[58, 96] Sizeable differences in the I.Q.'s of separated identical twins are only found when their educational backgrounds are highly dissimilar. On the basis of these small differences in I.Q. when heredity is held constant while the usual degree of environmental variability prevails, Woodworth concludes that "the differences found among the children of an ordinary community are not accounted for, except in small measure, by differences in home and schooling."[96]

Social Class Differences†

Prior to 18 months of age, zero or low negative correlations are found between scores on infant intelligence scales and various socioeconomic factors.[12] Thereafter the magnitude of correlational indices increases rapidly and at school age varies between .3 and .5 for different educational, occupational and economic criteria of social class status.[12] The early absence of

*Reviews of studies in this area are available.[15, 21, 31, 42, 58, 96]

†Reviews of studies in this area are available.[25, 27, 37, 42, 59]

relationship simply indicates that intelligence tests cannot possibly measure the same cognitive abilities during infancy as in later years. The increasing correspondence between I.Q. and socioeconomic variables as degree of test overlap increases may reflect either the cumulative impact of environmental influences or "an increasing manifestation of hereditary potentialities."[12]

Beginning with the preschool period, a range of about 20 I.Q. points separates children of the highest and lowest socioeconomic groups.[80] The relationship between children's relative intellectual status and father's position in the occupational hierarchy is practically linear[80] and, in correlational terms, varies between .20 and .43 for different tests of intelligence.[27] Upper socioeconomic groups also contribute a disproportionately large number of intellectually gifted and a disproportionately small number of mentally retarded children to the total population.[54] These relationships refer, of course, to group averages since differences within an occupational group are actually much larger than differences between the means of various groups. Although social class differences are greatest in the area of verbal abilities,[27] significant differences have also been found for all of Thurstone's primary mental abilities[37] as well as for other nonverbal tests.

The interpretation of these social class differences in intelligence has led to much heated controversy between hereditarians and environmentalists. Actually three different kinds of explanations based respectively on measurement, environmental, and genic factors seem equally plausible, but the evidence currently available is not sufficiently definitive to establish their relative weight. The measurement argument stems from a certain amount of middle-class bias in the construction of most intelligence tests. This creates test disadvantage for the lower-class child and results in an underestimate of his true level of cognitive functioning. In order to derive a valid and fair estimate of intellectual capacity from test performance it is necessary (a) that intelligence scales measure a representative cross-section of cognitive functions that is nondiscriminatory in terms of social class emphasis; (b) that specific test items be based on experiences and symbols that are equally available and familiar to individuals from all social class strata; and (c) that test materials arouse comparable degrees of interest and motivation in persons of different social class origin.[25, 27]

Most present-day tests are heavily weighted with specific items that are more familiar to middle- than lower-class children, and with the kinds of cognitive functions (e.g., vocabulary, linguistic skills) that are particularly emphasized in middle-class environments.* The tests are thus "unfair" in the sense that they do not give the lower-class child a fair opportunity to

---

*As noted above, however, large socioeconomic differences also prevail for other nonverbal tests.

demonstrate his *attained* level of cognitive capacity. But since intelligence tests do not purport to measure either genic potentialities per se or non-cognitive abilities, they are *not* unfair because they fail to measure level of functioning in those noncognitive abilities in which lower-class children excel or because the middle-class environment is experientially or motivationally more propitious for the development of native cognitive endowment.

Acceptance of the test bias explanation of social class differences by no means rules out the genic or environmental interpretations.* Insofar as environmental factors contribute to some of the variance in intelligence test scores (see pp. 598 and 600), it would not be unreasonable to expect that differential social class levels of stimulation and motivation affect extent of actualization of genic endowment. Evidence for this type of mediation of environmental influence comes from the finding that children's I.Q.'s are more highly correlated with parents' education than with the economic status of their homes.[50] Social class environment also selectively influences the differentiation of intellectual and other abilities as shown by the fact that middle-class children are superior to their lower-class contemporaries in both verbal *and* mechanical abilities at age 10 but are only superior in the former ability at age 16 (see p. 110). The environmentalist position is weakened by the existence of large social class differences in the preschool period,[80] by the failure of social class differentials to increase with advancing age,[72] and by the significantly greater correlation of foster children's I.Q.'s with true mothers' than with foster parents' educational status.[75, 76]

The hereditarian position rests on the assumption that (a) since there is indisputable evidence of substantial genic contribution to individual differences in I.Q. and (b) since more intelligent persons on the average choose and are selectively successful in the intellectually more demanding occupations it is reasonable to ascribe at least part of the consistently obtained social class differences in I.Q. to genic variability in cognitive potential. The tendency for more highly endowed individuals to reach the higher rungs of the occupational ladder is especially evident in a society characterized by a fair degree of social mobility; and since such persons also tend to marry at their own intellectual level,[42] their offspring acquire a genic advantage from both parents. Although logically tenable, it is understandably difficult to put this hypothesis to empirical test. It is supported in part by the applicability of the principle of filial regression to social class differences, i.e., children of professional parents tend to have a lower I.Q.

---

*The finding that approximately the same social class differentials appear on the Davis-Eells "culture fair" test as on the Kuhlmann-Finch test[20] casts doubt on the claim that the Davis-Eells test is culturally more fair but does not necessarily invalidate the test bias hypothesis of social class differences.

than their parents whereas the reverse holds true for children of unskilled laborers.[61]

Urban-Rural Differences

The mean I.Q. of rural children is consistently lower than that of urban children and also tends to diminish with increasing age.[5, 19, 94] As in the case of lower-class children this inferiority is most marked on verbal and speed items and is undoubtedly attributable in part to test bias.[42] Intelligence scales are typically devised by urban-reared psychologists and are validated on urban school children. However, since rural children also do more poorly on items presenting no special experiential or motivational handicap it is unwarranted to ascribe all urban-rural differences to test disadvantage. Equally plausible are explanations based either on the cumulative impact of a low level of intellectual stimulation or on the selective migration of more highly endowed individuals to urban areas.

Intelligence and Family Size

In most investigations of the relationship between I.Q. and number of siblings in the family a negative correlation of .2 to .3 is reported.[2] Since there is no evidence whatsoever of any intrinsic relationship between I.Q. and procreative ability only two other explanations seem plausible. First, the presence of a large number of children in the family may reduce the amount of cognitive stimulation available for each child. The per capita expenditure on education, recreation, housing, medical care, etc. is ordinarily lower when there are many siblings in the family; and even more important in terms of language development (see p. 529), the extent of parent-child contact is restricted.[59] Second, I.Q. and size of family are indirectly related by virtue of a common relationship to social class status, i.e., persons in the upper economic strata tend to have both a higher I.Q. and to raise relatively small families. To the extent that the intellectual superiority of their children is a function of either measurement or environmental factors (see p. 602), the inverse relationship between fertility and social class status obviously has no implications for eugenics. However, insofar as persons in the upper occupational strata may be presumed to possess a superior genic endowment with respect to cognitive capacity (see p. 603), their relatively low fertility rate may be expected over the course of many generations (in the absence of compensatory genic factors) to contribute to a national decline in the genotypic basis of intelligence.

In spite of the ominous prediction predicated on this line of reasoning, there is some evidence of a slight but significant gain in the mean I.Q. of Scottish children from 1932 to 1947.[69] Furthermore, despite the tremendous increase in high school enrollment from 1916 to 1940, with a corresponding elimination of the intellectual selectivity that formerly operated, there has been no drop in the mean I.Q. of the high school population.[29] The maintenance of phenotypic levels of intelligence under these circumstances can be explained perhaps by (a) compensatory changes in such environmental determinants of intelligence as the general standard of public education, (b) greater test sophistication on the part of children, and (c) a trend in recent years toward a higher birth rate among upper socioeconomic groups.[2]

Deprivation and Enrichment

Because of the great practical importance of the possibility of modifying intellectual capacity, a voluminous and highly controversial literature dealing with the effects of environmental deprivation and enrichment has arisen during the past two decades. Interpretation of this literature is extremely difficult since very few studies have been sufficiently well controlled to exclude many non-environmental sources of measured change in I.Q. (see pp. 599-600). In general, the weight of the evidence suggests two tentative conclusions. First, serious and prolonged deprivation, especially during late infancy and the preschool years, seems capable of inflicting permanent damage on intellectual growth. Second, enrichment of the existing environment can only effect substantial improvement of intellectual status in young children with a prior history of serious deprivation.

Effects of Deprivation. We have already considered evidence of the immediate (see p. 121) and long-term (see pp. 122 and 956) detrimental effects of early cognitive and emotional deprivation on neuromuscular, sensorimotor, language, and intellectual development. Such studies are obviously vulnerable to criticism on the grounds of unreliability of the infant scales employed and of inadequate matching of control and experimental groups.[64] Unqualified dismissal of these findings, on the other hand, is unwarranted when they are considered in the larger context of related evidence. In the first place, the very grossness of the findings and their consistent replication by many independent investigators in different parts of the world compensate in part for their methodological weaknesses. Second, they are consistent with observational and clinical data on the children concerned, with studies of animal deprivation, and with studies of older children growing up in orphanages and in depressed rural areas.

It seems probable that the longer children remain in substandard environmental conditions, i.e., orphanages[73, 74] or with mentally retarded mothers,[78] the progressively lower their I.Q. becomes in comparison with the I.Q. of control children placed in more favorable environments. These findings are consistent with reports of progressive decline in the intelligence test scores of isolated mountain and canal boat children who also grow up in non-stimulating and non-demanding intellectual environments.[5, 36, 71, 94] Some of this loss, however, is attributable (a) to relatively poor genic endowment (as a result of selective adoption or migration) which, for psychometric reasons, can first be manifested in later tests of intelligence, and (b) to progressively greater test disadvantage as intelligence tests place increasing emphasis on verbal abilities. Furthermore, despite the so-called "leveling effect" of the institutional environment, variability in intelligence test scores does not decline with advancing age.[3]

When orphanage children from relatively poor hereditary and social backgrounds are placed at an early age in superior foster homes there is evidence of either improvement in I.Q.[31] or of maintenance of an above-average rate of intellectual growth that is sustained over many years.[75, 76] Although part of these changes may reflect the influence of an improved environment, any complete explanation must also take into account the effects of filial regression and selective adoption as well as the greater probability of test disadvantage and unfavorable test conditions at the time of initial testing.

The provision of an enriched (experimental) nursery school environment to orphanage children has much the same effects as placement in a good foster home: It raises intelligence level only in the very young among those who have been seriously deprived.[67] In comparison with corresponding groups of control children, experimental children who initially test relatively high do not lose ground after a period of one-half to two and one-half years, and experimental children who initially test relatively low make larger gains.[74] Nevertheless, the fact that duller *control* children also gain in I.Q. and that brighter experimental children gain less than duller experimental children points to the large element of statistical regression in the improvement of the experimental group (see p. 599). In general, these findings are supported by the gain in mean I.Q. shown by Hawaiian[77] and East Tennessee mountain[94] children coincident with long-term improvement in substandard school conditions.

Effects of Enrichment. Quite unlike its effects on children reared under substandard home or school conditions, a program of school enrichment cannot be expected to increase intelligence test scores when provided to children who already enjoy reasonably adequate educational opportunities. Although children attending preschool tend to have a slightly higher mean I.Q. than non-preschool children,[93] the difference is small enough to be accounted for on the basis of dissimilarity in parental I.Q., errors of measurement, and the advantage of superior test rapport.* In support of this inter-

---

*The same general conclusion applies to studies of curriculum enrichment at the elementary school level.[35]

pretation is the fact that children who initially test high tend to make lower scores on retesting despite the intervening nursery school experience,[35] and that no significant differences are found when experimental and control groups are carefully matched with respect to home background.[35, 60] Kindergarten children who receive an intensive program of training in activities related to the Primary Mental Abilities tests make larger gains than control children on these latter tests but not on a different and more general test of intelligence.[40] This suggests that the improvement in mental test scores following such training is largely a specific practice effect rather than a genuine gain in intellectual status.

Prolonged schooling[42] also probably does not modify an individual's basic cognitive capacity. Follow-up studies of children matched for I.Q. in the eighth grade indicate that even 20 years later reliable differences in intelligence test scores appear in favor of those who completed more grades in school.[53] Nevertheless, gains are proportional to initial status and are rarely great enough to alter the relative positions of individuals in the original ranking of I.Q. Improvement in I.Q. accompanying college attendance is largely a function of test advantage accruing from continued academic pursuits and of selective factors (e.g., high academic aptitude) associated with admission to and success in college.[42] Continued schooling, in turn, further enhances the differentiation of general intellectual ability along those abstract verbal lines making for high scores on intelligence tests.

REFERENCES

1. Aldrich, C. G., and Doll, E. A.: Comparative intelligence of idiots and of normal infants. *J. Genet. Psychol. 39*: 227-257, 1931.

2. Anastasi, A.: Intelligence and family size. *Psychol. Bull. 53*: 187-209, 1956.

3. Anderson, J. E.: The limitations of infant and preschool tests in the measurement of intelligence. *J. Psychol. 8*: 351-379, 1939.

4. Anderson, L. D.: The predictive value of infancy tests in relation to intelligence at five years. *Child Develop. 10*: 203-212, 1939.

5. Asher, E. J.: The inadequacy of current intelligence tests for testing Kentucky mountain children. *J. Genet. Psychol. 46*: 480-486, 1935.

6. Baldwin, A. L., Kalhorn, J., and Breese, F. H.: Patterns of parent behavior. *Psychol. Monogr. 58*: No. 268, 1945.

7. Bayley, N.: Mental growth during the first three years. A developmental study of 61 children by repeated tests. *Genet. Psychol. Monogr. 14*: 7-92, 1933.

8. ——: Mental growth in young children. In *Thirty-ninth Yearbook, Nat. Soc. Stud. Educ.* Chicago, University of Chicago Press, 1940, part 2, pp. 11-47.

9. ——: Consistency and variability in the growth of intelligence from birth to eighteen years. *J. Genet. Psychol. 75*: 165-196, 1949.

10. ——: On the growth of intelligence. *Am. Psychologist 10*: 805-818, 1955.

11. ——: Individual patterns of development. *Child Develop. 27*: 45-74, 1956.

12. ——, and Jones, H. E.: Environmental correlates of mental and motor develop-

ment: a cumulative study from infancy to six years. *Child Develop. 4*: 329-341, 1937.

13. ——, and Oden, M. H.: The maintenance of intellectual ability in gifted adults. *J. Gerontol. 10*: 91-107, 1955.

14. Bliesmer, E. P.: Reading abilities of bright and dull children of comparable mental ages. *J. Educ. Psychol. 45*: 321-331, 1954.

15. Burks, B. S.: The relative influence of nature and nurture upon mental development: a comparative study of foster parent-foster child resemblance and true parent-true child resemblance. In *Twenty-seventh Yearbook,* Nat. Soc. Stud. Educ. Chicago, University of Chicago Press, 1928, part 1, pp. 219-316.

16. ——: On the relative contributions of nature and nurture to average group differences in intelligence. *Proc. Nat. Acad. Sci. 24*: 276-282, 1938.

17. Burt, C.: *Mental and Scholastic Tests.* London, King, 1928.

18. ——: The evidence for the concept of intelligence. *Brit. J. Educ. Psychol. 25*: 158-177, 1955.

19. Chapanis, A., and Williams, W. C.: Results of a mental survey with the Kuhlmann-Anderson intelligence tests in Williamson County, Tennessee. *J. Genet. Psychol. 67*: 27-55, 1945.

20. Coleman, W., and Ward, A. W.: A comparison of Davis-Eells and Kuhlmann-Finch scores of children from high and low socio-economic status. *J. Educ. Psychol. 46*: 465-469, 1955.

21. Conrad, H. S., and Jones, H. E.: A second study of familial resemblance in intelligence: environmental and genetic implications of parent-child and sibling correlations in the total sample. In *Thirty-ninth Yearbook,* Nat. Soc. Stud. Educ. Chicago, University of Chicago Press, 1940, part 2, pp. 97-141.

22. ——, Freeman, F. N., and Jones, H. E.: Differential mental growth. In *Forty-third Yearbook,* Nat. Soc. Stud. Educ. Chicago, University of Chicago Press, 1944, part 1, pp. 164-184.

23. Cornell, E. L., and Armstrong, C. M. Forms of mental growth patterns revealed by reanalysis of the Harvard growth data. *Child Develop. 26*: 169-204, 1955.

24. Cunningham, K. S.: *The Measurement of Early Levels of Intelligence.* New York, Teachers College, Columbia University, 1927.

25. Davis, A.: *Social Class Influences Upon Learning.* Cambridge, Harvard University Press, 1948.

26. Dunn, L. M.: A comparison of the reading processes of mentally retarded and normal boys of the same mental age. *Monogr. Soc. Res. Child Develop. 19*: 8-99, 1954.

27. Eells, K., Davis, A., et al.: *Intelligence and Cultural Differences. A Study of Cultural Learning and Problem-Solving.* Chicago, University of Chicago Press, 1951.

28. Escalona, S.: The use of infant tests for predictive purposes. *Bull. Menninger Clin. 14*: 117-128, 1950.

29. Finch, F. H.: Enrollment increases and changes in the mental level of the high-school population. *Appl. Psychol. Monogr.* No. 10, 1946.

30. Freeman, F. N., and Flory, C. D.: Growth in intellectual ability as measured by repeated tests. *Monogr. Soc. Res. Child Develop. 2*: No. 2, 1937.

31. ——, Holzinger, K. J., and Mitchell, B. C.: The influence of environment on the intelligence, school achievement, and conduct of foster children. In *Twenty-*

seventh Yearbook, Nat. Soc. Stud. Educ. Chicago, University of Chicago Press, 1928, part 1, pp. 103-217.

32. Garrett, H. E.: A developmental theory of intelligence. *Am. Psychologist 1*: 372-378, 1946.

33. ———, Bryan, A. I., and Perl, R. E.: The age factor in mental organization. *Arch Psychol.* No. 175, 1935.

34. Gesell, A., and Amatruda, C. S.: *Developmental Diagnosis: Normal and Abnormal Child Development.* New York, Hoeber, 1941.

35. Goodenough, F. L.: New evidence on environmental influence on intelligence. In *Thirty-ninth Yearbook,* Nat. Soc. Stud. Educ. Chicago, University of Chicago Press, 1940, part 1, pp. 307-365.

36. Gordon, H.: Mental and scholastic tests among retarded children: an enquiry into the effects of schooling on the various tests. *Educ. Pamphlets, Bd. Educ., London* No. 44, 1923.

37. Havighurst, R. J., and Breese, F. H.: Relation between ability and social status in a mid-Western community. III. Primary mental abilities. *J. Educ. Psychol. 38*: 241-247, 1947.

38. Hobson, J. R.: Sex differences in primary mental abilities. *J. Educ. Res. 41*: 126-132, 1947.

39. Honzik, M. P., Macfarlane, J. W., and Allen, L.: The stability of mental test performance between two and eighteen years. *J. Exper. Educ. 17*: 309-324, 1948.

40. Holloway, H. D.: Effects of training on the SRA Primary mental abilities (primary) and the WISC. *Child Develop. 25*: 253-263, 1954.

41. Jones, H. E.: The pattern of abilities in juvenile and adult defectives. *Univ. California Publ. Psychol. 5*: 47-61, 1931.

42. ———: The environment and mental development. *In* L. Carmichael, Ed., *Manual of Child Psychology,* ed. 2. New York, Wiley, 1954, pp. 631-696.

43. ———, and Conrad, H. S.: Mental development in adolescence. In *Forty-third Yearbook,* Nat. Soc. Stud. Educ. Chicago, University of Chicago Press, 1944, part 1, pp. 146-163.

44. Koch, H. L.: The relation of "primary mental abilities" in five- and six-year-olds to sex of child and characteristics of his sibling. *Child Develop. 25*: 209-223, 1954.

45. Kolstoe, O. P.: A comparison of mental abilities of bright and dull children of comparable mental ages. *J. Educ. Psychol. 45*: 161-168, 1954.

46. Laycock, S. R., and Clark, S.: The comparative performance of a group of old-dull and young-bright children on some items of the Revised Stanford-Binet Scale of intelligence, Form L. *J. Educ. Psychol. 33*: 1-12, 1942.

47. Leahy, A. M.: Nature-nurture and intelligence. *Genet. Psychol. Monogr. 17*: 235-308, 1935.

48. Lillienfeld, A. M., and Pasamanick, B.: The association of maternal and fetal factors with the development of mental deficiency. II. Relationship to maternal age, birth order, previous reproductive loss and degree of mental deficiency. *Am. J. Ment. Def. 60*: 557-569, 1956.

49. Lightfoot, G. F.: *Personality Characteristics of Bright and Dull Children.* New York, Teachers College, Columbia University, 1951.

50. Loevinger, J.: Intelligence as related to socio-economic factors. In *Thirty-ninth*

Yearbook, Nat. Soc. Stud. Educ. Chicago, University of Chicago Press, 1940, part 1, pp. 159-210.

51. ———: On the proportional contributions of differences in nature and nurture to differences in intelligence. *Psychol. Bull. 40*: 725-756, 1943.

52. Lord, F. E.: A study of spatial orientation of children. *J. Educ. Res. 34*: 481-505, 1941.

53. Lorge, I.: Schooling makes a difference. *Teachers College Rec. 46*: 483-492, 1945.

54. McGeehee, W., and Lewis, W. D.: The socio-economic status of the homes of mentally superior and retarded children and the occupational rank of their parents. *J. Genet. Psychol. 60*: 375-380, 1942.

55. MacRae, J. M.: Retests of children given mental tests as infants. *J. Genet. Psychol. 87*: 111-119, 1955.

56. Maurer, K. M.: Intellectual status at maturity as a criterion for selecting items in preschool tests. *Univ. Minnesota Child Welf. Monogr.* No. 21, 1946.

57. Merrill, M. A.: On the relation of intelligence to achievement in the case of mentally retarded children. *Comp. Psychol. Monogr.* No. 11, 1924.

58. Newman, H. H., Freeman, F. N., and Holzinger, K .J.: *Twins: A Study of Heredity and Environment.* Chicago, University of Chicago Press, 1937.

59. Nisbet, J.: Family environment and intelligence. *Eugenics Rev. 45*: 31-40, 1953.

60. Olson, W. C., and Hughes, B. O.: Subsequent growth of children with and without nursery school experience. In *Thirty-ninth Yearbook,* Nat. Soc. Stud. Educ. Chicago, University of Chicago Press, 1940, pp. 237-244.

61. Outhit, M. C.: A study of the resemblance of parents and children in general intelligence. *Arch. Psychol.* No. 149, 1933.

62. Owens, W. A.: Age and mental abilities: a longitudinal study. *Genet. Psychol. Monogr. 48*: 3-54, 1953.

63. Pasamanick, B., and Knobloch, H.: Early language behavior in Negro children and the testing of intelligence. *J. Abnorm. Soc. Psychol. 50*: 401-402, 1955.

64. Pinneau, S. R.: The infantile disorders of hospitalism and anaclitic depression. *Psychol. Bull. 52*: 429-452, 1955.

65. Purvis, A. W.: An analysis of the abilities of different intelligence levels of secondary-school pupils. Unpublished doctor's dissertation, Harvard University, 1938.

66. Ramaseshan, R. S.: A note on the validity of the mental age concept. *J. Educ. Psychol. 41*: 56-58, 1950.

67. Reymert, M., and Hinton, R., Jr.: The effect of a change to a relatively superior environment upon the IQ's of one hundred children. In *Thirty-ninth Yearbook,* Nat. Soc. Stud. Educ. Chicago, University of Chicago Press, 1940, part 2, pp. 255-268.

68. Rust, M. M.: The effect of resistance on intelligence test scores of young children. *Child Develop. Monogr.* No. 6, 1931.

69. Scottish Council for Research in Education: *Social Implications of the 1947 Scottish Mental Survey.* London, University of London Press, 1953.

70. Segel, D.: *Intellectual Abilities in the Adolescent Period.* Washington, D. C., Federal Security Agency, 1948.

71. Sherman, M., and Key, C. B.: The intelligence of isolated mountain children. *Child Develop. 3*: 279-290, 1932.

72. Shuttleworth, F. K.: The cumulative influence on intelligence of socio-economic differentials operating on the same children over a period of ten years. In *Thirty-ninth Yearbook*, Nat. Soc. Stud. Educ. Chicago, University of Chicago Press, 1940, part 2, pp. 275-280.

73. Skeels, H. M., and Fillmore, E. A.: Mental development of children from under-privileged homes. *J. Genet. Psychol. 50*: 427-439, 1937.

74. ——, Updegraff, R., Wellman, B. L., and Williams, H. M.: A study of environmental stimulation: an orphanage preschool project. *Univ. Iowa Stud. Child Welf.* No. 4, 1938.

75. Skodak, M.: Children in foster homes: a study of mental development. *Univ. Iowa Stud. Child Welf. 16*: No. 1, 1939.

76. ——, and Skeels, H. M.: A final follow-up of one hundred adopted children. *J. Genet. Psychol. 75*: 85-125, 1949.

77. Smith, S.: Language and non-verbal test performance of racial groups in Honolulu before and after a fourteen-year interval. *J. Gen. Psychol. 26*: 51-93, 1942.

78. Speer, G. S.: The mental development of children of feeble-minded and normal mothers. In *Thirty-ninth Yearbook*, Nat. Soc. Stud. Educ. Chicago, University of Chicago Press, 1940, part 2, pp. 309-314.

79. Stover, N.: The child's learning difficulty as related to the emotional problem of the mother. *Am. J. Orthopsychiat. 23*: 131-141, 1953.

80. Terman, L. M., and Merrill, M. A.: *Measuring Intelligence: A Guide to the Administration of the New Revised Stanford-Binet Tests of Intelligence.* Boston, Houghton Mifflin, 1937.

81. ——, and Oden, M.: *The Gifted Child Grows Up: 25 Years' Follow-up of a Superior Group.* Stanford, Stanford University Press, 1949.

82. ——, and Tyler, L. E.: Psychological sex differences. *In* L. Carmichael, Ed., *Manual of Child Psychology,* ed. 2. New York, Wiley, 1954, pp. 1004-1114.

83. Thompson, C. W., and Magaret, A.: Differential test responses of normals and mental defectives. *J. Abnorm. Soc. Psychol. 42*: 285-293, 1949.

84. Thorndike, E. L., et al.: *The Measurement of Intelligence.* New York, Teachers College, Columbia University, 1926.

85. Thorndike, R. L.: Growth of intelligence during adolescence. *J. Genet. Psychol. 72*: 11-15, 1948.

86. ——, et al.: Retest chances in the IQ in certain superior schools. In *Thirty-ninth Yearbook*, Nat. Soc. Stud. Educ. Chicago, University of Chicago Press, 1940, part 2, pp. 351-361.

87. Thurstone, L. L.: *Primary Mental Abilities.* Chicago, University of Chicago Press, 1938.

88. ——, and Ackerson, L.: The mental growth curve for the Binet tests. *J. Educ. Psychol. 20*: 569-583, 1929.

89. ——, and Thurstone, T. G.: *Tests of Primary Mental Abilities for Ages Five and Six.* Chicago, Science Research Associates, 1946.

90. Vernon, P. E.: *The Structure of Human Abilities.* New York, Wiley, 1950.

91. Wechsler, D.: *The Measurement of Adult Intelligence,* ed. 3. Baltimore, Williams & Wilkins, 1944.

92. ——: Intellectual development and psychological maturity. *Child Develop. 21*: 45-50, 1950.

93. Wellman, B. L.: IQ changes of preschool and nonpreschool groups during the preschool years: a summary of the literature. *J. Psychol. 20*: 347-368, 1945.

94. Wheeler, L. R.: A comparative study of the intelligence of East Tennessee mountain children. *J. Educ. Psychol. 33*: 321-334, 1942.

95. Wiseman, S.: Symposium on the effects of coaching and practice in intelligence tests. IV: The Manchester Experiment. *Brit. J. Educ. Psychol. 24*: 5-8, 1954.

96. Woodworth, R. S.: *Heredity and Environment: A Critical Survey of Recently Published Materials on Twins and Foster Children.* New York, Social Science Research Council, 1941.

Author Index

Subject Index

A